This book was made possible by the support from many organizations and individuals. The primary funders include:

Water and Post-Conflict Peacebuilding

Edited by Erika Weinthal, Jessica Troell, and Mikiyasu Nakayama

First published 2013
by Earthscan
2 Park Square, Milton Park, Abingdon, Oxon OX14 4RN

Simultaneously published in the USA and Canada
by Earthscan
711 Third Avenue, New York, NY 10017

Earthscan is an imprint of the Taylor & Francis Group, an informa business

Earthscan publishes in association with the International Institute for Environment and Development

© 2014 Environmental Law Institute and United Nations Environment Programme

The right of the editors to be identified as the authors of the editorial material, and of the authors for their individual chapters, has been asserted in accordance with sections 77 and 78 of the Copyright, Designs and Patents Act 1988.

All rights reserved. No part of this book may be reprinted or reproduced or utilised in any form or by any electronic, mechanical, or other means, now known or hereafter invented, including photocopying and recording, or in any information storage or retrieval system, without permission in writing from the copyright holders.

Trademark notice: Product or corporate names may be trademarks or registered trademarks, and are used only for identification and explanation without intent to infringe.

British Library Cataloguing-in-Publication Data
A catalogue record for this book is available from the British Library

Library of Congress Cataloging-in-Publication Data
Water and post-conflict peacebuilding / edited by Erika Weinthal, Jessica Troell, and Mikiyasu Nakayama.
   p. cm.
   Includes bibliographical references and index.
   ISBN 978-1-84971-232-3 (pbk. : alk. paper) – ISBN 978-1-84977-580-9 (ebook : alk. paper)   1. Water-supply–Political aspects.
2. Infrastructure (Economics)   3. Peace-building–Economic aspects.   4. Postwar reconstruction.   I. Weinthal, Erika.   II. Troell, Jessica.   III. Nakayama, Mikiyasu.   IV. Title: Water and post conflict peace building.
   HD1691.W3197 2012
   333.91–dc23

2012024239

Typeset in Times and Helvetica
by Graphicraft Limited, Hong Kong

Table of contents

List of figures and tables	vii
Preface	ix
Foreword	xiii
Acknowledgments	xvii
Shoring up peace: Water and post-conflict peacebuilding *Jessica Troell and Erika Weinthal*	1

Part 1: Basic services and human security — 25

Introduction	27
The role of informal service providers in post-conflict reconstruction and state building *Jeremy Allouche*	31
A tale of two cities: Restoring water services in Kabul and Monrovia *Jean-François Pinera and Robert A. Reed*	43
Conflict and collaboration for water resources in Angola's post-war cities *Allan Cain*	63
Thirsty for peace: The water sector in South Sudan *Sam Huston*	85
Community water management: Experiences from the Democratic Republic of the Congo, Afghanistan, and Liberia *Murray Burt and Bilha Joy Keiru*	95
Environmental management of the Iraqi marshlands in the post-conflict period *Chizuru Aoki, Ali Al-Lami, and Sivapragasam Kugaprasatham*	117

Part 2: Livelihoods — 137

Introduction	139
Irrigation management and flood control in post–World War II Japan *Mikiko Sugiura, Yuka Toguchi, and Mona Funiciello*	141
Refugee rehabilitation and transboundary cooperation: India, Pakistan, and the Indus River system *Neda A. Zawahri*	163

iv Water and post-conflict peacebuilding

Despite the best intentions? Experiences with water resource
management in northern Afghanistan   189
Jennifer McCarthy and Daanish Mustafa

Water's role in measuring security and stability in Helmand
Province, Afghanistan   211
Laura Jean Palmer-Moloney

Part 3: Peace processes, cooperation, and confidence building   **237**

Introduction   239

The Jordan River Basin: A conflict like no other   243
Munther J. Haddadin

Transboundary cooperation in the Lower Jordan River Basin   265
Munqeth Mehyar, Nader Al Khateeb, Gidon Bromberg,
and Elizabeth Koch-Ya'ari

The Sava River: Transitioning to peace in the former Yugoslavia   271
Amar Čolakhodžić, Marija Filipović, Jana Kovandžić, and Stephen Stec

Transnational cooperation over shared water resources in the
South Caucasus: Reflections on USAID interventions   297
Marina Vardanyan and Richard Volk

Water security and scarcity: Potential destabilization in western
Afghanistan and Iranian Sistan and Baluchestan due to transboundary
water conflicts   305
Alex Dehgan, Laura Jean Palmer-Moloney, and Mehdi Mirzaee

Water resources in the Sudan North-South peace process and the
ramifications of the secession of South Sudan   327
Salman M. A. Salman

Part 4: Legal frameworks   **357**

Introduction   359

Management of waters in post-Dayton Bosnia and Herzegovina:
Policy, legal, and institutional aspects   361
Slavko Bogdanovic

The right to water and sanitation in post-conflict legal mechanisms:
An emerging regime?   383
Mara Tignino

Table of contents v

Part 5: Lessons learned 403

Harnessing water management for more effective peacebuilding:
Lessons learned 405
Jessica Troell and Erika Weinthal

Appendices

List of abbreviations 471

Author biographies 475

Table of contents for *Post-Conflict Peacebuilding and Natural Resource Management* 487

Index 503

List of figures and tables

FIGURES

Water availability in countries affected by major conflict, cubic meters per year, 1990–2013 (Map)	2
Water resources in Kabul, Afghanistan (Map)	47
Population and water supply in Kabul, Afghanistan	48
Water resources in Monrovia, Liberia (Map)	49
Population and water supply in Monrovia, Liberia	51
Formal and informal settlements in the greater metropolitan area of Luanda, Angola (Map)	70
Value chain model of the water supply system in Luanda, Angola	71
Tanker trucks filling up from the River Bengo at the ANGOMENHA filling station at Kifangondo, Angola	74
Street vendors reselling water in plastic bags in Luanda, Angola	76
Location of the southern Iraq marshes, 2008–2009 (Map)	119
Agricultural productivity in Japan, 1880–1995	150
National agricultural water projects launched in 1947, Japan (Map)	151
Map of the Indus River Basin, 1947 (Map)	166
Regional command and control in Afghanistan prior to July 2010 (Map)	212
Separation of Regional Command (RC) South into RC South and RC Southwest (Map)	213
Helmand River watershed, Afghanistan (Map)	216
Map of mineral and freshwater springs of Afghanistan, mid-1970s (Map)	218
Civilian priorities in the city of Lashkar Gah, Afghanistan, 2010 (Map)	223
Spatial and temporal aspects of water complexity questions and answers	226
Location of wells monitored by the Danish Committee for Aid to Afghan Refugees in Helmand Province, Afghanistan (Map)	228
The Sava River and its tributaries (Map)	275
Organizational structure of the International Sava River Basin Commission	284

viii   Water and post-conflict peacebuilding

Kura-Araks River Basin (Map)	300
Watersheds of Afghanistan (Map)	307
Rivers of Afghanistan and Iran feeding into the Sistan Basin (Map)	309
Close-up of the Sistan Basin *hamuns* (lakes), the four Chahnimeh reservoirs, and main irrigation and drainage canals (Map)	310
Projected percent change in precipitation, soil moisture, runoff, and evaporation in 2080–2099 relative to 1980–1999 (Map)	316
Nile River Basin (Map)	334

TABLES

Countries and territories affected by major conflict since 1990, with and without transboundary basins	3
Major water network rehabilitation projects in Kabul, Afghanistan	52
Major water network rehabilitation projects in Monrovia, Liberia	53
Household water sources in Luanda, Angola	67
Distance to main water source for households in Luanda, Angola	67
Carriers of water in urban areas, Angola	77
Types of negative effects on surveyed Iraqi marshland villages during the Saddam Hussein regime	119
Transition of the legal framework in Japan for flood-control and irrigation management	148
Number of dams, their purpose, and their available storage capacity, Japan, 1900–1993	153
Water complexity definitions	215
Sava River Basin shares by country	276
Potential for hydropower in the Sava River Basin	288
Source contributions to the waters of the Nile River	336
Waters of Bosnia and Herzegovina that belong to the watersheds of the Black Sea and the Adriatic Sea	363
Objectives of water provisions in peace agreements, 1990–2013	431
Countries affected by major conflict between 1990 and 2013 that adopted constitutional provisions related to water	439
Approaches to managing water in post-conflict situations	451

Preface

Decades of civil wars, international wars, and wars of secession demonstrate the strong relationship between natural resources and armed conflict. Disputes over natural resources and their associated revenues can be among the reasons that people go to war. Diamonds, timber, oil, and even bananas and charcoal can provide sources of financing to sustain conflict. Forests, agricultural crops, and wells are often targeted during conflict. Efforts to negotiate an end to conflict increasingly include natural resources. And conflicts associated with natural resources are both more likely to relapse than non-resource-related conflicts, and to relapse twice as fast.

Immediately after the end of a conflict, a window of opportunity opens for a conflict-affected country and the international community to establish security, rebuild, and consolidate peace—or risk conflict relapse. This window also presents the opportunity to reform the management of natural resources and their revenues in ways that would otherwise be politically difficult to achieve. Capitalizing on this opportunity is particularly critical if natural resources contributed to the onset or financing of conflict—and, if this opportunity is lost, it may never reappear. Moreover, poorly informed policy decisions may become entrenched, locking in a trajectory that serves the interests of a limited few.

Since the end of the Cold War, and particularly since 2000, substantial progress has been made in establishing institutional and policy frameworks to consolidate peacebuilding efforts. In 2005, the United Nations established the Peacebuilding Commission to identify best practices for peacebuilding. The commission is the first body to bring together the UN's humanitarian, security, and development sectors so that they can learn from peacebuilding experiences.

The Peacebuilding Commission has started to recognize the importance of natural resources in post-conflict peacebuilding. In 2009, along with the United Nations Environment Programme, the commission published a pioneering report—*From Conflict to Peacebuilding: The Role of Natural Resources and the Environment*—that framed the basic ways in which natural resources contribute to conflict and can be managed to support peacebuilding. Building on this report, the commission is starting to consider how natural resources can be included

x   Water and post-conflict peacebuilding

within post-conflict planning and programming in Sierra Leone, the Central African Republic, Guinea, and other countries.

Since the establishment of the Peacebuilding Commission, the policies governing post-conflict peacebuilding have evolved rapidly. In his 2009 *Report of the Secretary-General on Peacebuilding in the Immediate Aftermath of Conflict*, UN Secretary-General Ban Ki-moon articulated five priorities for post-conflict peacebuilding, all of which have natural resource dimensions. In his 2010 update to that report, Ban Ki-moon noted the pressing need to improve post-conflict natural resource management to reduce the risk of conflict relapse, and urged "Member States and the United Nations system to make questions of natural resource allocation, ownership and access an integral part of peacebuilding strategies." The Secretary-General's 2012 report on the topic highlighted progress over the previous two years and called on UN entities to more effectively share knowledge and leverage expertise on post-conflict natural resource management. And a 2011 UN report, *Civilian Capacity in the Aftermath of Conflict*, highlighted approaches for mobilizing civil society to support peacebuilding in many realms, including natural resources.

The World Bank has also begun focusing on natural resources: the Bank's 2011 *World Development Report*, for example, placed the prevention of fragility, conflict, and violence at the core of the Bank's development mandate. Drawing on the Bank's experiences around the world, the report focuses on jobs, justice, and security, and highlights the contribution of natural resources to these goals.

Despite growing recognition of the importance of post-conflict natural resource management, there has been no comprehensive examination of how natural resources can support post-conflict peacebuilding. Nor has there been careful consideration of the risks to long-term peace caused by the failure to effectively address natural resources. Practitioners, researchers, and UN bodies have researched specific resources, conflict dynamics, and countries, but have yet to share their findings with each other at a meaningful scale, and limited connections have been drawn between the various strands of inquiry. As a result, the peacebuilding community does not know what works in what circumstances, what does not, or why.

Given the complexity of peacebuilding, practitioners and researchers alike are struggling to articulate good practice. It is increasingly clear that natural resources must be included as a foundational issue; many questions remain, however, regarding opportunities, options, and trade-offs.

Against this backdrop, the Environmental Law Institute, the UN Environment Programme, the University of Tokyo, and McGill University launched a research program designed to examine experiences in post-conflict peacebuilding and natural resource management; to identify lessons from these experiences; and to raise awareness of those lessons among practitioners and scholars. The program has benefited from broad support, with the government of Finland—one of the few donor governments to explicitly recognize the role of natural resources in both conflict and peacebuilding efforts—playing a catalytic role by providing core financing.

Preface xi

The research program has been guided by the collective experiences of the four members of the Steering Committee: as the coordinators of the program and the series editors, we have drawn on our work in more than thirty post-conflict countries. Our experiences—which include leading environmental assessments in Afghanistan, developing forest law in Liberia, supporting land reform in Mozambique, and fostering cooperation around water in Iraq—have led to a shared understanding that natural resource issues rarely receive the political attention they merit. Through this research program and partnership, we hope to catalyze a comprehensive global effort to demonstrate that peacebuilding substantially depends on the transformation of natural assets into peacebuilding benefits—a change that must occur without mortgaging the future or creating new conflict.

Since its inception in 2007, the program has grown dramatically in response to strong interest from practitioners, researchers, and policy makers. Participants in an initial scoping meeting suggested a single edited book consisting of twenty case studies and crosscutting analyses. It soon became clear, however, that the undertaking should reflect a much broader range of experiences, perspectives, and dimensions.

The research program yielded 150 peer-reviewed case studies and analyses written by 225 scholars, practitioners, and decision makers from fifty countries. The case studies and analyses have been assembled into a set of six edited books, each focusing on a specific set of natural resources or an aspect of peacebuilding: high-value natural resources; land; water; resources for livelihoods; assessment and restoration of natural resources; and governance. Examining a broad range of resources, including oil, minerals, land, water, wildlife, livestock, fisheries, forests, and agricultural products, the books document and analyze post-conflict natural resource management successes, failures, and ongoing efforts in sixty conflict-affected countries and territories. In their diversity and number, the books represent the most significant collection to date of experiences, analyses, and lessons in managing natural resources to support post-conflict peacebuilding.

In addition to the six edited books, the partnership has created an overarching book, *Post-Conflict Peacebuilding and Natural Resources: The Promise and the Peril*, which will be published by Cambridge University Press. This book draws on the six edited books to explore the role of natural resources in various peacebuilding activities across the humanitarian, security, and development sectors.

These seven books will be of interest to practitioners, researchers, and policy makers in the security, development, peacebuilding, political, and natural resource communities. They are designed to provide a conceptual framework, assess approaches, distill lessons, and identify specific options and trade-offs for more effectively managing natural resources to support post-conflict peacebuilding.

Natural resources present both opportunities and risks, and postponing their consideration in the peacebuilding process can imperil long-term peace and undermine sustainable development. Experiences from the past sixty years provide many lessons and broad guidance, as well as insight into which approaches are promising and which are problematic.

xii   Water and post-conflict peacebuilding

A number of questions, however, still lack definitive answers. We do not always understand precisely why certain approaches fail or succeed in specific instances, or which of a dozen contextual factors are the most important in determining the success of a peacebuilding effort. Nevertheless, numerous discrete measures related to natural resources can be adopted now to improve the likelihood of long-term peace. By learning from peacebuilding experiences to date, we can avoid repeating the mistakes of the past and break the cycle of conflict that has come to characterize so many countries. We also hope that this undertaking represents a new way to understand and approach peacebuilding.

Carl Bruch
Environmental Law Institute

David Jensen
United Nations Environment Programme

Mikiyasu Nakayama
University of Tokyo

Jon Unruh
McGill University

Foreword

Mikhail Gorbachev

Former president of the Union of Soviet Socialist Republics
Founding president of Green Cross International

I am delighted to write the foreword for *Water and Post-Conflict Peacebuilding*, the title of which aligns with objectives I have worked on for the past twenty years through Green Cross International. Since its founding in 1993, Green Cross and its worldwide network have worked on seemingly divergent goals: security, poverty eradication, and the environment. Yet the ongoing struggles in the Horn of Africa and Sudan, as well as the cases examined in this book, make clear that the links among conflict, water, human rights, and development are many and multifaceted. This book provides clear evidence of the need for more integrated action between the fields of water management and peacebuilding, as well as guidance on how to achieve such collaboration.

WATER AND SANITATION AS A HUMAN RIGHT

Access to safe drinking water and sanitation is a human right. However despite the adoption of this vital principle by the United Nations in 2010, the deficit of fresh water is becoming increasingly severe and widespread. And, unlike other resources, there is no substitute for water.

When I addressed the Sixth World Water Forum in Marseille in March 2012, I stressed that the water problem should not be considered in isolation from other global challenges and from the overall international context. Politics has often exacerbated water crises, and water crises have also had a reciprocal impact on politics that should not be overlooked. It is high time for us to help the 800 million people without access to potable water and the 2.5 billion people lacking access to basic sanitation, and to prioritize these issues at all levels. If this deprivation remains unchecked, the water crises can overstretch many societies' adaptive capacities in the coming decades.

The problems caused by inadequate water supplies and water mismanagement tend to be dramatically accentuated in post-conflict situations. In the aftermath of war, ensuring access to water and sanitation services is vital not only for meeting basic human needs and maintaining public health, but also for restoring economic livelihoods and alleviating poverty over the long term. The provision

xiv   Water and post-conflict peacebuilding

of water and sanitation services requires establishing, or reestablishing, cooperation at the community level, which may have been interrupted by conflict. The need for cooperation extends to the many institutions and stakeholders involved with water, since the absence of a formal mechanism to work together can lead to misuse of resources and missed opportunities to build capacity and social capital at many levels.

Access to water as a human right is not merely a theoretical matter; it also has very real implications for implementation. A rights-based approach to water services means that governments and other actors are obliged to ensure that clean water is widely available. We must clarify this obligation and enable governments to finance and carry out projects and policies that bring water and sanitation to people who need them most. Such a rights-based approach must also translate into national, regional, and local policies that foster access to sufficient water, support sustainable livelihoods in post-conflict situations, and maintain governance mechanisms to promote transparent and accountable water management practices that prevent corruption.

The UN General Assembly's resolution that declared access to water to be a human right also urged states and international organizations to secure that right by providing financing, capacity building, and technology transfer through international assistance and cooperation, especially to developing countries. Efforts should now be targeted at enforcing those rights in national legislation and action plans. This is particularly important for post-conflict countries because a rights-based approach, accompanied by the requisite assistance to realize that right, can provide a platform for redressing historical inequalities and discrimination in access to water as well as a means for fostering reconciliation and accountability.

TRANSBOUNDARY WATER

Water management across borders, especially during and immediately following conflicts between states, has been a key mechanism for promoting ongoing cooperation between riparian neighbors despite their differences. Many times third parties, notably NGOs and international organizations, have played a critical role in facilitating cooperation over shared waters. Indeed, civil society has consistently played a vital role in all post-conflict cooperation over cross-border water management. Green Cross is implementing the ideal of water as a human right through its work on many transboundary water issues around the world— from the Volga and the Indus to the Amazon and the Jordan rivers.

We often think of the environment and sustainable livelihoods in terms of how our grandchildren will be affected. There are about 1 million schools around the world, but less than half have access to clean drinking water and sanitation. Providing water and sanitation services to schools is an important step in engaging children and communities to improve their water security and to work for transformational change. The cases in this book highlight the importance of community-level projects in post-conflict, cross-border basins such as the Jordan River. Education programs, in particular, provide unique opportunities to enhance environmental and health awareness in children and their communities, and ultimately to build trust and confidence among the broader communities in post-conflict societies.

Green Cross has also been instrumental in promoting the 1997 Convention on the Law of the Non-Navigational Uses of International Watercourses (generally referred to as the UN Watercourses Convention), the only global treaty governing the use, management, and protection of international watercourses. The convention aims to establish basic standards and rules for cooperation between states for the sustainable and mutually beneficial management of transboundary waters. While it has not yet entered into force, the convention is widely considered to be an umbrella instrument to reinforce regional agreements and foster cooperation where basin treaties are absent. In post-conflict situations, adherence to the convention's governance principles of equitable use, access to information, technical cooperation, and accountability around shared waters could help facilitate reconciliation and provide a baseline for deepening relations among parties that share a basin.

CLIMATE CHANGE AND WATER

Climate change is affecting all of our lives. I experienced this firsthand in Moscow when, in the summer of 2010, the city was choked for weeks by the heavy smog from wildfires in nearby regions. The city seemed immersed in a different reality. People, plants, and animals all bore the imprint of suffering, frustration, and fear. Until then, many in Russia, including members of the ruling elite, were skeptical about global warming, and held the scientific data in disdain. Since the summer of 2010, the number of skeptics has shrunk. Of course, that Moscow summer was just one weather anomaly among many—mudslides in China, unprecedented drought and flooding in Australia and Pakistan, further deluges in Central Europe, more ferocious and frequent storms and cyclones in the Western Pacific and Gulf of Mexico. The list goes on, and almost all of the effects can be mediated through effective management of water resources.

The rising number of incidents of climate-induced disasters serves to underline the urgency. Each disaster once again raises the question of the costs of *not* taking action on climate change. What if the 2010 Russian heat wave and drought, which caused more than seventy deaths and indirectly affected thousands through the destruction of one-third of the country's wheat crop, or the catastrophic floods in Australia, China, and Pakistan, are just glimpses of future havoc from unchecked global warming? Everyone seems to understand that the climate problem cannot be wished away.

It may be that climate change, through its effects on water resources, will act as an additional stressor to harnessing water's peacebuilding potential. Steps to improve access to safe drinking water and sanitation in post-conflict situations

xvi   Water and post-conflict peacebuilding

will need to build resilience to climate impacts on the water sector. This will be vital for post-conflict countries such as Afghanistan and Sudan as they strive to meet the 2015 Millennium Development Goal targets for water and sanitation, as well as those in the forthcoming Sustainable Development Goals.

Despite disappointments among some who advocate urgent action to save humanity, we cannot afford failure or pessimism. There are enough people in civil society who have not succumbed to defeatism and are ready to act to make governments listen. This instinct of global self-preservation must finally force world leaders to consider the role of water in post-conflict peacebuilding if we are to build a sustainable and peaceful future. I am delighted that this book goes a long way toward furthering those goals.

Acknowledgments

This book is the culmination of a six-year research project. It would not have been possible without the efforts and contributions of many individuals and institutions.

The volume editors are grateful to our managing editor Peter Whitten and our manuscript editors Amanda Morgan, Mary Sebold, and Meg Cox for their editorial assistance. We are also thankful for the support of our assistant managing editors Annie Brock, Heather Croshaw, and Gwendolyn Brown in overseeing the development of this book. Nick Bellorini and Charlotte Russell provided guidance through the process; Matt Pritchard, Arthur Green, and Elan Spitzberg created the maps; and Joelle Stallone proofread the manuscript and Katarina Petursson, Eva Richardson, and Alyssa Casey coordinated the proofreading and publication process. We are also grateful to our colleagues at Duke University and the University of Tokyo for their comments, discussion, and support.

Research and publication assistance was provided by numerous research associates, interns, legal interns, and visiting attorneys at the Environmental Law Institute, including Elliott August, Andrew Beckington, Susan Bokermann, Marion Boulicault, Katja Bratrschovsky, Simonne Brousseau, Kyle Burns, Elizabeth Euller, Emanuel Feld, Akiva Fishman, Tristana Giunta, Adam Harris, Farah Hegazi, Katelyn Henmueller, Alex Hoover, Brian Judge, Rachel Kenigsberg, Amber Kim, Sonia Ledwith, Vrinda Manglik, Mark McCormick-Goodhart, Joseph Muller, Ayushi Narayan, Laetitia N'Dri, Vicki Nee, Delphine Robert, Aisha Saad, Lydia Slobodian, Sarah Stellberg, Whitney Stohr, Janna Wandzilak, Louise Yeung, Joel Young, and Danica Yu.

Peer reviewers were essential to ensuring the rigor of this book. The authors would like to acknowledge the professionals and scholars who contributed anonymous peer reviews.

One chapter in this book has been adapted with permission from an earlier published version. The editors wish to thank John Wiley and Sons for permission to reprint a revised version of "A Tale of Two Cities: Restoring Water Services in Kabul and Monrovia," by Jean-François Pinera and Robert Reed.

Financial support for the project was provided by the United Nations Environment Programme (UNEP), the government of Finland, the U.S. Agency

xviii   Water and post-conflict peacebuilding

for International Development, the European Union, the University of Tokyo Graduate School of Frontier Sciences and Alliance for Global Sustainability, the John D. and Catherine T. MacArthur Foundation, the Canadian Social Science and Humanities Research Council, the Philanthropic Collaborative, the Center for Global Partnership of the Japan Foundation, the Ploughshares Fund, the Compton Foundation, Zonta Club of Tokyo I, the International Union for Conservation of Nature's Commission on Environmental Law, the Nelson Talbott Foundation, the Jacob L. and Lillian Holtzmann Foundation, and an anonymous donor. In-kind support for the project was provided by the Earth Institute of Columbia University, the Environmental Change and Security Project of the Woodrow Wilson International Center for Scholars, the Environmental Law Institute, the Global Infrastructure Fund Research Foundation Japan, the Japan Institute of International Affairs, McGill University, the Peace Research Institute Oslo, the United Nations Environment Programme, and the University of Tokyo.

The cover was designed by Nikki Meith. Cover photography is by Roberto Schmidt/AFP/Getty Images.

Except as otherwise specifically noted, the maps in this publication use public domain data originating from Natural Earth (2009, www.naturalearthdata.com).

The designations employed and the presentations do not imply the expressions of any opinion whatsoever on the part of UNEP or contributory organizations concerning the legal status of any country, territory, city or area or its authority, or concerning the delimitation of its frontiers or boundaries.

When available, URLs are provided for sources that can be accessed electronically. URLs contained in this book were current at the time of publication.

Shoring up peace: Water and post-conflict peacebuilding

Jessica Troell and Erika Weinthal

Water is essential to human health, poverty alleviation, sustainable livelihoods, and food security. Yet 780 million people worldwide still lack access to safe drinking water, and 2.5 billion live without access to basic sanitation (UNICEF and WHO 2012). Of the approximately 2 million people who die each year from waterborne and water-washed illnesses, the majority are children under five (Water Aid 2011). In 2012, addressing the United Nations General Assembly on the culture of peace, UN Secretary-General Ban Ki-moon observed that "[p]eople intuitively understand that there can be no military solution to conflicts . . . that the world's scarce resources should be spent to help people flourish, not to fund weapons that cause more suffering. . . . $1.7 trillion dollars was spent last year on weapons. That is an enormous cost to people who go to bed hungry . . . children who die because they lack clean water . . ." (UN 2012).

For countries emerging from conflict, access to water and sanitation plays an integral role in meeting basic human needs, maintaining public health, and supporting livelihoods at the household and community levels. As these countries embark on the arduous pathway to peace, the provision of safe water is among the highest priorities for government and humanitarian efforts.

Freshwater is unequally distributed, spatially and temporally, both within and across states, resulting in seasonal and geographic scarcity (see figure 1, which depicts renewable water resources per capita in countries affected by major conflict between 1990 and 2013). Global water use nearly tripled during the second half of the twentieth century, far outstripping population growth during that period and placing increasing stress on water resources (CRS 2009). The Food and Agriculture Organization of the United Nations estimates that by 2025, approximately 1.8 billion people will be living in areas with absolute water

---

Jessica Troell is a senior attorney and director of the International Water Program at the Environmental Law Institute. Erika Weinthal is an associate professor of environmental policy at the Nicholas School of the Environment, Duke University.

2 Water and post-conflict peacebuilding

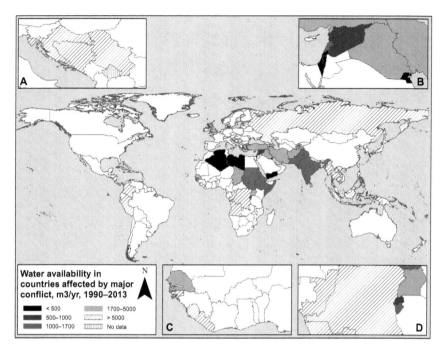

Figure 1. Water availability in countries affected by major conflict, cubic meters per year, 1990–2013
Source: FAO (2013).
Notes: A = Southeastern Europe; B = West Asia; C = West Africa; and D = Central Africa.
Major conflict is a conflict resulting in more than 1,000 battle deaths (Bruch et al. 2014; UCDP n.d.).

scarcity, and approximately two-thirds of the world's population will be experiencing some form of water stress (UNDESA n.d.; UN Water and FAO 2007).[1]

But the global water crisis is not simply a matter of physical scarcity: it is also a crisis of governance. Institutional and management failures, lack of financial and technological capacity and investment, and corruption are often to blame for inequities in access to water (TI 2008). The challenges associated with governing water wisely are particularly problematic in post-conflict countries, where governance and institutional frameworks are often weak or nonexistent, and the technical, financial, and infrastructural capacity to provide water and sanitation services is lacking.

Of the fifty-five countries affected by major conflict during or since 1990, fifty-one share at least one basin with one or more other nations; of the remaining four, two are island states (see table 1). During conflict, countries are often unable to (or fail to) engage in international dialogue regarding the allocation and development of shared waters. And during post-conflict recovery, the imperative to develop

---

[1] *Absolute water scarcity* is defined as annual water availability below 500 cubic meters per person; *water stress* is defined as annual water availability below 1,700 cubic meters per person.

Shoring up peace: Water and post-conflict peacebuilding 3

Table 1. Countries and territories affected by major conflict since 1990, with and without transboundary basins

With transboundary basins		*Without transboundary basins*
Afghanistan	Liberia	Kuwait
Algeria	Libya	Philippines
Angola	Mozambique	Sri Lanka
Azerbaijan	Myanmar	Yemen
Bangladesh	Nepal	
Bosnia and Herzegovina	Nicaragua	
Burundi	Pakistan	
Cambodia	Palestine†	
Chad	Peru	
Colombia	Republic of Congo	
Croatia		
Democratic Republic of the Congo	Russia	
	Rwanda	
El Salvador	Senegal	
Eritrea	Serbia	
Ethiopia	Sierra Leone	
Georgia	Somalia	
Guatemala	South Sudan†	
Guinea-Bissau	Sudan	
India	Syria	
Indonesia	Tajikistan	
Iran	Thailand	
Iraq	Timor-Leste†	
Israel	Turkey	
Kosovo	Uganda	
Laos	United Kingdom	
Lebanon		

Sources: Bruch et al. (2014); Institute for Water and Watersheds (n.d.).
Note: *Major conflict* is a conflict resulting in more than 1,000 battle deaths (Bruch et al. 2014; UCDP n.d.).
† Denotes countries whose transboundary waters are not recorded in Institute for Water and Watersheds (n.d.).

4   Water and post-conflict peacebuilding

water resources as a means of supporting livelihoods and economic development goals can strain relations among countries that share basins. For example, in response to drought in the Helmand River Basin, Afghanistan has made unilateral decisions that reduced the flow of the river to Iran, increasing tensions between the two states (Dehgan, Palmer-Moloney, and Mirzaee 2014*).[2] This situation also exemplifies the interplay among the post-conflict imperative to develop, other pressures on water resources (such as climate variability and change), and regional politics.

Of the many high-level political commitments made over the past decades to provide water and sanitation services to the world's poorest people, the most prominent are the UN Millennium Development Goals (MDGs), established in 2000, which include global targets for expanding access to safe drinking water and sanitation (UN 2009). The critical role of water in ensuring human health and well-being was reinforced in 2010, when the UN recognized access to clean water and sanitation as a fundamental human right, ratcheting up pressure to meet and surpass the MDGs and increasing emphasis on the social and political dimensions of access to safe water (UNGA 2010).

Progress toward meeting the MDGs has been mixed. One water-related goal was to halve the proportion of people lacking access to safe drinking water by 2015. As of 2010, more than 2 billion people had gained access to improved water sources—five years ahead of the target date (UNICEF and WHO 2012). However, many of the countries with the lowest levels of access still lag. Of the thirty-four countries farthest from reaching the MDGs, twenty-two are experiencing or emerging from conflict (ECOSOC 2010). As of 2010, no conflict-affected country had met a single MDG, although by 2013 Afghanistan, Myanmar, and Nepal reported meeting the target on improved access to water (World Bank 2011, 2013).

The populations of conflict-affected countries are twice as likely to lack clean water as those in other developing countries (World Bank 2011). In sub-Saharan Africa in the early 2000s, the percentage of the population with improved access to water was 15 percent higher in countries that had not experienced conflict than in those that had (Schwartz, Hahn, and Bannon 2004). Since the MDGs were put in place, only a few post-conflict countries have made significant improvements in access to water. Between 1990 and 2010, for example, Ethiopia increased the percentage of the population with access to improved water from 13 to 66 percent (World Bank 2011).

Water resources play a critical role in post-conflict recovery and peacebuilding: restoring livelihoods, supporting economic recovery, and facilitating reconciliation. The goal of this book is to examine how and under which conditions water can be effectively harnessed to contribute to peacebuilding in post-conflict situations. The nineteen chapters that follow explore diverse water-related interventions from twenty-eight conflict-affected countries and territories in Africa, Asia, Europe, and the Middle East (see map on page 5). The book draws on experiences in these and other locations to create a framework for understanding how decisions and activities related to water resources can facilitate, undermine, or otherwise influence

---

[2]   Citations marked with an asterisk refer to chapters within this book.

Shoring up peace: Water and post-conflict peacebuilding 5

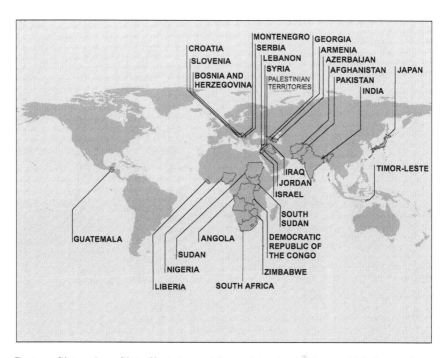

Post-conflict and conflict-affected countries and territories from which lessons have been drawn in this book, either through case studies or broader thematic analyses
Notes: UN member states are set in bold. During the time under consideration in this book, the Palestinian territories were known as the occupied Palestinian territories.

peacebuilding processes. (For an overview of key terms and concepts related to natural resources and post-conflict peacebuilding, see sidebar.)

The rebuilding of conflict-affected societies entails a large number of actors, including post-conflict governments at the national and local levels, humanitarian and aid organizations, civil society organizations, armed forces (including both civilian and military personnel), and the citizens of the country. The thirty-five authors who have contributed to this book have had wide-ranging experiences—from negotiating treaties to overseeing humanitarian and development interventions in rural communities—and offer diverse perspectives on post-conflict water management.

This book provides a series of snapshots of specific contexts at particular moments. Because post-conflict situations often evolve rapidly, later developments may influence the lessons drawn from the experiences detailed in these chapters. Nevertheless, it is valuable to document these efforts in order to create a more systematic framework for understanding the ways in which water management can be more effectively integrated into peacebuilding.

The remainder of this chapter is divided into five parts: (1) a discussion of the direct and indirect impacts of conflict on water resources, highlighting connections between hydrogeological, social, economic, and political factors and their influences on the post-conflict context; (2) an examination of the role of water

6 Water and post-conflict peacebuilding

Post-conflict peacebuilding and natural resources: Key terms and concepts

Following conflict, peacebuilding actors leverage a country's available assets (including natural resources) to transition from conflict to peace and sustainable development. Peacebuilding actors work at the international, national, and subnational levels and include national and subnational government bodies; United Nations agencies and other international organizations; international and domestic nongovernmental organizations; the private sector; and the media. Each group of peacebuilding actors deploys its own tools, and there are a growing number of tools to integrate the peacebuilding efforts of different types of actors.

A post-conflict period typically begins after a peace agreement or military victory. Because a post-conflict period is often characterized by intermittent violence and instability, it can be difficult to pinpoint when the post-conflict period ends. For the purposes of this book, the post-conflict period may be said to end when political, security, and economic discourse and actions no longer revolve around armed conflict or the impacts of conflict, but focus instead on standard development objectives. Within the post-conflict period, the first two years are referred to as the *immediate aftermath of conflict* (UNSG 2009), which is followed by a period known as *peace consolidation.*

According to the United Nations, "Peacebuilding involves a range of measures targeted to reduce the risk of lapsing or relapsing into conflict by strengthening national capacities at all levels for conflict management, and to lay the foundations for sustainable peace and development" (UNSG's Policy Committee 2007). In many instances, this means addressing the root causes of the conflict.

There are many challenges to peacebuilding: insecurity, ethnic and political polarization (as well as marginalization), corruption, lack of governmental legitimacy, extensive displacement, and loss of property. To address these and other challenges, peacebuilding actors undertake diverse activities that advance four broad peacebuilding objectives:*

- *Establishing security,* which encompasses basic safety and civilian protection; security sector reform; disarmament, demobilization, and reintegration; and demining.
- *Delivering basic services,* including water, sanitation, waste management, and energy, as well as health care and primary education.
- *Restoring the economy and livelihoods,* which includes repairing and constructing infrastructure and public works.
- *Rebuilding governance and inclusive political processes,* which encompasses dialogue and reconciliation processes, rule of law, dispute resolution, core government functions, transitional justice, and electoral processes.

Although they are sometimes regarded as distinct from peacebuilding, both peacemaking (the negotiation and conclusion of peace agreements) and humanitarian assistance are relevant to peacebuilding, as they can profoundly influence the options for post-conflict programming. Peacemaking and humanitarian assistance are also relevant to this book, in that they often have substantial natural resource dimensions.

Successful peacebuilding is a transformative process in which a fragile country and the international community seek to address grievances and proactively lay the foundation for a lasting peace. As part of this process, peacebuilding actors seek to manage the country's assets—as well as whatever international assistance may be available—to ensure security, provide basic services, rebuild the economy and livelihoods, and restore governance. The assets of a post-conflict country include natural resources; infrastructure; and human, social, and financial capital. Natural resources comprise land, water, and other renewable resources, as well as extractive resources such as oil, gas, and minerals. The rest of the book explores the many ways in which natural resources affect peacebuilding.

---

* This framework draws substantially from the *Report of the Secretary-General on Peacebuilding in the Immediate Aftermath of Conflict* (UNSG 2009), but the activities have been regrouped and supplemented by activities articulated in USIP and U.S. Army PKSOI (2009), Sphere Project (2004, 2011), UN (2011), UNSG (2010, 2012), and International Dialogue on Peacebuilding and Statebuilding (2011).

Shoring up peace: Water and post-conflict peacebuilding 7

at war's end in meeting basic human needs, and of the sociopolitical challenges that accompany this task; (3) a consideration of the multiple pathways through which investments in water management can help to rebuild livelihoods and revitalize economies, especially by helping to restore the agricultural sector; (4) an exploration of water management in post-conflict peacebuilding, highlighting the role of governance mechanisms and international water law in fostering effective cooperation and reconciliation at both the national and transboundary levels; and (5) a brief description of the organization of the remaining chapters in the book.

IMPACTS OF CONFLICT ON WATER RESOURCES

Historically, water resources and infrastructure have been strategic targets during conflict, and opposing sides have targeted water infrastructure and water to disrupt troop movements and compromise livelihoods. In fact, the deliberate destruction of water services and infrastructure has led to some of the most damaging direct and collateral impacts of modern warfare (Haavisto 2003). During World War II, for example, Allied bombing inflicted severe damage on Germany's water supply and treatment facilities (Jones et al. 2006). Decades later, in order to cripple local economies, the Soviet army deliberately destroyed one-third of all the traditional irrigation systems (*karez*) in Afghanistan (Formoli 1995). Attacks on water resources and infrastructure were also widespread during Liberia's first civil war (1989–1996): in 1990, Charles Taylor's rebel forces seized control of the Mount Coffee Water Plant, the country's only hydroelectric facility, thereby cutting off all water and electricity flowing to the capital, Monrovia (UNEP 2004; IRIN 2006). Over the course of the war, the plant was completely destroyed, forcing Monrovia's residents to rely on individual wells, which drew groundwater that was often contaminated (UNEP 2004).

In post-conflict situations, the destruction of water infrastructure and the contamination of water supplies present pressing challenges for meeting basic human needs and protecting public health. During Liberia's protracted civil wars, many of the country's community-based water and sanitation facilities were damaged: in 1989, before the first civil war began, 45 percent of urban populations and 23 percent of rural populations had access to pipe-borne water; by 1999, only 25 percent of urban residents and 4.1 percent of rural residents had such access. At the end of the second civil war (1999–2003), pipe-borne water was essentially unavailable, leaving the population dependent on ponds, rivers, and untreated wells as their primary source of drinking water (ROL and UNDP 2006). Since the end of the last war, Liberia has struggled to provide its citizens with access to safe water and sanitation. As of 2009, the government reported that 75 percent of its population had sustainable access to improved water sources and that 44 percent of its population had access to improved sanitation. However, 63 percent of those with improved access to sanitation were urban residents, and only 27 percent of those with improved access were rural residents (ROL and UNDP 2010).

8 Water and post-conflict peacebuilding

Even where water resources are not directly targeted during conflict, water infrastructure often suffers from neglect. For example, years of international war and civil strife severely damaged Iraq's water and sanitation networks: by 2008, less than half of Iraq's population had access to potable water, and less than 10 percent of urban households outside of Baghdad were connected to sewage systems (Dhayi 2008).

Perhaps most distressing is the socioeconomic harm that results from the lingering and indirect impacts of war: when the institutions that oversee the management and provision of water services are weak or nonexistent, the population is vulnerable to increased risks of disease, food insecurity, and death. Thus, even as the fighting stops, mortality rates may continue to rise, as unsanitary living conditions and the lack of safe drinking water lead to outbreaks of diarrheal and other waterborne and water-washed illnesses (Ghobarah, Huth, and Russett 2003). High mortality rates from water contamination and lack of sanitation have been documented in a number of post-conflict countries, including the Democratic Republic of the Congo (DRC), Liberia, and Sierra Leone (IRC 2008; Ghobarah, Huth, and Russett 2003). In the DRC, the International Rescue Committee estimates that 2.1 million of the 5.4 million deaths that occurred between 1998 and 2007 took place after the war had formally ended in 2002 (IRC 2008).

During wartime, basic maintenance of water supply systems in urban areas is often neglected. In addition, rural populations in search of safety and employment often flee to cities during and immediately after war, placing tremendous additional stress on already weakened water and sanitation systems (Jacobsen 2010). In Afghanistan, for example, violence, drought, and food shortages have driven many rural citizens to urban areas (Sharp et al. 2002): since 2001, Kabul's population has tripled in size (to approximately 4.5 million), and 80 percent of this increase has come from migrants and returning refugees (Setchell and Luther 2009). Such rapid growth often takes the form of informal urban or peri-urban settlements, in which basic services are minimal or nonexistent. Residents who have no direct access to piped water must buy water from private vendors, often at much higher prices than they would pay for water from public utilities. In some areas of the country, the monthly cost of domestic water supplies (twenty-five liters per person per day) for a family of eight is equivalent to approximately one-quarter of a government employee's monthly salary (CPHD 2011).

Another concern is potential conflict between displaced populations and local communities over water resources. In eastern Chad, where arable land is scarce and groundwater hard to access, local communities are finding it increasingly difficult to coexist peacefully with the 250,000 Sudanese refugees who have fled conflict in Darfur (IRIN 2009a). While international standards require that refugees receive between ten and fifteen liters per person per day of freshwater, many camps in eastern Chad cannot even supply ten.

As noted earlier, in addition to destroying physical infrastructure, armed conflict takes a critical toll on the institutional capacity of the water sector—the governance frameworks that make effective water management possible. Many

MEETING BASIC HUMAN NEEDS THROUGH HUMANITARIAN INTERVENTIONS

post-conflict countries lose human capital when qualified staff flee or are killed during conflict; moreover, new staff often lack training and technical capacity, further impeding recovery and reconstruction. In Afghanistan, for example, by 2001, nearly all of the 400 staff of the Central Authority for Water Supply and Sewerage had fled or been killed, and all of the authority's equipment and vehicles had been destroyed (Pinera and Reed 2014*).

MEETING BASIC HUMAN NEEDS THROUGH HUMANITARIAN INTERVENTIONS

The shattered landscape described in the previous section is the remnant upon which war-torn societies must rebuild the water services and infrastructure that will provide the basis for domestic life, public health, and livelihoods, as well as for sustainable economic development and poverty alleviation. When peace arrives, efforts to provide basic services are among the highest priorities of governments, citizens, humanitarian organizations, and donors. Almost invariably, however, mechanisms for ensuring that post-conflict interventions in the water sector are coordinated and sustainable are lacking. Moreover, the destruction of both formal and informal institutions for water management during conflict poses particular challenges for post-conflict water sector interventions. In Afghanistan, for example, violent disputes over water increased even after post-conflict recovery efforts began—because, as one Oxfam representative explained, "[t]hirty years of war has left sources of water co-opted, stolen and contaminated" (Vidal 2010). A 2008 Oxfam survey in Afghanistan found that, after land, water was the second-most-contentious issue at the local level, owing to its domestic and agricultural importance (Waldman 2008). Understanding how damage to both the physical and institutional aspects of water services has affected relationships among users is critical when attempting to rebuild institutions for water management.[3]

Once conflict has ended, one of the first tasks is to locate clean water sources for refugees, internally displaced persons (IDPs), and residents of communities whose water supplies were affected by the conflict or have yet to be connected to improved water sources. However, when humanitarian organizations attempt to accommodate populations that have migrated away from war-torn or water-scarce areas to places where water is available, limited water supplies are subject to additional stress, which may lead to competition over these resources. Water scarcity can also constrain efforts to resettle or facilitate the return of refugee populations. In Afghanistan, for example, the Office of the United Nations High Commissioner for Refugees is making a concentrated effort to assist IDPs and returning refugees by increasing access to safe drinking water, especially in the drought-affected northern part of the country (UNHCR 2009).

---

[3] See, for example, McCarthy and Mustafa (2014*).

10 Water and post-conflict peacebuilding

Immediate interventions are likely to take the form of temporary, short-term efforts to protect human health. Such efforts must be undertaken with care, however: installing camps in water-scarce regions without assessing water availability or monitoring use and impacts can result in overuse of the resource, as was the case in Darfur, where the aquifer was overdrawn and the water table fell (Tearfund 2007).

In most post-conflict settings, the government lacks the necessary financial and technical capacity to effectively deliver water and sanitation services, so the international community provides assistance.[4] Increasingly, such efforts include interventions that involve a wide variety of actors, including humanitarian organizations, bilateral development agencies, nongovernmental organizations (NGOs), international financial institutions, military personnel, agencies of foreign governments, and the formal and informal private sector. Such efforts raise a number of questions, however, during the various phases of post-conflict water-related interventions. For example, to what extent are nonstate actors able to establish viable and effective water and sanitation systems in post-conflict countries? And might the provision of public services by nonstate actors create problems of access, affordability, or quality? These are among the questions addressed in this book.

Water services and infrastructure are generally regarded as essential public goods that the state must provide for its population. The state's ability to do so (or to create enabling conditions for others to do so) is a key peace dividend and an indicator of progress in building peace after conflict. To maintain security and achieve credibility in the peacebuilding process, new governments often make promises designed to meet heightened expectations, including improved access to land, medical services, and education, as well as water and sanitation. Liberian president Ellen Johnson Sirleaf, for example, made numerous high-profile commitments to improving access to water and sanitation that were in line with the MDGs. Nevertheless, by 2006 (three years after Liberia's second civil war had ended), the "percentage of people with access to basic social services such as clean and safe drinking water . . . averaged about 40 percent of their pre-war levels" (ROL and UNDP 2006, 40). Moreover, in 2012, NGOs working in the water sector stated that they had yet to develop even 5 percent of the improved sources promised in Liberia's Poverty Reduction Strategy (Boley 2012). Thus, even with high-level political commitment, the rebuilding of water and sanitation infrastructure and delivery systems can take many years, especially where state institutions have been devastated by war and resources must be allocated among many competing redevelopment goals.

Continued violence and high insecurity further complicate the delivery of water and sanitation services in post-conflict situations. As a result, humanitarian and aid organizations often cede a certain amount of their role in recovery and

---

[4] See, for example, Welle (2008).

Shoring up peace: Water and post-conflict peacebuilding **11**

reconstruction to members of the military, who may be ill-equipped to undertake such activities. In Iraq, for example, after the 2003 bombing of the UN headquarters in Baghdad, UN agencies that had been involved in the early repair and rehabilitation of the water and sanitation sectors were forced to pull out. In addition to its original mandate to secure peace and help rebuild governance capacity, the Coalition Provisional Authority was then tasked with overseeing reconstruction efforts, including basic service provision and economic development (Jones et al. 2006). Ongoing violence, however, has rendered water infrastructure repair in urban areas an insurmountable challenge: during a few years in the mid-2000s, over 600 workers from the Ministry of Municipalities and Public Works were killed attempting to repair water and sanitation networks (Dhayi 2008). Similar difficulties in Afghanistan have led military units to integrate humanitarian interventions into counterinsurgency operations by establishing provincial reconstruction teams, which consist of civil affairs staff, members of the U.S. National Guard, and Afghan civilians (Palmer-Moloney 2014*; Civic 2014).

Despite the need for large influxes of capital to restore infrastructure, security risks have led the private sector to shy away from investing in the water sector in post-conflict countries (Schwartz, Hahn, and Bannon 2004). Often, in both urban and rural post-conflict environments, local communities (frequently with the support of NGOs) and the informal private sector have stepped in to fill the gap in water services (Pinera and Reed 2014*; Burt and Keiru 2014*). While such efforts meet a critical need, reliance on unregulated community-based institutions and the informal sector can lead to inequitable tariffs and uneven water quality and service. In Angola, for example, much of the water provided by the informal sector is neither treated nor tested for compliance with domestic water quality standards (Cain 2014*). In the DRC, however, in the absence of government delivery of safe drinking water, community-based groups built and managed small, piped-water networks (UNEP 2011). In this case, the assistance of an international NGO was instrumental in ensuring the necessary institutional and technical capacity to build and sustain the systems. Such efforts, often undertaken with limited resources, target specific underserved communities or locations. Whether such an approach might be scaled up to restore basic water and sanitation services to a large number of communities, or at the national level, and the extent to which such efforts can be integrated into national-level planning and policy making are questions for further research.

Finally, both interventions to improve water and sanitation, and peacebuilding activities more broadly, can significantly impact scarce water resources. A UN peacekeeper, for example, requires eighty-four liters of water per day; it is therefore essential for peacebuilding actors to take into account the possibility that they are competing with surrounding communities for water resources (Waleij et al. 2014; UNEP 2012). Recognizing the potential competition, peacekeepers have started to implement measures to conserve water. For example, to meet water requirements for UN peacekeeping operations in Sudan, Bengali troops are harvesting rainwater (Waleij et al. 2014).

12   Water and post-conflict peacebuilding

REBUILDING LIVELIHOODS AND REVITALIZING ECONOMIES

As post-conflict countries transition from short-term humanitarian assistance toward longer-term recovery and development, the sustainability of water supply, sanitation, irrigation, and other water sector interventions depends on strengthening state capacity to manage initiatives and build them into national policies and programs. Although the international community often tries to distinguish humanitarian efforts from development efforts, both are actually part of a development continuum that begins after war's end. Thus, even when decisions over water allocation and use are designed as humanitarian interventions, policy makers must recognize that such decisions will have implications for medium- and long-term development. For example, in addition to meeting basic needs, provision of immediate access to water creates a foundation for rebuilding livelihoods and the economy. Determining how water will be allocated and used for household consumption, agriculture, and industry is also key to development. The restoration of agricultural economies, for example, depends not only on access to fertile land but also on access to water resources.

Decisions about water allocation and use must also take environmental sustainability into account. In the case of humanitarian interventions, there is rarely time to assess the potential medium- to long-term impacts on water resources; nevertheless, those impacts may ultimately constrain options for livelihoods and sustainable development. Rapid impact assessment is one tool for overcoming such obstacles, as is better coordination among UN agencies undertaking post-conflict assessments (Conca and Wallace 2012; Kelly 2012). Moreover, interventions designed to rebuild livelihoods will need to reinforce social and environmental resilience—particularly with respect to climate variability. Such a comprehensive approach will help ensure post-conflict countries can cope with uncertainty and with increasingly frequent shocks to and stresses on water systems, including floods and droughts (Matthew and Hammill 2012).

Because interventions to support reconstruction and recovery occur in both urban and rural environments, various levels of government must coordinate in order to ensure policy coherence. Coordination is further complicated by the cross-sectoral nature of water; thus, decisions about water allocation and use must balance competing demands for water across sectors. Finally, it is important to ensure that short-term interventions lay the groundwork for (or at least do not create obstacles to) water governance frameworks that will provide an enabling environment for both sound resource management and sustaining the peace. For instance, ensuring food security at war's end is critical for facilitating the return and resettlement of refugees, IDPs, and demobilized soldiers. Such initiatives often entail infrastructural and institutional support for farmers' efforts to rekindle an agricultural sector devasted by conflict. But to succeed, land distribution and irrigation programs must take water rights and availability into account. Post-World War II Japan and post-partition India and Pakistan, for example, enhanced food security, rebuilt the agricultural sector, and fostered economic growth by

Shoring up peace: Water and post-conflict peacebuilding **13**

focusing early recovery efforts on the construction of irrigation and drainage systems in tandem with broader land and agricultural reforms (Sugiura, Toguchi, and Funiciello 2014*; Zawahri 2014*).

Choosing among various paths for post-conflict economic development invariably entails trade-offs. Because energy supply is often one of the greatest constraints to rebuilding post-conflict economies, construction or rehabilitation of large hydroelectric dams have been a common donor-supported initiative to foster economic development. Dams can also diversify energy resources: pumped-storage hydroelectric dams can store the potential energy from a mix of renewable sources.[5] Moreover, by storing excess water when it is plentiful and releasing water in times of scarcity, dams can also help regulate flows and facilitate flood and drought management.

A number of states faced with rapidly growing populations—including Afghanistan—continue to promote dam construction as a means of providing stable water supplies and electricity in the short term and bringing their populations out of poverty in the long term (Dehgan, Palmer-Moloney, and Mirzaee 2014*). It should be noted, however, that the construction of large-scale dams has also been associated with adverse social and environmental impacts, leading to local and regional conflict (Conca 2005). Dam construction and water storage require large tracts of (often arable) land; as a result, people living near the dams must be resettled. Dams also affect aquatic ecosystems, in many cases damaging the resource base on which local livelihoods depend. As countries emerge from conflict, decisions as to whether dams should be used to foster economic growth must take into account both domestic politics and the broader regional context. In some instances, such as in the Great Lakes region of Africa, hydroelectric production has provided a platform for regional cooperation (Westerkamp, Feil, and Thompson 2009).

Decision makers must also weigh the costs and benefits of various water tariff structures and the role of privatization in water management and service delivery. In the 1980s and 1990s, faced with rampant urban growth compounded by declining water quality and diminishing water supplies, many countries experimented with privatizing water services. By the end of the 1990s, more than fifty cities in twenty-seven developing countries had either privatized their water systems (through concessions or contracts with companies that paid the up-front costs of improving water supply and sanitation systems, in return for the profits from the operation) or leased them to nongovernmental entities for operation and maintenance (Noll, Shirley, and Cowan 2000).[6]

---

[5] Pumped-storage hydroelectric dams store energy from renewable sources for use when generating capacity might be low (for example, at night for solar power, or on calm days for wind power). When demand for electricity is low, a pumped-storage dam pumps water into a higher reservoir; when demand increases, water is released into a lower reservoir to generate power.

[6] See also McKenzie and Mookherjee (2005).

14 Water and post-conflict peacebuilding

Where state-owned water utilities have failed to maintain and retrofit infrastructure, various forms of public-private partnerships have also been seen as a viable solution (del Castillo 2008). If foreign investors are to recover the initial costs of connecting new users to the network, however, they often need to raise water tariffs—but because there are no alternatives to water, critics have noted that the negative impacts of such price increases fall disproportionately on the poor (Shiva 2002). Such price increases may further disenfranchise local populations in post-conflict countries, because even a minimal increase may make it prohibitively expensive for the very poor to reap welfare gains during the recovery period.

Another critical challenge is the dearth of hydrological data, including basic information on water quality and availability, which heightens uncertainty for interventions designed to restore livelihoods and the economy. Some gaps in data can be traced to the destruction caused by conflict; in many cases, however, baseline data never existed. In Afghanistan, for example, no hydrometeorological data has been collected for Helmand Basin—one of country's largest watersheds —since the late 1970s, before the Soviet invasion (Palmer-Moloney 2014*).

WATER, CONFLICT, AND PEACEBUILDING

Since the early 1990s, a great deal of literature in the field of international water management has focused on the relationship between conflict and water scarcity (both natural and human induced).[7] A number of highly publicized statements from world leaders further fueled the notion that water scarcity is an enduring source of conflict. Most notably, Boutros Boutros Ghali, an Egyptian politician and diplomat who later became UN Secretary-General, warned in 1985 that "the next war in the Middle East will be fought over water, not politics" (Vesilind 1993, 53).

As international water management has matured over the past few decades, more nuanced studies have examined the ways in which water can lead to conflict, as well as the ways in which it can facilitate peace (Conca and Dabelko 2002). Indeed, at the interstate level, scholars have found that cooperative behavior is more likely than conflict: of the 1,800 interactions that occurred in transboundary basins between 1946 and 1999, none led to formal war (Wolf, Yoffe, and Giordano 2003; Wolf et al. 2005). Even in the Middle East, most of the international tension over water has stayed at the level of heated rhetoric.

Researchers have found that the greatest likelihood for interstate conflict over water occurs during periods of institutional change (Wolf, Yoffe, and Giordano 2003). Since the 1990s, the collapse of the Soviet empire and the breakup of various states led to the formation of a number of new states in the Balkans, East-Central Europe, the former Soviet Union, and Africa. New political borders can wreak havoc on water-sharing arrangements—and can, at times, create new

---

[7] See, for example, Gleick (1993).

Shoring up peace: Water and post-conflict peacebuilding **15**

transboundary basins, as was the case with the Aral Sea Basin, in Central Asia, and the Sava Basin, in the former Yugoslavia (Weinthal 2002; Čolakhodžić et al. 2014*). In other cases, the breakup of states can change the number of riparians in an international river basin, as was the case in the Nile Basin after South Sudan's 2011 referendum vote for independence (Salman 2014*).

The securitization of water as a source of conflict, however, continues to pervade the field of international water management, particularly when it comes to arid regions in Africa and the Middle East. Studies of hydro-hegemony have emphasized that the structural and bargaining power of the riparians, which depends largely on whether a country is located upstream and on the extent of its economic and military resources, can determine whether water is more likely to lead to cooperation or conflict (Zeitoun and Warner 2006).

Although issues of conflict and scarcity have overshadowed the potential role of water management in peacebuilding, some studies (Conca and Dabelko 2002), as well as the chapters in this book, focus on the role of institutions and international water law in helping to foster cooperation and reconciliation. Some researchers have also begun to examine the role of transboundary treaties and water basin institutions as mechanisms that may help resolve conflict by building trust and confidence through joint management and technical cooperation (Conca, Wu, and Mei 2006). Others have looked at the relationship between international water management and state building to understand the ways in which international actors can help foster peaceful relations, regarding water, during transitional periods (Weinthal 2002). Still others have looked at the role of local institutions and approaches in negotiation and conflict resolution (Wolf 2000).

The specter of climate change, and its potential impact on the availability and distribution of freshwater resources, has compounded the fear that so-called water wars are inevitable. Through a large-scale study of rainfall variability and political conflict in Africa, Cullen Hendrix and Idean Salehyan found a robust relationship between social unrest and extreme deviations in rainfall (Hendrix and Salehyan 2012). Thomas Bernauer and Tobias Siegfried have argued that climate-change-induced shifts in river runoff will likely exacerbate interstate tensions over water in Central Asia, particularly between Kyrgyzstan and Uzbekistan (Bernauer and Siegfried 2012). Other observers, however, caution that accounts seeking to link climate change to conflict should avoid hyperbole, and should instead focus on the channels through which climate change is likely to interact with other variables, such as governance, in exacerbating both climate- and non-climate-related vulnerabilities and thus acting as a potential conflict multiplier (Raleigh and Urdal 2007; Matthew et al. 2010; UN 2009; Mayoral 2012; Dabelko 2009).

There is no question that in some parts of the world, water scarcity has indeed led to local conflicts. In northeastern Kenya, for example, recurrent droughts have forced the Turkana people—a pastoralist population in East Africa—to travel farther and more frequently to find water and pasture for their livestock.

16   Water and post-conflict peacebuilding

Often, other pastoralist groups interpret such movement as aggression. Meanwhile, in the absence of state protection, pastoralist communities have obtained small arms, and violent localized conflicts have led to dozens of deaths (IRIN 2009b, 2009c).[8]

Climate variability can also have cross-border effects. For example, protracted drought throughout the Horn of Africa and decades of internal conflict in Somalia have overwhelmed efforts to deal with widespread famine, forcing large-scale migrations of Somalis into Kenya and Ethiopia (Afifi et al. 2012).

Nevertheless, the effects of climate change on water availability do not necessarily lead to conflict. Because water is a shared resource, scholars have argued that a collective desire for survival renders cooperation over shared water basins viable (Meinzen-Dick and Nkonya 2005). In northern Kenya, for example, a sense of mutual dependence may account for the strength of some local institutions —which, instead of engaging in the widespread conflicts over resources in that area, have cooperated to cope with issues of water scarcity and drought (Adano et al. 2012). Furthermore, some international institutions and treaties may be better able to accommodate water variability in international river basins, and thereby mitigate conflict (De Stefano et al. 2012). However, most water treaties lack the flexibility necessary to cope with the uncertainty engendered by climate variability and change (Carius 2009).

ORGANIZATION OF THE BOOK

This book explores options for improving post-conflict peacebuilding by integrating water into the peacebuilding process. Part 1 focuses on the challenge of providing clean water and sanitation in post-conflict settings in order to alleviate humanitarian crises. The chapters in this part explore the ways in which access to water and sanitation services can provide peace dividends by addressing the immediate and basic needs of the population. Given that armed conflict disrupts traditional social norms and coping mechanisms, forcing communities to migrate and to compete for water access even when seeking refuge, part 1 examines an array of interventions to resolve conflict over access to water and sanitation in the face of weakened state capacity. Finally, the chapters address the critical role of informal water suppliers, especially in urban and peri-urban centers where state institutional capacity is lacking.

The chapters in part 2 examine the ways in which water can be harnessed to help restore livelihoods, foster sustainable development, reduce poverty, and attain food security. Taken together, the analyses show that success depends on the quality of the water data and on the extent to which (1) affected populations are involved in the design and maintenance of water systems and (2) decisions

---

[8]   For an analysis of livestock management, conflict, and peacebuilding in the Karimojong Cluster, see Lind (2014).

take account of the broader institutional context. In particular, the chapters emphasize that coordination between the water and agricultural sectors is necessary to reinvigorate the agricultural sector, which in post-conflict countries is the sector that most supports livelihood restoration.

Part 3 explores the ways in which water management can foster cooperation, build confidence, and increase trust among former adversaries. The chapters show that where water is a source of tension, it is essential to include discussions of the water sector in the formal peace process and to institutionalize this cooperation through formal governance mechanisms, such as joint water commissions (at the international level) or domestic mechanisms to address multilevel and intersectoral water governance.

The chapters in part 3 also highlight the importance of civil society engagement in international waters—specifically, the ways in which face-to-face meetings between citizens can further strengthen trust and confidence across borders. Another theme that runs through part 3 is the importance of incentives, typically provided by third parties, to encourage states that share water basins to build cooperative water governance institutions, as a first step in the larger process of regional reconciliation. (Here, too, the chapters show that a dearth of reliable water data can impede cooperation.) Finally, chapters examining countries that have undergone partition consider water management in relation to changing political borders, within the broader context of state building and regional water management.

Building on part 3, which considers how the design of treaties can be used to support regional cooperation, part 4 examines the domestic legal frameworks that undergird water management. Although there is no single path for effective water management, whatever legal framework is chosen will set the initial institutional context for how water is allocated and used. For example, including a right to water and sanitation in a constitution can both address past discrimination in access to water and facilitate reconciliation and trust building.

While the parts focus on basic services, economic development, cooperation, and legal institutions, the chapters also highlight the many feedback mechanisms and connections between these domains. Cooperation, for example, is essential not only for building trust but also for ensuring that allocation of water among sectors can be accomplished equitably and effectively. Water governance and institutional frameworks—also central to all chapters—allow for sound resource management and can foster reconciliation in post-conflict situations.

CONCLUSION

The chapters that follow demonstrate that restoring water services and infrastructure is critical to the transition from conflict to peace, and must be integrated into programs designed to reestablish security, governance, reconciliation, and economic reconstruction. Taken as a whole, the book demonstrates the urgency of finding more integrated and effective mechanisms for addressing water

18 Water and post-conflict peacebuilding

resources as part of the broader peacebuilding process—that is, as a means of ensuring that basic human needs are met, that economic development progresses, and that peace is sustained.

REFERENCES

Adano, W. R., T. Dietz, K. Witsenburg, and F. Zaal. 2012. Climate change, violent conflict and local institutions in Kenya's drylands. *Journal of Peace Research* 49 (1): 65–80.

Afifi, T., R. Govil, P. Sakdapolrak, and K. Warner. 2012. Climate change, vulnerability and human mobility: Perspectives of refugees from the East and Horn of Africa. Report No. 1. Bonn, Germany: Institute for Environment and Human Security, United Nations University. www.ehs.unu.edu/file/get/9951.pdf.

Bernauer, T., and T. Siegfried. 2012. Climate change and international water conflict in Central Asia. *Journal of Peace Research* 49 (1): 227–239.

Boley, T. 2012. In Liberia, political battles center on water access. PBS Newshour, April 25. www.pbs.org/newshour/rundown/2012/04/in-liberia-political-battles-center-on-water -access.html.

Bruch, C., D. Jensen, M. Nakayama, and J. Unruh. 2014. *Post-conflict peacebuilding and natural resources: The promise and the peril.* New York: Cambridge University Press.

Burt, M., and B. J. Keiru. 2014. Community water management: Experiences from the Democratic Republic of the Congo, Afghanistan, and Liberia. In *Water and post-conflict peacebuilding*, ed. E. Weinthal, J. Troell, and M. Nakayama. London: Earthscan.

Cain, A. 2014. Conflict and collaboration for water resources in Angola's post-war cities. In *Water and post-conflict peacebuilding*, ed. E. Weinthal, J. Troell, and M. Nakayama. London: Earthscan.

Carius, A. 2009. Climate change and security in Africa: Challenges and international policy context. Paper commissioned by the United Nations Office of the Special Adviser on Africa for the expert group meeting "Natural Resources, Climate Change and Conflict in Africa: Protecting Africa's Natural Resource Base in Support of Durable Peace and Sustainable Development," New York, December 17–18.

Civic, M. A. 2014. Civil-military coordination and cooperation in peacebuilding and natural resource management: An enabling framework, challenges, and incremental progress. In *Governance, natural resources, and post-conflict peacebuilding*, ed. C. Bruch, C. Muffett, and S. S. Nichols. London: Earthscan.

Čolakhodžić, A., M. Filipović, J. Kovandžić, and S. Stec. 2014. The Sava River: Transitioning to peace in the former Yugoslavia. In *Water and post-conflict peacebuilding*, ed. E. Weinthal, J. Troell, and M. Nakayama. London: Earthscan.

Conca, K. 2005. *Governing water: Contentious transnational politics and global institution building.* Cambridge, MA: MIT Press.

Conca, K., and G. D. Dabelko, eds. 2002. *Environmental peacemaking.* Washington, D.C.: Woodrow Wilson Center Press; Baltimore, MD: Johns Hopkins University Press.

Conca, K., and J. Wallace. 2012. Environment and peacebuilding in war-torn societies: Lessons from the UN Environment Programme's experience with post-conflict assessment. In *Assessing and restoring natural resources in post-conflict peacebuilding*, ed. D. Jensen and S. Lonergan. London: Earthscan.

Shoring up peace: Water and post-conflict peacebuilding 19

Conca, K., F. Wu, and C. Mei. 2006. Global regime formation or complex institution building? The principled content of international river agreements. *International Studies Quarterly* 50 (2): 263–285.

CPHD (Center for Policy and Human Development). 2011. *Afghanistan human development report 2011. The forgotten front: Water security and the crisis in sanitation.* Kabul, Afghanistan: Kabul University. www.cphd.af/nhdr/nhdr2010/Complete%20 NHDR%202011%20final.pdf.

CRS (Catholic Relief Services). 2009. *Water and conflict: Incorporating peacebuilding into water development.* Baltimore, MD. www.crsprogramquality.org/storage/pubs/ peacebuilding/waterconflict.pdf.

Dabelko, G. D. 2009. Avoid hyperbole, oversimplification when climate and security meet. *Bulletin of the Atomic Scientists*, August 24. http://thebulletin.org/avoid-hyperbole -oversimplification-when-climate-and-security-meet.

Dehgan, A., L. J. Palmer-Moloney, and M. Mirzaee. 2014. Water security and scarcity: Potential destabilization in western Afghanistan and Iranian Sistan and Baluchestan due to transboundary water conflicts. In *Water and post-conflict peacebuilding*, ed. E. Weinthal, J. Troell, and M. Nakayama. London: Earthscan.

del Castillo, G. 2008. *Rebuilding war-torn states: The challenge of post-conflict economic reconstruction.* New York: Oxford University Press.

De Stefano, L., J. Duncan, S. Dinar, K. Stahl, K. M. Strzepek, and A. T. Wolf. 2012. Climate change and the institutional resilience of international river basins. *Journal of Peace Research* 49 (1): 193–209.

Dhayi, B. 2008. Iraq's water and sanitation crisis adds to dangers faced by children and families. Unicef.com, March 19. www.unicef.org/infobycountry/iraq_43232.html.

ECOSOC (Economic and Social Council, United Nations). 2010. Joint special event of the Economic and Social Council (ECOSOC) and the peacebuilding commission (PBC) on "MDGs in countries emerging from conflict." Issues note. New York, July 19. http://esango.un.org/event/documents/ISSUES%20NOTE%20-%20FINAL.doc.

FAO (Food and Agriculture Organization of the United Nations). 2013. AQUASTAT database. www.fao.org/nr/water/aquastat/data/query/index.html?lang=en.

Formoli, T. A. 1995. Impacts of the Afghan-Soviet war on Afghanistan's environment. *Environmental Conservation* 22 (1): 66–69.

Ghobarah, H. A., P. Huth, and B. Russett. 2003. Civil wars kill and maim people—Long after the shooting stops. *American Political Science Review* 97 (2): 189–202.

Gleick, P. H. 1993. Water and conflict: Fresh water resources and international security. *International Security* 18 (1): 79–112.

Haavisto, P. 2003. Conflict and the environment: Lessons learned. *Environment House News* 8:1–3.

Hendrix, C., and I. Salehyan. 2012. Climate change, rainfall, and social conflict in Africa. *Journal of Peace Research* 49 (1): 35–50.

Institute for Water and Watersheds. n.d. International river basins of the world. Table 4: International river basin register. Oregon State University. www.transboundarywaters .orst.edu/publications/register/tables/IRB_table_4.html.

International Dialogue on Peacebuilding and Statebuilding. 2011. A new deal for engagement in fragile states. www.oecd.org/dataoecd/35/50/49151944.pdf.

IRC (International Rescue Committee). 2008. Mortality in the Democratic Republic of Congo: An ongoing crisis. IRC and Burnet Institute. www.rescue.org/sites/default/files/ migrated/resources/2007/2006-7_congomortalitysurvey.pdf.

20 Water and post-conflict peacebuilding

IRIN (Integrated Regional Information Networks). 2006. *Running dry: The humanitarian impact of the global water crisis*. Nairobi, Kenya. www.irinnews.org/pdf/in-depth/Running-Dry-IRIN-In-Depth.pdf.

———. 2009a. Chad: Daily needs squeeze dwindling resources in east. April 24. www.irinnews.org/Report.aspx?ReportId=84107.

———. 2009b. Kenya: Drought exacerbating conflict among pastoralists. February 2. www.irinnews.org/Report.aspx?ReportId=82683.

———. 2009c. Kenya: The dangers of pastoralism. July 13. www.irinnews.org/Report.aspx?ReportId=85252.

Jacobsen, K. 2010. Internal displacement to urban areas: The Tufts-IDMC profiling study; Case 1: Khartoum, Sudan. Geneva, Switzerland: Feinstein International Center, Tufts University, in collaboration with Internal Displacement Monitoring Centre. www.scribd.com/fullscreen/5502724?access_key=key-dpm84w1o18p0ojbyj5s.

Jones, S. G., L. H. Hilborne, C. R. Anthony, L. M. Davis, F. Girosi, C. Benard, R. M. Swanger, A. D. Garten, and A. Timilsina. 2006. *Securing health: Lessons from nation-building missions*. Santa Monica, CA: RAND Center for Domestic and International Health Security.

Kelly, C. 2012. Mitigating the environmental impacts of post-conflict assistance: Assessing USAID's approach. In *Assessing and restoring natural resources in post-conflict peacebuilding*, ed. D. Jensen and S. Lonergan. London: Earthscan.

Lind, J. 2014. Manufacturing peace in "no man's land": Livestock and access to natural resources in the Karimojong Cluster of Kenya and Uganda. In *Livelihoods, natural resources, and post-conflict peacebuilding*, ed. H. Young and L. Goldman. London: Earthscan.

Matthew, R. A., J. Barnett, B. McDonald, and K. L. O'Brien. 2010. *Global environmental change and human security*. Cambridge, MA: MIT Press.

Matthew, R., and A. Hammill. 2012. Peacebuilding and adaptation to climate change. In *Assessing and restoring natural resources in post-conflict peacebuilding*, ed. D. Jensen and S. Lonergan. London: Earthscan.

Mayoral, A. 2012. Climate change as a conflict multiplier. Peace Brief No. 120. Washington, D.C.: United States Institute of Peace. www.usip.org/publications/climate-change-conflict-multiplier.

McCarthy, J., and D. Mustafa. 2014. Despite the best intentions? Experiences with water resource management in northern Afghanistan. In *Water and post-conflict peacebuilding*, ed. E. Weinthal, J. Troell, and M. Nakayama. London: Earthscan.

McKenzie, D., and D. Mookherjee. 2005. Paradox and perception: Evidence from four Latin American countries. In *Reality check: The distributional impact of privatization in developing countries*, ed. J. Nellis and N. Birdsall. Washington, D.C.: Center for Global Development.

Meinzen-Dick, R., and L. Nkonya. 2005. Understanding legal pluralism in water rights: Lessons from Africa and Asia. Paper presented at the international workshop "African Water Laws: Plural Legislative Frameworks for Rural Water Management in Africa," Johannesburg, South Africa, January 26–28.

Noll, R., M. M. Shirley, and S. Cowan. 2000. Reforming urban water systems in developing countries. In *Economic policy reform: The second stage*, ed. A. O. Krueger. Chicago, IL: University of Chicago Press.

Palmer-Moloney, L. J. 2014. Water's role in measuring security and stability in Helmand Province, Afghanistan. In *Water and post-conflict peacebuilding*, ed. E. Weinthal, J. Troell, and M. Nakayama. London: Earthscan.

Shoring up peace: Water and post-conflict peacebuilding   21

Pinera, J.-F., and R. A. Reed. 2014. A tale of two cities: Restoring water services in Kabul and Monrovia. In *Water and post-conflict peacebuilding*, ed. E. Weinthal, J. Troell, and M. Nakayama. London: Earthscan.

Raleigh, C., and H. Urdal. 2007. Climate change, environmental degradation and armed conflict. *Political Geography* 26 (6): 674–694.

ROL (Republic of Liberia) and UNDP (United Nations Development Programme). 2006. *National human development report 2006: Liberia*. Monrovia. http://hdr.undp.org/en/reports/nationalreports/africa/liberia/LIBERIA_2006_en.pdf.

———. 2010. *Republic of Liberia: Progress, prospects and challenges towards achieving the MDGs; Millennium Development Goals 2010 report*. Monrovia.

Salman, S. M. A. 2014. Water resources in the Sudan North-South peace process and the ramifications of the secession of South Sudan. In *Water and post-conflict peacebuilding*, ed. E. Weinthal, J. Troell, and M. Nakayama. London: Earthscan.

Schwartz, J., S. Hahn, and I. Bannon. 2004. The private sector's role in the provision of infrastructure in post-conflict countries: Patterns and policy options. Social Development Papers, Conflict Prevention & Reconstruction Paper No. 16. August. Washington, D. C.: World Bank. http://siteresources.worldbank.org/INTCPR/214578-1111996036679/20618754/WP16_Web.pdf.

Setchell, C. A., and C. N. Luther. 2009. Urban displacement and growth amidst humanitarian crisis: New realities require a new strategy in Kabul. *Monday Developments*. October. http://transition.usaid.gov/our_work/humanitarian_assistance/disaster_assistance/sectors/files/urban_displacement_kabul_09.pdf.

Sharp, T. W., F. M. Burkle Jr., A. F. Vaughn, R. Chotani, and R. J. Brennan. 2002. Challenges and opportunities for humanitarian relief in Afghanistan. *Clinical Infectious Diseases* 34 (supplement 5): S215–S228.

Shiva, V. 2002. *Water wars: Privatization, pollution, and profit*. Cambridge, MA: South End Press.

Sphere Project. 2004. *Humanitarian charter and minimum standards in disaster response*. Geneva, Switzerland. http://ocw.jhsph.edu/courses/refugeehealthcare/PDFs/SphereProjectHandbook.pdf.

———. 2011. *Humanitarian charter and minimum standards in humanitarian response*. Geneva, Switzerland. www.sphereproject.org/resources/download-publications/?search=1&keywords=&language=English&category=22.

Sugiura, M., Y. Toguchi, and M. Funiciello. 2014. Irrigation management and flood control in post–World War II Japan. In *Water and post-conflict peacebuilding*, ed. E. Weinthal, J. Troell, and M. Nakayama. London: Earthscan.

Tearfund. 2007. Darfur: Relief in a vulnerable environment. Middlesex, UK. www.tearfund.org/webdocs/website/Campaigning/Policy%20and%20research/Relief%20in%20a%20vulnerable%20envirionment%20final.pdf.

TI (Transparency International). 2008. *Global corruption report 2008: Corruption in the water sector*. New York: Cambridge University Press.

UCDP (Uppsala Conflict Data Program). n.d. UCDP database. www.ucdp.uu.se/gpdatabase/search.php.

UN (United Nations). 2009. *The Millennium Development Goals report 2009*. New York.

———. 2011. *Civilian capacity in the aftermath of conflict: Independent report of the Senior Advisory Group*. New York. http://civcapreview.org/Default.aspx?tabid=3735&ctl=Details&mid=6436&Itemid=3148&language=en-US.

22 Water and post-conflict peacebuilding

———. 2012. Secretary-General's remarks to Opening Session of the General Assembly High-Level Forum on the Culture of Peace. www.un.org/sg/statements/index.asp?nid =6292.

UNDESA (United Nations Department of Economic and Social Affairs). n.d. Water scarcity. www.un.org/waterforlifedecade/scarcity.shtml.

UNEP (United Nations Environment Programme). 2004. *Desk study on the environment in Liberia.* Geneva, Switzerland.

———. 2011. *The Democratic Republic of Congo: Post-conflict environmental assessment—Synthesis for policy makers.* Nairobi, Kenya.

———. 2012. *Greening the blue helmets: Environment, natural resources and UN peacekeeping operations.* Policy Paper No. 3. Nairobi, Kenya. http://postconflict.unep.ch/ publications/UNEP_greening_blue_helmets.pdf.

UNGA (United Nations General Assembly). 2010. Resolution 64/292. A/RES/64/292 (2010). August 3. www.un.org/ga/search/view_doc.asp?symbol=A/RES/64/292.

UNHCR (Office of the United Nations High Commissioner for Refugees). 2009. Update on UNHCR's water programme. February 16. www.unhcr.org/49b4eb802.html.

UNICEF (United Nations Children's Fund) and WHO (World Health Organization). 2012. *Progress on drinking water and sanitation: 2012 update.* New York. www.unicef.org/ media/files/JMPreport2012.pdf.

UNSG (United Nations Secretary-General). 2009. *Report of the Secretary-General on peacebuilding in the immediate aftermath of conflict.* A/63/881–S/2009/304. June 11. New York. www.unrol.org/files/pbf_090611_sg.pdf.

———. 2010. *Progress report of the Secretary-General on peacebuilding in the immediate aftermath of conflict.* A/64/866–S/2010/386. July 16 (reissued on August 19 for technical reasons). New York.

———. 2012. *Peacebuilding in the aftermath of conflict: Report of the Secretary-General.* A/67/499–S/2012/746. October 8. New York.

UNSG's (United Nations Secretary-General's) Policy Committee. 2007. Conceptual basis for peacebuilding for the UN system. May. New York.

UN Water and FAO (Food and Agriculture Organization of the United Nations). 2007. Coping with water scarcity: Challenge of the twenty-first century. www.unwater.org/ wwd07/downloads/documents/escarcity.pdf.

USIP (United States Institute of Peace) and U.S. Army PKSOI (United States Army Peacekeeping and Stability Operations Institute). 2009. *Guiding principles for stabilization and reconstruction.* Washington, D.C.: Endowment of the United States Institute of Peace.

Vesilind, P. J. 1993. Water: The Middle East's critical resource. *National Geographic* 183 (5): 38–70.

Vidal, J. 2010. Kabul faces severe water crisis. *Guardian*, July 19. www.guardian.co.uk/ world/2010/jul/19/kabul-faces-severe-water-crisis.

Waldman, M. 2008. Community peacebuilding in Afghanistan: The case for a national strategy. Oxford, UK: Oxfam International. www.oxfam.ca/news-and-publications/ publications-and-reports/community-peacebuilding-in-afghanistan-the-case-for-a -national-strategy.

Waleij, A., T. Bosetti, R. Doran, and B. Liljedahl. 2014. Environmental stewardship in peace operations: The role of the military. In *Governance, natural resources, and postconflict peacebuilding*, ed. C. Bruch, C. Muffett, and S. S. Nichols. London: Earthscan.

Shoring up peace: Water and post-conflict peacebuilding   23

Water Aid. 2011. Off-track, off-target: Why investment in water, sanitation and hygiene is not reaching those who need it most. www.wateraid.org/~/media/Publications/water -sanitation-hygiene-investment.pdf.

Weinthal, E. 2002. *State making and environmental cooperation: Linking domestic and international politics in Central Asia.* Cambridge, MA: MIT Press.

Welle, K. 2008. Improving the provision of basic services for the poor in fragile environments: Water supply, sanitation and hygiene; International literature review. London: Overseas Development Institute. www.odi.org.uk/sites/odi.org.uk/files/odi-assets/publications -opinion-files/3603.pdf.

Westerkamp, M., M. Feil, and A. Thompson 2009. Regional cooperation in the Great Lakes region: A contribution to peacebuilding? Brussels, Belgium: Initiative for Peacebuilding. www.adelphi.de/files/uploads/andere/pdf/application/pdf/us_038_-_regional _cooperation_in_the_great_lakes_region.pdf.

Wolf, A. T. 2000. Indigenous approaches to water conflict negotiations and implications for international waters. *International Negotiation* 5 (2): 357–373.

Wolf, A. T., A. Kramer, A. Carius, and G. D. Dabelko. 2005. Managing water conflict and cooperation. In *State of the world 2005: Redefining global security*, ed. M. Renner, H. French, and E. Assadourian. New York: Norton.

Wolf, A. T., S. B. Yoffe, and M. Giordano. 2003. International waters: Identifying basins at risk. *Water Policy* 5 (1): 29–60.

World Bank. 2011. *World development report: Conflict, security, and development.* Washington, D.C.

———. 2013. Twenty fragile states make progress on Millennium Development Goals. May 1. Washington, D.C. www.worldbank.org/en/news/press-release/2013/05/01/twenty -fragile-states-make-progress-on-millennium-development-goals.

Zawahri, N. A. 2014. Refugee rehabilitation and transboundary cooperation: India, Pakistan, and the Indus River system. In *Water and post-conflict peacebuilding*, ed. E. Weinthal, J. Troell, and M. Nakayama. London: Earthscan.

Zeitoun, M., and J. Warner. 2006. Hydro-hegemony—a framework for analysis of trans-boundary water conflicts. *Water Policy* 8 (5): 435–460.

PART 1

Basic services and human security

Introduction

The provision of safe drinking water and adequate sanitation is essential for helping war-torn societies avert a humanitarian crisis in the wake of conflict. War often takes a heavy toll on basic services and infrastructure, including water and sanitation systems. Thus, obtaining safe water is one of the most pressing issues facing post-conflict populations—including refugees and former combatants, whether they are returning home at conflict's end or remaining in refugee or displacement camps. From the perspective of public health, ensuring access to water in post-conflict situations is a high priority because the lack of potable drinking water and sanitary living conditions exposes populations—many of which are unsettled and migratory—to an increased risk of disease and death.

How countries choose to rebuild water and sanitation infrastructure and provide the associated services greatly influences human security in post-conflict situations. For deeply divided societies, the mere construction of a water and sanitation system can foster unity by deepening interdependence and requiring cooperation in the management of the infrastructure. At the same time, determining where to locate such services without ensuring that stakeholders are involved in decision making and fully understand the factors informing the decisions can exacerbate tensions and undermine the legitimacy of the post-conflict government.

The restoration of water and sanitation services or the extension of those services to new populations is also essential to mitigating high levels of mortality from the spread of waterborne and water-washed illnesses—notably cholera and typhoid—in post-conflict countries. Furthermore, improving access to clean water and sanitation can generate a wide array of welfare gains—by, for example, reducing the time spent searching for water on a daily basis. As a result, adults can invest more time engaged in (or looking for) productive work, and children —especially young girls, who are most likely to bear responsibility for having to procure water—can spend more time in school.

To generate both health and economic welfare gains immediately after conflict ends, humanitarian organizations have identified the provision of basic services as an essential early intervention. In "The Role of Informal Service Providers in Post-Conflict Reconstruction and State Building," Jeremy Allouche argues that the provision of basic services in post-conflict states, especially the restoration of water and sanitation, does not occur in an institutional vacuum but is instead part of the larger political process of reconstituting state institutions. Having situated the process of restoring service delivery within the state-building process, Allouche further argues that state builders in post-conflict situations cannot assume that a centralized state is necessary for service delivery. During conflict, when state institutions are often absent, informal institutions tend to occupy the space that the state is normally presumed to hold as the provider of public goods.

28 Water and post-conflict peacebuilding

Thus, Allouche sets forth an innovative alternative model of state building that focuses on the role of the informal sector in post-conflict reconstruction. In doing so, he also shows that service delivery is not a benign process of public goods provision, but a highly political process in which political leaders can use the provision of water and sanitation not only to establish the legitimacy of the state, but also as a political tool to defeat or co-opt rivals.

In addition to facing the immediate need to avert a humanitarian crisis at war's end, international organizations and political leaders in post-conflict countries must focus on reestablishing security and stability—both of which are central to the state-building process, and involve, among other actions, (1) the disarmament, demobilization, and reintegration of former combatants and (2) the restoration of the political process by means of elections. Because international organizations and domestic leaders are largely preoccupied with reestablishing security and stability, civil society (including humanitarian organizations) must often step in to help provide basic services, and may even play a central role in helping countries (1) expand services to peri-urban and rural populations and (2) make progress toward the water- and sanitation-related Millennium Development Goals (MDGs). (Target 10 of the MDGs, established in 2000 by the member states of the United Nations, calls for halving the proportion of the world's population that lacks sustainable access to safe drinking water and basic sanitation by 2015).

In rural and, less often, peri-urban areas, nongovernmental organizations (NGOs) carry out projects focused on specific poor communities. In "A Tale of Two Cities: Restoring Water Services in Kabul and Monrovia," Jean-François Pinera and Robert A. Reed suggest that such community-based projects may not be best suited, however, for large urban areas. By examining different strategies for rehabilitating urban water services in Kabul, Afghanistan, and Monrovia, Liberia, Pinera and Reed find that the ability to provide water services depends largely on the interactions between aid agencies, water utilities, and local communities. Whereas the state and development organizations often prefer "legibility" and formality in water service systems,[1] Pinera and Reed stress the importance of recognizing and working with the informal sector—including illegal water vendors —to ensure that the poorest segments of urban populations have access to water.

Populations in post-conflict situations are likely to be in flux; often, significant numbers of people have fled the countryside for the relative safety of urban and peri-urban environments. Once conflict has ended, many displaced persons seek to remain in urban areas, in search of greater security and economic opportunity. But because the urban infrastructure is already crippled or overtaxed, these

---

[1] As Jamie Linton explains in *What Is Water? The History of a Modern Abstraction*, "James C. Scott uses the term 'legibility' to describe the means and apparatus by which the state has sought command of a vastly complex field, reducing it to a framework and to terms that are actionable by government agencies so as to bring things under control" (Linton 2010, 152).

Basic services and human security **29**

informal settlements often lack safe water and sanitation. In "Conflict and Collaboration for Water Resources in Angola's Post-War Cities," Allan Cain draws on decades of the NGO Development Workshop's experience in Angola to reveal a stark link between water services and poverty: as migrants flowed into peri-urban settlements in Luanda, Angola, they were forced to spend increasing amounts of their household income on more expensive and poorer-quality water from tanker trucks. In keeping with the perspectives of Allouche, and Pinera and Reed, Cain underscores the role of the informal economy as the main provider of water services to post-conflict populations, while also demonstrating the importance of community-based management for improving access to water; they also note that governments have been forced to accept the reality of the informal sector as the main supplier of water beyond the official network of household connections. Cain thus argues that the residents of informal settlements must be included in decision making and in negotiations with local authorities and the state water company, precisely because these residents are the conveyers of knowledge and capacity.

The provision of basic services is not disconnected from interventions designed to secure water resources for other sectors of the economy. In "Thirsty for Peace: The Water Sector in South Sudan," Sam Huston explores intersectoral coordination. Since the 2005 Comprehensive Peace Agreement, the MDGs for water, sanitation, and hygiene have provided the basis for the newly established government of South Sudan to extend water services to its population.[2] Huston argues, however, that such initiatives can also generate new conflicts by failing to take into account other water uses. In South Sudan, for example, the government and humanitarian organizations had to provide water under emergency situations, both during and in the years immediately following conflict; as a result, they overlooked the provision of water for livestock, which not only sparked local conflicts over water but also undermined longer-term capacity development by failing to engage communities in decisions about how and where to provide water services. On the basis of his experiences as the program coordinator for Pact Sudan's Water for Recovery and Peace Program, the author demonstrates the importance of fostering conflict-sensitive dialogue among communities about water, as a means of both reducing tensions and improving community members' understanding of the factors underlying local or national decisions about water allocation.

Because women and girls are primarily responsible for water collection and management in both rural and urban settings, tailoring basic service interventions to empower women and girls can generate important welfare gains, including improved health, economic revitalization, reduced gender-based violence, and the restoration of peace. In "Community Water Management: Experiences from the Democratic Republic of the Congo, Afghanistan, and Liberia," Murray Burt

---

[2] In July 2011, Southern Sudan seceded from Sudan and became South Sudan. Huston's chapter focuses on activities that occurred before independence.

30 Water and post-conflict peacebuilding

and Bilha Joy Keiru draw upon the experience of Tearfund, an international NGO, in improving water management in war-torn societies. In their fieldwork in three post-conflict countries, Burt and Keiru found that women were the most likely to be concerned about poor water quality, to advocate for safe drinking water, and to lead reconciliation efforts. Moreover, empowering women in donor-related water interventions can provide a critical opportunity for women to take on leadership roles in post-conflict reconstruction. Burt and Keiru note, however, that to facilitate the restoration of basic services and to strengthen capacity building for water management, gender inequality and gender-based violence must be addressed.

Many post-conflict countries are still marred by violence and insecurity, hampering the provision of basic services. The level of violence in countries such as Afghanistan and Iraq has restricted UN and other humanitarian operations to certain areas and forced the military and local entities to assume a larger role in basic service provision. In "Environmental Management of the Iraqi Marshlands in the Post-Conflict Period," Chizuru Aoki, Ali Al-Lami, and Sivapragasam Kugaprasatham reflect on the efforts of the United Nations Environment Programme (UNEP) to improve the welfare of populations that returned to the Iraqi marshlands after having been displaced for more than a decade. UNEP developed a project that would provide drinking water and rehabilitate the wetlands, but because UN staff were barred from entering the country to oversee the project, Iraqi personnel were charged, almost from the outset, with implementation. The authors demonstrate that in this case, a smaller role for an international organization bolstered both local capacity and trust between local communities and public authorities.

The state's ability to provide clean water and sanitation or to create enabling conditions for others to provide them are key indicators of progress in building peace after conflict. The chapters in part 1 stress the amount of time and the array of actors and interventions that are required to rebuild infrastructure and service delivery systems. The chapters also highlight the importance of engaging the informal sector and local communities in the reconstruction of delivery systems and services.

REFERENCE

Linton, J. 2010. *What is water? The history of a modern abstraction.* Vancouver, Canada: UBC Press.

The role of informal service providers in post-conflict reconstruction and state building

Jeremy Allouche

Violent conflict has a strong impact on individuals' livelihoods, well-being, and security. Post-conflict reconstruction priorities include ensuring that citizens' fundamental needs are met and restarting economic activity. Reducing poverty, promoting social welfare, and facilitating economic growth are three important steps in any such agenda. In this respect, restoring service delivery (or establishing it for the first time) is central to reconstruction (UNDP and UNDESA 2007). There is a need for more research on governance models for the post-conflict delivery of basic services such as health, education, electricity, water, and sanitation.

War, conflict, and violence reconfigure the state's authority, monopoly of power, and legitimacy. War diminishes the state's taxation capacity; many government departments and state agencies have been destroyed or seen their technical and human capacities weakened. In regions where state authority has been contested during civil war, in particular, the end of violence does not guarantee that the state will be accepted as a legitimate institution.

These issues give rise to two separate agendas: post-conflict reconstruction and state building. This chapter analyzes the relationship between the two, using the example of service delivery as an essential aspect of state (re)legitimization. Delivery of services is seen by donors as a way both to improve citizens' lives and to enhance the state's legitimacy and authority (Eldon and Gunby 2009). This view underpins the liberal peace model (Paris 2010) that serves as the normative basis for both agendas in post-colonial countries.

This chapter argues that current debates on state building are flawed because they employ a European and Weberian conception of state building premised on the conception of the state as a legal personality, an ordering power, and a set

---

Jeremy Allouche is a research fellow at the Institute of Development Studies at the University of Sussex in Brighton, United Kingdom.

32   Water and post-conflict peacebuilding

of formal arrangements that institutionalize power.[1] This conception is not well adapted to service delivery and state building in most contemporary post-conflict situations, because it does not take informal governance and service provision into account.[2]

Informal systems or institutions may arise either to oppose state authority or to provide services when the state fails to do so. In the first case, state building requires restoring the legitimacy of the state (Lemay-Hébert 2009); in the second case, it entails creating more effective state institutions (Brinkerhoff 2005).

Providing access to water services in post-conflict situations does not just improve citizens' lives but also represents an important instrument for state building and enhancing state legitimacy. Political legitimacy derives from the government's right to govern and from the explicit and implicit consent of the governed. The governance of formal and informal water systems may either support or undermine state building. This chapter argues that donor approaches to state building (including the first such efforts in Afghanistan and Iraq) have often failed to consider informal service providers as potential partners in post-conflict reconstruction.

This chapter is divided into two parts. The first focuses on donors' conceptions of the state and argues that the predominant discourse on state building focuses on creating the security and stability needed to control the territory and to lay the basis for international and regional trade. This often leads to a very centralized state, and causes state-building policies to deal with reconstruction and service delivery in a way that views informal institutions and providers as resisting state authority and the formalization of its institutional power.

The second part of the chapter explores the nexus between service delivery and state building through the specific example of water services. It examines the extent to which service delivery can strengthen the legitimacy of the state and highlights the limits of the dominant discourse, which links service delivery to state legitimacy. Lastly, it looks at alternative models of state building that focus on post-conflict reconstruction, the informal sector, and regulatory governance (Brinkerhoff 2005; Schwartz, Hahn, and Bannon 2004), and at the important role of nonstate providers in the delivery of services.

---

[1]   In *Economy and Society* (1968), Max Weber identified the following characteristics of a state: (1) the claim to the monopoly of the legitimate use of physical force within a given territory; (2) centralization of the material and the means to rule; (3) distribution of the powers of command among various organs (a rational constitution); (4) an administrative and legal order that claims binding authority over all within its jurisdiction; (5) subjection of this order to change through legislation; (6) organized enforcement and realization of this order (an administrative staff); and (7) regulation of the competition for political office according to established rules.

[2]   A number of interesting studies have looked at the coexistence of informal institutions with those of the state; see, for example, Unruh and Williams (2013).

DOMINANT VIEWS OF THE STATE

The dominant vision of state building is based on security and stability concerns (U.S. DOD 2005), leading to the emergence of a centralized Weberian state that treats informal institutions as a barrier to economic governance and service delivery (Lister and Wilder 2005).

Post-conflict reconstruction and state building have sparked interest among policy makers (DFID 2009; OECD 2007) and academics (Caplan 2004; Menkhaus 2007; Rubin 2006; Tripp 2004), essentially as a result of the major powers' involvement in conflict and post-conflict situations such as the Balkans, Somalia, Iraq, and Afghanistan. Donors and policy makers are now faced with the question of how state institutions can best be recreated and legitimized.

One approach has been to look back to European history. The influential work by Charles Tilly on the link between war and state building provided an interesting entry point to thinking and perhaps rethinking these issues in the post-colonial context (Tilly 1990). Tilly showed that the formation of nation-states in Western Europe was strongly linked to wars and the accumulation of capital to finance them, and that nation-states did not arise as a product of a linear evolution but from a particular historical and international context. This vision of state building has not been adapted to the current, broader context but remains rooted in the European experience (Taylor and Botea 2008). Experiences of post-conflict reconstruction in the post-colonial context, from Cambodia to Zimbabwe, have largely been ignored in the current debates (Clapham 2002).

Since economic deprivation may have been a cause of conflict (particularly if associated with ethnic, religious, or other kinds of social differentiation), donors active in post-conflict environments consider it vital to quickly stimulate economic development that can improve the general welfare of the population and thus weaken support for political violence. Service delivery appears to be an ideal way to achieve this. This vision of state building is very narrow, tends to focus on technical aspects of building state capacity, and ignores, to a certain extent, identity issues (Allouche 2008).

This dominant vision of state building affects the way the informal sector is approached. As pointed out by Simon Chesterman, Michael Ignatieff, and Ramesh Thakur, the international community with its interventions is trying to build a particular type of bureaucratic state: "a manifestation of political power that has been progressively depersonalized, formalized, and rationalized" (Chesterman, Ignatieff, and Thakur 2005, 2). So while policy makers and international donors may see state building as institution building, it may be more helpful to think of state-building initiatives in a multi-institutional context. As such, they may be seen as an attempt to replace one set of rules with another, so that formal bureaucratic rules of the Weberian type take precedence over informal rules (Lister 2007). This may create a tension in the liberal peacebuilding model, which promotes liberal democratic systems and market-oriented economic

34 Water and post-conflict peacebuilding

growth (Paris 2010). As the following paragraphs will show, local (informal) private providers are seen as part of the problem rather than the solution.

SERVICE DELIVERY AND STATE BUILDING

Despite the explosion in size of the literature on state building (Caplan 2005; Chandler 2006; Chesterman 2004; Fukuyama 2004; Zaum 2007), very little research explicitly addresses the role of public service provision in state building (Waldman 2007). Most of the literature that has addressed this issue (Eldon, Waddington, and Hadi 2008; Van de Walle and Scott 2009) emerged from research that was predominantly concerned with building the state's authority and legitimacy.

Legitimizing the state

The potential of service provision to act as a nonviolent vehicle for territorial penetration is attractive to international donors aiming to build capable states with a controlling presence, authority, and widespread visibility. The state has been understood as a centralized and public institution in which public services may contribute to (1) the integration of peripheries and the consolidation of territory; (2) standardization that facilitates exchange, mobility, equity, power-brokering, and pacification; and (3) accommodation of rebels in positions in public institutions to prevent the development of competing centers of power within the state (Migdal 2001).

This dominant centralized, securitized conception of state building focuses on state penetration and definition of boundaries. In its territorial sense, a boundary is the demarcation of a state territory. In its social sense, it separates "the state from other non-state, or private, actors and social forces" (Migdal 2001, 17).

Zimbabwe provides an interesting example of ways that the dominant discourse on state building can affect service delivery, especially as it pertains to access to water. Service delivery in Zimbabwe following independence in 1980 was used both as a tool of state legitimacy and as a weapon against competing forms of governance (Eldon and Gunby 2009; Musemwa 2006).

As a post-conflict country (from 1980 onward), Zimbabwe has usually been portrayed as a successful example of service delivery, state building, and state penetration, especially in the 1980s (Eldon and Gunby 2009). During the Zimbabwe Conference on Reconstruction and Development in 1981, the international community promised large-scale financial and technical support to help address capacity constraints. This international support was backed by strong political will by the new government, which was determined to eradicate inequalities in access to basic services, including water (Eldon and Gunby 2009).

Water and sanitation were seen during early planning as part of a wider state-led community development strategy to provide "increased access to safe and reliable water and sanitation facilities and improved health and hygienic practices" (Eldon and Gunby 2009, 106). But water and sanitation also played

The role of informal service providers 35

an important political role. Service delivery was a way of showing that the new Mugabe government was going to address the large inequalities developed during the colonial era and was a key part in establishing the credibility of the ruling political party, the Zimbabwe African National Union (ZANU). Rural areas were a priority for the newly formed government, as peasants and other rural groups had been central to the armed struggle and were the backbone of ZANU legitimacy. The nomination of district administrators for rural water supply and sanitation services gave the central government formal influence over even the most remote local authority (Eldon and Gunby 2009).

This rural policy successfully improved the health and well-being of rural people. As reported by the WHO/UNICEF Joint Monitoring Programme for Water Supply and Sanitation (Nicol and Mtisi 2003), 84 percent of Zimbabwe's population had access to safe drinking water by 1988. Politically, it was also a success, as a majority of these rural communities felt that they had the same rights as urban elites and that they were part of the nation-building process. As a result, service delivery, especially in rural areas, became a successful tool of state building and created a sense of legitimacy for the ruling party, at least during the 1980s.

Service delivery, and in particular the access to and administration and distribution of water, also became, under President Robert Mugabe, a political tool for managing rivalry and ethnic divisions (especially tensions with the Ndebele minority). In some ways, as soon as the state conceives service delivery as a tool for establishing legitimacy, reconstruction becomes highly political. This is what happened in the Matabeleland region, and especially the city of Bulawayo, where water services were used as a tool for political and social control. Research by Muchaparara Musemwa revealed that all development projects were suspended in the region in the early 1980s because of insecurity and political considerations on the part of the government (Musemwa 2006). Indeed, the region was seen as supporting the Zimbabwe African People's Union (ZAPU), and the early 1980s were marked by violence and uprisings against the ZANU-dominated government.

At the conclusion of the December 1987 Unity Accord between ZANU and ZAPU, people in Bulawayo and the province of Matabeleland had high hopes. "Many in the region expected to be rewarded for accepting Unity, and anticipated a program of reconstruction to compensate for the years of violence" (Alexander, McGregor, and Ranger 2000, 232). Water supply was critical in Bulawayo due to the droughts in 1982–1984 and 1986–1987 and the city's growing population, which included people displaced by violence from rural areas in Matabeleland North. However, the government viewed Matabeleland as a dissident region, as a result of uprisings there in the early 1980s and ZAPU's electoral victories in the 1980, 1984 (local), and 1985 (national) elections, a source of humiliation and anger for ZANU. The ZANU government used the withholding of water services as a weapon against these perceived dissidents despite the 1987 Unity Accord.

36 Water and post-conflict peacebuilding

Musemwa documented how the central government managed to block initiatives by the Bulawayo City Council during the late 1980s and early 1990s (Musemwa 2006). The Matabeleland-Zambezi Water Project (MZWP), proposed in the early 1990s, illustrates the competition between the Bulawayo City Council and the central government. This project was repeatedly turned down by the central government, despite the return of drought in 1991. The plan was shelved partly because it was costly but partly for political reasons.

As soon as Matabeleland's political leadership and Bulawayo residents, business people, and municipal officials came together to form the MZWP in 1991, the government created an alternative lobby, the Matabeleland-Zambezi Water Trust, duplicating the MZWP's functions (Nel and Berry 1993; Musemwa 2006). The government's manipulation of the MZWP served as a potent political weapon in the contest for the votes of Bulawayo residents. The project did not materialize in the early 1990s. The failure by the central state to construct a single water reservoir between 1980 and 1992 created water scarcity, exposing the people of Bulawayo to harmful social and environmental conditions.

Musemwa's 2006 discussion of this issue paid insufficient attention to local power struggles and the way they shaped the state's penetration in Bulawayo, a penetration that was mediated through the state's local representatives, who were either locally elected or appointed by a government agency in a technical and political capacity (Eldon and Gunby 2009). But overall it still holds that water was used as a weapon against what was viewed as contested and informal governance against state authority and legitimacy.

The Zimbabwe experience shows that water services may be used as a tool for increasing the state's presence and legitimacy in remote and rural areas. Donors should not assume that service provision is an apolitical, noncontroversial starting point for state building (Batley 2004) and conflict prevention (Vaux and Visman 2005). The delivery of public services is inherently political and has been used for political ends throughout history (Van de Walle and Scott 2009). Zimbabwe is a good example of how service delivery may become a weapon in the context of a challenge, real or perceived, to state authority. There are, of course, many other examples. In Mostar, Bosnia, for example, the Bosnian Croats sought to obstruct the implementation of an agreement to rehabilitate and integrate the city's divided water and sewage system (ICG 2000), as this measure was perceived by some ultranationalists as reuniting contested areas in the city that they saw as ethnic territorial spaces.

The link between public services and state legitimacy is not limited to their potential for use as a political tool by the ruling party. Public services provide one of the most direct links between the state and its citizens; they contribute to state visibility and serve as a symbol of state presence. Numerous studies have shown how public services diffuse cultural symbols of statehood and nationhood (Shils 1975). Nonetheless, the argument that state legitimacy will automatically follow from service delivery ignores complex issues such as political participation and representation (Lister 2007). Its understanding of state legitimacy is narrow, and in post-conflict situations, it assumes that conflict was the principal agent in undermining service delivery in peri-urban and rural areas. It ignores conditions existing prior to conflict in which service delivery to the urban and rural poor was already a major issue.

Conflict clearly has an impact on service delivery, but the ideal vision of state building and service delivery described above may have not existed prior to the conflict. Informal governance, as discussed in the introduction to this chapter, is more closely linked to the absence of state institutions for service delivery, especially in peri-urban and rural areas, than to challenges to state authority. The absence of clear and reliable data on the impact of conflict on service delivery (Schwartz, Hahn, and Bannon 2004), and the fact that data on access to water by definition exclude informal providers, limit our understanding of service delivery in post-conflict situations and how it compares with the situation prior to the conflict. Current assumptions regarding the effect of conflict on infrastructure in post-colonial countries are based on an understanding of conflict as a highly technological battlefield (Collier and Hoeffler 2007). This reflects a Western bias that is disconnected from recent conflicts in post-colonial countries, most of which have involved irregular warfare, which favors indirect approaches (rather than military battles) to erode an adversary's power, influence, and will. In this type of conflict, large elements of the infrastructure are difficult to destroy since the weapons used are not large, technologically sophisticated weapons such as tanks.

Service delivery might contribute (within the limits highlighted above) to state legitimacy. However, in many situations, informal governance is not a post-conflict challenge to state legitimacy but the continuation of a pre-conflict strategy to cope with lack of services.

Reconstructing society

The current debates on Afghanistan and Iraq, and more generally on state building, tend to focus exclusively on strengthening state institutions (by enhancing their authority or legitimacy) and are disconnected from the reconstruction agenda. However, improving the well-being of citizens will reinforce state building and the legitimacy of state institutions. With this alternative approach to state building, informal governance becomes a central issue in service delivery.

In poor rural and peri-urban communities, the provision of water is dominated by largely unregulated, small-scale, informal private water providers, also referred to as small-scale independent providers or small water enterprises (Sansom 2006). In many parts of the world, piped water is available only to a minority of urban dwellers. In 1999, Tova Maria Solo estimated that in Latin American cities, "25 percent of residents depend on independent providers for water and 50 percent for sanitation. In Africa, the figures rise to 50 percent for water and 85 percent for sanitation" (Solo 1999, 118). As a result, private sector participation in water services in post-conflict countries is important. In many African cities, informal providers are the predominant or only providers of water that have continued to function during periods of conflict (Sansom 2006).

38   Water and post-conflict peacebuilding

Outside investments in the water sector in post-conflict situations are often considered too risky. A study by the World Bank, for example, has shown that private investment in water supply and sanitation tends to come later and is much more limited than investment in other types of infrastructure:

> All of the investment, collection, tariff and regulatory risks found in the other sectors are exacerbated by the uncertainties of local political, administrative and contractual arrangements. The health concerns associated with water, the uncertainty of investment needs given the importance of underground assets and the intensely emotional manner in which many people view their right to water, further raise the risk profile of water investments in post-conflict countries (Schwartz, Hahn, and Bannon 2004, 15).

The provision of water and sanitation is of utmost priority in post-conflict states. Unsafe water equates directly with worse health, but the lack of adequate public revenues, government capacity, and investor interest often results in failure to reestablish access to basic infrastructural services.

In fragile post-conflict states, nonstate providers play a substantial role.[3] Their willingness to collaborate with government agencies is likely to depend on the prevailing political climate. Some resistance movements in fragile states, such as the Maoists in Nepal and Hamas in the Palestinian territories (before it won the parliamentary elections in 2006), have also provided basic social services. Collaboration with such organizations by the established government would clearly be difficult while they remain resistance movements.

Besides political considerations, the major challenge to post-conflict reconstruction is to identify mechanisms to reconcile informality with conventional procedures. The regulation of nonstate water providers (such as informal private providers and community groups) presents challenges due to their small-scale and informal nature, which makes them difficult to contract and monitor.

A number of states are recognizing the informal market and introducing new regulatory arrangements that acknowledge and legitimize these private providers. Their strict economic regulation is not viable; market-based approaches (such as permits) and voluntary self-regulation agreements have been developed. For example, in Malawi, the Blantyre Water Board has developed a system to support community groups and private providers by sharing construction procedures and advice on planning, implementation, and monitoring of their projects (Sansom 2006). Efforts to coordinate unregulated providers (for example, the setting up of bulk water supply contracts) become de facto state-building measures.

Lack of formal government recognition of nonstate providers has a number of consequences, especially in terms of pricing and public health. In Delhi, India, and Dhaka, Bangladesh, informal water providers who operate illegally charge

---

[3] The examples of nonstate water providers given in this section are not exclusive to post-conflict states; however, the approaches discussed can be—and increasingly are—deployed in post-conflict situations.

six to ten times more than state-subsidized utilities. In Cebu, Philippines, and Ho Chi Minh City, Viet Nam, where informal water providers have received official recognition, the multipliers are much lower: 2.6 and 1.7 (McIntosh 2003). The lack of recognition of informal private providers also has important public health implications, especially because of the inability to control water quality. This is why the government provided filling points for the 200-plus private water tankers in Enugu, Nigeria, to encourage tanker operators to use only authorized water sources. In Lagos, Nigeria, the state water corporation has allowed licensed water vendors to connect to its pipe system.

Community water watch groups have been used to compare different water providers' services. In Zambia, for example, water watch groups have been delegated powers from the national water regulator to monitor the performance of a variety of water and sanitation providers and deal with complaints (Franceys and Gerlach 2008). Benchmarking, flexibility in service standards, and reliance on community water watch groups have all helped to facilitate transitions from informal to formal governance.

Role of donors

Donors have the potential, within limits, to directly support nonstate providers delivering services to underserved groups. Donors rely on international and national nongovernmental organizations (NGOs) in post-conflict situations to provide services. Direct donor funding to NGOs bypasses government structures and often occurs when the government is unable to deliver services or unwilling to do so for reasons such as ongoing conflict or the fragility of the state. The risk for donors is that this approach can effectively disenfranchise the government, causing it to become uncooperative and thereby restricting opportunities for donors to influence broader government policies, plans, and programs. In the longer term, the government must play an important role in supporting the development of key services (such as electricity and water) as donors and international NGOs withdraw.

The example of Uganda is quite revealing. In the mid-1990s, Uganda was in a recovery phase as it emerged from previous conflicts, although fighting has continued in the north of the country. During this period, many NGOs, including faith-based organizations, were working to improve water supply and sanitation in rural Uganda. Uganda has a variety of water service providers, including international and local NGOs, the Church of Uganda, and informal private providers. Most water projects bypassed the government's Directorate of Water Development, which created resentment among government officials and tensions with the international aid community.

The international donor community and the government of Uganda addressed this issue by creating a program called the Sector Wide Approach. Water and sanitation were identified as priority sectors, which meant that more resources and efforts were devoted to the water sector by the government of Uganda. In a decentralization and capacity-building effort, young engineers were employed in

40　Water and post-conflict peacebuilding

district water offices to provide technical assistance, but the private sector and NGOs remained the implementing agents in providing water services. This new form of collaboration between the government, donors, and the informal private sector considerably improved access to water and sanitation from 2003 to 2005 (Sansom 2006).

Given the importance of informal water providers, the state-building discourse clearly needs to take them into account and arrange for an effective transition from informal governance to regulatory governance. A state-building discourse that emphasizes a strong state with full control does not seem to be very helpful in reconstructing the delivery of services after a conflict. It also limits the options for donors who are obliged to deal with nonstate actors in post-conflict situations.

CONCLUSION

There are multiple pathways to post-conflict state building and reconstruction. Both agendas are now dominated by a discourse that emphasizes authority, legitimacy, and formality. State-building and reconstruction practices use service delivery as a tool for strengthening the legitimacy and authority of state institutions. However, the relevance of a European concept of state building is questionable in post-conflict countries in which informal governance plays a strong role. Current state-building discourses and practices have not addressed the major issues of change from informal governance to state empowerment and are often inadequate to explain the current realities of water provision in peri-urban and rural areas.

This does not discredit the normative ideal of a strong state, especially with regard to service delivery. On the contrary, a reconstruction agenda that gives priority to service delivery and regulatory governance will enhance the state's legitimacy over the long term and give it greater authority over the management of public affairs. Regulatory governance emerges as a way to deal with the formal and informal sectors as two complementary realms rather than antagonists. The major challenge in terms of state building and service delivery lies in recognizing the importance of the informal sector and the tensions between formalization, state control, and success or failure in providing services to the people who need them the most.

REFERENCES

Alexander, J., J. McGregor, and T. Ranger. 2000. *Violence and memory: One hundred years in the "dark forests" of Matabeleland.* Portsmouth, NH: Heinemann.

Allouche, J. 2008. *State building and U.S. foreign policy.* Audit of the Conventional Wisdom. Cambridge, MA: MIT Center for International Studies.

Batley, R. A. 2004. The politics of service delivery reform. *Development and Change* 35 (1): 31–56.

The role of informal service providers 41

Brinkerhoff, D. W. 2005. Rebuilding governance in failed states and post-conflict societies: Core concepts and cross-cutting themes. *Public Administration and Development* 25 (1): 3–14.

Caplan, R. 2004. International authority and state building: The case of Bosnia and Herzegovina. *Global Governance* 10 (10): 53–65.

———. 2005. *International governance of war-torn territories: Rule and reconstruction.* Oxford, UK: Oxford University Press.

Chandler, D. 2006. *Empire in denial: The politics of state-building.* London: Pluto Press.

Chesterman, S. 2004. *You, the people: The United Nations, transitional administration, and state-building.* Oxford, UK: Oxford University Press.

Chesterman, S., M. Ignatieff, and R. Thakur, eds. 2005. *Making states work: State failure and the crisis of governance.* Tokyo: United Nations University Press.

Clapham, C. S. 2002. *Africa and the international system: The politics of state survival.* Cambridge, UK: Cambridge University Press.

Collier, P., and A. Hoeffler. 2007. Civil war. In *Defense in a globalized world.* Vol. 2 of *Handbook of defense economics*, ed. T. Sandler and K. Hartley. Amsterdam, Netherlands: Elsevier North Holland.

DFID (Department for International Development, United Kingdom). 2009. *Building the state and securing the peace.* London.

Eldon, J., and D. Gunby. 2009. *States in development: State building and service delivery.* London: HLSP Institute.

Eldon, J., C. Waddington, and Y. Hadi. 2008. *Health system reconstruction: Can it contribute to state-building?* London: Health and Fragile States Network.

Franceys, R., and E. Gerlach, eds. 2008. *Regulating water and sanitation for the poor—Economic regulation for public and private partnerships.* London: Earthscan.

Fukuyama, F. 2004. *State-building: Governance and world order in the twenty-first century.* Ithaca, NY: Cornell University Press.

ICG (International Crisis Group). 2000. *Reunifying Mostar: Opportunities for progress.* Balkan Report 90. Brussels, Belgium.

Lemay-Hébert, N. 2009. Statebuilding without nation-building? Legitimacy, state failure and the limits of the institutionalist approach. *Journal of Intervention and Statebuilding* 3 (1): 21–45.

Lister, S. 2007. Understanding state-building and local government in Afghanistan. Working Paper 14. London: Crisis States Research Center.

Lister, S., and A. Wilder. 2005. Strengthening subnational administration in Afghanistan: Technical reform or state-building? *Public Administration and Development* 25 (1): 39–48.

McIntosh, A. C. 2003. *Asian water supplies—reaching the poor.* Manila, Philippines: Asian Development Bank; London: IWA Publishing.

Menkhaus, K. 2007. Governance without government in Somalia: Spoilers, state building, and the politics of coping. *International Security* 31 (3): 74–106.

Migdal, J. S. 2001. *State in society: Studying how states and societies transform and constitute one another.* Cambridge, UK: Cambridge University Press.

Musemwa, M. 2006. Disciplining a "dissident" city: Hydropolitics in the city of Bulawayo, Matabeleland, Zimbabwe, 1980–1994. *Journal of Southern African Studies* 32 (2): 239–254.

Nel, E. L., and B. B. Berry. 1993. Bulawayo's water crisis: An update. *Development Southern Africa* 10 (1): 79–83.

42   Water and post-conflict peacebuilding

Nicol, A., and S. Mtisi. 2003. The politics of water policy: A Southern Africa example. Sustainable Livelihoods in Southern Africa Research Paper No. 20. Brighton, UK: Institute of Development Studies.

OECD (Organisation for Economic Co-operation and Development). 2007. Principles for good international engagement in fragile states and situations. Paris.

Paris, R. 2010. Saving liberal peacebuilding. *Review of International Studies* 36 (2): 337–365.

Rubin, B. R. 2006. Peace building and state-building in Afghanistan: Constructing sovereignty for whose security? *Third World Quarterly* 27 (1): 175–185.

Sansom, K. R. 2006. Government engagement with non-state providers of water and sanitation services. *Public Administration and Development* 26 (3): 207–217.

Schwartz, J., S. Hahn, and I. Bannon. 2004. The private sector's role in the provision of infrastructure in post-conflict countries: Patterns and policy options. Social Development Papers, Conflict Prevention and Reconstruction Paper No. 16. Washington, D.C.: World Bank.

Shils, E. 1975. *Center and periphery: Essays in macrosociology*. Chicago, IL: University of Chicago Press.

Solo, T. M. 1999. Small-scale entrepreneurs in the urban water and sanitation market. *Environment and Urbanization* 11 (1): 117–132.

Taylor, B. D., and R. Botea. 2008. Tilly tally: War-making and state-making in the contemporary third world. *International Studies Review* 10 (1): 27–56.

Tilly, C. 1990. *Coercion, capital, and European states, AD 990–1990*. Cambridge, MA: Blackwell.

Tripp, C. 2004. The United States and state-building in Iraq. *Review of International Studies* 30 (4): 545–558.

UNDP (United Nations Development Programme) and UNDESA (United Nations Department of Economic and Social Affairs). 2007. *The challenges of restoring governance in crisis and post-conflict countries*. New York.

Unruh, J., and R. C. Williams. 2013. Lessons learned in land tenure and natural resource management in post-conflict societies. In *Land and post-conflict peacebuilding*, ed. J. Unruh and R. C. Williams. London: Earthscan.

U.S. DOD (United States Department of Defense). 2005. Military support for stability, security, transition, and reconstruction (SSTR) operations. Directive 3000.05 (November).

Van de Walle, S., and Z. Scott. 2009. The role of public services in state- and nation-building: Exploring lessons from European history for fragile states. Research paper. Birmingham, UK: Governance and Social Development Resource Centre.

Vaux, T., and E. Visman. 2005. *Service delivery in countries emerging from conflict*. London: Department for International Development.

Waldman, R. 2007. Health programming for rebuilding states: A briefing paper. Washington, D.C.: United States Agency for International Development.

Weber, M. 1968. *Economy and society*. Ed. G. Roth and C. Wittich. Trans. E. Fischoff, H. Gerth, A. M. Henderson, F. Kolegar, C. W. Mills, T. Parsons, M. Rheinstein, G. Roth, E. Shils, and C. Wittich. New York: Bedminster.

Zaum, D. 2007. *The sovereignty paradox: The norms and politics of international statebuilding*. Oxford, UK: Oxford University Press.

A tale of two cities: Restoring water services in Kabul and Monrovia

Jean-François Pinera and Robert A. Reed

Kabul and Monrovia are two very different cities with little in common apart from being the capitals of their respective countries, Afghanistan and Liberia. Yet they share a tragic similarity: both have suffered, almost simultaneously, from years of conflict. The parallels are remarkable:

- In 1992, mujahideen fighters entered Kabul after the withdrawal of the Soviet army. Almost immediately, a four-year power struggle between rival factions began that left 20,000 people dead and large portions of the city destroyed (Johnson 2004). In the same year, Monrovia came under attack by rebel forces led by Charles Taylor, causing destruction and generating mayhem among the thousands of displaced people who had fled conflict in the provinces.
- In 1996, the Taliban (a Sunni Islamist, predominately Pashtun movement)[1] took Kabul, and Taylor's forces again attacked Monrovia. In the following months, peace returned to both countries, at least to the capitals. In Liberia, a presidential election resulted in a landslide victory for Taylor.
- In 2001, Kabul was bombed again, this time by the United States. The city fell in only a few days, and the Taliban regime collapsed. In 2003, Taylor's opponents took over Monrovia, forcing the president into exile.

Since then, Afghanistan and Liberia have each experienced a transition toward democracy under the guidance of the United Nations. However, while Liberia seems to be on the pathway to stability, Afghanistan remains in conflict.

Prolonged conflicts such as those in Afghanistan and Liberia affect cities in many ways. The damage to urban infrastructure is the most apparent result, but communities and institutions also suffer. A common consequence is disruption

---

Jean-François Pinera is a water engineer specializing in emergency response and rehabilitation. Robert A. Reed is a researcher, trainer, and consultant in public health engineering. This chapter is based on an article with the same title published in 2009 in *Disasters: The Journal of Disaster Studies, Policy and Management*. Some information for this chapter was drawn from the authors' professional and personal experiences in the field.

[1] The Pashtun word *talib* means student.

44 Water and post-conflict peacebuilding

to urban services such as the water supply. Armed rebellion may result from a wide range of factors, including miserable living conditions. Alleviating the consequences of conflict by restoring access to basic services, including water supply, can give people hope and thus diminish support for the insurgency and promote peace.

In Kabul and Monrovia, a number of humanitarian organizations contributed to the partial restoration of water supplies, and then worked to more fully rehabilitate the water networks in both cities. This chapter draws a parallel between those two efforts. Its aim is to show that, in addition to aid agencies and water utilities, communities of consumers have important roles to play in the delivery of water in an environment transformed by conflict. Access to basic services by the poorest portion of the population is particularly critical. This is a fundamental target in terms of peacebuilding, because this is where armed insurgents are the most likely to find followers. Low-income populations, whether rural or urban, often have little confidence in political settlements and may see violence as the only way forward. This chapter explores how interaction between aid agencies, water utilities, and local communities influence project outcomes. Restoration of tolerable living conditions can help facilitate community involvement and strengthen trust in institutions. The chapter concludes by suggesting ways to improve aid agency strategies to maximize the benefits of their intervention.

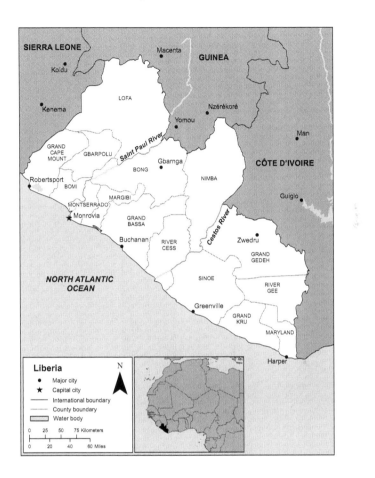

RESEARCH METHODOLOGY

Kabul and Monrovia were part of a wider case-study research project that also looked at interventions in cities and towns in Chechnya, the Democratic Republic of the Congo, Haiti, and Sri Lanka (Pinera 2006). The project offered an opportunity to explore numerous aspects of emergency situations, including type and intensity of armed conflict, geography, types of aid agencies involved, and types of assistance. The interventions that were studied had various levels of involvement by water utilities and communities of consumers. Their outcomes were evaluated in terms of service sustainability and coverage, in particular for areas sheltering the most vulnerable. The data were taken primarily from unpublished reports and from field visits carried out in 2005. During the field visits, water utility officials, community leaders, and members of aid agencies were interviewed. Interview questions concentrated on the consequences of the conflict

46   Water and post-conflict peacebuilding

for the water supply; interactions among aid agencies, water utilities, and communities; and the quality of assistance provided.

WATER SUPPLY IN KABUL AND MONROVIA

Reginald Herbold Green described rehabilitation as restoring "the same level of functionality as before the crisis" (Green 2000, 343). In Kabul and Monrovia, this task seems virtually impossible, because conflict has transformed these cities' appearance, infrastructure, institutions, population, and size. A more appropriate goal for rehabilitation in these cases would be a level of functionality that is appropriate to the new situation.

This section describes the transformation of Kabul and Monrovia, concentrating on the water supply and on how aid agencies responded to the emergency.

Kabul

Although Afghanistan has been at war since 1978, Kabul was spared until the withdrawal of Soviet troops on February 15, 1989. At that time, its population numbered approximately 1.3 million (CSO 2005). A water network, fed mainly by boreholes (water wells of reduced diameter) and surface water, supplied about 60 percent of Kabul residents. The boreholes were either located in one of three main well fields on the southern fringe of the city or were individual wells. Certain neighborhoods, inside the city and on its periphery, were not connected to the main water network and had independent water systems. Total water production in 1988 was estimated at 86,000 cubic meters per day (m^3/day) (Banks and Hamid 2002). The network had 30,000 individual connections, half of them metered. Water was available for between six and eight hours a day, on a regular schedule. Households not supplied with piped water relied on public and private shallow wells. The development of the water network was guided by a master plan designed in 1974 for a population of less than 1 million people (Brinkhoff 2010).[2] Figure 1 shows the urban area supplied by the central water network, according to this master plan; it also shows the nearby water resources.

The Central Authority for Water Supply and Sewerage (CAWSS) was responsible for developing the Kabul water network, according to the master plan. CAWSS was almost self-financing, with only 10 percent of its budget coming from the central government.

When fighting erupted around Kabul soon after the Soviet withdrawal in 1989, the Afshar and Logar well fields were looted almost immediately. Water production fell sharply to 25,000–30,000 m^3/day (Banks and Hamid 2002). The situation worsened after April 1992, when the mujahideen took the city. The power supply was then halted totally and the pumping stations plundered. People could only obtain water from shallow wells and from the Qargha Karez, an underground

---

[2] Kabul's population was given as 913,000 by the 1979 census (Brinkhoff 2010).

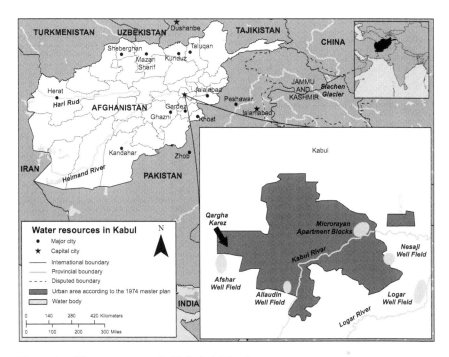

Figure 1. Water resources in Kabul, Afghanistan
Source: Based on a map by the Afghanistan Information Management Service (AIMS 2005).

canal, which was producing less than 5,000 m³/day. Heavy fighting continued intermittently until 1994, and some 500,000 people abandoned the city.

From 1994, a reduction in the intensity of hostilities allowed aid organizations including CARE, Solidarités International, and the United Nations Human Settlements Programme to intervene (Solidarités International 1995). Their operations initially consisted of trucking in water and constructing more than 2,000 shallow public wells, most of which were boreholes equipped with hand pumps (Pinera 1999). Essential repairs to the Afshar and Allaudin well fields and to some individual wells supplying the network were later carried out, allowing water production to reach approximately 15,000 m³/day. This level of production was maintained until the fall of the Taliban at the end of 2001. The CAWSS, which used to employ 400 staff in Kabul, including thirty-four engineers before 1992, lost most of its qualified personnel and all of its equipment and vehicles.

Kabul's infrastructure suffered heavy damage during the conflict; its southwest quarter was literally flattened. When a large number of people returned home from abroad after the removal of the Taliban, many found their homes damaged or destroyed and began to rebuild. Some settled in abandoned buildings or in improvised camps. The construction of new houses on the outskirts of the capital

48　Water and post-conflict peacebuilding

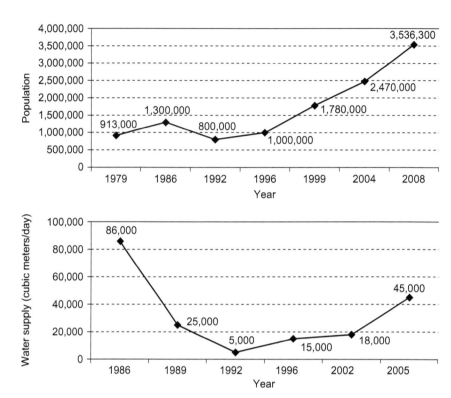

Figure 2.   Population and water supply in Kabul, Afghanistan
Sources: Population data drawn from CSO (2000, 2005); Grinnell and Troc (2004); Brinkhoff (2010). Water supply data drawn from Bank and Hamid (2002); Salim Karimi, former manager at Central Authority for Water Supply and Sewerage and employee of Kreditanstalt für Wiederaufbau, personal communication, April 2005.

contributed to the city's expansion, while the hills in the center were covered with more houses. Most of these areas were not included in Kabul's master plan. New and densely populated neighborhoods were created where some of the poorest people lived. In less than two years, the city's population grew from almost 1.8 million under the Taliban (CSO 2000) to approximately 2.8 million in 2004 (Grinnell and Troc 2004) and an estimate of more than 3.5 million in 2008 (Brinkhoff 2010). (Figure 2 shows changes to Kabul's population and water supply.)

Monrovia

Liberia became politically unstable in the mid-1970s, when it was affected by a severe recession, and suffered a bloody coup in April 1980. Even under these difficult conditions, the Liberia Water and Sewer Corporation (LWSC) managed

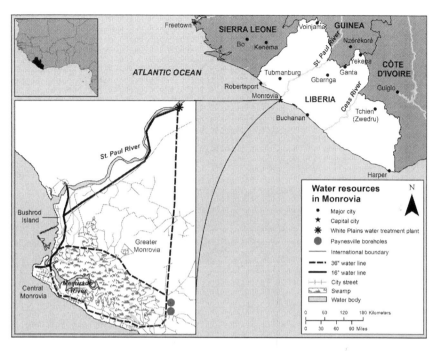

Figure 3. Water resources in Monrovia, Liberia
Source: Smith and Kpakolo (2004).

to serve 75 percent of the Monrovia area, using 17,900 individual connections, of which 45 percent were metered (Willson 2003). Households not connected to the water network relied on a few public taps and a large number of shallow private wells. The average daily production of the White Plains treatment plant, fifteen kilometers northeast of the capital on the Saint Paul River, was 61,000 m^3/day (Willson 2003). (Figure 3 shows Monrovia's main water resources.)

When a rebellion against the government reached the surrounding areas of Monrovia in April 1990, the water supply from White Plains was among the first services to shut down. Organizations including the International Committee of the Red Cross (ICRC), Médecins Sans Frontières–Belgium (MSF–Belgium), and the United Nations Children's Fund (UNICEF) intervened to support LWSC and managed the resumption of water production, which reached 22,500–37,500 m^3/day (Ockleford 1993; Smith et al. 2001). Along with other organizations, they constructed a large number of public wells equipped with hand pumps.

A new interruption to the water supply occurred during the October 1992 attack by Charles Taylor's troops and was not restored until the end of 1993, when the Deutsche Gesellschaft für Technische Zusammenarbeit (GTZ) installed power generators at White Plains. The same year, MSF–Belgium, supported by GTZ, drilled two boreholes in Paynesville, east of the city (Smith and Kpakolo

50 Water and post-conflict peacebuilding

2004). Damage to the transmission line did not allow the water supply from White Plains to be restored beyond Bushrod Island, a densely populated area located north of central Monrovia, to which 7,100–7,500 m^3 of water was delivered daily (Smith et al. 2001; Geoscience 1998). Since then, water trucks and wheelbarrow vendors have distributed a large portion of the drinking-water supply to areas not served with piped water. They obtained water either from the network through Bushrod Island outlets or from Paynesville boreholes.

In 2003, production at White Plains dropped further, to slightly more than 3,500 m^3/day, due to a lack of fuel (Smith and Kpakolo 2004). The LWSC, like the CAWSS, lost most of its qualified personnel and assets during the troubled years between 1992 and 1996. The situation changed in mid-2006 when the newly elected government carried out major repairs to the transmission line, resulting in a substantial increase in water production and allowing water to reach central Monrovia again after almost fifteen years of interruption (Alegre 2006). Since then, daily volume of water production has varied between approximately 9,800 and 18,000 m^3/day (Alegre 2006; AWF 2007). In 2010, average production was 14,000 m^3/day.[3]

Conflict caused far less destruction in Monrovia than in Kabul, because rockets were used only for a short time in 2003. But Monrovia, like Kabul, experienced a sudden population rise, from 500,000 in 1988 (Perry 1988) to approximately 1 million in 2003 (Smith and Kpakolo 2004), as Liberians fled conflict and devastation in the countryside and settled in the capital and the camps surrounding it. These camps received 200,000 people between 1992 and 1995 (Atkinson and Mulbah 2000). A large proportion of newcomers to Monrovia went to the shantytowns located next to a swamp along the Mesurado River. They also built houses in the peripheral area, contributing to the extension of the city beyond its original limits. These new settlements are part of what is known as Greater Monrovia. The city's population did not vary significantly between 2003 and 2008, the year of the last census (Brinkhoff 2010). (Figure 4 shows changes in Monrovia's population and water supply.)

WATER SUPPLY REHABILITATION

Once the situations in Kabul and Monrovia became somewhat more stabilized, a number of organizations began work to rehabilitate the cities' water supply systems. Strategies in both cities were primarily of two types:

1. Large-scale rehabilitation projects, supported by bilateral or multilateral donor organizations, were initiated as soon as the political environment was considered suitable. Sponsors of these projects adopted a global approach, aiming to sustainably improve the whole system of water production, distribution, and management. They also supported institutional reforms.

---

[3] John Kpakolo, manager at LWSC, personal communication, August 2010.

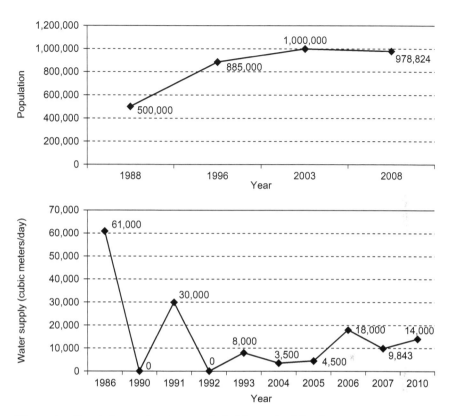

Figure 4. Population and water supply in Monrovia, Liberia
Sources: Population data drawn from Perry (1988); Atkinson and Mulbah (2000); Smith and Kpakolo (2004); Brinkhoff (2010). Water supply data drawn from Smith Kpakolo (2004); Alegre (2006); AWF (2007); John Kpakolo, manager at Liberia Water and Sewer Corporation, personal communication, August 2010.

2. More modest rehabilitation projects, mostly carried out by international nongovernmental organizations (NGOs), had as their main objective to avoid outbreaks of communicable disease caused by reduced access to water, sanitation, and health services, especially in the most congested areas.

Kabul

Essential repairs to the water network started in Kabul in 1995 when CARE, Oxfam, and Solidarités International repaired pumping stations, part of the main water network, and some of the independent water systems. Starting in 2002, the ICRC and the German government–owned development bank Kreditanstalt für Wiederaufbau (KfW), working through the German consulting firm RRI Beller/Kocks, became involved. By 2005, water production had been restored to 45,000 m³/day, and the number of house connections had returned

52   Water and post-conflict peacebuilding

to the pre-conflict level of 43,000. (Table 1 provides more details on these operations.)

Beginning in 2003, planning began on the large-scale rehabilitation of the Kabul water network. This started with a feasibility study funded by KfW and carried out by RRI Beller/Kocks. Based on its conclusions, KfW, together with the World Bank, funded a €100 million rehabilitation of the water network, which included drilling and equipping twenty-six new deep wells with the objective of producing a daily average of 121,000 m^3 of water once completed (Fischaess 2003). The project also planned to turn CAWSS into a state corporation, accountable to a board of directors instead of to the Ministry of Urban Development and Housing. Its branches, in thirteen cities and towns, were meant to acquire greater autonomy, and it was envisaged that independent service providers that were publicly, privately, or cooperatively owned would take part in the service (MUDH 2005).

In parallel with these large-scale rehabilitation and institutional development plans, a number of organizations, primarily NGOs, carried out community-based projects expected to have a swift impact on living conditions in the poorest areas. They targeted neighborhoods outside the master plan since, in the short and medium term, it was not expected that the main water network would supply them (Pinera and Rudge 2005). Some of these neighborhoods were served by

Table 1.   Major water network rehabilitation projects in Kabul, Afghanistan

Organization	*Operation*	*Period*	*Results*
CARE	Rehabilitation of pumping stations in Afshar well field	1995 (six months)	Handed over to Solidarités
CARE	Rehabilitation of two well fields	1996–2006	Handed over to CAWSS
ICRC, British Red Cross Society	Logar well field electrification	2002–2003	Completed
ICRC, Spanish Red Cross Society	Projects in five areas of the Kabul network	2002–2003	Completed
KfW, RRI Beller/Kocks	Urgent repairs to the Kabul network	2002–2005	Completed
Oxfam	Logar well field rehabilitation	1997–1999	Not completed
Solidarités	Operation, repair, and maintenance of pumping stations and independent networks in Kabul and along its periphery	1995–1998	Not completed

Sources: Cosgrave (1999); Diago and Arnalich (2004); Elliott (2002); KfW (2003); Solidarités International (1995).
Notes: CAWSS: Central Authority for Water Supply and Sewerage; ICRC: International Committee of the Red Cross; KfW: Kreditanstalt für Wiederaufbau; Solidarités: Solidarités International.

independent water systems, usually consisting of a borehole and a number of tap stands. While theoretically the responsibility of CAWSS, these water systems were in practice left to the communities to manage. Only a small proportion of the population living in unplanned areas benefited from water systems, with the majority relying on shallow public or private wells, sometimes equipped with hand pumps.

Organizations such as ICRC and the French NGOs Action Contre la Faim and Solidarités International ran the following projects:

- Constructing water-access points and water systems, usually boreholes equipped with hand pumps, and rehabilitating existing water systems.
- Training mechanics to repair water systems.
- Building or rehabilitating private latrines.
- Organizing hygiene promotion through house-to-house visits, sessions in schools and mosques, and focus-group sessions.
- Encouraging the establishment of water committees to manage the operation and maintenance of hand pumps and small-scale water systems.

Kabul municipal government and CAWSS had little or no interest in these projects.

Monrovia

GTZ, ICRC, MSF–Belgium, and UNICEF were involved initially in making essential repairs to the water supply system in Monrovia. This task was continued beginning in 1996 by the Florence-based consulting firm Geoscience, funded by the European Development Fund. (Table 2 provides more details.)

Table 2. Major water network rehabilitation projects in Monrovia, Liberia

Organization	Operation	Period	Results
European Development Fund, Geoscience	Essential repairs on water network and support for the LWSC	1996–2003	Completed
European Development Fund, GTZ, MSF–Belgium	Drilling of Paynesville boreholes, repairs and installation of generators at White Plains water treatment plant	1993	Completed
ICRC	Support to the water utility, repairs to the power supply, support for water production	1991 (six months)	Completed
MSF–Belgium, UNICEF	Support to the water utility, repairs to the power supply	1990–1991	Handed over to the ICRC

Sources: Geoscience (1998); Ockelford (1993); Smith (2001, 2004); Smith et al. (2001).
Notes: GTZ: Deutsche Gesellschaft für Technische Zusammenarbeit; ICRC: International Committee of the Red Cross; MSF–Belgium: Médecins Sans Frontières–Belgium; UNICEF: United Nations Children's Fund.

54   Water and post-conflict peacebuilding

While these repairs and the support provided to LWSC helped slow the deterioration of Monrovia's water production capacity, they failed to reverse the trend.

After the fall of Taylor's regime in August 2003, a large-scale rehabilitation of the water supply was envisaged. A number of studies, among them a water demand and market study (Browne and Tsikisayi 2004), were carried out and led to the launch of a €3 million rehabilitation project, funded by the European Union (EU) and awarded to the German consulting firm Hydroplan. One of the main objectives of this project was a complete overhaul of the water treatment plant and of the transmission lines carrying water to the city. The project also foresaw the drilling of new boreholes in the Paynesville area.

The EU's project recommended that LWSC delegate the management of the city's water supply to the private sector through concessions. This option would involve making private companies responsible for the operation and maintenance of the utility's assets as well as for necessary investments in the infrastructure (World Bank 2006). LWSC would, however, remain responsible for water production, quality control, and primary distribution through the transmission line. It would also distribute water in areas of Monrovia where the concession would not be viable because of low income levels or insufficient population density. The process was initiated in March 2005, but the new government that came to power in February 2006 opted to halt it. It questioned the process of privatization and decided to test the project in the richest areas. Community-based management of public stand-posts was preferred in low-income neighborhoods. In 2010, a number of stand-posts were running and the process of assigning concessions was ongoing—with other actors involved, including the African Development Bank and Japan International Cooperation Agency.[4]

Community-based projects aimed at preventing outbreaks of cholera were also carried out in Monrovia by organizations such as Action Contre la Faim, Concern, ICRC, Oxfam, and UNICEF. In the peri-urban areas of Monrovia, their activities were similar to those implemented in Kabul, with the difference that in Monrovia, community-based organizations played a prominent role in community mobilization. The relief agencies active in central areas of Monrovia tended to focus on ensuring fair access to the water sold by trucks and small vendors. For this purpose, Oxfam and UNICEF distributed water reservoirs, ranging in volume from about 1,000 to 11,000 liters, to be managed by communities that purchased water from bulk suppliers and agreed on a selling price.

Oxfam's project in Clara Town, a densely populated low-income area of Bushrod Island, deserves special attention since it dealt with illegal water vendors. In 2004, it was estimated that up to 60 percent of White Plains' water was unaccounted for (Smith and Kpakolo 2004). Leaks were part of the problem, but the main cause was water sellers illegally connecting to the network. Low pressure

---

[4]   John Kpakolo, manager of LWSC, personal communication, August 2010.

in the network obliged them to fill water vessels from the bottom of holes they dug to pierce the pipes. The conditions in which they sold water were very unhygienic. Since the network was not constantly under pressure, it could be contaminated through seepage from surface water accumulating in the holes.

Criminal gangs often controlled these vendors, and, for an international NGO, it was difficult to work in such an environment. Oxfam, though, had been able to intervene in Clara Town since mid-2005, in partnership with a community-based organization. The agency selected thirty of these illegal vendors and signed an agreement with LWSC under which they were recognized and equipped with water meters. Water sellers received plastic water tanks from Oxfam, allowing them to sell water throughout the day. The connections to the network were also improved to avoid contamination (Oxfam 2005). The project was designed to run in collaboration with LWSC. This choice was surprising, because it was in contradiction with the strategies adopted in NGOs' other community-based projects in Monrovia, which, like those in Kabul, tended to promote autonomous water sources such as community wells that were independent of the municipal water supply. These projects were beneficial in terms of social cohesion, which is particularly important in post-conflict societies, but they did not increase the coverage or the quality of municipal services.

ACHIEVING SUSTAINABLE SERVICE FOR ALL CONSUMERS

The concept of quality applied to the delivery of humanitarian assistance has gained momentum in the past fifteen years, along with the related notion of accountability. This is mostly due to the increase in the number of emergency operations and relief agencies and in the amount of funds spent during this period (Macrae 2002). As mentioned earlier, the interventions in this study were measured in terms of their sustainability and coverage. Sustainability refers to the capacity of the activity to continue producing outputs when external assistance is withdrawn. Coverage refers to the portion of the targeted population that actually receives assistance. Analyzing these parameters is particularly relevant for the rehabilitation of water systems in urban areas affected by armed conflict, because they are reflected in the two types of intervention mentioned above. Large-scale interventions often prioritize sustainability, while community-based projects prioritize coverage.

Sustainable services and privatization

Strengthening the capacity of water utilities weakened in conflict is essential for obtaining sustainable results. Through institutional development initiatives, they may acquire the financial, managerial, and technical capacity to run the service and to make appropriate strategic choices.

M. Sohail, Sue Cavill, and Andrew P. Cotton divide the sustainability of an urban service into three components:

56   Water and post-conflict peacebuilding

1. Technical sustainability is linked to the capacity to operate and maintain its assets.
2. Financial sustainability depends on a water utility's capacity to recover costs.
3. Institutional sustainability depends on a water utility's credibility as a service provider to both consumers and local administrations (Sohail, Cavill, and Cotton 2005).

Institutional development requires close collaboration with governmental agencies, which is only possible when aid agencies and donors accept them as partners. It can be a difficult task, and corruption often adds to the problem. In spite of these challenges, institutional reforms of water services were launched in Kabul and Monrovia. In Kabul, where they are most advanced, it took three years to conceptualize a vision for the institutional development of the water utility (MUDH 2005). The strategy chosen for improving the efficiency of water services was to rely on service providers to carry out certain functions, thereby restricting the tasks to be conducted by a water utility with limited capacity. Policy makers considered involving different types of service providers, but according to the manager of the KfW-funded project, the likely option considered at the time was a management contract granted to a private company.[5]

In Monrovia, the choice of operating through concessions is even more daring, and was largely objected to by the new management of LWSC that took over after February 2006. In the short term, it is hard to imagine a Liberian company capable of running the service at acceptable standards, let alone investing in the infrastructure. International water companies are hardly an option, since they are unlikely to be inclined to invest in a country beginning to emerge from civil war. Assuming that companies are found to run concessions in Monrovia, there is a risk that they will neglect less profitable low-income areas, which will remain the territory of vendors who sell water at prices up to twenty times higher than those paid by LWSC's private customers.

Private-sector participation in urban water supply is a common practice in the developed world. It has been tested in Africa with mixed results (Hall, Bayliss, and Lobina 2002; Stren 2001; Batley 2001). In countries affected by conflict or long-lasting political instability, obstacles seem even greater. With increased urban poverty, shattered infrastructure, and weak institutions, achieving profitability is certainly a greater challenge for a private company than it is in countries that may have weak economic prospects but are not recovering from violent conflict.

Opponents of privatization argue that it would result in a substantial rise in water tariffs and, as in the case of Monrovia, only well-off families in a limited number of areas would be covered and could afford the service (Balanyá et al. 2005). Others, however, contend that well-designed privatization can also benefit the poor (Alexander, Rosenthal, and Brocklehurst 2002). The debate is unresolved,

---

[5] Bernt Fischaess, RRI Beller/Kocks, personal communication, Kabul, April 2005.

and Kabul is a perfect illustration of what is at stake. A majority of its inhabitants live in areas not covered by the master plan and consequently not supplied by the central network. So far, the public water utility has mostly ignored them, and no global solution is envisaged to address the problem. It seems unlikely that the residents of these areas would be able or willing to meet the costs of connecting to the network. An increase in water tariffs in 2005 by the public utility—even before any privatization was officially envisaged—was received with complaints, in a country where water is considered by most as a gift of God.

Reaching those with the greatest need

Community-based projects carried out by aid agencies in low-income areas aim to respond to those with the greatest needed. However, most projects are not adapted to the urban environment and may have limited benefits in the long term. The organizations running these projects are usually experienced in emergency operations or rural water supply, but most of them lack experience in dealing with local institutions. Instead, they tend to prefer locally maintained individual systems. These systems have the advantage of being quick to install, and they sometimes offer much-needed instant relief. But there is no guarantee of quality and continuity of service beyond what communities are able to ensure. Furthermore, a community-based approach that works in rural areas or in a displaced persons camp is not necessarily applicable in urban neighborhoods that have been traumatized by violence. Monrovia and Kabul each have diverse populations with different ethnic, religious, and political backgrounds in which confrontation, violence, and gang culture have sometimes replaced solidarity and mutual trust.

Agencies willing to work in such contexts cannot always expect community participation, but they may help extend municipal water services to low-income communities. This may involve helping to establish a working relationship between informal vendors and the water utility, as Oxfam did in Clara Town, Monrovia. Another possibility is helping communities to set up and manage their own neighborhood water distribution systems.

This model has been applied in another city affected by armed conflict: Port-au-Prince, the capital of Haiti (Colin and Lockwood 2002). Its water utility, Centrale Autonome Métropolitaine d'Eau Potable, never considered supplying the 800,000 people living in the city's shantytowns, until the intervention of the French NGO Groupe de Recherche et d'Echanges Technologiques (GRET). Between 1995 and 2005, the organization extended the city water network to these areas, building a number of kiosks from which water was sold to residents. Water management committees were elected in each neighborhood and were put in charge of running these kiosks, paying the sellers and buying water in bulk quantities from the Port-au-Prince water utility, thereby maintaining affordable tariffs (Matthieussent and Carlier 2004). This operation helped not only to

58 Water and post-conflict peacebuilding

improve water access but also to restore a sense of citizenship among shantytown residents as they gained access to this municipal service.

Achieving universal access to basic services entails selecting the most appropriate mode of management according to the environment of the targeted area. In the case of water supply, the main options to consider are the following:

- Mode of delivery—private or collective connections.
- Involvement of the private sector, ranging from water vendors to international water companies.
- Role of the community, which may be directly involved in management or only represented on regulatory boards.

The choice may depend on the following variables:

- Income levels in the community.
- Social capital—links within the community, across social cleavages, and between communities and formal institutions.
- Relative strength of the water utility and of the informal sector.
- Level of violence, which is related to social capital and, in certain cases, to the efficiency of a disarmament process.
- Physical constraints such as the geography of the neighborhood, underground conditions, and level of sanitation.

In a city, water systems tend to be complex and therefore expensive to build, operate, and maintain. The strength of water sector institutions is therefore one of the main parameters affecting the efficiency of water services. Large rehabilitation projects usually entail large funds and a number of private companies. Where corruption is an issue, institutional development may become extremely difficult for the agencies involved.

There is no obvious solution to this problem. In such contexts, all stakeholders should take part in decisions about how the service should be managed, for instance through the creation of a management board in which consumers would have a voice. This is especially important when it comes to allocating markets and deciding on a mode of management.

CONCLUSION

This tale of two cities reveals comparable approaches to the rehabilitation of water supply despite very different cultures, natural environments, and historical backgrounds. The two cases have many elements in common: a run-down water utility, a new government, bilateral and multilateral donors, commercial consulting firms, emergency aid agencies—NGOs, the ICRC, or UN bodies—and divided communities. Both have adopted similar strategies: large-scale rehabilitation projects, funded by KfW and the World Bank in Kabul and by the EU in Monrovia, alongside community-based projects run by NGOs, ICRC, and UNICEF. Similar accounts could be given of many other cities emerging from conflict.

In both Kabul and Monrovia, the sustainability and coverage of interventions are important issues. Large-scale rehabilitation projects may contribute to the institutional development of the water utility, which should ensure sustainability, but their coverage is limited; they are unlikely to cover disenfranchised neighborhoods in the foreseeable future. In this respect, the prospects are even worse under privatization. Community-based projects, on the other hand, target disenfranchised areas but usually rely on locally maintained systems, with no guarantee of quality or long-term sustainability.

How agencies channel their support appears to be linked more to whether they are skilled and capable of action than to the actual needs of the community. Private consulting firms such as RRI Beller/Kocks in Kabul and Hydroplan in Monrovia are more at ease with conventional water distribution with individual connections than with custom-made solutions for areas forgotten or neglected by large-scale reconstruction projects. Water utilities tend to think along the same lines, since individual connections are, in principle, more likely to generate income. In contrast, humanitarian agencies prefer to deal with communities, as they do in rural areas or in camps, rather than with governmental institutions. They also rely on funding schemes designed to support short-term, quick-impact interventions with a limited long-term perspective.

In these conditions, little can be done to reduce the gap in access to water services that has been widened by conflict. A more holistic approach requires a much-needed paradigm shift.

It is essential that interventions simultaneously target hardware, institutional development, and social issues. Working efficiently at the neighborhood level requires dealing with all stakeholders. This means not only rehabilitating infrastructure and ensuring that the water utility has the capacity to run it—or even to manage a delegated service—but also taking care of social aspects such as community consultation and hygiene promotion.

There is no single solution. Certain neighborhoods may benefit from a particular level of private-sector participation, while in others, a different model, such as community management, may be the answer.

Finally, an appropriate leadership that coordinates the inputs of all organizations, whether involved in large-scale or community-based projects, is necessary. Ideally, this is a task for governments and public utilities. Unfortunately, they are often too weak to play this role unless genuine efforts are made to strengthen them. Donors, which often fund both large-scale and community-based water supply rehabilitation projects, are in the best position to encourage this cooperation, provided that they are aware of the problem.

This paradigm shift was partly achieved in Port-au-Prince, where the city water utility, with the intermediation of GRET, has managed to provide a water supply to many of its shantytowns. Could this occur in Kabul and Monrovia? It

60   Water and post-conflict peacebuilding

is hard to answer this question with certainty. Long years of poor service and weak institutional capacity have made the task difficult, but success was just as improbable in Port-au-Prince before GRET started its program.

It may be time for aid agencies, consulting firms, and major donors to establish a dialogue, under the auspices of the water utility, on how to extend the benefits of municipal water services, whether through community-based initiatives or private management. In addition to benefiting the health and well-being of the population, universal access to water services could help consolidate peace by building trust between local government and low-income communities, within which armed insurgencies often find followers. Aid agencies would then be addressing a situation described in Port-au-Prince as one in which needs that would be typical of an emergency situation remain over the long term (Braïlowsky, Boisgallais, and Paquot 2000), a characteristic that could apply to almost any city emerging from armed conflict.

REFERENCES

AIMS (Afghanistan Information Management Service). 2005. Kabul city map. Kabul. www.aims.org.af/maps/urban/kabul.pdf.

Alegre, S. 2006. Community-based management of urban water supply services in post-conflict environments: Case-study of Monrovia, Liberia. Master's thesis, Loughborough University, Loughborough, UK.

Alexander, I., S. Rosenthal, and C. Brocklehurst. 2002. Making the contract work for the poor. In *New designs for water and sanitation transactions: Making private sector participation work for the poor*, ed. C. Brocklehurst. Washington, D.C.: Water and Sanitation Program / Public-Private Infrastructure Advisory Facility.

Atkinson, P., and E. Mulbah. 2000. NGOs and peace building in complex political emergencies: Agency survey from Liberia. Working Paper No. 10. Manchester, UK: Institute for Development Policy and Management, University of Manchester.

AWF (African Water Facility). 2007. Project appraisal report: Liberia: Monrovia expansion and rehabilitation of three county capitals water supply and sanitation project: Appraisal report. www.africanwaterfacility.org/fileadmin/uploads/awf/projects-activities/24-Liberia%20 WSS%20Study%20Final%20%20Appraisal%20and%20TOR-%2013dec2007.pdf.

Balanyá, B., B. Brennan, O. Hoederman, S. Kishimoto, and P. Terhorst, eds. 2005. *Reclaiming public water: Achievements, struggles and visions from around the world.* Amsterdam, Netherlands: Transnational Institute, Corporate Europe Observatory.

Banks, D., and M. H. Hamid. 2002. *Water assessment mission to Afghanistan, January–February 2002. Part F: Urban water supply systems in Afghanistan.* Oslo: Norwegian Church Aid.

Batley, R. 2001. Public-private partnerships for urban services. In *The challenge of urban government: Policies and practices*, ed. M. Freire and R. E. Stren. WBI Development Studies. Washington, D.C.: World Bank; Toronto, Canada: Centre for Urban and Community Studies, University of Toronto. www-wds.worldbank.org/servlet/WDSContentServer/ WDSP/IB/2001/02/02/000094946_01011905315240/Rendered/PDF/multi_page.pdf.

Braïlowsky, A., A. Boisgallais, and E. Paquot. 2000. Intermédiation sociale et construction institutionnelle: Démarche du programme d'approvisionnement en eau des quartiers

Restoring water services in Kabul and Monrovia 61

populaires de Port-au-Prince en Haïti. Coopérer Aujourd'hui Report No. 15. Paris: Groupe de Recherche et d'Echanges Technologiques. www.gret.org/wp-content/uploads/cooperer15.pdf.

Brinkhoff, T. 2010. City population. www.citypopulation.de.

Browne, D., and S. Tsikisayi. 2004. *Water demand and market study in Monrovia, Liberia, draft final report.* Wamel, Netherlands: Quest Consult for Project Management Unit, European Commission Office–Liberia.

Colin, J., and H. Lockwood. 2002. *Making innovation work through partnerships in water and sanitation projects.* London: Business Partnerships for Development. www.aguaconsult.co.uk/uploads/pdfs/agua_bpdinnovation.pdf.

Cosgrave, J. 1999. *Watering thorns, version 0.90.* Oxford, UK: Oxfam.

CSO (Central Statistics Office of Afghanistan). 2000. Population 1999, Kabul City. In *Population survey project: AX/ZTQ/6/017/ACC – CSO.* Kabul: United Nations Regional Coordination Office.

———. 2005. Kabul city census by districts and age groups 1986. In *1382 (2003) Afghanistan statistical yearbook.* Kabul.

Diago, J. L., and S. Arnalich. 2004. *Intervención para la rehabilitación y mejora de las instalaciones de agua del cuadrante noroeste de Kabul, Afghanistan.* Madrid: Spanish Red Cross.

Elliott, M. J. 2002. *Feasibility study for the re-electrification of the Logar water supply scheme in Kabul, Afghanistan.* London: British Red Cross; Geneva, Switzerland: International Committee of the Red Cross.

Fischaess, B. 2003. *Summary of the feasibility study for the extension of the Kabul water supply system.* Entlingen, Germany: RRI Beller/Kocks.

Geoscience. 1998. *Water supply for Monrovia and rural areas, Liberia.* Report LBR/6ACP/29-20. Florence, Italy.

Green, R. H. 2000. Rehabilitation: Strategic, proactive, flexible, risky? *Disasters* 24 (4): 343–362.

Grinnell, E., and H. Troc. 2004. *Kabul vulnerability mapping.* Paris: Action Contre la Faim. www.internal-displacement.org/8025708F004CE90B/(httpDocuments)/34F66E2 7EE6CA19C802570B700587B57/$file/ACF_Kabul_vulnerability_mapping_jan04.pdf.

Hall, D., K. Bayliss, and E. Lobina. 2002. Water privatization in Africa. Paper presented at the Municipal Services Project Conference, Witswatersrand University, Johannesburg, South Africa.

Johnson, C. 2004. *An Oxfam country profile: Afghanistan.* 2nd ed. Oxford, UK: Oxfam.

KfW (Kreditanstalt für Wiederaufbau). 2003. *Afghanistan: Challenges after 23 years of civil war.* Frankfurt, Germany.

Macrae, J. 2002. The political dimension. In *Forum: War and accountability.* Geneva, Switzerland: International Committee of the Red Cross.

Matthieussent, S., and R. Carlier. 2004. Le cas de l'approvisionnement en eau potable des quartiers défavorisés de Port-au-Prince. Document de travail. In *Séminaires sur les politiques publiques de lutte contre la pauvreté et les inégalités,* ed. Groupe de Recherche et d'Echanges Technologiques. Paris: Reseau Impact-Politique Africaine. http://reseauimpact.org/spip.php?article82.

MUDH (Ministry of Urban Development and Housing, Islamic Republic of Afghanistan). 2005. *Urban water supply and sewerage sector institutional development plan.* Kabul.

Ockelford, J. 1993. How do we work with host government and other NGOs for the good of the refugees (workshop 3). Discussion paper: Coordination of emergency relief in

62　Water and post-conflict peacebuilding

Liberia. In *Technical support for refugees: Proceedings of the 1991 international conference,* ed. B. Reed. Loughborough, UK: Water Engineering and Development Centre, Loughborough University.

Oxfam. 2005. *Public health rapid needs assessment report urban programme, January and May 2005.* Monrovia, Liberia.

Perry, J. A. 1988. Networking urban water supplies in West Africa. *Journal of the American Water Works Association* 80 (6): 34–42.

Pinera, J. 1999. *Kabul 99 public health survey: Water and sanitation situation in Kabul, final report.* Report No. Kab 99/2182. Kabul, Afghanistan: International Committee of the Red Cross.

———. 2006. Partnerships between water sector institutions and aid agencies in urban areas affected by armed conflicts. Ph.D. dissertation, Loughborough University, Leicestershire, United Kingdom.

Pinera, J.-F., and R. Reed. 2009. A tale of two cities: Restoring water services in Kabul and Monrovia, Liberia. *Disasters: The Journal of Disaster Studies, Policy and Management* 33 (4): 574–590.

Pinera, J., and L. Rudge. 2005. Water and sanitation assistance for Kabul: A lot for the happy few? WEDC International 31st Conference, "Maximizing the Benefits from Water and Environmental Sanitation," Kampala, Uganda. http://susana.org/lang-en/library?view=ccbktypeitem&type=2&id=821.

Smith, C. 2001. *1st and 2nd rehabilitation programmes, water supply and sanitation, inputs/achievements (April 1998 to June 2001—39 months).* Florence, Italy: Geoscience.

———. 2004. *Reintegration programme for returnees and displaced people in Liberia: Water supply for Monrovia and rural areas, Liberia.* Report No. LBR/8ACP/02/2-3. Florence, Italy: Geoscience.

Smith, C., and J. Kpakolo. 2004. *Water supply in Monrovia, Liberia.* Florence, Italy: Geoscience.

Smith, C., A. Petters, R. Conti, and P. Smets. 2001. Cities in war: Thirsty cities. Monrovia (Liberia): Water supply for Monrovia during and after the civil war. Occasional Paper No. 4. Geneva, Switzerland: Geneva Foundation.

Sohail, M., S. Cavill, and A. P. Cotton. 2005. Sustainable operation and maintenance of urban infrastructure: Myth or reality? *Journal of Urban Planning and Development* 131 (1): 39–49.

Solidarités International. 1995. *Strategies for water supply and sanitation in Kabul city.* Paris.

Stren, R. E. 2001. Private involvement in the provision of public services: Editor's introduction. In *The challenge of urban government: Policies and practices,* ed. M. Freire and R. E. Stren. WBI Development Studies. Washington, D.C.: World Bank; Toronto, Canada: Centre for Urban and Community Studies, University of Toronto. www-wds.worldbank.org/servlet/WDSContentServer/WDSP/IB/2001/02/02/000094946_01011905315240/Rendered/PDF/multi_page.pdf.

Willson, N. 2003. Water and sanitation priority sector (community and infrastructure), December 2003. Monrovia, Liberia: United Nations / World Bank.

World Bank. 2006. *Approaches to private participation in water services: A toolkit.* Washington, D.C.: International Bank for Reconstruction and Development / World Bank. http://rru.worldbank.org/Documents/Toolkits/Water/Water_Full.pdf.

Conflict and collaboration for water resources in Angola's post-war cities

Allan Cain

Since 2002, Angola has been recovering from four decades of civil war. The conflict resulted in mass displacement of people, destruction of infrastructure, and diversion of investments away from maintenance and infrastructure development, producing chronic public health problems for the population at large. Social exclusion, inequality, and poverty—problems that originally seeded the conflict— are still problems in the post-war era. Access to water mirrors the biased distribution pattern of other resources in Angola. The majority of low-income, urban communities still have no access to affordable potable water and are mainly served by informal water vendors.

In Development Workshop's twenty years of implementing practical projects in Angola, it has gathered knowledge on the functioning of the informal water economy that continues to provide the bulk of water services to Luanda's population. Development Workshop estimates that the annual value of this informal water economy grew over a period of twelve years from about US$60 million during the civil war to almost US$250 million in 2009 (Development Workshop 2009).[1]

Allan Cain is the director of Development Workshop and has worked for nearly thirty years in Angola, implementing projects for community water supply, school building and planning, environmental sanitation, land rights, and public participation. This chapter draws on research carried out by Development Workshop Angola, which is supported by the International Development Research Centre's regional office for eastern and southern Africa in Nairobi, Kenya, under the project Post-Conflict Transformation in Angola's Informal Economy. The chapter also is partly abstracted from the International Institute for Environment and Development monograph by Allan Cain and Martin Mulenga (Cain and Mulenga 2009).

[1] Development Workshop was contracted by the World Bank in 1995, 1998, and 2008 to carry out water surveys, with the objectives of describing the water distribution system in the peri-urban areas of Luanda and other provincial cities, identifying the stakeholders, investigating the extent of their involvement, assessing water consumption and prices, and understanding consumers' priorities for improvement (Development Workshop 1995, 1998, 2008).

64   Water and post-conflict peacebuilding

In this environment of uneven and inequitable access to scarce urban water resources, conflict born of competition for access to water is inevitable. However, poor communities in Angola's capital city, Luanda, have found collective solutions and have built on neighborhood cooperation and social solidarity to improve their access to water. These experiences demonstrate the important role that community water management can play in promoting a more equitable distribution of water resources at affordable prices in the poor peri-urban *musseques* (informal settlements) of Luanda.

This chapter begins by outlining the structure of water services in Angola after more than forty years of conflict and then, focusing on Luanda in particular, discusses the importance of the informal water market, the main water provider for most of the urban poor. Based on the knowledge gathered by the Development Workshop, the chapter examines Luanda's peri-urban water value chain and uses value chain analysis to assess Luanda's water economy. Several factors affecting success in promoting post-conflict access to water are highlighted, including the need for cooperation with informal water service providers, addressing unresolved issues with those providers, and the importance of social capital in the informal water sector. The chapter examines key elements of community-based water management, particularly robust and low-cost technology, sustainability strategies, and water committees and associations, and concludes with recommendations for national post-war strategies.

WATER SERVICES IN POST-CONFLICT ANGOLA

Angola won independence from Portugal in 1975 after waging a war of independence that lasted almost fourteen years. At that time, Luanda had a population of about 500,000 people, many of whom were Portuguese settlers and urbanized Angolans. After independence and the flight of many Portuguese nationals, the country was immediately plunged into a brutal and protracted civil war that ended only in early 2002. The last decade of conflict was punctuated by a series of ceasefires that invariably broke down and were followed by a return to conflict.

These cease fires were lost opportunities to build peace by making politically divided communities and national economic actors into stakeholders in social reconstruction. The government of Angola did not implement the expected economic and administrative reforms that were considered to be preconditions for major local and international investment. The nascent national private sector, which was born out of the previously socialist state apparatus, emerged very slowly because the government failed to carry out the promised monetary, banking, and legal restructuring, which would have stimulated local small- and medium-scale private-sector development. Local entrepreneurs lacked confidence due to the slow movement of the peace process and the failure to guarantee the free movement of people and commodities around the country and between the cities and rural areas.

Water in Angolan cities 65

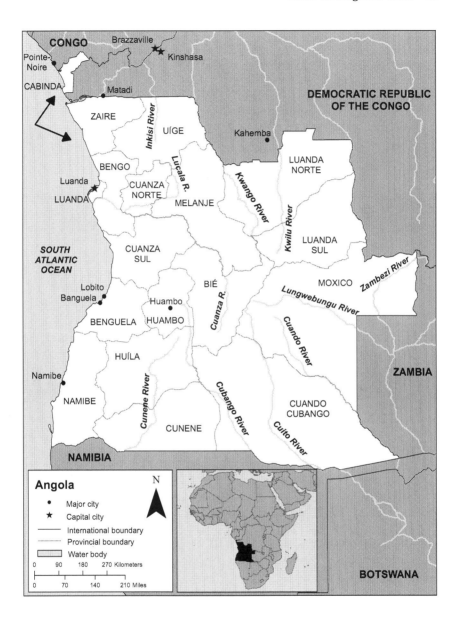

Peace was achieved only following the death of Jonas Savimbi, the president of the insurgent liberation movement UNITA (União Nacional para a Independência Total de Angola): in April 2002 a definitive cease fire was signed between the rebel army and the government of Angola. The peace agreement corrected some of the errors of earlier accords, which had not adequately demobilized the opposition's military forces. The 2002 Luena Memorandum of Understanding,

66 Water and post-conflict peacebuilding

an addendum to the previously concluded Lusaka Protocol, treated the former rebels with magnanimity, allowing UNITA to operate as a parliamentary political party and offering former combatants a dignified decommissioning and the opportunity to reintegrate into their former communities. However, reintegration into rural settlements that had been devastated during decades of conflict was only partially successful. Many former combatants, some of whom had perpetrated acts of terror in their areas of origin, joined a new wave of migration to the capital region in search of employment.

As control of the rural areas fell to one or the other contesting party during the civil war, government in those areas was nearly absent. There were massive shifts in population as people in rural areas sought refuge from the fighting and fled to the relative safety of the cities. Most of the internally displaced persons concentrated in Luanda. After forty years of conflict, Angola's landscape was heavily mined; its infrastructure had been neglected, sabotaged, or destroyed; state administration was weak; about 4 million persons were internally displaced; and the economy was barely functioning and had little productive capacity.

By the end of the conflict, only about 17 percent of households in the country reported having adequate access to water, and only 10 percent of total households had in-home connections. Of the households with a tap in their residence, only half received water every day; 35 percent received water most days; and 14 percent received water only once or twice per week (Pinto and Ribeiro 1998). A 1998 Development Workshop survey of peri-urban Luanda revealed that one-third of households with domestic water connections did not receive water through them. Only 5 percent of households reported that their connections provided water at least two or three times a week, and just three of the forty-three zones in the survey had more that 20 percent of households reporting domestic connections that provided water at least two or three times a week (Development Workshop 1998; see table 1).

In Luanda the water network was originally built for a colonial population of a half-million people. At independence, poor neighborhoods (musseques) in Luanda were served by about 300 standposts connected to the treated-water network. These standposts were distributed so that water could be fetched in buckets and jerry cans and carted or head-loaded back home. Water carting was traditionally the burden of women and children. During the conflict years, many standposts fell into disrepair; however, a number of nongovernmental organizations and international donors working with the state-owned water service corporation Luanda Provincial Water Company (Empresa de Aguas de Luanda, or EPAL) promoted standpost construction as a strategy to provide at least a basic supply of water to the musseques. By the end of the war, the network was stretched to its breaking point, with piped water reaching only a quarter of the city's households. Most of Luanda's population rely on water purchased from tanker trucks, with prices varying from the equivalent of US$4 per cubic meter

Water in Angolan cities 67

Table 1. Household water sources in Luanda, Angola

	1996		2002
	Main water source %	*Secondary water source* %	*Main water source* %
Tap in residence linked to network	6.0	1.1	6.2
Tap in building or neighbor's building	16.3	9.3	14.3
Tap in yard or garden	NA	NA	5.1
Public standpost	12.2	8.2	16.4
Borehole with pump	3.5	2.5	6.9
Spring or well	22.3	17.9	29.9
Surface water	1.3	3.5	0
River water	16.4	19.9	12.2
Lorry or tanker	11.2	25.2	6.5
Other	10.8	12.4	2.5

Sources: UNICEF (1997, 2002).

in an area close to a water company distribution tank to US$20 in an area distant from the river and from any piped water connection. (Table 2 shows distance of water source from Luanda households.)

One of the important challenges of post-war reconstruction is to provide more and better-quality basic services, including access to water. Attempts during the conflict years to improve peri-urban water supply were hampered by the government's lack of capacity to maintain the infrastructure that already existed, much less upgrade these systems or build and manage new ones.

Since the conflict, projects aimed at upgrading the main water supply systems to accommodate peri-urban areas have been overwhelmed by explosive population growth in Angola's major cities. The amount and quality of water available in most areas (and especially in peri-urban areas) is significantly below recommended levels. It appears that Angola will have difficulty in reaching the Millennium Development Goal (MDG) targets related to water and sanitation.

Table 2. Distance to main water source for households in Luanda, Angola

	1996 %	2002 %
Tap in residence	5.7	7.2
Less than 100 meters from residence	47.3	51.0
100 to 500 meters from residence	30.3	28.6
500 to 1,000 meters from residence	12.2	7.7
More than 1,000 meters from residence	4.4	5.5

Sources: UNICEF (1997, 2002).

68   Water and post-conflict peacebuilding

Water is costly and of poor quality, representing both a significant household expenditure for the urban poor and a growing health hazard, as evidenced by several post-war outbreaks of highly communicable diseases, including cholera, whose incidence is known to correlate with poor water quality and restricted access. In 2006, there were over 50,000 cholera cases in Angola and over 5,000 deaths from the illness. Cholera remains endemic in Luanda and several other urban centers.

The MDGs map out the ambitious target of reducing by half the number of people who lack minimal access to potable water by 2015. The government of Angola has incorporated the MDGs into its short- and medium-term plans for the water sector, and it has worked with bilateral and multilateral donors to draft large-scale plans for increasing water supply to Luanda and other cities through increased pumping and pipeline capacity. In 2008 the government launched the Agua para Todos, or Water for All, program. At its launch, the national water director made a public commitment to provide water to communities "wherever they are," signaling a new, more inclusive government policy to bring water to poor, previously excluded communities.

Official attitudes favor the participation of an organized private sector in water provision. However, the existing private sector is disorganized and needs to develop in its capacity to be a reliable partner with the government in the provision of essential services, including water. Provincial water authorities in both Luanda and Benguela have shown interest in franchising standposts to private-sector operators, but in the few cases where private operators have taken up franchises, they have proved unreliable and unable to guarantee the maintenance of those water systems (Development Workshop 1997).

In the meantime, the overwhelming majority of Angola's peri-urban population continues to rely for its water supplies on an informal system of water sellers and transporters that was developed by poor people who had been displaced from rural areas affected by the conflict. Residents of Luanda typically purchase water from tank owners, who have bought their water from lorry owners, who have transported water from the nearest river or have filled up at official or unofficial stations where water comes from the piped supply.

The mechanisms that poor people in Luanda use to access water are not merely economic arrangements. In the aftermath of conflict, it is important for neighborhoods to build social solidarity, especially in communities where social capital was severely eroded during the conflict. Rather than provoking competition, water scarcity has nurtured cooperation among neighbors in many of Luanda's *bairros*, or neighborhoods.

The informal sector has demonstrated its capacity to fill the service gap left by an under-capacitated government, but it lacks the regulatory controls necessary to ensure the provision of sustainable and safe supplies of water to a population in need. Therefore, Development Workshop partnered with local communities to develop the Community Management Model for water delivery— a model that promotes both sustainable enterprise and social solidarity between consumer-stakeholders. The Angolan government has incorporated these principles of community management into a national strategy under the banner of the national Water for All program.

IMPORTANCE OF THE INFORMAL WATER MARKET

The national post-war rehabilitation program in Luanda and other cities has included the rebuilding and extension of formal water systems. However, these programs are still at an early stage. It will take time to rebuild the core of systems that have not been maintained sufficiently for over thirty years or that were sabotaged during the conflict. It will also take time to develop new extensions to the formal water system. It is expected that the rehabilitated systems will supply piped water to households in the urbanized districts of the cities, but government planners envisioned that the peri-urban peripheries will still be supplied by community standpost water points.

The public utility, EPAL, manages water production and the distribution cycle through a vertically integrated monopoly. During the years of conflict, the growth of EPAL's water distribution system and the maintenance of the existing infrastructure did not keep pace with the growth of the urban population. Since the end of the civil war, EPAL has benefited from access to new Chinese and Brazilian loans and lines of credit, which have been used to install a new plant and other infrastructure. However, EPAL still suffers from weak management capacity and draws technical assistance and management advice from Portuguese firms that are familiar with the colonial-era systems left over from before independence but do not necessarily bring knowledge and experience appropriate to developing-country contexts where innovative solutions are required to meet the urgent needs of the urban poor.

Large areas in Angolan cities are likely to continue relying on informal water suppliers for some time. The government has tended to regard informal providers as economic opportunists who are filling the supply gap while the government develops its full capacity. Some people argue that small-scale water service providers give poor service to consumers, failing to meet both technological and quality standards. Recently, however, these suppliers have gained recognition as a viable alternative for communities that are not connected to the water grid, though this recognition has not yet translated into a legal or institutional framework within which informal service providers can operate.

Those government officials in charge of water distribution who recognize the important role of informal suppliers acknowledge that the informal sector is the main water supplier for most of the urban poor and that this segment of the population would go unserved if small-scale water service providers stop working. They also know that the provincial government's plan to extend the water supply system to all of the new and informal settlements is unattainable in the immediate future. (The extent of Luanda's informal settlements is shown in figure 1.) Finally, there is a growing recognition that urban water management in Luanda is not

70 Water and post-conflict peacebuilding

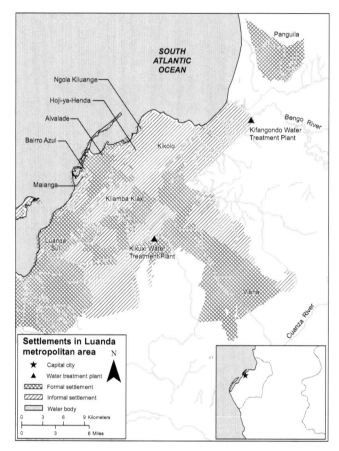

Figure 1. Formal and informal settlements in the greater metropolitan area of Luanda, Angola
Source: Created by Mathieu Cain for Development Workshop.

solely a government mandate and that its successful functioning is supported by a strong interaction of formal and informal activities.

LUANDA'S PERI-URBAN WATER VALUE CHAIN

Development Workshop has used various value chain tools to obtain a clearer picture of Luanda's informal peri-urban water market, which turns over more than US$250 million annually and provides almost twenty liters of water per person per day to almost 4 million people at a price of US$0.01 per liter. It has asked questions about the market itself (What is the main source of supply? Where is value added? Where is money made?), about market chain participants (What are the relationships between the formal and informal institutions involved? Where do they fit in the process of delivery?), and about consumer end points (What are the levels of access, satisfaction, affordability, and willingness to pay?).

Value chain analysis is a tool that involves the mapping of sequential commodity transactions. It has proved to be particularly useful for assessing the water economy in Luanda, where water services can be unbundled, with various components of the distribution chain operated by different entities (see figure 2). In the informal market, most water is supplied through a simple vertical structure:

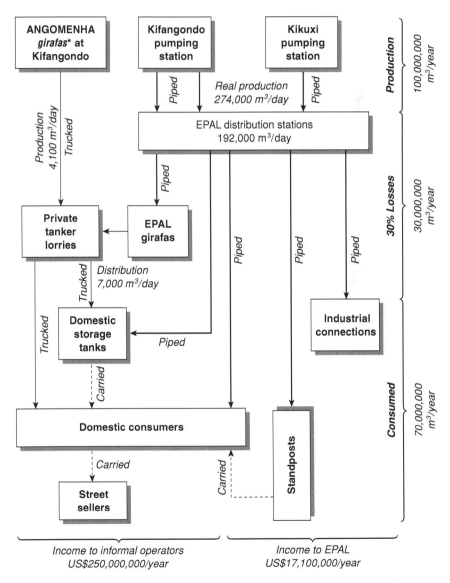

Figure 2. Value chain model of the water supply system in Luanda, Angola
Source: Development Workshop (2008).
Notes: EPAL is the state-owned water service corporation Empresa de Aguas de Luanda.
* Water truck filling stations

72   Water and post-conflict peacebuilding

water is pumped from the river, transported by tanker trucks, treated, stored in tanks, and distributed by street vendors. In contrast to the formal water supply system in which water is treated at riverside pumping and treatment stations, in the informal system water is treated later in the process, if at all. In the informal system, treatment involves introducing chlorine into tanked water being transported by tanker truck drivers. Public health officials encourage people who buy water from informal suppliers to disinfect the water before consuming it.

The key actors within the informal water supply market chain include the government of Angola, represented by the National Directorate for Water Supply and Sanitation; EPAL, the public company responsible for the production and distribution of water in Luanda; ANGOMENHA, an association of operators who pump river water for their tanker truck–driver members and transport it with tanker trucks to the informal supply network; water truck operators; home tank owners; and finally, consumers. The tanker truck operators are responsible for transporting water to unconnected consumers, and the home tank owners sell water at retail from underground tanks.

EPAL, the formal-sector water service provider, has a facility in place to produce 255,000 cubic meters of water per day, but it is currently operating at 35 percent below capacity (at 165,500 cubic meters per day) as a result of leakages in the distribution system and other technical and managerial constraints, such as weak consumer tracking and billing and a lack of authority to set economic tariffs. If it were operating at full capacity, in 2008 EPAL could have provided Luanda residents an average 57 liters of water per person per day, but given its reduced capacity, the amount of water per person is only 37 liters per day. Highly unequal distribution exacerbates this scarcity for many residents: most citizens who are not connected to the network receive nothing, while the fortunate few receive an unlimited supply. The amount of water that reaches connected consumers has been estimated at only 64,000 cubic meters per day; the remaining 101,500 cubic meters are distributed to unconnected consumers through standposts, water truck operators, and home tank owners (Cain and Mulenga 2009).[2]

As a short-term solution to the water distribution problem, EPAL had planned, on the basis of recommendations made by Development Workshop in its 1995 report, to build water truck filling stations *(girafas)* at sites on the periphery of the city where an underground pipe network did not exist (Development Workshop

---

[2] The amount of water that reaches connected and unconnected consumers cannot be determined with certainty because there are many illegal connections to the pipeline in bairros that lack a secondary network distribution system to the households. In addition, because water supply to households with connections is intermittent, those households also buy water from the informal distributors at various times during the year. Unconnected households close to the better served urbanized bairros, like Alvalade, Maianga, and Bairro Azul, can access piped water via clandestine connections to officially served households.

1995). Water truck operators would be able to buy water at the filling stations and resell it to unconnected households. However, EPAL constructed most of the filling stations adjacent to the EPAL water treatment centers within the city, where water pressure was higher and EPAL believed that the girafas could be more easily controlled. Underserved households are still ten to twenty kilometers away from the filling stations, and the farther a household is from a filling station, the more it pays for water. This is the case even if the price of water at the filling station is set at a low, subsidized level.

New water systems that are funded with foreign loans and serve individual households have only been built to serve the commercial, high-income, low-density areas in the southern extension of the city (Luanda Sul). These new systems often bypass high-density, low-income neighborhoods en route between the water source and the distribution point. Water provision to the newly developed subdivisions greatly enhances the value of land plots there, and it therefore benefits commercial developers, but it brings little income to EPAL. Yet EPAL still sells water at the official subsidized price to the relatively small number of consumers living in these low-density residential areas.

FACTORS AFFECTING SUCCESS IN PROMOTING POST-CONFLICT ACCESS TO WATER

Several factors affect the likelihood of success in promoting post-conflict access to water, including cooperation with informal water service providers, unresolved issues with those providers, and the role of social capital in the informal sector.

Cooperation with informal water service providers

Because the formal water service sector has been unable to meet the water needs of so many of Luanda's residents, officials have been obliged to accept the role of informal-sector water truck operators. The difference between the formal and informal water sectors is not clearly defined. The informal sector is often regarded as an extension of the formal because it fills a critical gap in the formal sector's capacity to extend services beyond the official network of household connections. Informal water service operators, some of whom are military officers or relatives of government functionaries, see themselves as partners of the government, and they seek government officials' recognition of the important service they provide. However, they are often identified as black marketeers and exploiters of the poor because of the high costs of transport, which they are obliged to pass on to consumers.

One of the official filling stations in Luanda is owned by water truck operators who have organized themselves into the association called ANGOMENHA. The association interacts with EPAL and the provincial government on behalf of its members. The ANGOMENHA filling station, located adjacent to the Bengo River, is the main source of water sold by trucks in Luanda. It serves about 550 trucks per day, each of which has a capacity of between five and twenty-five cubic meters (Development Workshop 2009). Because ANGOMENHA has the most efficient filling system, drivers at its station do not need to wait in long queues (see figure 3).

Each pump owner and water truck operator who is a member of ANGOMENHA is expected to contribute toward a monthly maintenance fee and to pay a 1 percent monthly tax on revenue to the Ministry of Finance. An additional fee that covers maintenance of the road leading to the station is paid on ad hoc basis.

Although ANGOMENHA's members are informal operators, the creation of the association is a clear attempt to formalize and rationalize their role and to establish themselves as a legitimate part of the market chain. The informal operators' willingness to pay taxes and water fees is a demonstration of their acceptance of some degree of regulation. Recognition of these operators, then licensing and regulation by the state, would reduce the risks they face by giving them some protection from (sometimes off-duty) law enforcement officers who seek illicit fees by providing operators with official business licenses.

Unresolved issues with informal services providers

Water vending is exceptionally profitable for operators who pump water from the river. They can earn a return on investment in two years or less. Profits are

Figure 3. Tanker trucks filling up from the River Bengo at the ANGOMENHA filling station at Kifangondo, Angola
Photo: T. Hetherington (2005).

lower for truck operators, for whom high fuel and labor costs are exacerbated by traffic congestion on Luanda's overcrowded roadways. The most significant cost is depreciation of vehicles, which is estimated to consume over half of an operator's margin. The reason for the high price of water delivered by tanker trucks is not unreasonable profits for truck owners, but the cost of the vehicles and their operation.

Another problem in the informal sector is unsafe drinking water. The water sold at the ANGOMENHA filling station is untreated at the source and therefore poses serious health risks to consumers. All drivers are expected to stop at a small nearby station for chlorine treatment, which costs only US$0.12 per cubic meter, but there is no system of enforcement to ensure that the water has been successfully treated. Most of the time no one verifies whether the driver has added chlorine to the tank.[3] During one cholera epidemic, Development Workshop piloted a community-based water-testing program (Development Workshop 1994). It trained community volunteers and equipped them with simple chlorine test kits. Volunteers targeted tank owners and water resellers in bairros where the cholera risk was high. The program raised the awareness of intermediary sellers about the need for water treatment and provoked them to boycott negligent water truckers who failed to avail themselves of the free water chlorination stations set up by the public health service during the crisis.

The role of social capital in the informal sector

Water selling in its various forms is probably the largest subsector of Luanda's extensive informal economy, and the interface between transporters and retailers is central to the informal water supply system. The retail price of water is set by household-based resellers. When they can buy bulk water cheaply, they normally pass these savings on to consumers. Focus groups organized by Development Workshop reported that vendors do not sell for profit at all, but rather to cover their own water-consumption costs. Only rarely did groups say that they felt exploited by the water vendors in their neighborhoods (Development Workshop 1995).

Neighborhood water access and prices are not determined solely by commercial factors. Social relationships and community solidarity play an important role. Householders who possess a water tank are in a position to choose not only the price but also the neighbors to whom they wish to sell. The price of water often varies, depending on the relationship between the owner of the tank and the water buyer. The owners of water tanks often sell water for a lower price to people with whom they have built a relationship or mutual solidarity (Lindblom 2010).

---

[3] EPAL takes weekly samples of water to its labs for chlorine analysis, but only from the cisterns of trucks that have voluntarily stopped for chlorination.

Home tank owners often do not have sufficient capital on hand to buy a truckload of water every time their tank becomes empty. Until they can accumulate a lump sum to purchase a complete load of water, they may become consumers of water from other tank owners in the neighborhood. Social networks evolve locally among neighbors who may be buyers and sellers at different times. It thus becomes essential for each water consumer in a poor, unserviced musseque to maintain amicable social relationships with a range of water suppliers within walking distance of their homes.

A secondary level of retailing within the informal market is sometimes practiced by street vendors who sell water in small containers or plastic bags (see figure 4). These vendors usually receive their water from home tanks and standposts and sell in units of half liters for US$0.06 to US$0.12 each. These ambulant traders are considered to be at one of the lowest rungs of the water market, and they make very small profits. For the poor and for women and youth, street vending is often seen as an entry point into the informal market that requires little capital or skill.

Water carrying by women and children is rarely factored into the price of water after it is delivered by truck to the neighborhood reseller or by pipe to the standpost. Significant time and therefore value is added by women and girls who head-carry jerry cans, basins, and buckets of water sometimes hundreds of meters

Figure 4. Street vendors reselling water in plastic bags in Luanda, Angola
Photo: T. Hetherington (2005).

Water in Angolan cities 77

Table 3. Carriers of water in urban areas, Angola

Carriers of water in urban areas	%
Women, age 18 and up	62.2
Female youth, age 12–17	16.6
Children, age 5–11	5.9
Male youth, age 12–17	5.3
Men, age 18 and up	4.7
Unspecified	5.3

Source: UNICEF (2002).

to their homes, and by children who haul water carts often weighing forty to fifty kilograms for even longer distances (see table 3).

A NEW PARADIGM: COMMUNITY-BASED WATER MANAGEMENT

With support from the Luanda Urban Poverty Programme (LUPP),[4] Development Workshop's Sustainable Community Service Project was developed to build partnerships with the provincial and national water authorities to develop robust systems for community-based water management in a city with rapid population growth, high levels of poverty, numerous informal settlements, and weak local government.

It was clear from Development Workshop's research, including its affordability and willingness-to-pay studies, that low-income households were prepared to pay for a public water supply service if they received reliable service and the price was less than that charged by private water vendors. A model was therefore developed to provide such a service at a price affordable to consumers. The costs of the water as well as standpost maintenance would be covered, and revenues for EPAL, the water company, would encourage it to provide a continuous supply to the standposts.

Water committees were formed to operate the standposts, collect revenue, oversee operations and maintenance, monitor and register the number of days of water flow, and ensure that records of all payments and expenses were kept. This meant developing community organizations that were accountable to residents, something for which there was little precedent. The new community organizations also had to manage finances and deal with conflict, including conflict related to enforcement of the prohibition against illegal connections.

Associations were developed through which committees involved in managing standposts could share their experiences and work together in seeking better services from EPAL and from local authorities. EPAL also recognized that it did not have the capacity to manage water supply at the community level and that it should concentrate on improving bulk water supply—that is, improving the

---

[4] LUPP is a consortium of nongovernmental organizations (NGOs) supported by the United Kingdom's Department for International Development. Participating NGOs include Development Workshop, CARE, Save the Children, and One World Action.

78   Water and post-conflict peacebuilding

process of extracting water from the river, treating it, and distributing it through water mains. The Sustainable Community Service Project is thus building local institutions from the bottom up and seeking to create trust and working partnerships between community organizations, local governments, and EPAL, in which each has defined roles and performance standards.

This type of long-term, local institutional development is not something that most international funding agencies support. Their support is more often for capital investments in time-bound projects. Many external agencies also promote privatization as the solution, but privatization would be inappropriate for Luanda. Angola's national private sector is weak, its public institutions are not strong enough to regulate privatization, and Luanda's large population has incomes too low to be attractive to private enterprises.

Key elements of sustainable basic service models

Development Workshop and its LUPP partners have refined the Community Management Model of sustainable community water management, have rigorously tested its components in practice, and have allowed adequate time for learning and feedback, with the aim of replication and scaling up to serve a larger target group. The project can be seen as a low-cost experimentation phase in advance of major investments that are eventually likely to be made in peri-urban Luanda by the World Bank, the European Union, the African Development Bank, and the Angolan government through commercial credit lines such as those now available from China and Brazil.

The Community Management Model has three key components: hardware that is based on robust and low-cost technology; a sustainability, or cost-recovery, strategy; and a community management system.

Robust, low-cost technology

Development Workshop programs supply water through public standposts constructed by joint EPAL and Development Workshop construction teams and linked to the main water supply. Communities suggest the sites, which are then rigorously screened to prevent the selection of sites where water pressure will diminish over time.

The program promotes the construction of standposts in areas where water pressure is insufficient to supply household connections. The aim has been to bring water to within 200 meters of every house because a number of studies have shown that when water is supplied at a distance of less than 200 meters, water consumption increases. To date this has never been possible in Luanda because water pressure has rarely been sufficient to allow this coverage. The Angolan government continues to work toward the commitment made in its Water for All project to increase water supply in order to reach at least 80 percent of slum dwellers with this minimal level of service.

Sustainability strategies

The Community Management Model employs a number of strategies to ensure that the water supply system will be sustainable. It starts by addressing a priority need that the community has identified during meetings to which representatives of each household were invited. It uses appropriate technologies that are accessible, affordable, and accepted by the users, and for which users can manage the ongoing maintenance.

As each water supply project progresses, the Community Management Model applies an informed-stakeholder analysis. Stakeholders are encouraged to dialogue and collaborate as they perform and monitor their respective roles in service provision. The project supports them in the development of their capacity to carry out their responsibilities and to deal with the conflicts that can arise from provision of basic services. The project also assists with the development of consumer associations, provides the legal support necessary for their registration with municipal administrations, and trains and supports community residents to help them reach their potential as user-managers of water services. The project also raises community awareness about ways to improve access to basic water services, and it urges policy makers to consider community management of resources as a viable option.

In this water supply model, users are client-consumers. They make fair payments for services provided, look after their community's investment, and put pressure on other stakeholders to be accountable for the performance of their roles. The money collected is divided proportionally to pay for water from EPAL, to pay local authorities for police protection, and to fund water committees and associations of water committees. Maintenance funds are managed by the associations through bank accounts that are audited annually to ensure the quality and transparency of the management of community money. This strategy helps to guarantee the financial sustainability of the standposts, helps people to become accustomed to paying for public services, and strengthens the capacity of local structures in management and accountability.

Finally, the Community Management Model establishes monitoring systems to track progress, identify technical and systemic problems, and identify new opportunities. Problems are addressed promptly and in a transparent fashion with the stakeholders. It pursues new opportunities in water service management when doing so does not compromise ongoing commitments.

Currently families participating in community management projects buy from standposts an average of five buckets of water per day (a hundred liters) at a cost of US$0.13 per day. This corresponds to US$1.30 per cubic meter, which is 12 percent of the price charged by private vendors selling water from tanks supplied by trucks. The amount charged at standposts has proved to be adequate for maintaining and repairing the standposts, paying a monitor, and contributing to EPAL for the cost of water supplied. Users may be willing to pay more for a household or yard tap, and this would yield health benefits because

80 Water and post-conflict peacebuilding

people with such water connections tend to use more water. Currently, however, not enough water is supplied to the city to serve a large number of consumers with household connections.

Community management through water committees and associations

The Community Management Model increases local responsibility and develops reciprocal actions between consumers, local administrations, and water provision companies. The beneficiaries of the model must be involved in the process from the beginning. The community management committee has decision-making authority to select locations and to plan for the standposts, the water distribution system, and maintenance.

The Community Management Model was developed over a fifteen-year partnership between Development Workshop and EPAL. This partnership has been progressively consolidated, with the objective of improving EPAL's capacity to construct community standposts and of developing systems of community management that can be expanded and replicated across all of Luanda.

The management and maintenance of this model is carried out at the local level by community groups—water committees, associations of water committees, and area-based organizations—elected by the users of the service. Community management requires constant investment in training and capacity building for all participants in the process, with special attention being given to the community groups. Central to the model is local groups' participation in the negotiation and management of public assets, so the model involves local authorities and EPAL as well as the representative community groups.

Cooperation between the water sector and communities involves the joint identification of problems that need to be resolved and linkage with appropriate technologies that need to be promoted. In accordance with the fundamental principles of community management, the community must take on the process of change, and if it is possible it must develop its own management associations. Angola's water sector authority, the National Directorate for Water Supply and Sanitation, has set up national and provincial departments to promote community water management under the recently launched Water for All program. Training materials created by Development Workshop are now used widely by the directorate.

Overall impact

LUPP has implemented the Community Management Model in the communes of Ngola Kiluange, Hoji-ya-Henda, Kikolo, and Kilamba Kiaxi. Seventy-three standposts were constructed that supply 74,000 people with water. It was necessary to rehabilitate 4,250 meters of the principal water distribution pipeline to ensure that the community standposts would function. Construction of the standposts increased water consumption from 7.6 to 14.58 liters per person per day;

reduced the average distance to collect water from 200 to 89 meters; reduced the price of water, making it five times cheaper than water purchased from private sellers; and considerably improved the quality of water from the public network (Development Workshop 2004).

Increased access to water reduces the time spent in water collection, which provides people—particularly women—with more time to pursue educational or income-generating activities. The increased proximity of the standposts to homes has had a positive impact on social inclusion because access is now easier for the most vulnerable groups.

The participating communities are not passive recipients of a technical asset; they are actively involved. They contribute and expand their knowledge and capacity, and they are accountable for their actions. The implementation of the Community Management Model has stimulated reflection among LUPP, local authorities, and EPAL about the capacity of communities to manage their own standposts.

The Community Management Model thus promotes the creation of social capital and of local structures that allow communities to participate in the resolution of their own problems, more independently of external experts than might otherwise be the case. Water management groups represent a mechanism for exercising citizenship at a local level and for promoting active civic participation focused on the importance of the rights and duties of citizens. The model also promotes an entrepreneurial spirit locally as demonstrated by several community water committees who have reinvested surplus funds earned into extending the basic water network and initiating social projects such as day care services for working mothers who have businesses in the informal marketplaces. Home-based retail sellers and street vendors still operate in places where the Community Management Model has not reached. At the time of writing, large parts of Luanda are not served by EPAL's water network. Trucked-water sellers, being by definition mobile, have shifted their services to these otherwise unsupplied neighborhoods, where they are still in great demand.

RECOMMENDATIONS

During wartime, state structures are usually underfunded and often ignored, and a lack of accountability often becomes embedded in the structures, so they need to be thoroughly reformed. The conflict in Angola weakened the state's capacity to deliver basic necessities such as water, and it provided an excuse for the state and the political elite to sever the link between their responsibilities and society's needs. The state became strong and weak at the same time: the conflict strengthened the security and command-oriented aspects of the state while weakening institutions that function through trust, dialogue, and accountability (Development Workshop 2006).

National post-war strategies need to address the rebuilding not only of physical infrastructure but also of human and social capital. Strategies should assist in consolidating peace and overcoming the legacies of war by addressing

82   Water and post-conflict peacebuilding

the root causes of conflict, such as inequitable access to essential services and resources, including water. Stabilizing fragile and vulnerable post-conflict transitions includes supporting the return of displaced people, promoting livelihoods strategies, and rebuilding essential public services.

Until the state-managed Water for All program is able to deliver potable piped water in adequate quantities and at affordable prices to virtually all Angolan households, or at least to construct standposts within close walking distance of every home, a transitional strategy needs to be adopted with a policy and operational framework that defines a role for small-scale water service providers. Such a framework needs to set standards of quality and efficiency and must not ignore the role of important participants in the existing delivery system.

Angolan politicians have often defended the position that basic services should be provided free of charge, and as a result insufficient funds have been available for the maintenance of existing services. Informal settlements are considered difficult to provide for, and official planners see such settlements as impermanent even though the majority of the urban population lives in them. Central-government income from the country's extractive industries has rarely trickled down to basic service provision in peri-urban and rural areas,[5] so poor people must pay a high price for essential services delivered by the private sector or lose income because of frequent illness from contaminated water.

International financial institutions have promoted privatization. As implemented in Angola, this has meant an obsession with profitability, with little attention being paid to affordability, accountability for funds collected, and inadequate preparation of public institutions for effective regulation of private-sector participation. When the privatization model has been applied in post-conflict Angola, operators have attempted to extract short-term gains, prices have risen, demand has been suppressed, and there has been a lack of clarity about how profits are used.

Those advocating for privatization assume that competition will provide accountability. They believe that holders of concessions to supply water will compete among each other to provide better services at cheaper prices. However, the institutions required to manage this sort of competition do not yet exist in Angola, and when concessions are based on geographical districts, they operate local monopolies; consumers cannot readily choose among services from competing providers.

This chapter demonstrates that in post-conflict Angola the unregulated informal private sector has stepped in to meet a basic need that state water service providers have not met. Although informal water service providers are unable to deliver adequate quantities of water of sufficient quality at affordable prices, they have, with narrow profit margins, enabled the survival of people living in the peripheral musseques where basic services from the state have not yet reached.

---

[5] Angola rivals Nigeria as sub-Saharan Africa's principal oil producer. Diamond mining is Angola's second most important extractive industry.

Contrary to classic privatization models, the informal private water economy, operating in an environment of scarcity, has been sustained on the basis of complex collaboration and social solidarity rather than on the basis of competition. Slum dwellers are often both buyers and sellers of water at different times and therefore are obliged to maintain amicable social and economic relationships with their neighbors, who may also be alternatively water suppliers and customers.

In an urban center like Luanda, its population swollen by people who have fled decades of civil conflict, the Community Management Model promotes the development of social capital. It builds on the strengths of the informal sector while improving the accessibility, quantity, quality, and price of water. Its collaborative approach can be adapted by other post-conflict urban societies where physical water infrastructure has broken down and community networks need to be rebuilt.

REFERENCES

Cain, A., and M. Mulenga. 2009. Water service provision for the peri-urban poor in post-conflict Angola. Human Settlements Working Paper Series: Water, No. 6. London: International Institute for Environment and Development.

Development Workshop. 1994. Cholera preparedness project report. Prepared for One World Action. Luanda, Angola.

———. 1995. *Water supply and sanitation in Luanda: Informal sector study and beneficiary assessment.* Luanda, Angola: World Bank.

———. 1997. *Managing public water standposts: Privatisation or community based management? Lessons from five case studies in Angola.* Luanda, Angola: University of Guelph.

———. 1998. *Community consultation and willingness-to-pay for basic water services.* Luanda, Angola: World Bank.

———. 2004. Estudo sobre o consumo de água nos chafarizes em Luanda. May. Luanda, Angola.

———. 2006. What to do when the fighting stops: Challenges for post-conflict reconstruction in Angola. Development Workshop Occasional Paper No. 7. Luanda, Angola.

———. 2008. Beneficiary assessment and willingness-to-pay study for five cities. Luanda, Angola: World Bank / National Directorate for Water Supply and Sanitation.

———. 2009. Informal peri-urban water sector research in Luanda. Report for the International Development Research Centre's Eastern and Southern African Office, Nairobi, Kenya. June.

Lindblom, H. 2010. Access to water through the informal water supply system in Luanda, Angola. Luanda: Development Workshop Angola; Bergen, Norway: Christian Michelson Institute, University of Bergen.

Pinto, E., and G. Ribeiro. 1998. *Relatório da pesquisa qualitativa preliminar sobre a disposição e capacidade no pagamento de serviços sociais básicos de água, saneamento, saúde e educação.* Luanda, Angola: United Nations Children's Fund and Instituto Nacional de Estetisticas.

UNICEF (United Nations Children's Fund). 1997. *Inquérito de indicadores múltiplos, MICS, INE-GMCVP/UNICEF.* Luanda, Angola.

———. 2002. *Multi indicator cluster survey (MICS).* Luanda, Angola.

Thirsty for peace: The water sector in South Sudan

Sam Huston

After more than two decades of civil war in Sudan ended with the 2005 signing of the Comprehensive Peace Agreement (CPA), the then-newly established government of Southern Sudan (GOSS) faced the massive task of providing basic services to an extremely underserved population. This challenge continues for the government of South Sudan.[1] Trying to meet high expectations for peace dividends—including much-needed access to water—in a large and conflict-devastated land with extremely poor infrastructure is an overwhelming task for an emergent government with limited capacity.

The effort has been complicated by a scarcity of data on where the biggest needs are in a region in which almost everyone lacks water for at least part of the year, and only 48.3 percent have improved water access, which is often defined in the South Sudan context as a community well with a hand pump (MOH 2006).

Attempts to provide equitable access to improved water sources—in the form of boreholes, small peri-urban water systems, and household water connections in urban areas—across what was then the southern part of Sudan (now South Sudan) have been further confused by emergencies, including frequent cholera outbreaks and mass displacement accompanying severe intertribal fighting that may have killed up to 2,500 people in 2009 (ICG 2009). These emergencies have diverted attention and funding from the establishment of longer-term systems

---

Sam Huston has worked in Southern Sudan as program coordinator for Pact Sudan's Water for Recovery and Peace Program and as a water and sanitation advisor to the U. S. Agency for International Development (USAID) in Sudan. He currently works for Tetra Tech ARD on the USAID-funded Afghan Sustainable Water Supply and Sanitation Project.

[1] The CPA contained a provision allowing Southern Sudan the right of self-determination. This right was exercised through a referendum held on January 9, 2011, with Southern Sudanese voting for secession. The Republic of South Sudan was declared a sovereign state on July 9, 2011. In this chapter, the term *Southern Sudan* refers to the southern region of Sudan prior to July 9, 2011, and the term *South Sudan* refers to the sovereign state.

86 Water and post-conflict peacebuilding

and institutional strengthening. Partly as a result, the government systems needed to build and maintain water sector infrastructure have yet to be fully established.

In the eyes of many, improved water access has had and will have a crucial role to play in peacebuilding and calming both North-South tensions and tribal conflict within South Sudan. South Sudan is divided in complex ways. Although efforts by both government and international actors to support its stabilization have had limited success, it is widely accepted that improved water access must be part of the solution.

However, most implementing partners in the sector are concentrating on the Millennium Development Goals for water, sanitation, and hygiene (WASH), which focus not on peacebuilding but on improving public health. This orientation is in line with the 2007 GOSS water policy, which stipulates: "Access to sufficient water of acceptable quality to satisfy basic needs is considered a human right and shall be accorded highest priority in water resources development" (GOSS 2007, sec. 4.1.1).

This approach largely overlooks the provision of water for livestock, which is the most important context for conflict over water. Some attempts have been made to provide water for communities as part of peacebuilding efforts. Given the complexity of competing interests in the region, a wider conceptual framework is needed to address how exactly water-for-peace programs should work. Little research has been done on the links between water and conflict in South Sudan. This lack of readily available information and examples of best practices, and in some cases the lack of detailed understanding of local social realities, have also discouraged practitioners from undertaking peace-oriented water programming, despite the obvious connection between water issues and violence.

CONFLICT-SENSITIVE APPROACHES: SOUTH SUDAN'S WATER SECTOR

When the CPA was signed, access to improved water sources for human consumption in the rural areas of Southern Sudan was estimated at 25 to 40 percent (Sudan Joint Assessment Mission 2004). Getting water to conflict-devastated communities that are vulnerable to a wide range of waterborne diseases was a major priority, which became even more pressing as hundreds of thousands of refugees returned to the region. Even before the CPA, a conflict analysis of Southern Sudan suggested that the acute shortage of water access was not only a humanitarian concern but also a threat to security (Pact Sudan 2002). In fact, local competition over access to scarce water resources and improved water points had contributed to local conflict across Southern Sudan, most infamously between the region's large pastoralist groups (Pact Sudan 2002).

Recommendations from intertribal peace conferences and a variety of conflict analyses have suggested that the lack of access to water for cattle during the height of the dry season is still a major driver of these local conflicts. Lack of

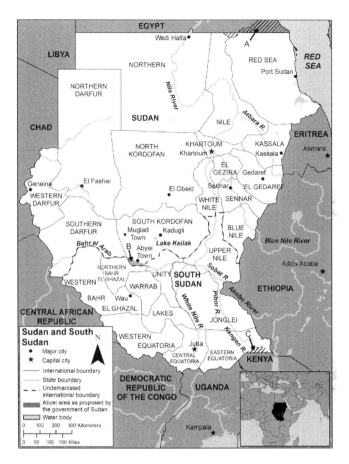

Notes: A – The Hala'ib Triangle is claimed by Sudan and de facto administered by Egypt.
B – The disputed Abyei area; shaded area depicts the Abyei area as proposed by the government of Sudan.
C – The Ilemi Triangle is claimed by Ethiopia, South Sudan, and Kenya, and de facto controlled by Kenya.

water and ample grazing land forces pastoralist cattle camps to migrate further, pushing them into conflict over limited environmental resources with other pastoralist groups and neighboring, sedentary farming communities. Competition between ethnic groups and subgroups has a long history, but in many cases grudges were much worsened by fighting within Southern Sudan during the civil war, which also armed many communities. As a result, cattle raiding and fighting over a water point or other resources frequently ends in a bloodbath, as was seen in 2009 conflicts between the Bor Dinka and the Lou Nuer in Jonglei State.

Ongoing intertribal fighting in large parts of the south has undermined real peace and stymied development. Peacetime has emphasized some problems, in part because herd numbers have increased and it is now possible to move cattle

88   Water and post-conflict peacebuilding

longer distances. This, together with the return of tens of thousands of people to the south, has created additional burdens on the water resource base in areas distant from large, all-season rivers. Populations in agricultural and more built-up areas have also swollen, putting pressure on the limited number of improved water points in large villages and towns and often increasing local tensions over access.

As stated above, while the importance of water for peace in South Sudan is widely acknowledged, a conceptual framework for how water is related to peace and conflict there has not fully evolved. The GOSS Water Policy of 2007 started its general principles section with the statement, "Water must be a lever for peace and not a source of conflict" (GOSS 2007, sec. 2.3). Yet, as of May 2012, there is still no vision about how this might be achieved, and there has been little research into efforts by nongovernmental organizations to provide water to resolve disputes.

Pact Sudan's Water for Recovery and Peace Program (WRAPP), funded by the Office of Foreign Disaster Assistance of the U.S. Agency for International Development (USAID), was one of the rare programs that consistently targeted water service delivery for peacebuilding, conflict prevention, and stabilization. The approach that WRAPP used entailed sending a representative to local peace conferences to follow any dialogue related to water. These peace conferences, often held in provincial towns and villages with tribal leaders and local officials, sought to encourage dialogue and facilitate a negotiated resolution of grievances. If the outcomes of a peace conference called for increasing access to community water points, WRAPP would offer to build the necessary wells and assist with community training and infrastructure improvements. This approach yielded a more sustainable investment, as communities engaged through the conflict-sensitive approach displayed more willingness to take ownership of the long-term care and maintenance of their water points.

Although the connection between water and peace is widely accepted, it is not surprising that so little has been done in this field, given how many areas still lack basic services. Despite the GOSS attempt to push for a longer-term approach to water development, the water sector in South Sudan has until recently largely confined its approach to basic, and sometimes unsustainable, service delivery. The government and water sector service providers, who still face continuing emergencies, have also been unable to wholly shift from the emergency mind-set that became deeply entrenched during the civil war. The focus of their work has largely been on infrastructure and other physical outputs, rapid responses to emergencies, and overcoming immense logistical challenges to quickly provide potable water. Additionally, international efforts have undermined capacity development, longer-term peacebuilding, and recovery: international organizations sidestep local authorities and traditional leaders by not addressing capacity gaps and by not effectively engaging stakeholders in consultative processes that do not meet their short-term emergency objectives.

With a view to decreasing resource-based conflict, Southern Sudanese politicians and traditional authorities from pastoralist areas have lobbied hard for both donor and government funding for water for cattle. However, due to financing, implementation, and bureaucratic constraints, most water sector actors have instead focused on drinking water for humans, paying little attention to cattle. Many international donors and implementing partners are constrained by mandates that limit their focus to drinking water for humans. Practitioners have also found that building *hafirs* (water pans) for cattle is extremely expensive and technically difficult, and little progress has been made in this area. Moreover, water providers are sometimes unwilling or unable to do other peacebuilding work, such as encouraging dialogue, that should take place in parallel.

When conflict-sensitive approaches have been applied to the water sector (consciously or unconsciously), two principles have consistently driven water sector decision making: equity and consensus building at the local level. Informally but widely accepted, these two principles are the basis of the conflict-sensitive approach to water programming in the south. Although local authorities, traditional leaders, and implementing partners sometimes interpret these concepts differently, which can be a problem, their use in planning for water point construction has greatly reduced destructive competition over access to a new or improved water point. The provision of new water points in growing villages and towns, for example, without aggravating existing tensions or provoking anger over perceived unfairness, was especially important in the conflict-bruised, fragile, and often-divided Southern Sudan, and continues to this day in South Sudan.

Equity is a significant principle behind macrolevel decision making within the water sector as well as at the community and intercommunity levels. Representatives of regions, states, and counties, as well as local communities, are often of the opinion that their areas are worse off than others. This is witnessed at sector coordination meetings, where local authorities often suggest that their particular region is acutely underserved. Regionalism and tribalism are important aspects of South Sudan's political fragility.

The GOSS was very careful to ensure that government (and, when possible, international) resources were evenly distributed across the ten states of Southern Sudan. This equity principle was often followed to a fault by the GOSS and continues under the government of South Sudan. Extremely high-need and historically underserved areas receive only their quota of limited sector resources. For example, the GOSS ministerial water budget was divided evenly among the ten states. The tendency toward even division of the water sector budget was compounded by a lack of statistics about which areas were really the worst off, and thus the default position was an even allocation that does not target the highest-need regions. This lack of data, combined with insufficient government capacity and the desire to avoid accusations of unfairness, has hindered the development of a system to prioritize water sector investment distribution by need. Instead, the primary goal has been to eliminate potential conflicts within the allocation process.

Consensus building among authorities and communities, usually operating at the local level, is the second primary principle guiding the few organizations applying conflict-sensitive approaches. This is often best illustrated during site

90 Water and post-conflict peacebuilding

selection for new water points at the county or community level—during which, ideally, local authorities, traditional leaders, peace committees, and community-based organizations allocate sites in a collective, transparent, and collaborative process (Welle, Malek, and Slaymaker 2008). Experience in South Sudan has shown that collective consensus building at the local level has reduced tensions, improved transparency, and improved understanding of the allocation of water points. Besides such peace dividends, consensus building lays the foundation for community ownership, and therefore sustainability, of improved water points. Lack of consensus building before new water points are created has often resulted in local tensions and competition over access, which can be witnessed in hundreds of communities across the south that often received their water points from emergency water programming during the more than two decades of civil war.

Even though the principles of equity and consensus building are often innately understood by South Sudanese, not enough international attention has been placed on using these simple conflict-sensitive approaches to water service delivery. International nongovernmental organizations and UN agencies implementing emergency programming often face short funding cycles and immense logistical challenges, and have ended up implementing water programming where and when they could, based on ease of access and seasonal limitations. They have also often done this work without building sufficient links with government or grassroots traditional leaders.

Lack of coordination between implementing organizations and authorities has also made it difficult for the government to completely understand international agencies' water sector activities. The water sector is extremely complex, and emergency programming is often run in parallel to recovery and development efforts, as local conflicts, floods, and other emergencies emerge. Although the sector's coordination systems have greatly improved since the signing of the CPA, these ad hoc responses have often not been well integrated, and general understanding remains poor.

As South Sudan begins its transition from emergency to recovery, the government will need to be able to better oversee longer-term, sustainable development work. Better government control and understanding are crucial, even though both could hamper the process of local consensus building.

Until now, international agencies working in the water sector have had to address a wide range of development needs, which have often complicated their goals and objectives. Supporting health, livelihoods, economic development, and other goals in such an extremely high-need environment has made it difficult to set priorities and to focus on peacebuilding. As donors move from emergency to development funding, and prioritize water for health clinics, schools, or guinea worm eradication programs, the water allocation process may come to rely less on community decision making, which would make it more difficult to leverage water sector investments for peace with collaborative, transparent, demand-driven, and locally led processes.

FROM RECOVERY TO DEVELOPMENT: ESTABLISHING WATER GOVERNANCE

A significant challenge for the water sector in post-conflict South Sudan remains the establishment of government systems that can provide a solid foundation for water sector investment and sustainability. Increasing government and institutional capacity with respect to the water sector, particularly WASH, is a critical challenge for long-term sustainability.

The capacity of the Ministry of Water Resources and Irrigation and the Southern Sudan Urban Water Corporation has grown since the CPA. However, significantly more progress is needed if these two institutions, which are the foundation for sustainable investments in the WASH sector, are to be able to fully take on the responsibility for policy, regulation, and coordination of WASH services for South Sudan. This is critical to the long-term performance of the WASH sector, a highly visible metric for overall government performance. Improved systems would bring immediate benefits to a government struggling to prove its effectiveness to a population greatly concerned about access to clean drinking water after years of conflict.

Following the signing of the CPA, the GOSS started to establish its structures and systems from scratch. The water sector, like all sectors, lacked trained professionals at all levels of government. Finding capable and literate government staff has been a challenge. Identifying the massive cadre of trained engineers, administrators, and managers needed to establish the functioning bureaucracy required to expand WASH services has not been possible. This deficiency has resulted in the prevalence of informal government systems, weak structures resulting in poor communication between different levels of government and ineffective decision making. Many water sector actors recognize this problem and understand that alternative approaches, such as more decentralized governance structures or the use of more appropriate technologies, will not by themselves resolve all the challenges.

Despite these challenges, the Ministry of Water Resources and Irrigation saw early on the need to begin to strengthen the policy environment for the sector. With assistance from international development partners, the ministry began developing a water policy for Southern Sudan in 2005. The policy was finalized in late 2007 (GOSS 2007) and formally launched in early 2009. A milestone for the sector, it outlined overall objectives and foundational principles for sector operations. However, partially due to consultations with local authorities and public stakeholders, the policy took a significant amount of time to develop during the critical post-conflict period, when the severely underserved population was thirsty for service delivery and had limited appreciation for the value of policy development.

The Ministry of Water Resources and Irrigation is now developing its sector strategy and investment plan. It is hoped that this process will help formalize the government's approach to prioritizing and actualizing the objectives laid

92   Water and post-conflict peacebuilding

out in the GOSS Water Policy in a systematic manner, while taking into account the realities of financing.

International donors, the GOSS, and now the government of South Sudan have made significant investments in the water supply infrastructure, both for humanitarian reasons and to provide tangible peace dividends. However, several years after the signing of the CPA, those humanitarian WASH peace dividends lack sustainability, and there is a clear need to shift focus away from high-visibility service provision and engage with the messy business of systems strengthening and sector governance in order to maintain and preserve the gains that have been made. Water sector actors are now beginning to understand that it is easy to drill a borehole but very difficult to establish the community and government structures that are needed to be able to finance, operate, and maintain that borehole, thereby securing the benefits of the improved water points over the long term. This is further compounded by the challenges of environmental degradation and the impacts of climate change, which until now have been beyond the planning and preparation horizon of the sector.

Prior to South Sudan's independence, a 2009 report published by the World Bank estimated that between 40 and 65 percent of all boreholes in Southern Sudan were not operational (Water and Sanitation Program 2009). Systems that would make it possible to locate nonfunctioning water points and help communities to repair them are badly needed. These services will have to be improved, expanded, and maintained over the long term if they are going to have the desired impacts of promoting peace and forming the core of the development agenda in South Sudan.

Donors have set aside efforts to stabilize peace by postponing the implementation of these kinds of systems and have focused instead on quick-impact projects that increase basic service delivery. They have also tended to spend more funds on emergency-prone areas, which often also have the weakest foundation for successfully absorbing development investments. Even in more stable areas, the host government and communities have been unable to operate and maintain old and new water points. Citing stabilization as the primary objective, agencies have avoided the challenge of sustainability, choosing to drill more boreholes and dig more latrines even as many remain unused because they are broken or unsuitably placed. This has, of course, limited the impact of their work.

South Sudan needs flexible funding mechanisms that take into consideration the length of time and the amount of money needed to achieve both stabilization and development. U.S. agencies have been able to complement each other and provide this type of flexibility. The Office of Transition Initiatives, the Office of Foreign Disaster Assistance, the USAID Sudan mission, and the Bureau of Population, Returnees, and Migration have all been engaged in the water sector in Southern Sudan (and now South Sudan), since the signing of the CPA. Researchers recently noted, however, that "there is concern within the agency that a progressive shift towards developmental funding for basic services may deprive USAID of the responsiveness allowed so far by the Office of Foreign

Disaster Assistance and the Office of Transition Initiatives funding. Flexibility to reorient programming is crucial to enable interventions to address tensions around access to water when they arise" (Pantuliano, Fenton, and Herrmann 2010, 22). Flexibility is even more important in the case of complex pooled funding mechanisms that involve inputs from multiple donors and government stakeholders.

Funding for the water sector has been considerable, but it has not been flexible enough to engage the complex post-conflict context; to consider development, stabilization, emergency, governance, and peacebuilding issues simultaneously; and to promote a comprehensive, government-led, sector-wide approach. Nongovernmental organizations and UN agencies have their own agendas, often not considering longer-term development issues or the government's needs for institutional strengthening. While dealing with these many challenges, the water sector has not often been able to prioritize the water-for-peace approach.

CONCLUSION

Meeting the needs of the population of South Sudan for improved water access is a long-term challenge that requires decades of progress on systems strengthening, capacity building, improvement of sector governance, infrastructure investment, and ending dependency on aid.

Stabilization, on the other hand, is a shorter-term objective that has been the priority of both GOSS and the international community since the signing of the CPA, and will remain so with the government of South Sudan. During this period, it is likely that international funding for expanding water access will continue as one of the many tools that development partners use to leverage their assistance in support of maintaining the peace. Yet it is critically important that the government-led water sector has a vision for itself and collectively encourages programming that can meet many of the competing long-term priorities for the water sector in a conflict-sensitive manner.

Some research on and implementation of conflict-sensitive approaches to water services in South Sudan have been carried out;[2] further focus on the links between water and conflict are needed. However, the main focus of the water sector must be on establishing and strengthening government systems in a manner that ensures that foundational structures are functioning and able to maintain investments and satisfy the population of South Sudan's long-term thirst for water and peace.

---

[2] See Euroconsult Mott MacDonald (2009); Harvey (2009); and Management Systems International (2009).

94 Water and post-conflict peacebuilding

REFERENCES

Euroconsult Mott MacDonald. 2009. *Report on Ministry of Water Resources and Irrigation, Directorate of Rural Water and Sanitation, Rural Water Supply and Sanitation Project capacity building assessment.* Juba, Southern Sudan.

GOSS (Government of Southern Sudan). 2007. *Government of Southern Sudan water policy.* Juba.

Harvey, P. 2009. *E.C. and U.S. approaches to linking relief, rehabilitation and development: A case study on South Sudan.* Draft. Berlin, Germany: Global Public Policy Institute.

ICG (International Crisis Group). 2009. *Jonglei's tribal conflicts: Countering insecurity in South Sudan.* Africa Program Report No. 154. Brussels, Belgium.

Management Systems International. 2009. *Government of Southern Sudan: Functional capacity prioritization study.* Consultative Draft No. 3. Juba.

MOH (Ministry of Health, Government of Southern Sudan). 2006. *Sudan household health survey.* Juba.

Pact Sudan, Sudan Peace Fund Program. 2002. *Summary of initial finding from the peace and conflict mapping exercise undertaken in SPLM controlled areas of southern Sudan.* Juba.

Pantuliano, S., W. Fenton, and K. Herrmann. 2010. Multi-donor evaluation of support to conflict prevention and peace-building activity in Southern Sudan since 2005: Report of Team Two focused on basic services and livelihoods. Unpublished manuscript. (On file with author.)

Sudan Joint Assessment Mission. 2004. *Sector note: Rural water supply and sanitation, SPLM areas of southern Sudan.* Draft. (On file with author.) Juba.

UNDFS (United Nations Department of Field Support). 2011. Sudan. Map No. 4458. October. www.un.org/Depts/Cartographic/map/profile/sudan.pdf.

Water and Sanitation Program. 2009. *Country status overview on water supply and sanitation, Southern Sudan.* Washington, D.C.: World Bank.

Welle, K., B. Malek, and T. Slaymaker. 2008. *Water for Recovery and Peace Programme: PACT Sudan external evaluation.* London: Overseas Development Institute.

Community water management: Experiences from the Democratic Republic of the Congo, Afghanistan, and Liberia

Murray Burt and Bilha Joy Keiru

Water is essential for life. Competing demands and poor management of scarce water resources can create or exacerbate conflict, while equitable and sustainable management can contribute to peacebuilding through economic revitalization, public health improvement, and the restoration of cooperation at all levels of society. A 2009 report from the United Nations Secretary-General highlighted four peacebuilding objectives that lay the foundation for sustainable peace and development—establishing security, building confidence in a political process, delivering initial peace dividends, and expanding core national capacity—and said, "If countries develop a vision and strategy that succeeds in addressing these objectives early on, it substantially increases the chances for sustainable peace— and reduces the risk of relapse into conflict" (UNSG 2009, 1). The report pointed to five priority areas for international support to help post-conflict countries achieve these objectives:[1]

- Support to basic safety and security, including mine action, protection of civilians, disarmament, demobilization and reintegration, strengthening the rule of law and initiation of security sector reform
- Support to political processes, including electoral processes, promoting inclusive dialogue and reconciliation, and developing conflict-management capacity at national and subnational levels
- Support to provision of basic services, such as water and sanitation, health and primary education, and support for the safe and sustainable return and reintegration of internally displaced persons and refugees
- Support to restoring core government functions, in particular basic public administration and public finance, at the national and subnational levels

---

Murray Burt manages Tearfund UK's Global Water, Sanitation, and Hygiene Programme. Bilha Joy Keiru is a policy and learning officer with Tearfund. Some information for this chapter was drawn from the authors' experiences in the field.

[1] Mine action, mentioned in the first objective, includes clearance of mines and unexploded ordnance, as well as victim assistance, mine-risk education, and advocating for a mine-free world.

96   Water and post-conflict peacebuilding

- Support to economic revitalization, including employment generation and livelihoods (in agriculture and public works) particularly for youth and demobilized former combatants, as well as rehabilitation of basic infrastructure (UNSG 2009, 6).

Effective water resource management is fundamental for the last three items on this list: provision of basic services, good governance, and economic revitalization.

Through its activities in post-conflict rural and peri-urban environments, Tearfund, a UK–based relief and development organization, has helped to empower communities to manage water resources effectively and provide basic water and sanitation services. This chapter presents case studies from three post-conflict states—the Democratic Republic of the Congo (DRC), Liberia, and Afghanistan—that explore the ways in which effective community water resource management can contribute to peacebuilding. These case studies show the positive contribution empowered communities can make to public health improvement, good water governance, economic revitalization, and the restoration of peace.

CASE STUDY 1: SWIMA VILLAGE, SUD KIVU PROVINCE, DEMOCRATIC REPUBLIC OF THE CONGO

Eastern DRC has experienced more than a decade of conflict. The Second Congo War (1998–2003) ended when a transitional government took power. The war caused a major exodus of refugees from DRC into neighboring countries and the destruction of much of the country's infrastructure.

Eastern DRC is now in a post-conflict phase in which a fragile peace agreement holds the region together in a climate of uncertainty about lasting peace. The war created huge capacity gaps, especially in the areas of management and technical knowledge. Ongoing conflicts, weak government institutions, and poor infrastructure linking the provinces to the capital city have hampered the provision of adequate water and sanitation facilities. At the same time, under the United Nations High Commissioner for Refugees (UNHCR) Voluntary Repatriation Programme, many Congolese refugees are returning daily from neighboring countries (UNHCR 2010). These refugees are returning to an environment with inadequate, war-damaged infrastructure and a lack of water and sanitation services. Since the beginning of the 1990s, Nord and Sud Kivu provinces have been identified as among the most active areas for cholera in the world (Bompangue et al. 2009).

Background

The village of Swima sits on the shore of Lake Tanganyika in Sud Kivu. In 1997, just before the Second Congo War, the government's rural water department, Service National d'Hydraulique Rurale (SNHR), in conjunction with Action Contre la Faim, built a spring-fed piped-water scheme for Swima's 25,000

Experiences in community water management 97

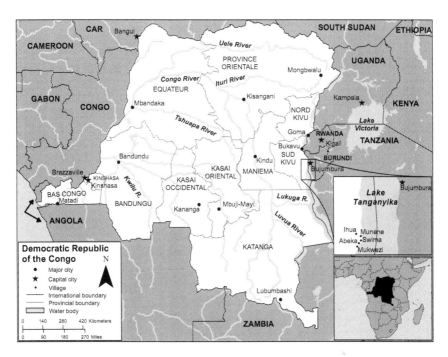

Note: The constitution of the Democratic Republic of the Congo, which was ratified in 2005 and came into effect in 2006, mandated that within three years the eleven provinces be redivided into twenty-six. As of June 2013, the redivision had not yet taken place.

residents. Customary, local-level water-user groups were mobilized to take a role alongside government in managing the scheme. However, the 1998–2003 conflict resulted in damage to the water scheme and massive loss of human capacity, both in the government and the community, as villagers sought refuge in neighboring countries or other parts of the DRC, and the water scheme became dysfunctional.

In 2003, Tearfund began work in the village of Swima, which is located in an area severely affected by the conflict. This area also had a high incidence of cholera, with an annual average of 17.75–33.43 cases per 10,000 inhabitants (Bompangue et al. 2009). During initial community meetings in Swima, villagers, especially women, identified rehabilitation of the water scheme as one of their highest priorities. SNHR did not have the capacity to operate and maintain the scheme over the long term. The community expressed a keen desire to build its own capacity to manage the system, and SNHR endorsed the establishment of a local, community-based organization for this purpose. This was on the understanding that Tearfund would help this organization to build its capacity to become a registered water association and recognized as an official partner of the government in provision of water services. In 2003, a local water management organization was established in Swima: Committee for Clean Water (Kamati ya Maji Safi, or KMS).

98 Water and post-conflict peacebuilding

Kamati ya Maji Safi's institutional framework

The community developed an institutional framework for KMS, based on customary water management methods, which was approved by SNHR. It had a three-tier structure: (1) a general assembly composed of all water users; (2) an administrative council, elected by the general assembly (eleven members, five of whom must be women); and (3) a management team, appointed by the administrative council (seven members, three of whom must be women). It is led by a program coordinator and includes accounting and finance staff and senior technical staff who supervise technical staff members, currently numbering fifty-nine, who handle system operations, maintenance, revenue collection, and hygiene and sanitation.

Building local capacity

From 2003 to 2007, Tearfund helped to build KMS's capacity to plan and manage the rehabilitation, expansion, and ongoing operation of the piped water supply network, which now provides safe water to more than 60,000 people. The capacity-building program focused on engineering and technology, economics and finance, management and administration, hygiene and sanitation promotion, and social and environmental responsibility. During this process there was effective collaboration with SNHR, and Tearfund and SNHR jointly organized many of the technical training sessions. Capacity-building support was intensive for the first two years and reduced in the following two years.

On March 20, 2007, KMS was officially registered as a water association under the Local Non-Governmental Organization Act. As an official association, KMS is recognized as an official partner of the government in provision of water services, and has legal authority to manage water supply and sanitation systems and collect the required revenue for this purpose. At this point, Tearfund's direct engagement ended. KMS, in collaboration with SNHR, has managed local water and sanitation services and has raised capital to extend the water supply network due to increasing demand from returnees.

Women's changing role

The war has produced a large number of widows and female-headed households. Widows make up 9 percent of the population and 43.9 percent of the female-headed households (Sow 2006). In Sud Kivu, the number of female-headed households increased from 8 percent in 1996, before the war, to 12 percent in 2007, after the war (Humphreys 2008).

Women in the region were not passive victims of the war and the subsequent humanitarian crisis; they exerted agency at all levels of society. The conflict created some fluidity in social ordering in the region, and gender power structures are beginning to change. In many cases, women have been the first to cross ethnic and political divides and begin to bridge community divisions (Sow 2006).

Women are also benefiting from the political transformation taking place in the region and are making significant gains in political participation. The constitution adopted by referendum in December 2005 is a major breakthrough for Congolese women in that it guarantees parity between men and women in state institutions (Sow 2006).[2]

In Swima, women bear the primary responsibility for domestic water collection and management. Therefore, water management is a critical issue for women and has become a focus for their interest and an area in which they have asserted leadership. Swima's recognition of women's role in water management was made clear in the provisions for balanced representation in the KMS institutional framework.

Women's leadership in reconciliation

In post-conflict situations with transient populations, frequent displacement and resettlement often result in resource-based conflicts. The unity and leadership of women in Swima is a testimony to the important role women can play in sustainable water resource management and reconciliation in such situations. Many of the women in Swima had learned about the link between contaminated water and disease while living in refugee camps in Tanzania and Burundi. On returning to Swima, they advocated first for the right to safe water and then for the rehabilitation and extension of the water scheme to realize that right. Women were concerned about the poor quality of water provided by the existing system due to waste discharges upstream by residents of the village of Ihua, and they suggested sourcing water instead from six protected springs they had identified.

The water quality issue, combined with the pressure of returning refugees, reignited a deep-rooted conflict between the Swima and Ihua villages over allocation of shared river water. The upstream community, Ihua, incited conflict by dumping waste close to the water system intake and then insulting the downstream community in Swima, calling them "consumers of Ihua waste." These actions were fueled by jealousy of the gravity-driven, piped-water scheme that the village of Swima had developed, and the tension between the two villages was rapidly escalating to a point where open conflict was imminent.

The six protected springs identified by women from Swima as an alternate water source were upstream of Ihua, and so the conflict between the two villages had to be resolved before the water scheme could be extended. Women from the two villages met to discuss the issue. Women from Swima highlighted the benefits of allowing access to the upstream springs, which would enable extension of the piped-water scheme to include the village of Ihua. These initial discussions were successful and signaled the beginning of reconciliation between the two villages.

---

[2] For the complete text of the Constitution of the Democratic Republic of the Congo, see www.constitutionnet.org/files/DRC%20-%20Congo%20Constitution.pdf.

100   Water and post-conflict peacebuilding

The women then brought the men into the discussion, and a consensus was reached that the water scheme development should proceed.

KMS managed the extension of the piped-water scheme, and villagers from the two communities worked side by side, digging trenches, transporting materials, and carrying out other tasks. The water system has been successfully completed, and peace has been restored between the communities.

Once the women from Swima and Ihua villages had access to clean piped water, they united with women from the nearby villages of Abeka, Mukwezi, and Munene, and organized meetings with KMS to advocate for further extension of the water scheme to service a total of 60,000 people.

During the extension, Tearfund offered technical support to the village members and KMS in the construction and rehabilitation of the system. As initiators of the extension and water quality–improvement projects in the Swima area, women actively participated in the decision-making and advocacy processes. This further raised their profile as decision makers and managers for water projects in the community. One villager, Mama Rehema, commented on the benefits of the scheme: "I am now able to collect three to four jerricans of clean water each morning, and the same number again in the evening. The amount of water we use at home has gone up a lot, and collecting it is much easier."[3]

With the time she saves fetching water, Mama Rehema is able to help her husband on the farm. He, too, appreciates the extra time his wife has on her hands: "For the first time in the thirty years of my marriage, I am now eating early since my wife is able to prepare food well before darkness; and this means, as a family, we have more time together to talk."

At the completion of the Swima-Ihua extension, the community and KMS acknowledged the important role of women in the water project. During the restructuring of KMS to become a formally recognized water association, it was agreed that women had to be well represented. By the end of 2009, women held nine out of eighteen senior positions on the administrative council and management team, including the key roles of vice president and accountant.

Sustainability

KMS continues to successfully manage the Swima water scheme and its ongoing expansion program, which now includes seven neighboring villages. Moreover, the success of KMS has inspired and challenged other communities in Sud Kivu Province to adopt similar models for water resource management.

Swima's experience is a good example of how successful empowerment of women and capacity development of communities to effectively, efficiently, and equitably manage water resources has made possible the provision of basic water

---

[3] Villagers quoted in this chapter were interviewed between June 1, 2008, and May 5, 2010, in Swima, DRC; Bako Kham, Afghanistan; and Henry Town, Liberia.

Experiences in community water management 101

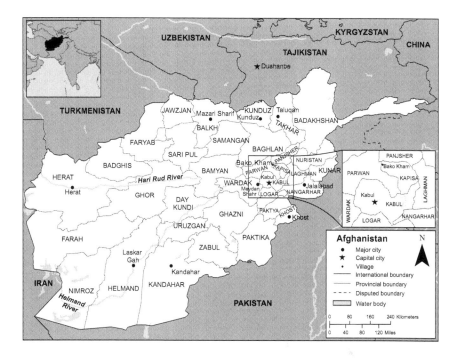

services to support the safe and sustainable return and reintegration of internally displaced persons and refugees, as well as a level of economic revitalization that has contributed to post-conflict recovery and peacebuilding in Sud Kivu, DRC.

CASE STUDY 2: BAKO KHAM VILLAGE, KAPISA PROVINCE, AFGHANISTAN

Afghanistan has seen more than three decades of sustained conflict, beginning with the Saur Revolution of 1978 and occupation by the Soviet Union from 1979 to 1989. During this period, the Islamic mujahideen resistance grew in strength, ultimately taking control of the government from 1992 to 1996. The Taliban wrested control and ruled from 1996 to 2001. At the same time, the Northern Alliance formed in opposition and continued the civil war until the United States and its allies joined forces with it to defeat the Taliban in 2001. Since 2001, many refugees and internally displaced persons have returned to their homes and set about restarting agriculture and other livelihoods.

As part of the peacebuilding process, external donors have provided assistance to the Afghan government and communities to restore and improve much of the infrastructure, including irrigation systems, which had been damaged or fallen into disrepair during the years of conflict.

102 Water and post-conflict peacebuilding

Tearfund currently operates programs in three provinces, Kapisa, Kandahar, and Jawzjan, all areas that have a high number of returnees as part of UNHCR's Assisted Voluntary Repatriation to Afghanistan program (UNHCR 2008). Tearfund's programs are based on an assessment of the priority needs of the most vulnerable communities in these areas.

Background

The village of Bako Kham is located in Kohistan District at the center of Kapisa Province. Like most Afghan villages, it has a community development council (CDC), which is responsible for managing the ongoing government-funded National Solidarity Programme as well as other development projects funded by organizations such as Tearfund. Like many Afghan villages, Bako Kham lies in mountainous terrain. It enjoys an abundant but seasonal water supply, which is strongest during the spring snowmelt. Nonetheless, effective water management has been a challenge. Two key water issues are crop irrigation and safe water and sanitation. Tearfund has worked with Bako Kham since 2006, focusing on capacity development of the CDC to effectively, efficiently, and equitably manage water resources.

The main livelihood in Bako Kham is agriculture; crops include wheat, corn, onions, tomatoes, and cotton. During the decades-long conflict, many irrigation systems fell into disrepair as people fled from the fighting. When they returned, restarting agriculture was one of their highest priorities. Without irrigation, they would only achieve meager harvests; however, with sufficient water for irrigation, more land could be cultivated. With this in mind, the CDC, with assistance from the government and funding from international donors, mobilized the community to rehabilitate and extend the irrigation canal system to ensure maximum coverage.

The canals that irrigate the fields also pass through the residential areas and are used as a primary drinking-water source. Contamination of the water has resulted in significant health issues in the community. As Quand Agha, a Bako Kham villager, explained, "Half our income every year is spent on doctors and medicine because we are always getting sick with stomach complaints and diarrhea. We believe this is because God is unhappy with us and can only be solved by sincere prayer." Due to the high incidence of diarrheal disease, Tearfund targeted this village as part of its wider water, sanitation, and hygiene (WASH) promotion program to provide basic water and sanitation services to support the safe and sustainable reintegration of the villagers, a majority of whom were returnees.

Social marketing approach

Tearfund's program was based on social marketing, which is the application of marketing techniques to achieve behavioral changes for a social good. Both women and men were involved in the process, although due to the cultural context, events tended to be held separately for men and women. Tearfund employed female facilitators to work with the women and girls, and male facilitators to work with the men and boys. The aim of the program was to create demand for household water treatment systems, sanitation facilities, and hygiene behavior improvement by achieving three key objectives.

The first objective was for the community to understand how contaminated water and poor hygiene and sanitation contribute to poor health, including the diarrheal disease prevalent in the village. Tearfund staff worked closely with the mullahs (religious leaders) to explain these issues, and assist them in carrying the message to the larger population. In many communities, faith-based institutions are central to the social fabric of a community; and in Afghanistan, the support of religious leaders validated Tearfund's work in the community.

Evidence compiled by the United Nations Children's Fund (UNICEF) indicates that programs that combine household-level water treatment interventions with sanitation and hygiene behavior change are more likely to result in the greatest reduction in diarrheal disease (van Maanen 2009). Based on this, Tearfund's second objective was to stimulate demand for household water treatment systems, sanitation facilities, and hygiene-behavior improvements. This was achieved through a number of hygiene promotion techniques, together with a hand-washing campaign that stimulated demand for hand washing with soap or ash, a community-led total sanitation (CLTS) campaign that stimulated demand for household latrines, and an advertising campaign that stimulated demand for household water treatment systems, of which the bio-sand filter—a household-size slow sand filter—proved most popular.

The third objective was to train and equip local artisans to manufacture items to meet the new demand, thus creating livelihood opportunities as well as addressing the health issue.

Outcome of the social marketing program

The social marketing approach stimulated demand for household latrines. After only three months, a survey revealed every household in the village of Bako Kham had a latrine. Most householders opted for an elevated vault latrine design, with a sealed waste collection chamber above ground that is periodically emptied. Ash is added to the waste to control odor and accelerate the composting process. Householders built their latrines themselves with help from local masons and carpenters who already had the necessary skills and knowledge.

Demand for hand-washing facilities was also stimulated; local steel workers, who were already producing small steel drums with a faucet designed for hand washing, largely met the increased demand.

The bio-sand water treatment filter was a new technology, and local artisans needed special training to enable them to meet the growing demand for it. Tearfund, together with the government, CDCs, and the targeted communities, selected trainees based on agreed criteria. After training, the technicians

104   Water and post-conflict peacebuilding

started producing filters and holding demonstrations in mosques and schools, where the religious leaders and teachers promoted the product and explained its health benefits to community members. Many community members bought the filters; all buyers received detailed training on how to operate and maintain them.

As demand increased, many of the trained technicians opened bio-sand filter shops. The first shop was established in Bako Kham and operated on a preorder basis. Popular government officials, religious leaders, and community leaders were invited to endorse each shop at a well-publicized opening ceremony; this proved to be very helpful for the promotion and marketing of the filters. Local television and radio stations and newspapers covered many of the opening ceremonies; during interviews, local government officials advised communities to consider using the filters.

During this introductory phase of the project, Tearfund signed a memorandum of understanding with local artisans, with various subsidies and price controls to enhance availability and accessibility of the filters to consumers to test the product. The retail cost of one filter during the introductory period was US$6, which included a US$2 profit for the shop owner. During this period, 2,100 filters were sold. Since the memorandum of understanding expired, product-pricing controls have been removed. Artisans have been able to sell a further 4,400 filters at a higher cost of US$22, which includes a profit margin of US$9 per filter. A technician with two molds can produce four bio-sand filters per day, casting two in the morning and two in the evening, and still carry out other profitable tasks during the day—effectively adding US$36 to daily income.

The high demand for filters in Kapisa District has resulted in interest from other technicians to receive training on the manufacturing process. In response, Tearfund—in conjunction with UNICEF, the Danish Committee for Aid to Afghan Refugees, and the Centre for Affordable Water and Sanitation Technology—has conducted additional bio-sand filter technician trainings. Many graduates of these workshops are now training others.

Surveys carried out in the area have shown that knowledge of public health issues has improved and that the health benefits of the bio-sand filter program, coupled with the CLTS and hygiene promotion campaigns, have become apparent within the community. Bibi Fatema, a villager from Bako Kham, said, "The money that we previously spent on expensive medication to treat water-related diseases, we now use to buy fruit for our children." The head of the village CDC, Noorullah Ahmed, said, "Before, I was always sick. Now with filtered water from the bio-sand filter, I am well."

Additional evidence collected by Tearfund from district health clinics indicates that water- and excreta-related diseases have been reduced by 61 percent for adults and children in target communities in Kapisa since the start of the program (Tearfund 2009).

The obvious health benefits and enhanced dignity, especially for women, as a result of the WASH program has stimulated a strong demand for sanitation and water filtration systems. Local artisans benefiting from the increased demand have become enthusiastic champions for this technology. This is especially true in the case of bio-sand filters, where the rapid growth of businesses manufacturing the filters has contributed significantly to economic revitalization in the village of Bako Kham and the wider Kapisa District.

Sustainability

Based on the success observed in Bako Kham and Kapisa Province, Tearfund, in collaboration with UNICEF and the Afghanistan Ministry of Rural Rehabilitation and Development, is encouraging other agencies implementing WASH programs to use social marketing. Tearfund has also successfully lobbied the government to amend the national WASH policy to include CLTS and household water treatment as acceptable WASH interventions. This change has enabled donors to increase funding to scale up similar demand-led WASH interventions across Afghanistan.

CASE STUDY 3: HENRY TOWN, GBARPOLU COUNTY, LIBERIA

During the fourteen-year civil war in Liberia (1989–2003), sexual and gender-based violence (SGBV) was used repeatedly as a weapon of war, and it is estimated that two-thirds of women were subjected to SGBV during the conflict (WHO 2009).

The terrible violence experienced by many Liberian women and girls during wartime still occur. The Gbarpolu County Development Committee noted:

> Currently, rape is the most frequently reported serious crime in Liberia. In 2007, 38% of the protection cases [abuse, exploitation, neglect, and violence] reported by UNHCR/NRC [United Nations High Commissioner for Refugees and Norwegian Refugee Council] monitors were SGBV related and reports from 2008 show a similar trend. Domestic violence is endemic (26% of all reported protection cases) and Liberia has among the highest rates of teenage pregnancy in the world. Of the 155 protection incidents reported in the County during January–May 2008, 25.2% and 19.4% relate to SGBV and domestic violence respectively (Gbarpolu County Development Committee 2008, 20–21).

During the conflict, most perpetrators (89.2 percent) were combatants (UN 2009). However, since the conflict ended, perpetrators have included not just excombatants but community and family members, teachers, and husbands or partners. "For fear of safety, they cannot collect water. For fear of stigmatization, their families cannot remain in their community. For fear of repercussions, they cannot report their violation. In short, sexual violence has become one of the greatest threats to the security of any community . . ." (Wallström 2009). The UN Secretary-General notes, when referring to United Nations Security Council Resolution

106 Water and post-conflict peacebuilding

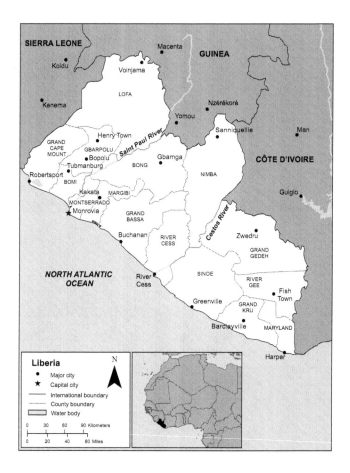

1820, that "persistent violence, intimidation and discrimination are obstacles to women's participation and full involvement in post-conflict public life, which can have a serious negative impact on durable peace, security and reconciliation, including post-conflict peacebuilding" (UNSG 2009, 8).

Led by President Ellen Johnson Sirleaf, the first elected female head of state in Africa and the first elected black female head of state in the world, Liberia tackled the issue of gender violence and discrimination with the 2008 National Action Plan for combating sexual violence, and the Truth and Reconciliation Commission with its mandate to promote national peace, security, unity, and reconciliation. The final report of the Truth and Reconciliation Commission, released in December 2009, contains a special section titled "Recommendations Related to Women's Rights, Protection and Empowerment" and another titled "Recommendations Relating to the Environment, Natural Resources and the Equitable and Sustainable Use and Management of Land and Other Natural Resources" (Truth and Reconciliation Commission of Liberia 2009). This recognizes

the important role that women play in post-conflict reconciliation and the importance of effective natural resource management in the peacebuilding process.

In the early post-conflict period, Liberian women seized the opportunity to
address past issues of conflict, gender imbalance, and gender exploitation, and
are actively working to change past imbalances and restore peace. Mama Morris,
a middle-age woman from Voinjama, told a UN interviewer in 2004 that sexual
violence was common during the civil war years and that men were used to being
in charge. "Traditionally women do not argue with men here in Liberia, that
needs to change," she said. "We want it to be a 50-50 arrangement in future"
(IRIN 2004).

This case study from Henry Town, Gbarpolu County, Liberia demonstrates
the complex set of relationships between gender equality and gender violence,
water resources, and peacebuilding.

Background

Gbarpolu is a county in the north of Liberia, rich in mineral resources such as
diamonds and gold. It has a population of approximately 83,758 (Gbarpolu County
Development Committee 2008). The main economic activities are small-scale
gold and diamond mining and subsistence farming. Gbarpolu has very poor roads
and lacks basic infrastructure. The government and nongovernmental organizations working in the county, including Tearfund, are focusing on rehabilitating
roads and basic infrastructure.

Henry Town is the largest town in Koninga Chiefdom, a subdistrict within
Gbarpolu County. In Koninga Chiefdom, the civil war resulted in an exodus of
refugees and the destruction of the meager infrastructure that existed. In the
post-conflict period, development of water resources, including rebuilding of
wells and irrigation systems, has enabled resettlement of returning refugees in
rural areas, and has contributed to the reestablishment of livelihoods. Empowerment of women and advancement of gender equality are also key components
in equitable and sustainable community water resource management and
peacebuilding.

In October 2007, Tearfund and its local partner, the Association of Evangelicals
of Liberia (AEL), started humanitarian interventions in Henry Town under the
guidance and direction of the county district superintendent.

Women, SGBV, and development

In Henry Town, women have traditionally collected water from a small creek in
the forest close to the village, which is surrounded by dense vegetation. The
location of the water supply makes women collecting water vulnerable to attack.
Evidence gathered during focus group discussions suggests that the incidence of
SGBV in this location increased significantly during and after the conflict. Tie
Kawoh, from Henry Town, said, "This is a mining town where men come and go.

108   Water and post-conflict peacebuilding

The forest surrounding the creek is a dangerous place for women and girls, and some have been raped when collecting water. It is especially dangerous after dark."

Due to the social stigma surrounding SGBV, many women are reticent to speak about their fears and the serious risks they face when collecting water each day. For this reason, many men are unaware of the issue and each day force women into dangerous situations. Many men have a totally different perspective about collecting water from the creek. Johnson Kolle said, "I prefer the water that comes from the small creek in the forest close to the village. This creek is important for the whole town; our ancestors left it for us. That is why the water is very cool and clean. It gives you a natural taste of water if you are drinking it."

In response to SGBV and other problems faced by women in Henry Town, four women—Janga Sherriff, Soko Koluba, Yamai Mansally, and Tie Kawoh—began to advocate for the construction of hand pumps in town. They mobilized the other women from Henry Town to join together to advocate, through their local church, which is a member of AEL, for Tearfund and AEL to help their community construct these pumps at safe locations. Soko Koluba explained the need for nearby hand-pump wells: "The water problem is on our shoulders, we the women. When my husband comes from the mining field he asks for hot water to take a bath and water to drink. He does not care or know where the water comes from, all he needs is water. Even at night I have to go for the water when he needs it. I am afraid to collect water from the creek after dark. But imagine if I have a pump near my house it would be a great help for me. This is why I want Tearfund and AEL to help us build a pump." At the invitation of women from Henry Town, Tearfund and AEL mobilized community members to consider their water resource management issues. Using a number of participatory techniques, AEL and the community explored the issues surrounding integrated water resource management, including water sources, water uses, health impacts, economic considerations, environmental considerations, and social, cultural, and gender considerations. Through this process, the women who had been mobilized advocated for consideration of women's views in the implementation of future water projects. Traditional gender prejudices were challenged, and the community began to realize that gender inequality and gender-based violence were hindering women's participation in water resource management and obstructing progress toward peace, security, reconciliation, and development.

Discussions of the risks faced by women collecting water from the creek and the ongoing SGBV issues within the community brought about a realization of the negative impacts SGBV was having on families in the community. The community began to understand the risks faced daily by women and girls collecting water from the creek, collecting firewood from the forest, and working in the fields, and how this affected the town's progress in peacebuilding and economic revitalization. The community is now committed to take action to stop SGBV, in line with the national priorities set by the Ministry of Gender and Development and the National Action Plan for combating sexual violence (ROL 2008).

Like most Liberian villages, Henry Town has a community development council (CDC), which is responsible for managing the ongoing development of the village. The CDC is an official body, linked to central government through district and county development councils. The Henry Town CDC decided to ensure a fifty-fifty representation of men and women. After the restructuring, a woman named Yamai Mansally was elected as chairperson.

Capacity building for community water resource management

Tearfund worked with the CDC on a leadership training and capacity development program to enable efficient, equitable, safe, and sustainable management of local water resources. Tearfund provided training for development of irrigation systems to improve food security, and economic revitalization to support the return and reintegration of refugees. Capacity was also developed for hand-pump well construction and household water treatment equipment (bio-sand filters) in order to meet drinking-water needs and address basic service provision and the health needs of the returnees.

Tearfund also assisted with capacity building in the areas of health and hygiene promotion and community sanitation, through training of community health volunteers, promotion of latrine building and hand washing, and establishment of child health clubs—weekly meetings attended by children in which they learn songs, play games, watch puppet shows, and participate in other activities that teach them about good hygiene.

The CDC and District Development Committee were involved from the outset, and a memorandum of understanding was signed between Tearfund, the CDC, and the District Development Committee to define the relationship and obtain mutual commitment from all relevant parties, and to ensure the scope of the project fit within the County Development Agenda, which prioritized security and provision of basic services (Gbarpolu County Development Committee 2008).

Hand-pump wells

Taking into account the significant SGBV risks faced by women while collecting water from the creek, and the biological contamination issues related to water from a surface source, the Henry Town CDC decided unanimously to construct hand-pump wells in safe locations within the town.

Women from Henry Town were keen to be involved from the outset of the project; they played a crucial role in undertaking social impact studies to decide on the most appropriate and safest locations for the hand-pump wells by carrying out transect walks and community mapping. These activities were carried out in conjunction with hydrogeological and environmental impact studies to determine the most sustainable locations for the wells. The women then volunteered their time and mobilized the community to help AEL staff construct the hand pumps by providing locally available raw materials and labor. Tie Kawoh, one of the

110   Water and post-conflict peacebuilding

original advocates for hand pumps in Henry Town, remarked, "We are so far from Monrovia; people do not easily come here to see us, let alone to help us. Most towns in this country have three or four water pumps, but we have none. Why then should I not embrace such a good help? Indeed, I need help, and I appreciate this help very much. One good thing I believe is that, if we get these hand pumps, it will reduce the running stomach [diarrhea]."

The CDC appointed a water committee to oversee the operation and maintenance of the hand pumps. The water committee has an equal representation of men and women; all members were involved in construction of the hand pumps and were trained in hand-pump operations, maintenance, and financial management.

Improved health and security

With the Henry Town water resource management project, Tearfund mobilized community members to take responsibility for their own health and hygiene by training a team of community health volunteers to conduct hygiene and sanitation promotion and lead the child health clubs. The availability of safe drinking water, together with improved sanitation and hygiene behavior, have resulted in observable health improvements for the whole community. Statistics from health centers in the area show a reduction in water- and excreta-related diseases of 48 percent for adults and 30 percent for children since the start of the program (Tearfund 2009). Installation of the hand pumps reduced the need for women to collect water from the creek, and evidence gained during focus group discussions and targeted interviews suggests that the incidence of SGBV in this location has diminished.

LESSONS LEARNED

The case studies in this chapter illustrate a number of common themes related to post-conflict community water resource management, which have been observed to contribute to the success of peacebuilding in these communities. While these case studies focus on rural and peri-urban communities, many of the same principles apply to urban communities.

The important role of women in water resource management and peacebuilding

The three case studies highlight the important role of women during post-conflict recovery of sustainable water resource management systems. Women often take the lead in restoring the fractured psyche of communities, starting at the foundational level of resolving domestic conflict and gender-based violence in the home and reestablishing functioning and peaceful family groups and communities (Schirch and Sewak 2005). Their role as peacemakers, educators, and communicators extends to water management, as women bear the burden of water collection.

Community water management is therefore a key priority for women, and any community-based approach should ensure their inclusion in water projects.

The DRC and Liberia case studies clearly show the positive impact that empowered women can have in dispute resolution and reconciliation at the community level, and illustrate the valuable role women play in water resource management. The Liberia case study illustrates especially clearly how gender inequality and gender-based violence can have a serious negative impact on women's participation and full involvement in water resource management, and how addressing these issues can contribute to a more durable reconciliation and post-conflict peacebuilding, as well as better community health and productivity through improved water management. These findings are consistent with experiences elsewhere. Indeed, the UN Secretary-General reported:

> The early post-conflict period offers a critical opportunity for women to capitalize on the changes in gender relations that may occur during conflict where women may have taken on community leadership roles or non-traditional employment. A tendency by outsiders to work with and acknowledge the leadership of men in governance and the economy, however, can mean that women's capacities to engage in public decision-making and economic recovery may not receive adequate recognition or financing. Women's marginalization can be exacerbated in contexts where sexual violence has been a major feature of the conflict, eroding public safety and women's social standing (UNSG 2009, 7–8).

The importance of engagement with communities at the grassroots level

Communities are central to post-conflict recovery and peacebuilding. They interact directly with the ecosystem and natural resources in their environment; and in the aftermath of conflict, with its initial paralysis of official systems and structured roles, key community members become the backbone of immediate post-conflict relief and response. This is especially true with regard to development and management of water resources, which are essential to all aspects of life and community development. Importantly, in all of the case studies presented, basic service provision and economic revitalization did not in themselves build peace. Instead, something changed within the communities themselves during the process of achieving these objectives. Individuals changed their mindsets, traditional prejudices were broken down, and communities were unified.

In the DRC, some wise women took the initiative, challenged long-standing tensions between two villages, and promoted reconciliation in order to ensure the effectiveness of a much-needed water supply project. In Afghanistan, community members who could see the benefit of economic development and health improvement were prepared to work together to make it happen. In Liberia, a group of women challenged traditional attitudes toward gender roles and SGBV, and as a result the community saw improvement in basic water services and water resource management.

112 Water and post-conflict peacebuilding

Change starts with individuals. As traditional prejudices are challenged and broken down, individual mindsets change, communities change, disputes are resolved, relationships are restored, and peacebuilding begins. It is important to focus on providing opportunities for dialogue, confidence building, and reconciliation at the community level as the first step toward peacebuilding at the national level. Capacity building and empowerment at the grassroots level is crucial.

In all the case studies presented in this chapter, a strong sense of ownership and responsibility was created by strengthening and empowering existing local groups to manage and resolve their own water resource issues, rather than by creating new groups.

The importance of capacity development to bridge gaps at the state level

Experience from the field has shown that there are often huge capacity gaps in the post-conflict environment, especially in the areas of management and technical knowledge, and this often severely hampers effective, efficient, and equitable water resource management during the time it takes to reestablish national capacity.

Building communities' capacity to take responsibility for their own water resource management in the immediate aftermath of conflict can effectively fill the gap until the government can rebuild its institutional capacity. Evaluations carried out in Liberia showed that engagement and capacity building of communities enhanced community cohesion and social inclusion, especially for marginalized groups, and reinforced democratic values and practices (Fearon, Humphreys, and Weinstein 2009).

Developing local community capacity for water resource management is also critical for project sustainability. In post-conflict environments in which capacity has been depleted, community capacity building should be a priority and should be viewed as a means to help ensure sustainability and contribute to peacebuilding. Donors need to realize that this takes a significant investment of time and cannot be achieved in short funding cycles. In Swima in the DRC, it took four years of sustained effort for the community to overcome the obstacles and build the confidence and skills required to sustainably manage a water supply network.

The importance of engaging with government and policy makers

It is important to establish formal links between government institutions and grassroots community organizations involved in water resource management. In this way, local initiatives contribute to the national objectives for integrated water resource management and support a unified and coordinated approach to nation building in the post-conflict setting, thereby laying the foundations for sustained national development and peace.

Experiences in community water management 113

This also prevents overreliance of communities on nongovernmental organizations, and instead helps them to understand the role of government in ensuring the right to basic services and to hold their government to account. All the case studies show how positive links can be established between grassroots organizations and the government, through water associations in DRC and CDCs in Afghanistan and Liberia.

Civil society groups should also be encouraged to engage with national-level policy makers in order to link policy with practice and shape peace and reconciliation initiatives and the future development of the country. The case study from Afghanistan illustrates how raising government awareness about the success of community-level water and sanitation initiatives led to a change in the national WASH policy. In a similar way, the Truth and Reconciliation Commission in Liberia has influenced policy development in that country by making the voices of individuals and communities heard at the national level.

The importance of livelihoods-based, demand-led interventions for sustainability

In the post-conflict context, economic revitalization is a key contributing factor to peacebuilding. Therefore, interventions that promote sustainable livelihoods should be favored. In the Afghanistan case study, resources were invested in promotion of household-level water and sanitation interventions. At the same time, artisans were trained and livelihoods were developed to meet the new demand for bio-sand filters and household latrines. This approach has created sustainable livelihoods for many artisans, while also addressing health issues relating to water quality and sanitation. In a similar way, the water scheme in the DRC was developed as the result of demand from the local community. As a result, community members are willing to pay for improved access to safe water, ensuring an economically sustainable system and creating new livelihoods for the growing number of staff employed to operate and manage the water scheme.

CONCLUSION

In a post-conflict environment, the well-planned and effective management of water resources is essential for economic revitalization through energy provision, irrigation, and flood management, which improve living conditions and stimulate employment and economic growth. At the same time, water and sanitation services reduce the incidence of infectious disease and contribute to a healthier and more prosperous society, with direct beneficial impacts on the health of women and children. In these ways, the efficient and equitable management of water resources can support the safe return and sustainable reintegration of internally displaced persons, refugees, and demobilized soldiers, and positively contribute to collective efforts to deliver peace, justice, and economic well-being in any post-conflict community.

114   Water and post-conflict peacebuilding

Development of women's capacity is especially critical during post-conflict recovery to ensure the establishment of sustainable water management systems. Women often take the lead in restoring peace in a community, beginning by addressing domestic conflict and gender-based violence in the home, and re-establishing functioning and peaceful family groups, communities, and nations.

In the aftermath of conflict, local communities are often motivated (and in the best position) to take a leadership role in water resource management, at a time when government capacity is limited. Therefore, capacity development and empowerment of communities to develop and manage their water resources efficiently, equitably, and sustainably should be a central element of peacebuilding activities from the outset.

However, it is also important to link community water management organizations with national institutions, so that local initiatives can contribute to national objectives and strengthen national capacity, thereby beginning to lay the foundations for sustained national development and lasting peace.

REFERENCES

Bompangue, D., P. Giraudoux, M. Piarroux, G. Mutombo, R. Shamavu, B. Sudre, A. Mutombo, V. Mondonge, and R. Piarroux. 2009. Cholera epidemics, war and disasters around Goma and Lake Kivu: An eight-year survey. *Public Library of Science Neglected Tropical Diseases* 3 (5): e436. doi:10.1371/journal.pntd.0000436. www.plosntds.org/article/info%3Adoi%2F10.1371%2Fjournal.pntd.0000436.

Fearon, J., M. Humphreys, and J. Weinstein. 2009. Evaluating community-driven reconstruction—lessons from post-conflict Liberia. *Development Outreach*, October, 50–53. Washington, D.C.: World Bank Institute. http://siteresources.worldbank.org/WBI/Resources/213798-1253552326261/do-oct09-fearon.pdf.

Gbarpolu County Development Committee. 2008. *Gbarpolu County development agenda 2008–2012*. In collaboration with the Ministries of Planning and Economic Affairs and Internal Affairs. Monrovia: Republic of Liberia.

Humphreys, M. 2008. *Community-driven reconstruction in the Democratic Republic of Congo*. Baseline report. New York: Columbia University.

IRIN (Integrated Regional Information Networks). 2004. Our bodies—their battle ground: Gender-based violence in conflict zones; Liberia: Working on rebuilding lives and trust. IRIN Humanitarian News and Analysis, September. www.irinnews.org/InDepthMain .aspx?InDepthId=20&ReportId=62830&Country=Yes.

ROL (Republic of Liberia). 2008. The Liberia national action plan for the implementation of United Nations Resolution 1325. Monrovia.

Schirch, L., and M. Sewak. 2005. *The role of women in peacebuilding*. The Hague, Netherlands: Global Partnership for the Prevention of Armed Conflict.

Sow, N. 2006. *Gender and conflict transformation in the Great Lakes region of Africa*. London: International Alert.

Tearfund. 2009. DFID WASH interim report 2: Capacity building to improve humanitarian action in the water sanitation and hygiene (WASH) sector. Unpublished paper. Teddington, UK.

Experiences in community water management 115

Truth and Reconciliation Commission. 2009. *Consolidated final report.* Vol. 2 of *Truth and Reconciliation Commission final report.* Monrovia: Republic of Liberia. http://trcofliberia.org/resources/reports/final/trc-of-liberia-final-report-volume-ii.pdf.

UNHCR (Office of the United Nations High Commissioner for Refugees). 2008. Assisted voluntary repatriation to Afghanistan: Return by province of destination—02 Mar 02–31 Oct 08. www.unhcr.org/4918660b2.html.

———. 2010. Repatriation fact sheet for Democratic Republic of Congo. www.humanse curitygateway.com/documents/UNHCR_UNHCRDemocraticRepublicofCongo _RepatriationFactSheet_30Sep2010.pdf.

UN (United Nations). 2009. *Combating sexual and gender based violence in Liberia.* http://reliefweb.int/sites/reliefweb.int/files/resources/3AE3B27002BF12A24925760C00 2BCEB4-Full_Report.pdf.

UNSG (United Nations Secretary-General). 2009. *Report of the Secretary-General on peacebuilding in the immediate aftermath of conflict.* A/63/881-S/2009/304. June 11. New York. www.unrol.org/files/pbf_090611_sg.pdf.

van Maanen, P. 2009. *Evidence base: Water, sanitation and hygiene interventions.* Literature review. New York: United Nations Children's Fund.

Wallström, M. 2009. Stop gender-based violence NOW! Speech delivered at the "Equality Between Women and Men in a Time of Change Seminar," organized by DG Employment of the European Commission, Brussels, Belgium, June 15–16. http://europa.eu/rapid/ pressReleasesAction.do?reference=SPEECH/09/297&format=HTML&aged=0&language =EN&guiLanguage=en.

WHO (World Health Organization). 2009. *Liberia country cooperation strategy 2008–2011* www.who.int/countryfocus/cooperation_strategy/ccs_lbr_en.pdf.

Environmental management of the Iraqi marshlands in the post-conflict period

Chizuru Aoki, Ali Al-Lami, and Sivapragasam Kugaprasatham

As part of United Nations assistance for the reconstruction of Iraq, the United Nations Environment Programme (UNEP) implemented a large-scale initiative —the Iraqi Marshlands Project—in the Iraqi marshlands to address critical environmental degradation that hampered the stability and livelihoods of the marshland communities. The project demonstrated environmentally sound technologies (ESTs) and management practices for rehabilitating wetlands and maintaining water quality, supplied safe drinking water to residents in selected rural communities, and provided pilot-scale sanitation services.

This chapter summarizes two types of natural resource management activities undertaken within the project: drinking-water provision and wetland rehabilitation. The period examined is from the inception of the UNEP project in mid-2004 to 2008, during the reconstruction phase after the fall of the Saddam Hussein regime. It covers a period in which significant changes occurred in the institutional landscape, from the transfer of sovereignty to the establishment of a permanent government.

THE IRAQI MARSHLANDS

The Iraqi marshlands, the largest wetland ecosystem in the Middle East, have environmental, historical, and sociocultural significance. Located in the areas surrounding the confluence of the Euphrates and Tigris rivers in the governorates of Basra, Maysan, and Dhiqar in southern Iraq, the Iraqi marshlands consist of

---

Chizuru Aoki is a senior technology transfer officer and cluster coordinator for climate change mitigation at the Global Environment Facility. Ali Al-Lami is the acting technical deputy minister for the Ministry of Environment in Iraq. Sivapragasam Kugaprasatham is a former project officer at UNEP's International Environmental Technology Centre. The discussion herein of project impacts draws on and expands upon two UNEP publications (UNEP 2009a, 2009b).

118 Water and post-conflict peacebuilding

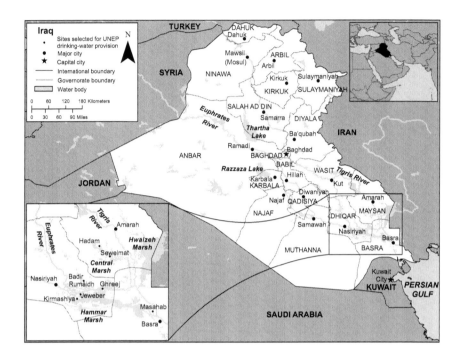

the interconnected wetland systems of the Central Marsh, Hammar Marsh, and Hwaizeh Marsh (see figure 1).

In 2001, UNEP alerted the world about the marshlands' destruction when it released satellite images showing that 90 percent of the marshlands had already been lost (UNEP 2007b). By the time the regime of Saddam Hussein collapsed in 2003, these marshlands were almost entirely destroyed. Numerous engineering structures, including more than thirty large dams, had been built along the Tigris and Euphrates rivers over the previous hundred years to control water flow and for irrigation, public water supply, and hydroelectric power generation (MOE, MWR, and MMPW 2006). During the 1990s, extensive drainage structures were built for the primary purpose of drying out the marshes. For example, initiatives were carried out to divert water for irrigation, to build railways and other transportation infrastructure by filling wetland areas, and to build canals and dikes to control water flow, limiting the number of water release points to the wetland system and reducing the overall flow.

The destruction of the area is also attributed in large part to deliberate acts by the regime of Saddam Hussein, who was retaliating against political factions in the area that opposed his regime. In order to tighten security and control, the regime sought to destroy natural landscapes that provided hiding places and to force migration away from the marshlands. A significant number of Iraqis suffered oppression and persecution, and the regime's actions led to systematic

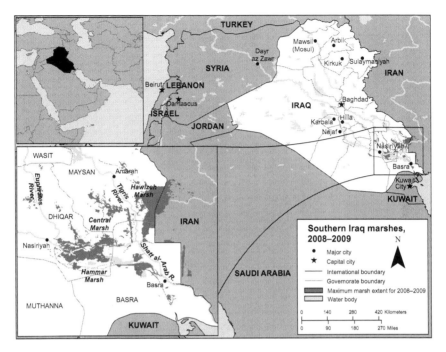

Figure 1. Location of the southern Iraq marshes, 2008–2009
Source: CIMI (2010).

shrinkage of the marshlands' area and to associated damage to the ecosystem and to the livelihoods of the local residents.

A socioeconomic survey that UNEP conducted with Thi-Qar University in 2007 assessed specific negative effects that the marshland villages faced during the Saddam Hussein regime (UNEP 2007a). More than half of the 199 villages surveyed experienced intentional negative effects, including destruction, bombing, and burning. Eighty-two percent of the villages experienced displacement, 37 percent experienced destruction, and 12 percent were bombed (see table 1). More than a third of the marshland villages were affected by multiple negative effects,

Table 1. Types of negative effects on surveyed Iraqi marshland villages during the Saddam Hussein regime

Governorate	Number of villages affected			
	Destruction	*Bombing*	*Burning*	*Displacement*
Dhiqar	19	3	3	37
Maysan	24	16	4	64
Basra	30	4	1	62
Total	73	23	8	163
Percentage	37%	12%	4%	82%

Source: UNEP (2007a).

120   Water and post-conflict peacebuilding

with nearly two-thirds of the surveyed villages in Dhiqar affected by multiple negative effects.

UNEP'S IRAQI MARSHLANDS PROJECT

Natural resource management concerns in the marshlands area, particularly marshland degradation and the lack of safe water and sanitation, along with the displacement of a large percentage of the indigenous population, were identified as critical problems in a joint needs assessment conducted by the United Nations and the World Bank (UN and World Bank 2003) and were considered priority reconstruction needs (UN 2003; USAID 2004). The Iraqi authorities requested help from UNEP, identifying management of the marshlands, provision of water and sanitation, and capacity building as priorities for reconstruction.

With this background and motivation, the United Nations Development Group's Iraq Trust Fund endorsed UNEP's Iraqi Marshlands Project in July 2004. The United Nations and the World Bank had established the Iraq Trust Fund under the International Reconstruction Fund Facility for Iraq (IRFFI), in 2004, in response to international requests for coordination of donor support for reconstruction and development in Iraq, and in close consultation with Iraqi authorities and donors. The IRFFI emphasized supporting projects that addressed Iraqi priorities, including those identified in the 2003 joint needs assessment.

The development goal of the first phase of the UNEP project was

> to support the sustainable management and restoration of the Iraqi marshlands, with the following immediate objectives:
> 1. To monitor and assess baseline characteristics of the marshland conditions, to provide objective and up-to-date information and to disseminate tools needed for assessment and management
> 2. To build capacity of Iraqi decision-makers and community representatives on aspects of marshland management including: policy and institutional aspects; technical subjects; and analytical tools
> 3. To identify . . . EST options suitable for immediate provision of drinking water and sanitation as well as wetland management, and to implement them on a pilot basis
> 4. To identify needs for additional strategy formulation and coordination for the development of a longer-term marshland management plan based on pilot results and cross-sectoral dialogue (UNEP 2009b, 15).

Although the primary focus of the project was on environmental management and basic service provision, the project also played an important role in socio-economic reconstruction for the local population because traditional livelihood activities in the area—such as agriculture, fishing, livestock rearing, and handicraft production—rely significantly on the marshlands.

Iraq's Ministry of Environment took the lead on the project, and cooperation was established with the Ministry of Water Resources and the Ministry of

Municipalities and Public Works. The Ministry of Environment had been established for the first time in 2003 under the Iraqi Governing Council. Previously, environmental management had been assigned to the Environmental Protection and Improvement Directorate within the Ministry of Health. The new ministry was staffed by personnel from the directorate and additional personnel who had been reassigned from various other ministries. Due to the newness of the environmental field in Iraq and limited access to outside educational opportunities during the sanctions, human and institutional capacity were in need of robust support.[1] Other main actors for the project included governorate councils from Basra, Maysan, and Dhiqar, local groups such as the Marsh Arab Forum, local universities, and nongovernmental organizations.

Provision of drinking water

Access to safe drinking water was the top priority for residents of small rural communities in the marshlands. Many rural residents depend on traditional activities such as agriculture, fishing, animal rearing, reed harvesting, or making of reed products for their livelihoods. These activities are small in scale, and residents tend to live in small tribal clusters along the fringe of the marshlands.

Lack of access to safe drinking water resulted from the presence of brackish water in some areas of the reflooded marshlands and the absence of infrastructure for water provision there.[2] Safe water was available only in nearby town centers, and treated water had to be transported by trucks if it was to reach the marshland villages. The supplies that reached the villages in this mode tended to be of inadequate quantity and unreliable quality due to the debilitation of the infrastructure for water treatment and transport. In addition, these supplies were too costly for many residents.

Surface water and tanker trucks are classified as unimproved drinking-water sources. Replacing them with improved drinking-water sources is necessary for movement toward meeting target 10 of the Millennium Development Goals (MDGs), which calls for cutting in half the proportion of the world's population without sustainable access to safe drinking water and basic sanitation by 2015 (WHO and UNICEF 2006). One of the main challenges addressed by the UNEP project was to provide access to a safe and improved drinking-water supply in an environmentally sound manner. Pilot projects on drinking-water provision were implemented through the UNEP project to address this challenge.

---

[1] The United Nations Security Council imposed economic sanctions against Iraq in response to Saddam Hussein's invasion of Kuwait. The sanctions were in place from August 1990 until Saddam Hussein was removed from power in May 2003.

[2] Significant efforts have been undertaken by various institutions to assess the water quality in different parts of the marshlands since the project commenced. For instance, water quality and other parameters in four marshes were monitored from 2003 to 2005 with support from the U.S. Agency for International Development (Richardson and Hussain 2006).

122 Water and post-conflict peacebuilding

To identify intervention areas that could be covered by the resources available, project personnel began by adopting a process by which stakeholders could participate in the selection of communities for intervention. First, they solicited proposals from the Iraqi ministries of Environment, Water Resources, and Municipalities and Public Works, and from community groups from the three governorates, such as the Marsh Arab Forums, which consist of nominated representatives of tribes in each area. Next they applied technical selection criteria developed by UNEP, including community size, physical stability of sites, road access, and existence of similar facilities. The project leaders also consulted external data on service availability and lists of communities receiving support, and considered geographical distribution over the three southern governorates. Finally, the project personnel and stakeholder representatives reached a consensus on site selection on the basis of discussions.

The selections were finalized at the Technical Meeting on Pilot Project Implementation held with Iraqi stakeholders in Amman, Jordan, in February 2005. The selection procedure and criteria were communicated clearly to the Iraqi stakeholders, and no issues arose with the process or the representation. Iraqi institutions assumed the responsibility of collecting documentation and presenting the candidate sites.

Six communities for pilot implementation were selected from the eighteen candidates proposed: Kirmashiya, Badir Rumaidh, Masahab, Jeweber, Hadam, and Sewelmat. The community representatives from the Marsh Arab Forums in the three governorates pledged to facilitate access to the sites and provide security for the facilities. Such active participation of local communities was one of the key factors in the successful implementation of the pilot project.

The provision of clean drinking water commenced in early 2006. Distribution pipelines and common taps were installed in the six villages to improve access. The facilities, worth US$4.7 million, have the capacity to serve up to 22,000 residents (UNEP 2007b), making a tangible contribution toward target 10 of the MDGs. The project provided operator training, as well as support for operation and maintenance for a one-year period following installation. In June 2007 the completed facilities were officially handed over to the Ministry of Municipalities and Public Works, which is responsible for public water service provision and management in Iraq. To prepare for the handover and ensure sustainability of operations, technical dossiers were created to enable the ministry's water directorate to continue operation and maintenance of the facilities. The plant manufacturer also organized technology and management training for ministry officials. Finally, UNEP handed over a warehouse with spare parts and chemicals necessary for maintenance.

In response to a request for further support from Iraqi stakeholders, UNEP implemented drinking-water provision in a seventh community, the village of Ghreej in Dhiqar Governorate. This facility, which utilizes diesel-powered generators and photovoltaic panels to meet its energy needs, serves approximately 3,000 people and was transferred to the Ministry of Municipalities and Public

Environmental management of the Iraqi marshlands 123

Works in 2009 (UNEP 2009b). The water treatment technologies are the same as for the six facilities in the first phase of the project; this allows for ease of continued operation and maintenance by the Ministry of Municipalities and Public Works.

Wetland rehabilitation

When displaced residents returned to the marshlands following the collapse of Saddam Hussein's regime, some people breached dikes to reintroduce water into dried areas. Such reflooding of the marshlands took place in a haphazard manner, until the Ministry of Water Resources assumed control of the reflooding process. Although the reflooding brought back life in some areas in 2003 and 2004, the extensive decade-long drying had resulted in accumulation of salts and other substances, causing degradation of the wetlands in many areas. Human settlements without adequate sanitation facilities also caused contamination of reflooded areas. Furthermore, upstream hydrological infrastructure reduced water flow, and there were seasonal variations in the amount of water available for flooding the marshlands.[3]

As the reflooding continued and the residents resettled, the need to study optimal hydrological options for reflooding with the available quantity of water emerged. Such an analysis was carried out by Iraqi authorities with international support from Italy and the United States. The New Eden Project, supported by the Italian Ministry for the Environment, Land and Sea beginning in 2003, evaluated the state of the marshlands, developed water allocation strategies, and identified actions, priorities, and costs related to development of the region. The Italian-developed New Eden Master Plan for Integrated Water Resources Management in the Marshlands Area was presented in 2006 to assist Iraqi policy makers by providing sound data analysis and analytical tools to make choices regarding water resource allocation and environmental management (MOE, MWR, and MMPW 2006). Also, a U.S. Agency for International Development initiative developed a hydrological model of the Tigris and Euphrates river basins to simulate water allocation and flood control, and it supported development and monitoring of an integrated marsh management plan (USAID 2005).

With this background, the UNEP project investigated the feasibility of ESTs to rehabilitate the degraded wetlands, improving water and wetland quality, while other donors pursued activities related to hydrology and water quantity. A donor coordination mechanism facilitated periodic assessment of gaps and sharing of experiences and data between Iraqi and international institutions. Recognizing the need to coordinate initiatives, several donors had begun meeting in 2003; at the third such meeting, organized by the government of Italy and held in October 2004, UNEP was nominated as a liaison for donor coordination. UNEP then

---

[3] For more information on the varying extent of the Iraqi marshlands and on efforts to restore the marshlands, see Lonergan (2012).

124   Water and post-conflict peacebuilding

organized a ministerial donor coordination meeting in November 2005 in Paris and participated in subsequent meetings held in 2006 and 2007.

The pilot project for marshland management and wetland restoration was implemented under an agreement with the Center for Restoration of the Iraqi Marshlands (CRIM) of the Iraqi Ministry of Water Resources. The project conducted field surveys and assessments at the six pilot drinking-water facility sites, analyzing water quality, water flow and volume, vegetation, soil quality, and erosion conditions. For each site, CRIM identified key work required for rehabilitation, including restoration of marshland interconnections, flow regulation through channel connection and irrigation management, application of phyto-technology for replanting and water-quality improvement, separation of domestic wastewater, and dredging and cleaning of canals to manage water flow and quantity. On the basis of discussions with experts, the project identified two sites for in-depth investigation, developed detailed designs of pilot work, and held discussions with local residents to solicit their views on wetland rehabilitation. CRIM then selected one community for the pilot project site.

The selected site, Jeweber, had been dewatered, with 80 percent of the original marsh area remaining dry. Options for marshland rehabilitation included regulating the flow of water through an existing outlet from a nearby marsh, constructing dikes, and replanting the area with *Phragmites australis*. Although most local residents and community leaders extended positive support and cooperation, a small faction threatened the CRIM staff near the end of the project in 2006. It is unclear whether this security incident was related to the specifics of the project. Such security problems temporarily halted the project's implementation, but by the time project management was handed over to CRIM, the project was functioning well, though at less than the intended design capacity. The Iraqi implementing partners continued dialogue with local stakeholders for longer-term management. This illustrated the importance of stakeholder engagement in the selection of suitable locations for intervention.

A second pilot project commenced in early 2008 with the purposes of identifying and demonstrating options to minimize further damage to the wetlands, and of assessing the feasibility of increasing the availability of water for longer-term marshland restoration using constructed-wetland technology. The pilot project targeted the Main Drain, which drains wastewater from Baghdad and upstream areas and has diverted water that used to flow into the marshlands. Pilot project activities included monitoring Main Drain water quality at several locations.

On the basis of preliminary surveys of potential sites, Auda Marsh in Dhiqar Governorate, which was being reflooded with Main Drain water, was selected as a pilot site. The Ministry of Environment took the lead in implementing the pilot work of using constructed-wetland technology for water-quality and wetland improvement. The project also provided targeted capacity building to support project implementation.

The results of the Main Drain water-sampling surveys showed that the quality of Main Drain water would need to be improved before its flow could be used as a source for marshland reflooding. Pilot activities in water-quality and wetland improvement showed a reduction in concentrations of some pollutants, such as nitrates, phosphates, and suspended solids. The study concluded that longer-term monitoring and control of operating conditions would be needed before researchers could reach definitive conclusions. Also, such wetland improvement activities would need longer-term, sustained availability of water flow, with the cooperation of and coordination with the Ministry of Water Resources. The Ministry of Environment requested such cooperation.

PROJECT IMPACTS

Overall, the interventions generated the impacts originally intended, and in some areas surpassed expectations. As operating conditions worsened during the conflict and media coverage of Iraq focused more on violence, the project was seen as a rare case of good news. The project impacts summarized here have also been articulated in UNEP reports (UNEP 2009a, 2009b).

The project improved living conditions in local communities by providing drinking water to up to 25,000 rural residents, and through demonstration of sanitation and wetland management practices for replication. Tangible contributions to target 10 of the MDGs were made. The terminal project evaluation found that the drinking-water facilities were functioning after the handover, with Iraqi financing of operations and maintenance. The project pioneered the use of modular reverse osmosis container units for water purification in rural areas, and the number of such units funded by the Iraqi government and donors in the marshlands increased significantly. On the other hand, the two-year drought in 2008 and 2009 exacerbated water flow problems and worsened marshland conditions, negatively affecting the sanitation and wetland management pilot projects (UNEP 2011).

The project also generated data on marshland conditions. Water-quality and biodiversity monitoring established baseline data and made possible limited trend analysis of marshland conditions. UNEP's 2007 socioeconomic survey collected previously unavailable data that government ministries used to inform policy making and intervention planning. The relevant ministries were directly engaged in developing the data-collection and analysis methods, and in preparing the survey report.

Because the project contributed to the redevelopment of local communities, anxiety about rebuilding life in the marshlands was reduced, according to third-party monitors. Community-level initiatives that were planned and implemented with local residents and organizations involved over 2,000 participants and enhanced the level of community engagement in marshland management.

Capacity-building activities increased the expertise of Iraqi personnel and institutions, and the project encouraged trained personnel to develop and use their new skills by taking part in pilot projects, data management, and policy assessments. Also, university personnel who participated in training planned and

126　Water and post-conflict peacebuilding

executed secondary training courses in Iraq. This linkage between capacity building and project implementation generated various employment opportunities. Altogether, the project held fourteen international training sessions with 314 participants, ten in-country training sessions with 141 participants, and two study tours with twenty-two participants.

Validation of results and impacts

Third parties commissioned by UNEP carried out independent monitoring of the pilot projects. The monitoring and evaluation report for six drinking-water plants was released in September 2006. It concluded that the project, which was successfully implemented under very difficult circumstances, had made "a tremendous impact in confidence building within the communities" (Prodev 2006, 13). The report authors wrote that "the contribution and support given to the returning families of the Iraqi Marshlands through this project is deeply appreciated by the beneficiaries and has to a great extent alleviated suffering and covered the basic humanitarian need for sustaining life" (Prodev 2006, 2). The report also found that the project had encouraged many households to return to their home villages and to reestablish their livelihoods. The number of livestock increased, as did the production of dairy products and of reed-related crafts that could be sold in the urban market centers, "adding to the income generation, employment and generally, the prosperity of the community" (Prodev 2006, 12).

The project team was awarded a 2007 UN21 Award from the UN Secretary-General.[4] The project was also honored as "a model of international environmental cooperation" by the Iraqi Minister of Environment in 2008.[5] Community groups indicated in official correspondence that "UNEP is one of the few organizations that has made a real effort at engaging the local communities."[6]

An assessment of pilot components on sanitation provision and wetland restoration was released in January 2008, with positive evaluations overall (Stars Orbit Consultants 2007). The evaluators concluded that the concepts and technology selected for the project were appropriate and that similar projects might be implemented in other parts of Iraq. The short-term benefits identified included the enhancement of water quality and the marshland environment, and reduction of water-related diseases and infections. The long-term benefits included return of original marshland residents, increased biodiversity, rehabilitation of the agricultural sector, an economic boost, creation of job opportunities, enhancement of the marshland environment, and restoration of the original wetlands.

---

[4] The UN21 Award recognizes UN staff members for innovation, efficiency, and excellence in the delivery of programs and services.

[5] Minister of Environment, official correspondence to United Nations Environment Programme, 2008.

[6] Personal communication from community groups to United Nations Environment Programme.

Environmental management of the Iraqi marshlands **127**

To assess the project results and impacts, UNEP organized several project evaluation meetings with stakeholders and donors. In particular, a meeting was held in Kyoto, Japan, in September 2008 to review the outcomes and results achieved in all project phases, and to formulate recommendations for future work to be undertaken by the Iraqi government and the international community to mainstream environmental issues in a sustainable development agenda for Iraq. Other participants in the meeting included high-level officials from the Ministry of Environment and the Ministry of Municipalities and Public Works, and the ambassador of the Republic of Iraq to Japan. The workshop was also attended by representatives from the government of Japan, the government of Italy, the United Nations Educational, Scientific and Cultural Organization (UNESCO), and other institutions. The Iraqi Minister of Environment indicated satisfaction with the project outcomes and benefits, especially concerning the development of ESTs in the marshland ecosystem and capacity building for ministry staff.

Finally, the terminal evaluation of the project, conducted in 2010 and 2011, found that all project activities appear to have been fully implemented with almost no shortcomings. Across the project phases, all of the project components were assessed as "highly satisfactory" except one, which was assessed as "satisfactory" (UNEP 2011).

Factors supporting and preventing positive outcomes

The UNEP project team has concluded that the factors contributing to the positive outcomes are primarily associated with project design, the addressing of immediate needs, involvement of local stakeholders in project decision making, and political will.

The project included multiple activity components, including support for strategy development and coordination, data collection and baseline analysis, capacity building, pilot implementation, and awareness raising and follow-up. Drinking-water provision addressed the immediate needs of the local communities, helping to generate their support and trust. Such support and trust facilitated the implementation of other field-based activities, including the data collection and monitoring that are necessary for effective natural resource management. Capacity building, awareness raising, and other initiatives addressed both immediate and medium-term needs.

The project discussed community needs extensively with stakeholders to incorporate them into project decisions. For example, during an early technical meeting to discuss EST pilot project implementation, stakeholders expressed the overwhelming need for drinking-water provision, and they reiterated this concern during follow-up discussions. As a result, the project allocated a larger share of resources than originally planned to the provision of drinking water to seven communities.

The project prioritized activities that were visible to and had direct benefits for local residents. Resentment was growing during the post-conflict period as

128 Water and post-conflict peacebuilding

residents continued to suffer and as their leaders expressed concern that there was insufficient help from international organizations and domestic sources. Therefore, expedited action was fundamental in mobilizing and maintaining local support for the project.

Finally, the government of Iraq demonstrated political will when it recognized the project as a national environmental and humanitarian priority for reconstruction and redevelopment. The Ministry of Environment demonstrated political will when it facilitated the allocation of human and technical resources within the ministry to support the project and took the lead in key activities, such as water-quality and biodiversity monitoring and pilot project implementation. Also, the Ministry of Environment took charge of interministerial and local coordination for the project and presented the project phases to the Iraqi Strategic Review Board, which has the final approval authority on recommendations from the Ministry of Planning and Development Coordination for allocation of international assistance to Iraq.

On the other hand, a number of factors negatively affected the project outcome. They include security concerns; limited availability of human, financial, technical, and other resources; and infrastructure and governance constraints.

Continued terrorism and worsening security at the local level presented unprecedented security and accountability challenges for all actors, including UNEP. For example, UN staff could not enter the country or directly oversee activities on the ground. Ensuring the safety of Iraqi personnel became an overwhelming priority. Moreover, continuing violence during the case study period necessitated prolonged humanitarian relief activities, slowing the move toward development activities in the transition phase. Many interventions related to basic services, such as water treatment, electricity generation, and construction, were halted due to security concerns, and in some cases they were destroyed by terrorism.

Human, financial, and technical resources were limited; this was in part due to the decade-long sanctions against Iraq, which eroded the capacity of Iraqi experts and institutions by restricting their exposure to international practices. In addition, threats, kidnappings, assassinations, and bombings within ministry premises preceded or resulted in the deaths of key partners, drove some to leave their government positions, and compelled others to flee the country altogether. The security risks also limited the number of available and willing contractors, and restricted the availability of goods and services for procurement. Personnel and procurement expenses increased significantly during the project period. Border closings and curfews complicated personnel movement and the transport and installation of equipment, and they caused negative financial impacts associated with stowage fees, contract extensions, and reluctance of vendors in subsequent procurements.

The project implementation period coincided with a period during which the Iraqi governance and institutional landscapes changed significantly. Although the reestablishment of democracy and participatory governance is a welcomed

Environmental management of the Iraqi marshlands 129

necessity, the emergence of or changes in multiple institutions and their sometimes competing mandates made it difficult at times for the project to learn which institution was responsible for what.

When Iraq's military and intelligence services were dissolved in May 2003, de-Baathification removed senior officials from government posts. The insurgency and criticism of uneven implementation of the de-Baathification policy led to the gradual partial return of vetted ex-Baathists to government and security positions beginning in 2004. Escalating violence also targeted government workers and public buildings, undermining stabilization. The sustenance of institutional knowledge about the project was hampered by frequent changes in personnel, including elected officials and senior-level managers. Because the worsening security situation restricted personnel movement, the project relied increasingly on mobile telecommunications and the internet, which quickly became available in the post-conflict period. However, the fragility of the telecommunications infrastructure and limitations on electricity supply caused communication difficulties at times (UNEP 2009a, 2009b).

Finally, although the new government had various regulations in place concerning pollutant release, water quality, and environmental impacts of new construction, the level of enforcement appeared to be low, possibly because of security concerns, competing priorities, difficulty accessing laboratories, and staffing limitations.

LINKS TO PEACEBUILDING

The Iraqi Marshlands Project made primary contributions to the socioeconomic dimension of peacebuilding by providing relief and basic social services and by aiding the return of displaced populations. Moreover, the project addressed two vulnerability concerns. The first was the fear that the decimated ecosystem would no longer support the culture and lifestyle of the local residents. The second was that the insufficiency of basic services and natural resources would make the return of displaced persons to the area more difficult.

Access to safe drinking water has been the critical priority of the marshland residents as they reestablish their livelihoods. The project's drinking-water interventions, undertaken in the face of many major challenges, helped this rural area to accommodate the projected number of returning displaced persons.

The rationale for wetland rehabilitation was to revive life in the marshlands and to prevent further deterioration of the socioeconomic conditions of the people, as well as to improve the security and stability of the region. The wetlands are the backbone for sustaining both human and other life in the area, and reflooding was necessary for restoration. The project interventions focused on two specific aspects of wetland rehabilitation. In the first phase, the focus was on ESTs for restoring degraded areas of the wetlands; in the subsequent phase, the emphasis was on ESTs to improve the quantity and quality of water available for reflooding.

130   Water and post-conflict peacebuilding

Whereas the interventions for drinking water are of immense immediate value to the local communities, the impacts of wetland rehabilitation are realized only over the long term and therefore are not immediately visible to the local communities. Nevertheless, UNEP's rehabilitative interventions were generally welcomed and appreciated by Iraqi stakeholders and led to the leveraging of additional resources to continue the establishment of long-term sustainable management practices.

In addition to providing drinking water and rehabilitating the wetlands, the project's interventions contributed to peacebuilding by helping to address residents' frustration and desperation and by increasing trust and partnership between public authorities and local communities. Without the interventions, the basic need for the access to safe drinking water could not have been met in the pilot communities, and this lack would have worsened the suffering of the marshland residents and resulted in increased resentment and mistrust of public authorities. Instead, because local communities and public authorities worked together on the project from inception to completion, the interventions helped to increase the trust.

The success of the first phase of intervention in the six communities helped to strengthen cooperation and consultation between public authorities and community stakeholders in subsequent phases of the project. Community-level initiatives supported by the project also helped to foster partnerships. For example, project-funded environmental awareness campaigns in Basra for the Marsh Arab Forums stimulated the establishment of partnerships to engage the community from different angles, such as religious, scientific, and political perspectives. The common goal of conveying a coherent message that the Iraqi marshlands are an invaluable environmental resource was present throughout the campaign. The series of public meetings, followed by further discussions, provided the indirect benefit of making community members aware of the wide range of organizations with which they could work in the future. In Dhiqar, short training courses were given to tribal chiefs and religious leaders to help explain to local fisherfolk and their families the adverse effects of fishing with poison. The rationale behind the campaign was to begin to create an atmosphere in which using poison for fishing would become unacceptable within marshlands societies so that eventually this practice would be eliminated.

The dynamics between local groups and the government changed drastically after the fall of Saddam Hussein's regime. Between mid-2004 and 2008, the period examined in this chapter, the people of the marshlands were given the power to choose their local government representatives in democratic elections. Consequently, relations between local groups and the government improved significantly compared with the period under the former regime, when decisions were taken from the top without consultation with local groups. The central government now provides special allocations to the governorates, which are given the authority to decide on the priorities of reconstruction projects and other relevant matters. In addition, the trials of figures suspected of persecuting local

Environmental management of the Iraqi marshlands 131

residents during the Saddam Hussein regime may have helped to bring some sense of justice among the residents, according to the project's national coordinator.

Occasional disputes did arise, but they were largely resolved amicably during the implementation of the interventions. Many disputes stemmed from competition to benefit from project activities and resources, such as employment opportunities and water access. These disputes did not contest the interventions or the rationale for natural resource management. Maintaining dialogue with local communities and building trust through local presence from the inception of the project helped in the resolution of these disputes.

LESSONS LEARNED

On the basis of its experiences managing water and wetlands in southern Iraq in the post-conflict period, the project team learned a number of lessons that are generally applicable to other post-conflict situations.

The limited availability of reliable data hampered decision making for many institutions working in Iraq. This limitation compelled some to spend significant resources and time on assessment activities. Also the difficult security situation may have steered some institutions to favor safe activities, such as training and desk studies. Various community leaders complained of "assessment fatigue," voicing their frustration about having facilitated numerous studies and assessments that did not yield any form of improved local conditions.

Communities cannot prioritize saving the ecosystem when they face acute hardships from a lack of basic services. In a post-conflict situation where the population suffers from the disruption of basic services such as the provision of drinking water, interventions to address immediate basic needs should be given priority and carried out as soon as feasible and in an environmentally sound manner. Such interventions, when successful, have additional benefits, such as the building of a solid foundation for the trust and partnership that will be necessary for work toward long-term ecosystem management. These interventions also help practitioners to learn what works and does not work in a particular setting, especially in an ecologically sensitive area such as the Iraqi marshlands. On the other hand, if the immediate basic needs of a community are not adequately addressed first, other well-intentioned interventions that need longer-term commitments may fail to garner community support.

Natural resource management has many elements, participants, areas of intervention, and supporting measures. For the UNEP project, having a clear focus on EST implementation and the multifaceted measures necessary to support such implementation was beneficial because this approach enabled the project team and its partners to better understand linkages and consequences among actions and participants. For example, the data collection to identify and monitor pilot project sites was facilitated by community groups and used ministry and local personnel who had undergone project training. As pilot projects were implemented,

132 Water and post-conflict peacebuilding

the analyzed data informed national ministries' subsequent policy decisions on wetland management and were made available through the project information system to national and international partners. Such comprehensive and integrated programming, which encompassed data collection, training, implementation, and policy coordination was effective and had synergistic impacts among the participants and activities.

Projects should include targeted and coordinated measures to address the specific needs and roles of various people. Donor coordination is beneficial for identifying gaps in international cooperation, facilitating communication and cooperation, and preventing overlaps. Donor coordination initiatives under UNEP's leadership provided a forum for discussing the contributions and status of various Iraqi-led and donor-supported initiatives. This supported and facilitated policy coordination and the establishment of a longer-term marshlands management structure.

National-level initiatives are needed for policy establishment and implementation, coordination among relevant ministries, monitoring, and enforcement. Increasingly, governorate councils are entrusted to make decisions on resource allocation. Close cooperation and coordination are necessary to ensure that initiatives complement rather than undermine natural resource management efforts.

Local citizens and communities face the direct consequences of environmental degradation and of efforts to address the degradation. The necessity of their participation and support for the success of natural resource management initiatives cannot be overstated. Establishment of a local presence and management structure for the project implementation period and beyond is thus essential. Because of the severe security restrictions placed on UN personnel, the project relied significantly on national coordination and local implementation support by Iraqi partners, with overall coordination carried out by UNEP from outside. The national coordinator's presence in Iraq throughout the project period was a key factor in the successful maintenance of communications and project implementation modalities.

Major consultative meetings with stakeholders were primarily organized outside Iraq and were supplemented with regular dialogue and community visits by the national coordinator inside Iraq. While this setup had the obvious limitations and challenges of remote operations for UNEP, it had the positive effect of enhancing local management and responsibility taking, which translated into a greater sense of national and local ownership. To ensure representation in the stakeholder engagement process, representatives of local communities, governorates, and academic and civic institutions from the three governorates were engaged in the consultative process from the project kickoff in September 2004, with UNEP support. Notification and engagement of Iraqi stakeholders followed a transparent and systematic process to alleviate concerns over fairness and equity.

Donors and countries should recognize the need for long-term financial and programmatic support for ecosystem rehabilitation and management. Initiation of such efforts in the early phases of peacebuilding is absolutely necessary to prevent further damage, and sustained support should be provided over the long term, with realistic goals.

Natural resource management takes a long time to establish, and it has significant financial costs even in stable, developed countries where people are not competing for resources for survival and where adequate environmental laws and regulations are in place, enforced, and understood by communities. For example, the management plan for the Florida Everglades in the United States took approximately sixty years to develop, and it entails action for the next twenty years, with a budget of US$8 billion for implementation (CERP 2004). The master plan development for Lake Biwa, the largest lake in Japan, took over ten years to reach consensus among various stakeholders. For that plan, coordination and government engagement alone costs approximately US$1 million per year, not including expenses for lake management measures (Shiga Prefecture 2000). Countries emerging from post-conflict situations are unlikely to be able to mobilize such resources on their own; therefore, they need sustained international support for such programming and implementation over a long period of time.

For the Iraqi Ministry of Environment, the Iraqi Marshlands Project was one of the first and largest environmental management initiatives implemented with UN support after the ministry was established. The project therefore served as a platform for on-the-job training in environmental management, international cooperation, and domestic coordination for the ministry and its staff. It also provided a practical context for establishing cooperative working relations with the governorates, local groups, universities, and other ministries, as well as with nongovernmental organizations and international organizations.

The positive impacts of the project extended to the development of new water policy and law at the national level. For instance, efforts by the Ministry of Environment to establish and revise water quality–analysis standards have been informed by the UNEP project's experiences in water-quality management and have been supported by personnel and institutions that built relevant expertise through the project. Furthermore, the project's findings and recommendations, particularly those related to Main Drain water-quality management, have been shared through the interministerial meetings to facilitate consultations and policy making.

The project helped the Iraqi people and institutions to better recognize the global value of the Iraqi marshlands and the Iraqi environment in general, beyond local and national concerns. The project also influenced the Ministry of Environment's concentrated efforts for Iraqi accession to multilateral environmental agreements, such as the Convention on Biological Diversity; the Convention on Wetlands of International Importance, commonly known as the Ramsar Convention; and the United Nations Framework Convention on Climate Change. Such effective use of international cooperation initiatives is a universal lesson for countries emerging from conflicts (UNEP 2009a, 2009b).

134   Water and post-conflict peacebuilding

CONCLUSIONS AND NEXT STEPS

Although the specific initiatives described in this chapter were completed by 2009, there is a need to continue the process of bringing the Iraqi marshlands back to life. Ecosystem rehabilitation and redevelopment is a long-term process, and sustainable development in this area needs to be prioritized in the national development process.

Recognizing the need to transition from short-term post-conflict interventions in the marshlands toward longer-term sustainable redevelopment initiatives with potential for rural employment and income generation, UNEP and UNESCO launched a new initiative in 2009 to preserve and manage the cultural and natural heritage of the area (UNEP n.d.). Using the World Heritage site inscription process, the new project will identify and implement key sustainable production and consumption practices that use local materials and heritage. It will operate on a pilot basis and will build capacity and raise awareness among local institutions to ensure their participation in site preservation and ecosystem management.

The government of Iraq has added the marshlands area to a national tentative list of World Heritage sites because of its mixed natural and cultural heritage. This tentative listing of the marshlands marks the first recognition for the World Heritage program of natural heritage importance in Iraq. Recognizing the need to build experiences and capacity for natural resource and environmental management related to the World Heritage program, the Iraqi Ministry of Environment has endorsed this project as a priority.

Despite the emergence of promising longer-term initiatives, additional environmental threats could undermine the improvements in natural resource management that have been achieved to date. The marshlands area experienced a severe drought in 2008 and 2009, which significantly reduced water flow and vegetative cover in the wetlands and the availability of water nationwide. The drought and resulting desertification, attributed to climate change, are having a negative impact on economic development and the quality of life of Iraqi citizens.

A common country assessment conducted in 2009 stated that Iraq's environmental problems are defined by "declining quality and quantity of natural resources, exacerbated by unsustainable resource use" by a population which lacks awareness of environmental issues (UN 2009, 54). The assessment articulated additional factors contributing to environmental problems, including the drought, desertification and elevated soil salinity, increasing carbon emissions, loss of biodiversity, and an unsuitable rural water supply for agriculture, livestock raising, and drinking purposes. Although Iraq has only recently transitioned to the post-conflict and redevelopment phase, the country now experiences issues that are more common in middle-income and industrializing countries, such as urbanization-related air, noise, and water pollution; a lack of housing; limitations in industrial waste management and accident response; and chemical and other waste-related pollution. The assessment also highlighted the need to diversify

Environmental management of the Iraqi marshlands   135

Iraq's economy and to use the wealth arising from resources toward sustainable development.

In response, the United Nations Development Assistance Framework (UNDAF) for Iraq for 2011–2014 gives priority attention to water resource management, particularly where transboundary issues are involved, and the Iraqi marshlands. In addition, UN programming will address climate change by strengthening institutions and institutional frameworks, assessing Iraq's vulnerability to climate change, and identifying opportunities for climate change mitigation measures that will have economic, social, and environmental benefits, including potential for the development of green jobs (UN 2010). Iraq has also become a member of the Global Environment Facility and has been eligible for its financing in the field of climate change and biodiversity since 2010.

The government of Iraq has requested urgent assistance from the international community and cooperation from neighboring countries. Included in the July 2009 United Nations Economic and Social Council Substantive Session was a special agenda item on the Iraqi marshlands. And UNEP is committed to continue its work beyond 2011. It will be part of the United Nations Country Team for Iraq, which will implement interventions under the UNDAF process to address emerging environmental priorities, with targeted ecosystem management initiatives for the Iraqi marshlands.

Through the provision of basic services and support for the return of displaced populations, the Iraqi Marshlands Project made significant contributions toward peacebuilding. Working with Iraqi institutions and citizens to help bring the area back to life has been an act of peace.

REFERENCES

CIMI (Canada-Iraq Marshlands Initiative). 2010. *Managing for change: The present and future state of the Iraqi marshlands.* University of Victoria, Canada. www.lonergansleanings.com/ storage/Marshlands%20Book.pdf.

CERP (Comprehensive Everglades Restoration Plan). 2004. *Rescuing an endangered ecosystem: The journey to restore America's everglades.* West Palm Beach, FL.

Lonergan, S. 2012. Ecological restoration and peacebuilding: The case of the Iraqi marshes. In *Assessing and restoring natural resources in post-conflict peacebuilding*, ed. D. Jensen and S. Lonergan. London: Earthscan.

MOE (Ministry of Environment, Republic of Iraq), MWR (Ministry of Water Resources, Republic of Iraq), and MMPW (Ministry of Municipalities and Public Works, Republic of Iraq). 2006. *New Eden master plan for integrated water resources management in the marshlands area.* Baghdad.

Prodev (Prodev Resources and Associates). 2006. *Monitoring and evaluation services for UNEP project support for environmental management of the Iraqi marshlands.* Final report. http://marshlands.unep.or.jp/default.asp?site=marshlands&page_id=A30AC478 -C721-448D-9DCA-302C13874C22.

Richardson, C. J., and N. A. Hussain. 2006. Restoring the Garden of Eden: An ecological assessment of the marshes of Iraq. *BioScience* 56 (6): 477–489.

136 Water and post-conflict peacebuilding

Shiga Prefecture. 2000. *Mother Lake 21 plan: Lake Biwa comprehensive preservation and improvement project.* www.pref.shiga.jp/biwako/koai/mother21-e.

Stars Orbit Consultants. 2007. *External evaluation report on sanitation and wetland restoration components for UNEP support for environmental management of the Iraqi marshlands.* November. Amman, Jordan.

UN (United Nations). 2003. *United Nations inter-agency assessment of vulnerable groups: Part 1; Marsh Arabs.* New York: Office of the Humanitarian Coordinator for Iraq, Lower South.

———. 2009. *Common country assessment: Iraq.* New York.

———. 2010. *United Nations development assistance framework for Iraq: 2011–2014.* New York.

UN (United Nations) and World Bank. 2003. *United Nations/World Bank joint Iraq needs assessment.* New York.

UNEP (United Nations Environment Programme). 2004. Support for environmental management of the Iraqi marshlands. Project document. Submitted to UNDG Iraq Trust Fund in July. Shiga, Japan.

———. 2007a. *Summary report on survey on demographic, social, and economic conditions of marshlands in the south of Iraq.* December. Osaka, Japan.

———. 2007b. *UNEP in Iraq: Post-conflict assessment, clean-up and reconstruction.* Nairobi, Kenya. http://postconflict.unep.ch/publications/Iraq.pdf.

———. 2009a. *Lessons learned on mainstreaming pilot projects into larger projects.* DTI/1241/JP. Osaka, Japan.

———. 2009b. *Support for environmental management of the Iraqi marshlands, 2004–2009.* Osaka, Japan. www.unep.or.jp/Ietc/Publications/Water_Sanitation/Support_for_EnvMng_of_IraqiMarshlands_2004-9.pdf.

———. 2011. *Terminal evaluation of project "Support for Environmental Management of the Iraqi Marshlands."* Nairobi, Kenya.

———. n.d. UNEP-UNESCO joint project: Natural and cultural management of the Iraqi marshlands. www.unep.or.jp/ietc/IraqWH/index.html.

USAID (United States Agency for International Development). 2004. The United States and the Iraqi marshlands: An environmental response. Written testimony of Gordon West, acting assistant administrator, Asia and Near East Bureau, and Dr. John Wilson, senior environment and agriculture specialist, Asia and Near East Bureau. U.S. House of Representatives, International Relations Committee, Subcommittee on the Middle East and Central Asia, February 24.

———. 2005. *Our commitment to Iraq.* November. Washington, D.C. http://pdf.usaid.gov/pdf_docs/PDACG063.pdf.

WHO (World Health Organization) and UNICEF (United Nations Children's Fund). 2006. *Meeting the MDG drinking water and sanitation target: The urban and rural challenge of the decade.* Geneva, Switzerland.

PART 2

Livelihoods

Introduction

While part 1 of this book discusses the need to restore basic water and sanitation services to alleviate human suffering and avert a humanitarian crisis in the immediate aftermath of armed conflict, part 2 considers how water can be harnessed to restore livelihoods and foster sustainable development in the near to medium term. By destroying water infrastructure—including irrigation canals, flood control systems, and dams—armed conflict can devastate the economy, exacerbate poverty, and undermine food security. Violent conflict also often forces civilians to abandon their homes and seek refuge elsewhere, thereby losing access to their traditional livelihoods. Finally, during conflict, ensuring the sustainability of water use to support diverse or alternative livelihoods is not a priority, and short-term coping strategies may create the potential for pollution or overexploitation of water resources and use of unsafe water supplies, contributing to the spread of disease.

For peace to be durable, people must not only have a stake in the political process but must also see "peace dividends"—that is, tangible welfare gains that result from the end of conflict. Providing access to land and water resources is a first step that can enable large segments of the population, including those in the agricultural sector, to revive their livelihoods. In many post-conflict countries, agriculture constitutes the largest percentage of the gross domestic product and employs the largest percentage of the population; thus, a productive agricultural sector can help to reduce the threat of famine, both for civilians and for excombatants returning home after conflict. This was the case in post-war Japan, as Mikiko Sugiura, Yuka Toguchi, and Mona Funiciello highlight in "Irrigation Management and Flood Control in Post–World War II Japan." The authors describe how the Japanese government, in an effort to improve livelihoods, increase food security, and support land reform, elected to make the construction of irrigation and drainage systems a central component of early recovery efforts. One factor that the authors identify as key to the success of Japan's irrigation reforms was the persistence of strong social institutions throughout the conflict. This finding is in keeping with a point made by Jeremy Allouche, in part 1: informal institutions should not be viewed as either a challenge to the consolidation of the state or as barriers to economic recovery, but as mechanisms that policy makers can draw on to foster post-conflict economic recovery.

One point emphasized in part 2 is the importance of quickly jump-starting the agricultural sector in the wake of conflict—first to ensure food security, and second to facilitate the resettlement of refugees, displaced persons, and demobilized soldiers. In "Refugee Rehabilitation and Transboundary Cooperation: India, Pakistan, and the Indus River System," Neda A. Zawahri points to the crucial role of effective coordination between the land and water sectors in the revival of agriculture in post-conflict situations. Both land and water are generally highly contested resources; thus, if a state allocates land rights without access

140   Water and post-conflict peacebuilding

to water (or, conversely, allocates water rights without access to land), it may jeopardize its own attempts to generate welfare gains and stabilize the post-conflict economy. In her examination of the Indian government's efforts to restore the livelihoods of rural refugees in eastern Punjab by establishing an agrarian economy, Zawahri highlights the government's awareness of the importance of both secure property rights and access to water.

Each post-conflict situation is unique, and the mechanisms for harnessing water to improve livelihoods must be tailored to the political, cultural, economic, institutional, and ecological context. In "Despite the Best Intentions? Experiences with Water Resource Management in Northern Afghanistan," Jennifer McCarthy and Daanish Mustafa show that the history of water management in Afghanistan has been closely aligned with the nation-building attempts of various regimes. In their exploration of recent attempts to implement community-level water projects through the National Solidarity Programme (NSP), the main government initiative for facilitating local development and alleviating rural poverty, McCarthy and Mustafa point to the problematic use of an "idealized village democracy model" as the basis for intervention. Partly because of the persistent failure of such interventions, the donor community and NSP managers have failed to develop a thorough understanding of local water governance norms and practices; as a result, they have also failed to incorporate such norms and practices into their initiatives. The authors demonstrate that local water management is far more complex than is often acknowledged, and that local water governance in Afghanistan is often driven by power arrangements that are remnants of previous conflicts, during which warlords stepped in to fill power vacuums and seized authority over resources. Ultimately, the authors point to the critical need for conflict- and gender-sensitive approaches to local water management.

For countries emerging from protracted warfare, the paucity of reliable hydrologic data, compounded by the dearth of scientific and technical expertise and social capital, can hamper livelihood restoration. In "Water's Role in Measuring Security and Stability in Helmand Province, Afghanistan," Laura Jean Palmer-Moloney illustrates the difficulty of harnessing water resources for economic recovery when there is a thirty-year gap in hydrometeorological data. Although, as Palmer-Moloney notes, there is an urgent need to collect and share data, the security situation has made it extremely difficult for nongovernmental and humanitarian organizations to operate in Afghanistan. One consequence is that military entities and their contractors are assuming a larger role in the reconstruction of water infrastructure.

Taken together, the chapters in part 2 stress the critical importance of water-related interventions at the national, provincial, and local levels to ensure the post-conflict recovery of food security, livelihoods, and the broader economy. Moreover, such interventions cannot succeed without effective coordination across sectors; with local stakeholders; and, in many post-conflict situations, with domestic and foreign militaries. Finally, the authors stress the importance of collecting and sharing valid information in order to ensure that post-conflict water-related interventions are based on a sound understanding of both local hydrology and the social structures that are in place to manage water allocation and use.

Irrigation management and flood control in post–World War II Japan

Mikiko Sugiura, Yuka Toguchi, and Mona Funiciello

The Japanese government prioritized irrigation and flood prevention following World War II by establishing a new legal framework. In the new framework, irrigation and flood prevention were divided between two separate management systems, with irrigation management maintaining a bottom-up approach while flood prevention shifted to a top-down, government-directed approach. These two strategies increased agricultural productivity and decreased flood damage in the short term, and they enhanced economic development and food security in the long term. The differences between the two approaches yield several lessons for water resource management in a post-conflict period, particularly with regard to institutional capacity, effective management with limited supplies, consensus building between local populations and the government, and creation of membership incentives through collection of fees.

This chapter examines the legal framework for and management of irrigation and flood control in post–World War II Japan (1945–1952).[1] The analysis focuses on benefits brought about by maintenance of the village as a bottom-up management unit for irrigation following the separation of irrigation and flood-control programs after World War II. The first two sections present the background of water and land management in Japan, pre- and post-1945, respectively. The chapter then offers an overview of the legal framework for water management. The subsequent

---

Mikiko Sugiura is a visiting scholar in the Department of Civil Engineering and Engineering Mechanics at Columbia University. Yuka Toguchi is a graduate student in the Department of International Studies, Graduate School of Frontier Sciences at the University of Tokyo. Mona Funiciello holds a master's degree in urban and environmental policy and planning from Tufts University. The research for this chapter was funded in part by a scholarship from the Zonta Club of Tokyo I, and in part by Grant-in-Aid for Young Scientists (Start-up), Phase I of a project of the Japan Society for the Promotion of Science.

[1] The post-war period is defined here as the years from 1945, when the Potsdam Declaration was accepted by the Japanese government as unconditional surrender, and 1952, when the San Francisco Peace Treaty entered into force and diplomatic relations with the United States were restored. The year 1952 was the beginning of a period of high economic growth. From 1955 to 1972, Japan's real gross national product grew by an average annual rate of 9.4 percent (MIC 2000).

142   Water and post-conflict peacebuilding

two sections examine, respectively, irrigation management from the perspective of agricultural productivity, and the development of a new legal framework for flood control.

Irrigation management is examined through the lessons of the Ooi River National Agricultural Water Project, one of four national water projects implemented soon after World War II. The Ooi River project demonstrates the importance of enabling villages to retain their roles as local management units while the role of national authorities is simultaneously expanding. Maintaining consistent management units for irrigation was a key part of consensus building in Japan. The Ooi River project also highlights the links between land reform and water reform in post-war Japan. By contrast, Japan's flood-prevention program involved increasing government control and decreasing opportunities for local involvement. The latter experience shows that top-down management was essential for post-conflict restoration of flood-control facilities but also that beneficiaries' declining awareness can negatively affect future flood-control efforts.

LAND AND WATER MANAGEMENT BEFORE 1945

For centuries land and water management in Japan have been closely linked. Before World War II, water resources were managed by water associations responsible for both irrigation and flood control. These associations were based in local villages (Tanaka and Sato 2005). The origins of this method of governance date back to the Edo period (1603–1868), when feudal lords imposed a land tax on villages, rather than on individual villagers, with rice as the form of payment (Nagata 1994). Water was managed primarily for agricultural use, and water management areas were determined by the land-tax payment, which was based on the amount of rice each hectare was able to produce. Villagers collectively built, operated, and maintained the water infrastructure necessary to produce a sufficient quantity of rice to pay the tax; this included constructing networks of irrigation canals, ponds, and dams.

This process evolved into a tiered system, with individual villages, also called water user groups, occupying the lowest tier (Nagata 1994). Farmers became the labor force that carried out the tasks associated with the operation, maintenance, and management of these systems. The two most essential tasks were removing mud from canals and clearing vegetation from canal banks, which facilitated the flow of water through the irrigation systems. At an intermediate level, the water user groups were managed by a water management association that was responsible primarily for water distribution, operation and maintenance of irrigation facilities, and control of branch canals. At the highest level, a single water management association controlled the main canal and was responsible for water distribution among upstream and downstream users, facility maintenance, irrigation systems, and resolution of water disputes.

The Meiji Reformation, which began in 1868, sought to transform the feudal system of administration, based on the village unit, into a new system of individual

Irrigation and flood control in post–World War II Japan 143

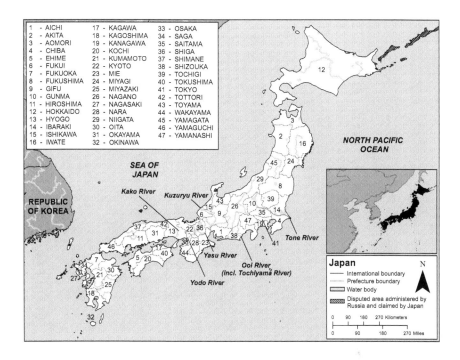

landownership. This supported the formation of cities, towns, and villages and required new administrative arrangements. Although in most cases the water management systems functioned as intended and met the water use needs of the villages, conflicts often arose over the distribution of water between upstream and downstream villages because upstream water users had the power to take water without accounting for downstream users (Nagata 1994; Tanaka and Sato 2005). This inequity led to the development of laws that reformed the management and distribution of water resources. The first of these was the Ordinance on Water Management Associations, enacted in 1890, which created new irrigation organizations that supported the land-reform process.

At the same time that land management policies were being transformed, a series of severe floods led to alterations in water management policy as well. The River Act, enacted in 1896, administered river controls for flood prevention and codified the customary water rights of water management associations. One year later, the Sabo Act addressed riverine erosion. These two acts and the Forest Act of 1897 were considered the "Three Laws for Flood Control" that covered the full extent of rivers from their mountain sources to the upper and lower reaches of the rivers (Sanbongi 2006).

A decade later additional legislation adjusted the legal regime governing arable land. In 1908 the Water Association Act confirmed the creation of new irrigation associations, which comprised individual landowners and often covered several cities, towns, and villages. This act supported shifting the responsibility

144 Water and post-conflict peacebuilding

for managing irrigation facilities from the village unit to individual landowners. Wherever a city, town, or village was not able to effectively operate and maintain irrigation facilities, the act provided for the establishment of a new irrigation association; in many instances, several water user organizations that had managed water collectively were replaced by a single irrigation association (Nagata 1994). The act also outlined coordination of responsibilities for agricultural water management. Arable-land-readjustment associations implemented irrigation and drainage works for land improvement, while the irrigation associations managed the operation and maintenance of water use facilities (Nagata 1994).

Because the organizations created by the Ordinance on Water Management Associations included only those that controlled main canals, almost all water management performed at the village level continued with traditional operation and maintenance of irrigation facilities and distribution of water (Nagata 1994). Through the Arable Land Readjustment Act of 1899, land was consolidated into more efficient paddy units, and revisions to the act in 1905 and 1909 focused on enabling the paddy units to manage irrigation, drainage projects, and reclamation, with the conversion of upland fields into paddy fields also taking place (Akino 1979). This act also created the arable-land-readjustment associations, local nonprofit organizations in charge of implementing land-improvement, irrigation, and drainage projects. Membership, leadership, and decision-making authority were limited to landowners only.

Although at the time these acts functioned well and met the needs of water users, political and economic changes following World War II resulted in their reexamination and modification—again in conjunction with ongoing land reforms.

OVERVIEW OF LAND AND WATER MANAGEMENT SINCE 1945

Following World War II, the General Headquarters of the U.S.-led Allied occupation force insisted that Japan reassign property titles from landlords to the renters working the farmland, with the specific intent of ending feudal oppression and addressing severe food shortages (McDonald 1997). Ownership of farmland was reorganized between 1946 and 1950, with the government purchasing uncultivated holdings and land belonging to absentee landlords for redistribution and sale to current tenants and other interested parties. Approximately 1.93 million hectares of farmland were purchased and sold to 4.75 million private farm households (Nagata 1994). Individual landownership was limited to the purchase of three hectares, and tenant farmers were limited to one hectare plots (Takemae 2002).

As farmland ownership reform came to a close, the Land Improvement Act was enacted in 1949. This act transformed the past property system, which dictated that most farmers rent land for cultivation, into a new system of landowner-farmers who purchased farmlands from the government at low rates and cultivated their land directly. Suggested by Allied General Headquarters, the act provided for the creation of land-improvement districts, which were charged with construction of irrigation and drainage facilities; land-improvement measures such as the building of farm roads and consolidation of farmland; and the operation and maintenance of canals, watercourses, reservoirs, pumping units, and other irrigation facilities (Nagata 1994; Mitra 1992). The districts had the additional benefits of providing a stable food supply to the country's burgeoning population and of ensuring that local stakeholders remained involved in irrigation management.

Land-improvement districts were incorporated bodies for a specific geographic area, and all members were farmer-cultivators. They were established when fifteen or more farmers with the prescribed qualifications wanted to implement a project for land improvement. The application required two-thirds agreement of potential beneficiary farmers, and the dissenting farmers were required to participate in the project once it was implemented. Because land improvement was considered beneficial to individual farmers, part of the cost of each project was assigned to the beneficiaries through a surcharge to the farmers involved (Nagata 1994).

World War II was also a major impetus for a shift of water resource management from local water associations to the national government. Water-related infrastructure (dams, canals, irrigation ditches, pipelines, and storage tanks) had been abandoned because of war-related financial deprivation and a severe labor shortage. Exactly how much of the infrastructure was destroyed or abandoned during the war is not documented; however, the many incidents of acute water shortage and serious flood damage that were recorded during the post-war period indicate the severity of the problem.

For instance, immediately following the war, conflicts over water availability erupted among irrigation farmers. Meanwhile, a series of major floods hit Japanese rivers almost every year during this same period, claiming more than a thousand lives per year and causing catastrophic damage (Musiake and Koike 2009; Aki and Takahasi 1956; Takahasi 1955). The severe effects of the flooding compounded the damage left in the wake of World War II and crippled reconstruction efforts (Takahasi 2009). These events led the government to prioritize flood prevention at the national level and coincided with the government's focus on increasing food production (Musiake and Koike 2009).

Food security had been tenuous during World War II, and during the occupation Japan was highly dependent on the food aid provided by the Allied General Headquarters. To reduce its reliance on foreign food aid and boost domestic food production, Japan sought to improve and develop farmland (Nishikawa and Latz 1981). On the basis of research by the National Resource Section of the Supreme Commander for the Allied Powers, the U.S. Committee on Foreign Affairs also emphasized the necessity of paying political attention to food and population problems (Ackerman 1948). The General Headquarters report enhanced Japanese economic recovery by leading to effective natural resource management (Ishimitsu 1986), in part by proposing the construction of irrigation and drainage systems as a viable path to food security.

The response to food security needs was an important dimension of an overall effort by the United States to generate reforms that would demilitarize the country and simultaneously help it to develop a peaceful, economically stable,

146 Water and post-conflict peacebuilding

and politically democratic society (Madsen and Samuels 2010; Iyori 2002; Kawagoe 1999). The priority placed on improving food security was a key consideration in the promulgation of the Land Improvement Act, which, along with related reforms, increased food production, specifically of rice, and augmented the amount of government funds devoted to further developing land and agricultural projects.

Because Japan was constrained by natural resource scarcity and a severe food shortage, effective natural resource management was essential for long-term social and economic stability (Ackerman 1948).[2] Under dire post-war conditions, characterized by deteriorating infrastructure, poor sanitation, and general social upheaval, water projects remained a significant political priority. Within five years of the end of the war, the government had launched four national irrigation projects as part of laying a foundation for peace and stability. Flood control was implemented simultaneously in a prompt and concerted response to recent flooding. Additionally, eleven river-development projects and multipurpose dams were completed during that same time period; these were necessary to repair damage caused by a series of typhoons that hit Japan in 1945 and 1947 (Takahasi 2009).

Because Japan is a collection of narrow and mountainous islands, the East Asian monsoon brings both abundant precipitation and occasional typhoons, which often result in natural disasters. One especially difficult issue in water management is the unpredictability of flooding and droughts resulting from fluctuating rainfall levels and extreme weather events. These cycles of flood and drought were prevalent in the post-war period, and people suffered from their effects on food and water supplies.

In the future, as climate change–related weather events escalate in quantity and severity across the globe, other post-conflict countries will increasingly be looking for ways to improve natural resource management. This chapter's analysis offers a number of useful insights and lessons for transitioning between different forms of governance.

The separation in administration of flood prevention and irrigation activities occurred in 1949 with the creation of the Flood Prevention Association Act. Flood management at the national level was required because of conflicts among land-improvement districts, particularly related to long-term land use planning and to transboundary management of water to prevent short-term flooding. Additionally, government intervention was necessary because of the high costs associated with flood prevention and maintenance, and because the irregularity of natural disasters lowered residents' perception of risk and thus made it difficult for flood-control associations to collect annual fees.

---

[2] Japan lacks reserves of many natural resources. There are multiple arguments about Japan's motivation for territorial expansion during World War II (Yasuba 1996), but the country's interest in decreasing its reliance on natural resource imports has been regarded as one of the driving factors behind the decision to send military forces into Southeast Asia in search of strategic materials such as petroleum, coal, copper, zinc, and rubber (Stranges 1993).

EVOLUTION OF THE LEGAL FRAMEWORK FOR WATER MANAGEMENT

This separation of irrigation and flood prevention aided short-term post-war economic recovery by leading to increased food production; however it weakened long-term stakeholder involvement because it removed local user groups from participation in flood prevention. Subsequent water management legislation continued the separation of these functions.[3]

EVOLUTION OF THE LEGAL FRAMEWORK FOR WATER MANAGEMENT

The evolution of the legal framework for water management in Japan is an important backdrop for the case studies on irrigation and flood control. The following section highlights key irrigation and flood control legislation that was enacted from the latter part of the Edo period (mid-nineteenth century) to the end of the post-conflict period in 1952. The changing roles of the management units, as detailed in table 1, provide important context for the pivotal legal changes that took place in 1949.

From the latter part of the Edo period through the early Meiji period, villages were responsible for the management of water resources (both flood control and irrigation), as well as for the collection of taxes on agricultural production. During this time water resources were held entirely in common.

At the beginning of the Meiji period, the established system did not change significantly. Although the village began to take on a broader number of administrative and management responsibilities, it did not have the legal authority to perform water management functions. However, because villages played a large role in irrigation and flood control, gradually those activities came to be accepted as village functions.

Several trends fueled shifts in water management. First, in order to meet the needs of projects that extended beyond the jurisdiction of villages, such as construction of water catchments that crossed village boundaries, water management responsibilities shifted from villages to larger administrative units under the Ordinance on Water Management Associations, which was the first significant legislation governing water use.

The 1908 Water Association Act established flood-prevention associations and consolidated flood-prevention and irrigation associations under a single law. Both irrigation and flood prevention were considered public goods, and both were subject to the same regulations under the legislation. The associations were also permitted to engage in water-usage and drainage projects. The Home Affairs Ministry was supposed to be the government agency that administered the act; however, administrative conflicts arose because the projects carried out by irrigation

---

[3] Following the post-war period that is the focus of this chapter, Japan continued to develop its legal regime governing water. Key legislation includes the Water Quality and Control Act (1958), the Industrial Effluent Control Act (1958), and the new River Act (1964, last revised in 1997) (Sanbongi 2006).

148   Water and post-conflict peacebuilding

Table 1.   Transition of the legal framework in Japan for flood-control and irrigation management

Period	Legislation	Flood control or irrigation management unit
Latter part of the Edo period (late-eighteenth century to mid-nineteenth century)	Not applicable	Village as management (control) unit.
Early part of the Meiji period (mid- to late-nineteenth century)	Not applicable	Village as administrative unit.
1890	Ordinance on Water Management Associations	Irrigation associations formed by private landowners, under Home Affairs Ministry.
1896–1897	River Act Sabo Act Forest Act	Flood-prevention associations and flood-fighting associations.
1908	Water Association Act (Ordinance on Water Management Associations abolished)	Irrigation associations and flood-prevention associations treated uniformly under the Home Affairs Ministry.
1909	Arable Land Readjustment Act	Two-track system: Agriculture and Commerce Ministry handled arable-land-readjustment projects; local government or irrigation associations handled maintenance after completion.
1949	Land Improvement Act Flood Control Act Flood Prevention Association Act (Water Association Act and Arable Land Readjustment Act abolished)	First, authorities under the Land Improvement Act and the Water Association Act; later, authorities under the Flood Control Act.

associations included elements that were essential to agricultural management and thus within the purview of the Agriculture and Commerce Ministry.

The Arable Land Readjustment Act of 1909 was designed to address these administrative conflicts and inconsistencies by creating a path for the arable-land-readjustment associations to carry out water usage and drainage projects under the Agriculture and Commerce Ministry. An inconsistency between the 1908 Water Association Act and the 1909 Arable Land Readjustment Act was resolved when local administrations or associations were allowed to take over management of completed projects. This resulted in the development of a separate administrative control structure under which irrigation and drainage projects would be handled by the Agriculture and Commerce Ministry, and the Home Affairs Ministry would then take over the maintenance and control functions once a project was completed. This structure later underwent major changes with the Land Improvement Act (Nishikawa and Latz 1981).

The Land Improvement Act and the Flood Prevention Association Act, both passed in 1949, had two objectives: (1) to reorganize the many laws dealing with irrigation and water use and drainage, and (2) to consolidate different associations with similar, overlapping functions. Irrigation and water-use activities were now under the purview of the Land Improvement Act, which replaced the 1909 Arable Land Readjustment Act, and flood prevention was governed by the 1949 Flood Prevention Association Act, which replaced the 1908 Water Association Act. These changes separated the management and administration of flood control and irrigation activities, which helped set in motion the economic recovery and stabilization of social systems that were essential to post-conflict peacebuilding efforts in the long term.[4] Unfortunately, the separation also resulted in a long-term lack of stakeholder involvement in water resource management.

IRRIGATION MANAGEMENT

Japanese irrigation projects from 1945 to 1952 reveal the historical significance of natural resource management systems in post-war Japan, particularly in relation to the prioritization of agricultural productivity and the development of a nationally designed and controlled system.

Figure 1 shows changes over time in agricultural productivity both per hectare and per person. Although Japan experienced economic and social turmoil following the end of World War II, there was also an immediate and sharp increase in agricultural productivity. Japan's signing of the San Francisco Peace Treaty in 1951, and thus its reemergence as a member of the international community, coincided with the implementation of its four national agricultural water projects.

Before 1945, Japanese food security had depended highly on rice imports from Korea and Manchuria; at the end of World War II a decline in rice imports to 10 percent below the pre-war level meant that food security required urgent attention (Johnston 1953). Besides the lack of agricultural facilities and a labor shortage, the level of imports was restricted by a worldwide grain shortage that made it impossible for food-deficit countries to fully satisfy their imports needs.

---

[4] The River Act of 1896 governed flood control in the pre-war period. In addition, it mandated the creation of both flood-fighting associations and flood-prevention associations. The difference between these associations was that the police had the right of command under the Home Affairs Ministry for the former, but not the latter. During the war, the flood-fighting associations became responsible for air defense and were transformed into voluntary guards. After the war, control of these groups passed from the police to local governments, and their focus shifted to firefighting and civil defense. Since passage of the Flood Control Act in 1949, both firefighting and flood-fighting units have worked on flood prevention, although they have differed in their degree of specialization.

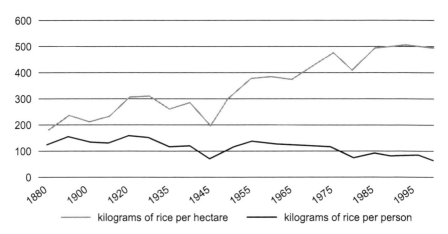

Figure 1. Agricultural productivity in Japan, 1880–1995
Source: MAFF (2007).

Additionally, food consumption greatly increased as demobilized soldiers and repatriates returned home, where most of the water resource infrastructure and food production facilities had been abandoned or destroyed.

A combination of post-war extrinsic factors and pre-war intrinsic and continuous conditions resulted in the prioritization of water reform, which made it possible to speedily implement an effective resource management strategy. Water and land reforms associated with Japan's response to food insecurity were key factors in the country's post-war stabilization. Policies for the establishment of landowner-farmers, introduced by the reforms, created an incentive for high productivity and secured the stability of farmers' households (Ōchi 1966).[5] Furthermore, because agricultural productivity was identified as a high priority by both the U.S. and the Japanese governments at an early stage of the post-conflict period, villages retained their roles as local management units while the role of the national authorities was expanding.[6] The governance structure introduced in 1949 enhanced the level of engagement between local, prefectural, and national stakeholders, which in turn contributed to the overall post-conflict peacebuilding process.

---

[5] Land reform contributed to Japanese economic development, but landlords, who were a link in a communication system joining the villages to the center of government, gradually became impoverished in the process of land reform (Dore 1959).

[6] The land reform established legal and administrative connections to the local committees. These connections, along with the use of bureau resources, helped to maintain the balance between villagers and the authorities. For example, five tenants, three landlords, and two owner-operators served on each committee (Montgomery 1972). In the case of irrigation projects, when there was no apparent tension between villagers and the authorities, retention of local management units was preferred as a low-cost approach.

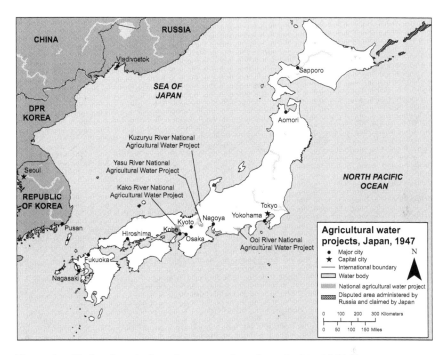

Figure 2. National agricultural water projects launched in 1947, Japan

The Ooi River project

The Ooi River National Agricultural Water Project was one of four national water projects implemented shortly after World War II that were called *kokuei-nogyo-suiri-jigyo*, or national reclamation works. The projects, which addressed food security by increasing agricultural productivity, were launched in 1947 by the Ministry of Agriculture, Forestry and Fisheries. They targeted four river basins: the Kako River Basin (Hyogo Prefecture, completed in 1951), the Yasu River Basin (Shiga Prefecture, completed in 1951), the Kuzuryu River Basin (Fukui Prefecture, completed in 1955), and the Ooi River Basin (Shizuoka Prefecture, completed in 1951) (see figure 2).

The Ooi River National Agricultural Water Project proposed to accomplish two things: first, to increase agricultural productivity and decrease the cost of irrigation-water intake by establishing new facilities or improving existing facilities located on both sides of the Ooi River; second, to create new jobs for the unemployed, including demobilized soldiers, repatriates, and families of war victims. While the second purpose, job creation, was specific to the post-war era, the first purpose, food security, existed both before and after the war. The project's plan included expanding existing water gates and building twelve new ones. Secondary and tertiary canals were built by local water association projects at

152 Water and post-conflict peacebuilding

the same time. The Ooi River National Agricultural Water Project took place between 1947 and 1951, with a total project budget of 36 million yen—in today's currency, about 530 million yen (US$5.85 million).

The Ooi River project was not the first irrigation project in the area. It had several predecessors from before World War II. One such project was the 1931 Tochiyama River Main Drainage Improvement Project, which involved construction of a discharge channel from the Tochiyama River to the Ooi River for the purpose of preventing rice paddies and agricultural facilities from flooding. Although it attained some positive results, many issues remained because of serious budget and labor shortfalls. Just as continuance of Japanese institutions or systems from pre-war to post-war periods has been mentioned in the literature with regard to trade unions (Tabb 1995) and bureaucracy (Dower 1993), coherence can be seen in the case of water issues that need to be dealt with as well.

The interaction between management units at the local, prefectural, and national levels played an important role in the success of the Ooi River project. A five-village meeting that was held on May 10, 1946, became the impetus for the project. One of the committee members was the governor of Shizuoka Prefecture, who identified water resource management as an urgent and crucial concern that required immediate attention. The number of concerned villages along the Ooi River expanded from the original five to a total of thirteen, and the group eventually submitted a petition for an irrigation water project to the prefecture governor.

The lobbying succeeded in generating an official response. A stakeholders' meeting was an essential next step in establishing a relationship between the villages and the authorities at the prefectural and national levels. In many post-conflict situations social networks are obliterated, but in post-war Japan the continuity of social networks and human capital provided an important foundation upon which to rebuild. Moreover, in contrast with some other post-conflict situations, including Iraq, two types of social capital required for viable governance—vertical social capital, which connects citizens to government, and bridging social capital, which links across different social, religious, and ethnic groups (Brinkerhoff 2005)—remained, barely but to a degree sufficient to transfer the remaining tasks of former projects to the new national water projects.

The maintenance of social networks and human capital was manifested in villages, which were the smallest water management units. Some village mayors were from local gentries called *tokuno-ka*, whose ancestors used their personal money to fund critical community development projects. The village mayors equally shared the burden of the project with the farmers, and their sense of responsibility played an important role in consensus building and negotiation. As their communication roles diversified with the progress of post-war reconstruction, some of the village mayors became local politicians, while others fell behind (Dore 1959).

As national developmental goals shifted toward agriculture, local stakeholders were affected by changes in both the scale and purpose of water-related

Irrigation and flood control in post–World War II Japan 153

Table 2. Number of dams, their purpose, and their available storage capacity, Japan, 1900–1993

Year of completion	Number of dams				Available storage capacity (1,000 cubic meters)	
	All dams		Dams for irrigation purposes			
	New	Total (accumulated)	New	Total (accumulated)	New	Total (accumulated)
1900–1925	200	788	161	749	85,618	183,202
1926–1945	412	1,200	289	1,038	623,682	806,884
1946–1955	219	1,419	139	1,177	1,220,263	2,027,147
1956–1965	355	1,774	150	1,327	5,180,546	7,207,693
1966–1975	327	2,101	150	1,477	3,218,732	10,426,425
1976–1985	267	2,368	97	1,574	2,421,685	12,848,110
1986–1993	188	2,556	88	1,662	3,666,213	16,514,323

Source: Adapted from Japan Dam Foundation (2005).

infrastructure, such as dams. The change in development scale and purpose coincided with a change of governance, as national authorities began to take over the management and implementation of large-scale water development projects. Dam building reached its peak in 1945, and available storage capacity peaked between 1956 and 1965 (see table 2). This indicates that the post-war period was a transitional time in terms of governance, stakeholders, development scale, and developmental purpose.

The Ooi River project was transitional not only from a historical perspective but also with regard to the type of irrigation projects. The targeted area was unusually large in relation to the length of the main canal, and the villages incorporated elements from both centralized and decentralized approaches into their project management practices.

It was more common at the time for irrigation-management projects to take a decentralized approach. In the local water system, water was provided by river diversion, which was traditionally supplemented by numerous small, local reservoirs that were interconnected to secure a reliable water supply. The water management unit was the village, the site of local demand. This demand-based approach was the most efficient and had the lowest cost under resource-limited conditions.

Robert Wade suggests that agricultural productivity is influenced by the manner in which irrigation water and water facilities are managed at the community and governmental levels (Wade 1982). His framework implies that as a project grows in scale the quality of management declines. This chapter shows that Japan's post-war water management practices led to an increase in irrigation productivity even though they represented a cross between a decentralized and a centralized system. Post-war Japan demonstrates that large-scale projects can be managed successfully and can have a positive impact on agricultural productivity,

154 Water and post-conflict peacebuilding

food security, economic revitalization, and other factors that contribute to post-war stabilization.

Official and unofficial interactions between the villages and the national government played an important role in these projects. Coordination between the national government and villages has been common since the beginning of the Meiji period in the 1860s. Several factors have facilitated effective and efficient communication between villages and the ruling elite.

First, family relationships aided efficient communication, coordination, and monitoring within villages despite the shift in management responsibilities from the villages to the national government. Conflicts of interest between villages concerning the quantity and timing of water intake could thus be addressed by the government authorities.

Second, sharing of accumulated knowledge about irrigation practices facilitated cooperation between villages, especially during abnormally dry periods (Sarker and Itoh 2001). When water is plentiful, the typical decentralized management system applies only minimal water controls because the need to limit water use does not exist. However, once water scarcity occurs, elaborate water-control techniques are required. Wade refers to this point as a "paradox" that characterizes decentralized irrigation water management (Wade 1982). Switching water-control techniques and placing limits on water use depending on the degree of water scarcity became common practice in Japanese water management.[7]

Finally, because expanding the land area affected by the project caused tension between the goals of land development and those of flood prevention, villages faced more risk of flooding and needed to request subsidies from the local government (Ooi River Land Improvement District 1976). The financial need necessitated effective communication on the part of local people.

Lessons from the Ooi River project

The Ooi River project had a positive impact on post-war peacebuilding and stabilization efforts. Most significantly, it involved the establishment of a continuous system of local governance that facilitated communication between national authorities and local communities throughout the series of projects. This bidirectional system of communication was important in building social capital, which yielded a flow of benefits to other development efforts. Because villages

---

[7] This concept is demonstrated in the STIM model (Sustainable Triangle for Irrigation Management). The model shows that the relationships among three substitutable factors influence how irrigation water is sustainably managed: quantity of water available, cost of improving facilities, and labor costs for operation and maintenance. When available water is sufficient, water travels to the ends of even poorly built and leaking canals. During these times, it is difficult to justify the need to incur the costs necessary to improve the irrigation facilities. However, when water is scarce, repair costs become reasonable because the investment can alleviate the water shortage (Sugiura 2007).

Irrigation and flood control in post–World War II Japan **155**

were included in the governance structure and the benefits of the project were shared, various stakeholders contributed to the building of consensus and to the achievement of post-war food security and economic development objectives.

Transition of the management of large-scale irrigation projects from the villages to the prefectures and national government was inevitable as economic development progressed, and it was crucial to maintain open channels of communication between the different levels. This stands in direct contrast to changes in flood prevention that occurred during the same period.

FLOOD PREVENTION

World War II was one of the triggers that produced two major changes in the management of flood prevention in Japan: flood prevention was split from irrigation management, and it shifted from the village to the national level. Flood prevention requires significantly more involvement from the national government than irrigation because of its high-maintenance technology and river-scaled development. In post-war Japan, the effective shift of management responsibilities from villages to the national government provided safeguards that protected residents from flooding in the short term and led to land use planning that enhanced agricultural productivity in the long term.

The shift of flood-prevention management from the village to the national level, however, weakened stakeholder involvement at the village level, which turned out to be a problem in the long term, particularly in the 1990s when integrated water resource management required an exchange of ideas between communities and the national administration.

Flood-prevention associations

Flood-prevention associations had four primary functions before World War II: to collect money from beneficiaries to meet part of the construction costs of flood-prevention works under prefectural management; to engage in urgent flood-prevention measures; to drive irrigation and drainage projects; and to petition national or local governments to implement flood-prevention works using public funds (Uchida 1994).

Of these four functions, the two most important after World War II were collecting money and managing urgent measures for flood prevention. According to a Chiba Prefecture representative, empirical knowledge about effective flood-management practices and a rapid-response plan were required during emergency situations, such as when water flowed from the cracked concrete of a dam.[8]

Under the Flood Control Act, three entities became responsible for managing flood prevention: municipalities, public flood-fighting associations, and flood-prevention associations. Flood-prevention associations originated at the village

---

[8] Interview with author, December 15, 2008.

156   Water and post-conflict peacebuilding

level. Flood-fighting associations were established where management by a single municipality was regarded as unnecessary because of land features; they were funded by the municipalities in a particular area. In addition, as management by a flood-prevention association became difficult—for example, when it had trouble collecting member fees from residents—it could be reorganized into a flood-fighting association.

The fluctuating number of flood-prevention associations is an indicator of the changing popularity of the village approach (Uchida 1994). Furthermore, there is a relationship between the change in the legislation and the number of associations. Most notable is that a significant decrease occurred between 1942 and 1960, the period when irrigation associations were legally split from flood-prevention associations. After the revision of the flood-prevention legislation in the 1950s, which simplified administrative procedures, the responsibility for flood control gradually shifted from flood-prevention associations to municipalities and flood-fighting associations.

National-level management was required to a greater extent for flood prevention than for irrigation due to the high costs associated with flood prevention. Such a shift offers financial advantages to local stakeholders as well as short- and long-term benefits, such as increased agricultural productivity and facilitation of land use planning. However, it also weakens the power of stakeholders at the local level.

Before 1900, governmental sources of financing for flood prevention in Japan were relatively limited. Local governments had to cover a significant portion of the costs, not only of maintenance of flood-prevention works on major rivers but also for the improvement and maintenance of such facilities on small and medium-sized rivers. This was impossible for local governments to sustain without additional financial resources. Therefore, the River Act of 1896 permitted local governments to request financing from the national government for the establishment of flood-prevention associations, which could in turn obtain national funding to build and maintain flood-prevention works. The flood-prevention plan for 1933 allowed for the implementation of flood-prevention works on some small and medium-sized rivers without encumbering the local populations with the projects' costs (Kikuchi 2004).

Following World War II, Japan faced land degradation and food shortages caused by a series of typhoons. The National Resource Section of the Supreme Commander for the Allied Powers conducted comprehensive research into the potential of using natural resource management to ameliorate post-war problems such as food shortages (Cohen 1987). Land planning was one of the critical tasks proposed in a report to the U.S. Committee on Foreign Affairs, which, as a result of indirect rule by the Allied forces, led the Japanese government to place a high priority on flood prevention as a way to address the labor and food-supply shortages (Ackerman 1948). It became crucial, therefore, for the national and local governments to engage with flood-prevention associations. Both the diversification of stakeholders involved in flood prevention and the difference between

Irrigation and flood control in post–World War II Japan   157

flood-prevention management and irrigation management then contributed to the diminishing importance of flood-prevention associations.

Flood-prevention projects such as dam construction and bank enhancement were remarkable improvements to flood-risk reduction. In the decade following the end of World War II, more than a thousand people a year were killed or reported missing due to floods. Since then, the number of people killed or missing due to floods has dropped to a few dozen annually (Takahasi 2011). The dramatic drop in the number of fatalities is considered a success of the legal changes that occurred during the post-war period.[9]

Resident participation

After the post-war period, residents' awareness of stakeholder issues related to flood prevention declined as a result of three factors: difficulties in gathering member fees, the change in collection methods, and the legal shift in management responsibilities from local governments to the national government. The decline of resident awareness meant the absence of stakeholder input, which was to be expected in the short term but turned out to be a problem in water management in the long term because stakeholder involvement is key to decision-making processes intended to secure water management coordination (Jønch-Clausen 2004). When local populations bear the cost burden, it increases the efficiency of flood-prevention works and raises the public awareness of stakeholders. But amid rapid economic growth and industrialization in post-war Japan, stakeholder interests shifted and diversified.

In 1981, the Ministry of Construction conducted a survey of people in the Tsurumi River Basin that focused on two concerns (Keihin Work Office 1981). The first was deteriorating awareness of flood prevention among those who had begun living in the river basin after World War II. The other was people's tendency not to share costs. In answers to questions measuring attitudes toward personal cooperation in three flood-prevention measures, fewer than 8 percent of residents displayed a favorable attitude toward cost sharing. This illustrates that residents regarded flood-prevention measures as a public work and considered there to be no need for local residents to bear the cost burden. Ultimately, the flood-prevention association in the area was dissolved.

Methodological changes in the gathering of member fees also resulted in residents having a diminished awareness of their stake in flood prevention. A hearing conducted on November 28, 2008, in Chiba and Osaka prefectures that

---

[9]   The most notable exception is the devastating tsunami that followed a 9.0-magnitude earthquake on March 11, 2011. In 1962 Japan began installing seawalls, banks, and protective structures with heights of approximately ten to twelve meters, although it was known that the seawalls were limited in their ability to protect the land from high waves and tsunamis (Isobe 1998). As it turned out, these seawalls and protective structures were ineffective against the force and height of the 2011 surge (MOFA 2011).

158   Water and post-conflict peacebuilding

focused on the Imba Tone River and Yodo River Left Bank flood-prevention associations uncovered several important issues (Imba Tone River Flood-Fighting Association 2008). The Imba Tone River flood-prevention association had collected member fees from each beneficiary until it was reorganized into a flood-fighting association in 1964. After the reorganization, the expenses for flood prevention were paid by a local municipal entity, which also took over responsibility for flood prevention. In a similar situation, the Yodo River Left Bank flood-prevention association reorganized into a flood-fighting association in 1958. The amount of money that had been gathered for flood prevention was so small that it was not worth the cost to collect a member fee from each person; high population turnover due to rapid economic growth had also made collecting member fees difficult.

When member fees were collected directly from local populations, residents were made aware of their stake in flood prevention. Also, when flood control was managed jointly with irrigation, residents had incentives not only for harvesting but also for coping cooperatively with natural disasters, such as floods and droughts. That system for flood prevention was efficient in pre-war Japan.

After World War II, however, due to the increase in population, the cost of flood-prevention works, and the increasing scale of construction, local participation in flood-prevention works was drastically reduced. Finally, the legal framework allowing local populations to bear the cost of projects through flood-prevention associations was eliminated in the 1964 revision of the new River Act. The flood-prevention and flood-fighting associations offer a number of lessons about the importance of local awareness of flood control and prevention. They also highlight the revenue effects of different types of governance.

Lessons from Japan's flood-prevention strategies

In post-war Japan, bottom-up associations for flood prevention were weakened while water users associations were not. Flood-prevention associations were undermined by beneficiaries' declining awareness of their stake in flood prevention— a decline that resulted from increasing government control and decreasing opportunities for local involvement. With regard to economic reconstruction, government control was an efficient short-term approach to urgent post-war problems such as flood control, although it was accompanied by a decline in beneficiaries' awareness in the long term.

Over time the necessity of bottom-up associations like flood-prevention associations became clear. Structures such as dams and banks are important for flood prevention, but they may not be sufficient in the event of an unexpected typhoon, when urgent measures are sometimes required to repair breached banks and evacuate flooded areas. Villagers and other local stakeholders are an important source of knowledge in such situations. Flood prevention thus requires involvement by both local and national governments.

Although top-down flood control was essential for post-conflict economic restoration in the immediate post-conflict period, over the long term it has not adapted well to new challenges. This first became evident in the 1970s when residents in many regions filed flood-damage lawsuits, claiming that government flood-prevention works had been insufficient. The series of lawsuits shows that local stakeholders' awareness of the importance of their role in flood prevention was returning.

In the 1990s Japan implemented integrated water resource management to increase public participation in flood control. The 1997 revision of the River Act included improvements to and conservation of river environments. This resulted in a new planning system for river development that includes a set of environmental standards in addition to flood-prevention and water-use standards, incorporating ideas put forth by local residents. The communication system created by the new River Act conveys opinions and input from local residents to prefectural and national authorities.

As a consequence of rising environmental interest and integrated water resource management, residential participation has increased significantly, although there are few local associations to convey people's ideas regarding flood prevention to the national government, and therefore few opportunities to apply innovative community-based approaches and experiential knowledge to flood-prevention measures.

CONCLUSION

Irrigation and flood prevention in post-war Japan were managed in significantly different ways. The government maintained a bottom-up approach to irrigation management after World War II but initiated a top-down approach for flood prevention, with the national government replacing villages as the management unit. These two approaches give rise to several conclusions.

First, during the post-war transition, it was critically important to maintain open communication channels between local populations, the prefectures, and the national government. When communication operated effectively, irrigation projects were successful in contributing to a post-war increase in agricultural productivity.

Furthermore, limited human and natural resources must be allocated efficiently to meet urgent needs during post-war periods. With flood prevention, a top-down, government-oriented approach was the most efficient. Different goals require different approaches. The goal of irrigation is to increase agricultural productivity, and the goal of flood prevention is to decrease harm. Irrigation results in tangible immediate benefits and therefore encourages interaction between local people and the prefectural and national governments. Prevention of irregular events such as floods does not encourage the same degree of interaction. Therefore, a top-down approach became necessary for flood prevention.

Keeping incentives high for stakeholders' participation in water resource management, however, is required even in post-conflict situations. Post-conflict legislative changes should be made in a way that alleviates the risk of decreasing

160 Water and post-conflict peacebuilding

the incentives for local stakeholders to be involved. One water user group in the Gifu Prefecture of Japan managed to maintain stakeholder involvement in spite of the legislative changes, continuing to function as both a flood-prevention and an irrigation group. It dissolved itself in 1951, at the end of the post-conflict period, but it was reestablished in 1978, shortly after the area suffered the effects of a 1976 typhoon. The group operates outside of legislative control because the present legal framework does not provide for general water groups to do both flood prevention and irrigation. This case demonstrates that a bottom-up approach to both major aspects of water management can be effective.

Post-war Japanese water projects have been commended in the international community for their effectiveness, particularly in India, where Japan's natural resource management practices have been considered a model for land and water management reforms (Mitra 1992). Overall, the lessons offered by Japan's experience with water and land reform efforts following World War II provide valuable insight into how shifting the legal framework for natural resource management can enhance post-conflict peacebuilding and economic recovery efforts.

REFERENCES

Ackerman, E. 1948. *Japanese resources and United States policy.* Washington, D.C.: United States Committee on Foreign Affairs.

Aki, I., and Y. Takahasi. 1956. *Some considerations on flood flow: Relation between storm rainfall and storm runoff on the Chikugo River.* Symposia Darcy, Publication No. 42. Dijon, France: Association Internationale d'Hydrologie.

Akino, M. 1979. Land infrastructure improvement in agricultural development: The Japanese case, 1900–1965. *Economic Development and Cultural Change* 28 (1): 97–117.

Brinkerhoff, D. W. 2005. Rebuilding governance in failed states and post-conflict societies: Core concepts and cross-cutting themes. *Public Administration and Development* 25 (1): 3–14.

Cohen, T. 1987. *Remaking Japan: The American occupation as new deal.* New York: Free Press.

Dore, R. P. 1959. *Land reform in Japan.* New York: Oxford University Press.

Dower, J. W. 1993. *Japan in war and peace: Selected essays.* New York: New Press.

Imba Tone River Flood-Fighting Association. 2008. Imba Tone River Flood-Fighting Association brochure. Chiba, Japan.

Ishimitsu, T. 1986. Dr. E. A. Ackerman and Japan's resource planning policy. *National Economy* 153 (1): 1–18.

Isobe, M. 1998. *Toward integrated coastal zone management in Japan.* Tokyo: Energy, Security and Environment in Northeast Asia.

Iyori, H. 2002. Competition policy and government intervention in developing countries: An examination of Japanese economic development. *Washington University Global Studies Law Review* 1 (1): 35–48.

Japan Dam Foundation. 2005. *Dam year book 2005.* Tokyo.

Johnston, B. 1953. *Japanese food management in World War Two.* Stanford, CA: Stanford University Press.

Irrigation and flood control in post–World War II Japan 161

Jønch-Clausen, T. 2004. *". . . Integrated water resources management (IWRM) and water efficiency plans by 2005" Why, what and how?* Mölnlycke, Sweden: Elanders. www.unep.org/civil_society/GCSF8/pdfs/IWRM_water_efficiency.pdf.

Kawagoe, T. 1999. *Agricultural land reform in postwar Japan: Experiences and issues.* World Bank Policy Research Working Paper No. 2111. Washington, D.C.: World Bank. www-wds.worldbank.org/external/default/WDSContentServer/IW3P/IB/1999/09/14/000094946_99060201522486/Rendered/PDF/multi_page.pdf.

Keihin Work Office. 1981. *The survey of prevention awareness in the basin of the Tsurumi River.* Yokohama, Japan: Ministry of Construction.

Kikuchi, S. 2004. A study about the formation and the change of traditional citizen organizations on river basins. *Doshisha University Policy and Management Review* 6:173–186.

Madsen, R., and R. Samuels. 2010. Japan LLP. *National Interest* 107:48–56.

McDonald, M. G. 1997. Agricultural landholding in Japan: Fifty years after land reform. *Geoforum* 28 (1): 55–78.

MAFF (Ministry of Agriculture, Forestry and Fisheries of Japan). 2007. Crop statistics data. www.e-stat.go.jp/SG1/estat/List.do?lid=000001061500.

MIC (Ministry of Internal Affairs and Communications, Japan). 2000. Statistical overview of Japan. www.stat.go.jp/english/data/chouki/03.htm.

MOFA (Ministry of Foreign Affairs of Japan). 2011. Press conference by the deputy secretary. March. www.mofa.go.jp/announce/press/2011/3/0317_01.html.

Mitra, A. K. 1992. Joint management of irrigation systems in India: Relevance of Japanese experience. *Economic and Political Weekly* 27 (26): A75–A82.

Montgomery, J. D. 1972. Allocation of authority in land reform programs: A comparative study of administrative processes and outputs. *Administrative Science Quarterly* 17 (1): 62–75.

Musiake, K., and T. Koike. 2009. Time for a change in Japanese water resources policy, part 1: Historical review of water resources management policy and challenges for the future. *International Journal of Water Resources Development* 25 (4): 555–564.

Nagata, K. 1994. *Evolution of land improvement districts in Japan.* Report No. 6. Colombo, Sri Lanka: International Irrigation Management Institute.

Nishikawa, O., and G. Latz. 1981. The role of land improvement districts (Tochi Kairyō Ku) in the modernization of Japan's agriculture sector: A preliminary research report. *Proceedings of the Department of Humanities, College of General Education, University of Tokyo, Series of Human Geography* 7:53–70.

Ōchi, T. 1966. The Japanese land reform: Its efficiency and limitations. *Developing Economies* 4 (2): 129–150.

Ooi River Land Improvement District. 1976. *History of Ooi River Land Improvement District.* Tokyo.

Sanbongi, K. 2006. Legislative arrangements of flood management in Japan. In *Legal and institutional aspects of integrated flood management: Case studies.* WMO-No. 1004. Geneva, Switzerland: Associated Programme on Flood Management. www.apfm.info/pdf/ifm_legal_aspects_casestudies.pdf.

Sarker, A., and T. Itoh. 2001. Design principles in long-enduring institutions of Japanese irrigation common-pool resources. *Agricultural Water Management* 48 (2): 89–102.

Stranges, A. N. 1993. Synthetic fuel production in prewar and World War II Japan: A case study in technological failure. *Annals of Science* 50 (3): 229–265.

162 Water and post-conflict peacebuilding

Sugiura, M. 2007. Water use practice in social aspect: A case of paddy field in Japan. Presentation at OECD expert meeting, "Sustainable Financing for Affordable Water Service: From Theory to Practice," Paris, November 15.

Tabb, W. K. 1995. *The postwar Japanese system: Cultural economy and economic transformation.* New York: Oxford University Press.

Takahasi, Y. 1955. Gradual alteration in the flow characteristics of the Chikugo-River flood. *Report of the Institute of Industrial Science, University of Tokyo* 5 (3).

————. 2009. History of water management in Japan from the end of World War II. *International Journal of Water Resources Development* 25 (4): 547–553.

————. 2011. Flood management in Japan during the last half-century. Institute of Water Policy Working Paper No. 1. www.spp.nus.edu.sg/iwp/WorkingPaper_Series/201106_Takahasi-IWP_WP_01.PDF.

Takemae, E. 2002. *Inside GHQ: Allied occupation of Japan and its legacy.* Trans. R. Ricketts and S. Swann. New York: Continuum.

Tanaka, Y., and Y. Sato. 2005. Farmers managed irrigation districts in Japan: Assessing how fairness may contribute to sustainability. *Agricultural Water Management* 77:196–209.

Uchida, K. 1994. *Flood prevention cooperatives in Japan.* Tokyo: Kokon-Shoin.

Yasuba, Y. 1996. Did Japan ever suffer from a shortage of natural resources before World War II? *Journal of Economic History* 56 (3): 543–560.

Wade, R. 1982. *Employment, water control and water supply institutions: South India and South Korea.* Bangkok, Thailand: International Labour Organization Asian Regional Team for Employment Promotion.

Refugee rehabilitation and transboundary cooperation: India, Pakistan, and the Indus River system

Neda A. Zawahri

At independence, in 1947, India and Pakistan experienced widespread communal violence, with the worst occurring in eastern and western Punjab.[1] As the states were engulfed in a war over Kashmir, people crossed the new border that now divided Punjab in an attempt to escape the bloodshed. To settle and rehabilitate the millions of refugees that entered eastern Punjab, India used the waters of the Indus River tributaries to establish an agrarian economy. India also employed refugees to build the hydrological infrastructure, including dams, canals, and irrigation networks, needed to support an agriculture-based economy. These policies also helped meet India's need to develop a border province threatened by the Indo-Pakistani conflict and to produce desperately needed grain to avert famine.

As India sought to restore sustainable livelihoods in conflict-torn eastern Punjab, it was drawing on the same water that was bringing Pakistan's arid lands to life. Conflict between India and Pakistan over the Indus River was averted by the direct mediation of the World Bank. After eight years of negotiation, India and Pakistan signed the Indus Waters Treaty (IWT) in 1960. The World Bank's mediation was also important to management of the two post-conflict societies because it coordinated the international donors who helped to underwrite the construction of the hydrological infrastructure that facilitated the reconstruction and economic development needed to build sustainable livelihoods.

Since signing the IWT, India and Pakistan have continued to confront the need to negotiate issues that arise as they develop the Indus River system. A commission established under the IWT has facilitated the management of many of these issues. For over fifty years, the riparian states have peacefully resolved their Indus River disputes using the conflict resolution mechanism specified in the IWT (Salman 2008).

This chapter analyzes the IWT and the effective use of the Indus River system's water to rebuild post-conflict eastern Punjab. First, the roots of the

---

Neda A. Zawahri is an assistant professor in the Department of Political Science at Cleveland State University.

[1] In this chapter, *eastern Punjab* refers to the portion of the Punjab region in India, and *western Punjab* refers to the portion in Pakistan.

164   Water and post-conflict peacebuilding

Indo-Pakistani conflict and the humanitarian disaster that erupted as these two countries came into being are considered. The Indian government's refugee rehabilitation and economic development policies in eastern Punjab are analyzed in the following two sections. The Indo-Pakistani water dispute is then evaluated, along with attempts to foster transboundary cooperation. Next, the factors that contributed to the successful outcome are considered, followed by a discussion of lessons learned for reconstructing conflict-torn societies and a conclusion summarizing the major findings.[2]

BACKGROUND OF THE CONFLICT

As Great Britain withdrew from the South Asian subcontinent in 1947, Pakistan and India gained their independence on August 14 and 15, respectively.[3] Due to the haphazard manner in which the decolonization process proceeded, Britain left behind some pernicious disputes that resulted in numerous Indo-Pakistani conflicts. These disputes included the interrelated conflicts over Kashmir and the Indus River system.

During the colonial era, 562 princely states were permitted to reign with some sovereignty, but at independence each had to accede to either India or Pakistan. Lord Mountbatten, the last British viceroy, specified that the accession should depend on the majority of the princely state's population and its geographic contiguity. Kashmir, a princely state, presented a special predicament. It had a Hindu monarch, Maharaja Hari Singh, while the majority of its population was Muslim. Kashmir's territorial contiguity to both India and Pakistan meant that it could accede to either state. The maharaja's indecisiveness and secret ambition for an independent state led him to waver and delay his decision (Dixit 2002; Schofield 2003). In October 1947, as communal violence overwhelmed Kashmir, tribesmen from Pakistan's North-West Frontier Province invaded. Fearing the collapse of his regime, the maharaja appealed to India for help. Under the advice of Lord Mountbatten, Jawaharlal Nehru—India's prime minister—refused to provide assistance until the maharaja acceded to India. Nehru also asked for a commitment to hold a plebiscite once order was restored to ascertain the people's wishes on the accession (Bose 2003; Schofield 2003).[4] As India came to the maharaja's rescue, it fought its first war with Pakistan, which culminated in the

---

[2] Many of the data for this chapter come from field research in India (January through June 2002), Jordan and Syria (January through July 2001), and Washington, D.C. (May 2006 and June 2007).

[3] In 1947, Pakistan consisted of two wings—west and east. After the 1971 civil war, eastern Pakistan became the independent nation of Bangladesh. Since the focus of this chapter is on western Pakistan, all references to Pakistan mean western Pakistan.

[4] Some scholars have argued that the maharaja signed the letter of accession prior to the Indian army's arrival (Bose 2003), but Alastair Lamb argued, after inspecting declassified British documents, that the maharaja signed the letter after the conflict (Lamb 1992).

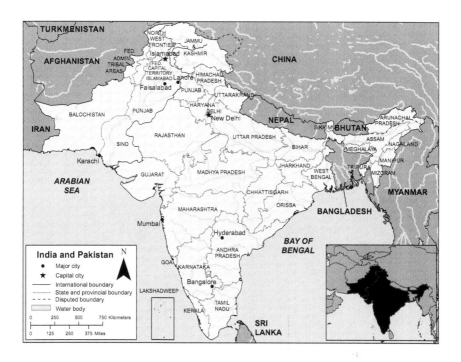

division of Kashmir between Indian-controlled Jammu and Kashmir and Pakistani-controlled Azad Kashmir.

Several factors contributed to the competition over Kashmir. The adversaries were divided along lines of ideology and national identity (Ganguly 2002). Pakistan's basis for existence was the two-nation theory, or the belief that the Muslims of South Asia constituted a distinct group and required their own independent state to guarantee their rights and freedoms. As a secular democracy, India was founded on ethnic and religious pluralism and a guarantee of religious freedom for all groups. The competition to secure Kashmir was further aggravated by the fact that several sources of freshwater, an essential livelihood resource, originated in or flowed through this territory (Mayfield 1955). To appreciate the significance of this often-overlooked issue, it is necessary to examine its origin.

The new Indo-Pakistani international border placed India upstream from an arid Pakistan, which lacked any alternative source of freshwater other than those originating from the Indus River system. The Indus River system consists of the main Indus River, two western tributaries, and five eastern tributaries, some of which are also shared by China and Afghanistan. India and Pakistan share six rivers of the Indus River system (see figure 1). Three of these rivers—the Chenab River, the Indus main stem, and the Jhelum River—flow through Jammu and Kashmir before entering Pakistan, and three—the Beas River, the Ravi River,

166   Water and post-conflict peacebuilding

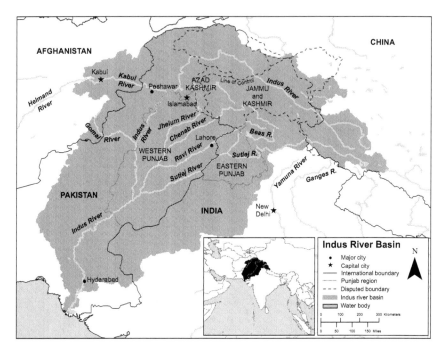

Figure 1.   Map of the Indus River Basin, 1947
Source: Adapted from Lowi (1993).

and the Sutlej River—flow through India's eastern Punjab before entering western Punjab in Pakistan.[5]

Demarcating the new Indo-Pakistani border in Punjab required a special commission because of its complexity. With little knowledge of the terrain and five weeks to delineate the border, Sir Cyril Radcliffe—the chairman of the commission—issued the award that divided greater Punjab in August 1947 (Butalia 2000). The Radcliffe Award bisected an elaborate canal system that relied on the Indus River to irrigate the granary of greater India during the colonial period. Britain had established canal colonies in Punjab to manage the famines that plagued the subcontinent, employ and settle the disbanded Sikh army, and develop crown wastelands (Michel 1967). The new Indo-Pakistani border left the headworks to several canals—the Upper Bari Doab, Dipalpur, and Eastern Grey canals—in India, but the irrigated farmlands went to Pakistan.

Once the states declared their independence and the Radcliffe Award was announced, the sporadic communal violence that had occurred prior to independence

---

[5] The IWT, which addresses the use of these six rivers, refers to the Chenab River, Indus main stem, and the Jhelum River as the "Western Rivers," because they are the westernmost of the six rivers shared between India and Pakistan. IWT refers to the Beas River, the Ravi River, and the Sutlej River as the "Eastern Rivers." This chapter similarly uses the terms *Western Rivers* and *Eastern Rivers* to refer to each set of rivers, respectively.

Indus River system **167**

grew dramatically, producing the single largest movement of people in history (Haque 1995). In Pakistan, some members of the Muslim majority massacred Hindus and Sikhs, while in India some Hindus and Sikhs slaughtered minority Muslims. The area that experienced the worst communal violence was greater Punjab; over 4 million Hindus and Sikhs fled to eastern Punjab and more than 5 million Muslims fled to western Punjab (Aiyar 1995).

Neither government was prepared for the onslaught of refugees, and their weak civil administrations collapsed when confronted with the humanitarian crisis (Haque 1995). An ineffective police force combined with an inadequate military and a collapsed civil administration contributed to widespread communal violence, torture, abduction and rape of women, and the slaughter of 1 million people throughout eastern and western Punjab (Hodson 1997; Keller 1975; Haque 1995; Butalia 2000). During the turmoil, homes, businesses, crops, and warehouses were set ablaze. In eastern Punjab alone, 90 percent of the homes in 1,800 villages were demolished (Randhawa 1954). Fires also destroyed basic infrastructure, which resulted in the disruption of electricity and water supplies. The inability to maintain proper sanitation services and distribute clean water contributed to the outbreak of cholera and other waterborne diseases (Talbot 2007). People escaped the violence in caravans or on foot, only to be attacked en route.

After the initial spontaneous wave of refugees, the national governments undertook their own evacuations of religious minorities via trains, airplanes, and foot columns that included 40,000 to 60,000 people each (Rao 1967).[6] On September 3, 1947, India and Pakistan agreed to establish the Military Evacuation Organization to secure the removal of minorities (Rai 1965). In planning these evacuations, the Indian government gave priority to civil servants and peasants. Civil servants were needed to operate the skeletal bureaucracy, and peasants were required to cultivate crops in farmlands vacated by Muslims (Rai 1965). These government-sponsored evacuations proved as dangerous as the spontaneous ones. Government-operated trains were derailed, their passengers killed, and their belongings looted. These trains often arrived at their destination "carrying only corpses" (Oberoi 2006, 51). Because food and water were in short supply, and at times deliberately withheld, many refugees also died of dehydration or starvation en route (Aiyar 1995).

As Sikh and Hindu refugees entered eastern Punjab, makeshift camps were established to provide temporary shelter and emergency relief. Approximately forty-five of these camps were created within the first few months of independence (Menon and Bhasin 1998). Refugees were also housed in schools, government offices, and military camps that were operated by the eastern Punjabi government with financial backing from the central government. Domestic and international nongovernmental organizations, such as the Red Cross, United Nations Children's Fund, Arya Samaj, and All India Women's Conference, assisted the government

---

[6] The largest convoys are estimated to have had 400,000 to 800,000 refugees (Oberoi 2006; Keller 1975).

168   Water and post-conflict peacebuilding

in the establishment and operation of these camps, which enabled a rapid response to the humanitarian disaster (Keller 1975; Menon 2003). In the camps, refugees received food, clothing, medical assistance, and a cash allowance of around Rs. 6 (approximately US$0.14) (Rai 1965; Oberoi 2006). Makeshift refugee camps tend to have improvised sewage systems and unsafe water supplies that can contribute to the outbreak of disease (Cernea and McDowell 2000). To minimize the spread of epidemics, eastern Punjabi refugees were inoculated against cholera and smallpox (Rao 1967).

In post-conflict situations, state capacity is usually low, which contributes to pervasive opportunities for corruption or the abuse of government office for personal profit (O'Donnell 2008). Since the potential financial gains outweigh any likely risks, corruption tends to be prevalent among civil servants, police officers, military personnel, and refugees (Bolongaita 2005; O'Donnell 2008). As in other conflict-torn societies, conditions in eastern Punjab created many opportunities for corruption. Reports indicated that during this period of chaos in the region some military and police officers participated in the looting of evacuee property and facilitated criminal activities, while others simply watched the slaughter (Hodson 1997; Rai 1965). The lack of an effective and sufficient police or military force to patrol the streets of eastern Punjab permitted young refugees to join local criminals and the police in looting evacuee properties, stealing cattle, and smuggling grain and ammunition (Rai 1965). Under these desperate conditions, India's central and provincial governments organized efforts to rehabilitate and settle refugees.

REBUILDING SUSTAINABLE LIVELIHOODS

To rebuild the lives of impoverished refugees, several factors appear to be important. A government's sense of urgency and its autonomy in the policy-making process seem to be essential to successful rehabilitation (del Castillo 2008). Experts have also suggested that a government needs to undertake a multilevel coordination effort (Cernea and McDowell 2000).

India's central government coordinated its efforts with those of the provincial government, various ministries and agencies, social workers, and voluntary organizations to integrate refugees into society by providing them with homes and stable livelihoods. It also formulated a three-tier plan that involved providing temporary shelter, guiding the settlement and rehabilitation of refugees in rural and urban areas depending on their place of origin, and rehabilitating displaced women and children (Rai 1965).

The Indian government felt an urgent need to settle refugees because post-conflict emergency aid to assist with the humanitarian disaster failed to arrive. Due to the financial drain inflicted on the young government, which totaled Rs. 10 million (at the time, in 1947, just over US$3 million) from 1947 to 1948, there was pressure to integrate refugees into society immediately (Randhawa 1954; Rao 1967; Oberoi 2006). The absence of the international donor community also meant that India was relatively autonomous in formulating its refugee policy.

Indus River system **169**

The majority of the refugees entering eastern Punjab were from rural areas (Randhawa 1954; Rao 1967; Kudaisya 1995). To rehabilitate rural refugees, it is essential to provide them with arable land that enables them to pursue a productive livelihood (Cernea and McDowell 2000; Unruh and Bailey 2009). Otherwise, a future of landlessness for rural refugees removes the foundation of their livelihood and productive system and threatens them with poverty. Along with providing rural refugees with arable land, experts have also noted the need to rebuild the social networks or communities that are essential to the provision of social capital in rural areas (Cernea and McDowell 2000).

Within months of their arrival, the government of eastern Punjab undertook land-based resettlement of rural refugees by settling them on farmlands evacuated by Muslims (Rao 1967; Randhawa 1954). To reconstruct social networks, the government distributed farmland to refugees in groups. Whenever possible, these groups included unattached women, such as widows or women who had been raped and then rejected by their families because of their perceived contamination (Randhawa 1954). The government also attempted to recreate the refugees' previous villages in eastern Punjab. These policies were designed to ease the psychological effect of resettlement, minimize the congestion of border areas, and enable refugees to pool their resources to improve agricultural production (Rao 1967; Kudaisya 1995; Keller 1975).

Initially, refugees were allocated six to ten acres on a temporary and equitable basis regardless of their previous holdings in what had become Pakistan (Rai 1965; Randhawa 1954; Rao 1967). To help these impoverished refugees to become viable farmers, the government provided loans to purchase agricultural inputs—seeds, fodder, and bullocks—and to feed their families until harvest time. Loans were also available for home improvements and the purchase of equipment such as tractors.

Irrigation water was available from canals or wells. Farmers received substantial subsidies on irrigation water from the few existing canals. The most reliable sources of water for farmers were shallow wells drawing from approximately twenty feet (Westley 1986). Wells allowed farmers to secure the right quantity of water at the exact time they needed it. Throughout this period, farmers had access to government loans to build or fix wells (Rao 1967). By the late 1950s, the central government had issued over Rs. 30 million (at that time, approximately US$6.3 million) in loans to farmers.

ECONOMIC DEVELOPMENT AND EMPLOYMENT GENERATION

Economic development and employment generation are essential to stabilizing post-conflict states (Bigombe, Collier, and Sambanis 2000; Obidegwu 2004). The success of economic rehabilitation policies undertaken immediately after a conflict depends partly on a commitment by the government and a belief that refugees are a resource for economic development (Voutira and Harrell-Bond 2000; del Castillo 2008). Not only was the Indian government committed to rehabilitating rural refugees, but it also perceived them as potential contributors to meeting its desperate need for national food security (Rai 1965). In fact, the decision to settle

170   Water and post-conflict peacebuilding

rural refugees immediately was driven by the desire to decongest refugee camps and the emphasis on cultivating all available farmland to manage the country's severe domestic food deficit (Kudaisya 1995).

As Nehru noted in a speech, "The question of food has become almost a nightmare and is pursuing us all the time" (Nehru 1995, 234). The independence of Burma (now Myanmar) and Pakistan decreased the supply of food grains in India by 200 million tons, which contributed to a chronic food shortage and threatened widespread famine (Central Board of Irrigation and Power 1992). This constant threat of famine was aggravated by the fact that 80 percent of India's rural population depended on subsistence agriculture but lacked access to irrigation (Kaushik 1998). Dependence on the monsoons resulted in an unstable agricultural sector because a failed, late, or heavy monsoon led to crop failure. For the government, therefore, the "taking up of irrigation schemes to increase food production became the top priority" (Central Board of Irrigation and Power 1992, 75).

Building an agriculture-based economy

In eastern Punjab, the government sought to establish an agrarian economy (Verghese 1994). Agriculture was also an effective approach to economic development for a border province in which substantial investment in industrialization would have been irrational because of the ongoing threat of war with Pakistan (Talbot 2007). Eastern Punjab was the most neglected part of greater Punjab in terms of agricultural development. In fact, of the 26 million acres of farmland irrigated by the Indus River system at independence, 21 million were in western Punjab and 5 million in eastern Punjab.[7] Eastern Punjab was arid, but with an adequate water supply it had the potential to become India's breadbasket. The Eastern Rivers flowed through eastern Punjab before entering Pakistan. They provided the Indian government with sufficient water to settle refugees, establish an agrarian economy, meet domestic food security needs, and generate hydropower to meet energy demands (Chadha 1986).

To deliver irrigation water from the Indus tributaries to farmers, the government undertook the construction of extensive hydrological infrastructure, which included the Nangal Barrage, Harike Barrage, Bhakra-Nangal Dam, Bhakra Canals, Bhakra Main Line, Madhopur-Beas Link, and Ferozepore Feeder. The largest of these projects was the multipurpose Bhakra-Nangal Dam along the Sutlej River. Initiated in 1948, the dam was designed to generate desperately needed hydropower to operate tubewells. These tubewells were needed because as farmers increased their reliance on shallow wells, the groundwater table fell. To encourage the use of tubewells, the government subsidized electricity and provided farmers credit to construct these much deeper and more reliable wells (Westley

---

[7] Official response to parliamentary discussion, "Statement referred to in reply to part (c) of Starred Question No. 35 to be answered in the Lok Sabha on 4-11-1965, regarding water supply to Pakistan under Indus Waters Treaty," on file at the Parliament Library, New Delhi, India.

Indus River system **171**

1986). The dam was also designed to distribute irrigation water to refugees settling in the area (Nehru 1988; Tan and Kudaisya 2000; Kudaisya 1995).

The government also undertook the remodeling and cleaning of existing irrigation systems to augment their capacity. Refugees were employed in the construction and remodeling of these irrigation systems, canals, barrages, and dams (Talbot 2007; Rai 1965; Rao 1967). Government-sponsored projects also employed refugees to expand farmland through the reclamation of wasteland and deforestation (Rao 1967). A number of researchers have suggested that these types of government-sponsored public employment programs are effective in lowering the unemployment rate among refugees and helping to stabilize post-conflict economies (McLeod and Dávalos 2008; del Castillo 2008).

After the temporary allocation of farmland, rural refugees in eastern Punjab pressured the government for a more permanent allocation that better reflected their previous landholdings. But permanent allocation was complicated by the insufficient quantity and quality of land in eastern Punjab. Sikhs and Hindus evacuated 5.7 million acres of farmland in western Punjab, while Muslims evacuated only 4.7 million acres in eastern Punjab (Rai 1965; Rao 1967). Moreover, the farmland of eastern Punjab varied substantially in soil quality, precipitation rates, and extent of desertification (Michel 1967; Gulhati 1973). To take into account the variance in the quantity and quality of land as it compensated farmers, the government formulated the measurement of a standard acre, in which each unit of land was evaluated based on its productivity.

Corruption during the rehabilitation process can minimize the intended benefits of any policy and complicate attempts to build a stable economic system (Bolongaita 2005; O'Donnell 2008; Unruh and Bailey 2009). But governments can implement preemptive policies to minimize the potential for corruption during the rehabilitation phase, a step that was taken by the Indian government.

To assess rural refugees' previous holdings of land, the Indian government asked them to submit claims for land in February 1948. It anticipated that some refugees would exaggerate their claims and took preemptive measures to discourage civil servants, elites, and refugees from lying or cheating on the claims.

The government sought to locate accurate information on refugees' previous landholdings by negotiating with Pakistan for the exchange of records. Complete records were received only from western Punjab. Due to the turmoil of the post-conflict environment in Pakistan, many records were missing, and other areas either failed to provide records at all or provided incomplete information (Rao 1967). To minimize exaggeration and misinformation, the Indian government decided to hold public meetings with refugees to ascertain the accuracy of the land claims they submitted. The objective of the public meetings was to allow disputes over the quantity of land claimed by each family. Those caught lying faced imprisonment or substantial reductions in the land allotted to them. Through these preemptive policies, the government was able to prevent corruption from derailing its rehabilitation program and undermining its effectiveness and legitimacy.

172   Water and post-conflict peacebuilding

Once the extent of a refugee's former landholdings was assessed, the government calculated it in standard acres and then subjected it to graded cuts that began at 25 percent and increased proportionally to the amount of land the family previously held (Rai 1965; Tan and Kudaisya 2000). Refugees received full ownership of the land once the government took legal possession of all evacuee property in 1954. By this time, eastern Punjab had settled 4.25 million refugee families on 20 million standard acres (Rao 1967). The government's efforts to rehabilitate refugees proved effective.

Consequences of the government's policies

Due to its commitment and strong interventions, the government was able to fulfill its objective of establishing an agrarian economy to rehabilitate refugees, contribute to the economic development of a border province, and generate food grains. Two months after the refugees' arrival in eastern Punjab, the government was able to allocate 2 million acres of land to settle them (Menon 2003). By the end of 1948, all refugee camps in northern India either had been closed or were about to close (Oberoi 2006). Due to the rapid expansion of hydrological infrastructure, the total irrigated area in eastern Punjab increased from approximately 33 percent at independence to 52.3 percent by 1950–1951 (Chadha 1986). When additional canals came into operation in the mid-1950s, the total irrigated area increased from 39.28 million acres in 1947–1948 to 66.50 million acres in 1956–1957 (Rai 1965). Farmers used government loans to transform marginal fields into productive farmland (Randhawa 1954).

Punjabi farmers received clear and secure property rights and clear access to water. Moreover, the Indian government subsidized agricultural inputs so that farmers paid minimum prices for irrigation water drawn from canals, electricity to operate tubewells, and fertilizer. On the output side, the government procured at premium prices all the grain produced by farmers. Farm property and profits were only lightly taxed. Due to this government support, Punjabi farmers had the economic incentive to produce as much as possible (Westley 1986).

The Indian government's efforts helped eastern Punjab make the transition from a grain importer to a surplus producer. At independence, eastern Punjab had an annual deficit of 35,000 tons of grain, but by 1950, the province provided 220,430 tons of grain to the central government (Rai 1965). In 1958, Punjab provided the central government with over 1 million bags of rice and other grains. Due to the development of the Indus River system to support the agricultural sector, by the mid-1980s the province was capable of contributing 1 million tons of grain to the national budget (Chopra 1981).

The standard acre measurement and graded cuts also helped minimize the number of landed elites and absentee farmers (Westley 1986). Due to the substantial graded cuts imposed on the landed elites and middle-class farmers, they were compelled to farm their allotted land more efficiently (Kudaisya 1995). Furthermore, the number of landless peasant refugees decreased because many received an

Indus River system **173**

allotment of land to cultivate. Thus, it can be concluded that the government's policy successfully achieved the integration of the rural refugee population, because by 1960 the former refugee population achieved a level of prosperity and success that would make Punjab India's breadbasket (Kudaisya 1995).

FOSTERING TRANSBOUNDARY ENVIRONMENTAL COOPERATION

Although these policies were essential to the post-conflict settlement of refugees in India's Punjab, the consumption of water from the Eastern Rivers to achieve these goals had a direct negative impact downstream. Predominantly agrarian Pakistan had a single source of water that brought to life its otherwise arid lands: the Indus River system. India's control of eastern Punjab and Jammu and Kashmir provided it with a strategic advantage to "encircle Pakistan militarily and strangle it economically" (Suhrawardy 1991, 36). Consequently, securing access to this water became essential to Pakistan's industrialization efforts and the stability of its agricultural sector (Spate 1948).

In the abstract, the Indus River system carried sufficient water to meet both India's and Pakistan's domestic demand, but closer inspection reveals a strong distributional conflict. In 1947, the Indus River carried 168 million acre-feet annually. Of this water, India was consuming 8 million acre-feet and Pakistan 63 million acre-feet, while the remaining 97 million acre-feet went into the Arabian Sea (Central Board of Irrigation and Power 1992). The water entering the sea came from two undeveloped sources, the monsoons and the Western Rivers (Gulhati 1973). The Indus River system received 60 percent of its water during the monsoon period, but storage facilities to capture this floodwater did not exist. The Western Rivers carried 80 percent of the river system's water, but they were much less developed. During this period, India and Pakistan depended on the same Eastern Rivers, which were not only in full use but also provided insufficient water for farmers in Sind, a province in southeastern Pakistan. As a result, India's plans to establish an agrarian economy in eastern Punjab directly affected the quality and quantity of water available to Pakistani farmers (Fowler 1950; Gulhati 1973).

In the absence of an international mediator to help them to share the canal waters and Indus tributaries, India and Pakistan were left to their own means. The states did reach an arrangement immediately after independence. On December 20, 1947, chief engineers from western and eastern Punjab signed a standstill agreement that maintained the status quo prior to independence, which was favorable to Pakistan because it was consuming more of the canal waters.

On March 31, 1948, the standstill agreement expired, and on April 1, 1948, eastern Punjab stopped the waters feeding the Upper Bari Doab and Dipalpur canals, which delivered water to Pakistan. This action deprived an important Pakistani city, Lahore, of municipal water and hydropower. It also deprived 1.66 million acres of farmland of irrigation water; consequently, "millions of people faced the ruin of their crops" (Ali 1967, 320). After intense negotiations, India

174　Water and post-conflict peacebuilding

reopened the canals on May 3, 1948 (Nehru 1994), but this experience resonated with Pakistani leaders as a constant reminder of their vulnerability and dependence on India (Khan 1967). Pakistani fears proved accurate when the flow of water in these canals was reduced in 1952 and 1953 (Nehru 1998).

On May 4, 1948, India and Pakistan signed the Delhi Agreement, covering a new arrangement for sharing the canals (Nehru 1994). Unlike the standstill agreement, the Delhi Agreement recognized India's right to increase its consumption of water from the Indus and required Pakistan to pay India for operating the canals. In spite of this agreement, the states continued to compete over access to the eastern tributaries of the Indus from 1947 until 1952. During this period, India and Pakistan undertook unilateral development of the Indus River system rather than negotiating over the design and construction of hydrological infrastructure.

Mediating international river disputes

States with a history of animosity and conflict can use the help of a single neutral mediator to facilitate the negotiation process leading to a treaty (Nakayama 1997; Alam 1998; Salman 2002). The contribution of a single mediator is especially important for post-conflict states. In these states, the mediator can facilitate the resolution of a transboundary dispute and help to coordinate the donor community's financing of reconstruction and economic development. Experts have noted that assistance for reconstruction and economic development can be more important for the future of conflict-torn states than immediate humanitarian aid, because most developing states lack the necessary financial resources to underwrite this critical phase (del Castillo 2008). For India and Pakistan in 1951, a mediator did offer its help with the Indus water dispute.

The former chairman of the Tennessee Valley Authority, David Lilienthal, asserted in a magazine article that the dispute over Kashmir was actually about control of the Indus River and, as the title of his article warned, this could be "[a]nother 'Korea' in the making" (Lilienthal 1951, 23). The article came to the attention of the World Bank's president, Eugene Black, and the U.S. Department of State. Both agencies feared an imminent war between India and Pakistan over the Indus River and Kashmir (Gulhati 1973). With the blessing of the United States, the World Bank provided its good offices to facilitate negotiations between the riparian states.

India and Pakistan accepted the World Bank's offer to mediate the Indus River dispute for several reasons. Both states were interested in developing the irrigation potential of the region watered by the Indus River system in order to support an agrarian economy, but they needed foreign aid to finance the construction of hydrological infrastructure. The states were also interested in stabilizing their future access to the water of the Indus River system (Alam 2002; Yamamoto 2008).

After a failed attempt to persuade the riparian states to embrace an integrated development of the river system, the World Bank asked each state to submit its own proposal. The two countries' October 6, 1953, proposals differed extensively.

The following year, the World Bank introduced its own proposal, which involved the allocation of tributaries between the two countries (Michel 1967; Nakayama 1997). Although India agreed to the essence of the World Bank's proposal, Pakistan was worried that the proposed replacement infrastructure was insufficient. Following a thorough examination of Pakistan's concerns and further negotiations, the World Bank conceded to Pakistan's request for dams along the main Indus and the Jhelum tributary. India, which agreed to finance the replacement work to transfer Pakistan's dependence from the Eastern Rivers to the Western Rivers, feared that the additional infrastructure would increase its expense. The World Bank was able to draw on a consortium of states in addition to India to finance the building of Pakistan's infrastructure (Gulhati 1973).

The next contentious issue was the amount of time Pakistan required to complete its replacement infrastructure. The World Bank's president met with India's prime minister; following intense negotiations, he agreed to a ten-year transition period. After eight years of negotiations, Jawaharlal Nehru and Field Marshal Mohammad Ayub Khan—India's prime minister and Pakistan's president, respectively—signed the Indus Waters Treaty (IWT) on September 19, 1960.[8]

Indus Waters Treaty

Consisting of twelve articles and eight annexures, the IWT allocated the Eastern Rivers to India. However, because some of these tributaries meander back and forth across the Indo-Pakistani border before making their final departure from India and receive additional tributaries from inside of Pakistan, the treaty permitted Pakistani farmers residing along these tributaries the right to use the water (in articles II and III, and annexure B). The treaty allocated the Western Rivers to Pakistan, but it preserved India's right to use the rivers in Jammu and Kashmir to generate hydropower, meet municipal demand for water, and support the agricultural sector (in article III and annexures C and E). Although the Western Rivers flow through the disputed territory of Kashmir, mediators and leaders were vigilant in writing a treaty that excluded discussion of this dispute. India and Pakistan were in effect able to separate this macropolitical conflict from the management of their international river (Lowi 1993).

Another unique feature of the IWT was the fact that the World Bank was a signatory to several provisions. The World Bank was responsible for operating the Indus Basin Development Fund, which coordinated funding from the donor community and India to construct the hydrological infrastructure specified in article V of the treaty. The World Bank was also involved in the provision, stipulated in article X, that permitted the extension of the transition period should war occur. It was a signatory to annexure H, which covered sharing the canal waters during the transition period. The IWT's mechanisms for conflict resolution in annexures F and G also included a role for the World Bank.

---

[8] For the complete text of the IWT, see http://siteresources.worldbank.org/ INTSOUTHASIA/Resources/223497-1105737253588/IndusWatersTreaty1960.pdf.

176   Water and post-conflict peacebuilding

April 1970 marked the end of the ten-year transition period and the termination of several of the World Bank's official roles under the IWT (Salman 2008). When Pakistan completed construction of its hydrological infrastructure, the World Bank fulfilled its obligation under article V. The transition period did not require an extension, so article X expired; annexure H, which specified the sharing of canal waters during the transition period, also ended. The only remaining role for the World Bank involved facilitating the conflict resolution mechanisms in annexures F and G. After 1970, the IWT became a purely bilateral agreement, and with the exception of facilitating the conflict resolution mechanisms, the World Bank's direct involvement ended (Salman 2008).

Permanent Indus Commission

An analysis of existing treaties revealed that the majority establish river basin commissions to implement the accord and facilitate future cooperation (Conca, Wu, and Mei 2006). These institutions are especially important for post-conflict states because they provide interested states with cooperation mechanisms to manage their disputes. The institutional capabilities needed to facilitate cooperation are the same in post-conflict states as in other riparian states. There is, however, a difference in that post-conflict and developing riparian states can use the help of a neutral mediator to design an effective river basin commission capable of facilitating negotiations and averting conflict.

With the assistance of the World Bank, the IWT (in article VIII) established the Permanent Indus Commission (PIC) to implement the treaty and negotiate issues that arise over the development of the shared river system. Headed by two commissioners, one Indian and one Pakistani, the PIC was given sufficient capabilities to perform its functions.

The commissioners have the ability to communicate directly with one another, which enables them to schedule meetings, arrange maintenance work, and exchange hydrological and meteorological data. Commissioners also hold meetings on a regular basis, which permits them to negotiate the design of hydrological infrastructure and coordinate their work in cleaning the river. The commission's work year ends on June 1, and it is required to submit an annual report summarizing its activities to member states. To complete this report, the PIC must hold its meeting by May 31 every year. Since 1960, the PIC has met every May to finalize and submit its annual report. Meetings have been held even when member states lacked any official diplomatic relations, which demonstrates the commission's resiliency and ability to avoid the frequent tensions in the macropolitical environment (Zawahri 2009).

States with a history of animosity and conflict tend to lack sufficient trust and confidence in one another to maintain long-term cooperation. Therefore, neoliberal institutionalist theory argues, states in an anarchic international system require institutionalized monitoring mechanisms to enable them to overcome their fear of cheating and cooperate (Mitchell 1994). In the case of river basin commissions, the capacity to monitor provides commissioners assurances against cheating and allows for transparency in managing the shared river system. It also provides adversarial states with mechanisms for long-term cooperation.

The IWT bestowed on the PIC the ability to monitor the entire river system. In fact, the treaty requires the commissioners to tour the river system every five years to ascertain the accuracy of exchanged information. Each commissioner can also ask for a special tour of any site along the river system, and this request must be granted.

As states develop a shared river system, they are likely to experience disputes (Zawahri 2008b). To manage these disputes and provide the commission with flexibility to address issues, states require conflict resolution mechanisms. The PIC commissioners are fortunate to have the capacity to draw on detailed conflict resolution mechanisms. The IWT indicates, in article IX, that when the commissioners are unable to resolve a question, they can send the issue to their two governments for further negotiations. Depending on the nature of the issue in question, it can also be sent to either a neutral expert or a court of arbitration. If the difference falls in one of twenty-three areas specified in the treaty, it can be sent to a neutral expert for resolution. The expert's decision is binding, as stipulated in annexure F. Should the neutral expert decide that the difference is actually a dispute, or should the difference not fall into one of the twenty-three designated categories, then it is sent to a specially established court of arbitration. In annexures F and G, the treaty outlines methods for the selection of the neutral expert, judges, and chair of the court, and the World Bank can facilitate the selection process.

During the 1960s, the PIC was busy implementing the treaty, managing the distribution of canal waters, exchanging hydrological data and flood warnings, maintaining drainage systems, and gathering data on the construction of hydrological infrastructure. The PIC conducted many tours of inspection, visiting hydroelectric plants, dams, drains, and flood embankments (PIC 1962, 1963, 1964). In response to requests from Pakistan, the commissioners negotiated the construction of wireless stations for transmitting flood warnings. The commissioners were responsible for maintaining India's extensive drainage systems inside both India and Pakistan. The Indian commissioner requested that Pakistan construct a drainage siphon under the Fordwah and Eastern Sadiqia canals along the Sutlej River in eastern Pakistan. Timber floating from India into Pakistan on the Ravi and Chenab tributaries was another issue the commissioners managed.

Over the years, the PIC's role has not changed. What did change was the increasing demand for it to negotiate issues as the riparian states increased their use of the shared river system. Commissioners negotiated the amount of agricultural land India is permitted to irrigate from the Western Rivers. For Pakistan, this was an important issue because it directly influenced the quantity and quality of water in these rivers. The more land India irrigated in Jammu and Kashmir, the less the quantity and quality of the water Pakistan would receive. The commissioners also negotiated the way flood warnings are delivered to Pakistan. In their 1989 agreement, India agreed to deliver them via broadcast,

178   Water and post-conflict peacebuilding

telephone, and wireless services (Gupta 2002). The commissioners negotiated, modified the design, and oversaw the construction of several major hydrological structures along the Indus River system. These structures include the Dulhasti (390 megawatts (MW)), Lower Jhelum (105 MW), Salal I and II (combined 690 MW), and Uri I (480 MW) dams in Jammu and Kashmir. As this book went to press, commissioners were overseeing the construction of two additional dams: Kishanganga (330 MW), which is to be completed by 2014, and Uri II (280 MW), which is to be completed in 2012.

The PIC has been relatively insulated from political pressure against cooperation. The deterioration in bilateral relations in 2001–2002 illustrates this point. After a series of terrorist attacks against India by militants suspected of being based in Pakistan, relations between the two states deteriorated significantly. Political and economic elites demanded that the Indian government abrogate the IWT or, at a minimum, cancel the PIC's annual meeting. Despite substantial domestic pressure, the PIC proceeded with its meeting (Zawahri 2009).

Since 1960, the PIC and the riparian states' foreign secretaries have succeeded in managing all but one issue. Recently, Pakistan invoked the neutral expert mechanism to address a difference that arose over India's construction of the Baglihar dam. Because the two states have accepted the expert's decision, it can be argued that the IWT has facilitated the peaceful management of the Indus River by India and Pakistan (Salman 2008).

FACTORS AFFECTING SUCCESS

A combination of factors affected the Indian government's ability to settle millions of rural refugees in eastern Punjab by using the waters of the Indus River system effectively. Within the Indian government, there was a general perception that the refugees in eastern Punjab were potential contributors to economic development (Rao 1967). There was also political will, strong intervention, and commitment on the part of the government at both the provincial and national levels, which was critical to securing the necessary financial resources and appropriate rehabilitation package (Voutira and Harrell-Bond 2000). In fact, the central government provided eastern Punjab with the most comprehensive rehabilitation program received by any Indian province (Menon and Bhasin 1998). The province also received the highest expenditure allocated for the development of infrastructure in the post-conflict setting (Chadha 1986). The government's willingness to expend these resources certainly facilitated the successful outcome, but the fact that many refugees came from the highly developed canal colonies in western Punjab meant that they were experienced farmers capable of cultivating their allotments efficiently.

Although the lack of international financial assistance for sheltering the millions of refugees was certainly a drain on the young Indian economy, it nevertheless provided the driving force to compel a rapid response. In other words, the high cost of housing refugees encouraged their rapid transfer to and settlement on lands vacated by Muslims, along with the expansion of farmland into areas of marginal quality. This policy allowed the government to cut the cost of sheltering refugees and to close the camps sooner. It was also consistent with the government's need to cultivate all available farmland in an attempt to meet growing demand for food, decrease grain import bills, and minimize the constant threat of famine. It can therefore be argued that the lack of international financial support provided the impetus and urgency needed to settle rural refugees.

As for the transboundary consequences of India's development of the Indus River system, several factors contributed to the successful management of this issue. One of the most important factors appears to have been the presence of a neutral and legitimate mediator (Nakayama 1997; Alam 1998; Biswas 1999; Salman 2002; Weinthal 2000, 2002; Wolf, Yoffe, and Giordano 2003; Giordano, Giordano, and Wolf 2005). Scholars agree that the World Bank's mediation from 1952 to 1960 and its use of carrot-and-stick approach to persuade India and Pakistan to compromise were critical to the signing of the IWT (Salman and Uprety 2002; Nakayama 1997; Alam 1998; Biswas 1999).

The World Bank also performed an important function in organizing the international donor community to underwrite the treaty's implementation and enable the construction of hydrological infrastructure to support the establishment of an agricultural sector in the post-conflict Indus River Basin (Gulhati 1973; Salman 2002). The donor community and India funded the necessary hydrological infrastructure that allowed Pakistan to draw on the Western Rivers to meet its domestic needs for water. India also received financial support totaling US$200 million to develop the irrigation potential of the Eastern Rivers (Swain 2004). Coordination of the donor community cut the transaction cost of locating donors to fund the treaty's implementation and assisted with the reconstruction of post-conflict economies. It also kept in check competing donor interests that might have prolonged, complicated, or even derailed the treaty's implementation. Therefore, it may be argued that the presence of a single agency with sufficient financial resources to fund the treaty's implementation facilitated the rapid and smooth development of hydrological infrastructure.

The fact that the IWT is clear, concise, and detailed could have contributed to the commissioners' ability to maintain peace. Negotiated and written by engineers, the treaty has meticulously detailed provisions for conflict resolution mechanisms, design limitations on hydrological infrastructure within Jammu and Kashmir, and the commission's ability to tour the entire river system. Moreover, the fact that the treaty focuses only on the Indus River system, and avoids discussion of Kashmir and other Indo-Pakistani disputes, might have also contributed to the commissioners' ability to manage water disputes.

The Israeli-Jordanian Joint Water Committee was not as fortunate. The Treaty of Peace between the State of Israel and the Hashemite Kingdom of Jordan, concluded on October 26, 1994, does not focus simply on water issues but on all Israeli-Jordanian political issues. The heavy participation of politicians in writing the treaty's water section also contributed to ambiguities and inconsistencies,

180 Water and post-conflict peacebuilding

which have complicated the commissioners' ability to perform their function (Zawahri 2008a). A clear and concise treaty likely contributes to cooperation, although scholars do argue that the simple presence of a treaty does not guarantee future cooperation (Downs, Rocke, and Barsoom 1996).

The mediator's presence during the first ten years of the treaty's implementation also had a positive impact. Scholars argue that a mediator's continued presence in the post-conflict environment is important for stabilizing the peacebuilding process (Walter 2002; Fortna 2004). A review of PIC minutes reveals that it was able to operate and perform its assigned task of sharing the canal waters and implementing the treaty without enlisting the World Bank's assistance (PIC 1961–1970). Nevertheless, the mediator's presence had an impact during one critical moment. In 1965, India and Pakistan fought their second war over Kashmir. During this conflict, India was still expected to deliver canal waters to Pakistan and make its annual installment to the Indus Basin Development Fund. Drought conditions plaguing the Indus River Basin contributed to domestic pressure from Punjabi farmers against making the deliveries to Pakistan. The 1965 war also created domestic pressure against making the annual installment. In spite of pressure, India delivered water in one canal and promptly paid the annual installment. However, India did fail to deliver water in the second canal, claiming that Pakistan did not submit the proper requisitions needed for making the delivery (Lok Sabha 1965a). An analysis of parliamentary debates provides a glimpse into the government's reasons for complying with most of its commitments, which included the need to preserve the treaty's integrity because of significant future gains in water and the need to avoid confrontation with the World Bank (Lok Sabha 1965a, 1965b).

In 1970, the World Bank completed the majority of its obligations under the IWT. Its only remaining role is to facilitate the selection process for the neutral expert or court of arbitration for the operation of the conflict resolution mechanisms. This remaining function is not sufficient to compel the states to alter their behavior to ensure cooperation. In fact, experts have noted that a mediator has "little power to prevent any of the signatories from defecting, that is becoming free riders, once [a] project is implemented" (Waterbury 1990, 7). Rather, India and Pakistan maintain cooperation with the IWT because it is in their interest. The treaty enables Pakistan to secure access to its only source of water, and India is able to develop the Eastern Rivers to support the agricultural sector in its northwestern provinces (Swain 2009; Zawahri 2009).

LESSONS LEARNED

There is no doubt that a committed government can use its resources effectively to provide refugees with livelihoods, integrate them into society, and bring peace and prosperity to a conflict-torn region. In the case of eastern Punjab, the Indian government was able to effectively use the waters of the Indus River system to establish an agrarian economy that permitted the settlement, employment, and future prosperity of millions of refugees. Several lessons may be drawn from this case regarding the management of natural resources in post-conflict societies, the sharing of international rivers, and the implementation of treaties.

During the turmoil that occurs in conflict and post-conflict situations, corruption is inevitable (Bolongaita 2005; O'Donnell 2008). Throughout the communal violence and the process of settling refugees, the government of eastern Punjab faced corruption among civil servants, military officers, police, local elites, and refugees. At times, the government accurately anticipated and prepared for attempts at corruption, such as refugees' exaggeration of their landholdings. The government failed to prepare for other types of corruption, such as military escorts starving evacuees by withholding food rations. Government policies were unable to eliminate another form of corruption: elites still managed to collude with civil servants to secure control of large and highly fertile landholdings.

Despite the prevalence of corruption in the conflict-torn society, the government was still able to rapidly rehabilitate refugees and contribute to the economic development of a border province. One may conclude, then, that although corruption is inevitable and certainly contributes to economic inefficiencies, it does not have to paralyze a government or prevent it from responding effectively in a post-conflict environment. Moreover, a government's anticipation of corruption, by formulating policies that increase the cost of rent seeking, can minimize its impact.

In post-conflict situations such as eastern Punjab in 1947–1948, a state's power to formulate public policy expands extensively compared to more stable periods, even if its bureaucratic structure is weak (Rosenberg 2011). Taking advantage of this expanded political power, the Indian government was able to minimize the prevalence of landed elites and absentee farmers and increase the number of landholding refugee peasants. This policy had both domestic and regional consequences. Regionally, it increased India's interest in reaching an agreement with Pakistan over the river system because of its dependence on the Eastern Rivers. Domestically, India's change of land tenure compelled farmers to cultivate their lands more efficiently, which increased overall productivity. The policy also increased the number of rural refugees that the government could rehabilitate and prevent from falling into poverty. This accomplishment is remarkable because, under normal political conditions, the restructuring of land tenure is a highly complex and contentious endeavor. States, such as Egypt and Iran, that have attempted to restructure their land tenure have failed because of the governments' inability to penetrate rural politics.

Rather than sequencing emergency relief, rehabilitation, and development policy, the Indian government undertook a holistic and concurrent approach in which, as some refugees were receiving emergency aid, others were immediately dispersed onto vacant farmland and provided with financial support to enable their economic development. These simultaneous policies allowed India to integrate refugees into society rapidly. Scholars have suggested that the rapid rehabilitation of farmers also appears to contribute to success (Green and Ahmed

182   Water and post-conflict peacebuilding

1999). Farmers can facilitate the rehabilitation and economic development of a conflict-torn society by helping to meet individual and urban food security needs along with providing the raw material needed for industrial development. The agricultural sector can also contribute directly and indirectly to revenue generation through exports and taxes (Green and Ahmed 1999).

The exact contribution of the donor community in providing emergency relief and aid to rebuild economies for conflict-torn states remains unclear (del Castillo 2008). Although donor assistance can help guide many countries through humanitarian disasters, their presence is not essential (Green and Ahmed 1999). Several factors interact to minimize the potential contribution of the donor community during this phase. Donors often have varying knowledge bases, competing goals, and even conflicting political agendas that can minimize the success of their efforts (del Castillo 2008). Moreover, the linkage between the donor community and the government in the policy-making process is often missing. As a result, lack of international financial assistance during a humanitarian disaster may actually contribute to a successful settlement of refugees because it enables host states to maintain their sovereignty over both the policy-making and implementation aspects of integrating refugees into society (Voutira and Harrell-Bond 2000). It may also serve to compel a rapid response by the government to minimize the financial burden generated by the crisis.

While donors tend to quickly pledge emergency humanitarian assistance, they rarely remain long enough in conflict-torn societies to support the economic development that is necessary to rebuild sustainable societies (del Castillo 2008). The Indus River system case, however, suggests that the presence of a single entity capable of mediating transboundary disputes, coordinating the donor community to implement an agreement, and providing the financial resources needed to reconstruct conflict-torn society appears to be important for peacebuilding. In fact, it might be argued that the function of a single mediator in providing the necessary financial aid is possibly more important for underwriting the long-term economic development in post-conflict societies than for providing short-term emergency aid.

The World Bank's direct mediation efforts facilitated the negotiations leading to a treaty (Salman and Uprety 2002; Nakayama 1997; Alam 1998; Wolf, Yoffe, and Giordano 2003). The accord contributed to the economic development of two post-conflict societies: it freed India to develop the Eastern Rivers of the Indus River to meet its need for irrigation water to develop eastern Punjab, and it enabled Pakistan to secure access to the river's Western Rivers to meet its domestic need for water. The lack of such an international mediator might have contributed to conflict in other basins. In the case of the Euphrates and Tigris rivers, which are shared by Turkey, Syria, and Iraq, the absence of a mediator might have contributed to an environment of competition and conflict (Naff and Matson 1984).[9]

---

[9]   It has also been suggested that in this case, the international community actually hindered cooperation because it repeatedly ignored requests from Syria and Iraq to mediate a treaty (Rubinstein 2001).

Indus River system 183

Implementation of a treaty is extremely complex, especially if there are any ambiguities in the agreement or if the signatories lack the financial means to underwrite the construction of planned infrastructure. States searching for donors to assist with implementing treaty commitments can confront difficulties as donors have divergent interests, objectives, and agendas. These difficulties can slow the implementation process or threaten the accord's integrity. A single donor can overcome these various obstacles and interests by collecting funding and co-ordinating the financing of projects. The World Bank's coordination of the donor community to underwrite the IWT also minimized the inefficiencies associated with the lack of coordination between donors.

The consequence of the absence of a single third party willing to coordinate the donor community to underwrite a treaty's implementation is evident in the Israeli-Jordanian peace treaty. The parties to that treaty spend precious time negotiating, arguing, and searching for donors to fund the various stages of projects—such as fact-finding, environmental impact assessment, design, construction, and operation and maintenance. A competitive and uncoordinated donor community has delayed the construction of some projects identified in the treaty.[10]

Concomitant with India and Pakistan's interest in cooperation is the fact that the World Bank was able to help the states design an effective river basin commission with appropriate conflict resolution mechanisms. Since states sharing a river are likely to experience continuous disputes, the availability of conflict resolution mechanisms is essential because they enable states to draw on standard operating procedures to settle these questions or disputes as they arise. These mechanisms also lend some predictability to the river's future development. To operate the conflict resolution mechanisms and facilitate the peaceful management of a jointly held river system requires a robust joint river commission. In the case of the Indus River system, India and Pakistan have been drawing on their conflict resolution mechanisms since 1960 as they developed the shared waters.

The Jordan-Israel peace treaty failed to provide sufficient conflict resolution mechanisms to the Joint Water Committee that was established to implement the treaty and manage the hydrological systems shared by Israel and Jordan. The absence of such mechanisms has meant that small disputes that could have been addressed through negotiations can flare up into bilateral disputes that require emergency meetings between national leaders (Zawahri 2008a).

Some experts have suggested that institutions require financial revenue, autonomy from member states, and authoritative decision making to manage the complexities inherent in sharing an international river (Waterbury 1997, 2002). River basin organizations certainly vary in their capacity to facilitate cooperation. Their success or effectiveness depends on the definition of cooperation. If cooperation is understood to require integrated water resource development of a river

---

[10] Officials of Jordan's Ministry of Water and Irrigation interviewed by the author, April and May 2001, Amman.

184 Water and post-conflict peacebuilding

basin, then it is likely to require a highly complex and empowered river basin commission. On the other hand, in this analysis of the Indus River system, cooperation was defined as states altering their behavior after negotiations to resolve their water disputes and avert conflict. The type of river commission required for this level of cooperation needs to have sufficient capacity to facilitate the management of disputes. The Indus River's PIC has been successful in managing India and Pakistan's river disputes since 1960 by providing the two countries with a means to negotiate their disputes (Salman 2002).

CONCLUSION

Due to the communal violence that plagued India and Pakistan in 1947–1948, millions of people crossed the border between the two new states in one of the largest exchanges of populations in history. The worst massacres occurred in western and eastern Punjab. To settle the more than 4 million refugees who crossed into eastern Punjab, the Indian government decided to use the waters of the Indus River's Eastern Rivers to enable it to rehabilitate its refugees through the establishment of an agrarian economy. India was able to effectively facilitate economic development and peacebuilding in this conflict-torn province. The government's successful policies and programs also permitted the employment of refugees to construct the infrastructure necessary for turning eastern Punjab into India's granary, which helped to meet the nation's growing demand for food. The long history since India's independence permits us to assess this case and conclude that it truly represents a successful example of the effective management of a livelihood resource to contribute to peacebuilding in a post-conflict society.

Yet to implement these policies and projects, India had to draw on the same resource that sustained Pakistan's agrarian economy, which resulted in a transboundary dispute. From 1947 to 1952, the two riparian states negotiated two temporary agreements, but these failed to provide a stable solution. The direct mediation of the World Bank from 1952 until 1960 enabled the two states to avoid conflict over this natural resource and sign the IWT, which allocated the Indus main stem and the five easternmost tributaries between the states. India received the Eastern Rivers and Pakistan the Western Rivers. To finance the construction of hydrological infrastructure to shift Pakistan's dependence from the Eastern Rivers to the Western Rivers, the World Bank coordinated funding from India and a consortium of donors. The World Bank also operated the Indus Development Fund, which financed the implementation of these projects. To oversee the treaty's implementation and manage disputes arising from the development of the shared river system, the IWT established the PIC and provided it with sufficient authority to fulfill its task. Should questions, differences, or disputes arise, the states have extensive conflict resolution mechanisms to draw upon. For over forty years, the parties to the IWT have used the negotiation path to peacefully address all their Indus River disputes (Salman 2008).

REFERENCES

Aiyar, S. 1995. 'August anarchy': The partition massacres in Punjab, 1947. *South Asia: Journal of South Asian Studies* 18:13–36.

Alam, U. 1998. Water rationality: Mediating the Indus Waters Treaty. Ph.D. diss., University of Durham, UK.

————. 2002. Questioning the water wars rationale: A case study of the Indus Waters Treaty. *Geographical Journal* 168 (4): 341–353.

Ali, C. M. 1967. *The emergence of Pakistan.* New York: Columbia University Press.

Bigombe, B., P. Collier, and N. Sambanis. 2000. Policies for building post-conflict peace. *Journal of African Economies* 9 (3): 323–348.

Biswas, A. K. 1999. Management of international waters: Opportunities and constraints. *International Journal of Water Resources Development* 15 (4): 429–441.

Bolongaita, E. 2005. Controlling corruption in post-conflict countries. Kroc Institute Occasional Paper No. 26:OP:2. Notre Dame, IN: Kroc Institute for International Peace Studies, University of Notre Dame.

Bose, S. 2003. *Kashmir: Roots of conflict, paths to peace.* Cambridge, MA: Harvard University Press.

Butalia, U. 2000. *The other side of silence: Voices from the partition of India.* Durham, NC: Duke University Press.

Central Board of Irrigation and Power. 1992. *History of irrigation in Indus Basin.* Publication No. 230. New Delhi, India.

Cernea, M., and C. McDowell. 2000. Reconstructing resettlers' and refugees' livelihoods. In *Risks and reconstruction: Experiences of resettlers and refugees*, ed. M. Cernea and C. McDowell. Washington, D.C.: World Bank.

Chadha, G. K. 1986. *The state and rural economic transformation: The case of Punjab, 1950–85.* New Delhi, India: Sage Publications.

Chopra, R. N. 1981. *Evolution of food policy in India.* New Delhi, India: MacMillan.

Conca, K., F. Wu, and C. Mei. 2006. Global regime formation or complex institution building? The principled content of international river agreements. *International Studies Quarterly* 50 (2): 263–285.

del Castillo, G. 2008. *Rebuilding war-torn states: The challenge of post-conflict economic reconstruction.* Oxford, UK: Oxford University Press.

Dixit, J. N. 2002. *India-Pakistan in war and peace.* London: Routledge.

Downs, G. W., D. M. Rocke, and P. N. Barsoom. 1996. Is the good news about compliance good news about cooperation? *International Organization* 50 (3): 379–406.

Fortna, V. P. 2004. Does peacekeeping keep peace? International intervention and the duration of peace after civil war. *International Studies Quarterly* 48 (4): 269–292.

Fowler, F. J. 1950. Some problems of water distribution between east and west Punjab. *Geographic Review* 40 (4): 583–599.

Ganguly, S. 2002. *Conflict unending: India-Pakistan tensions since 1947.* New Delhi, India: Oxford University Press.

Giordano, M., M. Giordano, and A. Wolf. 2005. International resource conflict and mitigation. *Journal of Peace Research* 42 (1): 47–65.

Green, R. H., and I. Ahmed. 1999. Rehabilitation, sustainable peace and development: Towards reconceptualisation. *Third World Quarterly* 20 (1): 189–206.

Gulhati, N. 1973. *Indus Waters Treaty: An exercise in international mediation.* Bombay, India: Allied Publishers.

186   Water and post-conflict peacebuilding

Gupta, A. C. 2002. Interview by author of India's commissioner to the Permanent Indus Commission. May 13. New Delhi, India.

Haque, C. E. 1995. The dilemma of "nationhood" and religion: A survey and critique of studies on population displacement resulting from the partition of the Indian subcontinent. *Journal of Refugee Studies* 8 (2): 185–209.

Hodson, H. V. 1997. *The great divide: Britain–India–Pakistan.* Karachi, Pakistan: Oxford University Press.

Kaushik, K. K. 1998. Food security and new economic policy: Issues and policy implications. In *South Asia: Democracy, discontent, and societal conflicts*, ed. G. Singh. New Delhi, India: Anamika Publishers.

Keller, S. 1975. *Uprooting and social change: The role of refugees in development.* New Delhi, India: Manohar Book Service.

Khan, M. A. 1967. *Friends not masters: A political autobiography.* London: Oxford University Press.

Kudaisya, G. 1995. The demographic upheaval of partition: Refugees and agricultural resettlement in India, 1947–67. *South Asia: Journal of South Asian Studies* 18:73–94.

Lamb, A. 1992. *Kashmir: A disputed legacy, 1846–1990.* Karachi, Pakistan: Oxford University Press.

Lilienthal, D. E. 1951. Another "Korea" in the making? *Collier's*, August 4.

Lok Sabha. 1965a. Motion re: Payment to World Bank and release of water under Indus Waters Treaty. November 10. New Delhi, India: Jawaharlal Nehru Library.

———. 1965b. Release of canal water supplies to Pakistan. November 4. New Delhi, India: Jawaharlal Nehru Library.

Lowi, M. 1993. *Water and power: The politics of a scarce resource in the Jordan River Basin.* Cambridge, UK: Cambridge University Press.

Mayfield, R. C. 1955. A geographic study of the Kashmir issue. *Geographical Review* 45 (2): 181–196.

McLeod, D., and M. Dávalos. 2008. Post-conflict employment creation for stabilization and poverty reduction. Bronx, NY: Economics Department, Fordham University. www.fordham.edu/economics/mcleod/PostConflictEmployment10.pdf.

Menon, R. 2003. Birth of social security commitments: What happened in the West. In *Refugees and the state*, ed. R. Samaddar. New Delhi, India: Sage Publications.

Menon, R., and K. Bhasin. 1998. *Borders and boundaries: Women in India's partition.* New Brunswick, NJ: Rutgers University Press.

Michel, A. 1967. *The Indus rivers: A study of the effects of partition.* New Haven, CT: Yale University Press.

Mitchell, R. 1994. Regime design matters: International oil pollution and treaty compliance. *International Organization* 48 (3): 425–458.

Naff, T., and R. Matson. 1984. *Water in the Middle East.* Boulder, CO: Westview Press.

Nakayama, M. 1997. Successes and failures of international organizations in dealing with international waters. *International Journal of Water Resources Development* 13 (3): 367–382.

Nehru, J. 1988. Letter to N. V. Gadgil, July 3, 1948. In vol. 7 of *Selected works of Jawaharlal Nehru*, ed. S. Gopal. Bombay, India: Oxford University Press.

———. 1994. Letter to Liaquat Ali Khan, October 27, 1950. In *Selected works of Jawaharlal Nehru.* New Delhi, India: Oxford University Press.

Indus River system **187**

————. 1995. A policy of self-sufficiency in food. Speech on the inaugural day of a two-day conference of the States' Food Ministries, February 19, 1952. In vol. 17 of *Selected works of Jawaharlal Nehru*, ed. S. Gopal. Bombay, India: Oxford University Press.

————. 1998. Letter to Bhimsen Sachar, March 18, 1953. In vol. 21 of *Selected works of Jawaharlal Nehru*, ed. S. Gopal. New Delhi, India: Oxford University Press.

Oberoi, P. 2006. *Exile and belonging: Refugees and state policy in South Asia.* New Delhi, India: Oxford University Press.

Obidegwu, C. 2004. Post-conflict peace building in Africa: The challenge of socio-economic recovery and development. African Region Working Paper Series No. 73. Washington, D.C.: World Bank.

O'Donnell, M. 2008. Corruption: A rule of law agenda? In *Civil war and the rule of law: Security, development, human rights*, ed. A. Hurwitz and R. Huang. London: Lynne Rienner.

PIC (Permanent Indus Commission). 1961. *Annual report for the year ended on 31st March 1961.* New Delhi, India.

————. 1962. *Annual report for the year ended on 31st March 1962.* Rawalpindi, Pakistan.

————. 1963. *Annual report for the year ended on 31st March 1963.* New Delhi, India.

————. 1964. *Annual report for the year ended on 31st March 1964.* Karachi, Pakistan.

————. 1965. *Annual report for the year ended on 31st March 1965.* Karachi, Pakistan.

————. 1966. *Annual report for the year ended on 31st March 1966.* New Delhi, India.

————. 1967. *Annual report for the year ended on 31st March 1967.* Lahore, Pakistan.

————. 1968. *Annual report for the year ended on 31st March 1968.* New Delhi, India.

————. 1969. *Annual report for the year ended on 31st March 1969.* Islamabad, Pakistan.

————. 1970. *Annual report for the year ended on 31st March 1970.* New Delhi, India.

Rai, S. M. 1965. *Partition of the Punjab.* New Delhi, India: Asia Publishing House.

Randhawa, M. S. 1954. *Out of the ashes: An account of the rehabilitation of refugees from West Pakistan in rural areas of East Punjab.* Bombay, India: C. N. Raman.

Rao, U. B. 1967. *The story of rehabilitation.* New Delhi, India: Ministry of Information and Broadcasting.

Rosenberg, J. 2011. Natural disasters, climate change, and recovery: The sustainability question in post-Ivan Grenada. In *Community disaster recovery and resiliency: Exploring global opportunities and challenges*, ed. D. Miller and J. Rivera. Boca Raton, FL: Auerbach Publications.

Rubinstein, D. 2001. Interview by author of official from United States Embassy's Economic Division. June 6. Damascus, Syria.

Salman, S. M. A. 2002. Good office and mediation and international water disputes. In *The International Bureau of the Permanent Court of Arbitration: Resolution of international water disputes.* The Hague, Netherlands: Kluwer Law International.

————. 2008. The Baglihar difference and its resolution process—a triumph for the Indus Waters Treaty? *Water Policy* 10:105–117.

Salman, S. M. A., and K. Uprety. 2002. *Conflict and cooperation on South Asia's international rivers: A legal perspective.* Washington, D.C.: World Bank.

Schofield, V. 2003. *Kashmir in conflict: India, Pakistan and the unending war.* London: I. B. Tauris.

Spate, O. H. K. 1948. The partition of India and the prospects of Pakistan. *Geographical Review* 38 (1): 5–29.

188 Water and post-conflict peacebuilding

Suhrawardy, A. H. K. 1991. *The incredible freedom flight*. Lahore, Pakistan. Quoted in V. Schofield, *Kashmir in conflict: India, Pakistan and the unending war* (London: I. B. Tauris, 2003), 39.

Swain, A. 2004. *Managing water conflict: Asia, Africa and the Middle East*. London: Routledge.

———. 2009. The Indus II and Siachen Peace Park: Pushing the India-Pakistan peace process forward. *Round Table* 98 (404): 569–582.

Talbot, I. 2007. A tale of two cities: The aftermath of partition for Lahore and Amritsar. *Modern Asian Studies* 41 (1): 151–185.

Tan, T. Y., and G. Kudaisya. 2000. *The aftermath of partition in South Asia*. London: Routledge.

Unruh, J. D., and J. Bailey. 2009. Management of spatially extensive natural resources in postwar contexts: Working with the peace process. *GeoJournal* 74 (2):159–173.

Verghese, B. G. 1994. *Winning the future*. New Delhi, India: Konark Publishers.

Voutira, E., and B. Harrell-Bond. 2000. "Successful" refugee settlement: Are past experiences relevant? In *Risks and reconstruction: Experiences of resettlers and refugees*, ed. M. Cernea and C. McDowell. Washington, D.C.: World Bank.

Walter, B. 2002. *Committing to peace: The successful settlement of civil wars*. Princeton, NJ: Princeton University Press.

Waterbury, J. 1990. Dynamics of basin-wide cooperation in the utilization of the Euphrates. Paper presented at the conference "Economic Development of Syria: Problems, Progress, and Prospects," Damascus, Syria.

———. 1997. Between unilateralism and comprehensive accords: Modest steps toward cooperation in international river basins. *International Journal of Water Resources Development* 13 (3): 279–289.

———. 2002. *The Nile Basin: National determinants of collective action*. New Haven, CT: Yale University Press.

Weinthal, E. 2000. Making waves: Third parties and international mediation in the Aral Sea Basin. In *Words over war*, ed. M. Greenberg and M. McGuinness. Lanham, MD: Rowman and Littlefield.

———. 2002. *State making and environmental cooperation: Linking domestic and international politics in Central Asia*. Cambridge, MA: MIT Press.

Westley, J. 1986. *Agriculture and equitable growth: The case of Punjab-Haryana*. Boulder, CO: Westview Press.

Wolf, A. T., S. B. Yoffe, and M. Giordano. 2003. International waters: Identifying basins at risk. *Water Policy* 5 (1): 29–60.

Yamamoto, S. 2008. The Indus water dispute and its relation with domestic policies. In *International water security: Domestic threats and opportunities*, ed. N. I. Pachova, M. Nakayama, and L. Jansky. Tokyo: United Nations University Press.

Zawahri, N. 2008a. Designing river commissions to implement treaties and manage international rivers: The story of the Joint Water Committee and Permanent Indus Commission. *Water International* 33 (4): 464–474.

———. 2008b. International rivers and national security: The Euphrates, Ganges-Brahmaputra, Indus, Tigris, and Yarmouk rivers. *Natural Resources Forum* 32 (4): 280–289.

———. 2009. India, Pakistan and cooperation along the Indus River system. *Water Policy* 11 (1): 1–20.

Despite the best intentions? Experiences with water resource management in northern Afghanistan

Jennifer McCarthy and Daanish Mustafa

The development and management of water resources has been part of the nation building projects of various Afghan regimes dating back to the beginning of twentieth century. Since 2001, the Afghan government has tried to enhance its legitimacy and reduce the influence of the insurgency by improving the living conditions of ordinary Afghans, but these efforts have not met expectations when it comes to water services for domestic use and irrigation, possibly because many of the water use and development initiatives have been shaped by national and international stakeholders without the full participation of the intended beneficiaries. At the national level, the key strategic frameworks informing Afghan development in the water sector and beyond, most notably the Afghanistan National Development Strategy (ANDS), are replete with references to participation, bottom-up development, and social equity (Farhadi 2008). At the local level, however, implementation of these concepts has proved problematic, and fulfillment of the basic need for water in rural areas has been difficult to achieve.

The case studies examined in this chapter highlight how some specific local Afghan experiences with water resource management programs and water infrastructure development have not been characterized by effective participation and equity in decision making. These water-related interventions have not met the basic need for water for irrigation, domestic water supply, and sanitation, but they have had implications for governance and the peacebuilding process at the local level.

The chapter begins with a history of water resource development in Afghanistan, identifying key features of traditional Afghan water management systems, which remained functioning at the local level despite decades of conflict, and providing an overview of water management systems dating back to the late 1800s. The chapter discusses the National Solidarity Programme, the implementing

---

Jennifer McCarthy is a Ph.D. student in geography at King's College, London. Daanish Mustafa is a senior lecturer in environment, politics, and development at King's College, London.

190   Water and post-conflict peacebuilding

mechanism of the ANDS, and examines the deficiencies of the program with respect to improving access to water in Afghan villages. Lessons from local resource management are then highlighted, and two case studies from northern Afghanistan are presented. The case studies demonstrate how local power dynamics can drive conflict related to the national government's initiatives for water resource management. The chapter provides recommendations for rescaling water resource management to the local level, including government recognition and understanding of local power dynamics, the use of village-level stakeholders as water resource managers, and greater government legitimacy.

HISTORY OF WATER RESOURCE DEVELOPMENT IN AFGHANISTAN

Water resource development has been a key conduit for imperial control and nation building in many colonial and post-colonial contexts, and Afghanistan is no exception (Cosgrove and Petts 1990; Gilmartin 1994; Swyngedouw 1999). Water sector interventions helped to consolidate government control over rural Afghan society throughout the nineteenth and twentieth centuries (Shah 2009; Abdullayev et al. 2009). However, water management and provision remains a local phenomenon, contrary to the popular notion that it was decimated during the three decades of conflict that began with the Soviet invasion of Afghanistan in 1979 (Abdullayev et al. 2009). There is not an institutional and infrastructural void in rural Afghan water resource management. Indeed, government and international efforts to superimpose water management structures on existing and functioning resource governance systems in rural villages have caused resentment and given rise to local-level conflict between elites, who are often accused of controlling resources to serve their own interests, and others, who are not equally benefiting from government water management programs.

Traditional Afghan water management systems have been characterized by four key features (Shah 2009):

1) Community-based management structures with elected or, more often, selected water masters (called *mirabs*), who oversee water infrastructure construction and maintenance, enforcement of local norms, and conflict resolution.
2) Community-level water rights and allocation regimes based primarily on landownership and levels of contribution to water infrastructure maintenance.
3) Water infrastructure built and maintained by the community, often requiring high levels of labor and other resource inputs for development and maintenance.
4) A minimal or absent state role in rural water management.

These key features are reflected in the oral history of water management systems in Faryab Province, where decisions of mirabs, along with landownership, have determined levels of access to water from a range of water systems, such as dams, streams, underground canal systems (*karez*), and traditional water tanks

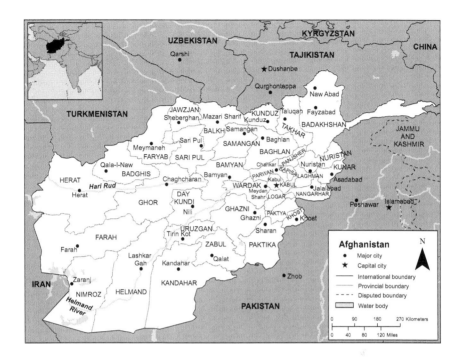

(*howz*).[1] For the most part, the state endorsed each mirab's selection by the most powerful elders in the community. This added legitimacy to the mirab's actions, which also drew legitimacy from tacit community endorsement gained through consensus or, sometimes, intimidation (Abdullayev et al. 2009).

Traditional water management systems were challenged by the state when, in the aftermath of the Second Anglo-Afghan War, Abdur Rahman (emir of Afghanistan from 1880 to 1901) initiated strong state intervention in local-level water management and infrastructure. Rahman was cognizant of the fragility of the nascent Afghan state and sought to undo the damage of the war by investing in the repair of water infrastructure; reclaiming vast swaths of territory in northern Afghanistan by constructing new canals; providing seed advances (known as *taqawi* loans) to farmers to increase productivity; and, most important, encouraging the settlement of ethnic Pashtuns and members of other loyal ethnicities in various parts of Afghanistan, particularly the north, in order to dilute ethnic divisions (Kakar 1979).[2] The settlement schemes, which continued through the early twentieth century, went hand in hand with the Afghan state's flirtation with the Soviets

---

[1] Interview with Faryab provincial government official, Meymaneh, 2009.
[2] Pashtuns are largely concentrated in the east and southeast of Afghanistan and have historically dominated Afghanistan politically. In the interest of national integration, the group was settled in the north and east by successive Afghan governments. The Taliban movement largely draws from the Pashtun ethnic group.

192 Water and post-conflict peacebuilding

and even with some of the Axis powers in the 1930s. Afghanistan sought the Axis powers' assistance with water development until the British and Soviet governments forced the Afghan government to evict all Japanese, German, and Italian advisors during World War II (Shah 2009).

After World War II, the Tennessee Valley Authority model from New Deal era in the United States was exported to Afghanistan, as it was to many other places in the developing world (Hirsch and Wyatt 2004; Lahiri-Dutt 2003; Sneddon 2002). This model entailed undertaking multipurpose water development projects across a river basin with the intention of using irrigation and power generation for regional development and poverty alleviation. The Helmand-Arghandab Valley Authority (HAVA) in southern Afghanistan was the product of this U.S. assistance to the water sector in the 1950s (Shah 2009). HAVA focused on the development of physical infrastructure and largely overlooked the social aspects of water management, which is likely why the project was a resounding failure. The affected communities, which were at times forcibly or otherwise involuntarily resettled, quickly abandoned the project area because of ethnic conflict and state mismanagement (Shah 2009). The inherent design problems of the project revealed insensitivity to the inequitable resource distribution in the valley. For example, many farmers at the tail end of canals and watercourses could not benefit from the irrigation schemes, nor could they gain access to remedial support in risk management and mitigation from the project or provincial authorities. Operation and management of the infrastructure was lacking, as was revenue generation from the projects, which severely limited HAVA's ultimate efficacy (Shah 2009).

Chastened by the failure of HAVA and driven by other geopolitical imperatives, particularly the close relationship between its chief rival, Pakistan, and the United States, the Afghan government started a phase of more intense interaction with the Soviet Union in the late 1950s. This increased interaction included activities in the water sector. Throughout the 1960s and early 1970s, the focus of Soviet assistance to Afghanistan was on water development planning, such as the Hari Rud irrigation project in the Herat region and irrigation expansion on the Kikcha River in Takhar Province, the Kunduz river in Kunduz Province, and the Pyanj River in Badakhshan Province. One of the more substantive Soviet contributions in the late 1960s and the 1970s was improving Afghan farmers' access to cotton mills and markets in the Soviet Union, which caused considerable expansion of irrigated cotton farming in the country, particularly in the northern plains (Dupree 1975).

The period from 1978 to 2001 was a time of external invasion, local resistance, and then civil war in Afghanistan. Despite an ongoing civil war and unprecedented destruction of infrastructure as a result, the last of the Soviet-supported governments, that of Mohammad Najibullah, undertook some important developments in the water sector, including creation of the Ministry of Irrigation and Water Resources in 1988, as well as programs of support to farmers that supplied seeds, loans, and machinery for canal cleaning.

Water resource management in northern Afghanistan 193

Soviet withdrawal in 1989 was followed by an era of civil war and dominance by warlords; in the second half of the 1990s the Taliban became the dominant force in most of the country. During the war, the role of the central state in the water sector was almost nonexistent. Water supply infrastructure was damaged throughout the country, and traditional elites with local control over water management were often replaced by predatory warlords. New political alliances allowed warlords and affiliated communities to violate customary water distribution agreements (Pain 2004). Traditional management systems in their purest form were not necessarily equitable or just, but the distortions spawned by civil conflict undermined what legitimacy they did have (Barfield 2007; Pain 2004). The Taliban tried to reverse some of the worst of the warlords' land and water appropriations, with limited success (Shah 2009).

In the present post-conflict era, international donors' ideas about the nature of development are often disconnected from the daily realities of rural Afghan life, and this sometimes has contradictory and problematic implications for peacebuilding.[3] The current peacebuilding efforts in Afghanistan began with the 2001 Bonn Conference, during which attendees together pledged billions of dollars in aid toward implementation of the Bonn Agreement, a plan laying out a three-year process of reconstruction (Barakat 2002; Montgomery and Rondinelli 2004). The Bonn Agreement resulted in the establishment of the Afghan Interim Authority, chaired by Hamid Karzai and charged with representing Afghanistan in external relations. Following the conclusion of the Bonn process, the Afghanistan Compact was created during a London conference in 2006. It outlined national and international stakeholders' political commitments to international cooperation in Afghanistan through 2011.

A key strategic document in the peacebuilding process, drawing together the goals of the Afghanistan Compact and the UN Millennium Development Goals, is the ANDS, which recognizes that post-conflict reconstruction must be undertaken in concert with long-term development initiatives. The ANDS lays out a strategy for putting Afghanistan on a "virtuous path towards peace, stability and prosperity . . ." (Farhadi 2008, 1). It states that the extent to which Afghanistan can be at peace with itself and its neighbors depends on the "effective utilization of all available human, natural and financial resources . . ." (Farhadi 2008, 4). However, when it comes to water, a comprehensive and sustainable management strategy is still in the formative stages. Preliminary benchmarks for rural water resource development are currently set at impressively optimistic levels: "Rural development will be enhanced for 90 percent of villages through the provision of safe drinking water, sanitation (50 percent) and small scale irrigation (47 percent) by the end of 2010" (Farhadi 2008, 83), but progress toward this

---

[3] The term *peacebuilding* in this chapter refers to "an endeavour aiming to create sustainable peace by addressing the 'root causes' of violent conflict and eliciting indigenous capacities for peaceful management and resolution of conflict" (Peacebuilding Initiative 2008, 2).

194   Water and post-conflict peacebuilding

objective has been slow. In August 2010 the World Bank reported that only 27 percent of Afghans have access to safe drinking water, and only 5 percent have access to sanitation (World Bank 2010).

Personal accounts of rural villagers, together with the findings from Usman Shah's and Iskandar Abdullayev and his colleagues' research on water management mechanisms in the northern province of Kunduz (Shah 2009; Abdullayev et al. 2009), suggest a widespread inability to provide adequate water through rural water supply projects. Research also points to the complexity of differential power arrangements in rural Afghanistan, which are rarely congruent with the idealized village democracy model that is the basis for the institutional design of the National Solidarity Programme, the key institutional mechanism for implementing the objects outlined in the ANDS from 2003 to 2008 (McCarthy 2011).

THE NATIONAL SOLIDARITY PROGRAMME

The Ministry for Rural Rehabilitation and Development (MRRD) was charged with the management of the National Solidarity Programme (NSP), which aims to improve rural infrastructure, create robust local governance mechanisms, and alleviate poverty throughout Afghanistan. The MRRD implements the NSP across the country through its provincial departments, with international and national nongovernmental organizations (NGOs) acting as facilitating partners. These facilitating partners work alongside community development councils (CDCs) to provide technical assistance in project implementation and to report to MRRD's provincial departments. The local CDC is charged with creating a community development plan that includes the community's top development priorities and also with managing the funds for projects initiated through the program. The formation of a CDC is a required element for a community to participate in the NSP, and its leaders are chosen in a closed-ballot election (MRRD 2009).

Each community is entitled to US$200 per family, up to a maximum of US$60,000, to use for its priority projects. These funds are given directly to the CDCs. The community is required to provide a 10 percent contribution to the overall cost of a project, which most often comes in the form of in-kind manual labor. Projects are managed and monitored by the CDC, often with technical assistance from a facilitating partner (MRRD 2009). The NSP is one of the few attempts to devolve governance and conflict resolution to the village level in order to establish development mechanisms that contribute to peacebuilding efforts in the country (Dennys and Zaman 2009).

The government of Afghanistan has identified the NSP as the principal mechanism for achieving reconstruction and peacebuilding within the Comprehensive Agriculture and Rural Development program (Farhadi 2008). As such, the NSP is intended to play an important role in the creation of conditions for a stable peace in rural Afghanistan. In a return to the traditional social structure, the mirab has become the key interface between the provincial water management department and the local communities under the NSP (Abdullayev et al. 2009; Shah 2009). Most national- and provincial-level stakeholders consulted in 2008 and 2009 during the research for this chapter believed that the NSP held great potential to bring peace to Afghanistan by increasing trust between the Afghan citizenry and the central government. As Barnett Rubin explains, building a legitimate and capable state requires "transitional governance institutions that incorporate the need for both national and international legitimacy" (Rubin 2006, 184). In addition, because it attempts to address the priority needs of the populace by devolving decision making to the village level, the NSP is believed to hold one of the keys to accountability and social cohesion, both nationally and locally. However, there has been widespread resentment over the fact that resources allocated to individual communities for infrastructure or livelihood enhancement projects have not actually achieved those goals. Water and related infrastructure are necessary for livelihoods in the agricultural economy of rural Afghanistan. Improved access to water for irrigation could thus be a litmus test of the efficacy not only of the NSP but also of the new Afghan government and the international community that stands behind it. Failure to improve access to water, either by improving infrastructure or by moderating the influence of powerful elements who appropriate water from the weak, undermines the confidence of the Afghan populace and reduces the potential of the internationally backed Afghan government to improve Afghans' lives.

The authors' interviews with several villagers suggest that projects affecting water resource management at the village level require much more scrutiny before the projects can provide a meaningful contribution to peacebuilding in northern Afghanistan. These findings demonstrate how water resource management in rural villages is not being effectively integrated into the Afghan peacebuilding strategy. Peacebuilding involves "identifying and alleviating the underlying sources of conflict within a war-shattered state, which [requires] a thorough understanding of local conditions" (Paris 2004, 3). During the fieldwork conducted for this research, the authors did not get a sense that the NSP managers and donors had a thorough understanding of local conditions, particularly of pre-NSP power structures and contemporary social dynamics. This lack of understanding has contributed to patchy service delivery and growing frustration on the part of Afghans.

In 2009, when the fieldwork informing a large part of this analysis was conducted, the government had six years of NSP implementation from which to draw lessons related to the program's impact on resource-based livelihoods, including water resource management. Issues such as local discrimination and insufficient financial and human resources still negatively affected access to water six years into program implementation. This suggests that the NSP's structure and implementation processes were not allowing for local experiences to be recognized and addressed as important barriers to peacebuilding. As a previous minister for MRRD explains, building trust between citizens and government

196   Water and post-conflict peacebuilding

takes time, particularly in the case of Afghanistan, which was not left with anything resembling a functioning government after the fall of the Taliban regime.[4] However, it seems that the potential to even begin building a foundation for this trust through effective and informed management of the NSP has not been realized.

LESSONS FROM LOCAL RESOURCE MANAGEMENT

In the cases described later in this chapter, the NSP did not directly cause conflict over water. However, the inability of the NSP programs to secure equitable access to water resources led to increased frustration and tension in the villages discussed. Rather than creating an environment in which Afghans could gain equitable and sustainable access to water, the NSP inadvertently created a space in these villages wherein either power dynamics or social processes were exercised in an exclusionary manner, or in which projects simply did not deliver on their promises. Although this is not the case in every NSP community and the authors do not intend to declare the entire program ineffective, the examples presented in this chapter from different areas of northern Afghanistan, along with examples the authors have gleaned from secondary research, suggest that there may be similar situations in other villages.

If NSP stakeholders have more informed engagement with existing power structures, Afghans will have more space to voice their concerns and take collective action, and the program may become more effective in reducing the likelihood of local, resource-based conflict. More sustainable and equitable access to water during years of drought and beyond can contribute significantly to the potential for a stable peace in Afghanistan.

On the basis of observations in rural areas and discussions with NSP participants since 2005, Jennifer McCarthy concluded that the rural population viewed the NSP as the single largest government intervention in their communities (McCarthy 2011). Thus government legitimacy was tied to how the NSP was managed. Acquiring the quality and quantity of human resources required to adequately implement the NSP was a challenge for the MRRD. A former minister explained that a lack of in-country experience and capacity has limited the degree to which the ministry can take practical measures to improve the NSP's impact.[5] Legitimacy should be improved not merely by the provision of more financial resources, but by the assignment of people to the project who possess the skills and knowledge necessary to ensure that funds are used effectively and to address programmatic shortfalls when they become apparent.

When citizens lack access to adequate and safe water for consumption and irrigation even though the government is managing a participatory development program that aims to lay a foundation for poverty alleviation, the government loses legitimacy with the people. There is a growing body of evidence suggesting

---

[4]   Interview with high-ranking MRRD official, Kabul, June 2009.
[5]   Interview, Kabul, June 2009.

Water resource management in northern Afghanistan 197

that frustration with ongoing vulnerability—which sustainable access to water would significantly alleviate—may be contributing to increased levels of violence in Faryab Province (McCarthy 2011). Perceptions of government legitimacy can thus be said to be a contributing element to building a stable peace in Afghanistan.

Power and CDCs: A combination for conflict resolution?

Noting that post-conflict development is not a conflict-free process, Christian Dennys and Idrees Zaman cite two examples from Badakhshan and Kunduz provinces in which the communal nature of NSP block grants created problems within the CDCs, largely because of shifting power structures (Dennys and Zaman 2009). They contend that the NSP has not sufficiently accounted for local dynamics, and that it shifted the social landscape by territorializing the rural areas into "communities."[6] Dennys and Zaman cite an example from Kunduz Province, where planning for reconstruction interventions disregarded the existing organizing feature of the province: an irrigation system that has survived the decades of conflict. They argue that there is "no real level of solidarity in the region and the NSP implemented through the Community Development Councils has not taken into account that identity is largely based on face-to-face interactions rather than through affiliation to a village" (Dennys and Zaman 2009, 28). The conflicting definitions of what constitutes "community" highlights the need for in-depth understanding of local dynamics and how they relate to water resource management.

In contrast to the 2009 findings presented by Dennys and Zaman, a high-level MRRD official cited social cohesion as the main benefit to come from creating NSP communities.[7] This perspective was also voiced by a representative of Faryab's Provincial Department for Rural Rehabilitation who explained that the NSP has enabled Afghans of different ethnicities to work together and share funds and information.[8] The representative cited a case in which multiple CDCs rallied together to complain about malfeasance by a facilitating partner organization's staff member. The staff member was dismissed, and the misappropriated funds were returned to the CDCs. This and other successes notwithstanding, the authors' ongoing research does not yield such sanguine conclusions about the benefits of the NSP.

People-centered strategy

As noted by key MRRD stakeholders at the national and provincial levels, the CDCs are demonstrating that they can undertake conflict resolution activities at

---

[6] McCarthy's wider research grapples with the issue of power structures in CDC "communities," both pre- and post-NSP, to analyze how power shifts due to the NSP have affected vulnerability to environmental hazards such as drought. See also Mielke and Schetter (2007).

[7] Personal communication, June 2009.

[8] Interview, Meymaneh, June 2009.

198   Water and post-conflict peacebuilding

the village level, preventing issues from being escalated to the district-level government.[9] The potential for CDCs to grow in this role could play a key role in future peacebuilding strategies. This would not necessarily involve centering power in local institutions or reinforcing existing power differentials because CDCs could become more transparent and inclusive. Until now, the Afghan peace-building project has been conceptualized at the national level and has addressed warlordism, corruption, and criminality (Waldman 2008). This top-down approach to peacebuilding, which includes the NSP, has largely failed to address many of the practical concerns of Afghan citizens at the village level. National peacebuild-ing, development, and water resource management strategies are vital, but the government of Afghanistan should also develop peacebuilding strategies at the village level that make effective use of the CDCs and other local institutions and that facilitate meaningful two-way communication.

CASE STUDIES

Governance mechanisms at the national level can be paired with local-level initiatives to improve the equitable and sustainable use and management of water resources. Such an approach touches on reconstruction and peacebuilding as well as development (Farhadi 2008). The following case studies reveal how local power dynamics can fuel conflict and frustration related to water resource man-agement efforts led by the national government.

Water management in Kunduz Province

Research on the Kunduz River Basin Programme (KRBP) offers insights into Afghanistan's domestic water supply and irrigation sectors, both of which are critical components a strong peacebuilding strategy (Shah 2009; Abdullayev et al. 2009). The KRBP is also a further example of an intervention that does not adequately integrate the structures and mechanisms of the social landscape that shape access to water in the target area. The weaknesses of the approach employed in the KRBP can thus be said to mirror those of the NSP—neither project realizes its objectives of improving resource availability and equitable access at the com-munity level.

The river basin management approach used in the KRBP is based on the establishment of water user associations (WUAs) at the community level. The WUAs liaise with provincial governments' water management departments and their district-level officers. The water management departments report to the Ministry for Energy and Water at the central level. The KRBP is the authority at the river-basin level, with a mandate that crosses provincial and district boundaries. Its role is to formulate a basin management plan, undertake infrastructure im-provements, regenerate upper watersheds, strengthen regional Ministry for Energy

---

[9]   Personal communication, June 2009.

Water resource management in northern Afghanistan 199

and Water offices, and improve water-use efficiency through community-based management and attention to the social aspects of water management (Shah 2009).

According to Shah, the KRBP project had so far failed to live up to its promises for a number of reasons (Shah 2009). To begin with, there was a lack of clarity about the mandates of two of the ministries involved: the Ministry of Energy and Water, and the Ministry of Agriculture, Animal Husbandry, and Food (now called the Ministry of Agriculture, Irrigation, and Livestock). Furthermore, the traditional mirab system was weakened during the conflict. Traditionally, there had been a single mirab from a community at the tail end of a canal who was charged with managing water along the entire length of the canal. However, social fragmentation that occurred during the conflict period resulted in the establishment of a separate mirab for each community. Coordination along the entire canal became more difficult than it had been before, and the KRBP did very little to address this conflict-related social development.

When the social organizers employed by the KRBP mobilized the WUAs, they typically interacted with and legitimized only larger farmers and other influential individuals, to the almost complete exclusion of smaller farmers and landless people. The project therefore reinforced existing social and financial hierarchies and inequities. Another problem was the considerable antipathy between the government and the international NGOs and other organizations running the KRBP. The international organizations controlled the resources for the projects, and the Afghan government departments were competing among themselves for a share of the finances. This led to obstructionist behavior, rather than facilitative roles for the relevant departments, further undermining the potential for building credibility with the local populace (Abdullayev et al. 2009; Shah 2009).

Water access and social marginalization in Faryab Province

In the course of research regarding the availability of water in rural areas and the impact of the NSP on villagers, McCarthy used participatory photography to understand the everyday lives of people in two villages in Faryab Province in northern Afghanistan, Lower Charvak and Khumsan.[10] Accounts from a couple and a young man in the two villages reinforce Shah's 2009 findings regarding the KRBP and further illustrate how local power relations and the idealistic

---

[10] Participatory photography is a research method in which participants use photographs to communicate their perceptions and experiences (Clover 2006; Crang and Cook 2007). After initial meetings in villages to recruit volunteers, McCarthy held workshops to familiarize participants with digital cameras, then left the cameras with them for one or two weeks so they could work in small groups to take photographs that communicated the most important issues in their lives. Lower Charvak, Khumsan, and Upper Charvak are fictitious names given to protect the research subjects profiled in this chapter, and they correspond to actual villages located approximately five to fifteen kilometers to the southeast of Meymaneh.

200 Water and post-conflict peacebuilding

institutional design of the NSP have sometimes impeded meaningful improvement in access to water resources for economically or socially marginalized households in rural Afghanistan.

The research for these case studies was conducted over five months in 2008 and 2009. Group discussions about the villagers' photographs provided the bulk of data from which the main findings were drawn. The two villages had been participating in the NSP since 2003. Each has between sixty and eighty households and is situated less than ten kilometers from the provincial capital of Meymaneh. A mix of agriculture, livestock raising, teaching, and manual labor constitutes the majority of livelihoods in these villages. As is typical in Faryab Province, many households in these villages have a subsistence lifestyle; villagers depend upon what food they can grow and must barter goods or borrow money to meet their remaining needs.

Rural Afghanistan is full of female-headed households and members of ethnic minority groups who, for assorted reasons, are marginalized within the rural society. Despite the presence of the CDC, a supposedly representative body, power dynamics have prevented some of the most marginalized families from accessing water. Because of this, their livelihoods have faltered, and these rural Afghans have been frustrated with the development process and with the government of Afghanistan, which is responsible for managing the implementation of the NSP. The first of the two stories, focusing on Lower Charvak village, illustrates how the process of marginalization and exclusion plays out and how, within the participatory model, powerful elements that cause marginalization can use the idealized participatory structure of the CDCs.

Lower Charvak is the second largest of the three villages that make up the NSP community of Khumsan/Charvak.[11] It is nearly one kilometer off the main road, on the banks of the Meymaneh River. The Meymaneh was almost entirely dry from 2004 to 2009, and then the river reached its highest level in twenty years and threatened to flood the lower part of the village, according to village residents. Lower Charvak has worked with the other two villages in the community to implement three NSP projects, which include graveling roads, carpet weaving, and digging shallow wells for drinking water. Of these, Lower Charvak received one shallow well and graveled part of the main road through the village.

Seema's story

Seema, a Tadjik mother of three in a landless family living in Lower Charvak, and her husband, an Uzbek, are estranged from their extended family.[12] They are

---

[11] Charvak village is actually two separate villages, Lower Charvak and Upper Charvak. However, in the NSP documentation they are considered to be only one village that shares a CDC with Khumsan. The authors were unable to ascertain why the two villages were not kept separate in the program documentation.

[12] The names of the case study subjects and their villages have been changed to protect their identities.

tenants of the garden that is the main source of livelihood for them. As payment for the use of the land, they must relinquish half of the garden's yield. They feel a significant amount of financial pressure because they are responsible for purchasing all the seed, water, and fertilizer to be used on the land. If there is no yield, the landowner demands financial compensation in lieu of the expected food, a demand that has resulted in the swift accumulation of debt.

Access to water is obviously vital in such a situation. The lack of water during the 2008 growing season meant that the cost of irrigation was very high. Seema and her husband access irrigation water from a stream that is controlled by a mirab. Five or six privately owned gardens are fed by this stream, and each owner must pay for using the water. The mirab determines which gardens are irrigated and at what time. During the five-year drought the price of this water climbed until it was out of reach for many of those whose livelihoods depend on gardens, including Seema and her husband.

Most of the plants and trees in Seema's garden died due to the couple's inability to pay for sufficient water in 2008, and the landowner demanded a payment of approximately US$60 in compensation. In addition to investing money in the garden and paying the penalty imposed on them by the landowner, Seema's family also had to rely entirely on food purchased from markets for most of that year.

In the 2009 growing season, Seema and her husband faced a different situation but similar stresses. The rains had returned and there was plenty of water in the stream for all the gardens, and thus the price of water was much more affordable.[13] However, Seema and her husband were still unable to pay for sufficient water due to outstanding loans from previous years. Even when they do pay for water, their supply can be interrupted because of a long-standing family conflict in which some family members manipulate the irrigation stream to prevent the water from reaching Seema's garden.

These events led Seema and her husband to dig a water storage hole. They took out a small loan to purchase an electric water pump and some piping, which they hid from sight during the day. Late at night during the summer months, when everyone else was sleeping, Seema and her husband woke up to direct some stream water into the storage hole. Once the hole had enough water, they lowered the water pump from the tree where it was hidden and pumped water from the hole to irrigate their garden.

The extent of this couple's vulnerability to water stress was related to their relative position of power in relation to their neighbors, extended family members, and landowners. These power dynamics were key elements in Seema's differential access to water even though the village was participating in the NSP and she supposedly had access to a representative development council.

---

[13] Elders in other villages in Faryab Province indicated that spring 2009 brought more rain than people had seen in twenty years.

202   Water and post-conflict peacebuilding

In an attempt to regain some control over her livelihood, Seema ran for deputy chair of the CDC's women's subcommittee in March 2009, and she won. However, the men's committee deputy chair refused to recognize her official position, and a number of other council members, including other female members, neglected to advise Seema about forthcoming CDC meetings. Though she was popular enough within the village to muster the majority of female votes, the NSP structure of electoral democracy was trumped by the preexisting power structures, and the results of the election were annulled to deny her the opportunity to have a formal voice in the community or a claim to benefits that accrued from NSP projects in the village.

Seema's story illustrates that although the NSP states that it aims to facilitate a representative voice and access to resources for Afghan women, it may not be effective in doing so (MRRD 2009). The degree to which marginalized women can exercise their agency to represent the concerns of fellow women is limited by male power holders.

It would be unreasonable to expect the NSP to confront and undo every local-level configuration of differential power and marginality. But it is reasonable to expect the program to identify these issues and to modify its interventions in individual communities accordingly. The insurgency in Afghanistan is carried out not by men belonging to traditional rural elites or the middle class, but by those belonging to the most marginalized segments of society. If the NSP cannot facilitate the most marginalized people's access to resources, then it has failed in one of the most elementary of its missions and perhaps even undermined the peacebuilding process.

Dennys and Zaman contend that the NSP draws on a formulaic approach to participatory development that was pioneered by Akhtar Hamid Khan in the Comilla District of Bangladesh in the 1950s and was subsequently taken up by the Aga Khan Foundation as a model of participatory development in its project areas across Asia and Africa (Dennys and Zaman 2009). This approach involves the establishment of elected community councils to manage development projects, but has been criticized for being based on an idealized conceptualization of "community" and for not anticipating or addressing the potential outcomes of coercive expressions of power within communities.

A more effective participatory intervention would not necessarily eliminate all power imbalances; there will always be injustices that the more vulnerable members of a community will need to overcome. However, with regard to water resource management, more meaningful participation in development planning and implementation could enable vulnerable people to gain a more powerful or representative voice in decision-making processes that affect their ability to pursue and achieve sustainable livelihoods. The imposition of structures of accountability in a context that is rife with existing prejudices and hierarchies is a risk with the NSP and can be a cause for concern (Escobar 1995; Peet and Hartwick 1999). However, it is a necessary risk if the aim is to enable the less powerful people in a village to exercise their agency in accessing resources.

Mohsen's story

Home to approximately one hundred families, Khumsan is the largest village in the Khumsan/Charvak community, and it is the closest to the provincial center of Meymaneh. Despite the presence of an NSP-funded shallow well, at the time of the study the village was still relying on a traditional water pool, or howz, for drinking water because the water of the NSP-funded well had high salinity levels and was not potable. The saline intrusion was most likely caused by a lack of precipitation, which prevented the aquifer from sufficiently recharging (Alim 2006).

Uncovered and fed by rainwater and an open stream, Khumsan's howz did not provide safe drinking water either, but villagers perceived the water as more palatable.[14] Mohsen, a local villager, explained that the contamination of their sole source of drinking water had a debilitating impact on the health and livelihoods of some families in the village due to increased incidence of waterborne diseases.

Research in other areas of Faryab indicates that children and elderly individuals are particularly susceptible to infection by the bacteria in contaminated water and many of them have chronic diarrhea (Petri et al. 2008; Walker et al. 2007). The availability of safe drinking water in all villages, including Khumsan, is of great importance to those whose livelihoods require them to remain healthy and strong enough to work.

The community was extremely frustrated with the failure of the government to provide safe drinking water, whether through the NSP or other means. In focus group discussions in Khumsan in May 2009, Mohsen explained that the CDC had approached the provincial governor about the problem: "All the time the people go to the government. . . . They say their problem but they didn't pay attention. They say, 'OK, we will try,' but they didn't pay attention."

Mohsen stated that people in Khumsan did not trust that the government or international agencies would be willing to work toward a solution for their water access problem. The international NGO that was acting as facilitating partner in Pashtun Kot District had visited and had seen the state of their drinking-water source, but nothing was done to rectify the situation. Even the body elected to represent the village and address such issues, the CDC, was not trying to solve the drinking water problem. In the May 2009 focus group discussion, Mohsen reported that members of the CDC believed that if they "trouble themselves and dig the well, [the water] will be salty," and they therefore preferred not to dig another well at all.

With exasperation, Mohsen further explained that if the government decided to dig a well, it would take five or six years to complete the task because of bureaucratic hurdles and systemic corruption. Those in Khumsan with whom

---

[14] This situation was occurring during a year when the rains had been the heaviest in approximately twenty years, according to village elders in this area. During years of severe drought, people from another village traveled to this howz to collect their drinking water as well.

204 Water and post-conflict peacebuilding

Mohsen spoke no longer trusted that their government would take action to address their water problems. They perceived the government as unwilling and unable to work through the NSP to provide them with sustainable access to safe water. Mohsen was scathing in his critique of how local and regional power structures within the Afghan government and the NSP worked against equal access to resources.

LESSONS AND RECOMMENDATIONS

This overview of water management issues in post-conflict Afghanistan suggests that the rescaling of water resource management to the local level across Afghanistan has not been without friction in the rural areas. The villagers' experiences recounted here are not unique to them, to their villages, or to their region. Although each NGO facilitates the NSP differently, and although each CDC operates differently, the NSP's operational framework and structure is common throughout Afghanistan, and key managerial and operational details are identical across all projects. Also, the severe water scarcity of the region studied is a widespread issue in the country. The findings of these case studies are symptomatic of how the Afghan peacebuilding strategy is failing to effectively engage local water resource management as a central element in moving toward a stable peace.

Government learning and action

In order for there to be substantial progress in the provision of equitable access to water for all Afghans, engagement with Afghan water users and decision makers needs to be at a much deeper level than it has been thus far, and commitments to international paradigms of water management and development need to be much less formulaic. A key structural weakness of the NSP is the foundational assumption that it would be implemented upon a social tabula rasa. It is true that conflict reconfigures social and institutional power relations, but it does not eliminate them. Therefore, a sound knowledge of the history of local and national developments leading to such a reconfigured social reality—one that incorporates thorough gender analysis—is key to the success of any reconstruction and peacebuilding effort.

Recognizing the potentially harmful impact of introducing a new power structure in Afghan villages is a vital first step in making gains in local water resource management. Using evidence from India and Pakistan, Nicholas Hildyard and colleagues, and Daanish Mustafa, respectively, discuss the futility of exercising participatory development without due attention to differential and gendered power structures at the village level (Hildyard et al. 2001; Mustafa 2002). Concrete action to address unequal and sometimes exploitative power relations, coupled with an enhanced understanding of current and pre-conflict local practices of water management in various provinces and districts, will enable more informed

Water resource management in northern Afghanistan 205

decision making by those who facilitate water resource management at the village level.

Local ownership of national peacebuilding strategies and activities

The institutional focus of development and governance interventions must shift in order for Afghanistan to move toward a stable peace. Village-level stakeholders can become effective water resource managers and can shape peacebuilding strategies through more effective processes of consultation and government learning. Peacebuilding analysts in Afghanistan strongly recommend building the capacity of local councils—including CDCs and the village-level decision-making groups called *shuras*, which existed before the NSP—in mediation, negotiation, and conflict resolution so they can resolve disputes peacefully and effectively (Dennys and Zaman 2009; Waldman 2008).

Contextually informed mediation of water-related conflict could be a useful first step in ensuring that decision-making and management authority is not further skewed in the direction of power holders—either those from the conflict period or those in power at present. Care must be taken to prevent a depoliticized conceptualization of peacebuilding from taking hold at the policy level. As Jonathan Goodhand and Mark Sedra argue, working toward an ideal of peace that is not infused with Afghan politics at various scales "succeeds in reducing the opportunity for alternative or indigenous approaches to reconstruction. As a result, donors and a narrow clique of Afghans 'own' the bureaucratic façade of reforms, while real ownership is exerted by local power holders, leading to very different outcomes from those intended" (Goodhand and Sedra 2010, 97).

Government legitimacy

An Afghan government that is aware of the relationship between water resource management and peacebuilding initiatives at the local level and that takes steps to afford Afghan citizens greater ownership of peacebuilding strategies is more likely to hold greater legitimacy in the eyes of its citizenry. Finding a balance between top-down, national-level interventions and bottom-up, village-level participation is a challenging task in the best of circumstances, and certainly seems a tall order in a complex and deeply troubled context such as Afghanistan. However, a government that is accountable to its citizens must recognize the challenges they face with regard to water resource management and must resolve to take concrete action and commit to real progress toward equitable and sustainable access to water for all of its citizens.

Another stumbling block along the road to government legitimacy relates to the role of international NGOs in the funding and implementation of water management interventions. Because these organizations have a relatively large wealth of human and other resources compared to the Afghan government departments, tensions can arise between them and with the populace (Ghani,

206   Water and post-conflict peacebuilding

Carnahan, and Lockhart 2005; Goodhand and Sedra 2010; Howell and Lind 2008). Salaries are sometimes as much as twenty times higher for employees of international organizations than for civil servants, so the international organizations draw in many highly skilled staff, leaving the government with a lack of professional human resources (Howell and Lind 2008).

Achieving improvements in water resource management is as much a social process as a physical one, so professionals with skills in facilitation, conflict resolution, and mediation also play an important part in the realization of peacebuilding objectives related to water (Goodhand and Sedra 2006). If, as some research argues, peacebuilding efforts in Afghanistan need to be national rather than international, as well as legitimate, the necessary human resources must be accessible to the national institutions involved (Goodhand and Sedra 2006; Suhrke et al. 2002; Suhrke, Harpviken, and Strand 2002).

North Afghanistan: Struggling to move on from a legacy of conflict

The situation in Afghanistan continues to shift, with different regions experiencing varying degrees of conflict, post-conflict adjustment, and reconstruction and development activities (Donini 2007). Until mid-2009, Faryab Province seemed to be quickly moving on from a legacy of conflict. Peacebuilding objectives, including much work in water resource management, were incorporated into development interventions, and in most districts continuing armed conflict was sporadic rather than systemic.[15] However, it became clear during late 2009 that these interventions were not sufficient to prevent the growth of the Taliban in Faryab. An NGO staff member explained to the authors that young Uzbek men throughout the province were being lured into Taliban forces by a monthly salary of US$300.[16] Persisting poverty and vulnerability seem to be a contributing factor to the spread of the Taliban in Faryab. If this is so, then in order to prevent further expansion of the Taliban in the province, development interventions such as the NSP need to be more effective in enabling people to access and control the resources necessary for meeting their basic needs and generating income.

An engineer working for an NGO in Faryab explained to the authors in August 2010 that Taliban advances from the western provinces had begun to impede progress in reconstruction, with attacks against government authorities and attacks against and kidnapping of NGO staff working in the villages. These

---

[15]   The exception here is Ghormach District, which was formerly within Badghis Province. When the district became part of Faryab Province in 2008, it carried with it a growing Taliban presence that has since spread across most other southern districts of the province.

[16]   Personal communication, August 11, 2010; see also Giustozzi and Reuter (2010).

actions undermine the peacebuilding processes implemented in Faryab Province to date and also raise concerns about the future of any improvements in water resource management that may facilitate those processes. Growing insecurity will prevent government and nongovernmental institutions from carrying out further work on improving water resources and their management.

CONCLUSION

Afghanistan has suffered a host of local governance distortions as a result of three decades of conflict. The enhanced power of former warlords, breakdown of the traditional moderating influence of communities, and greater interethnic resentment all contribute to the political and social challenges facing the country. Ultimately the issue of differential power and its effects in the water sector cannot be ignored. CDCs and water user associations (WUAs) will not be able to deliver sufficient, safe water to the vast majority of poor and disenfranchised Afghans if they continue to represent only the rural elites. Interventions such as the NSP and the KRBP need to provide the necessary space for learning, growth, and change so CDCs and WUAs can more effectively address inequities experienced by rural Afghans.

Beyond functioning as a simple conduit for disbursement of international development aid and a testing ground for Western peacebuilding paradigms, the CDCs and WUAs could appropriate institutional vehicles for addressing the anomalies and distortions that have crept into the Afghan body politic during thirty years of conflict. Different relations between the international community and the Afghan government, and between the Afghan government and its people, based on mutual respect, willingness to admit mistakes, and a commitment to undoing the perverse legacies of the conflict in Afghan society are essential for movement toward relevant and responsive water management mechanisms within Afghanistan's larger peacebuilding project.

REFERENCES

Abdullayev, I., K. Mielke, P. P. Mollinga, J. Monsees, C. Schetter, U. Shah, and B. Ter Steege. 2009. Water, war and reconstruction irrigation management in the Kunduz region, Afghanistan. In *Water, environmental security and sustainable rural development: Conflict and cooperation in Central Eurasia*, ed. M. Arsel and M. Spoor. New York: Routledge.

Alim, A. K. 2006. Sustainability of water resources in Afghanistan. *Journal of Developments in Sustainable Agriculture* 1:53–66.

Barakat, S. 2002. Setting the scene for Afghanistan's reconstruction: The challenges and critical dilemmas. *Third World Quarterly* 23 (5): 801–816.

Barfield, T. 2007. Weapons of the not so weak in Afghanistan: Pashtun agrarian structure and tribal organization for times of war and peace. Hinterlands, Frontiers, Cities, and States: Transactions and Identities, Agrarian Studies Colloquium Series. New Haven, CT: Yale University.

208   Water and post-conflict peacebuilding

Clover, D. E. 2006. Out of the dark room: Participatory photography as a critical, imaginative, and public aesthetic practice of transformative education. *Journal of Transformative Education* 4 (3): 275–290.

Cosgrove, D., and G. Petts. 1990. *Water, engineering and landscape: Water control and landscape transformation in the modern period.* London: Belhaven.

Crang, M., and I. Cook. 2007. *Doing ethnographies.* London: Sage Publications.

Dennys, C., and I. Zaman. 2009. Trends in local Afghan conflicts: Synthesis paper. Kabul, Afghanistan: Cooperation for Peace and Unity.

Donini, A. 2007. Local perceptions of assistance to Afghanistan. *International Peacekeeping* 14 (1): 158–172.

Dupree, L. 1975. Settlement and migration patterns in Afghanistan: A tentative statement. *Modern Asian Studies* 9 (3): 397–413.

Escobar, A. 1995. *Encountering development: The making and unmaking of the Third World.* Princeton, NJ: Princeton University Press.

Farhadi, A. 2008. Afghanistan National Development Strategy 1387–1391 (2008–2013): A strategy for security, governance, economic growth, and poverty reduction. Kabul.

Ghani, A., M. Carnahan, and C. Lockhart. 2005. Stability, state-building and development assistance: An outside perspective. Working paper, Princeton Project on National Security. Princeton, NJ: Princeton University.

Gilmartin, D. 1994. Scientific empire and imperial science: Colonialism and irrigation technology in the Indus Basin. *Journal of Asian Studies* 53 (4): 1127–1149.

Giustozzi, A., and C. Reuter. 2010. The Northern Front: The Afghan insurgency spreading beyond the Pashtuns. Afghanistan Analysts Network Briefing Paper No. 3. Kabul: Afghanistan Analysts Network.

Goodhand, J., and M. Sedra. 2006. *Bargains for peace? Aid, conditionalities and reconstruction in Afghanistan.* The Hague: Netherlands Institute of International Relations.

———. 2010. Who owns the peace? Aid, reconstruction, and peacebuilding in Afghanistan. *Disasters* 34 (1): S78–S102.

Hildyard, N., P. Hegde, P. Wolvekamp, and S. Reddy. 2001. Pluralism, participation, and power: Joint forest management in India. In *Participation: The new tyranny?* ed. B. Cooke and U. Kothari. London: Zed Books.

Hirsch, P., and A. Wyatt. 2004. Negotiating local livelihoods: Scales of conflict in the Se San River Basin. *Asia Pacific Viewpoint* 45 (1): 51–68.

Howell, J., and J. Lind. 2008. Civil society with guns is not civil society: Aid, security, and civil society in Afghanistan. NGPA Working Paper No. 24. London: London School of Economics and Political Science.

Kakar, H. K. 1979. *Government and society in Afghanistan: The reign of Amir ‘Abd al-Rahman Khan.* Austin: University of Texas Press.

Lahiri-Dutt, K. 2003. People, power and rivers: Experiences from the Damodar River, India. *Water Nepal* 9/10 (1/2): 251–267.

McCarthy, J. A. 2011. *Reframing knowledges of participatory development and livelihoods in Afghanistan's rural north: A power analysis to understand complex realities of vulnerability.* London: I.B. Tauris Academic Studies.

Mielke, K., and C. Schetter. 2007. "Where is the village?" Local perceptions and development approaches in Kunduz Province. *Asien* 104:71–87.

Montgomery, J. D., and D. A. Rondinelli. 2004. Introduction. In *Beyond reconstruction in Afghanistan: Lessons from development experience,* ed. J. D. Montgomery and D. A. Rondinelli. New York: Palgrave Macmillan.

Water resource management in northern Afghanistan 209

MRRD (Ministry for Rural Rehabilitation and Development, Islamic Republic of Afghanistan). 2009. *National Solidarity Programme (NSP) operational manual.* Kabul, Afghanistan.

Mustafa, D. 2002. To each according to his power? Participation, access, and vulnerability in irrigation and flood management in Pakistan. *Environment and Planning D: Society and Space* 20 (6): 737–752.

Pain, A. 2004. Understanding village institutions: Cases studies on water management from Faryab and Saripul. Case Studies Series: Afghanistan Research and Evaluation Unit. http://ageconsearch.umn.edu/handle/14639.

Paris, R. 2004. *At war's end: Building peace after civil conflict.* Cambridge, UK: Cambridge University Press.

Peacebuilding Initiative. 2008. History. http://peacebuildinginitiative.org/index.cfm?pageId=1764.

Peet, R., and E. R. Hartwick. 1999. *Theories of development.* New York: Guilford.

Petri, W. A., J. M. Miller, H. J. Binder, M. M. Levine, R. Dillingham, R. L. Guerrant. 2008. Enteric infections, diarrhea, and their impact on function and development. *Journal of Clinical Investigation* 118 (4): 1277–1290.

Rubin, B. R. 2006. Peace building and state-building in Afghanistan: Constructing sovereignty for whose security? *Third World Quarterly* 27 (1): 175–185.

Shah, U. 2009. Bringing order to the jangal: State building, social change, and international intervention in Afghanistan's Kunduz River Basin. MA Thesis, School of Geography and Environmental Science, Monash University, Melbourne, Australia.

Sneddon, C. 2002. Water conflicts and river basins: The contradictions of comanagement and scale in northeast Thailand. *Society and Natural Resources* 15 (8): 725–741.

Suhrke, A., K. B. Harpviken, A. Knudsen, A. Ofstad, and A. Strand. 2002. *Peacebuilding: Lessons for Afghanistan.* Bergen, Norway: Chr. Michelsen Institute.

Suhrke, A., K. B. Harpviken, and A. Strand. 2002. After Bonn: Conflictual peace building. *Third World Quarterly* 23 (5): 875–891.

Swyngedouw, E. 1999. Modernity and hybridity: Nature, "regeneracionismo", and the production of the Spanish waterscape, 1890–1930. *Annals of the Association of American Geographers* 89 (3): 443–465.

Waldman, M. 2008. Community peacebuilding in Afghanistan: The case for a national strategy. Oxfam Research Report. Kabul, Afghanistan: Oxfam International. www.oxfam.de/files/20080228_communitypeacebuildinginafghanistan_359kb.pdf.

Walker, S. P., T. D. Wachs, J. M. Gardner, B. Lozoff, G. A. Wasserman, E. Pollitt, J. A. Carter, and International Child Development Steering Group. 2007. Child development: Risk factors for adverse outcomes in developing countries. *Lancet* 369 (9556): 145–157.

World Bank. 2010. Afghanistan country overview 2010. Washington, D.C.

Water's role in measuring security and stability in Helmand Province, Afghanistan

Laura Jean Palmer-Moloney

Clear. Hold. Build. According to counterinsurgency (COIN) doctrine employed in Operation Enduring Freedom by the International Security Assistance Force (ISAF) in Afghanistan, these operational stages lead to the security, stability, and sustainable economic growth necessary for building peace.[1] The application of COIN doctrine has temporal and spatial dimensions depending on the operational environment—ranging from relatively simple tactical decisions and actions to more complex strategic planning. In Afghanistan, such operations range from close personal dialogue between soldiers, marines, the civilian workforce, and local Afghan leaders to collaboration involving ISAF, U.S. government agencies (such as the Department of Defense, Department of State, Agency for International Development, and Department of Agriculture), and the government of the Islamic Republic of Afghanistan (GOIRA). From a U.S. military perspective, COIN operations are population-centric by design and demand action different from traditional "kinetic" military response (Flynn, Pottinger, and Batchelor 2010; Petreaus 2010; USACAC n.d.).

Despite the irreversible trajectory implied by the phases of COIN operations, Clear does not always lead to Hold, nor Hold to Build, as the ebb and flow of the post-conflict period in Helmand Province illustrate. Helmand is part

---

Laura Jean Palmer-Moloney works with the U.S. Army Corps of Engineers Engineer Research and Development Center in Alexandria, Virginia. She is a senior research geographer and serves as the principal investigator of the Civil-Military Operations–Human Environment Interaction research team.

[1] According to the counterinsurgency field manual (U.S. DOD 2009), a counterinsurgency (COIN) operation typically includes the following phases:
(1) Clear: Create a secure physical and psychological environment.
(2) Hold: Establish firm (host nation) government control of the populace and area, and gain the populace's support.
(3) Build: Progress in building support for the host nation government requires protecting the local populace. People who do not believe they are secure from insurgent intimidation, coercion, and reprisals will not risk overtly supporting COIN efforts. The populace decides when it feels secure enough to support COIN efforts.

212   Water and post-conflict peacebuilding

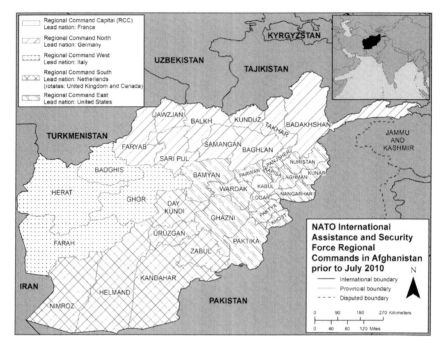

Figure 1. Regional command and control in Afghanistan prior to July 2010
Source: ISAF (2010b).

of Afghanistan's Taliban stronghold and was originally one of the six provinces comprising Regional Command (RC) South (see figure 1). As of July 2010, Helmand became one of the two provinces comprising RC Southwest (see figure 2).[2]

Since December 2009, ISAF has worked to oust the Taliban from areas determined to be the province's key districts. Water's significance in the economic development of Helmand is understood and clearly linked to numerous ISAF and U.S. government interagency activities. However, water's significance in near-term COIN operations and as a "proxy observable" (that is, indicator) to measure COIN operational success is underappreciated, if it is considered at all. The purpose of this chapter is to assess the role of water in peacebuilding, cooperation, and confidence building in the early phases of COIN operations when security and stability are not guaranteed.

---

[2] As part of the ISAF design, the regional commands in Afghanistan coordinate regional civil-military activities conducted by the military elements of the provincial reconstruction teams. In May 2010, the North Atlantic Council of the North Atlantic Treaty Organization gave the go-ahead for the reorganization of Regional Command (RC) South into RC South and RC Southwest. Since July 2010, RC South has included Uruzgan, Zabul, Day Kundi, and Kandahar provinces, and RC Southwest has included only Helmand and Nimroz provinces.

Water, security, and stability in Helmand Province 213

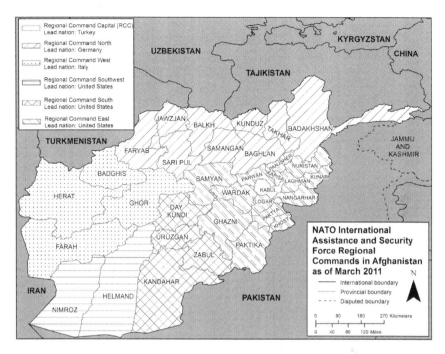

Figure 2. Separation of Regional Command (RC) South into RC South and RC Southwest
Source: ISAF (2011).

The chapter focuses on Helmand Province from summer 2009 to autumn 2010, just before and during the U.S. military surge of forces. During this time, efforts to consolidate peacebuilding were linked to three overarching areas—security, governance, and development. Yet in the midst of peacebuilding, for many, the conflict was still ongoing. This chapter highlights the fragility, instability, insecurity, and violence that characterize many post-conflict areas. Though Afghanistan (and Iraq) pose unique cases, as long as the U.S. military uses COIN doctrine, the type of war fought there may increasingly become the norm: militaries and their contractors may undertake work that was once delegated to humanitarians. This chapter provides insight into some of the challenges faced when traditional roles become blurred and change to fit this new paradigm.[3]

BACKGROUND

The Bonn Agreement, signed in December 2001, created a framework for the transition of Afghanistan from Taliban rule to a new Afghan national government and effectively began Afghanistan's post-conflict period. Delegates at the United

---

[3] For an analysis of civil-military activities broadly, see Civic (2014).

214   Water and post-conflict peacebuilding

Nations–sponsored event in Germany did not address the country's natural resource base or natural resource management issues. Seven years later, the Afghan National Development Strategy, 2008–2013 (GOIRA 2008),[4] which outlined the country's reconstruction goals (security, governance, economic growth, and poverty reduction), did not address natural resources or resource management (U.S. GAO 2010). Though the Water Strategy for Afghanistan, 2009–2014 links water to the Afghan National Development Strategy's reconstruction goals, most decision makers fail to appreciate water's importance to near-term governance, security, and development success in Afghanistan (USG 2010).

Water is one of Afghanistan's most important resources. But the unequal distribution of water leads to regional loss of livelihoods and population displacement. As archaeological and historical records show, the country's unequal distribution of water has created what may be termed "environmental refugees" and internally displaced persons as affected populations move in search of basic needs during times of drought and severe flooding (Adamec 1973; Breshna 1988; Whitney 2006). Unequal distribution of potable water can be seen in the economic disparities of Afghanistan's population. Generally speaking, densely populated urban centers, such as Herat, Lashkar Gah, Kandahar, and Mazari-Sharif, are relatively wealthy and are populated by people whose most basic needs are met to some degree.

But in Afghanistan's relatively poor rural areas and in the country's informal urban squatter settlements, where essential services are often lacking, people may not have access to potable water, one of the most fundamental human needs (USAID 2010). In these poor, underserved areas, Afghanistan's insurgents have had the most influence (Gallup 2009).

In September and October 2009, Gallup conducted a survey in ISAF's key terrain areas, including accessible districts of Helmand Province. Local Afghans, trained to conduct the survey, questioned individuals to determine the population's view of the job market, standard of living, and perceptions of the strength and momentum of the local and national economies. The Gallup research showed that individuals in Helmand Province who regarded the Taliban positively had a much more pessimistic opinion of the country's condition. Though safety and security topped their list of concerns, access to health care, trash collection, and potable water were also significant (Gallup 2009).

The Gallup research revealed two types of insurgents, differentiated as Type One and Type Two. Type One insurgents are ideologically based, elitist, intolerant, lack confidence in government, thrive in areas where hardship or

---

[4] The Afghan National Development Strategy, 2008–2013 was replaced in 2010 by the Afghan National Development Strategy: Prioritization and Implementation Plan, 2010–2013 (GOIRA 2010). Both water resources and general natural resource management are mentioned in the newer document. However, for nine years (2001–2010), natural resource management was not addressed.

Water, security, and stability in Helmand Province   215

concern for safety exists, and are not demographically distinct. Type Two insurgents search for leaders, accept violence, seek gains in economic and social status, and view themselves as victims. Some are heads of households trying to support families, and some are young men who want to prove themselves to their communities as they come of age.

Gallup's findings can be linked to water's role in post-conflict peacebuilding in Helmand. If there is hardship or illness caused by lack of water or poor water quality, the environmental circumstances could give Type One insurgents an opportunity to sway the affected population to their side. Lack of potable water could also reinforce Type Two insurgents' feelings of victimization and further limit their livelihoods and alternatives.

Water resource management unites the ISAF and GOIRA through diplomacy and development. As noted in the Water Strategy for Afghanistan, 2009–2014, water is essential for the country's development and has "a dramatic and every day effect on agricultural productivity, economic growth, health, education, quality of life, and political and social stability" (USG 2010, 3). Water must move beyond resource management if it is to advance post-conflict peacebuilding efforts in Helmand Province. Knowledge of district and provincial water complexities is needed to gain a rich contextual insight into the area's security and stability. *Water complexities*, as used here, relate to intricacies that must be understood in order to critique water's role in a given area of interest. The intricacies, or characteristics, are water supply, water quality, water availability, and water accessibility (see table 1). All are interrelated: changes in any one characteristic often affect the others, and all are linked to security and stability in peacebuilding.

By 2009, the civilian and military leaders of ISAF realized that successful COIN operations must include positive interaction with the local population in the Hold and early Build phases of an engagement. As 2010 drew to a close, water-complexity questions were just beginning to be used to analyze security and stability situations in areas of interest (Palmer-Moloney et al. 2010).

Table 1.   Water complexity definitions

Characteristic	Definition
Supply	The quantity of water necessary for a variety of uses.
Quality	The chemical, physical, and biological characteristics of water, usually with respect to its suitability for the variety of uses.
Availability	The capability of the water source to meet the variety of uses.
Accessibility	The socio-cultural and transaction cost (time, distance, money) of acquiring water supply, for example, ability of community to travel spatially and temporally as well as percentage of monies spent.

Source: Palmer-Moloney et al. (2010).
Note: Each definition is subject to spatial-temporal variability.

THE GEOGRAPHIC SPACE

Helmand Province is located in southwestern Afghanistan and shares a border with Pakistan. Except for the mountainous northern reaches of the province, which receive snow, Helmand is a plateau with rocky outcroppings averaging 1,000 meters in elevation with steppe and desert climate zones.

The Helmand River drains approximately 40 percent of the country (Whitney 2006), and snowmelt in the upper reaches of the watershed supplies the river with most of its water (see figure 3 for location of Helmand River watershed). In a normal hydrological year, the Helmand River flows at its fullest between March and June, but the river system has experienced dramatic declines in flows in recent years (Chirico 2009). Satellite data show that, on May 9, 2010, the snow water–equivalent volume of the Helmand watershed was below normal compared to volumes during the twenty-two-year period of 1987–2009, confirming that drier than average conditions prevail.[5]

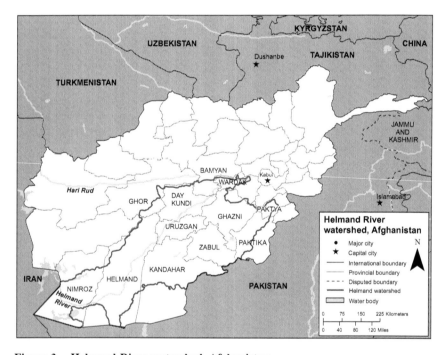

Figure 3. Helmand River watershed, Afghanistan
Source: Adapted from base map of Helmand watershed provided by U.S. Army Corps of Engineers, Army Geospatial Center.

---

[5] U.S. Army Geospatial Center's Hydrologic Analysis Team (AGC-HAT), personal communication, October 20, 2010.

Water, security, and stability in Helmand Province   217

Because of drought conditions and poor water management practices, the amount of available surface water in the system remains below normal.[6] Field reports and remote-sensing analysis indicate an increase in the number of groundwater wells dug for water consumption and irrigation since 1998 (USAGC 2009).

Generally, when studying a watershed, the presence or absence of surface water and the location of wells can be seen and mapped using traditional field methods and remote sensing–image techniques. The amount of surface water in the system can be quantified relatively quickly using any number of measuring devices in field or geospatial modeling–image analysis. But the quality of water is more challenging to gauge because of the numerous physical, chemical, and biological factors considered and because the tests are more labor and time intensive.[7]

Poor water quality is a problem across Afghanistan (Berkley 2010; Bonventre 2010), and most concerns relate to bacterial contamination caused by untreated wastewater and high levels of dissolved solids. Bacterial contamination in Afghanistan is particularly vexing because wastewater treatment is almost nonexistent. The shallow wells commonly used in villages access water from the unconfined water-table aquifer, which may be contaminated by wastewater leaching from the surface.[8]

Today, most of the information available on the quantity and quality of well water from villages in Helmand Province is from nonscientific observations or ad hoc testing.[9] The limited available scientific data substantiate anecdotal reports that water drawn from the unconfined water-table aquifer is contaminated not only with bacteria but also with a high concentration of dissolved salts. According to a 2002 report from the U.S. Army Corps of Engineers, well water with values above 1,500 milligrams per liter (mg/L) total dissolved solids can be expected in many parts of Helmand Province,[10] in marked contrast to the mid-1970s when the area was known for its fresh, sweet well water (USAGC 2002; see figure 4).

---

[6]   S. R. Kikkeri, environmental program manager, Trans-Atlantic Division of the U.S. AGC-HAT, personal communication, October 20, 2010.

[7]   The physical, chemical, and biological characteristics of water quality include temperature, pH, turbidity, total dissolved solids, and presence or absence of microbes, as well as color, taste, and odor.

[8]   An aquifer is a rock unit that will yield water in a usable quantity to a well or spring. (In geologic usage, *rock* includes unconsolidated sediments.) Where water only partly fills an aquifer, the upper surface of the saturated zone is free to rise and decline. The water in such aquifers is said to be unconfined, and the aquifers are referred to as *unconfined aquifers*, or *water-table aquifers*. Unconsolidated deposits important in groundwater hydrology include, in order of increasing grain size, clay, silt, sand, and gravel (Heath 2004). Surface water and shallow groundwater are prone to exhibit poor quality. Generally, groundwater from deep wells in confined aquifers is free from disease-causing microorganisms.

[9]   S. R. Kikkeri, personal communication, October 20, 2010.

[10]   Water is considered fresh if the concentration of dissolved solids is less than 1,500 mg/L, brackish if between 1,500 and 15,000 mg/L, and saline if greater than 15,000 mg/L.

218 Water and post-conflict peacebuilding

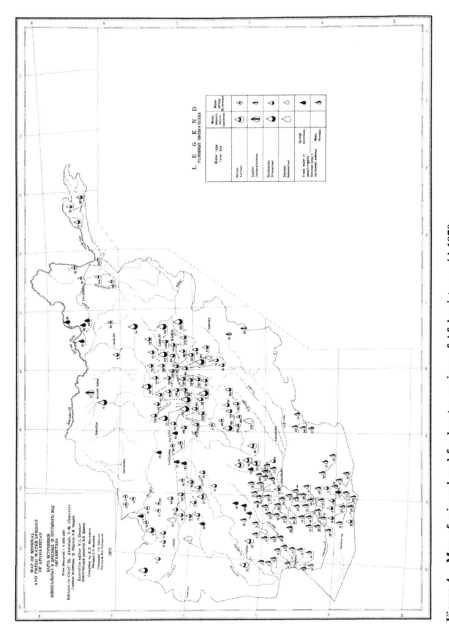

Figure 4. Map of mineral and freshwater springs of Afghanistan, mid-1970s
Source: Abdullah and Chmyriov (1977), reprinted with permission from East View Geospatial, Inc.

Water, security, and stability in Helmand Province 219

For Helmand Province, there is no comprehensive record of the number of wells that have been dug or drilled; no documentation of changes in the water table over time; and, at the time of writing, no scientific, ongoing collection and sharing of groundwater-quality data. Hand-dug wells require no permits, and there are hundreds of hand-dug wells—some producing potable water, some not producing any water at all.[11] High-capacity wells drilled by nongovernmental organizations (NGOs) and by ISAF contractors often pull water from local wells and frequently cause them to run dry. Across the study area, groundwater levels are dropping because of drought conditions and water withdrawn from aquifers that cannot be recharged quickly enough by the hydrological cycle.[12] Thus, groundwater is an unsustainable solution to water-scarcity problems.

HELMAND PROVINCE: POST-CONFLICT PEACEKEEPING IN THE MIDST OF A TROOP SURGE

In February 2010, ISAF and Afghan National Security forces began Operation Moshtarak in an effort to clear the Taliban from the region southwest of Lashkar Gah, the provincial capital of Helmand. The operation was supposed to be "the first blow in a decisive campaign to oust the Taliban from their spiritual homeland in adjacent Kandahar province, one that [General] McChrystal [commander of ISAF] had hoped would bring security and stability to Marjah and begin to convey an 'irreversible sense of momentum' in the U.S.-led campaign in Afghanistan" (Nissenbaum 2010). Still, "[t]here aren't enough U.S. and Afghan forces to provide the security that's needed to win the loyalty of wary locals. The Taliban have beheaded Afghans who cooperate with foreigners in a creeping intimidation campaign. The Afghan government hasn't dispatched enough local administrators or trained police to establish credible governance, and now the Taliban have begun their anticipated offensive" (Nissenbaum 2010). Whether the peace accord was signed in 2001 or not, reports by Dion Nissenbaum and others illustrate that, at the time of writing, those living in Helmand Province may challenge declarations that they are living in a post-conflict environment (Chandrasekaran 2010; Dominguez 2010).

Bringing water to the table: A Washington perspective

On July 2, 2009, the U.S. Marines launched Operation Khanjar in Helmand Province, and one month later, the U.S. Department of Defense initiated the Helmand Deep Dive research project. The goal of the project was to develop a "rich contextual understanding" of Helmand Province that could be used to

---

[11] U.S. AGC-HAT, personal communication, October 20, 2010; S. R. Kikkeri, personal communication, October 20, 2010.

[12] U.S. AGC-HAT, personal communication, October 20, 2010; S. R. Kikkeri, personal communication, October 20, 2010.

220 Water and post-conflict peacebuilding

strengthen and support COIN operations. From August 2009 to February 2010, experts from U.S. government agencies and academia worked with coalition forces in the field to answer fundamental questions about the operational environment and those individuals ISAF was trying to "protect and persuade" (Flynn, Pottinger, and Batchelor 2010). Originally, the research plan focused on human factors—behavioral psychology, sociology, cultural anthropology, history, economics, and political science—with no regard to human geography, water, or human-environment interactions. By the end of the research and reporting period, however, the briefings presented to the civilian and military decision makers laid out the significance of water to the security and stability of the region. This shift occurred as a result of the work done by an interagency geography and geoscience research team composed of scientists from the U.S. Army Corps of Engineers Engineer Research and Development Center (USACE-ERDC), in Alexandria, Virginia; the U.S. Geological Survey, in Reston, Virginia; and the U.S. Department of State Office of the Science and Technology Advisor to the Secretary. The interagency team joined Helmand Deep Dive in November 2009 (Palmer-Moloney et al. 2009).

The rapid turnaround time set for the Helmand Deep Dive, combined with travel constraints and the limited amount of data available, defined the research parameters. Nevertheless, the interagency research team was able to review and analyze archival records (written documents and aerial photography, circa 1950–1978), satellite images (1975–present), geospatial information collected by U.S. forces, and maps of the Helmand River watershed. Ground-level empirical work during the research timeframe was restricted because, for all intents and purposes, Helmand Province was at war.

The conclusions reached by the geography and geosciences research team are as follows:

- Water has a determinative impact on the drug trade, population movement, agriculture and livestock, energy, and public works in the region.
- Increases in economic activity, employment, and livelihood opportunities, which are critical to improving confidence in and popular support for the GOIRA, will most likely occur through agriculture. Humanitarian assistance supported by NGOs, the U.S. Agency for International Development (USAID), and ISAF require a reliable supply of water. Economic and assistance programs must be supported by investment and improvements in water infrastructure and sustainable watershed management.[13]
- Though many institutions (for example, NGOs, USAID, U.S. Military Command, and the international community) are involved in water projects in the province, there is no coordinated watershed management to monitor

---

[13] Helmand Province's water infrastructure was built with U.S. support (1950–1978), destroyed by the Soviets (1980s), and left in disrepair during the civil war and Taliban regime (1989–2001).

Water, security, and stability in Helmand Province 221

and assess water quantity and quality in the basin. There are innumerable ad hoc projects and little oversight of project effects and outcomes. Consequently, water sector projects upstream can divert water, adversely affecting downstream communities. High-capacity wells may draw water from smaller capacity wells, and overall withdrawal rates may be unsustainable.

- ISAF efforts to stabilize Afghanistan must balance near-term gains in agricultural production with the potential for increased transboundary conflicts over water and exhaustion of Afghanistan's water resources. Actions must focus on improving resource policy and management capacity and effectiveness, with special attention to increasing efficiency of water quantity and quality monitoring and assessment.[14]

- There is sparse, uncoordinated data collection on the depth of groundwater. In unconfined and confined aquifers, the water level is dropping as a result of drought and groundwater overdraft. In northern Helmand Province, the decrease is evidenced by the number of traditional *karez* wells that have run dry in recent years.[15] Augmenting reduced surface-water flow by tapping the unconfined water-table aquifer and withdrawing from the deeper, confined groundwater sources is not a sustainable alternative when the amount of withdrawal is greater than the rate of groundwater recharge. From environmental-security and population-stability perspectives, the recharge rates of the aquifers need to be established and monitored, and plans need to be in place for what to do if or when the wells run dry.

- There is no coordinated, cross-ministry, ongoing, watershed-scale water quality data collection and dissemination or analysis. Data about water quality are more difficult to come by than surface-water and groundwater supply data (Uhl 2003). Little information is found in the literature; most reporting is anecdotal. Water quality is fundamental to public health in the province. Those who collect, disseminate, and analyze water-quality data can support post-conflict peacebuilding by working with communities to build an environmental baseline, track water contamination, and examine the socio-cultural (power and control) factors and transaction costs (time, distance, and money) related to accessing potable water. Watershed-data collection and sharing are needed for integrated water resource management, which is part of the foundation for dialogue on and resolution of water issues.

---

[14] For a more complete discussion on this topic, see Alex Dehgan, Laura Jean Palmer-Moloney, and Mehdi Mirzaee, "Water Security and Scarcity: Potential Destabilization in Western Afghanistan and Iranian Sistan and Baluchestan Due to Transboundary Water Conflicts," in this book.

[15] A karez is a hand-dug water supply system (also known as *qanat*) common in arid regions of central and southwest Asia. It taps underground mountain-water trapped in and beneath the upper reaches of alluvial fans and channels the water downhill through a series of tunnels, often several kilometers long, to the places where it is needed for irrigation and domestic use.

222 Water and post-conflict peacebuilding

- Efforts need to be focused on gathering and disseminating accurate information on the current water budget (surface and groundwater demand versus available supply) of the Helmand watershed because *water cannot be managed if it cannot be measured.* At present, the only water data regularly collected in Afghanistan are on the Kabul River Basin,[16] which is located in northeastern Afghanistan and formed by the Paghman Mountains to the west and the Kohe Safi Mountains to the east.

Bringing water to the COIN operational environment: A perspective from Operation Enduring Freedom, Afghanistan

ISAF civilian and military commanders in Helmand Province have had difficulty finding measurements that can be used to determine the degree of success of COIN operations. As seen in the examples that follow, water can serve as a proxy observable to gauge headway (or lack thereof) in operations related to security, governance, and development.

Water and provincial reconstruction teams, civilian-military operations, and the Tactical Conflict Assessment and Planning Framework (TCAPF)

After the signing of the Bonn Agreement in 2001, provincial reconstruction teams (PRTs) of military civil affairs soldiers, National Guard members, and Afghan civilians were set up in key Afghan provinces. But the civilian-military effort was inconsistent, unplanned, and lacked overarching goals and strategic guidance for nearly nine years. Since COIN doctrine was adopted in Afghanistan in 2009, every PRT commander has been given a copy of the *Provincial Reconstruction Team (PRT) Handbook.* According to the guiding principles, a PRT should "[f]ocus upon improving stability by seeking to reduce the causes of instability, conflict, and insurgency while simultaneously increasing the local institutional capacity to handle these on their own" (ISAF 2010a, 4). Furthermore, a PRT must work to reduce the destabilizing threats and their underlying causes while building the capacity of local institutions to counteract the destabilizing causes with minimal ISAF support (ISAF 2010a). Water supply, quality, availability, and accessibility were not included as destabilizing threats, and civilians selected and sent to the PRT commands were not chosen because of their hydrology or water resource management skills (MRRD-NABDP n.d.; Leppert 2010).

By April 2010, the role of the Helmand PRT was understood—to support the GOIRA.[17] The PRT leaders were aware that the GOIRA was susceptible to appearing incompetent if the locals had unrealistic expectations regarding the

---

[16] V. Schneider, senior research scientist, International Water Unit, U.S. Geological Service, personal communication, June 30, 2010, and March 22, 2011.

[17] R. Donohoe, USAID agriculture program manager, Helmand Province, personal communication, April 19, 2010.

level of basic services the government was able to offer them. However, they were sure that the Afghan government could not afford to fail if called upon for dispute resolution pertaining to landownership and particularly issues involving water rights (USAID 2009). To address the PRT's goals and meet the expectations that came with COIN doctrine, the Helmand PRT encouraged use of a survey instrument developed by USAID to help determine local stability (Whittington 2009; Baranick and Wilkinson 2010; Montgomery 2010; U.S. MCCLL 2010). The Tactical Conflict Assessment and Planning Framework (TCAPF) tool was designed to help users understand complex situations from a people-centered perspective, recognize and target sources of instability, and determine ways to gain traction with local populations (Whittington 2009; Baranick and Wilkinson 2010; USAID 2010).

In 2009, a Marine Corps Civil Affairs Group was charged with taking TCAPF surveys of Helmand Province (Whittington 2009). They determined that in the rural countryside and squatter settlements of Lashkar Gah, most local Afghans' requests for assistance centered on water, with specific calls for digging wells and reconstructing canals to improve irrigation. Most appeals were for help acquiring potable water for consumption (Baranick and Wilkinson 2010) (see figure 5). As a result, wells have been dug and pumps installed, but the question

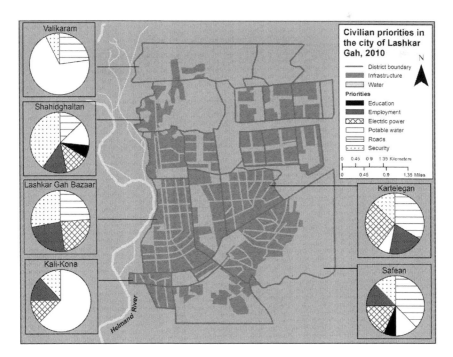

Figure 5. Civilian priorities in the city of Lashkar Gah, Afghanistan, 2010
Sources: USAID (2010); Baranick and Wilkinson (2010).

224 Water and post-conflict peacebuilding

remains: Did the response yield sustainable potable water for communities in need? Drilling wells in areas with dropping water tables requires digging ever deeper. Drilling deeper for water calls for money, as does the energy needed to pump water from deep wells, and money is a critical limitation for the people of Helmand Province.

Afghan Sustainable Water Supply and Sanitation project

The USAID-funded Afghan Sustainable Water Supply and Sanitation (SWSS) project is meant to assist national and local government agencies, PRTs, and other stakeholders in the design, installation, and operation of sustainable potable water systems, sanitation facilities, and hygiene-education programs. The goal of SWSS is to apply a holistic approach to providing clean drinking water and improved sanitation for communities in parallel with their engagement in Community-Led Total Sanitation (CLTS) interventions (USAID 2009). According to the USAID program description, CLTS will be carried out through a network of experienced NGOs mandated to provide the Afghan Basic Package of Health Services on the provincial and community levels.[18] SWSS's activities primarily focus on rural areas, but may reach urban areas. Because SWSS is a demand-driven mechanism, it serves no specific province or district.

Potable water supply and sanitation projects for consideration under SWSS are identified by the PRTs and USAID field program officers (FPOs), based upon the requests of the receiving populations. The FPOs work closely with the communities, local authorities, and other stakeholders in their areas of operation to identify and nominate subprojects, which can include education and awareness-raising activities.[19]

The main limitations to SWSS's success in Regional Command (RC) South and RC Southwest are procuring reliable construction subcontractors and the operation and maintenance follow-up to engage poor communities in the upkeep of their newly installed infrastructure. The restraints are directly related to the nonpermissive, insecure environment and the threat level for all those working with ISAF and GOIRA projects.[20]

As summer 2010 progressed, Taliban influence and control in many Helmand districts continued. Even with financial backing from USAID, SWSS had not moved into Helmand Province because of security concerns. In the meantime,

---

[18] More information on the Afghan Basic Package of Health Services can be found online on the Afghanistan Ministry of Public Health web site, www.msh.org/afghanistan/pdf/Afghanistan_BPHS_2005_1384.pdf, and on the USAID/Afghanistan web site, http://afghanistan.usaid.gov/en/USAID/Activity/125/Health_Services_Delivery_Grant_Partnership_Contracts_for_Health_PCH.

[19] G. Saleh, water program manager, USAID Afghanistan, personal communication, May 31, 2010.

[20] M. Gottlieb, program expert, USAID-contracted Afghan SWSS project, personal communication, May 31, 2010.

water needs continued to mount in the province's rural areas. "Tipping-point" communities wait for someone to deal with their water needs, and they may not have the patience to wait for SWSS/USAID and GOIRA to bring solutions. In the meantime, the Taliban do not have the capacity to step in and offer these services, although they can point out services GOIRA has failed to provide.

Water-sector proxy observables for ISAF Joint Command metrics

In the spring of 2010, to formulate metrics for the COIN effort, the ISAF Joint Command identified eleven key objectives. Among them were increasing the availability of essential services and improving agricultural development and productivity.[21] Water is a crosscutting resource that affects programs and projects of the PRTs, the ISAF Joint Command, and GOIRA national and subnational government entities (for example, the Ministry of Agriculture, Irrigation, and Livestock; the Ministry of Rural Rehabilitation and Development; the National Solidarity Programme; and the Community-Based Natural Resources Management Program). Water connects the COIN lines of operation, linking governance, development, and security.

By the fall of 2010, a growing number of policy makers and decision makers designing COIN metrics understood that water sector data (for example, water supply, quality, availability, and accessibility) could be used as tangible proxy observables to measure COIN operational progress. Though the ISAF Joint Command's intelligence center was briefed on the significance of water to short-term, midterm, and long-term success in Afghanistan, ISAF leaders in Helmand Province were captivated by higher-visibility items, such as increasing electricity supply in Kandahar. Though community leaders and GOIRA ministers were also anxious to expand the electric grid to support economic growth (Palmer-Moloney 2010; MRRD-NABDP n.d.), many communities in RC South and RC Southwest continued to live without reliable water supplies, potable water sources, and wastewater treatment.

As COIN doctrine drove operations in Afghanistan, the USACE-ERDC in Alexandria, Virginia, became involved in developing a methodology to examine the interaction of people and the environment at the cultural (human) and hydro-physical (watershed) local levels. The goals of the Civil-Military Operations–Human Environment Interaction (CMO-HEI) research are to address water issues specific to time, place, and culture and generate context-rich information for analysis and produce methodology and models that support actionable analysis for decision making. The CMO-HEI pilot program for Helmand Province was aimed at district-level analysis of water's relationship to environmental security and regional stability. To assist with community support and situation analysis, the CMO-HEI team developed a comprehensive list of questions on water

---

[21] Access to water is but one essential service. Others include electricity, transportation, communication, infrastructure, education, water and sewage treatment, and health care.

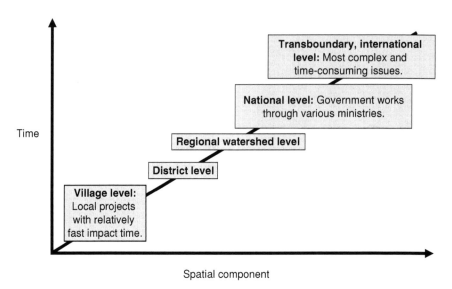

Figure 6. Spatial and temporal aspects of water complexity questions and answers
Source: Palmer-Moloney et al. (2009).
Note: At the national level, the government of the Islamic Republic of Afghanistan worked with the Independent Directorate of Local Governance; the Ministry of Agriculture, Irrigation, and Livestock; the Ministry of Energy and Water; the Ministry of Public Works; and the Ministry of Rural Rehabilitation and Development.

and a conceptual model that linked questions to ISAF goals, COIN metrics, and associated development indicators.

At the time of writing, the impact of the pilot program was yet to be determined. As of December 2010, the U.S. Marines in RC Southwest, U.S. Army National Guard Agribusiness Development teams in RC South, and the Kandahar City Water Project team were preparing to initiate water complexity–data collection. As ISAF commanders and Afghan government officials prepare to shift from ISAF to GOIRA lead in Afghanistan, answers to questions on water can be used to help determine district and province readiness for transition. Iterative use of the questions and answers can also support post-conflict peacebuilding by helping decision makers connect water complexities to local and regional security and stability (see figure 6).

IDENTIFIED CONSTRAINTS AFFECTING WATER AND PEACEBUILDING IN THE HELMAND BASIN

There are four identified constraints affecting water and peacebuilding in the Helmand Basin: weather variation and climate change–related uncertainties, unsustainable groundwater withdrawal, water contamination, and Helmand Province's insecure and nonpermissive environment.

Weather variation and climate change

Weather variation and climate change–related uncertainties will affect water quantity and quality in Helmand Province. For the ten-year period (1998–2008), Afghanistan was seriously affected by drought conditions, which led to critical shortages of surface water, falling groundwater tables, substantially below-average agricultural yields, and increased concentrations of contaminants in the available water supply. The drought destroyed fragile coping mechanisms in rural communities and, according to a report from the Danish Committee for Aid to Afghan Refugees (DACAAR 2002), it—at least temporarily—undermined many rehabilitation and development achievements of the past decade. Furthermore, hotter temperatures and lower water in the snowpack associated with regional climate change set back the region's food security, stability, and economic development water sector initiatives (LLNL 2009). Adaptive management techniques need to be incorporated so that affected plans and communities have a number of options for climate adaptation and information on which to base their decisions (UN 2010; USAID n.d.).

For surface-water management and natural resource planning, knowledge of the magnitude and time distribution of streamflow is essential. The agencies responsible for the development and management of Afghanistan's surface-water resources need these data for making environmentally sound water resource–planning decisions. Though the U.S. Geological Survey—in cooperation with USAID—computed streamflow statistics for data collected at historical gauging stations within the Helmand Basin, no consistent, reliable streamflow data have been collected since September 1980 (Williams-Sether 2008). During many of the years without records, Afghanistan and other countries of Central Asia were in the throes of a drought that devastated the natural environment.

Unsustainable groundwater withdrawal

The current rate of groundwater withdrawal is not sustainable. The last surface-water gauging of the Helmand Basin was in the late 1970s, before the Soviet invasion. As revealed through extensive research of historic records, there has never been a coordinated collection of data on groundwater levels or quality (Palmer-Moloney et al. 2009, 2010). Recent drought conditions in the Helmand Basin caused the unconfined groundwater table to drop. The drop has been compounded by ad hoc pumping projects implemented by NGOs and ISAF to supply water to communities in need.

DACAAR reports illustrate uncoordinated and possibly unsustainable groundwater solutions in Helmand Province (DACAAR n.d.). DACAAR involved communities in planning and maintenance of new wells, but because no one officially oversaw the water sector—demonstrating the governance vacuum in the country—there was no indication that DACAAR coordinated pump installations effectively with any public works office or any water resource–oversight

228 Water and post-conflict peacebuilding

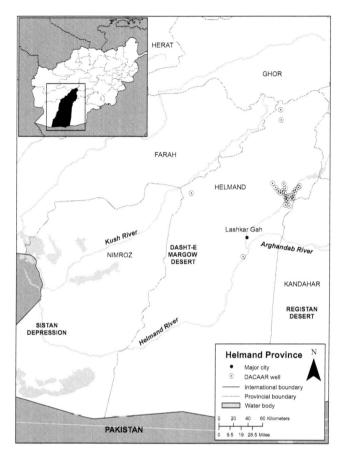

Figure 7. Location of wells monitored by the Danish Committee for Aid to Afghan Refugees in Helmand Province, Afghanistan
Source: DACAAR (n.d.).

group (DACAAR 2005, 2000, n.d.; see figure 7 for the locations of DACAAR-monitored wells). Although there are national laws in place to regulate well drilling and groundwater withdrawal, the control mechanisms are insufficient to require provinces to adhere to the laws.[22] As a result, neither Afghanistan nor the international community was able to manage these efforts, and groundwater extraction has continued in an unmanaged—and ultimately unsustainable—manner.

---

[22] North Atlantic Treaty Organization (NATO) officials and Afghan ministry officials, NATO System Analysis and Studies COIN metrics workshop, NC3A, The Hague, Netherlands, personal communication, December 6–10, 2010.

Water, security, and stability in Helmand Province **229**

The challenges of sustainably managing Afghanistan's groundwater are exacerbated by an ongoing drought, which has led to falling water tables and substantially below average agricultural yields.[23] The drought has destroyed fragile coping mechanisms in rural communities and temporarily undermined many of the achievements of the rehabilitation and development efforts during the past decade. As a result, assistance resources have had to be moved away from development programs into a comprehensive relief effort. The continuation of this drought could have significant impacts on the assistance strategies of humanitarian and development agencies. Digging a well does not guarantee water, and putting in wells with no watershed-level coordination or accountability can lead to tension and exponential complications.

Water contamination

Levels of surface and groundwater contamination must be monitored. Many wells are dug to yield a clean alternative to water from bacterially contaminated surface-water sources. However, shallow groundwater from unconfined aquifers is likely to be polluted due to lack of proper waste disposal and sewage treatment in the study area.

Insecure and nonpermissive environment of Helmand Province

As long as significant portions of Helmand Province are considered insecure and nonpermissive, water sector work will involve ISAF forces to some degree. The northern and eastern regions of Afghanistan are the most studied because of easy access and relatively secure conditions for water (quantity and quality) analysts. There must be a way to measure water quantity, quality, availability, and accessibility in RC South and RC Southwest so that water in Helmand Province can be managed.

LESSONS LEARNED: WATER'S WAY FORWARD IN HELMAND PROVINCE AND COIN OPERATIONS BEYOND AFGHANISTAN

In order for water to play a part in post-conflict peacebuilding, the following lessons from experiences in Helmand Province, Afghanistan, need to be addressed:

1. **Water cannot be managed if it cannot be measured.** Because of the paucity of available data on Helmand's surface water and groundwater resources, local and national officials lack data they need to make informed decisions

---

[23] Using limited available data, the U.S. Army Geospatial Center's Hydrologic Analysis Team determined that the water table in most of Helmand Province was dropping.

230 Water and post-conflict peacebuilding

about water supply and quality in Helmand Province. Scientific and authoritative stream-gauging stations and groundwater-observation wells are needed to determine the supply and quality of water in the watershed. These "authoritative" data must be complemented by "nonauthoritative," community-collected water information to gain a rich contextual understanding of water's relationship to security, stability, and peacebuilding in the region (Nicholson, Ryan, and Hodgkin 2002).

2. **Focus on water complexities rather than water resource management is required.** Water resource management is most often associated with infrastructure development. Though infrastructure development is linked to agricultural development and is critical to post-conflict peacebuilding, it misses the water quality, availability, and accessibility aspects of water complexities–resource management. Social-impact assessment is as consequential as water-resource assessment. A conflict-sensitive approach to analysis of water complexities in the post-conflict context can give insight into a region's environmental security and stability and can enhance options for using water management as a peacebuilding and reconstruction tool.

3. **Water's spatial and temporal aspects must be considered when accounting for water complexities.** From the local community level to national ministers and from weeks to years, the spatial and temporal circumstances of water-sector concerns must be considered.

4. **Data sharing is critical to post-conflict peacebuilding.** Data need to be collected and shared at the lowest level of security classification possible. The unclassified level best facilitates collaboration among all coalition forces and Afghan ministries, as well as local communities (Batson 2008). Data sharing continues to be problematic. If this is not resolved, data collection is of little use.

5. **There will be participation and support of local populations when water sector projects have a local face.** Community-focused and Afghan-led water-complexity projects need to have meaningful and active participation and support from the local population and will need to produce results quickly if local leaders are to maintain credibility in their communities. ISAF and international NGO counterparts should work in the background.

6. **The Helmand PRT civilian-military and USAID water sector projects and programs can be the seeds of a provincial public works department.** According to the U.S. Department of Defense's field manual on COIN operations, "Essential services provide those things needed to sustain life. Examples of these essential needs are food, water, clothing, shelter, and medical treatment. Stabilizing a population requires meeting these needs. People pursue essential needs until they are met, at any cost and from any source. People support the source that meets their needs. If it is an insurgent source, the population is likely to support the insurgency. . . . If the HN [host nation] government provides reliable essential services, the population is more likely to support it" (U.S. DOD 2009, II:7, VIII:11). If the goal of the PRT is to

support the GOIRA and if one of the obligations of the GOIRA is to provide essential services to the Afghan people, establishment of public works in Helmand Province would help sway people to support the GOIRA. Water-treatment and water-quality testing are needed to support public health (Berkley 2010; Bonventre 2010). Water-sector projects and programs can tie together goals of the Ministry of Rural Rehabilitation and Development/National Area-Based Development Programme; the Ministry of Energy and Water; and the Ministry of Agriculture, Irrigation, and Livestock to bring essential services to the population. The Afghan National Development Strategy, 2010–2013 indicates that movement in this direction is underway (GOIRA 2010).

7. **Near-term water projects are at risk as the civilian-military command cycles.** Empirical research is needed to develop recommended courses of action for commanders and staff directors to consider when engaging the Afghan population and identifying points of friction and opportunities for collaboration and support. Change of command—from the regional military and civilian leaders to the provincial and district teams—often causes lack of continuity in water sector and public-works projects because not all commanders understand or have time to consider water's importance. Though critical to post-conflict peacebuilding, water is seldom appreciated for the game changer it can be in the Hold and early Build phases of COIN operations. An understanding of water's significance in COIN operations can be garnered by predeployment training of civilian and military leaders for the command and control levels, as well as by development of tactics, techniques, and procedures for soldiers, marines, and civilians who will participate in civilian-military operations.

8. **Military involvement in water is an indication of a paradigm shift at the U.S. Department of Defense.** Afghanistan may represent the new norm: militaries and their contractors may increasingly undertake work once delegated to humanitarians. Though COIN doctrine's population-centric goals and objectives demand attention to humanitarian issues, the military is taking the lead at the Hold and early Build phases of actions, and then transitioning operations to the civilian agency (USAID) and its NGO contractors.

   Implementation of TCAPF by the U.S. Marine Civil Affairs Group in Helmand had less than the hoped-for results (Montgomery 2010). In order to consider water's role in environmental security and regional stability, Civil Affairs and PRTs need to be not only well trained in the use of TCAPF but also familiar with water supply and quality issues. To understand how water affects security and stability, those administering the survey and those analyzing the results need to be able to weave in the sociocultural aspects and transaction costs of water availability and accessibility.

9. **Climate change and the need for adaptive mechanisms must be addressed as water complexities are analyzed.** There is a need for improved adaptive practices to confront increasing variability of the water supply resulting from climate change. USAID and U.S. Department of Agriculture–sponsored

232 Water and post-conflict peacebuilding

agriculture programs in Afghanistan—programs that depend on water—are not required to incorporate a plan for climate change. Is the recurring drought in southwestern Afghanistan no longer a weather anomaly but the new normal? If so, groundwater levels will continue to drop as recharge of the system continues to fall behind demand. As crops other than poppy are encouraged, as infrastructure for irrigation is repaired and expanded, as more and more wells are dug, adaptive practices for water conservation and use reduction must be implemented (UN 2010; USAID n.d.).

REFERENCES

Abdullah, S., and V. M. Chmyriov, eds. 1977. Annex 9: Map of mineral and fresh water springs of Afghanistan. In *Mineral resources*. Book 2 of *Geology and mineral resources of Afghanistan*. Moscow, USSR: Nedra.

Adamec, L. W., ed. 1973. *Farah and southwestern Afghanistan*. Vol. 2 of *Historical and political gazetteer of Afghanistan*. Graz, Austria: Akademische Druck-u. Verlagsanstalt.

Baranick, M., and T. Wilkinson. 2010. *Afghanistan institution building*. Briefing by the Center for Technology and National Security Policy, National Defense University. www.thecornwallisgroup.org/cornwallis_2010/Wilkinson.pdf.

Batson, D. E. 2008. *Registering the human terrain: A valuation of cadastre*. Washington, D.C.: National Defense Intelligence College Press. www.dtic.mil/cgi-bin/GetTRDoc?AD =ADA485498&Location=U2&doc=GetTRDoc.pdf.

Berkley, V. 2010. The future direction of the United States Department of Health and Human Services in Afghanistan. Briefing at the symposium on Afghanistan and Pakistan, "The Challenges and Opportunities of Governance and the Role of Regional Actors," March 26. University of South Florida, Tampa.

Bonventre, E. 2010. Civil-military cooperation on health matters: Past, present, and future directions. Briefing at the symposium on Afghanistan and Pakistan, "The Challenges and Opportunities of Governance and the Role of Regional Actors," March 26. University of South Florida, Tampa.

Breshna, A. 1988. Shelter for the homeless after a flood disaster: Practical experience in southwestern Afghanistan. *Disasters* 12 (3): 203–208.

Chandrasekaran, R. 2010. As Marja assault progresses, coalition considers challenges in rebuilding area. *Washington Post*, February 21. www.washingtonpost.com/wp-dyn/content/article/2010/02/20/AR2010022002331.html?nav=emailpage.

Chirico, P. 2009. Preliminary report: An evaluation of the 1952 Fairchild Aerial Photography of the Helmand Valley, Afghanistan. Briefing to InterAgency Water Resources Working Group. October 6. Reston, VA: United States Geological Survey.

Civic, M. A. 2014. Civil-military coordination and cooperation in peacebuilding and natural resource management: An enabling framework, challenges, and incremental progress. In *Governance, natural resources, and post-conflict peacebuilding*, ed. C. Bruch, C. Muffett, and S. S. Nichols. London: Earthscan.

DACAAR (Danish Committee for Aid to Afghan Refugees). 2000. Ground water potential and development of water supply facilities in Helmand Province, Afghanistan.

———. 2002. Terms of reference for mid-term review of the DACAAR programme in Afghanistan. Annex 1. www.alnap.org/pool/files/erd-3172-tor.pdf.

Water, security, and stability in Helmand Province   233

————. 2005. Annual report 2005. Kabul, Afghanistan. http://reliefweb.int/sites/reliefweb.int/files/resources/4BFBA386F30FFD25492571AF001FC6B4-dacaar-afg-18jun.pdf.

————. n.d. Water supply section: Groundwater survey of Helmand Province. On file with the author.

Dominguez, C. 2010. Hearts and minds vs. killing people and breaking things. *Silent Majority* (blog). http://web.archive.org/web/20101221052305/http://silentmajority09.com/2010/12/15/korea-afghanistan/.

Flynn, M. T., M. Pottinger, and P. Batchelor. 2010. Fixing intel: A blueprint for making intelligence relevant in Afghanistan. Washington, D.C.: Center for a New American Security. www.cnas.org/node/3924.

Gallup. 2009. Survey of key terrain districts in Helmand Province. Paper presented at the "Helmand Deep Dive Conference," Office of Secretary of Defense, Strategic Multi-Layer Assessment, December 11, Arlington, VA.

GOIRA (Government of the Islamic Republic of Afghanistan). 2008. *Afghan national development strategy 1387–1391: A strategy for security, governance, economic growth, and poverty reduction.* www.undp.org.af/publications/KeyDocuments/ANDS_Full_Eng.pdf.

————. 2010. *Afghan national development strategy: Prioritization and implementation plan, 2010–2013.* www.cfr.org/afghanistan/afghanistan-national-development-strategy-prioritization-implementation-plan-2010-2013/p22679.

Heath, R. C. 2004. *Basic ground-water hydrology.* Water Supply Paper No. 2220. Reston, VA: United States Geological Survey. http://pubs.er.usgs.gov/djvu/WSP/wsp_2220.pdf.

ISAF (International Security Assistance Force). 2010a. *ISAF provincial reconstruction team (PRT) handbook.* 4th ed. www.cimicweb.org/Documents/PRT%20CONFERENCE%202010/PRT%20Handbook%20Edition%204.pdf.

————. 2010b. International Security Assistance Force (ISAF): Key facts and figures. www.isaf.nato.int/images/stories/File/Placemats/100607Placemat.pdf.

————. 2011. International Security Assistance Force (ISAF): Key facts and figures. www.isaf.nato.int/images/stories/File/Placemats/Revised%206%20June%202011%20Placemat%20%28Full%29.pdf.

Leppert, M. 2010. Agribusiness development teams in Afghanistan: Seeding freedom. Briefing to the InterAgency Water Resources Working Group, United States Army Geospatial Center, June 1, Ft. Belvoir, VA.

LLNL (Lawrence Livermore National Lab). 2009. Unpublished preliminary report of climate change/hydrology coupling model for Helmand watershed. Presented at the Water Resources Working Group meeting, December 10, United States Army Corps of Engineers Engineer Research and Development Center, Alexandria, VA.

Montgomery, G. 2010. Memorandum for record: Meeting with Fourth Civil Affairs Group (4th CAG), USMCR. Unpublished meeting report from United States Army Corps of Engineers Engineer Research and Development Center meeting with United States Marines' Fourth Civil Affairs Group at United States Marine Corps Drill Center, Anacostia Naval Base, Washington, D.C.

MRRD-NABDP (Ministry of Rural Rehabilitation and Development–National Area-Based Development Programme, Islamic Republic of Afghanistan). n.d. *Provincial development plan: Helmand; Provincial Profile.* Kabul.

Nicholson, E., J. Ryan, and D. Hodgkin. 2002. Community data—where does the value lie? Assessing confidence limits of community collected water quality data. *Water Science and Technology* 45 (11): 193–200.

234 Water and post-conflict peacebuilding

Nissenbaum, D. 2010. McChrystal calls Marjah a "bleeding ulcer" in Afghan campaign. McClatchy, May 24. www.mcclatchydc.com/2010/05/24/94740/mcchrystal-calls-marjah -a-bleeding.html#.

Palmer-Moloney, L. J. 2010. COIN ties to water: Examples of water complexity indicators to support development metrics. Briefing to the Development Syndicate, NATO System Analysis and Studies workshop, NATO Consultation, Command, and Control Agency (NC3A), December 8, The Hague, Netherlands.

Palmer-Moloney, L. J., B. Graff, R. Karalus, S. Veeravalli, D. Voyadgis, M. Tischler, and M. Campbell. 2010. Human-water complexities: "Smart questions" to discern water's role in COIN operations. Interagency briefing prepared by United States Army Corps of Engineers Engineer Research and Development Center. Alexandria, VA.

Palmer-Moloney, L. J., B. Graff, D. Voyadgis, J. Young, P. Holeva, J. Jarrett, M. Collins, and F. R. Griggs. 2009. Gauging water security and scarcity in southwest Afghanistan: A cultural, geographic, and environmental perspective on Afghanistan's Helmand River watershed. Paper presented at the "Helmand Deep Dive Conference," Office of Secretary of Defense, Strategic Multi-Layer Assessment, December 11, Arlington, VA.

Petreaus, D. H. 2010. For the soldiers, airmen, marines, and civilians of NATO ISAF and U.S. Forces-Afghanistan: COMISAF's counterinsurgency guidance. http://graphics8. nytimes.com/packages/pdf/world/2010/COMISAF-MEMO.pdf.

Uhl, V. 2003. Afghanistan: An overview of groundwater resources and challenges. www.vuawater.com/pages/Afghanistan_GW_Study.pdf.

United Nations Office to Support the International Decade for Action "Water for Life" 2005–2015. 2010. *Water and climate change reader.* www.un.org/waterforlifedecade/ eventsarchive_2010.shtml.

USAID (United States Agency for International Development). 2009. Afghanistan Sustainable Water Supply and Sanitation (SWSS) Project ARD Contract No. EPP-I-00-04-00019-00. http://afghanistan.usaid.gov/en/Activity.151.aspx.

———. 2010. Tactical Conflict Assessment and Planning Framework (TCAPF). Office of Military Affairs, United States Agency for International Development.

———. n.d. Global climate change: Climate science for decision-making. On file with author.

USACAC (United States Army Combined Arms Center). n.d. Counterinsurgency Knowledge Center. http://usacac.army.mil/cac2/coin/KC.asp.

USAGC (United States Army Geospatial Center). 2002. Water resources areal appraisal of Afghanistan. Alexandria, VA. On file with the author.

———. 2009. Provincial water resources data summary of Helmand (Province), Afghanistan. Alexandria, VA. On file with the author.

U.S. DOD (United States Department of Defense Joint Command). 2009. *Counterinsurgency operations.* Joint publication No. JP3-24, October 5. www.dtic.mil/doctrine/new_pubs/ jp3_24.pdf.

U.S. GAO (United States Government Accountability Office). 2010. The strategic framework for U.S. efforts in Afghanistan. Washington, D.C. www.gao.gov/new.items/d10655r.pdf.

USG (United States Government). 2010. Water strategy for Afghanistan, 2009–2014. Kabul, Afghanistan.

U.S. MCCLL (United States Marine Corps Center for Lessons Learned). 2010. *Civil affairs detachment operations in support of Marine Expeditionary Brigade: Afghanistan; Lessons learned from 4th CAG, Detachment L Afghanistan deployment, May–December 2009.* http://info.publicintelligence.net/MCCLL-AfghanCA.pdf.

Whitney, J. W. 2006. Geology, water, and wind in the lower Helmand Basin, southern Afghanistan. U.S. Geological Survey Scientific Investigation Report No. 2006–5186. Reston, VA: United States Geological Survey. http://pdf.usaid.gov/pdf_docs/PNADH905.pdf.

Whittington, S. 2009. *RCT-3 marines implement methodology to understand local problems.* www.marines.mil/unit/iimef/2ndmeb/Pages/RCT-3Marinesimplementmethodologytoun derstandlocalproblems.aspx#.UAnZBo4lfHh.

Williams-Sether, T. 2008. *Streamflow characteristics of streams in the Helmand Basin, Afghanistan.* Data Series No. 333. Reston, VA: United States Geological Survey. http://pubs.usgs.gov/ds/333/pdf/ds333_v1.1.pdf.

PART 3

Peace processes, cooperation, and confidence building

Introduction

Unlike many high-value natural resources (such as oil, diamonds, and gold) and resources for livelihoods (such as pasturage, charcoal, and bananas), which are generally situated within national borders, water often traverses such borders, creating a natural physical boundary that can both bind and divide states. For example, the disconnect between political borders and hydrologic systems often divides upstream and downstream users who have competing interests and differing capacities with respect to the use and allocation of water, complicating cooperation both across and within states. Although it is difficult to generalize, upstream states or regions often have a stronger interest in hydropower development, recreation, and tourism, whereas downstream states tend to be more interested in navigation and in agricultural and industrial development. The chapters in part 3 explore the ways in which joint management of shared water resources can provide opportunities, in the wake of conflict, for former adversaries to build mutual trust and confidence.

Despite hyperbolic statements in the popular press about "water wars"—particularly in the Middle East, where water has been a source of tension between Israel and its Arab neighbors for over half a century—several of the chapters in part 3 focus on the extent to which states that border the same body of water use the shared waters as an important (and sometimes the sole) platform for interstate cooperation. In "The Jordan River Basin: A Conflict Like No Other," Munther J. Haddadin draws on his decades of experience in water negotiations between Israel and Jordan to illuminate the ways in which shared water can foster peacebuilding. Haddadin notes that earlier informal meetings between water managers established trust and communication between Israelis and Jordanians, and thereby helped to facilitate the inclusion of the water section in the 1994 Jordan-Israel peace treaty. Moreover, the establishment of a joint water commission in the treaty institutionalized direct communication between the countries, particularly between their respective water managers. Haddadin observes that even in the face of deteriorating political relations, which were compounded by a regional drought in the 2000s, the joint water commission has continued to provide a venue for conflict resolution and has strengthened respect and trust between prior adversaries.

Although political leaders and legislative bodies may sign and ratify peace treaties that include sections on water resources, such treaties are unlikely to sustain peace in the absence of broad societal acceptance. Thus, one of the challenges facing negotiators is to ensure that treaties are implemented in such a way as to achieve their intended societal benefits, fulfill the expectations of the other parties, and provide peace dividends. In "Transboundary Cooperation in the Lower Jordan River Basin," Munqeth Mehyar, Nader Al Khateeb, Gidon Bromberg, and Elizabeth Koch-Ya'ari argue that strong engagement on the part of civil

240   Water and post-conflict peacebuilding

society can facilitate the implementation of water-related provisions in peace agreements—and, in particular, can strengthen cooperation on water management despite political intransigence at the national level. Focusing on the Lower Jordan River, the authors demonstrate the importance of community engagement, both to improve the quality of the Lower Jordan River and to generate economic welfare gains for neighboring communities. They describe an array of community-level projects administered by the Good Water Neighbors project of Friends of the Earth Middle East, and they note that educational and public awareness campaigns focusing on the Lower Jordan River have helped to change public perceptions and build trust among Israeli, Jordanian, and Palestinian communities.

Effectively incorporating water into the post-conflict peacebuilding process may depend on the active and prolonged involvement of third-party actors. In "The Sava River: Transitioning to Peace in the Former Yugoslavia," Amar Čolakhodžić, Marija Filipović, Jana Kovandžić, and Stephen Stec argue that without the sustained intervention of the European Union (EU), which designated the Sava River Basin as one of thirteen pilot projects for the implementation of the EU Water Framework Directive, cooperation over the basin would never have developed after the breakup of the former Yugoslavia. When states share a water system, third parties can provide incentives to cooperate. In the case of the Sava River Basin, the prospect of EU membership was a particularly effective inducement because joint management of the river was not only a low-profile, low-stakes issue but was also considered essential for reestablishing navigation, which would yield economic benefits for the states and communities in the basin. The circumstances surrounding the Sava River example contrast sharply with those in an example cited by Haddadin, who notes that in the 1950s, U.S. attempts to use water to broach political negotiations in the Middle East floundered precisely because water was an extraordinarily contentious and high-stakes issue throughout the region.

Technical cooperation on water issues provides an important entry point for strengthening post-conflict peacebuilding—but to succeed, such initiatives must be sustained and geared toward longer time horizons. In "Transnational Cooperation over Shared Water Resources in the South Caucasus: Reflections on USAID Interventions," Marina Vardanyan and Richard Volk provide a firsthand account of efforts by the U.S. Agency for International Development to promote dialogue and capacity building for integrated water resource management as a means of initiating broader political cooperation in the South Caucasus. Although such programs may seem modest in relation to the larger political landscape, when donors introduce them immediately after the end of conflict, they can provide an initial means of improving dialogue among adversaries and create a foundation for economic recovery and eventual political engagement.

One of the greatest impediments to capitalizing on opportunities for water-related cooperation in post-conflict situations is the lack of transparent and up-to-date scientific data. Many chapters in the book highlight donors' efforts to improve the collection and sharing of data—but in "Water Security and Scarcity:

Peace processes, cooperation, and confidence building 241

Potential Destabilization in Western Afghanistan and Iranian Sistan and Baluchestan Due to Transboundary Water Conflicts," Alex Dehgan, Laura Jean Palmer-Moloney, and Mehdi Mirzaee argue that the dearth of reliable hydrological data has not only hampered efforts to foster cooperation between Afghanistan and Iran but could also aggravate existing tensions between the two countries, particularly in the border regions of Iran that depend on the Helmand River, which flows from Afghanistan to Iran. The authors focus on the importance of rebuilding Afghanistan's national capacity for water monitoring and data collection as a means of mitigating potential conflict, and note that climate change will likely make it even more difficult to predict water availability in the future. Finally, given that reconstruction efforts in Afghanistan will largely depend on stabilizing relations with Iran, efforts to engage Iran in water coordination could provide an important entry point for post-conflict peacebuilding.

Post-conflict changes in political borders can have tremendous implications for the management of transboundary water resources. Although it may be too early to tell how the independence of South Sudan will affect water sharing in the Nile Basin, "Water Resources in the Sudan North-South Peace Process and the Ramifications of the Secession of South Sudan," by Salman M. A. Salman, establishes the historical context in which decisions about the use of the tributaries of the White Nile will likely be made. Unlike the Jordan-Israel peace treaty, which explicitly laid out mechanisms for water sharing, the Comprehensive Peace Agreement that created the blueprint for the secession of South Sudan only briefly addressed water resource issues. Whereas many other chapters in this book emphasize the peacebuilding potential of water, this chapter highlights the potential of the newly created state of South Sudan to aggravate tensions between upstream and downstream riparian countries within the Nile Basin, especially if South Sudan chooses to unilaterally develop the waters of the White Nile to support its own economic recovery.

Taken together, the chapters in part 3 demonstrate that the physical interdependence associated with water, which binds societies both within and across national borders, provides unique opportunities for building trust and confidence in the post-conflict period. Many of the experiences analyzed in part 3 describe water sharing in regions where violence has yet to fully recede and water remains a high-stakes issue. Nevertheless, the authors find that small, discrete projects that are technical in nature and that engage civil society may generate support for expanding peacebuilding efforts to the regional level. Without question, however, fostering trust and confidence among former adversaries will require a long-term and active commitment on the part of donors.

The Jordan River Basin: A conflict like no other

Munther J. Haddadin

The Jordan River has been marked by conflict between the countries on its banks —Israel on one hand, and Lebanon, Syria, Jordan, and the Palestinian Authority on the other. The Arab states resented the United Kingdom's 1917 Balfour Declaration supporting the establishment of a national home for the Jews in Palestine.[1] The League of Nations granted Great Britain a mandate over Palestine and empowered it to implement the pledge made in the Balfour Declaration. Arab resentment developed into violent conflict in Palestine in the late 1920s.

Jewish immigration to Palestine began in 1882 in the aftermath of anti-Jewish violence following the assassination of Czar Alexander II of Russia, in which 200 Jews who had nothing to do with the assassination were beaten to death. The Palestinians feared the consequences of Jewish immigration into their land, supported after 1897 by the Zionist Organization (now the World Zionist Organization) and facilitated by the British Mandate government, including the acquisition of land by the immigrants.

The conflict peaked in 1936 with a six-month Palestinian revolt. The British government dispatched a royal commission headed by Lord Earl Peel to look into the grievances of the Palestinians. The Peel Commission recommended the partition of Palestine between its indigenous population and the immigrant Jews, with the Jerusalem enclave to remain under international jurisdiction (PRC 1937). This plan, later modified by the Woodhead Commission, was not accepted by

---

Munther J. Haddadin is a consultant based in Amman, Jordan. He was the chief water negotiator on the Jordanian delegation to the Middle East peace process and has served as Jordan's minister of water and irrigation. In this chapter, he draws on his extensive experience involving the technical and transnational issues relating to the development of the Jordan River Basin.

[1] The Balfour Declaration stated: "His Majesty's Government view with favour the establishment in Palestine of a national home for the Jewish people, and will use their best endeavors to facilitate the achievement of this object, it being clearly understood that nothing shall be done which may prejudice the civil and religious rights of existing non-Jewish communities in Palestine, or the rights and political status enjoyed by Jews in any other country" (Yapp 1987, 290).

244 Water and post-conflict peacebuilding

the Palestinians, and the conflict continued. The United Nations General Assembly (UNGA) adopted a partition plan in 1947 based largely on the earlier British plan (UNGA 1947), and the State of Israel was proclaimed on the evening of May 14, 1948, despite Arab resistance, immediately after the British withdrawal from Palestine. The first Arab-Israeli war erupted the next day. Armistice agreements were concluded under the auspices of the United Nations, in 1949, between Israel and Egypt, Lebanon, Jordan and Syria; and the United Nations Truce Supervision Organization (UNTSO) was set up to maintain peace between the parties.

The parts of Palestine not taken over by Israel in 1948 were the Gaza Strip, which came under Egyptian military administration but was kept separate from Egypt, and the West Bank, which in 1950 became part of the Hashemite Kingdom of Jordan. The Palestinians in the West Bank, including those from other parts of Palestine who had taken refuge there, became Jordanian citizens.

Perhaps the worst consequence of the proclamation of the State of Israel and its aftermath has been the displacement of hundreds of thousands of Palestinians who fled the fighting and took refuge in the West Bank and Gaza Strip, and in the surrounding Arab states—the majority in Jordan, and others in Lebanon, Syria, Iraq, and Egypt.

Despite the armistice agreements, recurring violence erupted between Israel and its Arab neighbors in the early 1950s and thereafter. Several wars also broke out: one waged by Israel against Egypt in 1956, in collaboration with Great Britain and France; another in 1967, waged by Israel against Egypt, Syria and Jordan; a third waged by Egypt and Syria against Israel, in 1973, to recover territories Israel had held since the preceding war; and a fourth by Israel against Lebanon in 1982. Peace talks started between Egypt and Israel in 1978. Until a peace treaty between them was concluded in 1979, in which the two states exchanged explicit political recognition, none of the Arab states had recognized the legitimacy of the State of Israel, despite its admission to the United Nations. The Arab states based their rejection on the argument that Israel's statehood was proclaimed on territories belonging to the indigenous Palestinian people and that Israel was a foreign implant on Arab soil. That position gradually transformed in the wake of the successive wars. The acceptance by the Arab states of United Nations Security Council (UNSC) resolutions 242 and 338, which brought to an end the wars of 1967 and 1973 respectively (UNSC 1967, 1973), could be considered an implicit recognition of Israel.

Conflict between the indigenous populations of the region, Jews and Arabs, can be traced to the decision of the First Zionist Congress in Basel, Switzerland, in 1897, to target Palestine as a national home for the Jews. As a conflict between states, it surfaced in 1947, when Arab and other states voted against UNGA Resolution 181, which called for the partition of Palestine between Jews and Arabs. The post-conflict era can be said to have begun between Israel and Egypt in 1979 and between Israel and Jordan in 1994, when each of these Arab countries concluded a peace treaty with Israel. (The latter treaty is discussed in more detail, later in this chapter.) Conflict still simmers between Israel and the Palestinians, Syria, Lebanon, and the rest of the Arab countries.

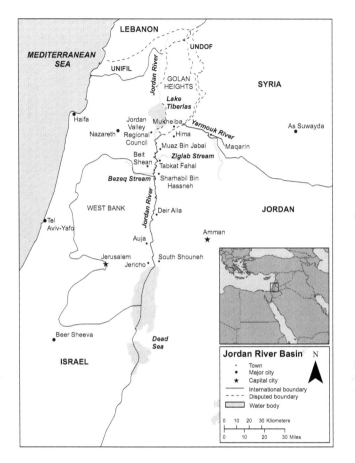

Note: The Sea of Galilee is also known as Lake Kinneret and Lake Tiberias.

WATER ISSUES DURING THE CONFLICT

The different territories that shared the Jordan River Basin developed conflicting plans for its utilization. Abraham Bourcart, a German engineer, assessed Palestine's water resources for the Zionist Organization in 1901 (Haddadin 2001). In 1915, the Ottoman Empire's director of public works for Palestine, George Franjieh, initiated an effort to utilize the water of the Yarmouk River, the largest tributary to the Jordan River, for irrigation and power development; his efforts were aborted by the outbreak of World War I and the demise of the Ottoman Empire. Plans developed in 1944 and 1947 for the Jewish Agency, the pre-state Jewish government and the executive arm of the Zionist Organization, conflicted with plans developed for the Emirate of Transjordan in 1939 and for its successor, the Hashemite Kingdom of Jordan, in 1951 (Haddadin 2001). The Jewish Agency's Lowdermilk Plan of 1944 called for the utilization of the Jordan River and the

246 Water and post-conflict peacebuilding

transfer of water from Palestine's humid north to its arid south, and the transfer of Mediterranean Sea water to the Dead Sea to compensate the latter for the loss of inflow from the Jordan River. Israel's Seven Year Plan of 1953 also addressed water issues.

Water plans for Jordan included the Ionedis Plan of 1939, which envisaged two canals, one on each side of the Jordan River, and allowed for the use of Lake Tiberias (also known as the Sea of Galilee and Lake Kinneret) as a reservoir, with a feeder canal conveying water from there to the eastern canal, which would also be fed by the Yarmouk River. This plan was further elaborated in 1951. Both Jordanian plans conflicted with a Syrian-Lebanese plan for the use of the Jordan River's upper tributaries. This plan, created in 1951 and revised in 1959, called for the diversion of the two upper tributaries of the Jordan, the Banias and the Hasbani rivers, to the Baqa'a Valley in Lebanon for irrigation.

When Israel implemented its plan to divert water from its semihumid north to the arid south in 1951, it unilaterally attempted to divert Jordan River water from a point in the demilitarized zone that had been established between Syria and Israel in their armistice agreement of 1949 (Haddadin 2001). To prevent the Israeli earthmoving equipment from operating there, Syria fired at the equipment operators as they approached the diversion point. Israel responded by expelling Syrian citizens from their villages of Bekara, Naymeh, and Mazra'at al Khouri. (Syrian citizens in the demilitarized zone and nearby areas lived within the range of the rifles of Israeli soldiers.) This in turn triggered Syrian shelling of Israeli equipment and settlements inside Israel. UNTSO intervened and determined that the Israeli diversion works were contrary to the provisions of the armistice, and on October 27, 1953, the UNSC adopted Resolution 100, suspending the diversion (UNSC 1953).

At the same time the Israeli military made incursions into the West Bank, then part of Jordan, in response to what Israel claimed were Palestinian incursions into Israeli territory. These were mostly civilian raids carried out by disenchanted Palestinian refugees seeking access to their former homes inside Israel, during which they sometimes looted Israeli property, mostly livestock. The Arab Legion, Jordan's army, responded to the Israeli military incursions, and tensions in the region escalated. Other military clashes took place between Israeli military and Egyptian patrols on account of Palestinian incursions from the Gaza Strip.

These military clashes in the early 1950s created political tensions in the Middle East at the beginning of the Cold War. The Korean War had just ended, and the confrontation between East and West in Indochina had begun. The Near East—which includes the Middle East, Turkey, and Iran—was becoming increasingly unstable: Iran was just returning to normal after the Mossadegh government nationalized the oil companies; a series of military coups had taken place in Syria and one in Egypt, creating tremors in the wake of the Arab failure to rescue Palestine from Zionist control. Frequent military clashes along ceasefire lines with Israel added to the political and social tensions in the region. Coupled with the growing needs of Palestinian refugees and their hopes of returning to their homes in Israel, it was feared that these tensions would fuel a popular drive toward communism as a reaction to Western support for Israel.

In response to these tensions, the president of the United States, Dwight D. Eisenhower, appointed Eric Johnston as a U.S. envoy to the Middle East in October 1953. Johnston's mission was to try to defuse the conflict over water, create calm in the region, promote economic and social development, settle Palestinian refugees in Jordan, and induce the Arab riparian states to communicate and cooperate with Israel over water.

It was believed that poverty and want invited the spread of communism and that a fight against them would curb its spread. The social and political plight of refugees, especially in a poor economy like Jordan's, could not be alleviated without outside help. If water was brought to the arid Jordan Valley, irrigated agriculture could provide livelihoods for a good portion of the Palestinian refugees. Water works and irrigation could create jobs and help refugees resettle in the Jordan Valley. This was expected to be an attractive proposition for Israel and an incentive to cooperate with American objectives.

THE JOHNSTON MISSION

Ambassador Johnston was to work out a plan for the development of the Jordan Valley in which the Jordan waters would be fully harnessed for the benefit of all riparian states. He had to pursue shuttle diplomacy between the Arab states and Israel. Lebanon, Syria, and Jordan (including the West Bank) were all members of the League of Arab States (Arab League), established in 1945, and none were prepared to recognize or deal directly with Israel.

A plan for the development of the Jordan Valley had been prepared by the American consulting firm Chas. T. Main on request of the Tennessee Valley Authority, which in turn had been commissioned by the United Nations Relief and Works Agency for Palestinian Refugees (UNRWA). This plan, also known as the Unified Plan for the Development of the Jordan Valley, "describes the elements of an efficient arrangement of water supply within the watershed of the Jordan River system. It does not consider political factors or attempt to set this system into the national boundaries now prevailing" (Clapp 1953). It was submitted to UNRWA and to the U.S. government on August 31, 1953, and a month after that to the relevant Arab states. Johnston met with the prime ministers of Lebanon, Jordan, and Egypt on his first trip. The Egyptian prime minister, Gamal Abdel Nasser, was receptive and advised the Arab League to form a committee to negotiate the plan with Johnston.

The agreement addressed water storage, distribution, and supervision. It allowed the impoundment of Yarmouk River waters, with U.S. financing, by a 126-meter dam to be built on the river at Maqarin on the border between Jordan and Syria. The dam could be made higher than that, but without any additional U.S. financial contribution. Lake Tiberias was designated as another storage location,

248   Water and post-conflict peacebuilding

which would regulate the river flow downstream. An international board would supervise the distribution of water and would rule, in five years, on the feasibility of storing Yarmouk waters in Lake Tiberias.

In assessing the total water resources of the Jordan River Basin, the Johnston technical team, led by Wayne D. Criddle, an American water specialist, assumed the average annual rate of return flow (after use for irrigation) at 112 million cubic meters per year (mcm/year).[2] Return flow augments the natural flow of the river. The natural flow in 1953 was estimated at 1,320 mcm/year, and the historic consumptive use prior to that year was estimated at 40 mcm/year. Thus the total resources available for sharing by the riparian parties (natural flow, consumptive use, and return flow) amounted to an estimated 1,472 mcm/year.

Water distribution to Arab countries was based on the irrigation of arable lands within the basin in the territories of each riparian party. The Israeli share was based mostly not on the irrigation needs of its arable lands within the basin but more on the residual flow after the arable lands in the basin, Arab or otherwise, had their needs for irrigation met. This was a clever approach by Johnston to strike a middle position between two contradictory demands: The Arab side insisted that basin water should be reserved for in-basin uses and not transferred out of the basin. Israel, on the other hand, demanded that water from the basin could be transferred outside the basin to irrigate the arid south. No water was allocated for municipal, industrial, or environmental uses.

Water sharing under the plan was negotiated in four shuttle rounds that Johnston conducted between 1953 and 1955. The final version, known as the Modified Unified Plan or the Jordan Valley Plan, was arrived at in September 1955.[3] That plan called for a dam on the Yarmouk River 126 meters high, more than twice the height originally envisioned. It allocated water from the Jordan River and its tributaries north of Lake Tiberias as follows:

- Lebanon: 35 mcm/year from the Hasbani River, the upper tributary that flows through Lebanon before it enters Israel to meet two other tributaries to form the Jordan River.
- Syria: 22 mcm/year from the Jordan River and 20 mcm/year from the Banias River, the tributary that originates in Syria and flows to join the Hasbani and Dan rivers inside Israel to form the Jordan River.
- Jordan (including the West Bank): 100 mcm/year from Lake Tiberias including a maximum of 15 mcm of brackish water emerging from saline springs on the western shore of the lake and on the lake bottom near the western shore.
- Israel: The residual flow of the Upper Jordan River (before it enters Lake Tiberias), estimated at 554 mcm/year.
- Estimated loss to evaporation: 300 mcm/year.

---

[2] Wayne D. Criddle, unpublished working documents (on file with author).
[3] For the complete text of the Jordan Valley Plan, see Haddadin (2001).

Water from the Jordan River tributaries south of Lake Tiberias was allocated as follows:

- Syria: 90 mcm/year from the Yarmouk River, the largest tributary to the Jordan River.
- Israel: 25 mcm/year from the Yarmouk River.
- Jordan (including the West Bank): The residual flow of the Yarmouk River, estimated at 377 mcm/year.
- Estimated loss to evaporation: 14 mcm/year.

The Jordan River itself would become a drain unfit for agricultural use after water shares were distributed for use by the riparian parties.

The West Bank share had to be separated from the Jordanian share after the disengagement of Jordan from the West Bank.[4] As will be shown below, the West Bank share of this estimated flow was 81 mcm/year, and Jordan's was 296 mcm/year.

The final plan was presented to Egyptian President Jamal Abdul Nasser on October 7, 1955. Nasser remarked that the plan had both an economic and a political character, that he was sure the technical side of it would be acceptable by the Arabs, and that he had to handle the political side in his own way (Haddadin 2001).

The Arab Technical Committee of the Arab League, which was entrusted by the Arab League Council to negotiate with Johnston, recommended that the Council accept the plan but try to increase Jordan's share from Lake Tiberias to 160 mcm/year. Meeting on October 11, 1955, the Political Committee of the Arab League failed to reach consensus on accepting the plan and instructed the Secretary General of the Arab League to inform Johnston that time was needed to perform more studies. The Israeli political leadership expressed its preparedness to ratify the agreement once the Arab side did (Haddadin 2001).

The United States distributed the Jordan Valley Plan to the parties in January 1956, and made it the cornerstone of its Jordan River Basin policy for the next decade. American emissaries visited the area and followed up on the water development projects there. For example, Wayne D. Criddle, advisor to Johnston and the chief technical member of his mission, made two trips to the region and verified the compatibility of the water projects financed by the United States in the basin with the Jordan Valley Plan. This lasted until Israel won the 1967 war against Egypt, Syria, and Jordan.

U.S. SUPPORT FOR WATER PROJECTS IN THE BASIN

Lebanon's foreign minister, Salim Lahoud, suggested in 1956 to the U.S ambassador in Beirut, Donald R. Heath, that a staged implementation of the

---

[4] The Hashemite Kingdom of Jordan disengaged with the West Bank on July 31, 1988, by a royal decree.

250   Water and post-conflict peacebuilding

water-sharing plan be adopted. Jordan, with assistance from the Food and Agriculture Organization of the United Nations, had prepared a project to divert unregulated flows of the Yarmouk River to irrigate land in the Jordan Valley. The idea of a staged implementation appealed to the United States. It offered assistance to Jordan, provided that Jordan would not draw from the Yarmouk more water than allocated to it under the Jordan Valley Plan. Jordan undertook to abide by that condition (Haddadin 2001; MOF 1958).

There were political reasons behind U.S. support for the Jordanian project. Jordan, a Western-leaning country, had a sizable number of Palestinian refugees and one of the weakest economies in the region. (Its per capita gross domestic product was US$100 in 1957, and its balance of payments deficit was the highest of any Middle Eastern country except Israel.) The U.S. role in the region had grown following the 1956 Suez crisis, which began with Egypt's nationalization of the British- and French-owned Suez Canal. British, French, and Israeli forces invaded Egypt but, following intense international pressure, soon had to withdraw. Jordan, which had been under British influence since its creation in 1921, terminated its treaty of alliance with Great Britain in 1957, although it maintained diplomatic relations. Meanwhile, the Soviet Union had established a foothold in Egypt and Syria by supplying weapons to both countries, and the United States was concerned about communist influence spilling over to Jordan and spreading in the region.

The United States adopted a staged approach to the implementation of the Jordan Valley Plan, in which it helped Jordan to develop the Jordan Valley, create jobs, and settle Palestinian refugees there. This was seen as fighting communism by fighting the poverty and need on which communist propaganda depended. In parallel to its assistance to Jordan, the United States also helped fund an Israeli pipeline that would convey some 70 mcm/year of water from Lake Tiberias, a Jordan River source, to the Beit She'an Valley. Thus the United States maintained a balance between the Arab parties and Israel in its approach to the implementation of the Jordan Valley Plan.

By 1966 Jordan, with U.S. funding, had brought some 11,400 hectares under perennial irrigation. A drop inlet dug on the southern bank of the Yarmouk River drew water by gravity toward an inlet structure on Jordanian territory. The inlet marked the beginning of the Jordanian main water carrier, the East Ghor Canal (renamed the King Abdullah Canal in 1987).

To improve diversion efficiency, the project needed a diversion weir across the Yarmouk River to direct water to the Jordanian inlet and on to the East Ghor Canal. Israel objected to the construction of this structure, arguing that it would give Jordan a military advantage as it could provide a crossing point for pedestrian intruders from Jordan to a demilitarized zone across the river from which they could enter Israeli territory. Contacts were made in the early 1960s through UNTSO and through the good offices of the United States, but none persuaded Israel to consent to this construction. Israel would not even agree to have a lip built from the Jordanian bank to midstream at the same location, which would have helped improve the diversion efficiency without giving Jordan a military advantage. Beyond its military implications, the issue also affected the Israeli water supply: The less efficient the water diversion to Jordan, the greater the flow to Israel. Also, the diversion structure would have been operated by Jordan alone, and that could have caused problems for water sharing with Israel.

The 1967 war and its aftermath stalled this development effort in Jordan and brought about further complications related to the diversion of Yarmouk waters to Jordan. Before the war, UNTSO patrolled the Yarmouk bank across from Jordan, aided on request by Syrian police. After the war Israel occupied the Golan Heights and the Yarmouk gorge inside Syria, and thus controlled that bank of the Yarmouk. The ceasefire line between Jordan and Israel extended up the midstream of the Yarmouk until the confluence of its principal tributary, Wadi Raqqad. Consequently, routine Jordanian maintenance work in the river's midstream, such as cleaning debris and deposits in the riverbed at the site of the drop inlet after each flood season, became impossible without the consent of Israel, which proved difficult and costly to obtain.

THE VALUE OF THIRD-PARTY INTERVENTION

The involvement of the United States in managing the conflict over the Jordan River proved to be very valuable, at least to Jordan. Without it the conflict, exacerbated by Arab grievances over the loss of most of Palestine to Israel and the plight of the Palestinian refugees, could have escalated into all-out war. Neither Jordan nor the other riparian Arab countries, Syria and Lebanon, were equipped to win such a war, and the loss would have devastated Jordan.

U.S. financial assistance to Jordan and Israel enabled the United States to create an indirect channel of communication between the two countries. Visiting American experts were dispatched to the region to follow up on the staged implementation of the Jordan Valley Plan and assure that no violations of it were committed. Through their deliberations with these U.S. technical missions, water officials in both Israel and Jordan learned about each other's views. Sometimes U.S. intermediaries conveyed professional proposals from one country to the other. Such indirect interactions helped avoid misunderstandings.

Third-party intervention proved very helpful. By 1979, twelve years without maintenance of the riverbed at the drop inlet location had allowed the formation of a sandbar that partially obstructed the diversion of water to the inlet. The United States worked with UNTSO in the summer of 1979, a low-flow year, to help obtain Israeli consent for Jordan to shave off as much of the sandbar as possible. The cleanup resulted in Jordan receiving more water than it was entitled to. When Jordan was slow to respond to Israeli requests to adjust the diversion ratio, Israeli soldiers moved into the river and adjusted the flow using rocks to recover what they thought was Israel's share. In so doing, the Israelis created an inverse imbalance, again diminishing the flow to Jordan. The Jordanian armed forces were mobilized, the Israeli forces responded in kind, and the two forces

252　Water and post-conflict peacebuilding

faced each other separated only by the Yarmouk gorge. The situation was defused only when the president of the Jordan Valley Authority of Jordan worked with the U.S. embassy in Amman and with UNTSO to arrange a meeting of the Truce Commission under UN auspices to settle the dispute and avoid a breakout of hostilities (Haddadin 2001).

After that incident, and because of the need to monitor the diversion rates to both parties, the UNTSO-sponsored meetings continued at almost regular intervals during the dry months, and during the winter months if there was a drought. Each party was represented by a military officer and a water systems expert. Discussion was limited to matters pertinent to the immediate diversion problems. However, the reaction of each side to the plight of the other helped cement informal ties between the two sides' representatives at the talks and even between their superiors.

Soon each party realized the importance of transparency, honesty, and credibility in living up to the commitments they had undertaken. Important operational transactions were agreed on verbally without a binding written document. The mutual respect that developed made it possible, during droughts, for Israel to help Jordan by allowing part of its share of the Yarmouk River water to be diverted to Jordan. This was particularly helpful to Jordan when large numbers of Jordanian citizens returned from the Gulf states in 1990–1991, after Iraq's invasion of Kuwait. Some 300,000 returnees took up residence in and around the capital city of Amman, raising the demand for municipal water there. A good part of Amman's municipal water supply came from the Yarmouk River via the King Abdullah Canal.

Between 1975 and 1990, several high-level U.S. missions tried to remove political barriers to the building of a dam for Jordan on the Yarmouk River at Maqarin. Donors made the approval of other riparian parties a prerequisite for funding to build the dam. Emissaries who shuttled between Jordan and Israel included Philip Habib (1978–1981); Richard Murphy (1984); and Richard Armitage (1988–1991), who continued his work as an intermediary until the Middle East peace process was launched in 1991. Bilateral negotiations then made it possible for Jordan to negotiate directly with Israel without the need for intermediaries.

Palestinian refugees, as well as other natives in the Jordan Valley, benefited from jobs created by U.S.-supported irrigation projects there. But third-party interventions did not resolve the water dispute between Jordan and Israel, and it continued to occupy center stage in the negotiations between the two countries from 1991 to 1994. By the end of the negotiations in October 1994, Jordan and Israel had come to agreement on water-related issues and resolved their bilateral conflict.

Direct bilateral negotiations achieved what the indirect talks could not. During Johnston's shuttle diplomacy (1953–1955), two political considerations stood in the way of ratification by the Arab League Council of the final version of the Jordan Valley Plan. One was the plight of the Palestinian refugees, whose return to their homes had been called for by the United Nations in 1948 (UNGA 1948);

The Jordan River Basin: A conflict like no other 253

the other was the fact that cooperation with Israel could be interpreted as political recognition of Israel when the issues that caused the Arab-Israeli conflict had not been resolved.

The staged development of the Jordan Valley in Jordan took a significant turn in 1973 when the integrated social and economic development approach was adopted. In this approach a single government organization was entrusted with the integrated development. The approach entailed the implementation of infrastructure projects for social and economic development and the creation of nongovernmental institutions to enhance such development. The backbone of Jordan Valley development was irrigated agriculture, around which population centers would be established or expanded. Schools, health centers, government buildings, and community centers, as well as housing units, streets, and parking lots were built. Municipal water, electricity, and telecommunications were provided. Highways, market centers, and tourism facilities were built. Farmers were organized into a farmers association. The outcome was very positive economically, socially, environmentally, and politically (Haddadin 2006). For the most part, Jordanians have supported the development drive and worked to protect its achievements. The Jordan Valley was never allowed to become a military front or a war zone because there were too many achievements and benefits there to protect.

CONFLICT WITH SYRIA

Jordan shares the Yarmouk River with Syria upstream and Israel downstream. It has always been inferior to its riparian neighbors in economic and military power and has chosen to resolve conflicts with them through peaceful means.

Jordan's relations with Syria have not been very brotherly. Since 1954, Syria has been ruled by leftist regimes that extended a hand to Jordan only intermittently in accordance with Syria's interests. Headaches for Jordan relating to Syria started immediately after the June war of 1967. While Jordan was preoccupied with the consequences of Israel's occupation of East Jerusalem and the West Bank, Syria started constructing earthen dams on the Yarmouk tributaries inside its borders, violating a 1951 treaty between the two countries. Syria also prepared plans to expand its use of the Yarmouk headwaters beyond the 90 mcm/year allocated to it both in this treaty and in the Jordan Valley Plan. It further allowed Syrian farmers to expand their use of the aquifer that feeds the Yarmouk springs allocated to Jordan under the bilateral treaty. Extensive pumping from the Yarmouk aquifer was and is being practiced by Syrian users.

Jordan and Syria held bilateral talks between 1976 and 1987,[5] interrupted from 1981 to 1986 due to tensions arising from Jordan and Syria's support for opposite sides in the Iraq-Iran War (1980–1989). During those talks, Syria represented to Jordan that its increased use of water from the Yarmouk River

---

[5] The Jordanian delegation was headed by the author.

254   Water and post-conflict peacebuilding

was meant to deny Israel, their common enemy, access to that water (Haddadin 2001). Jordan responded that, even if such action appeared legitimate, it caused appreciable harm to Jordan.

Political relations between Jordan and Syria, which deteriorated between 1980 and 1985, improved in 1986 as Prime Minister Zeid S. Al Rifai, known to be friendly to Syria, took office in Jordan. A new bilateral treaty on the Yarmouk, concluded in 1987, replaced the original 1953 treaty. From the Jordanian perspective, the new treaty was unfair because it conceded to Syria, whose consent was required for Jordan to build the dam at Maqarin, the right to impound floodwaters in its territory that would otherwise be stored at Maqarin. That dam was completed in 2005. By 2010 the Al Wahda Dam had impounded a cumulative total over five years of no more than 25 mcm of Yarmouk water, although it has a storage capacity of 125 mcm.

Hopes were high that the new treaty would define the rights and obligations of each party, and that the two parties would honor it. In reality, however, Syrian behavior in the Yarmouk catchment did not change, and Jordan continues to be adversely affected by Syrian actions. Conflict with Syria over the Yarmouk continues, and efforts are made intermittently to bridge the differences through joint assessments of the catchment yield.

OBSTACLES TO DEVELOPMENT

Jordan adopted a comprehensive plan in 1973 for the social and economic development of the Jordan Valley on the river's East Bank, as described above. Irrigated agriculture was the backbone of the plan, and the role of the Yarmouk River was and is pivotal. The plan called for the expansion of irrigated agriculture in two stages. The first would add 8,300 hectares and convert an additional 1,000 hectares to piped distribution networks, and the second would involve the construction of a dam at Maqarin and the expansion of irrigated agriculture to 36,000 hectares. Ambitious infrastructure projects were included, and a score of donor agencies assisted, led at first by the U.S. Agency for International Development.

By the time the first stage ended in 1979, the water supply from various sources, particularly the Yarmouk River, had diminished because of increased Syrian water use upstream. The efficiency of water diversion from the Yarmouk to the East Ghor Canal, the main water carrier for the Jordan Valley, was also diminished by deposits of sediment at the diversion point, which formed the sandbar described above. Thus the water supply to the Jordan Valley suffered both from Syrian overuse upstream and from diminishing diversion efficiency caused by the sandbar.

Israel saw in Jordan's need to clean the sandbar a chance to initiate top-level meetings between the water officials of the two countries, a political gain indeed at the time of the Arab boycott of Israel. Furthermore, Israel benefited from the reduced efficiency of water diversion to Jordan because whatever water Jordan could not divert became available for Israeli use. Israel responded slowly to UNTSO's requests for a meeting to address the problem. The impact on Jordan's water share was pronounced. Records show that on July 11, 1954, the Yarmouk flow at the diversion point was 7.32 cubic meters per second (Baker and Harza Engineering 1955). By July 1979, the flow at the same location was only 3.2 cubic meters per second (Haddadin 2001). Drought had some effect, but so did increased Syrian extraction upstream.

The sandbar at the diversion point made it more difficult to divide the reduced Yarmouk River flow between Jordan and Israel. The reduced flow also forced the Jordan Valley Authority to shift its irrigation development strategy from surface canals to more costly pressure pipe networks, and to urge farmers to adopt advanced on-farm irrigation methods with financing from the government's Agricultural Credit Corporation. Increased water use efficiency in the Jordan Valley made up for the reduction in water supply, but it required costly efforts by Jordan to mitigate the impact of both Syrian and Israeli water policies.

Although Jordanian and Syrian negotiators met frequently between 1977 and 1981, Jordan had practically no success in curbing Syrian water extraction or obtaining Syria's consent to build the Maqarin dam. High-level meetings between Jordan and Israel were a taboo at the time, and water issues could not be resolved. However, meetings of the Armistice Commission under the chairmanship of UNTSO, designed to look into transient problems, yielded an understanding with Israel on the mechanism and ratios of water diversion from the Yarmouk. Water diversion was controlled by sandbags set across the river by Jordanian and Israeli technicians overseen by UNTSO. UNTSO meetings took place at the diversion site, and although they were transient in scope, they contributed to Israel's understanding of the difficulties Jordan was facing in water supply, something that Syria did not display in its direct high-level talks.

Increased trust between water technicians from both countries finally paved the way for the removal of the sandbar discussed above. Political developments helped accelerate that step. Under President Ronald Reagan, the United States initiated a Middle East initiative after the Sabra and Shatila massacre of Palestinians during the Israeli invasion of Lebanon in 1982. U.S. Secretary of State George Schultz shuttled between Arabs and Israelis in an attempt to work out a platform for the resolution of the Middle East conflict. In the positive atmosphere this U.S. intervention generated in the mid-1980s, Israel finally agreed to have the sandbar removed. That step, implemented in September 1985, improved the efficiency of water diversion to Jordan and enhanced mutual understanding between the two countries.

THE JORDAN-ISRAEL PEACE TREATY

After the liberation of Kuwait in 1991 from Iraqi occupation, U.S. President George H. W. Bush resumed efforts started by his predecessor, Ronald Reagan, to make peace in the Middle East. Secretary of State James Baker designed a Middle East peace process that responded to the demands of the adversaries. It involved, first, a conference consisting of four separate and parallel bilateral negotiation tracks to settle fundamental political disputes between Israel on the

256   Water and post-conflict peacebuilding

one hand and Jordan, the Palestinians, Syria, and Lebanon on the other; and second, a multilateral conference, consisting of five working groups and a steering committee, in which thirty-eight countries participated. In the bilateral peace negotiations that commenced in Washington, D.C., in December 1991, Jordan met Israel face to face without the intermediaries who had played such an important role since 1953. The negotiations between Jordan and Israel lasted until October 1994, when the two countries concluded a peace treaty.

In the multilateral conference that opened in Moscow in January 1992, one working group was dedicated to water resources while others were dedicated to the environment, economic development, refugees, and regional security and arms control. The conference aimed to devise ways to consolidate the peace once it was reached. The multilateral working groups held intermittent sessions in different capitals of the world, but these were stalled in 1996 when difficulties, emanating from the ascent of the rightist Likud party to power in Israel, interrupted the bilateral negotiations between Israel and Syria, Lebanon, and the Palestinians.

In the bilateral negotiations between Jordan and Israel, water was an important agenda item. Before settlement of their dispute, the water demand in Amman, the capital city of Jordan, increased drastically because so many Jordanians had returned from the Gulf states after the Iraqi invasion of Kuwait in 1990. The Yarmouk River was a key water source for Jordan, and the Israeli delegation to the bilateral negotiations responded positively to a request from their Jordanian counterparts to temporarily augment Jordan's share in the Yarmouk with as much as Israel could afford to relinquish. Israel's response built confidence and helped create a positive atmosphere in the negotiations. By October 17, 1994, the two sides arrived at a peace treaty that was signed on October 26 and ratified on November 11. The Treaty of Peace between the Hashemite Kingdom of Jordan and the State of Israel became effective on that date.[6] Annex II to the treaty was devoted to water-related matters.

THE WATER ANNEX

Article 6 of the Jordanian-Israeli peace treaty committed both sides to recognize each other's rightful water shares, cooperate bilaterally and regionally, share information, and protect each party's water resources from degradation by using sound water management and development practices. These commitments were detailed in Annex II: Water-Related Matters, which was negotiated between March 1992 and October 1994.[7]

---

[6] For the complete text of the treaty, see www.kinghussein.gov.jo/peacetreaty.html.

[7] The author of this chapter drafted the Water Annex in September 1994 and negotiated its contents with two Israeli delegates the following month. The annex reflected the substance of negotiations between March 1992 and September 1994. Serious water negotiations started on August 8, 1994, and ended on October 17, 1994.

The Jordan River Basin: A conflict like no other   257

The Jordanian and Israeli sides agreed in March 1992 to negotiate simultaneously the issues of water, energy, and the environment. A common negotiating agenda was approved by both sides in late October 1992. Its ratification by the Jordanian government awaited similar progress on the Israeli-Palestinian track. Progress on that track surprised the world when the Oslo Accords between Israel and the Palestine Liberation Organization (PLO) were signed on September 13, 1993. Jordan and Israel signed their common agenda the following day.[8] Negotiators for Jordan and Israel on water, energy, and the environment reached similar agreement on agendas for negotiations on the three topics in June 1994. These agendas formed the basis for resolution of many aspects of the conflict.

Throughout the 1992–1994 water negotiations, Jordan's stance was based partly on the Jordan Valley Plan of 1955, endorsed by the Arab League's Arab Technical Committee but not ratified by the Arab League's Political Committee. This position was shielded against potential criticism by other Arab countries since it was identical to what the Arab Technical Committee had accepted in 1955. The resurrection of the Jordan Valley Plan in 1992 served Palestinian rights in the Jordan River. The Palestinians were engaged in negotiations with Israel over interim self-government arrangements, and negotiations over water were to be started three years after that. Bilateral talks between Israel and the Palestinians postponed negotiations over water, territories, refugees, and Jerusalem until the Final Status negotiations. Jordan would reach agreement with Israel before that time.

The Jordan Valley Plan had stipulated the water shares of Jordan, which prior to 1988 had included the West Bank. On June 1, 1994, Jordan's King Hussein bin Talal directed that the Jordanian delegation should negotiate only Jordan's share of the water, leaving the shares of the West Bank for the PLO to negotiate with Israel. The PLO and Israel had exchanged political recognition in September 1993. Guided by the Jordan Valley Plan, the Jordanian chief negotiator delineated the water shares of the West Bank and East Bank separately. The West Bank share, amounting to 241 mcm/year, was delineated as follows:

- 52 mcm/year from west-side wadis discharging into the Lower Jordan River within the West Bank.
- 8 mcm/year from groundwater in the Jordan Valley within the West Bank.
- 81 mcm/year from the Yarmouk River (calculated as part of Jordan's share, which was estimated at 377 mcm/year).
- 100 mcm/year from Lake Tiberias, including a maximum of 15 mcm/year of brackish water.

---

[8] Negotiations had been suspended between December 1992 and April 1993 because of Israel's deportation of 316 Palestinian activists to Marj Al-Zuhour in Lebanon. Another reason was the need to modify a sentence in the common agenda related to the occupied Palestinian territories. For details, see Majali, Anani, and Haddadin (2006).

258   Water and post-conflict peacebuilding

The share of the East Bank amounted to 479 mcm/year and was delineated as follows:

- 175 mcm/year from east-side wadis within Jordan.
- 8 mcm/year from groundwater in the Jordan Valley within the East Bank.
- 296 mcm/year from the Yarmouk River.

Based on the Jordan Valley Plan, the only water source for Jordan and Israel to negotiate was the Yarmouk River, which they also shared with Syria. The rest of the water sources awarded to Jordan were not contested and had been put to use in the development of the Jordanian side of the Jordan Valley by 1979.

The Jordan Valley Plan stipulated Jordan's share of the Yarmouk River as the residual flow after deducting annual allocations to Syria (90 mcm/year) and Israel (25 mcm/year, though Israel contested this allocation and claimed 40 mcm/ year). Jordan's annual share was calculated at 377 mcm/year. But by the time of the water negotiations in 1994, Israel was using between 70 and 95 mcm/year depending on the rainfall, and Syria was using about 265 mcm/year. Both had exceeded their allocations at the expense of Jordan and the Palestinians.

The water annex to the Jordanian-Israeli treaty contained seven articles. The first addressed water allocation; as discussed above, it echoed many of the provisions of the Jordan Valley Plan. Syria's violation of that plan was not on the agenda of Jordan's negotiations with Israel, but Israel's violations were. Jordan pressed for a greater share of the Jordan River than had been allocated under the earlier plan, based on municipal and industrial water needs that had not been taken into account by that plan but had become apparent over time. Agreement was reached to allow Israel to pump 20 mcm from the Yarmouk winter flow in return for a summer share for Jordan from Lake Tiberias. Full use by Jordan of the Yarmouk winter flow would be possible only by building a dam at Mukheiba in the lower catchment or by using Lake Tiberias as a storage facility for Yarmouk water. Building of a dam at Mukheiba would require the use of the opposite, Syrian bank of the river, which had been occupied by Israel since 1967. Any attempt to talk about building such a dam would be placed in political limbo. Syria would want to await liberation of its territories from Israeli occupation, and Jordan would not negotiate with Israel, the occupying power, over the use of Israeli-occupied Syrian territory.

The mutual concessions by Jordan and Israel amounted to free virtual storage for Jordan and a way to capture otherwise unregulated Yarmouk winter floodwaters. Physical storage of Yarmouk floods in Lake Tiberias had been envisaged in the Jordan Valley Plan and was then estimated at 90 mcm/year. This article of the water annex has been and is observed by both parties.

The water annex allocated an additional 50 mcm/year of water to Jordan over that allocated in the Jordan Valley Plan. This provision has been partially observed by Israel, which has been supplying Jordan with 25 mcm/year from Lake Tiberias since 1997. In other allocations that go beyond the Jordan Valley

Plan, the water annex allowed Israel to use 10 mcm/year of additional groundwater from Jordanian sources in Wadi Araba and committed Israel to supply Jordan with 10 mcm/year of water from a planned desalination plant to be built near Lake Tiberias. This provision has been observed since 1995. Israel is delivering 10 mcm/year to Jordan from Lake Tiberias until the desalination plant is built.

The second article of the water annex addressed water storage and stipulated the construction of two small dams on the Jordan River on the border between the two countries. Jordan was allocated a minimum of 20 mcm/year of the water so impounded, and Israel was allocated up to 3 mcm if additional storage is possible. The article also stipulated the construction of a diversion dam (also envisioned in the Jordan Valley Plan) to control water diversion from the Yarmouk River to both Jordan and Israel.

The water annex addressed additional issues that were not addressed in the Jordan Valley Plan, including water quality and protection, establishment of a joint water committee, bilateral cooperation, and groundwater outside the Jordan River Basin.

THE IMPACT OF THE WATER ANNEX

The progress achieved on water sharing facilitated the successful conclusion of the peace treaty as well as continued confidence building and peacebuilding after the treaty was signed and ratified. Despite the cold relations that have dominated the political scene between Israel and Jordan since 1999, the two countries have continued to implement the water agreement. This has been a primary factor in avoiding major water-related crises in the Jordan Valley and in Amman. The water that flows to Jordan from Israel has been key to Jordan's ability to mitigate the damage imposed by the drastic reduction in the Yarmouk River flow.[9]

The implementation of the water agreement thus far has enhanced the credibility of the peace treaty and the ability of the two parties to deliver on their commitments. Despite political turmoil in the region, the water agreement has remained almost intact, and its implementation has benefited both sides, particularly Jordan. It is hoped that water agreements will also be concluded between Israel, Lebanon, Syria, and the future Palestine state, and that a settlement will be reached between Jordan and Syria over the Yarmouk River in accordance with their treaties. The water agreements should address the Jordan River Basin as a whole, including the groundwater aquifers. Agreement over water could propel progress toward agreement on other issues of dispute.

---

[9] Jordan blames the reduction in flow on Syrian water use, while Syria argues that it is due to climate change.

260 Water and post-conflict peacebuilding

LESSONS LEARNED

Jordan and Israel's handling of their water conflicts, both before and since the conclusion of the peace treaty, has provided valuable lessons for conflict management and peacebuilding.

Period of conflict

Conflict between Jordan and Israel arose as soon as the State of Israel was established in 1948. Jordan, like all Arab countries, did not recognize Israel's legitimacy and participated in the war that ensued after the proclamation of the State of Israel in 1948. That war ended in an armistice supervised by the United Nations, but Israel and Jordan remained enemies. In the absence of mutual diplomatic recognition, it was not possible for Jordan to engage directly with Israel in negotiations to resolve disputes. The first lesson learned was the value of a third party, friendly to both sides, in mediating the conflict. The involvement of the United States beginning in 1953 in the water conflict between Jordan and Israel was a decisive factor in their ability to develop the water resources of the Jordan River system without a peace treaty or even mutual political recognition.

Throughout the years of conflict, it was important for each side to respect its adversary. Credibility, also crucial, was achieved by honoring commitments and by not promising more than one could deliver. Transparency and credibility were crucial in adversaries' dealings, not only with each other, but also with the intermediary.

It was important to make clear the impact of water on all sectors—economic, social, environmental, and political—to both adversaries and the intermediary. Just as water serves to extinguish fires, it should propel cooperation and not violent confrontation. This lesson was learned in the wake of the military response (i.e., the sandbar incident described above) of both Jordan and Israel (in that order) to their differences over water sharing in 1979.

Above all, particularly during negotiations, adversaries need to understand each other's point of view. In this respect, Israel on more than one occasion appreciated difficulties Jordan was facing in water supply and agreed to augment supplies to Jordan from its share in the Yarmouk River. Such gestures deeply affected Jordanian officials' attitudes toward Israel.

Negotiation

The 1991 negotiations were the first direct contact between the states of Israel and Jordan. An important lesson Jordanian negotiators learned at the outset was that the Israelis were not supermen but peers, no matter how impressive their repeated military victories over the Arabs had been since 1948. Another was the importance of negotiators being able to show that they had done their homework and were aware of the history of the conflict and its development. For example, after Jordanian negotiators proposed to save time and energy by adopting the Jordan Valley Plan, the Israelis cross-examined them on the details of that plan to make sure both sides had the same understanding of it.

Another important lesson was the importance of being honest with the adversary and clear about one's disagreements and the proposed solutions. "Beating around the bush" wastes time and energy.

Also important was the need to display respect and, whenever possible, understanding for the adversary's position. This is not a question of agreement or submission but simply of humanitarian consideration. Putting oneself in the shoes of one's adversaries and imagining how one would act in their position helps promote cooperation in finding a solution acceptable to both sides.

Water should be treated like the life-giving commodity that it is and should be considered in connection with other social, economic, and environmental issues. It was easy for Jordan and Israel to agree, almost without hesitation, to Jordan's proposal to negotiate water, energy, and environmental issues in one negotiation package.

Post-conflict period

The most important lesson learned since the treaty was concluded is the importance of transparency and credibility. Jordan has lived up to this standard.

An unfortunate factor has clouded Jordanian-Israeli relations since the ascent to power of the Israeli right in 1996 in the wake of the assassination of Israeli peacemaker Yitzhak Rabin. That factor is Israel's management of its affairs with the Palestinians and its deliberate delay of the Final Status negotiations between them. The goal of the Jordanian-Israeli negotiations as set out in their common agenda was "the achievement of just, lasting and comprehensive peace between the Arab States, the Palestinians and Israel as per the Madrid Invitation" (Haddadin 2001, 496). Also, the preamble to the Jordan-Israel peace treaty stated as a justification for the treaty "the achievement of a just, lasting and comprehensive peace [in the Middle East] based on Security Council resolutions 242 and 338 in all their aspects."

Violence between Israelis and Palestinians beginning in 1999, which peaked in an all-out war on Gaza in 2008 and continues intermittently, has hindered the growth of positive relations between Jordan and Israel. Despite this, the water annex has continued to be honored by both parties, a statement that cannot be made about other important agreements concluded under the treaty. There has been a lull in achieving the full implementation of the water annex provisions. Construction has not begun on the desalination plant near Lake Tiberias or the two dams on the Jordan River. Both require foreign assistance, which has not been forthcoming due to continuing hostilities in the region. The full delivery of the additional 50 mcm/year of water to Jordan hinges on the desalination plant installation. Until that is achieved, only half of that quantity is delivered by Israel from Lake Tiberias.

262   Water and post-conflict peacebuilding

A post-conflict development that has created a setback in the cooperative approach to peacebuilding has been the shift to the right in Israeli politics. This has been the result of the actions by extremists on both the Israeli and Palestinian sides. Each side wants peace according to its own terms, which are mutually contradictory. The Israeli political right aspires to have peace and keep territories, and the Palestinian extremists desire to have peace and more territory. The political clash inside Israel resulted in the assassination of Prime Minister Yitzhak Rabin, who was able to engineer a peace agreement with the Palestinians as he had done with Jordan. His demise diminished the chances for comprehensive peace in the region. Since the Israeli right ascended to power in 1996, the peace process has, for the most part, been stalled.

The Palestinian reaction to the political shift in Israel has been a shift toward the right. It looked like opponents to comprehensive peace were reinforcing each other on both sides. The return of Israeli moderates to power in 1999 did not help reverse the trend. A second Palestinian intifada in 2000 spread violence and bloodshed. The Israeli right returned to power and is still ruling Israel, and the Palestinian right ascended to power in 2006. There exists little chance for resumption of peace talks.

The Israeli peace talks with Syria were stalled in 2000; indirect talks through Turkey were terminated, and little hope exists today to resume peace talks on that front.

The involvement of the United States gives some hope for the resumption of peace talks. President George W. Bush announced U.S. support for a two-state solution: a Palestinian state next to Israel. President Barack Obama is trying through active engagement of the United States to initiate indirect talks in the hope that they will lead to bilateral negotiations between the Palestinians and Israel. Several bilateral and regional political factors stand in the way.

Even this troubled situation offers a lesson about the need for a comprehensive vision of water, which affects and is affected by every aspect of life, in ways that are not always obvious. The channel of communication over water has always been kept open between Jordan and Israel; mutual visits by high-ranking officials have been made, albeit not publicized.

The main lesson learned during and after the conflict is that water can promote cooperation between adversaries as well as between allies. Both Jordan and Israel realize that their water needs cannot be met even by the entire yield of the Jordan River system. They further realize that conflict would not bring about more water for them but would create a zero-sum game. Conversely, cooperation can yield a positive result from which all parties can benefit.

REFERENCES

Baker, Inc., and Harza Engineering Company. 1955. Appendix V-A: Hydrology and groundwater. In *Yarmouk–Jordan Valley Project master plan report*. Chicago.

Clapp, G. 1953. Letter by Gordon Clapp, chairman of the Tennessee Valley Authority, to Leslie Carven, acting director of the United Nations Relief and Works Agency, August 31. In *Water and power: The politics of a scarce resource in the Jordan River Basin*, 83. Cambridge, UK: Cambridge University Press.

Haddadin, M. J. 2001. *Diplomacy on the Jordan: International conflict and negotiated resolution*. Norwell, MA: Kluwer Academic Publishers.

———. 2006. *Water resources in Jordan: Emerging policies for development, the environment and conflict resolution.* Washington, D.C.: Resources for the Future.

Majali, A., J. Anani, and M. J. Haddadin. 2006. *Peacemaking: The inside story of the 1994 Jordanian Israeli Peace Treaty*. Reading, UK: Ithaca Press / Garnet Publishing.

MOF (Ministry of Foreign Affairs, Hashemite Kingdom of Jordan). 1958. Note number 58/14/6719, dated February 25, 1958, signed by Foreign Minister Samir Al Rifai and addressed to the U.S. chargé d'affaires in Amman.

PRC (Palestine Royal Commission). 1937. Palestine Royal Commission report. July. London: His Majesty's Stationery Office.

UNGA (United Nations General Assembly). 1947. Resolution 181 (II). A/RES/181 (II) (1947). November 29.

———. 1948. Resolution 194 (III). A/RES/194 (III) (1947). December 29.

UNSC (United Nations Security Council). 1953. Resolution 100. S/RES/100 (1953). October 27.

———. 1967. Resolution 242. S/RES/242 (1967). November 22.

———. 1973. Resolution 338. S/RES/338 (1973). October 22.

Yapp, M. E. 1987. *The making of the modern Near East, 1792–1923*. Harlow, England: Longman.

Transboundary cooperation in the Lower Jordan River Basin

Munqeth Mehyar, Nader Al Khateeb, Gidon Bromberg, and Elizabeth Koch-Ya'ari

EcoPeace/Friends of the Earth Middle East (FoEME) was founded in 1994 to foster regional peace through transboundary environmental projects. As one of only a few transboundary organizations working on environmental peacemaking today, its approach and experience in water resource management in conflict and post-conflict situations can serve as a model for both top-down and bottom-up efforts. One of FoEME's central areas of activity, the rehabilitation of the Lower Jordan River, illustrates key strategies by which water projects can facilitate transboundary cooperation.

The Lower Jordan River flowed freely for thousands of years from the Sea of Galilee (also known as Lake Tiberias and Lake Kinneret) to the Dead Sea. The river's location in the Great Rift Valley, at the meeting point of Asia, Africa, and Europe, creates a lush wetland ecosystem, rich in biodiversity and one of the most important migratory flyways on the planet with an estimated 500 million birds traveling its length twice annually (Turner, Nassar, and Al Khateeb 2005). This river has been immortalized in the holy texts of the three Abrahamic traditions and remains an important cultural anchor for half of the world's population.

Sadly, the mighty Jordan River has been reduced to a trickle—devastated by overexploitation, pollution, and a lack of regional management. According to recent studies conducted by Yale University (Anisfeld and Shub 2009), this important regional water resource once carried an average of 1.3 billion cubic meters of fresh water from the Sea of Galilee to the Dead Sea every year.

Friends of the Earth Middle East (www.foeme.org) is an association of Jordanian, Palestinian, and Israeli environmentalists working to promote cooperative efforts to protect the region's shared environmental heritage. Munqeth Mehyar, Nader Al Khateeb, and Gidon Bromberg are FoEME's Jordanian, Palestinian, and Israeli directors, respectively; Elizabeth Koch-Ya'ari is the Israeli coordinator of the organization's Jordan River Rehabilitation Project. An earlier version of this chapter was published in *Getting Transboundary Water Right: Theory and Practice for Effective Cooperation*, Stockholm International Water Institute Report No. 25, edited by A. Jägerskog and M. Zeitoun (Stockholm International Water Institute, 2009).

266   Water and post-conflict peacebuilding

The 1994 Treaty of Peace between the Hashemite Kingdom of Jordan and the State of Israel committed the two countries to work toward the ecological rehabilitation of the river, renewing hopes that they would act to restore the Lower Jordan River through coordinated management. Despite this formidable commitment, in the sixteen years that have passed since the signing of the treaty, neither government has taken concrete action to return any measure of fresh water to the river. On the contrary, a new dam—the Unity Dam, which was a joint Syrian and Jordanian undertaking—was built on the Yarmouk River, a tributary of the Jordan, to capture its remaining winter floodwaters.

In 2010, FoEME completed the first environmental flows study ever conducted on the Lower Jordan River, in a trilateral effort to identify its ecological needs. The study found that the river was in even worse ecological shape than previously estimated with just 20 to 30 million cubic meters (mcm) of annual discharge. This striking finding indicated that, in the absence of a formal regional management authority, Israel, Jordan, and Syria have diverted nearly 98 percent of the Lower Jordan River's historic flow for domestic and agricultural purposes. This big-grab approach to water management has effectively destroyed the Lower Jordan River, reduced biodiversity along its banks by over 50 percent, and transformed the culturally and historically important river into little more than an open channel of agricultural runoff, diverted saline waters, and wastewater, which has further resulted in the devastation of its terminal lake, the Dead Sea (Gafny, Talozi, and Al Shiekh 2010).

The story of the demise of the Lower Jordan River is hardly unique. Around the world, human activity has pulled massive quantities of water from the great rivers—the Indus on the Indian subcontinent, the Yellow in China, the Rio Grande along the U.S.-Mexico border—to the extent that they now either disappear before reaching the sea or contain long sections that seasonally run dry. The underlying reason is always the same: rivers are viewed, not as valuable in themselves, but as exploitable resources for human and economic development. The vital ecosystem services they supply, which support people, fish, animals, and plants as well as economic development, are overlooked until they are lost.

PROGRESS IS POSSIBLE

Despite this grim picture, FoEME has demonstrated that it is possible to reverse decades of deterioration on a river—even, as in the case of the Lower Jordan River, in the midst of animosity, sometimes erupting into violent conflict, between the countries that share it, and in spite of reduced precipitation due to climate change. Positive action, though still piecemeal and slow, is taking place at the grassroots level as well as at the national and regional levels due to increased public awareness and advancement of a strong regional coalition in support of efforts to rehabilitate the river.

At the grassroots level, support is growing in communities on both sides of the Lower Jordan River in Israel, Jordan, and Palestine, led by FoEME coordinators

Cooperation in the Lower Jordan River Basin 267

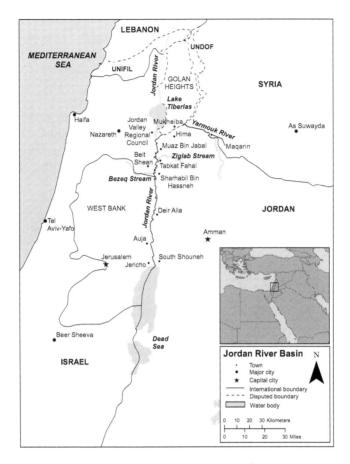

Note: The Sea of Galilee is also known as Lake Kinneret and as Lake Tiberias.

who run grassroots environmental education and public-awareness activities in twenty-five communities. These local leaders coordinate dozens of activities involving youth and adults and serve as direct links to municipal representatives. Thousands of Jordan Valley residents have participated in Neighbors Path Tours that educate them on the state of the river and its tributaries. Through these tours, many residents learn for the first time how the river's waters are being diverted, come to understand the effects of pollution, and see the economic opportunities that have been missed because of the unhealthy state of the river. Some tours actually cross the border, and all explore the water issues of neighboring communities. Media participation in these unique tours helps tell the story of the Lower Jordan River to the broader public, both local and international, effectively placing its plight at the center of the public debate and creating a constituency of local residents empowered to voice their concerns.

268   Water and post-conflict peacebuilding

Israeli, Jordanian, and Palestinian mayors were involved from the outset as necessary partners in support of regional water policy reform. The project identified mayors both as the most receptive to community residents' needs and perspectives and as key stakeholders with much to gain from the economic opportunities a rehabilitated river would create. Mayors have not only participated in tours in their own communities and neighboring cross-border communities but have also led municipal efforts to remove pollutants from the river. They have, on several occasions, literally jumped into the river together, in public events designed to express their commitment to regional water policy reform.

FoEME has created a Lower Jordan River Regional Advisory Committee, involving key government representatives and other stakeholders from Israel, Jordan, Palestine, and the international community. This forum is unique in bringing regional decision makers to the table to strategize how to achieve the shared goal of rehabilitating the Lower Jordan River. Through involvement in this forum, leading national figures have spoken out publicly, drawing public attention to the state of the Lower Jordan River and advancing plans for its rehabilitation, primarily at the national level but also in communication with their regional counterparts.

The cumulative results of these bottom-up and top-down strategies are starting to yield concrete results. All Jordan Valley mayors have signed memorandums of understanding with their neighbors, committing their communities to rehabilitate the river and identifying concrete actions that they can take. These commitments have enabled further financial support of joint projects such as the creation of a cross-border Israeli-Jordanian Park, the Jordan River Peace Park, at the confluence of the Jordan and Yarmouk rivers; the building of an environmental education center in Auja, Palestine; and the creation of a protected area, park, and visitor center on the Ziglab Stream, a tributary of the Jordan River in Jordan.

The current practice of allowing untreated sewage to flow into the Lower Jordan River will be significantly reduced with the upcoming activation of several new sewage treatment plants in the Jordan Valley. In Israel, a plant has been completed in the community of Beit She'an. The Jordan Valley Regional Council, also in Israel, has broken ground on a new plant that will treat the sewage of Tiberias and other Sea of Galilee communities. In northwestern Jordan, North Shuna—the largest community in the valley—has launched a project to collect sewage from cesspits for treatment rather than allowing it to seep into the ground and pollute the springs that flow into the Lower Jordan River.

Lower Jordan River champions are also hosting discussions on how to bring fresh water back to the river. In a joint initiative of the Israeli Ministry of Regional Cooperation and Ministry of Environmental Protection, the terms of reference for the ministries' program to rehabilitate the Lower Jordan River from the Sea of Galilee to Bezeq Stream have been drafted and presented to their Jordanian and Palestinian counterparts for feedback via FoEME's Regional Advisory Committee.

RESTORING AND REALLOCATING THE LOWER JORDAN RIVER

Returning fresh water to the river is the most important and most difficult issue. While Israeli, Jordanian, and Palestinian champions have made public statements committing to rehabilitating the river and drafted plans for how this will take place, freshwater resources have yet to be allocated to the struggling river.

To address this concern, the Jordan River Rehabilitation Project undertook two studies to inform a regional strategy for the Lower Jordan River. The environmental flows study mentioned earlier identified a target level of rehabilitation, and a related economic study identified tradeoffs and opportunities for national and regional water management reform to reallocate water to the Lower Jordan (Gorskaya, Rosenthal, and Harthi 2010). Both of these studies involved Israeli, Jordanian, and Palestinian experts working together and were overseen by FoEME's Regional Advisory Committee.

The environmental flows study (Gafny, Talozi, and Al Shiekh 2010) proposed a regional rehabilitation strategy that requires 400 to 600 mcm of flow annually, including one minor flood,[1] a salinity level of no more than 750 parts per million, and a base flow that consists of at least 75 percent fresh water with the remainder made up of high-quality treated effluents. This would remove most of the environmental disturbances, restore the river's structure and function, allow the natural riparian plant community to recover, and achieve fair to high ecosystem integrity, health, and stability.

This strategy would require substantial but achievable water and economic resources. The economic study (Gorskaya, Rosenthal, and Harthi 2010) identified between 463 and 1,053 mcm of freshwater resources that could be saved or produced from the Israeli, Jordanian, and Palestinian water economies and potentially allocated to the Lower Jordan River through the implementation of reasonably priced domestic and agricultural water demand management.

To further strengthen the national and regional political will required to implement the measures recommended in these studies, public hearings, parliamentary debates, and regional conferences are planned to educate the public and create political momentum.

The equitable sharing of the Lower Jordan River's water between people and nature in all countries bordering the river is of paramount importance. While Palestinians are presently denied the right to extract water from the river by Israel, they sit alongside their Israeli and Jordanian counterparts in FoEME's Regional Advisory Committee meetings to work for a new future for the Lower Jordan River. FoEME's experience has shown that a dual approach—an energetic

---

[1] All floodwaters are currently caught and stored rather than being allowed to flow into the Lower Jordan River. Floods are essential to healthy river ecology as they flush fine sediment and associated pollutants, reconnect the channel and floodplain, remove invasive plant and animal species, and provide biological cues for native migration and breeding. Therefore, flow variation, including at least one minor (artificial) flood, is a critical part of the rehabilitation plan.

270   Water and post-conflict peacebuilding

grassroots or bottom-up campaign that demonstrates local benefits for transboundary environmental rehabilitation projects, combined with top-down advocacy—is critical to creating concrete change. The international community is supporting this work in two ways: encouraging the three Lower Jordan River national governments to work together for water policy reform, and sharing other experiences of cross-border water resources management, for example from the Rhine River in Europe, the Great Lakes of North America, and the Nile River in Africa.

Decades of conflict and human arrogance have led to the near total demise of the Lower Jordan River. FoEME believes that cross-border cooperation to advance peace and sustainable development in the Lower Jordan River Valley is the only hope to restore the river to health, while creating economic and social opportunities for all communities along its banks.

REFERENCES

Anisfeld, S., and J. Shub. 2009. Historical flows in the Lower Jordan River. New Haven, CT: Yale School of Forestry and Environmental Studies.

Gafny, S., S. Talozi, and B. Al Shiekh. 2010. *Towards a living Jordan River: An environmental flows report on the rehabilitation of the Lower Jordan River.* Ed. E. Ya'ari. EcoPeace/Friends of the Earth Middle East.

Gorskaya, T., G. Rosenthal, and T. Harthi. 2010. *Transboundary diagnosis analysis of the Lower Jordan River.* EcoPeace/Friends of the Earth Middle East.

Turner, M., K. Nassar, and N. Al Khateeb. 2005. *Crossing the Jordan: Concept document to rehabilitate, promote prosperity and help bring peace to the Lower Jordan River Valley.* Ed. G. Bromberg. EcoPeace/Friends of the Earth Middle East.

The Sava River: Transitioning to peace in the former Yugoslavia

Amar Čolakhodžić, Marija Filipović, Jana Kovandžić, and Stephen Stec

The Sava River flows through Slovenia, Croatia, Bosnia and Herzegovina, and Serbia on its way to join the Danube in Belgrade. This formerly national river became international as a result of the 1991–1995 Yugoslav conflicts. Following the end of hostilities, the need for joint management of the river according to up-to-date management principles provided the formerly warring parties an opportunity to build new regional cooperative institutions. Multiyear negotiations with international support produced the Framework Agreement on the Sava River Basin (FASRB) and the Protocol on the Navigation Regime to the FASRB;[1] to implement these instruments, the International Sava River Basin Commission (ISRBC) was established in 2006 with headquarters in Zagreb, Croatia.

While armed hostilities have ceased between the countries of the former Yugoslavia, differences remain. For example, upstream countries have a strong interest in recreation and tourism, while for downstream countries, industry, agriculture, and navigation have higher priority. Slovenia, a European Union (EU) member state, has different concerns from the other states, which are still applying for EU membership. However, many of these differences are now addressed through the ISRBC.

This chapter examines the negotiations that led to the FASRB and the ISRBC and assesses their performance to date. Following an overview of the conflict and a description of the Sava River Basin, the chapter describes post-conflict

---

Amar Čolakhodžić implements sustainable green-building projects in Dubai. Marija Filipović works as an independent climate change consultant in New York City. Jana Kovandžić is a master's degree student in Environmental Science, Policy, and Management at Lund University. Stephen Stec is an adjunct professor at Central European University and directs the Environmental Security Program in its Center for Environment and Security; he worked on the chapter while a visiting scholar at Middlebury College and Monterey Institute of International Studies. The authors received valuable research assistance from Jelena Stanić and Miloš Milićević.

[1] For the complete text of the FASRB, see www.savacommission.org/dms/docs/dokumenti/ documents_publications/basic_documents/fasrb.pdf. For the complete text of the navigation protocol, see www.savacommission.org/dms/docs/dokumenti/documents_publications/ basic_documents/protocol_on_navigation_regime.pdf.

272 Water and post-conflict peacebuilding

challenges to joint management of the basin, earlier attempts at joint management, and the eventual establishment of the ISRBC—with the support of the international community, which saw the Sava River Basin as a key area for post-conflict cooperation and confidence building. The institutions and mechanisms that were established in this process are placed within the context of broader European and global processes. The chapter assesses the future prospects for the ISRBC's work and recommends some important next steps. Finally, factors affecting the success of peacebuilding efforts in this arena are reviewed, along with lessons learned.

BACKGROUND

The Yugoslav conflicts took place in a geographically and politically complex region. Its environment, already fragile due to decades of poor resource management, was further stressed during the conflict.

Dissolution of Yugoslavia

The conflicts in the 1990s that led to the dissolution of Yugoslavia were the deadliest hostilities in Europe since World War II. The conflicts in Croatia and Bosnia and Herzegovina from 1992–1995 alone left an estimated 300,000 people dead and 3 million displaced (Glenny 2000). The conflicts had their roots in the breakdown of the Cold War order, in which communist ideology was able to unify Yugoslavia's Serbs, Croats, Slovenes, Bosnians,[2] Albanians, and Macedonians (Carnegie Commission 2000). With the breakdown in support for the cosmopolitan socialist narrative that had defined the post–World War II period, nationalist narratives gained ascendancy (Bjelajac et al. 2007; Schwandner-Sievers and Fischer 2002; Prunk 1994). In the late 1980s, Serbian leader Slobodan Milošević consolidated his political power by exploiting fear over the Kosovo Serb minority's fate (Bjelajac et al. 2007).

In July 1991, Slovenia became the first part of the Socialist Federal Republic of Yugoslavia to secede successfully, after a ten-day war against the Yugoslav People's Army. Croatia had declared independence on June 25, 1991, but ethnic Serbs in the eastern Croatian districts of Krajina and Slavonia attempted to set up separate authorities and appealed to Belgrade for protection (Almond 1994). Paramilitary forces formed on ethnic lines throughout Croatia and Bosnia and Herzegovina (Almond 1994). In August, the Yugoslav People's Army entered Croatia to support the Serbs in Krajina and Slavonia, and conflict erupted (Glenny 2000). By the time Croatia was admitted to the United Nations in spring 1992, the Yugoslav People's Army occupied Krajina, Eastern Slavonia, and Western

---

[2] *Bosnian* refers to someone of any ethnic or religious group from Bosnia and Herzegovina. The term *Bosniak*, also used in this chapter, generally refers to Bosnian Muslims. Bosniaks are an ethnic South-Slavic group from the historical region of present-day Bosnia, characterized by adherence to Islam since the fifteenth and sixteenth centuries, with a common culture and language.

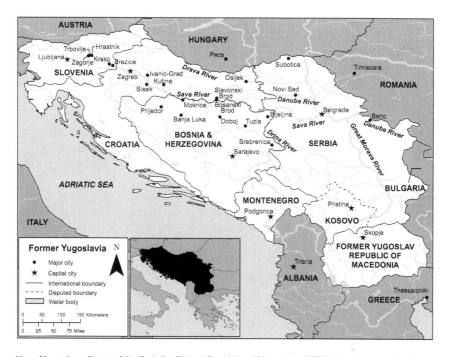

Note: Upon the collapse of the Socialist Federal Republic of Yugoslavia (SFRY, also known as the *former Yugoslavia*), the SFRY republics of Serbia and Montenegro joined to become the Federal Republic of Yugoslavia, which—in 2003—became the Union of Serbia and Montenegro. On June 2, 2006, Montenegro declared its independence from Serbia, and two states were formed: Serbia and Montenegro.

Slavonia, one-third of its territory (Almond 1994). In February 1992, the United Nations Protection Force was given a mandate to protect certain safe areas in Croatia; this mandate was gradually extended to further peacekeeping activities in Croatia and Bosnia and Herzegovina. From 1993 through 1995, Croatia's army pushed the Yugoslav People's Army and ethnic Serb residents out of Krajina and West Slavonia (Glenny 2000). When the conflict ended in 1995, an agreement was reached on the gradual reintegration of the remaining Serb-held areas of Eastern Slavonia into Croatia, a process that was completed in 1998.

Serb leader Milošević and Croatian leader Franjo Tudjman had agreed in March 1991 to divide Bosnia and Herzegovina between their two countries. In fulfillment of this agreement, Croatian forces in Bosnia and Herzegovina declared certain territories to comprise the Croatian Republic of Herceg-Bosna. In January 1992, Serb-dominated areas declared the existence of the Serbian Republic of Bosnia and Herzegovina, later renamed Republika Srpska. That April, the Bosnian parliament (with ethnic Serb representatives abstaining) declared independence and established the Army of Bosnia and Herzegovina. The Yugoslav army's military assets were transferred to the Army of Republika Srpska, which engaged in military action in concert with Bosnian Serb and Serbian militias in their attempts

274 Water and post-conflict peacebuilding

to partition Bosnia and Herzegovina along ethnic lines. In May, Radovan Karadžić, the leader of Republika Srpska, and Mate Boban, the leader of the Croatian Republic of Herceg-Bosna, signed the Graz Agreement, which divided Bosnia and Herzegovina, leaving a small Bosniak buffer state.

After this agreement, Croatian and Bosnian forces fought in what has been called the Croat-Bosniak War. This ended in early 1994 with the Washington Agreement, under which the Croats and Bosniaks agreed to form the Federation of Bosnia and Herzegovina. The Washington Agreement specified that the use of natural resources and the formulation of joint environmental policies within this federation, and its possible confederation with the Republic of Croatia, would be formulated jointly by the central government and the canton governments (USIP 1997).

Despite the Croat-Bosniak alliance, the government of Croatia reached a separate ceasefire with Serb forces in Bosnia and Herzegovina in March 1994, and shortly thereafter Serb forces began to attack the UN safe havens in eastern Bosnia and Herzegovina, prompting a bombing campaign by the North Atlantic Treaty Organization (NATO). In July 1995, Serb forces moved against the other safe havens, culminating in the Srebrenica massacre, in which approximately 8,000 Bosnian Muslims were killed—the largest act of genocide in Europe since World War II. Increasing pressure to settle the conflict in Bosnia and Herzegovina resulted in the General Framework Agreement for Peace in Bosnia and Herzegovina, known as the Dayton Peace Agreement, which was signed in December 1995. By the end of the conflict in Bosnia and Herzegovina, half of Bosnia and Herzegovina's population of 4 million had been killed, injured, or displaced (Glenny 2000). Renewed military activity in the Sava River Basin took place in spring 1999 with NATO bombing of Serbian infrastructure during the Kosovo conflict.

The countries that emerged from the dissolution of Yugoslavia (with the exception of Slovenia) suffered major disruption of their economic and social fabric and have continued to lag behind the rest of Central and Eastern Europe in various indicators of human development.[3] Long-term environmental damage resulted from the widespread use of landmines; the use of depleted uranium munitions, particularly in Serbia during the Kosovo conflict;[4] the destruction of chemical facilities and other critical infrastructure; and the impacts of refugees and displaced persons (UNEP and UNCHS 1999). More than 1 million landmines and 1 billion small-arms rounds remained scattered across Croatia after the conflict ended (GOC 1998). In the period 1990–1998, as much as 24 percent of

---

[3] In 1985 Yugoslavia had a UN Human Development Index (HDI) of 0.913. (The HDI is a composite index that measures development by combining indicators of life expectancy, educational attainment, and income, expressed as a value between 0 and 1.) Conflict caused the HDIs in the region to drop significantly. In 1995, Croatia's HDI was 0.759; in 1999, the HDI for the Federal Republic of Yugoslavia (then consisting of Serbia and Montenegro) was only 0.729. In 1985, Yugoslavia's per capita gross domestic product (GDP) was $2,480, and Hungary's was $2,240. By 2007, Hungary's per capita GDP had risen to $13,766, while Croatia's was $11,559 and Serbia's was $5,435 (UNDP 1990, 1991, 1998, 2000, 2009).

[4] During the Kosovo conflict, Serbia was a republic of the Federal Republic of Yugoslavia.

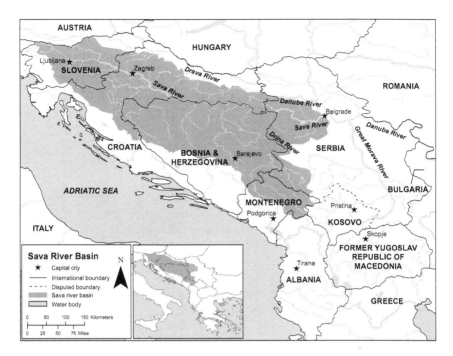

Figure 1. The Sava River and its tributaries
Source: Adapted from Zinke et al. (2007).

the population of former Yugoslavia and its successor states lacked access to safe drinking water (UNDP 2000).

The Sava River Basin

The Sava River and its tributaries connect the capitals of four basin states: Ljubljana, Slovenia; Zagreb, Croatia; Sarajevo, Bosnia and Herzegovina; and Belgrade, Serbia (see figure 1). It is the second largest tributary of the Danube and was the most important inland waterway in former Yugoslavia. The Sava River was a key component of a post–World War II economy based on heavy industrialization and collective farming. A total of 593 kilometers was navigable for vessels with a capacity of 1,500 tons, and approximately 15 million tons of goods were transported per year (Vukasovic 2006).

The Sava River Basin is the largest drainage area in the Western Balkans and a major water source for the countries through which the Sava River system flows. (See table 1 for each country's portion of the basin and the basin's share of national territory.) The basin is home to a wide variety of plants and animals; the river and its tributaries pass through recreational areas, national parks, forests, and other protected areas. Around 35 percent of the population of former Yugoslavia (8.5 million) lived in the Sava River Basin (Tomić and Budin 1989).

276 Water and post-conflict peacebuilding

Table 1. Sava River Basin shares by country

Country	Country's share of basin	Basin's share of national territory
Albania	0.2%	0.6%
Bosnia and Herzegovina	39.2%	75.8%
Croatia	26.0%	45.2%
Montenegro	7.1%	49.6%
Serbia	15.5%	17.4%
Slovenia	12.0%	52.8%
Total basin	**100.0%**	

Source: Komatina (2010).

The Sava River Basin is less developed than other river basins in Europe. Water retention capacity per capita for Bosnia and Herzegovina, Croatia, and Serbia is well below the world average; water management suffers from inadequate institutional structures, inefficient operations, lack of water and sewage treatment plants, outdated water pipelines and sewage systems, lack of assessment and planning, and reduced financial capacity (World Bank 2003). The Sava River Basin has unexploited potential for electricity production and irrigation and represents an important source of water and sanitation, and is thus vital to post-conflict reconstruction.

By the late 1980s, the Sava River, already heavily polluted from industry, agriculture, wastewater discharges, and navigation, was clean for only thirty kilometers in the upper flow (Meštrov et al. 1989). Parts of the basin, such as the basin's floodplain, were under heavy agricultural use, while mining in Bosnia and Herzegovina, construction of thermal plants, and other exploitation of natural resources had a huge impact on environmental quality (Čolakhodžić 2008). The industrial region downstream from Ljubljana, the mining complex of Zagorje, Trbovlje, and Hrastnik, as well as the industrialized region of Sevnica-Krsko (in southeastern Slovenia) overloaded the Sava River with wastewater. It was already highly polluted when it reached Zagreb, where a highly developed manufacturing industry polluted it further (Meštrov et al. 1989). Yugoslav water authorities were considering urgent action when the conflict erupted.

Environmental impact of the conflict

Yugoslavia was already suffering from the environmental effects of a centrally planned economy, lack of investment in the environment, and technological decay; conflict made a bad situation worse (UNEP and UNCHS 1999). Many industrial facilities are outdated and poorly maintained; many have been abandoned. The region is highly polluted in urban and industrial areas and in the mining sector; intensive agriculture and lack of adequate water technology and infrastructure compound the problem. While the United Nations Environment Programme concluded that the conflicts in Yugoslavia did not result in an environmental disaster,

The Sava River: transitioning to peace 277

the population perceives conflict-related environmental impacts as direct threats to the economy, health, and well-being (Čolakhodžić 2008). This situation is exacerbated by various factors including the migration of rural people to urban centers, driven by decades of policies favoring low food prices that continue today (Hopić 2009). During the 1992–1995 international embargo, authorities kept food prices artificially low, which—combined with delayed payments—led to huge financial losses for farmers, the abandonment of many farms, and migration to the cities (Zarić et al. 2005).

The conflicts' creation of large refugee populations has also put pressure on the environment. Illegal dump sites that sprang up near refugee camps could not be connected to existing sewage systems, leading to pollution of the water table (REC 1999). Many camps and their dump sites were located near rivers, including the Sava River (UNEP and GRID-Arendal 2000). Many refugees are still waiting to return home, especially in Serbia and Croatia. In 2009, approximately 165,000 refugees and 248,000 internally displaced persons remained in Serbia alone (UNDP 2009). This widespread displacement has caused considerable social change and left its mark on the economy and environment. In some cities, refugees almost doubled the population.

In many places, local residents and refugees alike still rely on rivers and streams near illegal dump sites for water, exposing themselves to health risks. UN and EU programs supporting the camps have been severely criticized for their failure to solve water issues (ECOSOC 2005). In 2008, approximately 8 percent of refugees still did not have access to clean drinking water, and 13 percent lacked access to sanitation (KIRS 2008). On average a refugee produces between four and ten kilograms of waste per day, much of it plastic and metal packaging from aid agencies' supplies (CBC News 2007). These and similar issues have affected the hydrological cycle and water quality (Kendrovski and Kochuboski 2001).

Military action, which was heavy in the Sava River Basin, also had a huge impact on rivers. Landmines were extensively used in the Sava River Basin. Where mines exploded, heavy metals (such as cadmium, lead, and mercury) are present in the soil at ten times background values and have increased groundwater pollution (Miko et al. 1995). The oil refineries at Sisak in Croatia and Bosanski Brod in Bosnia and Herzegovina were attacked several times, and approximately 12,000 tons of oil and oil derivatives found their way into the Sava River (Murphy 1997). At the river's confluence with the Danube in Belgrade, levels of certain dangerous substances were far above acceptable levels (Martinović-Vitanović and Kalafatić 2009). Serbian forces attacked the Petrochemia plant in Kutina, Croatia—a manufacturer of fertilizer and other petroleum products using ammonia, sulfur, nitric and phosphoric acids, and formaldehyde—on six occasions during 1993–1995 (Murphy 1997). Serbs also targeted a natural gas refinery in Ivanic-Grad and a chemical plant in Jovan; at the latter, seventy-two tons of anhydrous ammonia were released. In Republika Srpska Krajina, the destruction of power station transformers released PCBs, flame retardants, and explosives into the groundwater (Picer 1998).

278   Water and post-conflict peacebuilding

The NATO bombing of Serbia during the 1999 Kosovo conflict placed an additional burden on the already fragile and conflict-torn Sava River Basin. On a single occasion, approximately 150 tons of crude oil and gasoline entered the Sava River (Tošović and Šolaja 1999). As a result of the bombing of the Barič industrial complex, hydrogen fluoride, nitric acid, and liquid ammonia were released, killing all aquatic wildlife for thirty kilometers downstream (Tošović and Šolaja 1999). Since then, fishing has been abandoned and crop irrigation has become problematic. The river's sandy bed has trapped toxic heavy metals. In addition to Serbia, the downstream countries of Romania and Bulgaria were also affected (UNEP and UNCHS 1999).

Other incidents took place along the Sava's tributaries, polluting both surface and ground water that eventually entered the Sava River. Chronic bronchitis, asthma, eczema, diarrhea, and thyroid diseases were detected in the year after the NATO bombing (Popovska and Šopova 2000). Later, a significant growth (up to 400 percent) in the number of people with cancer was recorded (Ždrale et al. 2007; Jovanović 2007), which may be connected with these toxic spills (UNEP 2004). Scientists observed an increased frequency of colorectal cancer in areas where the population was exposed to depleted uranium (Ždrale et al. 2007). Contamination and poor water and hazardous waste management, already a problem before the conflict, worsened and created urgent problems (UNEP 2004). Releases of toxic, mutagenic, and cancerous chemicals have increased lung, skin, and other diseases among the population of Serbia and Bosnia and Herzegovina, affecting the entire food chain, from fruit and vegetables and livestock fodder to meat and dairy products (Ždrale et al. 2007; Jovanović 2007).

Conflict, economic decline, and neglect also affected the navigability of the Sava River through erosion, obstruction from bombed bridges, destruction of navigation infrastructure, and mines. Today the Sava River is navigable for large vessels (up to 1,500 tons) from Belgrade to Slavonski Brod, Croatia (377 kilometers), and for small vessels to Sisak, Croatia (583 kilometers) (ISRBC 2008). In the past it was navigable for large vessels up to Sisak. The estimated cost to restore large-vessel navigation to the entire 583-kilometer route is at least €79.4 million.

Deforestation had a significant impact on the river. Yugoslavia was under a tight oil embargo during the conflict, and any oil that slipped through was used for military purposes. Serbian settlements in particular had to find alternative sources of heating fuel and electricity, and usually relied on coal and firewood (Dimitrijević and Pejić 1995). This—combined with poor land use practices—caused severe deforestation, increasing soil erosion along the riverbanks. The Sava River has a low channel slope and low stream power, and the increased sediment load further reduced navigability.

When the Yugoslav conflicts erupted, the effort to protect the Sava River Basin was just getting under way. Until then, the river had been wholly within the jurisdiction of Yugoslavia, where water laws included the Regulations on

The Sava River: transitioning to peace 279

Water Communities of 1952, the Agricultural Land Utilization Act of 1959, and the Water Act of 1965, as well as water acts issued by individual republics and provinces within Yugoslavia (Bašić 1989). The first Sava River Basin Management Plan was developed by the Yugoslav government in 1972. Despite efforts to implement this plan, a 1987 scientific conference concluded that the river was no longer useable for drinking, recreation, tourism, industry, agriculture, or fishing (Bašić 1989). Water pollution was beginning to limit the potential for economic development (Petrik, Meštrov, and Brundić 1989).

Conflict put efforts to manage the river on hold for more than a decade. During this time, international standards for river basin management became highly developed, but scientists from some Sava countries were cut off from these advances due to sanctions that prevented their participation in international activities. When the conflict ended, some experts remained committed to out-of-date standards.

POST-CONFLICT SAVA RIVER BASIN MANAGEMENT

Sava River Basin countries came to the negotiating table with differing needs and priorities. Negotiations, which received strong international support, served not only to improve river basin management but also to promote regional cooperation. An incremental approach led to a basic framework being approved in 2002, followed by a number of specific protocols.[5] Several controversial issues were bypassed during the fragile early stages of the agreement process but will have to be addressed eventually. Chief among these is the need for greater transparency in river basin management.

Constraints on river basin management

At the end of the Yugoslav conflicts, the most urgent issues concerned establishment of civilian government, delineation of territory, decommissioning of armed forces, establishment of power-sharing agreements, and return of refugees. Natural resource management and environmental protection had been low priorities in the agreements ending the conflict. In the immediate post-conflict period, restoration of industry and agriculture, coupled with inadequate environmental policies and capacity for implementation, exacerbated pollution (World Bank 2003). After a long period of conflict, the prospect of the newly independent states cooperating on environmental matters was remote.

---

[5] When negotiations began, Serbia and Montenegro comprised one country and was considered one of the four riparian states (not counting Albania, which included a tiny proportion of the basin). When Montenegro seceded in 2006, Serbia remained a riparian state, and Montenegro became one of the six countries in the Sava River Basin. As of July 2012, Montenegro had not yet become a party to the basic framework or the subsequent protocols agreed to prior to its independence. In preliminary discussions, Montenegro has expressed an interest to join in due course.

280   Water and post-conflict peacebuilding

Once attention turned from stabilization to reconstruction, however, the economically and ecologically important Sava River was an obvious priority. Water is not scarce in the Sava River Basin, but the potential existed for disputes over water, especially given the lack of treatment systems and the outdated water and sewage systems. The reindustrialization of the basin appeared inevitable, and the return of refugees and emigrants was expected to exert pressure on water systems. The need for dialogue and coordination became apparent.

The riparian countries had different interests, experiences during the conflict, capacities, and internal political situations. Slovenia, the most removed from the conflict and the most economically and politically advanced, was not a hard negotiator and saw the Sava negotiation process as a way to improve stability on its borders as well as to show itself as a good European citizen. As an upstream country without a navigable stretch of the river, its interest in the Sava mainly related to tourism and environmental protection. Croatia was concerned with navigation, due to the status of Sisak as the main inland port in the vicinity of the capital, Zagreb. Croatia and Bosnia and Herzegovina also had an interest in flood control and hydropower. Serbia and Montenegro, as the downstream country, was concerned with water quality and quantity. Protection of the aquatic ecosystem was an issue during negotiations as well, because of the principles of sustainability derived from the Convention on the Protection and Use of Transboundary Watercourses and International Lakes (also known as the Helsinki Water Convention)[6] and the EU Water Framework Directive (WFD).[7]

Numerous obstacles stood in the way of cooperation. The resolution of the conflict was radically different for Bosnia and Herzegovina than for Slovenia and Croatia. In Slovenia and Croatia, existing republic-level authorities became national authorities. But in the case of Bosnia and Herzegovina, an entirely new constitutional order was established, with the Federation of Bosnia and Herzegovina, the Republika Srpska, and the special district of Brcko united under a national government with limited powers. These entities, not the national government, received responsibility for the environment. In the case of the Federation of Bosnia and Herzegovina, there were also potential overlapping responsibilities at the canton level. Lack of clear lines of authority, the unclear mandate of state-level negotiators, and power struggles between different ethnic blocs hampered efforts by Bosnia and Herzegovina to participate in international talks for some time.

---

[6] For the complete text of the Helsinki Water Convention, adopted by member states of the United Nations Economic Commission for Europe on March 17, 1992, see www.unece.org/fileadmin/DAM/env/water/pdf/watercon.pdf.

[7] The EU Water Framework Directive—formally, Directive 2000/60/EC of the European Parliament and of the Council of 23 October 2000 Establishing a Framework for the Community Action in the Field of Water Policy—was adopted on October 23, 2000. For the complete text of the directive, see http://eur-lex.europa.eu/LexUriServ/LexUriServ .do?uri=OJ:L:2000:327:0001:0072:EN:PDF.

International support for cooperation

The Sava River Basin provided an opportunity to foster cooperation in the region while also taking advantage of more than a decade of advances in river basin management. Efforts at regional cooperation found ready support from the international community. In 1999 the Stability Pact for South Eastern Europe opened the way to cooperation among the Sava riparian states. Under the pact's auspices, representatives of the riparian countries met several times in 2001 to discuss international cooperation on river basin management. In November, they agreed to work on an agreement on the Sava River.

In 2002, they formed two working groups, one to focus on a legal framework and the other on a technical action plan. The effort began to attract support from a number of international bodies: the Office of the High Representative in Bosnia and Herzegovina, the Organization for Security and Co-operation in Europe, the International Commission for the Protection of the Danube River (ICPDR), the European Commission, and the Regional Environmental Center for Central and Eastern Europe (REC). The REC received funding from the U.S. government to serve as an interim secretariat. Its long-standing presence in the region and record of neutrality helped facilitate negotiations. The Netherlands and Hungary also provided support through the Stability Pact.

Major advances had been made in river basin management since the last pre-conflict efforts at cooperation in the Sava River Basin. The Helsinki Water Convention, to which some experts from former Yugoslavia had contributed, provided a reference point for the Sava River negotiations. The convention encouraged the establishment of agreements at the river basin level. One such agreement is the Convention on Co-operation for the Protection and Sustainable Use of the River Danube, also known as the Danube River Protection Convention, which gave rise to the ICPDR.[8] The member states of the Framework Agreement on the Sava River Basin (FASRB) also agreed to be guided by the WFD, which set standards for river basin management and water quality. EU membership has been a goal for all Sava River Basin countries, and thus they have been committed to adopting EU standards.

The Danube River is also subject to a separate navigation regime under the Convention Regarding the Regime of Navigation on the Danube, also known as the Belgrade Convention.[9] Serbia and Croatia are parties to the Belgrade Convention; Slovenia and Bosnia and Herzegovina are not. Serbia only became a party to the Danube River Protection Convention in 2003, and Bosnia and Herzegovina in 2005.[10] Unsurprisingly, the post–World War II agreement and the

---

[8] The Danube River Protection Convention was signed on June 29, 1994, in Sofia, Bulgaria. For the complete text of the convention, see www.icpdr.org/icpdr-pages/drpc.htm.

[9] The Belgrade Convention was signed on August 18, 1948. For the complete text of the convention, see http://ksh.fgg.uni-lj.si/danube/belgconv/.

[10] Montenegro became a contracting party to the Danube River Protection Convention in 2008.

282 Water and post-conflict peacebuilding

agreements of the 1990s have different and sometimes conflicting priorities. The riparian countries' differing orientations to these agreements were reflected to some extent in the Sava negotiations.

An incremental approach to negotiations

The four states negotiating the Sava regime found themselves in very different positions from those they held, as constituent republics within Yugoslavia, at the beginning of the 1990s. Slovenia had escaped the devastation of the Yugoslav conflicts and was well on its way to EU membership. Croatia had the best prospects for EU membership of the other three countries, but had not progressed very far. Bosnia and Herzegovina suffered from strong internal divisions and unclear spheres of authority, while the Federal Republic of Yugoslavia was dominated by power struggles and an unresolved attitude toward the West. This was a far cry from the earlier situation, in which an overarching federal government provided the legal and political context for cooperation.

Nevertheless, there was a strong political will for the countries to agree. The Sava River itself was a unifying factor, in that each country had strong cultural associations with this river, an artery connecting the capitals of three of the four riparian states.[11] Because of their previous experience as part of Yugoslavia, they had a common body of experience and familiarity with each other's languages and dialects. While Slovenian is a separate Slavic language, the languages spoken by Croats, Serbs, and Bosnians are mutually intelligible and are considered by some to be dialects of a common South Slavic language. The delegations also had a common understanding of terminology.[12] There were, however, differing levels of appreciation for developments in integrated river basin management.

Negotiations adopted a step-by-step process involving a broad legal agreement (the FASRB), followed by a series of more specific protocols. This incremental approach allowed negotiators to gradually and methodically garner support within their national bureaucracies.

Negotiators agreed early on that the reestablishment of navigation on the Sava River and its navigable tributaries would be the subject of the first protocol. This protocol was negotiated in parallel with the parent treaty. Meanwhile, four subgroups were formed in late 2002 on specific issues of importance for the action plan.

---

[11] The fourth capital, Sarajevo, is on the Miljacka River, a tributary of the Sava River.

[12] Language issues did occasionally threaten to block progress. At one point the negotiations discussed whether official documents should be translated into all of the official languages of the riparian countries. Bosnia and Herzegovina alone has three official languages; conceivably it could have become necessary to translate a document written in Serbian into Bosnian Serb, Bosnian, Bosnian Croat, Croatian, and Slovenian, despite the fact that the document would have been completely understood by all parties. In the end, negotiators agreed to the use of English and of unnamed local languages in some circumstances.

The FASRB and the Protocol on the Navigation Regime to the FASRB were signed by the ministers of Bosnia and Herzegovina, Croatia, Serbia and Montenegro, and Slovenia on December 3, 2002. These instruments were the first (and, at the time of writing, are still the only) voluntary agreement among these countries in any field. The FASRB covers protection of water quality and quantity, protection and improvement of aquatic ecosystems, and navigation and other utilization of water resources. It defines three goals (ISRBC 2008):

1. An international regime of navigation on the Sava River.
2. Sustainable water management.
3. Measures to prevent or limit hazards and reduce and eliminate adverse consequences.

The FASRB calls for the drafting of at least nine further protocols. Besides the Protocol on Navigation, four other protocols were drafted with the help of the REC: the Draft Protocol on the Prevention of Water Pollution Caused by Navigation; the Draft Protocol on Transboundary Impacts; the Draft Protocol on Emergency Situations; and the Draft Protocol on Protection Against Flood, Excessive Ground Water, Erosion, Ice Hazards, Drought and Water Shortage. Later, a separate task force also drafted the Protocol on Sediment Management.

The agreement also established institutions to oversee its implementation and coordinate national-level activities: the International Sava River Basin Commission (ISRBC) and its permanent secretariat. (The organizational structure of the ISRBC is shown in figure 2.) Pending the entry into force of the agreement, an interim commission for the Sava River Basin, based in Bosnia and Herzegovina and supported by the REC, undertook preparatory activities, including the adoption of a work plan and establishment of working groups on sustainable water management and navigation. The FASRB entered into force on December 29, 2004; the permanent ISRBC was formally established in June 2005; and in January 2006, the secretariat of the ISRBC began work in Zagreb, Croatia (ISRBC 2009a).

Negotiations produced a strong sense of ownership of and responsibility for the regime. Croatia won the right to host the secretariat in Zagreb, the country of Serbia and Montenegro (and now Serbia) the right to nominate the head of the secretariat, and Bosnia and Herzegovina the chair of the ISRBC. Slovenia acted as depositary for the agreement. These agreements represented a major milestone but did not guarantee the ISRBC's success. According to Aaron T. Wolf, differences in the Sava countries' priorities, for example between navigation and protection, can create the potential for conflict when changes in capacity of water institutions do not keep up with changes in water use (Wolf 2003).

Significance of the Sava agreement

International river basin agreements can be instruments of peace in regions accustomed to conflict and can contribute to regional stability (Murphy 1997;

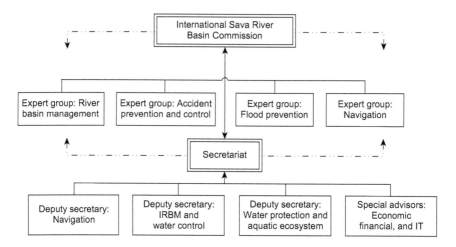

Figure 2. Organizational structure of the International Sava River Basin Commission
Source: Derived from the Framework Agreement on the Sava River Basin (FASRB), Annex I.
Notes: For the complete text of the FASRB, see www.savacommission.org/dms/docs/dokumenti/documents_publications/basic_documents/fasrb.pdf.
IRBM = integrated river basin management. IT = information technology.

Čolakhodžić 2008). The Sava countries had successful examples to draw from, including the Danube River Protection Convention and the Convention for the Protection of the Rhine.[13]

The ISRBC has been the main mechanism by which the four riparian countries have cooperated on river basin management. Harmonization of national regulations with EU regulations is especially important for the three riparian countries (Croatia, Bosnia and Herzegovina, and Serbia) that are closest to becoming EU member states.[14] The four FASRB member states are now integrating their river management systems—such as geographic information systems, river information services, monitoring, forecasting, and early warning systems (ISRBC 2008)—a process that is expected to be achieved by 2012.[15] This cooperative work has helped to establish constructive practical relationships between the riparian states.

The EU has supported this process by designating the Sava River Basin as the site of one of thirteen European pilot projects for implementation of the WFD. The existence of the ISRBC has made it possible for EU funding to be

---

[13] For the complete text of the Convention for the Protection of the Rhine, concluded on April 12, 1999, see www.ecolex.org/server2.php/libcat/docs/TRE/Multilateral/En/TRE001307.txt.

[14] Slovenia, as an EU member, is already obliged to conform to EU requirements, and Croatia largely closed the environmental chapter in its negotiations for membership in 2009 and is set to become the twenty-eighth member state of the EU on July 1, 2013. Serbia and Bosnia and Herzegovina are pre-candidate countries.

[15] Dejan Komatina, secretary of the ISRBC, personal communication, February 2009.

The Sava River: transitioning to peace   285

coordinated to address water quality at the basin level. Such projects depend on international funding, as the water institutions of riparian states generally lack development funds.

The international community has launched two projects in the basin. The United Nations Development Programme/Global Environment Facility Danube Regional Project, implemented from 2001 to 2007, focused on nutrient reduction and transboundary cooperation in the Danube Basin and its subbasins, including the Sava. The Sava EU-CARDS (Community Assistance for Reconstruction, Development and Stabilisation) project, extended under the Instrument for Pre-Accession, aims to develop a strategy for basin-wide water monitoring and test the capacities of Bosnia and Herzegovina, Croatia, and Serbia to implement the WFD.[16] Three Sava River subbasins were selected as pilot projects: Vrbas, Kupa, and Kolubara. Such initiatives would not have been conceivable without the FASRB in place to demonstrate the commitment of the riparian states to cooperation.

Yet the FASRB falls short in some areas when evaluated against accepted principles of integrated water resource management and the provisions of the WFD. It is silent on certain generally accepted principles, including decentralization, emissions limits, gender equality, poverty reduction, and stakeholder participation—issues that continue to be controversial in parts of the basin and thus could have interfered with the tentative first steps toward cooperation. Now that those first steps have been completed, however, it is important to remedy these deficiencies as soon as possible.

Perhaps the most important criteria for assessing the performance of the Sava institutions are transparency, exchange of information, and participation of stakeholders and the public—issues of prime importance in a region where trust has to be built slowly. Current practice in the Sava countries is an improvement over that of the previous socialist regime, largely because of the transition toward democracy; but it remains a sensitive issue and was largely avoided by the FASRB negotiators. The only provision in the agreement on stakeholder involvement is in article 21, section 2: "The implementation monitoring methodology will include timely provision of information to stakeholders and the general public by the authorities responsible for implementation of the Agreement."

Stakeholder participation was not provided for in the planning and implementation phases of the FASRB. During the operation of the Interim Sava Commission, the REC's attempt to build capacity through public communication and stakeholder involvement was rejected on the grounds that it was premature.[17]

---

[16]   When the EU-CARDS project was developed, Montenegro was not included. For more information on environmental considerations in EU-CARDS, see Bruch, Wolfarth, and Michalcik (2012).

[17]   Magdolna Toth Nagy, head of Public Participation Programme, REC/Hungary, personal communication, June 6, 2006.

286   Water and post-conflict peacebuilding

The main standard-setting instrument in Europe for this field is the United Nations Economic Commission for Europe's Convention on Access to Information, Public Participation in Decision-making and Access to Justice in Environmental Matters (also known as the Aarhus Convention).[18] The three pillars on which the convention is built—access to information, public participation, and access to justice—empower members of the public to play a greater role in environmental decision making, an important step in providing outlets for legitimate grievances and opportunities for resolution of potential conflicts that can assist in rebuilding trust among former adversaries. The Aarhus principles also contribute to improved decision making, greater transparency, and greater respect for decisions. All Sava River Basin countries are parties to the Aarhus Convention.

The ISRBC is seen to have the potential to aid the process of reconciliation by stimulating the acceptance of norms of transparency and participation. In its early stages, it was criticized by environmental nongovernmental organizations (NGOs) as being a top-down hierarchical organization much like those of the socialist era. The lack of transparency and participation has been attributed to the low environmental awareness and nontransparent water management practices carried over from the Yugoslav era (Čolakhodžić 2008). "One major obstacle," said Vladimir Lukić, a senior engineer with the Institute for Development of Water Resources in Serbia "is the evident lack of trust on both sides."[19] Many in the government see NGOs as incompetent, abusing the Aarhus Convention, and exaggerating the shortcomings of governmental agencies. Many NGO members perceive the government as incompetent, corrupt, and perpetuating a socialist mentality inherited from the previous Yugoslav regime.

THE ROLE OF THE SAVA COMMISSION

Improving navigation was an early focus of the ISRBC.[20] The Sava River is underused for river transport; transport in the area is currently dominated by road corridors. In Croatia, the Sava River flows parallel to Pan-European Transport Corridor X,[21] which continues through Serbia and is planned to become one of the main arteries of Europe, running from Salzburg, Austria, to Thessaloniki, Greece. The Sava River also crosses Corridor Vc at Slavonski Brod. Commercial traffic on the river, excluding sand and gravel operations, reached 408,000 tons during 2007 (ISRBC 2009a). As the Sava's potential is further developed, the

---

[18]   The Aarhus Convention was signed on June 25, 1998, in Aarhus, Denmark. For the complete text of the convention, see www.unece.org/fileadmin/DAM/env/pp/documents/cep43e.pdf.

[19]   Vladimir Lukić, personal communication, June 8, 2006.

[20]   Djordje Stefanović, former secretary of the Interim Sava Commission, personal communication, June 20, 2006.

[21]   Pan-European transport corridors involve rail, road, and river traffic and have been designated by European countries as major transport routes for further development.

The Sava River: transitioning to peace 287

expansion of transport on these routes is expected to result in increased river traffic. (Typically in Europe, inland water transport makes up 6–24 percent of total traffic.)

Transport on the Sava River faces several problems: lack of maintenance and investment, resulting in poor quality of infrastructure, poor road and railway connections, damaged ports and river infrastructure, and the presence of unexploded ordnance endangering navigation (ISRBC 2009a). Additionally, the depth, flow, and geography of the Sava River make navigation difficult, as do other problems such as limited width under bridges and insufficient marking (ISRBC 2008). The *Feasibility Study and Project Documentation for the Rehabilitation and Development of Transport and Navigation on the Sava River Waterway* provides the economic and organizational framework for restoring trade and navigation (ISRBC 2009a).

The ISRBC is mandated to make decisions on navigation issues and recommendations on other river-related issues such as natural resource management. Its permanent and ad hoc working groups employ experts from all member states and cover an array of multidisciplinary issues: navigation; river basin management; accident prevention and control; flood prevention; legal, hydrological, and meteorological issues; and the development of geographic information systems and river information services. But the process for transforming findings on these issues into decisions and recommendations is not yet clearly defined. Clarifying this process is an opportunity to strengthen mechanisms for regional cooperation within the Sava River Basin and throughout Europe.

The elaboration of ISRBC's first Sava River Basin Management Plan, a European Commission–funded project, was started in December 2009, and it has subsequently been finalized. It emphasizes the integrated planning approach required by the WFD, and provides guidelines for defining short-term, mid-term, and long-term policies on development of the waterway (ISRBC 2009b). Related procedures require public hearings to be held and, in accordance with EU standards, guarantee transparency of all ISRBC activities, increasing the legitimacy of this governance mechanism.

On March 9, 2010, the ISRBC hosted in Zagreb a meeting of stakeholders, who signed the Joint Statement on Guiding Principles for the Development of Inland Navigation and Environmental Protection in the Danube River Basin. The idea of the joint statement was launched in March 2008 by the ISRBC, ICPDR, and the Danube Commission, and involved a yearlong negotiation process among over fifty stakeholders. The statement calls for meetings to be held once a year to discuss the progress and strengthen the cross sectoral communication, and transboundary communication (ISRBC 2010). The March meeting concluded that the best intentions for mutual cooperation have been demonstrated so far, but that remaining post-conflict tensions should be kept in mind during planning in order to avoid reviving conflict, and river engineering projects should take all possible measures to minimize potential transboundary consequences.

288   Water and post-conflict peacebuilding

An integrated river basin management plan, flood risk management plan, and emergency preparedness plan are expected to be fully elaborated by 2015.[22] The river basin management plan is modeled on the WFD and the flood risk management plan on the EU Flood Directive (ISRBC 2008).

The ISRBC has the potential to play an important role in resolving water-related disputes. A 2004 dispute between two Sava countries—Bosnia and Herzegovina, and Serbia and Montenegro—over the potential construction of the Buk Bijela hydropower plant on the Drina River, a tributary of the Sava River, might have fallen under its authority if it had existed then. But it must work within the limits of the FASRB, although this mandate may be extended in the future as additional protocols are established.

NEXT STEPS AND FUTURE PROSPECTS

While currently limited in scope, the Sava regime offers the potential for enhancing cooperation on a wide range of issues. In April 2010, preliminary agreement was reached between the governments of Serbia, Bosnia and Herzegovina, and Italy to construct hydropower plants on the Sava River and its tributary the Drina. The potential of these plants is 380 to 450 megawatts, producing around 6 terawatt hours of electricity for Serbia and Bosnia and Herzegovina (Lazarevic 2011) and for export to the EU.

Table 2 summarizes data on the potential for developing hydropower in the Sava countries. Development of this potential would contribute to the riparian countries' energy independence and economic well-being, while providing another fruitful opportunity for building cooperation.

The ISRBC is regarded as the single authority over the management of the Sava River, despite the fact that only its navigation-related decisions are binding. It is expected to provide a basis for basin-wide environmental cooperation, and as such promote reconciliation and peacebuilding, among other objectives. Theoretically, the extent to which it can be regarded as cooperative depends on its ability to make legitimate decisions in a transparent manner and the degree to which it perceives environmental protection as a priority.

Table 2.   Potential for hydropower in the Sava River Basin

Country	Terawatt hours per year
Bosnia and Herzegovina	19.0
Croatia	8.0
Serbia and Montenegro	27.0
Slovenia	8.0

Source: Adapted from Schreyer and Mez (2008).
Note: Statistics are prior to Serbia and Montenegro becoming separate states.

---

[22]   Dejan Komatina, secretary of the ISRBC, personal communication, February 2009.

The environmental impacts of planned projects under the action plan should be carefully monitored and reported. The ISRBC has indicated that it will regard compliance with environmental commitments as mandatory for all navigation- and flood-prevention-related decisions. But it has also stated that compromises between the objectives of inland water transport projects and the goal of environmental protection might be necessary (ISRBC 2009a). It is considering the establishment of a special body to monitor environmental compliance on a day-to-day basis for those projects with the highest risk of negative impacts on the environment or economy, such as those involving riverbed dredging and flood prevention.

The ISRBC has worked hard to incorporate EU standards for sustainable river management into its practices. Though working documents are available online, there is a need for more intense publicity concerning ISRBC activities, including an environmental education campaign.

Hydropower plants are also an issue in the Sava River Basin. Such plants can provide a renewable source of electricity and improve flood control, water supply, and wastewater treatment, but they always lead to problems with a river's hydromorphology. Dams hold back sediments, depriving the river downstream of its normal sediment load, which triggers erosion and leads to the lowering of the riverbed, with impacts on vegetation and wildlife. Depriving riparian ecosystems of the annual flooding to which they are adapted also disturbs various species' life cycles and habitats. Dams built without a proper bypass system also disturb fish migration patterns; in many cases, this has led to extinction of entire species.

Besides existing hydropower plants, and plants currently under construction, nine new plants are expected to be completed in Slovenia by 2030 (Kryzanowski, Horvat, and Brilly 2008). This will be a huge step forward in Slovenia's renewable energy production, but it could have an adverse impact on the downstream states.

Restoration of navigation is currently the highest priority for the ISRBC. This involves removal of war debris and unexploded ordnance, and reconstruction of bridges and ports. It is expected to be costly and (given the ISRBC's reliance on funding from the limited budgets of the Sava countries) to limit the funds available to address other needs—such as protection of water quality and aquatic ecosystems, flood and pollution prevention and control, habitat preservation, community mitigation projects, rehabilitation of water and wastewater treatment systems, evaluation and monitoring of water quality, and further development of the capacity of water institutions.

The longer navigation takes precedence over these other needs, the more expensive eventual investments in them will be. This is particularly true for parts of the river passing through urban areas (such as Zagreb and Belgrade), where untreated wastewater could reach levels that destroy nature's ability to restore itself (Meybeck 2003). Needs for wetlands restoration could easily be multiplied if navigation improvement projects do not involve thorough measures to preserve

290   Water and post-conflict peacebuilding

them. Ecosystem water quality and habitat preservation should be at least as high a priority as navigation.

The major criticisms of the FASRB are that it fails to provide adequately for environmental protection and transparency. These are essential elements of widely accepted international standards and key indicators of the maturity and effectiveness of a river basin regime, based on analyses of other important regimes such as those governing the Rhine, Danube, Nile, and Jordan basins (Čolakhodžić 2008). However, in these other cases, environmental protection and transparency were often not given high priority in the initial agreements, but gained importance as the regimes developed over time and the basins stabilized economically and socially.

The FASRB is somewhat different from earlier agreements in that it was negotiated at a time when the importance of environmental protection and transparency was already well established. A comparative analysis reveals other differentiating factors that can help explain why the FASRB did not prioritize environmental protection and transparency (Čolakhodžić 2008). For example, the Sava River Basin does not suffer from water scarcity and does not have a history of unregulated economic activity and competition over scarce resources. It has been considered an international river for a relatively short time. Environmental advocacy groups have been active in the shaping of river regimes such as the Danube and Rhine since at least the 1970s, but in the Sava countries (with the possible exception of Slovenia), such groups' input in policy making was not recognized until well after the end of the Yugoslav conflicts (Atkinson and Stec 2009).

The fact that the FASRB involves all the riparian states gives it an advantage over some other international agreements (such as those for the Mekong and Jordan rivers), particularly in terms of its practicality and ability to evolve and mature. Fortunately, the FASRB and the ISRBC adhere to the provisions and principles of the WFD and integrated water resource management, opening a window to improvements in transparency and public participation. Both the agreement and the commission have also had an unusual amount of international and European support.

A drawback of the ISRBC is that it is not well known. For an organization to be successful, a wide range of stakeholders must be informed about its activities and their opportunities to play a role. The establishment of the ISRBC was not sufficiently publicized, especially among stakeholders such as NGOs, local businesses, and people who pursue traditional livelihoods. This was partially due to its initial (and current) focus on the technical and economic aspects of cooperation, which attract less widespread interest. In order to achieve broader support, the ISRBC could embark on more public awareness campaigns, on topics such as urban issues, traditional lifestyles, and cultural values.

The Sava River Basin is still characterized by fragile relationships among the countries and relatively serious security issues. The potential for conflict over water remains, particularly if mismanagement of hazardous activities, extreme flooding, uncontrolled industrial wastewater discharge, excessive agricultural water consumption, or uncoordinated development of hydropower occurs. As the downstream riparian states, Serbia and sections of Bosnia and Herzegovina would be the most affected. Sava River Basin management must take into account the competing interests of developers, the environment, and the public—the latter especially in terms of flood safety (James 2010). The four member states have agreed to manage the basin in accordance with European and international processes, requiring cooperation on important issues such as hydropower development, land use practices, and pollution. However, weak institutions and rule of law and a high level of corruption present a constant challenge; for example, a significant portion of the illegal exploitation of natural resources goes to support organized crime networks and competing nationalist organizations (Tilney 2009).

The risk of conflict in the basin still exists. The Serbian government filed a lawsuit against Croatia in the International Court of Justice in 2009, accusing it of genocide during the 1991–1995 Balkan War and seeking compensation. This was in response to a similar lawsuit filed by Croatia in 1999. This legal dispute renews tensions and threatens to undermine relations between Serbia and Croatia that are crucial to the stability of the region.

The prospect of eventual EU membership unites Sava countries in a common purpose. So long as steady progress is made throughout the region, and the EU door remains open, the idea of a federated Europe with open internal borders will help to lower tensions and prevent a resumption of conflict. Having successfully established a system for transboundary cooperation, the Sava countries now have the responsibility to seek lasting peace by promoting the conditions for sustainable development (Carius, Feil, and Switzer 2003).

LESSONS LEARNED

The connection between peacebuilding and the environment in fragile post-conflict communities has several aspects. The management of natural resources often serves as a starting point for reestablishing trust and cooperation. Post-conflict societies have also usually suffered heavy economic losses, and natural resources projects foster economic development through job creation, a key component of peacebuilding. Great care must be taken with this process, as poor choices made in the early stages can backfire and deepen mistrust. But the environment and natural resources cannot be neglected, and addressing them as part of peacebuilding is not merely a good idea but a security imperative (UNEP n.d.).

To overcome the legacy of conflict, it is important to establish a wide variety of cooperation mechanisms, from grassroots movements to governmental or intergovernmental initiatives. In post-conflict regions, international organizations have an important role to play, to identify mutually acceptable and beneficial objectives, provide guidance, and help bridge differing perspectives and interests. The initial negotiations to establish the ISRBC were driven predominantly by mutually perceived economic benefits, including improved navigation. However,

292   Water and post-conflict peacebuilding

the presence of experienced international organizations such as the Organization for Security and Co-operation in Europe, REC, and ICPDR broadened this perspective and created more opportunities for cooperation toward sustainable development.

The ISRBC is limited in terms of its objectives. One limitation is its prioritization of navigation over environmental protection. Low levels of stakeholder involvement and transparency in its early stages also limited its effectiveness. In 2010, as part of the ICPDR, the ISRBC participated in the work of the Platform for the Implementation of the NAIADES (Navigation and Inland Waterway Action and Development in Europe). The result of this cooperation was the release of the *Manual on Good Practices in Sustainable Waterway Planning*, which is intended to lead to further action (ICPDR 2010). Increasing transparency and legitimacy will be essential as the regime matures and the Sava states become more democratic. Active public participation is a core principle in the work of the ICPDR, and as of 2010, twenty-two organizations had been granted observer status, giving them the opportunity to get involved in ICPDR decision making (ICPDR n.d.).

Raising environmental awareness can also contribute to regional stability. The public in the Western Balkans shows a high level of environmental concern but a low level of environmental knowledge (Landau, Legro, and Vlašić 2008). In order to achieve adequate public support for ISRBC policies, consistent with EU standards, activities should have a high level of transparency, accompanied by a public education campaign. Given the lack of data on various aspects of the basin—including pollution levels and sources, biodiversity, and public demand for services—it can be argued that a strategy to involve local stakeholders and interest groups would have helped the ISRBC to develop a better sense of scale and needs at an earlier stage.

Both top-down and bottom-up approaches are needed. It is important to try to engage all stakeholders, creating a solid base for dialogue among communities. Cooperation on the joint management of the Sava River Basin can provide wider opportunities for peacemaking and capacity building within the riparian states, among relevant government institutions, local authorities, and civil society. The performance of the ISRBC in this area needs improvement, as poor marketing has left the public unfamiliar with its work.

In spite of its limitations, the ISRBC's example of cooperation in a region with a history of complex relations and diverse national identities, religions, languages, and cultures can serve as a model for cooperation in other cases, as long as careful attention is paid to the differences of each case. By helping the Sava countries to meet some of the major requirements of the WFD, it has helped Serbia, Bosnia and Herzegovina, and Croatia to move closer to the goal of EU membership. Many other initiatives involving different sectors of society, industry, and agriculture can also help promote stability and cooperation in the region and thus accelerate its process of association with the EU. Cooperation on environmental issues seems like a good step in that direction.

REFERENCES

Almond, M. 1994. *Europe's backyard war: The war in the Balkans.* London: Heinemann.

Atkinson, R., and S. Stec. 2009. Civil society turning 21—development of environmental civil society groups in the West Balkans. *Iustum Aequum Salutare* 5 (1): 67–84, reprinted in *Environmental Policy and Law* 39:162–170.

Bašić, M. 1989. Pravni aspekti korištenja i zaštite voda sliva rijeke Save. In *Rijeka Sava—zaštita i korištenje voda.* Proceedings of the Sava River conference, Yugoslavian Academy of Arts and Sciences, Zagreb, Croatia.

Bjelajac, M., O. Zunec, M. Boduszynski, R. Draschtak, I. Graovac, S. Kent, R. Malli, S. Pavlović, and J. Vuić. 2007. *The war in Croatia, 1991–1995.* The Hague, Netherlands: Center for History, Democracy and Reconciliation.

Bruch, C., R. Wolfarth, and V. Michalcik. 2012. Natural resources, post-conflict reconstruction, and regional integration: Lessons from the Marshall Plan and other reconstruction efforts. In *Assessing and restoring natural resources in post-conflict peacebuilding,* ed. D. Jensen and S. Lonergan. London: Earthscan.

Carius, A., M. Feil, and J. Switzer. 2003. *Environment and security: Transforming risks into cooperation; The case of Central Asia and South Eastern Europe.* Nairobi, Kenya: United Nations Environment Programme.

Carnegie Commission (Carnegie Commision on Preventing Deadly Conflict). 2000. *Preventing deadly conflict: Toward a world without war.* Washington, D.C.

CBC News. 2007. Anatomy of a refugee camp. June 19. www.cbc.ca/news/background/refugeecamp/#.

Čolakhodžić, A. 2008. *Environmental security and the role of river regimes in fostering (environmental) cooperation: Case of the International Sava River Basin Commission.* NATO Science for Peace and Security Series C: Environmental Security. Enschede, Netherlands: Springer.

Dimitrijević, V., and J. Pejić. 1995. UN sanctions against Yugoslavia (Serbia and Montenegro): Two years later. Unpublished manuscript, European University, Florence, Italy.

ECOSOC (Economic and Social Council, United Nations). 2005. *Concluding observation: Review report to the state parties submitted under article 16.1 17th of the pact.* New York and Geneva, Switzerland.

Glenny, M. 2000. *The Balkans: Nationalism, war, and the great powers, 1804–1999.* New York: Viking.

GOC (Government of Croatia). 1998. Danger of land mines, unexploded ordnance, and environmental consequences of the recent war on Croatia. Proceedings of the Chemical and Biological Medical Treatment Symposium, Dubrovnik, Croatia.

Hopić, S. 2009. *Ruralni razvoj u Republici Srbiji.* Belgrade, Serbia: Stalna konferencija gradova i opstina.

ICPDR (International Commission for the Protection of the Danube River). 2010. *Manual on good practices in sustainable waterway planning.* Vienna, Austria.

———. n.d. Observers. www.icpdr.org/main/icpdr/observers.

ISRBC (International Sava River Basin Commission). 2008. Strategy on implementation of the Framework Agreement on the Sava River Basin. Zagreb, Croatia.

———. 2009a. *Feasibility study and project documentation for the rehabilitation and development of transport and navigation on the Sava River waterway.* Zagreb, Croatia.

———. 2009b. *Sava River Basin analysis report.* Zagreb, Croatia.

294   Water and post-conflict peacebuilding

———. 2010. *Sava news flash: Official bulletin of the ISRBC.* May. Zagreb, Croatia.

James, J. G. 2010. *Sava River Basin: General considerations in defining goals for floodplain regulations and basin management plans.* Nashville, TN: U.S. Army Corps of Engineers.

Jovanović, S. 2007. Učešće karcinoma u stopi smrtnosti raseljenih lica opštine hadžići u periodu od 1996. do 2000. godine. Paper presented at the "First Congress of Medical Doctors of the Republic of Srpska," Banja Vručica, Bosnia and Herzegovina.

Kendrovski, V. L., and M. Kochubovski. 2001. Transboundary pollution of River "Lepenec" (One year after the Kosovo conflict). *Journal of Environmental Protection and Ecology* 2 (2): 380–383.

KIRS (Commissariat for the Refugees of the Republic of Serbia). 2008. *Stanje i potrebe izbegličke populacije u Republici Srbiji.* Belgrade, Serbia: Komesarijat za izbeglice Republike Srbije.

Komatina, D. 2010. Framework agreement on the Sava River Basin—a basis for sustainable development of the region. Presentation at International Sava River Basin Commission meeting on the contribution of small- and medium-enterprises sector to the Framework Agreement on the Sava River Basin, December 22, Zagreb, Croatia. http://ecpd.si/uploads/dokumenti/FASRB%20and%20SME%20sector.pdf.

Kryžanowski, A., A. Horvat, and M. Brilly. 2008. Hydro power plants on the middle Sava River section. Paper presented at the twenty-fourth conference of the Danubian Countries. IOP Conference Series: Earth and Environmental Science 4. http://iopscience.iop.org/1755-1315/4/1/012033/pdf/ees8_4_012033.pdf.

Landau, S., S. Legro, and S. Vlašić. 2008. *A climate for change: Climate change and its impact on society and economy in Croatia.* Zagreb, Croatia: United Nations Development Programme.

Lazarevic, N. 2011. Serbia and Italy sign energy deal. *Balkan Insight*, October 27. http://www.balkaninsight.com/en/article/serbia-italy-sign-energy-deal.

Martinović-Vitanović, V., and V. Kalafatić. 2009. Ecological impact on the Danube after NATO air strikes. In *Environmental consequences of war and aftermath*, ed. T. A. Kassim and D. Barcelo. Vol. 3 of *The handbook of environmental chemistry*. Berlin, Germany: Springer.

Meštrov, M., I. Habdija, B. Stilinović, Z. Žutić-Maloseja, V. Tavčar, M. Kerovec, B. Primić-Habdija, and N. Futač. 1989. Biološko-ekološka valorizacija kvaliteta vode rijeke Save. In *Rijeka Sava—Zaštita i korištenje voda.* Proceedings of the River Sava conference, Yugoslavian Academy of Arts and Sciences, Zagreb, Croatia.

Meybeck, M. 2003. Global analysis of river systems: From Earth system controls to Anthropocene syndromes. *Philosophical Transactions of the Royal Society of London [B]* 358 (1440): 1935–1955.

Miko, S., L. Palinkaš, B. Biondić, K. Namjesnik, and S. Stiglić. 1995. Groundwater pollution hazard by heavy metals following the explosion at an ammunition depot near Oštarije, Croatia. In *The effects of war on the environment: Croatia*, ed. M. Richardson. London: Spon Press.

Murphy, I. L. 1997. *The Danube: A river basin in transition.* Dordrecht, Netherlands: Kluwer Academic Publishers.

Petrik, B., M. Meštrov, and D. Brundić. 1989. Kvaliteta i mjere zaštite voda porječja rijeke Save. In *Rijeka Sava—zaštita i korištenje voda.* Proceedings of the Sava River conference, Yugoslavian Academy of Arts and Sciences, Zagreb, Croatia.

Picer, M. 1998. Jeopardized water with war wastes in Karst of Croatia. Proceedings of the Chemical and Biological Medical Treatment Symposium, Dubrovnik, Croatia.

The Sava River: transitioning to peace 295

Popovska, N., and J. Šopova. 2000. The pollution of the Balkans. *UNESCO Courier* 53 (5): 11–12. http://unesdoc.unesco.org/images/0011/001196/119663e.pdf#119666.

Prunk, J. 1994. *A brief history of Slovenia: Historical background of the Republic of Slovenia.* Trans. W. Tuttle and M. Klander. Ljubljana, Slovenia: Tiskana Tone Tomšič.

REC (Regional Environmental Center for Central and Eastern Europe). 1999. *Assessment of the environmental impact of military activities during the Yugoslavia conflict: Preliminary findings.* http://archive.rec.org/REC/Publications/YugoConflictAssessment/contents.html.

Schreyer, M., and L. Mez. 2008. *ERENE: European Community for Renewable Energy: A feasibility study.* Publication Series on Europe, vol. 3. Berlin, Germany: Heinrich Böll Foundation. www.fondacija-boell.eu/downloads/ERENE_study_EN.pdf.

Schwandner-Sievers, S., and B. J. Fischer. 2002. *Albanian identities: Myth and history.* Bloomington: Indiana University Press.

Tilney, L. 2009. Natural resource management in the absence of the rule of law: A case study from Bosnia and Herzegovina. In *Energy and environmental challenges to security*, ed. S. Stec and B. Baraj. Dordrecht, Netherlands: Springer.

Tomić, F., and T. Budin. 1989. *Poljoprivreda u melioracijskom području doline rijeke Save: Rijeka Sava zaštita i korištenje voda.* Zagreb, Croatia: Akademija Znanosti i Umjetnosti.

Tošović, S., and B. Šolaja. 1999. Aggression on Yugoslavia: Indirect chemical warfare. In *Environmental impact of the NATO bombing in Yugoslavia.* Geneva, Switzerland: Foundation Global Reflexion.

UNDP (United Nations Development Programme). 1990. *Human development report 1990: Concept and measurement of human development.* New York.

———. 1991. *Human development report 1991: Financing human development.* New York.

———. 1998. *Human development report 1998: Consumption and human development.* New York.

———. 2000. *Human development report 2000: Human rights and human development.* New York.

———. 2009. *Human development report 2009: Overcoming barriers; Human mobility and development.* New York.

UNEP (United Nations Environmental Programme). 2004. *From conflict to sustainable development: Assessment and clean-up in Serbia and Montenegro.* Geneva, Switzerland.

———. n.d. United Nations Environment Programme: Environment for development. www.unep.org/PDF/ABOUT_UNEP_ENGLISH.pdf.

UNEP (United Nations Environmental Programme) and GRID-Arendal. 2000. Environmental knowledge for change. www.grida.no/.

UNEP (United Nations Environment Programme) and UNCHS (United Nations Centre for Human Settlements). 1999. *The Kosovo conflict: Consequences for the environment and human settlements.* Geneva, Switzerland. http://postconflict.unep.ch/publications/finalreport.pdf.

USIP (United States Institute of Peace). 1997. *The United States and Croatia: A documentary history, 1992–1997.* Vienna, Austria.

Vukasovic, V. 2006. Međunarodnopravno regulisanje zaštite vodnih resursa. *Izvorni naučni rad*, January. www.doiserbia.nb.rs/img/doi/0025-8555/2006/0025-85550602157V.pdf.

296 Water and post-conflict peacebuilding

Wolf, A. T. 2003. The present and future of transboundary water management. In *Rethinking water management: Innovative approaches to contemporary issues*, ed. C. M. Figuéres, C. Tortajada, and J. Rockström. London: Earthscan.

World Bank. 2003. *Issues and direction*. Vol. 1 of *Water resources management in South Eastern Europe*. Washington, D.C.: International Bank for Reconstruction and Development.

Zarić, V., P. Muncan, Z. Vasiljević, M. Sevarlić, M. Bogdanov, and J. Malcom. 2005. *Agro-economic policy analysis of the new member states, the candidate states and the countries of the Western Balkans.* Belgrade, Serbia and Montenegro: Central and Eastern European Countries Appliance Policy.

Ždrale, S., T. Pleša, M. Šupić, I. Djokić, and S. Vuković. 2007. *Kolorektalni karcinomi na području Sarajevsko-Romanijske regije.* Paper presented at the "First Congress of Medical Doctors of the Republic of Srpska," Banja Vrućica, Bosnia and Herzegovina.

Zinke, A., G. Windhofer, R. Konecny, A. Schönbauer, T. Dworak, E. Interwies, N. Kranz, E. Kampa, and M. Edthofer. 2007. Development of the Sava River Basin management plan: Pilot project. Vienna, Austria: Hydro-Ingenieure, Umweltbundesamt, and Ecologic. www.icpdr.org/main/sites/.../1.1-9_SavaRBM_FR_23-04-07_inclAnx-f.pdf.

Transnational cooperation over shared water resources in the South Caucasus: Reflections on USAID interventions

Marina Vardanyan and Richard Volk

This chapter provides a brief history of major conflicts in the South Caucasus and highlights the peacebuilding potential of cooperation on management of shared water resources. The chapter discusses two regional water programs run by the U.S. Agency for International Development (USAID) in the South Caucasus and identifies the initiatives' successes and failures in implementing transboundary water resource management in the region. USAID's efforts demonstrate how donor support of technical cooperation can promote peacebuilding despite ethnic tension and political stalemate. Although relatively little progress was made by the countries at the political level, USAID's attempts to foster collaboration at the technical level on water resource management yielded several notable achievements. The chapter concludes by considering the next steps to facilitate continued cooperation on water resource management in the South Caucasus and the broader lessons learned about donor assistance in integrated water resource management in regions emerging from conflict.

CONFLICT AND THE POTENTIAL FOR COLLABORATION ON SHARED WATERS

Countries in the South Caucasus gained independence with the dissolution of the Soviet Union in 1991. But since independence, Armenia, Azerbaijan, and Georgia have grappled with economic and political instability, ethnic conflict, and environmental degradation. Major conflicts in the South Caucasus center on ethnicity, Nagorno-Karabakh's efforts to gain independence from Azerbaijan, and Abkhazia's and South Ossetia's attempts to separate from Georgia (Wittich and Maas 2009). The conflicts involving Nagorno-Karabakh are of most immediate

---

Marina Vardanyan is team leader for USAID (U.S. Agency for International Development)/ Armenia's water and energy portfolio and mission environmental officer. Richard Volk is a coastal and aquatic resources advisor for USAID's Water Team in Washington, D.C. In this chapter, the authors have drawn upon their experience in managing water projects in the South Caucasus.

298 Water and post-conflict peacebuilding

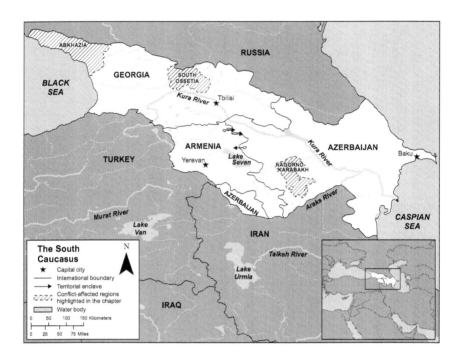

relevance to water resource management in the Kura-Araks Basin because the nonrecognized-entity status of Nagorno-Karabakh is a source of ongoing tension between Armenia and Azerbaijan, which share the basin.[1]

During the Soviet era, Nagorno-Karabakh was given the rank of autonomous oblast (region) in the Republic of Azerbaijan, but at the time, its population was comprised largely of ethnic Armenians. In 1988, the Nagorno-Karabakh legislature resolved to join the Republic of Armenia and secede from the Republic of Azerbaijan (Beehner 2005). The resolution strained relationships between Azerbaijan and Armenia, resulting in violent conflict in the Nagorno-Karabakh region from 1992 to 1994. Over the course of the violent struggle, approximately 25,000 lives were lost (Beehner 2005; BBC 2010). By 1993, Armenian military forces controlled Nagorno-Karabakh and approximately 20 percent of the land surrounding the region, as well as an area called the Lachin corridor, which links the region to Armenia (Beehner 2005). In 1994, Russia negotiated a ceasefire that remains in effect, and the Organization for Security and Co-operation in Europe (OSCE) Minsk Group—led by France, Russia, and the United States—began to mediate between Azerbaijan and Armenia. Still, as many as 700,000 Azeri and 235,000 Armenian refugees remain displaced (Beehner 2005). The stalled conflict and continuing tension between Armenia and Azerbaijan have undermined cooperation

---

[1] Neither Armenia nor Azerbaijan recognizes Nagorno-Karabakh as an independent state.

Transnational cooperation over water resources in the South Caucasus 299

on a number of critical regional issues, including management of and equitable access to water in the Kura-Araks Basin.

As the South Caucasus emerges from conflict, regional cooperation on water resource management will become increasingly important for economic recovery. The area faces many challenges related to water quantity and quality because of ineffective allocation of water resources and growing water-quality degradation from agricultural and urban pollution (Vener 2006; Vener and Campana 2010). Disputes over water quality and quantity grow in the absence of credible information and misinterpretation of existing data. Despite political tension, capacity building and technical cooperation on shared water resources can improve dialogue among states and be a stepping stone in establishing lasting peace in the region.

To begin building a foundation for peace, USAID implemented two programs in the 2001–2008 timeframe, namely, the Water Management in the South Caucasus program and the South Caucasus Water Program (SCWP). While helping to improve the understanding of issues pertaining to the larger Kura-Araks Basin, the programs focused much of their attention on two subbasins: the Alazani Basin, straddling the border of Georgia and Azerbaijan, and the Khrami-Debed Basin, bestride the border of Georgia and Armenia. The programs strengthened scientific and analytical capacity by establishing monitoring capabilities, supporting data collection on water quality and quantity, and providing technical training. The initiatives additionally facilitated dialogue on transboundary water resource management by convening workshops for water technicians and engaging nongovernmental organizations (NGOs) and state ministries with authority over water.

Regional water: The Kura-Araks Basin

Consisting of ten thousand tributaries, the Kura-Araks Basin supports over 16 million people (UNEP, UNDP, and OSCE 2004; Vener 2006). The basin encompasses northeastern Turkey, central and eastern Georgia, northwestern Iran, and most of Azerbaijan and Armenia (see figure 1). The Kura River originates in Turkey and flows through Georgia and Azerbaijan, into the Caspian Sea. The Araks River also begins in Turkey and flows along the border of Armenia and Iran, into the Kura River in Azerbaijan (Vener and Campana 2010). Over forty of the Kura-Araks Basin's tributaries and river segments are transboundary (Vener 2006). The basin covers approximately 188,000 square kilometers, and two-thirds of the area is located across Armenia, Azerbaijan, and Georgia (Vener and Campana 2010).

Demographics and national boundaries result in some inequities in water resource distribution. Georgia has the second-largest population of the three countries and the smallest watershed (Vener 2006; Vener and Campana 2010). In contrast, Azerbaijan has the highest population and the largest watershed (Vener 2006; Vener and Campana 2010). Azerbaijan has one of the lowest per capita water availabilities globally (Vener 2006). Although it has a greater per capita water

300 Water and post-conflict peacebuilding

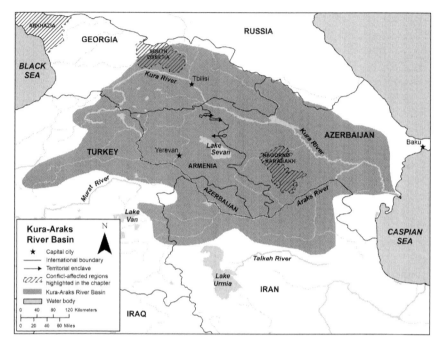

Figure 1. Kura-Araks River Basin
Source: Adapted from Vener (2006).

availability, Armenia periodically experiences surface-water shortages due to poor water management (Vener 2006; Vener and Campana 2010). The Kura-Araks Basin captures 100 percent of Armenia's storm-water runoff and sewage discharge. It also captures 60 percent of Georgia's and 50 percent of Azerbaijan's storm-water runoff and sewage discharge (Vener and Campana 2010).

Because it has been an area of agricultural and industrial significance since the Soviet period, the region suffers from inefficient allocation of water resources and poor water quality due to agricultural and urban pollution (Vener and Campana 2010; Vener 2006). Water resources are essential to health and economic growth, but countries in the region do not fully understand that hydropower development, management of sediment (and other water-quality issues), and flood control are among the economic benefits they can derive from cooperation on water resource management.

From bilateral to transboundary water cooperation

Despite international attempts to reconcile disagreements through formal diplomacy, ethnic tension and political stalemate remain. Donors see cooperation on shared water resources as an opportunity for countries in conflict to engage in regional dialogue. Because livelihoods in Armenia, Azerbaijan, and Georgia depend on improved water quality and sustainable water use, technical cooperation on water resource management, fostered through USAID's regional programs, led to political cooperation. USAID attempted to stimulate dialogue, problem solving, and capacity building for integrated water resource management.

USAID's regional investments built upon the work of two bilateral programs in Armenia—the Sustainable Water Management to Enhance Environmental Quality Program and the Institutional and Regulatory Strengthening of Water Management Program—which focused on national capacity building and benefited from the Armenian government's strong interest and will to reform the water sector. Following the government's creation of the Water Resources Management Agency (WRMA), with a mission to oversee decentralized water management in the country, USAID saw an important opportunity to help develop new policy and legal frameworks. Over several years, it supported a multi-sector process to develop the National Water Policy, the National Water Code, and the National Water Program. Capacity was built at the WRMA and other agencies to implement activities in support of decentralized and integrated water resource management. For example, efforts were made to develop and maintain the State Water Cadastre Information System to integrate multiagency data on water quality and quantity, catchment areas, water use and discharge permits, and water system–use permits. In an effort to standardize data sets, additional work concentrated on a national river network and a water resources–coding system. USAID also helped found basin-management organizations and offered specialized training to improve institutional capacities (Vardanyan et al. 2005). To round out its bilateral activities in Armenia, USAID backed improved monitoring of groundwater, which provides 95 percent of the drinking water in Armenia.

In 2002, USAID elected to expand its bilateral water programs in Armenia, Georgia, and Azerbaijan through the Water Management in the South Caucasus program, which addressed transboundary water resource management. USAID believed that countries in the region were ready for national management of water resources, an essential precursor for transboundary cooperation. In 2005, efforts were extended to two subbasins—the Alazani Basin and the Khrami-Debed Basin—through the SCWP. SCWP worked in close partnership with the three governments, particularly with Armenia's Ministry of Nature Protection, Azerbaijan's Ministry of Ecology and Natural Resources and Ministry of Agriculture, and Georgia's Ministry of Environment Protection and Natural Resources. Both regional programs focused broadly on strengthening scientific and analytical capacity and facilitating dialogue on transboundary water management in the region.

USAID selected the two subbasins because of their location between countries with less tense relations. Although the riparian countries involved conducted joint monitoring of water in the subbasins, the data and analyses were openly shared with all three countries and others interested in the Kura-Araks Basin. The approach offered a less controversial mechanism for bringing regional actors together and revealed the benefits of collaboration on transboundary water resource management. The SCWP was designed, in part, as a prelude

302   Water and post-conflict peacebuilding

to a larger program of the United Nations Development Programme/Global Environment Facility (UNDP/GEF). USAID cooperated closely with other donors, including the North Atlantic Treaty Organization (NATO) and OSCE, which also believed that technical cooperation on water by the three South Caucasus countries was important for the basin's immense development value and its peacebuilding potential.

Through the programs, several capacity-building initiatives were implemented in Georgia and Azerbaijan to complement bilateral programs in Armenia. For example, Georgia and Azerbaijan are completing national water resource–coding systems, which will allow more meaningful information coordination. The SCWP also helped establish regional monitoring and data sharing and national activities, such as institutional and regulatory strengthening of relevant ministries.

To further improve relations in the area and support efficient use of donor resources, USAID helped facilitate regular donor meetings. It also implemented joint activities, including programs sponsored by UNDP/GEF, OSCE, the European Commission, NATO, and the Regional Environmental Centre for the Caucasus. USAID cooperated with OSCE to cosponsor regional and national workshops on transboundary water priorities, including harmonization of water-related legislation. The workshops provided a valuable opportunity for networking and sharing information and data. Previously, in the absence of data collection and disclosure, many misperceptions existed (and open accusations were made) regarding sources of pollution and water use. Participation in data-sharing activities resulted in the three countries' deeper understanding of the causes and severity of water-quality and quantity problems and highlighted the need for regional cooperation. The program supported joint water quality–monitoring activities and passive exchange of water data through a new web portal. But misunderstanding and mistrust remain. To overcome them, further exchange of information, data analyses, and harmonization of monitoring procedures are required.

Finally, the USAID-supported SCWP offered small grants to local NGOs to facilitate their involvement in and coordination of water resource management. The NGOs helped raise public awareness by publishing the first-ever report card on the health of water in the Kura-Araks Basin. It provided, to the extent data were available, valuable baseline information on the biological, chemical, and physical parameters of the basin. The report card remains a layperson's tool for understanding what makes the basin important to decision makers and the public.

CONCLUSIONS AND LESSONS LEARNED

USAID's regional water programs in the South Caucasus present interesting lessons for regional cooperation and capacity building on water resources shared by post-conflict states. Multiyear efforts at the national and regional levels led to significant progress in water resource monitoring, national water planning and coordination, and integrated and decentralized river basin management. The

Transnational cooperation over water resources in the South Caucasus 303

strategic direction of USAID's investment was to develop national institutional capacity and political support as a critical precursor for regional cooperation. The cooperation—including political cooperation—intentionally focused in the early years on the technical staff of key ministries in the three countries. USAID's efforts were premised on the notion that cooperation at the technical level would enhance dialogue on the political level and ultimately serve regional peace and security.

Despite political tension in the region, USAID's South Caucasus water programs achieved many successes in transboundary water cooperation. The initiatives improved monitoring, data analysis, and information exchange, as well as dialogue between stakeholders on water resource management. Water resources are fundamental to national and regional development and stability; they sustain the health of communities and activities essential to economic growth. But lack of data, information, and agreement on what drives the subbasins' water quantity and quality still constrains consensus on the benefits of improved and collaborative water management at the regional level.

Because of the different stages of national water sector reform and the persistent tension between Armenia and Azerbaijan, several years will probably pass before SCWP gains traction at the political level. USAID's push for ministerial representatives to sit on the same panel at the 4th World Water Forum in Mexico, in 2006, is but one example of backing that should be strategically encouraged.

Although USAID supported the collection and sharing of data and information on water quality and quantity, additional work is needed to ensure that the data are fully analyzed and made available to decision makers and civil society. Investments in data analysis and application are necessary for capacity building and political commitment over the long term. Future efforts on transboundary water resource management in the South Caucasus should focus on evaluating available information, identifying the causes of water resource challenges, and determining joint solutions. Capacity building of national and subnational leaders and institutions must precede political acceptance of the mutual benefits of transboundary cooperation on water resource management.

Through its experience in the region, USAID is familiar with the stakeholders in and constraints to transboundary water resource management. Although some goals will be achieved rather quickly, others will be hindered by persistent tension between Azerbaijan and Armenia. Seemingly apolitical issues can quickly become political. Shifting long-held convictions takes time, so efforts such as the Water Management in the South Caucasus program and the SCWP should be supported with long-term funding and ongoing donor coordination.

REFERENCES

BBC. 2010. Regions and territories: Nagorno-Karabakh. January 10. http://news.bbc.co.uk/
2/hi/europe/country_profiles/3658938.stm#facts.

304   Water and post-conflict peacebuilding

Beehner, L. 2005. Nagorno-Karabakh: The crisis in the Caucasus. Council on Foreign Relations. www.cfr.org/publication/9148/nagornokarabakh.html#.

UNEP (United Nations Environmental Programme), UNDP (United Nations Development Programme), and OSCE (Organization for Security and Co-operation in Europe). 2004. *The case of the Southern Caucasus: Environment and security; Transforming risks into cooperation.* www.iisd.org/pdf/2004/envsec_transforming_risk_en.pdf.

Vardanyan, M., T. Lennaerts, A. Schultz, L. Harutyunyan, and V. Tonoyan. 2005. Towards integrated water resource management in Armenia. In *Sustainable development and planning II*, ed. C. A. Brebbia and A. Kunglolos. Southhampton, UK: WIT Press.

Vener, B. B. 2006. The Kura-Araks Basin: Obstacles and common objectives for an integrated water resources management model among Armenia, Azerbaijan, and Georgia. Masters thesis, University of New Mexico.

Vener, B. B., and M. E. Campana. 2010. Conflict and cooperation in the South Caucasus: The Kura-Araks Basin of Armenia, Azerbaijan, and Georgia. In *Water, environmental security and sustainable rural development: Conflict and cooperation in Central Eurasia*, ed. M. Arsel and M. Spoor. Oxford, UK: Routledge.

Wittich, A., and A. Maas. 2009. *Regional cooperation in the South Caucasus: Lessons for peacebuilding, from economy and environment.* Brussels, Belgium: Initiative for Peacebuilding. www.initiativeforpeacebuilding.eu/pdf/Regional_Cooperation_in_the_South_Caucasus.pdf.

Water security and scarcity: Potential destabilization in western Afghanistan and Iranian Sistan and Baluchestan due to transboundary water conflicts

Alex Dehgan, Laura Jean Palmer-Moloney, and Mehdi Mirzaee

Afghan stabilization and reconstruction efforts include agricultural development and water withdrawal, diversion, and containment projects in the middle and lower Helmand River and Hari Rud watersheds of Afghanistan.[1] The Iranian government sees these actions as undermining water security in the eastern part of its country. The concern is particularly relevant in the region known as Sistan and Baluchestan, the most desolate, most marginalized, and least stable of Iran's provinces. This region's instability is Iran's Achilles' heel, and Iran is sensitive to actions that may undermine its hold on the region.

Population growth and consumption patterns are at the root of near-term water challenges in both Iran and Afghanistan, and changes in climate are expected to exacerbate the situation. U.S. and Afghan efforts to harness or divert water from these watersheds without resolution of the water dispute between Afghanistan and Iran—which has festered intermittently since 1870—has encouraged Iran to adopt a paradoxical mixed strategy of destabilization and cooperation in Afghanistan. Its destabilization activities include support for the Taliban and direct action against water diversions. Failure to address water concerns has the potential to increase tensions between the two countries and to slow or prevent stability gains in Afghanistan's western provinces. However, handling water concerns adroitly could encourage closer cooperation on stability and development in Afghanistan, turning the challenge into an opportunity for post-conflict peacebuilding.

This chapter begins with a discussion of water relations between Afghanistan and Iran, focusing on the regional hydropolitics of Afghanistan's transboundary

---

Alex Dehgan is the chief scientist at the U.S. Agency for International Development. Laura Jean Palmer-Moloney is a senior research geographer for the U.S. Army Corps of Engineers' Engineer Research and Development Center, and former senior advisor on water with Regional Command Southwest in Helmand Province, Afghanistan (July 2011–May 2012). Mehdi Mirzaee is on the faculty of Islamic Azad University, Central Tehran Branch, and a research scholar at the Center for Water Conflict Management of the Department of Geosciences at Oregon State University.

[1] *Rud* means "river" in Dari and Farsi, forms of Persian spoken in Afghanistan and Iran, respectively.

306 Water and post-conflict peacebuilding

water basins; Iran's water insecurity and dependence on water originating from its upstream neighbor, Afghanistan; previous political negotiations over the waters of the Helmand watershed; and factors affecting future water availability in the region, including population growth, agricultural expansion, and climate change. The chapter then highlights how Iran's attempts at balancing its economic and political interests—interests that are conflicting at times—have collided with reconstruction projects for Afghanistan's water sector. Concentrating on Afghanistan's water-based development projects, the chapter concludes by outlining a five-part strategy to address the transboundary water issues. The strategy recommends developing monitoring systems and databases, identifying historic hydrometeorological baseline data, building capacity in water management and irrigation efficiency, creating an international support network for negotiations, and establishing a transboundary commission.

THE WATER DISPUTES BETWEEN AFGHANISTAN AND IRAN

Afghanistan's economic recovery requires reconsidering the definition of traditional security. With 80 percent of the population directly dependent on natural resource management (UNEP 2009), the strategy for reconstruction of the country after three decades of nearly continuous conflict requires incorporating historical resources that were the key to Afghanistan's greatness. This includes water.

Afghanistan's western neighbor, Iran, was forgotten after the initial days of the U.S. invasion of Afghanistan in October 2001 and the subsequent Bonn

Conference, when the United States, Iran, and Afghanistan had productively engaged on Afghanistan's reconstruction.[2] But any solution for post-conflict peacebuilding in Afghanistan requires consideration of its regional security and its economic and environmental context. This is particularly true with regard to Afghanistan's transboundary river basins.

Political hydrology

Worldwide, water is a commodity whose value varies according to locality, purpose, and circumstance (Grimond 2010). Within a specific river basin, it is more valuable in some locations than in others. Each of Afghanistan's five major river basins extends beyond its borders (see figure 1), and water use in each of

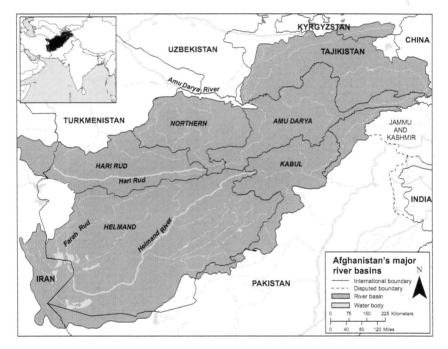

Figure 1. Watersheds of Afghanistan
Source: USACE-ERDC (2011).
Notes: The Helmand Basin, as referred to in this chapter, includes the Helmand, Upper Helmand, and Western Helmand, as shown on the map. The watershed extends into Iran's Sistan and Baluchestan Province, although that province is not shown on the map.

---

[2] The Bonn Conference took place in Bonn, Germany, in December 2001, under the auspices of the United Nations. The Bonn Agreement, formally known as the Agreement on Provisional Arrangements in Afghanistan Pending the Re-Establishment of Permanent Government Institutions, was concluded on December 5, 2001, and outlined the framework for the reconstruction of Afghanistan following the U.S. invasion. For the complete text of the agreement, see www.un.org/news/dh/latest/afghan/afghan-agree.htm.

308 Water and post-conflict peacebuilding

these transboundary basins has sparked tension with its neighbors (King and Sturtewagen 2010; Favre and Kamal 2004).

The Helmand River (known as the Hirmand River in Iran) is the longest river (1,150 kilometers) in Afghanistan, and its basin is among the most strategic of Afghanistan's river basins. With its waters originating in the Sia Koh Mountains in Herat Province and the Parwan Mountains northwest of Kabul, the river flows southwest through the desert of Dashti Margo, where it and the Farah Rud feed into the Sistan Depression at the Afghan-Iranian border (see figure 2). The Sistan Depression is divided into four separate shallow lakes of water—Hamun-i-Saberi, the deepest, is to the north; Hamun-i-Puzak is to the northeast, in Afghanistan; Hamun-i-Shapour is to the south; and Hamun-i-Helmand is a centrally located pool (Mojtahed-Zahed 2006; see figure 3).[3] These separate bodies of water can become one at flood times and can reach an area of approximately 3,200 square kilometers when the level of the combined lake rises (Favre and Kamal 2004). This large complex of wetlands, shallow lakes, and lagoons is world renowned as a haven for wildlife. The international community has designated the region a wetland of international importance under the Ramsar Convention (Ramsar Secretariat 2009).[4] For the past 5,000 years, the Hamun wetlands have been a major source of food and shelter for the people of Central Asia (Kakar 2011).

More than 7 million people inhabit the Helmand Basin, and they use the river and its tributaries extensively for irrigation (Favre and Kamal 2004). Most of the agriculture occurs in the lower reaches of the basin—in Kandahar, Helmand, and Nimroz provinces of Afghanistan, and in the Sistan and Baluchestan Province of Iran, which is part of the Persian granary. Ninety-five percent of the Helmand Basin is located in Afghanistan, but because of a lack of other economically feasible sources of potable groundwater, it is the only water resource for the main cities in Sistan and Baluchestan (van Beek and Meijer 2006).

Though Helmand River is a renewable water resource, it is vulnerable to overuse and seasonal exhaustion. The river and its tributaries are fed annually by melting snow from the highlands of central Afghanistan, and recent below-average snowfall and a reduction of water in the snow pack have led to a reduction of water in the overall drainage system (USACE-ERDC 2010). Two major dams that were constructed circa 1950 (the Kajaki Dam, capacity 2,720 million cubic meters; and the Arghandab Dam, capacity 435 million cubic meters) help control seasonal flooding and release water into the river during the seasonally dry times (FAO 1962; Caudill 1969; USAGC 2009; USACE-TEC 2002).

---

[3] These lakes are also known as Hamum-i-Saberi, Hamum-i-Puzak, Hamum-i-Shapour, and Hamum-i-Hirmand.

[4] For the complete text of the Ramsar Convention, formally known as the Convention on Wetlands of International Importance, see www.ramsar.org/cda/en/ramsar-documents-texts-convention-on/main/ramsar/1-31-38%5E20671_4000_0__.

Water security and scarcity in Afghanistan and Iran   309

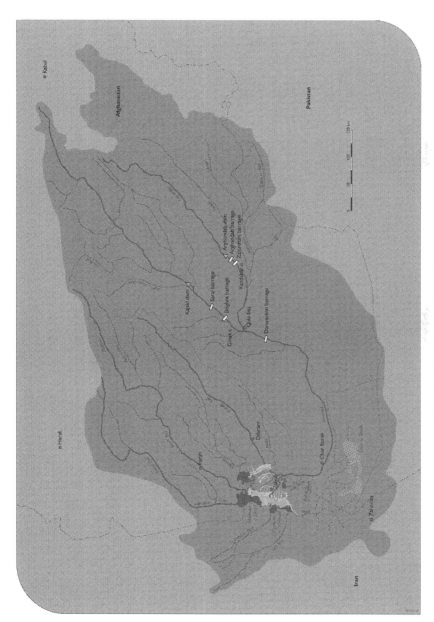

Figure 2. Rivers of Afghanistan and Iran feeding into the Sistan Basin
Source: van Beek and Meijer (2006).
Note: The Sistan Basin is shown in more detail in figure 3.

310   Water and post-conflict peacebuilding

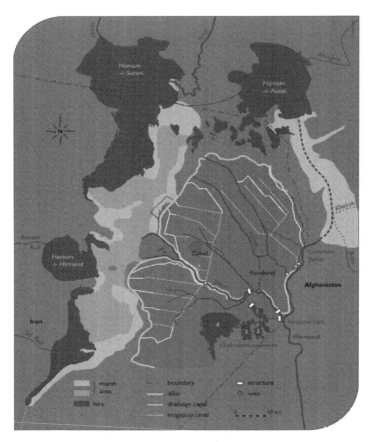

Figure 3.   Close-up of the Sistan Basin *hamuns* (lakes), the four Chahnimeh reservoirs, and main irrigation and drainage canals
Source: van Beek and Meijer (2006).

In Iranian Sistan and Baluchestan Province, the four Chahnimeh reservoirs hold water from the Helmand River. With an overall capacity of 700 million cubic meters, these reservoirs are a source of water for consumption in Sistan and Baluchestan (van Beek and Meijer 2006). Their primary function is to secure a public water supply for the cities of Zabul and Zahedan (located along Iran's eastern border with Afghanistan) and surrounding rural villages. However, when there is sufficient water available for public consumption, additional water is released for irrigation. Furthermore, the reservoirs supply water to the river system in times of drought (van Beek and Meijer 2006). This regulatory function is critically important in the lower Helmand and in the wetlands of the Sistan Basin, for if the river does not flow, few things can survive. When wetlands dry out, ecosystems diminish and the livelihoods that depend on the ecosystems vanish with them (Weier 2003).

Water security and scarcity in Afghanistan and Iran   311

Surface water in the Helmand system does not meet the basin's demands. Because a predictable year-round flow of surface water is not guaranteed, groundwater drawn from wells is the traditional and most reliable source of water for Afghan communities and agricultural fields in the area. When water is extracted faster than it is replaced, the groundwater level drops (Heath 1983). This situation, referred to as groundwater overdraft, leads to falling crop yields, higher costs (because additional power is needed to pump water out of the ground), and in some cases, greater debts for rural poor.

Water insecurity

Afghanistan's downstream neighbor, Iran, relies heavily on renewable water sources for its agricultural production and economy. More than 90 percent of the country's renewable water resources are used in agriculture (Alizadeh and Keshavarz 2005), but because of low efficiency in irrigation and transport, approximately 50 to 60 percent of the water is lost during the process (Keshavarz et al. 2005). These inefficiencies are not insignificant. Iran's agricultural sector accounts for approximately one-tenth of its GDP (World Bank n.d.), employs one-fifth of its workforce (UN n.d.), and is central to the country's goal of achieving food security.[5]

Strong population growth in recent decades has left Iran unable to grow enough food to feed its population despite the Iranian leadership's goals of achieving food self-sufficiency. Water scarcity continues to be a bottleneck. Urbanization, industrialization, and the development of irrigated agriculture to support population growth have raised the demand for water and simultaneously have reduced the supply (Ardakanian 2005). The increased demand has drawn down Iran's aquifers and has created conditions for water stress. As noted in the 2005 Iranian-American Workshop on Water Conservation, Reuse, and Recycling, sponsored by the U.S. National Research Council and the Academy of Sciences of the Islamic Republic of Iran, serious scientific, technical, ecological, economic, and social issues surrounding water are of concern to Iran now and will be for years to come (Alizadeh and Keshavarz 2005).

Less than 10 percent of Iran's water resources originate outside the country, but those regions dependent on transboundary water resources are highly susceptible to water scarcity (Frenken 2009). Iran uses 80 percent of the Helmand's current downstream flow for agriculture. This region is economically important to Iran, having frequently been referred to in historical documents as the "bread basket" of Central Asia. Remote sensing analysis of satellite images has identified approximately 150,000 hectares of farmland and forests and approximately 500,000 hectares of pastureland in the Helmand transboundary watershed (van Beek and Meijer 2006). Sistan Basin's traditional economic fortune has diminished as a result of the reduction of water flow from the Helmand River.

---

[5] See the Iranian Ministry of Agriculture web site, at www.maj.ir/english/main/default.asp.

312   Water and post-conflict peacebuilding

Iran also has concerns about Indian reconstruction of the Salma Dam on the Hari Rud (also known as the Harut Rud), which forms the border between Iran, Turkmenistan, and Afghanistan. Once reconstructed, the Salma Dam, which was originally built in 1976 but was damaged during the Afghan civil war, will regulate river flow during flood season and reduce the amount of water that flows from the Hari Rud to Iran and Turkmenistan from 300 million cubic meters to 87 million cubic meters per year, a reduction in water flow of 71 percent (Peter 2010). Iran perceives the reconstruction of the Salma Dam and current North Atlantic Treaty Organization and U.S. Agency for International Development efforts to rehabilitate the Kajaki Dam on the Helmand River as a direct security threat (Bagherpour and Farhad 2010; Peter 2010). Iran has put substantial political pressure on Afghanistan and India to halt dam construction (Christensen 2011).

Water is also essential for Afghanistan's stabilization and reconstruction efforts. In Afghanistan, 98 percent of the water being withdrawn from the Helmand Basin is used in the agricultural sector (UNEP 2008). Moreover, 80 percent of the Afghan population is directly dependent on natural resource management, primarily in animal husbandry and agriculture (UNEP 2009). Future agricultural development—a key portion of U.S. president Barack Obama's strategy to rapidly increase economic activity as a bulwark against the insurgency and the opium trade that helps fund it—will depend on the availability of sufficient water resources for expansion (Wegerich 2010; USG 2010).

Although Afghanistan theoretically has sufficient water for its needs, the country is hampered by poor infrastructure that has been damaged by thirty years of conflict. The Soviet invasion and civil wars, coupled with a weak central government, also have damaged traditional systems of management through the undermining of social norms and institutions; this has increased internal water stress and conflict (Kakar 2011). Finally, Afghanistan loses approximately two-thirds of its water to Iran, Pakistan, Turkmenistan, and other neighbors because it does not harness its rivers (Peter 2010; Babakarkhail 2009).

From 1999 to 2009, the Helmand Basin region in Afghanistan and Iran intermittently experienced drought conditions that lasted long enough to cause an imbalance in hydrologic processes (Mousavi 2005). The droughts greatly increased the fragility of the population and increased tensions between the two countries. Drought played an important role in the displacement that was prevalent in southwestern Afghanistan. According to the Kabul office of the United Nations High Commissioner for Refugees (UNHCR), the majority of Afghanistan's internally displaced persons—166,153 out of 235,833 individuals—were displaced for two reasons: the conflict in the period prior to and after the fall of the Taliban in 2001, or the drought of the 1990s, which severely affected Kuchi (nomads) in the north, west, and south (UNHCR 2008).

In 2002 alone, UNHCR registered 5,000 displaced persons from Nimroz who were arriving in other Afghan provinces (Ghashtalai 2003). Lack of potable water caused the population of Zaranj, Nimroz's capital city, located on the Helmand River at the Afghan-Iranian border, to plummet from 100,000 in 1997 to 60,000 in 2002. As water from the Helmand River vanished and wells dried up, residents who remained in the border city were faced with having to buy water imported from Iran to survive (Ghashtalai 2003; Sabir 2008).

The Taliban-led Afghan government's decision from 1999 to 2001 to cut off the flow of the Helmand River to Iran in the midst of the drought exacerbated tension with Iran (Press TV 2011). As a result of natural drought and human actions, Iran's *hamuns* (lakes) dried up, and sandstorms buried dozens of villages and destroyed farmland (Weier 2003; NASA MODIS 2003).

The drought has had direct and indirect effects on farmers in Afghanistan and Iran (Weier 2003). The direct effects include decreasing production in agriculture and rangelands; groundwater depletion; low flows in rivers and streams, which exposes all ecosystems to destruction and contamination; soil erosion; and mortality of livestock and wildlife (Grimond 2010; Asian Development Bank 2009; Bates et al. 2008; Mousavi 2005). Indirectly, the drought has lowered farmers' income, decreased the government's tax income, increased the cost of water and forage transport, and increased migration of farmers to small and big cities (Mousavi 2005). The drought also reduced yields and quality of grain and increased incidence of pests and diseases, exacerbating the impact to the agricultural sector.

The decreased surface water flow and decreased available water in the Helmand River system may have also led to increases in desertification (UN-Water and FAO 2007). Sandstorms that scoured southwestern Afghanistan from early June through September 2003—called the worst in living memory by residents of the area—buried villages, filled waterways, destroyed crops, and killed livestock (NASA MODIS 2003). Though locally strong winds known as the Wind of 120 Days occur annually (Whitney 2006), wind-generated sandstorms persisted longer than expected during the drought. Most of the windblown dust originated in the Sistan Basin wetlands, in the beds of dried out hamuns. Persistent drought conditions coupled with increased withdrawal of Helmand River water for irrigation have quickly turned these wetlands into arid salt pans (IRIN 2007; UNEP 2003, 2006).

Political negotiations over the Helmand

Although the headwaters of the Helmand watershed are within Afghanistan's territorial boundaries, Afghanistan's rights to the use of that water are limited under international law, state practice, and long-standing water-sharing agreements with Iran. Under customary international law, no riparian state has the exclusive right to the use of a transboundary river; instead each state's sovereign right to develop a river is limited by the rights of equitable apportionment and equitable utilization of other states. In relation to allocation of the waters of the Helmand River, these principles are supported by specific agreements in the region.

On August 19, 1872, the Goldsmid Arbitral Award allocated equal shares of the water in the lower reaches of the river to Afghanistan and Iran. A key

314 Water and post-conflict peacebuilding

portion of the award language states: "It is, moreover, to be well understood that no works are to be carried out on either side calculated to interfere with the requisite supply of water for irrigation on both banks of Hirmand" (Goldsmid 1876, 414). After the Helmand River changed its course in 1896 and after a severe drought in 1902, the two governments attempted through arbitration to reach new agreements in 1905 and again in 1938, but both attempts were unsuccessful.[6]

On September 7, 1950, the Afghan and Iranian governments signed the Terms of Reference of the Helmand River Delta Commission, which established the Neutral Technical Commission for the Helmand River Delta, with the assistance of the U.S. Department of State. This commission was designed to elaborate on the technical methods for sharing waters of the Helmand River and was to be composed of three technical experts from disinterested states who would have powers of recommendation only.[7] Afghanistan and Iran rejected the 1951 report of the commission at the Washington Conference of 1956, and the dispute over the division of water continued.[8] The variability in the course and seasonal flows of the river made division of the river's water challenging, even without considering the political pressures for control of its resources.

The building of the Kajaki Dam in 1953 increased instream flow during the dry season but reduced the flood waters on which pastoralists were dependent for fertilization. Removing water from the river system upstream from the historical point of measurement at Kamal Khan Dam complicated the water-sharing dialogue and alarmed Iran. In 1956, the government of Iran proposed that Iran be allotted 51.7 cubic meters per second, moving away from allotment by percentage to allotment by quantity. Afghanistan responded with a proposal that Iran be entitled to 22 cubic meters per second.[9] Iranian prime minister Amir Abbas Hoveida and Afghan prime minister Mohammad Musa Shafiq signed an accord in 1973 that was based on the Afghan counterproposal: Iran was allotted 22 cubic meters per second, with an option to purchase an additional 4 cubic meters per second in "normal" water years.

The 1973 agreement was never fully implemented due to the distractions caused by the Afghan coups d'état in 1973 and 1978, the Soviet invasion of Afghanistan, the Islamic revolution in Iran, and subsequent tensions between the Wahhabist Taliban and the Shia government in Tehran. Iran has held discussions with the Karzai government under the framework of the 1973 agreement, but these discussions have been inconclusive (King and Sturtewagen 2010). A common Afghan refrain is that Iran is taking as much as three-fourths of the water

---

[6] The McMahon Arbitration of April 10, 1905, recommended a one-third share for Iran; it was rejected by Iran. The Temporary Agreement for Distribution of Water of 1938 recommended a return to equal shares; it was rejected by Afghanistan.

[7] Helmand Commission Report, unpublished (on file with authors).

[8] John G. Laylin, counselor to the Iranian Minister of Foreign Affairs, unpublished working papers of the arbitration (on file with authors).

[9] John G. Laylin, unpublished working papers of the arbitration.

Water security and scarcity in Afghanistan and Iran 315

of the Helmand River by way of illegal canals and diversions (Babakarkhail 2009; Rasooli 2011).

The future of water availability

Predicted population growth, increased agricultural expansion, and climate change conditions are likely to exacerbate existing tensions between Afghanistan and Iran over dams and other water-control features on the Helmand River but may also provide opportunities for peacebuilding and for engagement that would prevent such tensions from escalating or provoking new conflicts that could impinge on Afghanistan's economic recovery and stability.

The region's climate is changing, and the exact impact of these changes is difficult to predict. According to a study by the Water Governance Facility of the United Nations Development Programme (UNDP), Afghanistan's glaciers have shrunk by as much as 50 to 70 percent (Granit et al. 2010). Although the shrinking of glaciers may increase runoff in the short term, the long-term effect is a decrease in water availability (U.S. Senate Committee on Foreign Relations 2011). Variability in the timing of water movements through the system may be as important a stressor as changes in the quantity of water moving through these river basins (van Beek and Meijer 2006).

Decreases in precipitation and increases in temperature will exacerbate changes that are already caused by glacial melt. Climate projections from the Intergovernmental Panel on Climate Change, coupled with downscaled modeling of its global predictions for the region, suggest that water stress caused by above average temperatures and below average rainfall will continue to increase in southeast Iran and southwest Afghanistan (Lawrence Livermore National Laboratory 2009; Alcamo, Florke, and Marker 2007; see figure 4). These estimates have been supported by the International Research Institute for Climate and Society (IRI 2011).

This situation has been made worse by the post-conflict reconstruction efforts in Afghanistan. On the recommendation of the U.S.-led coalition and with its assistance, Afghanistan is seeking to capture and use an increasing share of the Helmand River, Farah Rud, and Hari Rud and various tributaries through agricultural projects, new dam construction, and revitalization. It is doing so without conducting a comprehensive study on how these projects will affect overall water flow and availability, recharge rates for aquifers in Afghanistan, and transboundary water management and historical water negotiations (USAID 2008; USG 2010).[10]

Three decades of intermittent conflict in Afghanistan caused nearly one-third of the land in the country to be placed out of agricultural usage and many

---

[10] For further discussion on the water projects in Afghanistan, see Laura Jean Palmer-Moloney, "Water's Role in Measuring Security and Stability in Helmand Province, Afghanistan," in this book.

316 Water and post-conflict peacebuilding

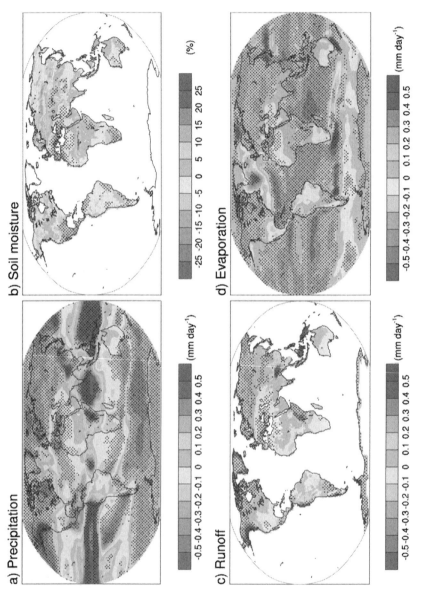

Figure 4. Projected percent change in precipitation, soil moisture, runoff, and evaporation in 2080–2099 relative to 1980–1999.
Source: Bates et al. (2008).

development projects to be placed on hold, and current reconstruction efforts could increase the amount of water used on the Afghan side just to bring agriculture back to pre-conflict levels through irrigation (Wolf and Haack 1993). These irrigation efforts may become a primary reason for decreased water supply in the future (van Beek and Meijer 2006). Population growth will be an additional stressor: as the population in the lower Helmand Basin grows, it will place more demands on water supply for domestic consumption, business, and food production.

The Afghan water sector projects have raised concerns in Tehran, Iran's capital, over the geopolitical use of water (Peter 2010). Iran is sensitive, given its past tensions with the Taliban and its concern over U.S. containment of its regional aspirations. Moreover, Baluchestan is one of Iran's most volatile regions, and Iran fears foreign interference that would destabilize the Baluch population. Sistan and Baluchestan Province is heavily Sunni in a majority Shia nation-state and remains Iran's most marginalized and least educated region. The population feels strongly that it has been disenfranchised by Tehran, and its isolation was made worse by the results of Iran's June 2009 elections (Cyrus 2010).

The marginalized Sunni population has reacted in radical ways against the central government. Since 2004, Sistan and Baluchestan Province has witnessed regular attacks, bombings, and kidnappings at the hands of Jundullah (soldiers of God), an ethnic Sunni Baluch group that Iran has accused the United States of supporting. One such attack was a double-suicide bombing, on December 12, 2010. The bombing targeted Shia worshipers at Imam Hussein Mosque in Chabahar, and it killed forty-one people, including women and children (Cyrus 2010).

Shared data and modeling is needed to increase understanding of the future impact of climatic and human-driven change in the water regime on management of the transboundary conflict, as well as on stabilization, reconstruction, and development efforts (U.S. Senate Committee on Foreign Relations 2011). There is insufficient systematic monitoring of groundwater tables, salinization, water flow, snowpack, and rainfall to establish baselines and understand how water flow and availability is changing in the Helmand Basin. Similar problems exist for the other Afghan river basins. The thirty-year gap in Afghanistan's hydrometeorological data will continue to undermine Afghanistan's ability to manage its water resources wisely (Kakar 2011; Williams-Sether 2008; Whitney 2006).

IMPACTS ON WATER SECTOR FROM CONFLICTING ECONOMIC AND POLITICAL INTERESTS

The water tensions between Iran and Afghanistan have led to a paradox. On one hand, Iran has sought to support development in Afghanistan, particularly where such funding would lead to benefits for Iran, such as improved efficiency in water use and transport, and in the past it has opposed the Taliban, which has historically been hostile to the Iranian government and Shiites. On the other hand, Iran provides ongoing support for multiple Taliban insurgent groups

318 Water and post-conflict peacebuilding

in Afghanistan, which have slowed or prevented U.S. reconstruction projects, including those around the water sector. It is difficult to determine whether this paradox is a reflection of the different interests in the cacophonous Iranian leadership or a manifestation of an Iranian hedging strategy toward Afghanistan that seeks to improve the efficiency of Afghanistan's water systems in amity while simultaneously undermining any attempt by the Afghans to divert a greater share of the water. Iran's interests are balanced between the political and the economic.

Iran has repeatedly tried to negotiate the status of the Helmand River, Farah Rud, and Hari Rud with Afghanistan—for example, it has called for the formation of a trilateral commission between Afghanistan, Tajikistan, and Iran—but Afghanistan has continued to demur, claiming that it lacks expertise, data, and capacity to participate in transboundary water negotiation (Xinhuanet 2010; EastWest Institute 2009). Although this is true, Afghanistan may be using the argument as a stalling tactic. Any negotiations with Iran could potentially result in a decrease in water retained by Afghanistan. Concessions by Afghanistan would also limit economic growth in its unstable region, which is largely driven by agricultural development. Therefore, Afghanistan possesses little incentive to seriously engage in talks based on the water issue alone.

Brokering such treaties may prove difficult for Afghanistan at the moment anyway. Being in the midst of a conflict and rebuilding, it is uncertain how much water Afghanistan needs or even how much it has (Peter 2010). Moreover, it is not clear—given the decentralized nature of power in Afghanistan and the split in reconstruction efforts between U.S. Agency for International Development, the U.S. military's Commander's Emergency Response Program, and other donors— whether a centralized Afghan development strategy on water would be carried out consistently and systematically.

U.S. activities and the threat to security posed by the reduction of water supplies have caused Iran to create perverse alliances counter to its normal interests. Although Iran nearly went to war with Taliban-controlled Afghanistan and the Taliban (who, as conservative Sunnis, see the Shia as apostates), Iran reportedly has been providing various factions of the Taliban with support in western Afghanistan. In March 2009, Afghan security forces found a cache of Iranian-made explosives and ammunition around the Bakhashabad Dam in Farah Province, and Iran continues to attempt to disrupt the dam project (Tabish 2011). Simultaneously Iran has allocated US$3.2 million for reconstruction of Afghanistan's water sector (MOE 2010). This competing strategy suggests that it may be possible to use concerns over water to build bridges for engagement and peacebuilding.

LESSONS LEARNED AND RECOMMENDATIONS

Any water-based development project in Afghanistan must take into account the water needs of Afghanistan's neighbors and the rights and obligations imposed on Afghanistan by international law, bilateral treaties, and state practice on the use of water from shared basins (EastWest Institute 2009). At the same time,

Water security and scarcity in Afghanistan and Iran 319

Afghanistan's immediate future economic growth will occur through agriculture, which requires using more water, improving irrigation and distribution systems, and increasing water efficiency. Water is necessary for Afghanistan's development, security, and stability (USG 2010).

Afghanistan cannot proceed to build new dams, restore old dams, and take an increasingly greater fraction of shared groundwater and surface water resources from the Helmand River and Hari Rud in Afghanistan without serious consequences if it does not equitably address the transboundary water issues with Iran. Because Afghanistan claims that it lacks the capacity and data to enter into negotiations, the United States should be focused on increasing Afghanistan's capacity on the technical level, creating monitoring systems that are transparent and shared, and building mechanisms for technical cooperation to the benefit of both countries. Finally, any agreement needs to take into account seasonal, year-to-year, and future climate-based changes in the quantity of water in the Helmand River. In any future agreement, the benefits of gains in water flow and the costs of shortages need to be shared.

This chapter outlines a five-part strategy for addressing the transboundary water issues between Afghanistan and Iran.[11] Transparent and shared monitoring systems and databases should be developed for Afghanistan's transboundary river basins to improve the scientific basis for any agreement. To create a better understanding of changes in water availability in Afghanistan's river systems, historical hydrometeorological baseline data need to be identified. Capacity building in water management and irrigation efficiency is required. An international support network must be created for negotiations on water. Finally, a transboundary commission between Afghanistan and Iran should be created to manage transboundary water resources.

Monitoring systems and databases

Though circumstances in western Afghanistan and southeastern Iran may make it difficult to perform measurements related to water, water cannot be managed if it cannot be measured. There must also be an understanding of the water budget. The major technological and knowledge deficit in the water sector restricts prospects for efficient management and use of water resources and hinders the policy development process (Arasteh and Tajrishy 2006; Homayoonnezhad, Amirian, and Piri 2008; Meybeck and Vörösmarty 2004; Rahimzadeh, Asgari, and Fattahi 2008; van Beek et al. 2008). Decision makers need to know the quantity and quality of water in transboundary river basins before moving forward with upstream projects that will affect both instream flow and groundwater levels.

The international community—possibly under the direction of the World Bank, the UNDP, the United Nations Environment Programme (UNEP), or

---

[11] U.S. counterinsurgency operations in Afghanistan would also benefit from the recommendations outlined in this section. For more information on these counterinsurgency operations, see Laura Jean Palmer-Moloney, in this book.

320 Water and post-conflict peacebuilding

the United Nations Educational, Scientific and Cultural Organization—should continue to help Afghanistan to put in stream gauges, map glacier melt, record changes in precipitation and snowfall, develop satellite monitoring tools, and monitor water-table depth and inflows and outflows to underground aquifers associated with transboundary river basins (USAGC 2009). On the basis of these data, dynamic models of water flow should be developed for each transboundary basin to predict the potential impacts of agricultural projects, population growth, climate change, and infrastructure projects on downstream water flow and quantity. Development of this knowledge base would allow the parties to negotiate water-sharing agreements that are more sensitive to seasonal, interannual, and long-term changes in water flow in Afghanistan and throughout the region. These data should be available online in close to real time and shared with surrounding countries. The monitoring stations and infrastructure should be opened to inspections by participating countries, as well as observer states and organizations.

The international community should look beyond aid delivery at just the national level and incorporate regional water strategies into policy development and aid programming, and it should work with the United Nations Assistance Mission in Afghanistan (UNAMA) to improve coordination of water-related donor aid. After the Taliban were removed and the Bonn Agreement was signed, Iran helped Afghanistan by establishing a water research institute in Kabul. This institute was equipped with tools and technology to train water experts, thereby increasing Afghanistan's capacity with regard to its water resources (van Beek and Meijer 2006). The existence of the institute could open doors for Iran to build or financially support the building of much-needed monitoring systems.

Historic hydrometeorological baseline data

Afghanistan's years of civil war and unrest have interrupted data collection on the amount of water moving through its river basins, data that had been collected since the agreements negotiated in the 1950s through the 1970s.[12] Discussions with scientists at the National Center for Atmospheric Research suggest that Afghanistan's river systems probably have less water in the last fifty years due to global warming, similar to patterns found in other transboundary river systems in the region, and may see further decreases in the future.

There are ways to develop proxies for past changes in water distribution and flow, including looking at past records of well depth; time series remote sensing imaging of glaciers, snow cover, and rivers; and preexisting river gauges. The United States should assist Afghanistan in establishing historical baseline information on water flow—for example, by obtaining the Fairchild Aerial Survey dataset and sharing commercial remotely sensed images of its critical watersheds.

---

[12] Helmand Commission Report, unpublished, and John G. Laylin, unpublished working papers of the arbitration.

It can also help with creating new baselines. Establishing the extent of previous water flow is important for adequate prediction of future changes, better understanding of the variability of water flow and the plasticity of its pathways, and adjustment of previous water-sharing agreements in light of current realities. In addition, Iran has data collections and expertise that could be shared and could prove useful to both countries.

Capacity building

The United States, partner states, and the United Nations and other international organizations should build capacity in Iran and Afghanistan to better understand international law and potential models governing shared water resources, as well as capacity for negotiations (Chavoshian, Takeuchi, and Funada 2005; McMurray and Tarlock 2005). Technical officials from these states should study the successes and failures of other regional water-sharing commissions, such as the Mekong River Commission, the Colorado River Commission, and the Nile River Basin Commission.

Because irrigation drives much of the demand for water, the United States, through its land-grant universities, should work with both Iran and Afghanistan on improving irrigation efficiency throughout the system, working closely with the Academy of Sciences of Iran, with which the United States has had active exchanges for more than ten years. The United States should also leverage its scientific assets in academia and in federal science agencies—such as the U.S. Geological Survey, the Department of Interior, the Army Corps of Engineers, the Environmental Protection Agency, and the National Oceanic and Atmospheric Administration—to build the capacity of Afghan scientists for gathering water-flow and volume information through remote sensing that would be shared among all basin partners.

International support network for negotiations

The United States is no longer a disinterested country in the water dispute between Iran and Afghanistan, nor is it necessarily a trusted partner for either party. Accordingly, the United States should continue efforts to build an international support network for resolution of the transboundary water dispute. It should push for expansion of the existing Water Sector Group, which includes the UNAMA, the Canadian International Development Agency, the U.S. Army Corps of Engineers, the U.S. Agency for International Development, the European Commission, the German development association Deutsche Gesellschaft für Internationale Zusammenarbeit (also known as GIZ), and the Dutch Embassy. Additional donors and implementing agencies may include UNDP, UNEP, the Organization for Security and Co-operation in Europe, the World Bank, and the Asian Development Bank, as well as key nongovernmental organizations, such as the Wildlife Conservation Society, that work in both countries on

322   Water and post-conflict peacebuilding

ecosystem management. Wider engagement of a larger donor community is needed to ensure the consistency and success of the water strategy. Engaging international agencies where Iran is a party, as opposed to working solely through the International Security Assistance Force and its member states, would help build Iranian trust.

Transboundary commission

A transboundary commission between Afghanistan and Iran should serve as a formal body that would negotiate water-sharing agreements, collect and share data, and build confidence and capacity on both sides. At the end of 2010, the government of Iran called for the creation of such a commission. It should have as its initial mandate the creation of a technical working group of three representatives from disinterested countries, agreed on by Iran and Afghanistan, to review the entire course of the Helmand and to assess existing and planned infrastructure, agriculture production, and population density and growth. The technical working group would oversee data collection, monitoring, and modeling of the Helmand River Basin, including the Farah Rud. It would assess future changes and make recommendations.

CONCLUSION

Afghanistan's plans for upgrading and developing its water infrastructure on each of its major river basins are aimed at exploiting the irrigation and energy potential of its rivers and at mitigating floods. Although these projects are crucial to the social and economic development of Afghanistan, they will also affect transboundary water flow and, as a result, Afghanistan's relations with its neighbors. Failure to address water concerns in the middle and lower Helmand River and the Hari Rud Basin has the potential to increase tensions between Iran and Afghanistan explosively, slowing or preventing stability gains in western Afghanistan and interfering with the success of important development projects in agriculture and energy generation. Moreover, Iran increasingly sees threats to its water supply as threats to its security, and it could seek to destabilize the region, possibly through support for its adversaries, such as the Taliban. On the other hand, adroit handling of water concerns could encourage closer cooperation with Iran on stability and development in Afghanistan and potentially even create a framework for U.S. cooperation with Iran.

REFERENCES

Alcamo, J., M. Flörke, and M. Märker. 2007. Future long-term changes in global water resources driven by socio-economic and climatic changes. *Hydrological Sciences Journal* 52 (2): 247–275.

Alizadeh, A., and A. Keshavarz. 2005. Status of agricultural water use in Iran. In *Water conservation, reuse, and recycling: Proceedings of an Iranian-American workshop*, ed.

Water security and scarcity in Afghanistan and Iran 323

Committee on U.S.-Iranian Workshop on Water Conservation, Reuse, and Recycling; Office for Central Europe and Eurasia Development, Security, and Cooperation; and National Research Council. Washington, D.C.: National Academies Press. www.nap.edu/openbook.php?record_id=11241&page=94.

Arasteh, P. D., and M. Tajrishy. 2006. Estimation of free water evaporation from Hamun wetlands using satellite imagery. *Atlantic Europe Conference on Remote Imaging and Spectroscopy* 1:1. http://ewrc.sharif.edu/pdf_folder/01%20Arasteh.pdf.

Ardakanian, R. 2005. Overview of water management in Iran. In *Water conservation, reuse, and recycling: Proceedings of an Iranian-American workshop*, ed. Committee on U.S.-Iranian Workshop on Water Conservation, Reuse, and Recycling; Office for Central Europe and Eurasia Development, Security, and Cooperation; and National Research Council. Washington, D.C.: National Academies Press. www.nap.edu/openbook.php?record_id=11241&page=18.

Asian Development Bank. 2009. Climate change threatens water, food security of 1.6 billion South Asians. Mandaluyong City, Philippines. http://reliefweb.int/node/322669.

Babakarkhail, Z. 2009. Afghan Iran water war. Asia Calling, October 31.

Bagherpour, A., and A. Farhad. 2010. The Iranian influence in Afghanistan. Frontline-Tehran Bureau, August 9. www.pbs.org/wgbh/pages/frontline/tehranbureau/2010/08/the-iranian-influence-in-afghanistan.html.

Bates, B., Z. W. Kundzewicz, S. Wu, and J. Palutikof, eds. 2008. *Climate change and water.* Technical paper of the Intergovernmental Panel on Climate Change, IPCC Technical Paper No. VI. Geneva, Switzerland: Intergovernmental Panel on Climate Change.

Caudill, M. 1969. *Helmand Arghandab: Yesterday, today, tomorrow.* Lashkar Gah, Afghanistan: United States Agency for International Development.

Chavoshian, S. A., K. Takeuchi, and S. Funada. 2005. An overview to transboundary and shared water resources management in Iran: Technical challenges and solutions. Paper presented at the "International Symposium on the Role of Water Science in Transboundary River Basin Management," Ubon Ratchathani, Thailand, March 10–12.

Christensen, J. B. 2011. *Strained alliances: Iran's troubled relations to Afghanistan and Pakistan.* Danish Institute for International Studies Report No. 2011 (3).

Cyrus, M. 2010. Iran's Jundallah problem. Frontline-Tehran Bureau, December 24. www.pbs.org/wgbh/pages/frontline/tehranbureau/2010/12/irans-jundallah-problem.html.

EastWest Institute. 2009. Symposium "Alternative Futures for Afghanistan and the Stability of Southwest Asia: Improving Regional cooperation on Water." Session 4: The Helmand River Basin and the Harirud and Murghab Rivers. EastWest Institute Brussels Centre, Brussels, Belgium, June 25.

FAO (Food and Agriculture Organization of the United Nations). 1962. Survey of land and water resources: Afghanistan general report. New York: United Nations Special Fund.

Favre, R., and G. M. Kamal. 2004. Watershed atlas of Afghanistan. Kabul: Afghanistan Information Management Services.

Frenken, K., ed. 2009. Irrigation in the Middle East region in figures: AQUASTAT Survey—2008. FAO Water Report No. 34. Rome: Food and Agriculture Organization of the United Nations.

Ghashtalai, H. 2003. Thirsty town taps into Iran: Drought-stricken border region looks around for vital water supplies. ReliefWeb, November 13, AAR #81. http://reliefweb.int/report/afghanistan/afghanistan-thirsty-town-taps-iran.

Goldsmid, F. J., ed. 1876. *Eastern Persia: An account of the journeys of the Persian Boundary Commission 1870-71-72.* London: Macmillan.

324 Water and post-conflict peacebuilding

Granit, J., A. Jägerskog, R. Löfgren, A. Bullock, G. de Gooijer, S. Pettigrew, and A. Lindström. 2010. *Regional water intelligence report Central Asia: Baseline report.* Regional Water Intelligence Report No. 15. Stockholm, Sweden: Water Governance Facility.

Grimond, J. 2010. For want of a drink: A special report on water. *Economist* 395 (8683): 1–20.

Heath, R. 1983. Basic ground-water hydrology. U.S. Geological Survey Water-Supply Paper No. 2220. Reston, VA: United States Geological Survey.

Homayoonnezhad, I., P. Amirian, and I. Piri. 2008. Investigation on water quality of Zabol Chahnimeh reservoirs: The effective means for development of water management of Sistan and Baloochestan Province, Iran. *World Applied Sciences Journal* 5 (3): 378–382.

IRI (International Research Institute for Climate and Society). 2011. Climate outlook: Middle East, February–July 2011. Palisades, NY. http://iri.columbia.edu/climate/forecast/net_asmt/2011/jan2011/text/MEast.html.

IRIN (Integrated Regional Information Networks). 2007. Afghanistan: Environmental crisis looms as conflict goes on. IRIN News.org, July 30. www.globalsecurity.org/military/library/news/2007/07/mil-070730-irin01.htm.

Kakar, K. 2011. *Afghanistan human development report 2011: The forgotten front; Water security and the crisis in sanitation.* Kabul, Afghanistan: Centre for Policy and Human Development, Kabul University.

Keshavarz, A., S. Ashraft, N. Hydari, M. Pouran, and E. A. Farzaneh. 2005. Water allocation and pricing in agriculture of Iran. In *Water conservation, reuse, and recycling: Proceedings of an Iranian-American workshop*, ed. Committee on U.S.-Iranian Workshop on Water Conservation, Reuse, and Recycling; Office for Central Europe and Eurasia Development, Security, and Cooperation; and National Research Council. Washington, D.C.: National Academies Press. www.nap.edu/openbook.php?record_id=11241&page=153.

King, M., and B. Sturtewagen. 2010. *Making the most of Afghanistan's river basins: Opportunities for regional cooperation.* New York: EastWest Institute.

Lawrence Livermore National Laboratory. 2009. Coupling climate change and hydrology in the Helmand watershed. Unpublished report presented to the InterAgency Water Resources Working Group, United States Army Geospatial Center, Alexandria, VA. December 1.

McMurray, J. C., and D. Tarlock. 2005. The law of later-developing riparian states: The case of Afghanistan. *New York University Environmental Law Journal* 12:711–763.

Meybeck, M., and C. J. Vörösmarty. 2004. The integrity of river and drainage basin systems: Challenges from environmental changes. In *Vegetation, water, humans, and the climate: A new perspective on an interactive system*, ed. P. Kabat et al. Berlin, Germany: Springer.

MOE (Ministry of Energy, Islamic Republic of Iran). 2010. Projects: Afghanistan reconstruction projects. *Iran Power and Water, Special Edition* 121:120–121.

Mojtahed-Zadeh, P. 2006. Hydropolitics of Hirmand and Hamun. In *Boundary politics and international boundaries of Iran: A study of the origin, evolution, and implications of the boundaries of modern Iran with its 15 neighbors in the Middle East, the Persian Gulf, the Caucasus, the Caspian Sea, Central Asia, and West Asia by a number of renowned experts in the field*, ed. P. Mojtahed-Zadeh. Boca Raton, FL: Universal Publishers.

Mousavi, S. F. 2005. Agricultural drought management in Iran. In *Water conservation, reuse, and recycling: Proceedings of an Iranian-American workshop*, ed. Committee

Water security and scarcity in Afghanistan and Iran 325

on U.S.-Iranian Workshop on Water Conservation, Reuse, and Recycling; Office for Central Europe and Eurasia Development, Security, and Cooperation; and National Research Council. Washington, D.C.: National Academics Press. www.nap.edu/openbook.php?record_id=11241&page=106.

NASA MODIS (National Aeronautics and Space Administration, Moderate Resolution Imaging Spectroradiometer). 2003. Image of the day: Dust storm over Afghanistan and Pakistan. August 21. http://earthobservatory.nasa.gov/IOTD/view.php?id=3724.

Peter, T. 2010. Afghanistan's woeful water management delights neighbors. *Christian Science Monitor*, June 15. www.csmonitor.com/World/Asia-South-Central/2010/0615/Afghanistan-s-woeful-water-management-delights-neighbors.

Press TV. 2011. Iran seeks its share of Hirmand water. April 15. www.presstv.ir/detail/174852.html.

Rahimzadeh, F., A. Asgari, and E. Fattahi. 2008. Variability of extreme temperature and precipitation in Iran during recent decades. *International Journal of Climatology* (29) 3: 329–343.

Ramsar Secretariat. 2009. The annotated Ramsar list: Islamic Republic of Iran. www.ramsar.org/cda/en/ramsar-pubs-annolist-annotated-ramsar-16557/main/ramsar/1-30-168%5E16557_4000_0__.

Rasooli, S. 2011. Water conflict with Iran needs professional negotiators. *Afghanistan Times*, April 13.

Sabir, A. S. 2008. Thousands of families in Zaranj are faced with water scarcity. *RAWA News*, June 21. www.rawa.org/temp/runews/2008/06/21/thousands-of-families-in-zaranj-are-faced-with-water-scarcity_9345.html.

Tabish, J. 2011. Iran faces renewed Afghan dam sabotage claims. Relief Web, February 1. http://reliefweb.int/node/382878.

UN (United Nations). n.d. Iran. United Nations Statistics Division. http://data.un.org/CountryProfile.aspx?crName=Iran%20(Islamic%20Republic%20of).

UNEP (United Nations Environment Programme). 2003. UNEP report chronicles environmental damage of the Afghanistan conflict. http://new.unep.org/Documents.Multilingual/Default.asp?DocumentID=277&ArticleID=3201&l=en.

———. 2006. *History of environmental change in the Sistan Basin: Based on satellite image analysis, 1976–2005*. Geneva, Switzerland.

———. 2008. *Freshwater under threat: South Asia*. Nairobi, Kenya.

———. 2009. *UNEP in Afghanistan: Laying the foundations for sustainable development*. Geneva, Switzerland.

UNHCR (United Nations High Commissioner for Refugees). 2008. *National profile of internally displaced persons (IDPs) in Afghanistan*. Kabul, Afghanistan.

UN-Water and FAO (Food and Agriculture Organization of the United Nations). 2007. Coping with water scarcity: Challenge of the twenty-first century. www.unwater.org/wwd07/downloads/documents/escarcity.pdf.

USAID (United States Agency for International Development). 2008. *Water atlas*. Washington, D.C.

USACE-ERDC (United States Army Corps of Engineers Engineer Research and Development Center). 2010. Assessment of the state of the snowpack in the major Afghanistan snow-impacted watersheds. Cold Regions Remote Snow Assessment Report. Hanover, NH: United States Army Cold Regions Research and Engineering Laboratory.

———. 2011. Assessment of the state of the snowpacks in the major Afghanistan snow-impacted watersheds, February 10, 2011. Alexandria, VA.

326 Water and post-conflict peacebuilding

USACE-TEC (United States Army Corps of Engineers Topographic Engineering Center). 2002. *Water resources areal appraisal of Afghanistan.* Alexandria, VA.

USAGC (United States Army Geospatial Center). 2009. *Provincial water resources data summary of Helmand (Province), Afghanistan.* Alexandria, VA.

USG (United States Government). 2010. Water strategy for Afghanistan, 2009–2014. Kabul, Afghanistan.

U.S. (United States) Senate Committee on Foreign Relations. 2011. Avoiding water wars: Water scarcity and Central Asia's growing importance for stability in Afghanistan and Pakistan. Majority staff report, 112th Congress, First Session, February 22. Washington D.C.: United States Government Printing Office.

van Beek, E., and K. Meijer. 2006. Integrated water resources management for the Sistan closed inland delta, Iran. Delft, Netherlands: Delft Hydraulics. www.wldelft.nl/cons/area/rbm/wrp1/pdf/main_report_sistan_irwm.pdf.

van Beek, E., B. Bozorgy, Z. Vekerdy, and K. Meijer. 2008. Limits to agricultural growth in the Sistan closed inland delta, Iran. *Irrigation Drainage Systems* 22:131–143.

Wegerich, K. 2010. *Water strategy meets local reality.* Afghanistan Research and Evaluation Unit Issues Paper Series. Kabul, Afghanistan.

Weier, J. 2003. From wetland to wasteland: The destruction of the Hamoun oasis. *NASA Earth Observatory*, December 13. http://earthobservatory.nasa.gov/Features/hamoun.

Whitney, J. W. 2006. Geology, water, and wind in the lower Helmand Basin, southern Afghanistan. U.S. Geological Survey Scientific Investigation Report No. 2006-5182. Reston, VA: United States Geological Survey. http://pdf.usaid.gov/pdf_docs/PNADH905.pdf.

Williams-Sether, T. 2008. *Streamflow characteristics of streams in the Helmand Basin, Afghanistan.* U.S. Geological Survey Fact Sheet No. 2008-3059. Reston, VA: United States Geological Survey. http://permanent.access.gpo.gov/LPS107281/LPS107281/pubs .usgs.gov/fs/2008/3059/pdf/fs2008-3059.pdf.

Wolf, J. M., and B. Haack. 1993. *Helmand-Arghandab Valley irrigation system: A change assessment, 1973–1990.* Bethesda, MD: Development Alternatives, Inc. / Earth Satellite Corporation.

World Bank. n.d. World development indicators. World DataBank. http://databank .worldbank.org/data/views/variableselection/selectvariables.aspx?source=world -development-indicators.

Xinhuanet. 2010. Iran calls for forming commission over water issue with Afghanistan, Tajikistan. China Economic Net. http://en.ce.cn/World/Middleeast/201012/28/t20101228 _22093646.shtml.

Water resources in the Sudan North-South peace process and the ramifications of the secession of South Sudan

Salman M. A. Salman

On January 9, 2005, after lengthy and complex negotiations, the government of the Republic of the Sudan and the Sudan People's Liberation Movement/Army (SPLM/A) signed the Comprehensive Peace Agreement (CPA),[1] which incorporated a number of separate protocols and agreements. This was a defining moment in the history of Sudan. It ended a devastating civil war that had lasted since 1983 following the collapse of the Addis Ababa Agreement.[2] It put in place radically new political structures for the division of power and wealth between the two parts of the country; and it recognized, for the first time, the right of the people of Southern Sudan to self-determination.

The CPA was signed by the then-first vice president of the Republic of the Sudan and the chairman of the SPLM/A, and was witnessed by envoys of thirteen countries and organizations—the presidents of Kenya and Uganda and representatives of Egypt, Italy, the Netherlands, Norway, the United Kingdom, the United States, the African Union, the European Union, the Intergovernmental Authority

---

Salman M. A. Salman is an academic researcher and consultant on water law and policy. Until December 2009, he served as the lead counsel and water law adviser with the Legal Vice Presidency of the World Bank. Some data in this chapter is drawn from the author's experience.

[1] The CPA is formally known as the Comprehensive Peace Agreement between the Government of the Republic of the Sudan and the Sudan People's Liberation Movement/Sudan People's Liberation Army. For the complete text of the CPA, see www.sd.undp.org/doc/CPA.pdf.

[2] The Addis Ababa Agreement on the Problem of South Sudan was concluded between the government of Sudan and the Southern Sudan Liberation Movement on March 12, 1972. The agreement ended Sudan's first civil war that erupted in 1955, and granted Southern Sudan limited regional autonomy. Its implementation, however, faced a number of difficulties, as well as major breaches by the government in Khartoum, and as a result, it collapsed in 1983. The SPLM/A was established that year and led the renewed civil war, and thereafter the negotiations that resulted in the conclusion of the CPA in 2005. For more information on the history, see Wai (1973); Alier (1990); and Bob (2009). For the complete text of the Addis Ababa Agreement, see www.goss-online.org/magnoliaPublic/en/about/politicalsituation/mainColumnParagraphs/00/content_files/file3/Addis%20Ababa%20Agreement.pdf.

328 Water and post-conflict peacebuilding

on Development (IGAD),[3] the Arab League, and the United Nations. This wide range of participants testified to the importance the world community had ascribed to the CPA and to the peaceful resolution of the conflict in Sudan. The CPA's main provisions are reflected in the Interim National Constitution of the Republic of the Sudan, which was adopted six months later, on July 6, 2005.[4]

As per the CPA, the people of Southern Sudan exercised the right of self-determination on January 9, 2011, and voted overwhelmingly to secede from the Sudan.[5] The new state of the Republic of South Sudan (also referred to as South Sudan)[6] formally came into existence on July 9, 2011, as the 193rd member of the global family of nations and the fifty-fourth African state, following the end of the interim period stipulated under the CPA and the interim constitution.

This chapter reviews the agreements that made up the CPA as they addressed water resources. It describes the political geography of South Sudan and the Nile Basin; examines the centrality of water resources to the Sudan North-South relations; and analyzes the implications of the secession of Southern Sudan and emergence of the new state of the Republic of South Sudan on the sharing and management of the Nile waters, both with Sudan as well as with the larger group of the other Nile riparian states.

AGREEMENTS AND PROTOCOLS UNDER THE CPA

The CPA consisted of the chapeau,[7] six protocols and agreements, and two annexures on the implementation of these instruments. The chapeau recorded the long and continuous negotiations process that took place from 2002 to 2004 in Kenya,[8] referred to the tragic losses resulting from what had become the

---

[3] IGAD is a regional organization consisting of the East african countries of Djibouti, Eritrea, Ethiopia, Kenya, Somalia, Sudan, Uganda, and (starting in 2011) South Sudan. Its vision is to achieve peace, prosperity, and regional integration. See www.igad.org for more information.

[4] For the complete text of the Interim National Constitution of the Republic of the Sudan, see www.mpil.de/shared/data/pdf/inc_official_electronic_version.pdf.

[5] The results of the referendum were announced on February 7, 2011, and showed that close to 99 percent of the Southern Sudanese voters opted for secession (Southern Sudan Referendum Commission 2011).

[6] This chapter generally uses the terms *Southern Sudan* and *Northern Sudan* to refer to the two parts of Sudan prior to South Sudan's secession. On February 13, 2011, about a week after the Southern Sudan referendum results were officially announced, the government of Southern Sudan decided to call the country "Republic of South Sudan." Accordingly, the chapter uses this term when referring to the new state.

[7] The chapeau is the umbrella agreement that was signed by the two parties and the thirteen witnesses on January 9, 2005, and to which the other agreements and protocols constituting the CPA are attached.

[8] Negotiations took place under the auspices of IGAD. They were held in the Kenyan towns of Karen, Machakos, Nairobi, Nakuru, Nanyuki, and Naivasha. Because five of the six main agreements of the CPA were concluded at Naivasha, the CPA is often referred to as the Naivasha Agreement. Kenya played a major role in the negotiations, and appointed General Lazaro Sumbeiywo as a mediator. For a description of the negotiations process and the role of General Sumbeiywo, see Waihenya (2006).

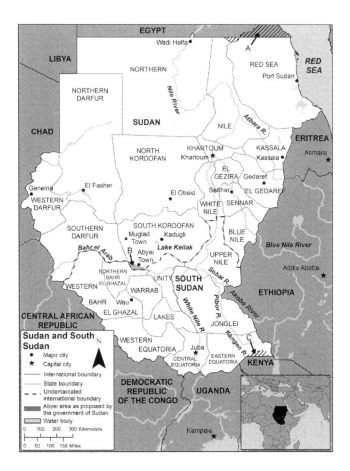

Notes:
A – The Hala'ib Triangle is claimed by Sudan and de facto administered by Egypt.
B – The disputed Abyei area; shaded area depicts the Abyei area as proposed by the government of Sudan.
C – The Ilemi Triangle is claimed by Ethiopia, South Sudan, and Kenya and de facto controlled by Kenya.

longest-running conflict in Africa, and emphasized the need for full adherence to the letter and spirit of the CPA to ensure lasting peace, security, justice, and equality in Sudan. The chapeau was followed by the six separately negotiated agreements and two annexures. The six agreements include:

1. The Machakos Protocol,[9] concluded on July 20, 2002, stated in paragraph 1.1: "The unity of the Sudan, based on the free will of its people democratic governance, accountability, equality, respect, and justice for all citizens of the Sudan is and shall be the priority of the parties and that it is possible to redress the grievances of the people of South Sudan and to meet their

---

[9] For the complete text of the protocol, see www1.chr.up.ac.za/chr_old/indigenous/documents/Sudan/Legislation/Machakos%20Protocol%202002.pdf.

330   Water and post-conflict peacebuilding

aspirations within such a framework." Yet paragraph 1.3 stated, "the people of South Sudan have the right to self-determination, *inter alia*, through a referendum to determine their future status." More specifically, paragraph 2.5 stated that "[a]t the end of the six (6) year Interim Period, there shall be an internationally-monitored referendum, organized jointly by the GOS [government of the Sudan] and the SPLM/A, for the people of South Sudan to: confirm the unity of the Sudan by voting to adopt the system of government established under the [CPA]; or to vote for secession." Incorporating these provisions, the interim constitution reconfirmed the six-year interim period, starting on July 9, 2005, with the referendum on the status of Southern Sudan to take place on January 9, 2011, six months before the end of the interim period on July 8, 2011.[10]

2. The Agreement on Security Arrangements was concluded on September 25, 2003. It provided for an internationally monitored ceasefire to come into effect upon the signing of the CPA,[11] and for the continued existence of two separate and equal armed forces during the interim period, the Sudanese Armed Forces and the Sudan People's Liberation Army (SPLA), along with a number of joint integrated units incorporating members from both forces.

3. The Agreement on Wealth Sharing, concluded on January 7, 2004, addressed land and other natural resources, including oil. It provided for the establishment of the National Land Commission, the Southern Sudan Land Commission, the National Petroleum Commission, the Fiscal and Financial Allocation and Monitoring Commission, and the Oil Revenue Stabilization Account. It established guiding principles for sharing oil and non-oil revenues,[12] and dealt with monetary policy, banking, currency, borrowing, and the establishment and operation of multi-donor trust funds.

4. The Agreement on Power Sharing was concluded on May 26, 2004.[13] It set forth principles of governance and human rights, and fundamental freedoms—including freedom of thought, conscience and religion, expression, assembly, and association. It called for a decentralized system of government with significant devolution of powers to Southern Sudan, the states, and local governments, and described the structure and institutions of the national,

---

[10] The first six months after the CPA was signed (January 9, 2005 to July 8, 2005) were referred to as the pre-interim period. This period was primarily devoted to agreeing on and adopting the interim constitution.

[11] A de facto ceasefire had begun to evolve after the conclusion of the Machakos Protocol.

[12] The Agreement on Wealth Sharing stipulated that the net revenue from the oil in Southern Sudan would be divided equally between the national government and the government of Southern Sudan, after the deduction of a certain amount for the Oil Revenue Stabilization Account and 2 percent for each of the oil-producing states or regions.

[13] For the complete text of the Agreement on Power Sharing, see www.splmtoday.com/docs/CPA%20Related/2004%20Power%20Sharing.pdf.

Southern Sudan, and state governments. Despite its detailed provisions on land and natural resources, the Agreement on Wealth Sharing did not address water resource issues. These issues were addressed briefly only by the Agreement on Power Sharing.

The Agreement on Power Sharing, and subsequently the interim constitution, granted the national government (in schedule A, paragraph 33 of both documents) exclusive jurisdiction over the "Nile Water Commission, the management of the Nile Waters, transboundary waters and disputes arising from the management of interstate waters between Northern states and any dispute between Northern and Southern states."[14] The agreement and the interim constitution also empowered the government of Southern Sudan to coordinate Southern Sudan services and establish minimum standards in a number of areas, including water provision and waste management (in schedule B, paragraph 9 of both documents). The government of Southern Sudan was also given jurisdiction over natural resources and forestry, as well as over disputes arising from the management of interstate waters within Southern Sudan. Thus, jurisdiction over the Nile and other transboundary waters was placed with the national government, while local water resource management became the responsibility of the government of Southern Sudan.

5. The Protocol on the Resolution of the Conflict in the Two States of Southern Kordofan and Blue Nile was also concluded on May 26, 2004. It dealt with those two states that are geographically part of Northern Sudan but inhabited by people who identify culturally and ethnically more with Southern Sudan. It called for the diverse cultures and languages of the people in these states to be developed and protected. It underscored the need for the development of the two states, and it set up special local structures, with significant powers devolved to them. It also stipulated carrying out popular consultations for achieving these objectives.

6. The Protocol on the Resolution of the Abyei Conflict (also known as the Abyei Protocol) was the third agreement concluded on May 26, 2004, and is the sixth agreement under the CPA.[15] Abyei, according to this protocol, is an area that was transferred from Southern Sudan to the North during the colonial era, and became a focus of a major dispute between the North and the South. The protocol established arrangements for defining the boundaries of the area and for a referendum, to be carried out simultaneously with the Southern Sudan referendum, to determine the area's future.

---

[14] The term *Nile Water Commission* should be understood to refer to the Permanent Joint Technical Committee, which was established in 1959 under the Agreement for the Full Utilization of the Nile Waters between Egypt and Sudan, as discussed later in this chapter.

[15] The title of the protocol was changed on December 31, 2004, to the Protocol between the Government of the Sudan and the Sudan People's Liberation Movement/Army on the Resolution of the Abyei Conflict. For the complete text of the protocol, see www.gossmission.org/goss/images/agreements/Abyei_protocol.pdf.

332   Water and post-conflict peacebuilding

On December 31, 2004, two annexures were concluded on the implementation of the six agreements, covering issues such as timing, executing authority, funding sources, and procedures. This brought to a successful conclusion the arduous negotiations that had spanned almost three years. The CPA was signed less than ten days later, on January 9, 2005. On July 6 of that year, the Interim National Constitution of the Republic of the Sudan was adopted, incorporating the basic provisions of the CPA.[16] Both documents addressed, in addition to the right of self-determination for the people of Southern Sudan, broad issues of governance, security, and power and wealth sharing. As mentioned earlier, water resources were dealt with not in the Agreement on Wealth Sharing but in the Agreement on Power Sharing. Jurisdiction over the Nile waters, which are the only transboundary waters in Southern Sudan, was granted exclusively to the national government.

POLITICAL GEOGRAPHY OF SOUTH SUDAN AND THE NILE BASIN

South Sudan covers an area of approximately 640,000 square kilometers, or about 26 percent of the total area of Sudan, which is approximately 2.5 million square kilometers. Parts of the borders between Sudan and South Sudan, which extend for more than 2,000 kilometers, had not been demarcated at the time of writing (January 2013).[17] Most of the border areas involve tributaries of the Nile River, such as Bahr el Arab and Bahr el Ghazal. A major complicating factor is the grazing and water rights of the tribal communities in those areas. Whether the disputed area of Abyei (about 10,500 square kilometers) belongs with Northern or Southern Sudan was supposed to be decided in a referendum scheduled to take place simultaneously with the referendum of Southern Sudan on January 9, 2011. However, as will be discussed later, the Abyei referendum did not take place. Water and grazing rights are central to the Abyei dispute.

According to the 2008 census, the population of Southern Sudan was 8.2 million, or 21 percent of Sudan's total population of 39.1 million (SSCCSE

---

[16] Article 225 of the interim constitution stated: "The Comprehensive Peace Agreement is deemed to have been duly incorporated in this Constitution; any provisions of the Comprehensive Peace Agreement which are not expressly incorporated herein shall be considered as part of this Constitution." This article attested clearly to the comprehensiveness and authority of the CPA, and came close to recognizing the supremacy of the CPA over the interim constitution. The government of Southern Sudan adopted its own interim constitution in December 2005. For the complete text of the Interim Constitution of Southern Sudan, see www.chr.up.ac.za/undp/domestic/docs/c_SouthernSudan.pdf.

[17] Sudan had boundary disputes with some of the countries now bordering South Sudan. The Ilemi Triangle, de facto controlled by Kenya, was disputed by Kenya, Ethiopia, and Sudan. Some border areas between Sudan and Uganda were also in dispute. The Republic of South Sudan has now inherited those disputes.

2009). The census figure representing the population of Southern Sudan was contested by the SPLM/A, which argued that the Southern Sudanese were grossly undercounted during this census, and that refugees were still steadily returning to Southern Sudan.

Southern Sudan has been devastated by the civil war that erupted in August 1955, a few months before Sudan gained independence in January 1956. The war took the lives of more than 2 million people and sent a larger number as refugees to neighboring countries as well as to Northern Sudan. A decade of relative peace emerged following the conclusion of the Addis Ababa Agreement between the North and the South in 1972 (see note 2). However, civil war erupted again in 1983 and continued until the conclusion of the CPA in 2005. Not much development took place in Southern Sudan during the six-year interim period that followed, and the new state of the Republic of South Sudan emerged in 2011 as a poor country with little infrastructure and with serious security problems in many areas. The new state borders Ethiopia in the east; Kenya, Uganda, and the Democratic Republic of the Congo in the south; the Central African Republic in the west; and Sudan in the north. It is a landlocked state, bordering three other landlocked states.[18]

The government of the Republic of South Sudan relies heavily on oil that was discovered in 1999, and which was shared under the CPA in equal percentages with the North during the interim period. About 75 percent of Sudan's proven oil reserves are now located in South Sudan, with some in disputed border areas. Oil revenue provides an estimated 95 percent of the total income of the government of the Republic of South Sudan. With the oil infrastructure—the pipeline, the refineries, the export facilities, as well as the ports—all situated in Sudan, the two parties have been locked in intricate and difficult negotiations on this matter, as well as other major issues.

As indicated earlier, the CPA and the interim constitution placed all issues related to the Nile waters within the exclusive jurisdiction of the national government, even though a large part of the Nile falls within Southern Sudan (and now South Sudan). As shown in figure 1, almost all of the important tributaries of the White Nile, including the Sobat River, either originate, or join the river in South Sudan (Collins 1996).

Upon exiting Lake Victoria, the river is called Victoria Nile. It passes through Lake Kyoga and then enters Lake Albert, after which it is renamed Albert Nile. Upon entry into South Sudan at the town of Nimule (in Eastern Equatoria State), Albert Nile is renamed Bahr el Jebel. Juba, the capital of South Sudan, is located next to this river. After passing through the city of Bor (in Jonglei State), the river spreads into the large swamps called the Sudd (after the Arabic word for

---

[18] For administrative purposes, Southern Sudan was divided into ten states, replacing the long-known division of the South into the three provinces of Upper Nile, Equatoria, and Bahr el Ghazal.

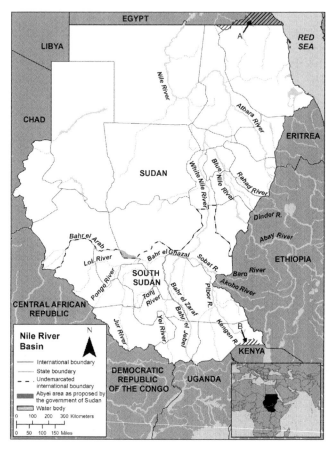

Figure 1. Nile River Basin
Notes:
A – The Hala'ib Triangle is claimed by Sudan and de facto administered by Egypt.
B – The disputed Abyei area; shaded area depicts the Abyei area as proposed by the government of Sudan.
C – The Ilemi Triangle is claimed by Ethiopia, South Sudan, and Kenya and de facto controlled by Kenya.

barrier), and branches into Bahr el Jebel and Bahr el Zaraf, to be joined by a number of tributaries flowing from the west and the southwest. The river Bahr el Arab originates in the border areas between Sudan and the Central African Republic, and flows eastward. It is fed by a number of tributaries, including the Lol, Yei, Jur, and Tonj rivers. The city of Wau, the capital of Western Bahr el Ghazal State, is situated on the Jur River. The Jur and Bahr el Arab merge to form Bahr el Ghazal, and after joining Bahr el Jebel at Lake No, the river is called the White Nile. The river Bahr el Zaraf, which branches off Bahr el Jebel, joins the White Nile a few kilometers after Lake No. The White Nile then flows eastward to the city of Malakal, the capital of Upper Nile State, where it is joined by the Sobat River. The White Nile contributes approximately 11.5 billion cubic meters (bcm) per year—or about 14 percent of the total flow of the Nile River, as measured at Aswan, in Egypt.

The Sobat River originates in Ethiopia as the Baro and Akobo rivers, which merge inside South Sudan. The Sobat River is then joined by the Pibor River, which originates within South Sudan. The river thereafter flows through the Machar marshes (sometimes referred to as the Sobat marshes) before joining the White Nile near the city of Malakal. The combined river, now called the White Nile,[19] flows for a considerable distance within South Sudan before entering Sudan, later merging with the Blue Nile at Khartoum, the capital of Sudan. As such, the White Nile dominates and is dominated by South Sudan. Indeed, South Sudan is where the White Nile loses and later consolidates itself.

The Blue Nile and its tributaries, including the Rahad and Dinder rivers, rise in the Ethiopian highlands. Upon their confluence at Khartoum, the White Nile and the Blue Nile form the Nile River.[20] The Nile is joined after that, still in Northern Sudan, by the Atbara River, which also originates in the Ethiopian highlands. The Atbara River is the last tributary to join the Nile, which thereafter flows through Northern Sudan and Egypt before emptying into the Mediterranean Sea.

The Sobat River contributes the same amount of water as the White Nile (approximately 11.5 bcm, or 14 percent of the Nile waters, as measured at Aswan). This brings the total flow of the White Nile to approximately 23 bcm, or 28 percent of the total Nile waters. (Table 1 summarizes the source contributions to the waters of the Nile River.) A large amount of the water of the tributaries of the White Nile evaporates and seeps in the huge swamps of South Sudan. It is estimated that about 20 bcm of water from those swamps could be conserved and added to the flow of the White Nile, almost doubling its flow (Collins 2002). Approximately 20 percent of the Nile Basin area falls in South Sudan, and more than 90 percent of South Sudan is part of the Nile Basin.[21] As mentioned above, the three main cities in South Sudan—Juba, Malakal, and Wau—are all situated on the White Nile or one of its main tributaries.

The remaining 72 percent of the flow of the Nile (approximately 61 bcm) comes from the Blue Nile (59 percent) and the Atbara River (13 percent)

---

[19] Some books and maps consider the White Nile as starting after the confluence with the Sobat River. Others call the entire river from Lake Victoria to Khartoum the White Nile, while still others consider the White Nile to start after the confluence of Bahr el Ghazal and Bahr el Jebel rivers. The latter approach, which this author subscribes to, is consistent with most of the literature on the Nile and helps in distinguishing the White Nile, with its Equatorial Lakes origin, from the Sobat River, which flows from Ethiopia. Yet, the author also subscribes to the use of the name *White Nile* to describe, in a generic sense, the whole river from Lake Victoria to Khartoum.

[20] For a detailed account of the political geography of the Nile, see Collins (2002).

[21] About 63 percent of the Nile Basin fell in Sudan before the secession of South Sudan. The secession leaves Sudan with about 43 percent of the Nile Basin, still the largest area of the basin in one country (Salman 2011).

336 Water and post-conflict peacebuilding

Table 1. Source contributions to the waters of the Nile River

	Annual water contribution (in billion cubic meters)	Percentage of total Nile River flow
Equatorial Lakes		
White Nile	11.5	14%
Subtotal	**11.5**	**14%**
Ethiopian Plateau		
Atbara River	11.0	13%
Blue Nile	50.0	59%
Sobat River	11.5	14%
Subtotal	**72.5**	**86%**
TOTAL	**84.0**	**100%**

(Waterbury 2002). Thus, the Ethiopian plateaus are the origin of about 86 percent of the waters of the Nile (72.5 bcm), while the Equatorial Lakes contribute about 14 percent (11.5 bcm). Despite the high contribution of the Blue Nile, its flow is largely seasonal, concentrated in the months of June through September. Conversely, the relatively smaller contribution of the White Nile remains steady throughout most of the year and provides for the critical water needs of Sudan and Egypt during the low-flow period of the Blue Nile.[22] Thus the two rivers complement each other to provide a perennial water flow in Sudan and Egypt.[23]

With the emergence of the Republic of South Sudan as a new state, the Nile is now shared by eleven states. Tanzania, Uganda, and Kenya share Lake Victoria, while the highlands of Burundi and Rwanda are the origins of the Kagera River, which is the major river flowing into Lake Victoria. The Democratic Republic of the Congo shares the Semliki River, which flows into Lake Albert (one of the sources of the White Nile), as well as Lake Albert, with Uganda. The White Nile consolidates itself after being joined by the Sobat River in South Sudan. Eritrea shares portions of the Setit River, which is a tributary of the Atbara River, with Ethiopia, the origin of the Blue Nile and almost all of its tributaries. Sudan and Egypt are the most downstream riparian states. The stakes and interests of Egypt, Sudan, and Ethiopia in the Nile are very high; those of Uganda as high; those of Tanzania, Kenya, Burundi, and Rwanda as moderate; and those of Eritrea and the Democratic Republic of the Congo as low (Salman 2011). Because of the size of the White Nile in South Sudan, the heavy water evaporation and seepage at the swamps there, and the possibility of conservation of a good part of such

---

[22] The Blue Nile also carries a heavy load of silt from the Ethiopian highlands, whereas the White Nile is almost silt-free.

[23] Since its completion in 1971, the Aswan High Dam has been regulating the flow of Nile waters in Egypt.

Water resources in the Sudan North-South peace process   337

water, the stakes of South Sudan can be classified as very high, almost on a par with Egypt, Ethiopia, and Sudan.

Despite this wide range of interests and contributions to the Nile River, Egypt and, to some extent, Sudan have long dominated the Nile River. In November 1959, Egypt and Sudan concluded the Agreement for the Full Utilization of the Nile Waters (known as the 1959 Nile Agreement).[24] This agreement established the total annual flow of the Nile (measured at Aswan) as 84 bcm, and allocated 55.5 bcm to Egypt and 18.5 bcm to Sudan. The remaining 10 bcm represents the evaporation and seepage at the large reservoir created by (and extending below) the Aswan High Dam in southern Egypt and northern Sudan. The agreement sanctioned the construction of the Aswan High Dam in Egypt and the Roseires Dam on the Blue Nile in Sudan. To ensure cooperation in research related to the management of the Nile waters, and the increase of the water supply, and in hydrological survey work in the Nile's upper reaches, the agreement established a Permanent Joint Technical Committee with an equal number of members from each country.[25]

Thus, the two countries allocated the entire flow of the Nile at Aswan to themselves. While they recognized the claims of the other riparian states to a share of the Nile waters if the other states so requested, they reserved to themselves the ultimate decision on whether those states would get a share, and if so, how much. This position is rejected by the other riparian states who consider it an infringement of their rights under international law as riparians of the Nile Basin.

Those states also reject the earlier 1929 Nile Agreement,[26] which gave Egypt veto power over any project in the then-British colonies of Uganda, Kenya, Tanganyika, and Sudan. They have argued that they are not bound by this agreement because they were not parties to it (Garretson 1967). Egypt and Sudan contend that their historic and existing rights are protected under international law and are not negotiable. The other riparian states also invoke international law in support of their claims to a share of the Nile waters. They argue that, since almost the entire flow of the Nile originates within their territories, they are entitled to an equitable and reasonable share of that flow. These countries also invoke the Nyerere Doctrine (named after Julius Nyerere, the first prime minister and later president of Tanganyika, later Tanzania), which gave countries emerging from colonialism two years to renegotiate treaties concluded during the colonial era, after which they would lapse (Makonnen 1984). Egypt, on the other hand,

---

[24] *United Nations Treaty Series* 453:64 (1963).

[25] The details regarding the committee are spelled out in the Protocol Concerning the Establishment of the Permanent Joint Technical Committee, 1960, *United Nations Legislative Series* B/12 (International Rivers).

[26] Exchange of Notes between Great Britain and Northern Ireland and Egypt in Regard to the Use of the Waters of the River Nile for Irrigation Purposes, Cairo, May 1929, *League of Nations Treaty Series*, No. 2103.

338 Water and post-conflict peacebuilding

invokes the principle of state succession to support its claim that the 1929 Nile Agreement remains valid and binding.

The 1959 Nile Agreement also addressed the water evaporation and seepage in the Sudd area of Southern Sudan and the other swamps and marshes, and the need for conservation and use of such waters. Under the 1959 agreement, the two parties would carry out projects to conserve some of the waters of these swamps in order to increase the flow of the Nile. The benefits and costs of such projects are to be shared equally between the two parties. The agreement gave Egypt the right to undertake this work by itself if it decided it needs the water before Sudan does. When Sudan is ready to use its share, it would reimburse Egypt for its share of the cost of the work. Thus, the Sudd and other swamps and marshes of Southern Sudan have been viewed by Egypt and Northern Sudan as a major potential source of additional water for their use, in addition to their full utilization of the existing amount of Nile waters.

NILE WATERS MANAGEMENT UNDER THE CPA

As stated earlier, the CPA and the interim constitution were explicit that the Nile waters were the exclusive responsibility of the national government. Given the size of the Nile Basin in then-Southern Sudan and the fact that most of the projects to augment the flow of the Nile would take place there, it may seem counter-intuitive that the SPLM/A would not push for a more active role in Nile water management during the interim period, as it did with oil, land, and other natural resources. In this author's view, there are two main reasons for this decision.

The primary reason relates to the wide and acute controversies surrounding rights to the Nile River waters described in the previous section, and concerning both the 1929 and 1959 Nile agreements. Attempting to bridge their differences, nine of the riparian states established the Nile Basin Initiative (NBI) in 1999.[27] One of the goals of the NBI has been to conclude a cooperative framework agreement among all the Nile riparian countries for regulating the sharing and management of the Nile Basin. Intense discussions since 2001 have failed to achieve this goal. During the CPA negotiations between 2002 and 2005, the SPLM/A leaders must have been keenly aware of these controversies and developments.[28] It seems

---

[27] The nine original NBI member states included Burundi, Democratic Republic of the Congo, Egypt, Ethiopia, Kenya, Rwanda, Sudan, Tanzania, and Uganda. Eritrea was, and continues to be, an observer. On July, 5, 2012, the Republic of South Sudan was admitted as the tenth member of the NBI during the twentieth annual meeting of the Nile Council of Ministers of Water (Nile-COM) in Kigali, Rwanda. The NBI has described its vision as achieving "sustainable socioeconomic development through the equitable utilization of, and benefit from, the common Nile Basin water resources" (NBI n.d.a, n.d.b).

[28] The late John Garang de Mabior, the leader of the SPLM/A, and one of his closest advisers, Mansour Khālid, addressed Nile water issues at length in their respective doctoral dissertations (Garang de Mabior 1981; Khālid 1966).

likely that they realized that Southern Sudan's hard-won right of self-determination could be jeopardized if it became entangled with the Nile politics, and could cause the other riparian states to fear the emergence of a new competitor for the Nile River waters, or at least a complicating factor in an already complex situation. The Organization of African Unity and its successor, the African Union, have opposed secessionist movements and have—since 1963—repeatedly called for the retention of the boundaries set during the colonial era. Under these circumstances, the SPLM/A choice not to demand a voice in Nile water management must have allayed the fears of the other Nile riparian states and made it easier for them to support, or at least remain neutral on, the issue of self-determination for Southern Sudan.

The second reason for the SPLM/A's decision not to pursue a role in Nile water management under the CPA is that there were no functional irrigation projects in Southern Sudan using Nile waters when the CPA was being negotiated. On the other hand, there are several large irrigation projects in the North,[29] but these have not exhausted Sudan's annual share of the 18.5 bcm under the 1959 agreement. Its average annual use has ranged between 14 and 15 bcm. The few existing agricultural projects in Southern Sudan—such as the Nzara (or Anzara) Agro-industrial Project, Tonj Kenaf factory, Melutt and Mongalla sugar projects, Wau Brewery, and Malakal Pulp and Paper project—either were not completed or were in need of major rehabilitation (Yongo-Bure 2007). Due to its unequal development, South Sudan's water needs remain limited. It must have also been realized during the negotiations of the CPA that the heavy rains that fall from June to October would be sufficient, for some time to come, to sustain the limited subsistence agriculture and livestock herds of communities in the South. Even if the projects in the South were completed or rehabilitated, Sudan's unused share of Nile waters could, for the near future, accommodate them.

Although the SPLM agreed to leave responsibility for the Nile waters during the interim period to the national government, the government of Southern Sudan, as will be discussed later, gradually started to assert itself on the Nile water issues from the early years of the interim period.

THE CENTRALITY OF WATER ISSUES IN THE NORTH-SOUTH RELATIONS

Water resources have been central to the relationship between Northern and Southern Sudan. As an indication of this centrality, the Southern Sudan Referendum Act of 2009 listed ten issues, including water resources, which were supposed to be resolved by the two parties immediately after the referendum. Those issues

---

[29] The Gezira Scheme in central Sudan is the largest user of Nile waters in Sudan, averaging about 8 bcm per year, or about 40 percent of Sudan's allocation under the 1959 agreement, and more than half of Sudan's total annual usage of Nile waters. Other projects include the Rahad Project, the New Halfa Scheme, the Suki Scheme, the White Nile and Blue Nile Pumps Schemes, and the Kenana Sugar Scheme.

340   Water and post-conflict peacebuilding

comprise: nationality; currency; public service; position of joint integrated units; international agreements and treaties; debts and assets; oil fields, production, and transport; oil contracts; water resources; and property. Attempts to resolve those issues during the period between the adoption of the Southern Sudan Referendum Act in December 2009 and the emergence of South Sudan as an independent state were not successful.[30] Indeed, a number of those issues were still pending resolution when this chapter was completed at the end of February 2013 and would now have to be dealt with by two sovereign nations.

Two examples, the Jonglei Canal Project and the Abyei territorial dispute, serve to show the centrality of water resources issues in the Sudan North-South relations. The Jonglei Canal Project, intended to conserve water from the Sudd and add it to the White Nile, foundered on the tensions between the North's and Egypt's desire for additional Nile waters, and the South's concerns about the canal's potential to harm local livelihoods and the environment. Water rights also play a central role in the territorial dispute over the Abyei area on the border between Sudan and South Sudan. In addition, allocation between the two parties of the Nile waters allotted to Sudan under the 1959 Nile Agreement between Egypt and the Sudan, and the relationship of the new state of South Sudan with the other Nile riparians, particularly Sudan and Egypt, emerge as major issues for the Sudan and South Sudan relations, as discussed below.

The Jonglei Canal Project

Describing the Sudd of Southern Sudan, Alan Moorehead wrote:

> There is no more formidable swamp in the world than the Sudd. The Nile loses itself in a vast sea of papyrus ferns and rotting vegetation. . . . This region is neither land nor water. Year by year the current keeps bringing down more floating vegetation, and packs it into solid chunks perhaps twenty feet thick and strong enough for an elephant to walk on. But then this debris breaks away in islands and forms again in another place, and this is repeated in a thousand indistinguishable patterns and goes on forever (Moorehead 2000, 88–89).

The Sudd area varies in size between 30,000 and 40,000 square kilometers, and can expand to double that size during the wet season, making it one of the

---

[30]   On June 21–22, 2010, representatives of the National Congress Party (NCP) and the SPLM met in Mekelle, Ethiopia, to discuss the post-referendum issues. On June 23, they signed the Mekelle Memorandum of Understanding between the NCP and SPLM on Post-Referendum Issues and Arrangements (*Sudan Tribune* 2010). For the complete text of the memorandum of understanding (MOU), see www.cmi.no/sudan/doc/?id=1283. The MOU stated that negotiations on post-referendum issues would be conducted by a joint negotiating team consisting of six members from each party, to be assisted by a joint technical secretariat. The MOU clustered the issues to be negotiated into four groups: (i) citizenship; (ii) security; (iii) financial, economic, and natural resources; and (iv) international treaties and legal issues.

Water resources in the Sudan North-South peace process 341

largest wetlands in the world. A large portion of its water is lost to evaporation and transpiration. Navigation through its thick vegetation has always been difficult, as attested to by explorers in the second half of the nineteenth century who passed through the Sudd looking for the sources of the Nile (Baker 2002). The Anglo-Egyptian colonial administration of Sudan, established in 1898, quickly recognized the potential of the Sudd as well as the other swamps of Southern Sudan to help augment the flow of the Nile. Water was needed to expand cotton production in Egypt to meet the growing needs of the textile industry in Lancashire (Tvedt 2004).[31] Thus, the search and planning commenced immediately after the conquest of Sudan for ways to bypass the swamps and deliver more water to the Nile.

In 1904, Sir William Garstin, the undersecretary of state for public works in Egypt, published an influential report on the Upper Nile (Garstin 1904), which included a thorough investigation of the White Nile and its tributaries. To bypass the Sudd, Garstin recommended excavating a new channel of about 340 kilometers to bring water from the upper Nile (Bahr el Jebel) at Bor directly to the confluence of the White Nile and the Sobat River. This proposal was the origin of what was later known as the Jonglei Canal Project.[32]

Garstin's proposal was reconsidered in the early 1920s but was shelved due to deterioration in relations between Britain and Egypt in the mid-1920s following the assassination of the governor-general of the Sudan, Sir Lee Stack, in Cairo (Gaitskell 1959). Interest revived in the mid-1930s, and again in 1946, when the colonial administration in Sudan established the Jonglei Investigation Team, which produced a report in 1953 (Howell, Lock, and Cobb 1988). However, by that time the attention of Egypt had shifted to the Aswan High Dam, and the Jonglei Canal Project took a back seat.

As discussed earlier, the 1959 Nile Agreement between Egypt and Sudan included detailed provisions on projects for preserving the waters of the swamps of Southern Sudan. Planning of the construction of the Jonglei Canal, however, did not start until 1974, after the temporary end of Sudan's civil war and conclusion of the Addis Ababa Agreement in 1972. The newly designed project, which still drew substantially on the 1904 Garstin proposal, consisted of a 360-kilometer canal from Bahr el Jebel at the village of Jonglei to the junction of the White Nile and the Sobat River. It also included development components for the project area: a large-scale irrigation scheme for sugar growing and

---

[31] Terje Tvedt noted "British banks supported increased cotton exports in order to buttress Egypt's ability to repay its debts. In 1882 Egypt's foreign debt had risen to £100 million, and annual debt service to £5 million, of which a large proportion went to Britain. The Lancashire textile industry wished to reduce its dependence on American cotton by increasing supplies of cheaper cotton from Egypt" (Tvedt 2004, 21).

[32] Under the design of this project, the canal would start at the village of Jonglei, not far from Bor, and extend for about 360 kilometers to the confluence of the White Nile and the Sobat River, following a similar route to the one suggested by Garstin. It would fall entirely within Jonglei State in Southern Sudan.

342   Water and post-conflict peacebuilding

processing; all-year roads, bridges, and river transportation links; and education and health services.

Under the 1959 Nile Agreement, Egypt had agreed to pay 15 million Egyptian pounds to Sudan in compensation for the inundation of Sudanese territory by the Aswan High Dam.[33] However, the agreement did not mention compensation to the people who may be adversely affected by projects in the swamps of Southern Sudan.

Sudan established a National Council for the Development of the Jonglei Canal Area in 1974. Nonetheless, the (Sudanese-Egyptian) Permanent Joint Technical Committee established under the 1959 Nile Agreement continued to have supervisory responsibility for the project. The cost of the project was estimated at US$260 million; costs and benefits were to be divided equally between Sudan and Egypt. When completed, the canal was expected to add close to 5 bcm to the flow of the White Nile. An equal amount of water is expected from a second canal that would drain a part of the remaining swamps in the Sudd area of Behr el Jebel and Bahr el Zeraf. Studies also indicated that a similar amount of water could be drained from the Bahr el Ghazal swamps and the Machar marshes. The four projects together could almost double the flow of the White Nile (Waterbury 2002).

The contract for the Jonglei Canal was awarded to the French consortium Compagnie de Constructions Internationales (generally known as CCI), which had excavated a similar project in Pakistan.[34] Its huge excavator was dismantled, brought by land and sea to the proposed canal site, and reassembled. Engineers and technicians from France, Pakistan, and Sudan were employed in addition to local laborers. The French-led foreign staff lived in a camp at the northern end of the canal site—ironically, just a few kilometers from the site from which French forces withdrew after they were confronted by the British in the 1898 Fashoda Incident.[35]

---

[33] More than 50,000 Sudanese Nubians living in the border town of Wadi Halfa and surrounding villages had to be relocated to northeastern Sudan (Dafalla 1975).

[34] The project that CCI constructed in Pakistan was the Chasma-Jhelum link canal, connecting the Indus River with the Jhelum River. The project was completed in 1964 (Collins 2002).

[35] A French battalion, under the leadership of Major Jean-Baptiste Marchand, arrived in the Fashoda area of the White Nile in Southern Sudan in July 1898. Following the conquest of the Sudan by the Anglo-Egyptian army in September 1898, Colonel Horatio Kitchener was ordered to move immediately to Fashoda to confront the French battalion. The incident represented the epic of the Scramble for Africa generally, and for the Nile in particular, by European colonial powers. After a brief encounter and frenzied communications between London and Paris, the French withdrew from Fashoda, resulting in the White Nile coming under the full control of the British. Fashoda, the village where that incident took place, was subsequently renamed "Kodok," perhaps as a gesture of conciliation with the French. The CCI camp was erected a few miles south of that village. For a detailed account of the Fashoda Incident, see Tvedt (2004).

Water resources in the Sudan North-South peace process 343

The Jonglei Canal Project faced some major opposition from the start in Southern Sudan because it was seen as serving the interests of Northern Sudan and Egypt. Local and international actors voiced concerns that the canal could have negative impacts on the Sudd ecosystem and on local livelihoods—specifically, on drinking water, pastures, fisheries, and access to either side of the canal by pastoral communities and their herds and by wildlife (Yongo-Bure 2007). Opposition was also fuelled by rumors about the impending settlement of 2 million Egyptian farmers in the canal area. Students in a number of cities in Southern Sudan rioted against the project, and three people were shot and killed during those riots.

The situation gradually quieted, and implementation of the project started in 1978.[36] By November 1983, about 260 of the canal's 360 kilometers were completed. However, in that month, the recently formed SPLM/A attacked the canal site. The SPLA carried out three major attacks on the Jonglei Canal site—on November 16, 1983, February 6, 1984, and February 10, 1984—and the final attack brought the project to a complete halt (ICCA 1988).[37] Since that time, the huge excavator has sat idle and rusting in the middle of the Sudd swamps about 100 kilometers north of the village of Jonglei. The completed portion of the canal has turned into a large ditch in which wildlife could easily be trapped and die and which has impeded the movement of people and animals in the region (Yongo-Bure 2007).

The SPLM/A's main complaint against the project was that its implementation concentrated on the excavation of the canal, which would benefit Northern Sudan and Egypt, and neglected the components of the project intended to help develop Southern Sudan. Such components had not even been started in 1983, although they had originally been presented as an integral part of the project (Oduho 1983).[38]

Environmental and social standards, particularly for water infrastructure projects, are far more strict and comprehensive today than they were when the Jonglei Canal Project was planned in the 1970s. Local, regional, and international civil society organizations concerned about the Sudd ecosystem and the rights of the people who live there are certain to keep a close eye on any plans for the revival of the project. Moreover, the Sudd was officially recognized on November 1, 2006, under the Ramsar Convention (Ramsar Convention Secretariat 2012b)

---

[36] For further discussion of the Jonglei Canal Project, see Collins (2002) and Alier (1990). Abel Alier was the president of the High Executive Council of Southern Sudan when those developments took place. He was a strong supporter of the Jonglei Canal Project, and was quoted as saying, in response to protests against it, "If we have to drive our people to paradise with sticks, we will do so for their own good and the good of those who come after us" (Collins 2002, 204).

[37] The SPLM/A also halted Chevron's oil operations in Southern Sudan as well as improvements to the airport at Juba, the capital of Southern Sudan (and now South Sudan), in the early months of 1984.

[38] The late John Garang de Mabior, leader of the SPLM/A, argued in his doctoral dissertation that the project, as designed and implemented, would perpetuate poverty, misery, and underdevelopment in the area (Garang de Mabior 1981).

344 Water and post-conflict peacebuilding

as an internationally important wetland.[39] It is the third largest Ramsar site in the world after the Okavango Delta in Botswana, and the Queen Maud Gulf in Canada.

As a Nile River project, the Jonglei Canal fell, during the interim period, under the jurisdiction of the national government as stipulated in the CPA and the interim constitution. However, from the very early days of the interim period, the government of Southern Sudan raised concerns about the political, economic, social, and environmental effects of the project.[40] The president of the government of Southern Sudan made it clear that the Jonglei Canal Project was not one of their priorities (Kiir Mayardit 2010). The emergence of the Republic of South Sudan as an independent state means that the issues of conservation and use of the waters of the swamps of South Sudan fall fully in the hands of the government of the Republic of South Sudan. The security situation in Jonglei State as well as other areas in the South, has been steadily deteriorating. Inter-tribal fights, food shortages, and military clashes have been regularly reported since early 2009 (UNHCR 2009; Schomerus and Allen 2010). Those circumstances are certain to make resumption of work on the Jonglei Canal Project more difficult.

The increasing assertiveness of the Nile upstream riparian states is also likely to complicate future negotiations on the resumption of work on the Jonglei Canal, or the work on any of the other three proposed canals. This is because the waters of the Sudd and of the Machar marshes of South Sudan could be viewed, due to the sources of those waters, as a wider Nile Basin issue, and not simply a South Sudanese-Sudanese-Egyptian concern (Salman 2008).

The Abyei dispute

The dispute over the Abyei area on the border between Sudan and South Sudan also raises important water issues for the local communities in the area. Although a number of steps were taken during the interim period in an attempt to settle this dispute, the issues are still far from resolved, and now have to be

---

[39] Article 2(2) of the Ramsar Convention—concluded in 1971 and formally known as the Convention on Wetlands of International Importance—states: "Wetlands should be selected for the List on account of their international significance in terms of ecology, botany, zoology, limnology or hydrology." Sudan became a party to the Ramsar Convention on May 7, 2005 (Ramsar Convention Secretariat 2012a). Article 4(1) of the convention requires each party to "promote the conservation of wetlands . . . by establishing nature reserves on wetlands, whether they are included in the List or not, and provide adequately for their wardening." For the complete text of the convention, see http://www.ramsar.org/cda/en/ramsar-documents-texts-convention-on/main/ramsar/1-31-38%5E20671_4000_0__.

[40] The minister of irrigation for the government of Southern Sudan expressed reservations in 2009 about the effects of the Jonglei Canal Project and called for a new feasibility study to be carried out by his ministry (*Sudan Tribune* 2009b).

Water resources in the Sudan North-South peace process   345

dealt with by two sovereign states, together with the United Nations Security Council.[41]

Abyei is defined by the Abyei Protocol, which is part of the CPA, as the area of the nine Ngok Dinka chiefdoms that was transferred from Southern to Northern Sudan by the colonial government in 1905 for administrative convenience.[42] However, the exact size and boundaries of the area were not agreed upon, and became the central issue in the dispute between the North and the South following independence of the Sudan in 1956. The Abyei Protocol placed Abyei temporarily in a special administrative status under the presidency. The protocol gave the area's residents citizenship in both Kordofan and Bahr el Ghazal, and provided for the creation of a local executive council, initially appointed by the presidency and to be later elected by Abyei residents. Once the boundaries of Abyei were demarcated, its residents would choose—in a referendum scheduled to be carried out simultaneously with the referendum on Southern Sudan's self-determination on January 9, 2011—between retaining their current status or becoming part of Bahr el Ghazal in Southern Sudan.[43] However, the referendum did not take place.

The major complication to the Abyei dispute is that, in addition to the national government and the SPLM/A, the dispute also involves the Southern tribe of the Ngok Dinka and the Northern tribe of the Misseriya, who share parts of, and have conflicting claims over, the Abyei area (Salman 2013). The discovery of oil in and around Abyei has added to the complication of the situation. The Abyei Protocol included detailed provisions on the sharing of oil revenues during the interim period.[44]

Based on the provisions of the Abyei Protocol, the Abyei Boundaries Commission (ABC) was established in March 2005 (Petterson 2008). The ABC was made up of five representatives each from the national government and the SPLM/A, and five international experts. Its report, issued in July 2005 (ABC 2005), set the boundaries of Abyei area in a way that was close to those claimed by the SPLM/A, legitimating Ngok Dinka dominant (permanent) and secondary claims well into Kordofan to the north, and assigned large areas to Abyei in the east and some areas in the west. It also established an area of shared seasonal rights for the Ngok Dinka and the Misseriya north of the dominant claims area

---

[41] For more information on the land and territorial aspects of the Abyei dispute, see Salman (2013).

[42] Abyei was transferred from the Southern state of Bahr el Ghazal to the Northern state of Kordofan. Both states have since been further divided; the Abyei issue concerns the states of South Kordofan and Northern Bahr el Ghazal.

[43] Most of the provisions of the Abyei Protocol, including the Abyei referendum, were reflected in article 183 of the interim constitution.

[44] The percentages were as follows: 50 percent for the national government, 42 percent for the government of Southern Sudan, and 2 percent each for Bahr el Ghazal, Kordofan, the Ngok Dinka, and the Misseriya.

346   Water and post-conflict peacebuilding

and divided it between the two parties. Thus, the ABC report included large areas of Kordofan within the Abyei area boundaries.

The SPLM/A accepted the report, but the government of Sudan immediately rejected it, claiming that the ABC had exceeded its mandate. A stalemate resulted and continued for the next three years. Following violent clashes in Abyei, the two parties agreed, in July 2008 to refer the dispute to the Permanent Court of Arbitration (PCA).

In October 2008, three months later, the arbitral tribunal of the PCA was constituted and issued its decision on July 22, 2009.[45] It validated the ABC's decision regarding the dominant claims of the Ngok Dinka on the northern boundary, but the PCA overturned the decision on the eastern and western boundaries and the shared secondary rights above the northern boundary. The tribunal's award reduced the Abyei area from that delimited by the ABC substantially in the east and slightly in the west. As a result of this reduction, some major oil fields reverted to Sudan. However, Bahr el Arab (also known as the Kiir River), the main river in the area, together with most of its major tributaries, would fall largely within the Abyei area as delimited by the arbitral award.[46]

The grazing and other traditional rights of the Misseriya and other communities within the Abyei area were confirmed in both decisions. The PCA tribunal's award stated: "The exercise of established traditional rights within or in the vicinity of the Abyei Area, particularly the right (guaranteed by Section 1.1.3 of the Abyei Protocol) of the Misseriya and other nomadic peoples to graze cattle and move across the Abyei Area (as defined in this Award), remains unaffected."[47] It further indicated that under international law, traditional rights are not extinguished by boundary delimitations. Thus, according to the award, the Ngok Dinka and the SPLM/A got land and water, while the government of Sudan got most of the oil fields around the area, and the Misseriya got confirmation of their grazing rights (Salman 2010).

The PCA tribunal's award was accepted by both parties, and was welcomed by the United Nations, IGAD, the European Union, and the United States. Although one of the arbitrators issued a powerful dissent, this did not dilute the wide welcome the award received. However, the Misseriya tribe rejected the award, claiming that it added too much of their own land and villages to the Abyei area, and limited their rights over the area to grazing rights (*Sudan Tribune* 2009a). The Misseriya leaders issued a series of strong statements that they would defend their

---

[45]   For the full text of tribunal's final award, see www.pca-cpa.org/showfile.asp?fil_id=1240.

[46]   For a map of the Abyei area as delimited by the PCA arbitral tribunal, see Terralink (2009); see also Salman (2013). The government of Sudan announced immediately after the PCA decision that the government of Southern Sudan would no longer receive any of the revenue from the oil in those fields, since they were no longer in the Abyei area as delimited by the PCA. The government of Southern Sudan responded that it would still claim those oilfields as part of Southern Sudan when the process of delimiting the complete border between the North and the South commenced.

[47]   Para. 770(e)(2).

rights in the Abyei area. Clearly, with the considerable expansion of the Abyei area, the Misseriya believe that they have a claim to more than just grazing rights in the area.

On its face the Abyei dispute concerns land, but oil and water are also critical aspects of the dispute. Revenues from oil in the Abyei area were shared mainly by the governments of Sudan and Southern Sudan and have not been a concern of the Misseriya or the Ngok Dinka. Water and grazing rights are the root cause of the dispute between the Misseriya and the Ngok Dinka. The Misseriya argue that their claims go beyond the right to move in the Abyei area in search for water and fodder. They believe that a good part of the area actually belongs to them. This point was highlighted in paragraph 203 of the dissenting opinion by Judge Awn Shawkat Al-Khasawneh when he asked who "gave the Experts or the Tribunal the right to reduce the Misseriya to second class citizens in their own land and to create conditions which may deny them access to water." The Misseriya welcomed the dissenting opinion and saw it as strengthening their rejection of the award. With the oil in this area expected to run out soon (ICG 2007), water emerges as the pivotal element of this dispute.

Because of the opposition of the Misseriya to the tribunal award, the demarcation of the area, as per the award, did not take place. Nonetheless, negotiations between the government of Sudan and the SPLM on the Abyei referendum commenced in late 2009. In December 2009, five months after the PCA tribunal's decision, the National Assembly passed both the Southern Sudan Referendum Act and the Abyei Area Referendum Act.[48] The Abyei Area Referendum Act confirmed the boundaries of Abyei area (as determined and delimited by the PCA) and the date for the Abyei referendum (January 9, 2011, as determined by the CPA). It called for the Abyei Area Referendum Commission to be established as a legally and financially independent entity with its head office in Abyei Town, and branch offices where the commission deemed necessary.

The Abyei Area Referendum Act was silent on who are considered residents of the Abyei area, and thus eligible to participate in the referendum. The Abyei Protocol, in paragraph 6.1, defined the residents of Abyei as the "Members of the Ngok Dinka community and other Sudanese residing in the area" and stated that the criteria for residence should be worked out by the Abyei Area Referendum Commission. The act did not reiterate the definition of residency, as it did with other provisions of the Abyei Protocol and other parts of the CPA. Perhaps the reason for this was the demand of the Misseriya tribe that they also be mentioned by name in the act, which was vehemently rejected by the SPLM. It seemed that the compromise the framers of the act reached was neither to reiterate the Abyei Protocol's definition (which specified the Ngok Dinka) nor to mention the Misseriya by name.

---

[48] For the major points raised during the discussion of the Abyei Area Referendum Act, and the Misseriya protest against the act, see *Sudan Tribune* (2009c).

348   Water and post-conflict peacebuilding

The adoption of the Abyei Area Referendum Act did not, however, pave the way for holding the referendum in Abyei on January 9, 2011, as envisaged under the Abyei Protocol. The Misseriya, with support from the government of Sudan, insisted that they are residents of the Abyei area, and thus are entitled to participate in the referendum. The SPLM and the Ngok Dinka rejected this demand, and are adamant that the Misseriya are not residents of the Abyei area, and accordingly are not eligible to participate in the referendum. Thus, on January 9, 2011, only the Southern Sudan referendum was undertaken, and its results were near unanimity for secession. Meanwhile, the situation deteriorated further in Abyei, and on May, 2011, Sudanese government forces took over Abyei area after some of their soldiers were killed by the SPLM a day earlier. After four tense weeks, the two parties signed an agreement in Addis Ababa on June 20, 2011, whereby the security in Abyei would be the responsibility of some 4,200 Ethiopian soldiers, with the administration of Abyei being jointly run by the government of Sudan and SPLM appointees. This agreement was incorporated and elaborated in United Nations Security Council Resolution 1990, issued on June 27, 2011. The resolution urged the parties to resolve peacefully the final status of Abyei (UNSC 2011; Salman 2013).

Those developments have not addressed the issue of who has the right to vote in the referendum. This issue, which is closely tied with the water and grazing rights of the Misseriya, has turned out to be the crux of the Abyei dispute, overshadowing the original issue of the borders of the Abyei area. With the emergence of the Republic of South Sudan as an independent state, the Abyei dispute has now turned into an international dispute involving two sovereign nations.

Allocation of the Nile waters

As indicated earlier, water resources had been listed in the Southern Sudan Referendum Act as one of the pending issues between the two parties. Consequently, the Republic of South Sudan is now demanding a share in the Nile waters allocated to the Sudan under the 1959 agreement. The issue might have been easier to negotiate and resolve before secession, when the two states were still one country. This is because negotiations between two states are generally more difficult than between two parts of the same state. While the six-month transitional period between the referendum vote and the establishment of South Sudan as a separate state (January to July 2011) provided some time to negotiate these issues, the issues are complex and require additional time to resolve. Moreover, it is possible that negotiations on water resources could be expanded to include the grazing rights of the border communities in the two countries.

The demand of South Sudan for a part of Sudan's share of the Nile waters under the 1959 agreement may seem easier to accommodate given the fact that Sudan has not been able to use more than 14 to 15 bcm of its share of 18.5 bcm

Water resources in the Sudan North-South peace process **349**

under the 1959 agreement.[49] However, this situation may be complicated by other new factors. One of the consequences of secession is the loss by Sudan of 50 percent of the income from the oil in Southern Sudan to which it was entitled under the CPA during the interim period (IMF 2011). This is a major economic and financial loss to Sudan, and has to be compensated from other sources. Thus, the government of Sudan has decided that it needs, and indeed plans, to pay more attention to agriculture to help make up for the loss of income from the oil of South Sudan. Sudan has large tracts of irrigable lands that have hitherto not been developed, and it has recently revived its four-decade-old slogan of Sudan being the bread basket of the Arab world. This in turn will mean the need for more waters than Sudan is currently using. In 2011, following completion of the Merowe Dam on the main Nile River in 2010, the government of Sudan started implementing a project to increase the height of the Roseiris Dam on the Blue Nile. The government has also started leasing large tracts of land to foreign investors and other countries for growing food crops (von Braun and Meinzen-Dick 2009).

On the other hand, South Sudan is claiming a share of the Nile waters, allotted to Sudan, to meet the demands of its agricultural projects that need rehabilitation or completion, the demands of its existing and planned projects, and the growing needs of the returning South Sudanese. Work on the Bedden Dam on Bahr el Jebel, south of Juba, is already underway. This would mean that the competing demands of the two countries may not be easy to meet within the current allocation to Sudan of 18.5 bcm.

The factors enumerated under the UN Convention on the Law of the Non-Navigational Uses of International Watercourses regarding utilization of shared watercourses should provide helpful guidance to the parties in deciding how to share the 18.5 bcm.[50] Such factors would include, inter alia, the current and planned uses of Sudan, and the expected future uses of South Sudan; the amount of Nile waters crossing from South Sudan into Sudan and Egypt; and the heavy

---

[49] It may be argued that any water allotted to the state of South Sudan out of the waters of the Nile could arguably fall under article 5(2) of the 1959 Nile Agreement, which states: "Since other riparian countries on the Nile besides the Republic of Sudan and the United Arab Republic claim a share in the Nile waters, both Republics agree to study together these claims and adopt a unified view thereon. If such studies result in the possibility of allotting an amount of the Nile water to one or the other of these territories, then the value of this amount as at Aswan shall be deducted in equal shares from the share of each of the two Republics." However, both parties are proceeding to address the claims of South Sudan from the allocation of the Sudan, and not under the provisions of this article. This is perhaps because South Sudan was part of the Sudan when the agreement was concluded in 1959.

[50] Although the UN Watercourses Convention has not yet entered into force, many of its provisions, including those on equitable and reasonable utilization, are considered as reflecting customary international water law (Salman 2007).

350 Water and post-conflict peacebuilding

rains in South Sudan as an alternative source of water for South Sudan.[51] Negotiations may also bring up the issue of conservation of the waters in the swamps of South Sudan and the need to complete the Jonglei Canal to augment the flow of the White Nile, providing more water for sharing. The fact that South Sudan does not share the Blue Nile River that provides the bulk of the Nile River waters is another factor. Thus, the negotiations on the reallocation of the 18.5 bcm allotted to the Sudan under the 1959 agreement are not expected to be easy.

RELATIONSHIP WITH THE OTHER NILE RIPARIAN STATES

The relationship between Sudan and South Sudan over the Nile waters reflects broader controversies across the basin surrounding rights to the sharing and management of its waters by the riparian states. As mentioned before, one of the goals of the Nile Basin Initiative (NBI) has been to have all Nile riparian countries to conclude the Nile River Basin Cooperative Framework Agreement (CFA), which would regulate the sharing and management of waters in the Nile Basin. Despite intense discussions and negotiations on the CFA since 2001, however, the Nile riparian states have failed to reach a final agreement on the CFA. Five of the riparian states—Ethiopia, Kenya, Rwanda, Tanzania, and Uganda— signed the CFA in May 2010. At that time, Burundi and the Democratic Republic of the Congo indicated their intention to sign, and Burundi did so on February 28, 2011. However, as of the time of writing in February 2013, the Democratic Republic of the Congo had not yet done so. Egypt and Sudan vehemently oppose the CFA, and Eritrea has remained an observer, and not a full member of the NBI, perhaps because of its limited interests and stakes in the Nile (Salman 2011). To enter into force and effect, the CFA requires ratification by six of the riparian countries.

One of the major differences over the CFA relates to the existing uses of, and rights over, water by Egypt and Sudan, for which the two countries demand recognition by the other riparians, as well as in the CFA. Another difference relates to the treaties concluded during the colonial era, particularly the 1929 agreement. Other differences concern notification for planned projects,[52] and

---

[51] In addition to the Nile waters, a number of groundwater basins fall across the borders between Sudan and South Sudan, largely fed and replenished by the White Nile and its tributaries, as well as the huge swamps there. The Upper Nile Basin is one such shared aquifer. However, technical knowledge and data about these basins is, at best, quite limited, and the borders between Sudan and South Sudan in some of these areas are still to be demarcated. Additionally, there is limited use of groundwater resources by the agro-pastoral communities in South Sudan. Thus, shared groundwater is not expected to be a major issue in the near future.

[52] Ethiopia claims that it was never notified by any riparian of any of the projects that have been constructed on the Nile, and thus feels no obligation other than to exchange data and information on its planned projects with the other riparians. On the other hand, Egypt and Sudan demand that notification for planned projects be a major part of the CFA.

Water resources in the Sudan North-South peace process 351

whether the CFA should be amendable by a majority or by consensus.[53] Differences on the first three issues have dominated the Nile discussions since the 1960s when the Nile Equatorial countries gained their independence, and when Ethiopia's request to be a party to the 1959 Nile negotiations was ignored by Egypt and Sudan. As such, major differences between the Nile riparian states have existed for a long time, and were brought to a head, and indeed exacerbated, by the negotiations over the CFA, resulting in heightened tension, accusations, and threats.[54]

The Republic of South Sudan was born at a time of tense relations among the then-ten Nile riparian countries, exacerbated by the acute differences over some basic principles and provisions of the CFA. The Republic of South Sudan applied for membership of the NBI during its ministerial meeting in Nairobi in July 2011, and was expected to be admitted as a full member during the Nile water ministers meeting in Kigali, Rwanda, in October 2011, after it was admitted as a full member of the African Union in August 2011. However, that meeting did not take place. Membership of South Sudan was eventually approved during the NBI ministerial meeting that took place on July 5, 2012. Membership of South Sudan in the NBI raises a number of critical questions. Will the new state of the Republic of South Sudan align itself with the equatorial lakes countries—as is widely expected based on common interests on the White Nile, ethnicity, geography, and history? Will it accede to the Nile Basin CFA, which has six signatories thus far, and needs six ratifications/accessions to enter into force? Will Sudan and Egypt claim that South Sudan is bound by the 1959 Nile Agreement, particularly with regard to construction of the water conservation projects in the swamps of South Sudan, as specified in that agreement? If Sudan makes that claim, how can it enforce it? Will Egypt claim that the new state is bound by the 1929 Nile Agreement, based on the same reasoning it argues vis-à-vis Kenya, Tanzania, and Uganda, and demand that any project in South Sudan be subject to its prior agreement? These are some of the difficult questions that may be posed now, adding more complexities to the already intricate relations within and among the Nile Basin states.

CONCLUSION

The emergence of a new state invariably carries with it a vast array of challenges. Some of these challenges relate to resolving outstanding issues with the mother state, and sharing and managing of common natural resources. This is certainly the case with Sudan and the new Republic of South Sudan. Indeed, the challenges in this case are compounded by the inability of Sudan and South Sudan to resolve thus far many of the outstanding issues, enumerated in the Southern Sudan Referendum Act of 2009, including water resources.

---

[53] Egypt and Sudan demand that the CFA be amendable by consensus (thus giving them veto power), while the other riparians insist that a simple majority should suffice for amending the CFA.

[54] See, for example, Reuters (2010a, 2010b).

352　Water and post-conflict peacebuilding

The Republic of South Sudan dominates and is dominated by the White Nile. About 90 percent of South Sudan falls in the Nile Basin, and about 20 percent of the Nile Basin falls in South Sudan. Approximately 28 percent of the Nile flow of 84 bcm measured at Aswan crosses South Sudan into Sudan and eventually Egypt. Yet, for reasons related to hydropolitics, the SPLM gave up, under the CPA, all responsibilities for the Nile waters during the interim period to the central government. The SPLM did not even demand representation in the Permanent Joint Technical Committee. Although this position might have facilitated acceptance by the Nile riparians of the right to self-determination, it has resulted in major delays in the decisions on the sharing and management of the Nile waters between the two parts of the country, and eventually between the two states.

Sudan and the new Republic of South Sudan now have to address the issue of sharing and managing the Nile waters allocated to the Sudan under the 1959 Nile Agreement. They also have to address the grazing and related water rights of the border communities in areas across some of the tributaries of the White Nile. Indeed, some of the disputed border areas that the two parties still have to resolve, including the dispute over the Abyei area, fall across the White Nile or some of its tributaries, thus extending the border disputes to water rights. The Jonglei Canal Project, as well as the other projects for conserving some of the waters of the swamps of South Sudan, could as well be on Sudan's agenda. Sudan may bring up completion of the Jonglei Canal Project as a way of providing more water for sharing with South Sudan. Aside from hydropolitics, the security situation in South Sudan may be an important factor in determining the future of the Jonglei Canal Project, as well as the other projects for conserving the waters of the swamps of South Sudan.

Moreover, South Sudan will also face the issue of its relationship with the other Nile riparians, and how to deal with the Nile Basin CFA. As indicated earlier, the six countries that have thus far signed the CFA will do their best to woo, perhaps even pressure, the Republic of South Sudan to become a party to the CFA so as to ensure that the CFA would enter into force and effect. On the other hand, Egypt and Sudan which vehemently oppose the CFA will do their best to court South Sudan to their side, or at least keep it neutral on this issue. It remains to be seen how South Sudan will address this matter.

The centrality of water resources in the issues that need to be addressed in post-conflict situations has been reconfirmed by the emergence of South Sudan as an independent state. In this case, the issues and their implications go well beyond Sudan and the new Republic of South Sudan, and extend to the other riparian states of the Nile Basin.

REFERENCES

ABC (Abyei Boundaries Commission). 2005. *Abyei Boundaries Commission report.* Djibouti: Intergovernmental Authority on Development. www.sudantribune.com/TEXT -Abyei-Boundary-Commission,11633.

Water resources in the Sudan North-South peace process   353

Alier, A. 1990. *Southern Sudan: Too many agreements dishonoured.* Exeter, UK: Ithaca Press.

Baker, S. W. 2002. *The Albert N'yanza Great Basin of the Nile and explorations of the Nile sources.* Torrington, WY: Narrative Press.

Bob, A. M. 2009. *Southern Sudan: The debate of unity and secession* [in Arabic]. Khartoum, Sudan: University of Khartoum.

Collins, R. O. 1996. *The waters of the Nile: Hydropolitics and the Jonglei Canal, 1900–1988.* Princeton, NJ: Markus Wiener Publishers.

———. 2002. *The Nile.* New Haven, CT: Yale University Press.

Dafalla, H. 1975. *The Nubian exodus.* London: C. Hurst.

Gaitskell, A. 1959. *Gezira: A story of development in the Sudan.* London: Faber and Faber.

Garang de Mabior, J. 1981. *Identifying, selecting and implementing rural development strategies for socio-economic development in the Jonglei projects area, Southern region, Sudan.* Ph.D. diss., Iowa State University.

Garretson, A. H. 1967. The Nile Basin. In *The law of international drainage basins,* ed. A. H. Garretson, R. D. Hayton, and C. J. Olmstead. New York: Oceana Publications.

Garstin, W. 1904. *Report upon the basin of the Upper Nile: With proposals for improvement of the river.* Cairo, Egypt: National Printing Department.

Howell, P., M. Lock, and S. Cobb, eds. 1988. *The Jonglei Canal: Local impact and opportunity.* Cambridge, UK: Cambridge University Press.

ICCA (International Council for Commercial Arbitration). 1988. 1988 report. The Hague, Netherlands: Kluwer.

ICG (International Crisis Group). 2007. Breaking the Abyei deadlock. Africa Briefing No. 47. October 12. www.crisisgroup.org/en/regions/africa/horn-of-africa/sudan/B047 -sudan-breaking-the-abyei-deadlock.aspx.

IMF (International Monetary Fund). 2011. *Regional economic outlook: Middle East and Central Asia.* Washington, D.C.

Khālid, M. 1966. *Le régime international des eaux du Nil.* Ph.D. diss., University of Paris.

Kiir Mayardit, S. 2010. Interview of the president of Southern Sudan, Mr. Salva Kiir Mayardit, by Sudanile, May 2 [in Arabic]. www.sudanile.com/index.php?option=com _content&view=article&id=14036:2010-05-02-18-05-53&catid=43:2008-05-30-16-11 -36&Itemid=67.

Makonnen, Y. 1984. *The Nyerere Doctrine of state succession and the new states of East Africa.* Arusha, Tanzania: Eastern Africa Publications.

Moorehead, A. 2000. *The White Nile.* New York: HarperCollins.

NBI (Nile Basin Initiative). n.d.a. About the NBI. www.nilebasin.org/newsite/index .php?option=com_content&view=article&id=71%3Aabout-the-nbi&catid=34%3 Anbi-background-facts&Itemid=74&lang=en.

———. n.d.b. South Sudan admitted to the Nile Basin Initiative. www.nilebasin.org/ newsite/index.php?option=com_content&view=article&id=127%3Asouth-sudanadmited &catid=40%3Alatest-news&Itemid=84&lang=en.

Oduho, J. 1983. Letters from Joseph Oduho, chairman of the Political and Foreign Affairs Committee of the SPLM, November 30, 1983, and December 7, 1983. *Horn of Africa Bulletin* 8 (1): 52–55.

Petterson, D. 2008. Abyei unresolved: A threat to the North-South agreement. In *Implementing Sudan's Comprehensive Peace Agreement: Prospects and challenges.* Washington, D.C.: Woodrow Wilson International Center for Scholars, Africa Program.

354 Water and post-conflict peacebuilding

Ramsar Convention Secretariat. 2012a. Contracting parties to the Ramsar Convention on Wetlands. May 31. www.ramsar.org/cda/ramsar/display/main/main.jsp?zn=ramsar&cp=1 -36-123^23808_4000_0__.

———. 2012b. The Ramsar list of wetlands of international importance. June 4. www .ramsar.org/cda/en/ramsar-documents-list/main/ramsar/1-31-218_4000_0__.

Reuters. 2010a. Egypt asserts right to block upstream Nile dams. May 18. www.reuters .com/article/2010/05/18/idUSLDE64G1D0.

———. 2010b. Ethiopia PM warns of Nile war. Nov. 24. http://english.aljazeera.net/news/ middleeast/2010/11/20101124152728280839.html.

Salman, S. M. A. 2007. The Helsinki Rules, the United Nations Watercourses Convention and the Berlin Rules: Perspectives on international water law. *International Journal of Water Resources Development* 23 (4): 625–640.

———. 2008. Water resources in the Sudan North-South peace process: Past experience and future trends. *African Yearbook of International Law* 16:299–328.

———. 2010. The Abyei territorial dispute between Northern and Southern Sudan and the decision of the Permanent Court of Arbitration. *Nature of Law Newsletter*, September. http://web.worldbank.org/WBSITE/EXTERNAL/TOPICS/EXTLAWJUSTICE/0,,conte ntMDK:22607203~pagePK:148956~piPK:149081~theSitePK:445634,00.html.

———. 2011. The new state of South Sudan and the hydro-politics of the Nile Basin. *Water International* 36:154–166.

———. 2013. The Abyei territorial dispute between North and South Sudan: Why has its resolution proven difficult? In *Land and post-conflict peacebuilding,* ed. J. Unruh and R. C. Williams. London: Earthscan.

Schomerus, M., and T. Allen. 2010. *Southern Sudan at odds with itself: Dynamics of conflict and predicaments of peace.* London: Development Studies Institute, London School of Economics. www.academia.edu/266877/Southern_Sudan_at_odds_with_itself _Dynamics_of_conflict_and_predicaments_of_peace.

Southern Sudan Referendum Commission. 2011. SSRC announces final referendum results. February 8. http://southernsudan2011.com/Sudan.

SSCCSE (Southern Sudan Centre for Census Statistics and Evaluation). 2009. *Statistical yearbook for Southern Sudan 2009.* Juba.

Sudan Tribune. 2009a. Sudan Misseriya community refuse to implement Abyei ruling. October 5. www.sudantribune.com/spip.php?article32687.

———. 2009b. Jonglei Canal Project needs to be revised, South Sudan says. August 7. www.sudantribune.com/spip.php?article32062.

———. 2009c. Sudan parliament adopts Abyei referendum law amid Messeriya protest. December 30. www.sudantribune.com/spip.php?article33635.

———. 2010. Sudan's SPLM & NCP sign MOU on post-referendum arrangements. June 27. www.sudantribune.com/spip.php?article35494.

Terralink. 2009. Abyei arbitration: Final award map. http://reliefweb.int/map/sudan/ sudan-abyei-arbitration-final-award-map-22-jul-2009.

Tvedt, T. 2004. *The River Nile in the age of the British: Political ecology and the quest for economic power.* London: I. B. Tauris.

UNHCR (United Nations High Commissioner for Refugees). 2009. Deteriorating security in parts of South Sudan hampers refugee returns. March 24. http://www.unhcr.org/ 49c908c92.html.

UNSC (United Nations Security Council). 2011. Resolution 1990. S/RES/1990 (2011). June 27.

von Braun, J., and R. Meinzen-Dick. 2009. "Land grabbing" by foreign investors in developing countries—Risks and opportunities. Policy Brief No. 13. Washington, D.C.: International Food Policy Research Institute. www.presentationsistersunion.org/_uploads/fcknw/Land_Grabbing.doc.

Wai, D. 1973. *The Southern Sudan: The problem of national integration.* London: Frank Cass.

Waihenya, W. 2006. *The mediator: Gen. Lazaro Sumbeiywo and the Southern Sudan peace process.* Nairobi, Kenya: Kenway Publications.

Waterbury, J. 2002. *The Nile Basin: National determinants of collective action.* New Haven, CT: Yale University Press.

Yongo-Bure, B. 2007. *Economic development of Southern Sudan.* Lanham, MD: University Press of America.

PART 4

Legal frameworks

Introduction

While many chapters in parts 1, 2, and 3 emphasize the customary institutions that sustain community management of water systems, the chapters in part 4 explore legal and institutional frameworks at the national and international levels. Such frameworks provide the enabling environment that is necessary in order for water management interventions to restore human dignity, build livelihoods, and sustain a lasting peace. Thus, the reconstitution of statutory water management institutions is an essential part of the post-conflict state-building process. These institutions may be centralized or decentralized to varying extents and can embody a range of ownership and management structures, from state to private. In essence, legal and institutional frameworks for water management set the rules for how water is allocated and used in post-conflict situations.

Although few peace agreements adequately address water use and allocation, this oversight—especially in areas where water was a source of tension before or during a conflict—can allow tensions to fester following the formal end of hostilities. In "Management of Waters in Post-Dayton Bosnia and Herzegovina: Policy, Legal, and Institutional Aspects," Slavko Bogdanovic addresses the consequences of the Dayton Peace Agreement for the water sector. Because the architects of the agreement were focused primarily on creating autonomous territorial control for each entity in the new nation, they gave little consideration to overlapping authority over water service provision and water resource management: in fact, the agreement contains no language pertaining to the water sector. In light of this shortcoming, Bogdanovic explores various domestic and international mechanisms, including the potential for integration into the European Union, for strengthening the legal framework and institutions responsible for water management in Bosnia and Herzegovina (BiH). Although BiH may be an unusual case, in that the post-conflict divisions of territory were made along ethnic lines, Bogdanovic's chapter does highlight the need to address water issues in the immediate post-conflict context, in order to avoid creating inefficient, ineffective, and ultimately unsustainable management structures.

Legal and governance reforms in the water sector can also help to facilitate reconciliation, especially where water resources, infrastructure, and services were targeted during hostilities, used as weapons of war, or intentionally denied to certain segments of the population during the conflict. In "The Right to Water and Sanitation in Post-Conflict Legal Mechanisms: An Emerging Regime?" Mara Tignino argues that acknowledging past discrimination in the water sector at the onset of the post-conflict period can foster accountability for past injustices and support trust building. Tignino observes that international water law has evolved to such an extent that not only is water recognized internationally as a human right, but governments are also incorporating a rights-based perspective into their domestic legal frameworks, including constitutional provisions recognizing the

360 Water and post-conflict peacebuilding

right to water. As Tignino notes, despite the importance of restoring basic services as soon as possible after the cessation of conflict, a number of political and physical obstacles prevent countries from both including the right to water and sanitation in their legal frameworks and taking steps to implement that right. Such obstacles are somewhat counterbalanced, however, by the increasing role of transitional justice mechanisms—including international criminal tribunals, human rights courts, and truth commissions—in defining the roles of states with respect to various social and economic rights, including the right to water. Greater clarity about what is required to implement the right to water, along with the necessary commitment of resources and capacity building on the part of the international community, may provide a strong impetus to raise the profile of water and sanitation in the realm of post-conflict reconstruction.

These two chapters highlight international and domestic legal developments that promote sound water resource management and service provision in post-conflict peacebuilding. In both chapters, the authors argue that to ensure basic needs are met and water conflicts are averted (especially in cases where political borders are redrawn), water resources—and their importance to human rights—must be addressed from the outset, through both domestic and international legal frameworks.

Management of waters in post-Dayton Bosnia and Herzegovina: Policy, legal, and institutional aspects

Slavko Bogdanovic

As Bosnia and Herzegovina (BiH) recovers from the devastating civil conflict of the early 1990s, the country is continuing to establish itself as a member of the international community. The collapse, in 1991, of the Socialist Federal Republic of Yugoslavia (SFRY) triggered disputes over territory and sovereignty—ultimately leading to a civil war that split BiH along ethnic lines. The region's infrastructure and economy were devastated as various ethnic groups fought to control portions of the former SFRY. The war in BiH came to a close in December 1995, with the signing of the Dayton Peace Agreement,[1] which divided the country into two individual political units, the Federation of Bosnia and Herzegovina (Federation of BiH) and the Republic of Srpska,[2] and a third small district— the Brčko District, an independently governed, multiethnic territory that links the two units and technically belongs to both. The agreement also included the constitution of BiH, which explicitly assigned exclusive rights and responsibilities (referred to as "competencies") to the state and to its political units.[3]

Respecting the extensive autonomy of each political unit was paramount, but the boundaries between the units were drawn without any consideration for the hydrological configuration of BiH. Thus, with respect to water management, governing authority was divided between the newly formed Federation of BiH and Republic of Srpska.

The results of the war—destruction of infrastructure, changes in society, and the establishment of a new government—required the state to reform its water management institutions and legal frameworks to meet the needs of the entities.

Slavko Bogdanovic is a professor of environmental law and water law at the University Business Academy in Novi Sad, Serbia.

[1] Republic of Bosnia and Herzegovina, Republic of Croatia, and Federal Republic of Yugoslavia, General Framework Agreement for Peace in Bosnia and Herzegovina, Paris, December 14, 1995 (referred to in this chapter as the Dayton Peace Agreement).

[2] These two units of government are collectively referred to as "the entities."

[3] In this chapter, *state* refers to the BiH government. The state represents national interests on the international stage, coordinates the activities of the entities, and ensures adherence to the rule of law throughout the territory.

362   Water and post-conflict peacebuilding

As the state and its political units continue to rebuild, they have collaborated on some aspects of water management, but real progress has been limited.

Many of the challenges facing BiH are similar to those faced by other countries transitioning from one-party rule and a socialist economy to democracy and a free-market economy; BiH faces the additional challenge of preserving the rights of its ethnic groups. Water sector reforms, however, are critical to all citizens of BiH and provide a potential platform for cooperation—and, ultimately, for achieving common goals as a unified nation.

As it continues to establish itself as a sovereign nation, BiH has been subject to both internal and external pressures. In addition to having entered into several treaties, the country is working to achieve membership in the European Union (EU), which mandates legislative and structural reforms to achieve compliance with the requirements of the *acquis communitaire*.[4] To meet these requirements, the political units of BiH must cooperate with each other and with the state government. However, the redundancies and gaps in water management authority created by the constitutional division of powers between the state and its political units have created barriers to achieving the EU legislative requirements. In sum, because the peace agreement and constitution that brought the war to an end lack the mandatory mechanisms for coordination and cooperation that are necessary for water sector reform, they are obstructing post-conflict peacebuilding.

This chapter considers the unique political organization of post-conflict BiH and its effect on water management. It is divided into five sections: (1) a brief background discussion; (2) a consideration of the constitutional and legal frameworks for water resource management in BiH; (3) a description of water management strategies for BiH; (4) a consideration of the impact of the Dayton Peace Agreement on water management in BiH; and (5) a brief conclusion.

BACKGROUND

BiH is a Western Balkan country that consists of three units of government: (1) the Federation of BiH and (2) the Republic of Srpska, which are collectively referred to as "the entities"; and (3) the Brčko District of BiH. As noted earlier, the Brčko District is formally a condominium of both entities; but in practical terms, it is an administratively independent region under BiH sovereignty. The principal ethnic groups in BiH are Bosniaks (referred to by the former, socialist regime as Muslims), Croats, and Serbs. The Federation of BiH is primarily made up of Bosniaks and Croats, and the Republic of Srpska is made up primarily of Serbs.

BiH has a total area of 51,212 square kilometers and a twenty-kilometer coastline along the Adriatic Sea (FMAWMF, SRBDA, and ASRBD 2012; Redžić

---

[4]   The acquis communitaire is a constantly evolving body of common rights and obligations that bind all EU member states; it includes but is not limited to treaties, legislation, decisions of the European Court of Justice, and policy measures. For more information, see EU (2012).

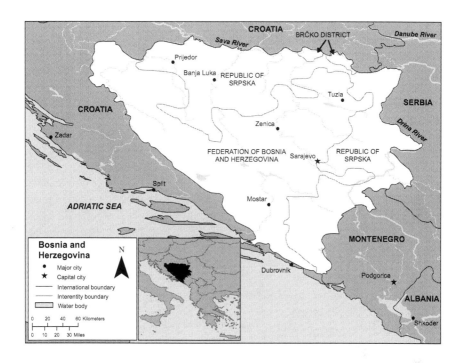

2007). Both entities share the waters of the Black Sea and Adriatic watersheds, which drain into either the Adriatic Sea or the Black Sea via the Sava River, a tributary of the Danube (DW 2006).[5] (See table 1.)

Table 1. Waters of Bosnia and Herzegovina that belong to the watersheds of the Black Sea and the Adriatic Sea

Territory	Land area		Black Sea watershed		Adriatic Sea watershed	
	Total area (km^2)	Percentage of country	Total area (km^2)	Percentage of territory within the watershed	Total area (km^2)	Percentage of territory within the watershed
Bosnia and Herzegovina (BiH)	51,212.00	100.00	37,849.00	73.91	13,363.00	26.09
Federation of BiH	26,086.00	50.94	17,304.00	66.33	8,782.00	33.67
Republic of Srpska	24,640.00	48.11	20,059.00	81.41	4,581.00	18.59
Brčko District	486.00	0.95	486.00	100.00	0.00	0.00

Source: Sarajevo Vodoprivreda (n.d.).

---

[5] For data and further information, see the Sarajevo Vodoprivreda web site: www.vodoprivreda.ba/ozavodu.php.

364 Water and post-conflict peacebuilding

The pre-war Socialist Republic of BiH, a federal unit of the SFRY, supplied raw materials, energy, and heavy-industry products throughout the SFRY, and the water resources of what is now BiH were exposed to intense pollution. Because water resources are unequally distributed throughout the country, the Socialist Republic of BiH constructed an extensive and complex infrastructure system to ration water use, safeguard against floods, and protect water quality (OSCE 2007).

The collapse of the SFRY in the early 1990s and the subsequent war left the Socialist Republic of BiH in ruins, both physically and economically, and had widespread effects on the water sector. Not only was much of the physical water infrastructure destroyed, but the war also prevented adequate maintenance of the remaining works. Municipal water supply facilities also suffered significant damage and deterioration, which led to major disruptions of operation and maintenance.[6] Perhaps most important, once the conflict had ended, the pre-war regulatory framework governing water was no longer adequate or appropriate, making it impossible to effectively manage water resources in the post-conflict era (CD&M and HEIS 1999).

Rehabilitation of the water and wastewater sectors in the newly independent BiH was a high priority for post-war reconstruction. In 1996, to support such efforts, international donors established the Emergency Water Construction Program, which was coordinated by the International Management Group, an ad hoc technical support entity created in 1994 at the behest of the United Nations High Commission for Refugees. The program had three goals: to initiate and support a wide variety of capital improvement and rehabilitation projects throughout the country; to assist with the fundamental reform of water management at both the local and national levels; and to strengthen the functioning and management of water and wastewater utilities in BiH's ten municipalities. Funded by the EU, the government of Finland, and the U.S. Agency for International Development (CD&M and HEIS 1999), the program provided vital support, throughout the country, for the recovery of basic municipal water infrastructure.[7]

CONSTITUTIONAL AND LEGAL FRAMEWORKS FOR THE MANAGEMENT OF BIH WATERS

This section of the chapter describes the constitutional and legal frameworks for the management of BiH waters: the Dayton Peace Agreement, BiH competencies with respect to the environment and natural resources, the relevant laws of

---

[6] In some cases, however, the war actually improved water quality—for example, by destroying many of the industrial plants that had previously been sources of pollution (Stoett 2005).

[7] See, for example, USAID and BiH (2012).

The Dayton Peace Agreement

The Dayton Peace Agreement brought the four-year armed conflict in BiH to an end. Negotiated through an extensive process supported by the international community, the agreement preserved the BiH state borders (which were wholly within the SFRY); established the boundaries between the two entities (51 percent of the total land area was included in the Federation of BiH, and 49 percent in the Republic of Srpska);[8] and left the status of the Brčko District to be determined at a later date by the Arbitral Tribunal.[9]

The Dayton Peace Agreement includes eleven annexes and two appendices. Annex 4 is the constitution of BiH, which establishes the rights and responsibilities (referred to as "competencies") of the state and the entities. Generally speaking, the state represents national interests on the international stage, coordinates the activities of the entities (in accordance with the constitution), and ensures adherence to the rule of law throughout the territory. According to article 3, sections 1–3 of the constitution, the entities retain all competencies that are not expressly assigned to state institutions. Article 3, section 5 of the constitution provides that the entities can agree to state appropriation of additional competencies for the following purposes: the use of energy sources; the implementation of joint economic projects; and the protection of the sovereignty, territorial integrity, and political independence of the state.

Although ethnic divisions formed the basis for the organization of the state and resulted in the establishment of the two entities, the constitution also established principles, objectives, and modalities for creating unity among the previously warring ethnic groups. Specifically, the preamble declares that all ethnic groups are constitutional "peoples" that should work alongside each other to build a shared community. The actions of the entities are to be guided by

---

[8] Dayton Peace Agreement, annex 2 (Agreement on Inter-Boundary Line and Related Issues). The negotiation process that led to the Dayton Peace Agreement was overseen by an arbitral tribunal that handed down a series of interim and supplemental awards that established boundaries before the issuance of the Brčko Final Award of 5 March 1999 (Schreuer 1999).

[9] In 1997, the Arbitral Tribunal established the Brčko Supervisor, a body of the UN Office of the High Representative, to oversee the implementation of the Dayton Peace Agreement in the Brčko District and to promulgate binding regulations and orders. Two years later, as provided for in the Dayton Peace Agreement, the tribunal finalized the Brčko District boundary line. Once the boundary had been established, what had once been the Municipality of Brčko came under the exclusive sovereignty of BiH, although it remained a condominium of both entities (Schreuer 1999). After the final award, the Brčko Supervisor was charged with furthering the development of governmental institutions in the Brčko District.

366　Water and post-conflict peacebuilding

principles of equality and reciprocity; at the same time, each group's distinct ethnic culture is to be respected (Sahovic 1996).

The emphasis on ethnicity is reflected in the relationship between the state and the entities. For example, under article 4, section 2, of the constitution, the Federation of BiH has two-thirds and the Republic of Srpska one-third of the total number of votes in the BiH Parliamentary Assembly. Article 4, section 3, also includes provisions intended to prevent a majority group from obstructing or dominating minority groups.

BiH competencies with respect to the environment and natural resources

The Dayton Peace Agreement, including the constitution, profoundly limits the ability of BiH to regulate the waters within its borders. Unlike some other peace treaties (such as the treaties of Versailles and Trianon, signed in 1919 and 1920, respectively), the Dayton Peace Agreement lacks any provisions that specifically apply to water resources or their management, except those regarding the inter-entity boundary line.[10] This scheme is substantially different from the system that was in place at the time of the Socialist Republic of BiH, when a single government office controlled water legislation, and issues related to waters that crossed or marked boundaries between socialist republics were within the competency of the federal state (SFRY), and were accordingly regulated by federal law (YLI 1979; Sparavalo 1982). In the absence of a constitutional mandate, the BiH Parliamentary Assembly has no power to regulate relations between the entities with respect to water. Furthermore, because there is no reliable institutional or procedural system for the coordination of the territorially divided water management systems, BiH has no legal means for resolving disputes over shared water (FMAWMF, SRBDA, and ASRBD 2012).

The state of BiH has constitutional competency over foreign policy and foreign relations, but the entities also have a constitutional right to establish special relationships with neighboring countries or international organizations, provided that such relationships do not interfere with the sovereignty and territorial integrity of BiH. However, under article 3, section 2, of the constitution, such agreements with foreign states or international organizations must be approved by the BiH Parliamentary Assembly.

In the realm of environmental protection and natural resources, the BiH Ministry of Foreign Trade and Economic Relations is responsible for setting policies and for ensuring the coordination and harmonization of the activities of the entities' authorities and institutions at the international level. Thus, the authority to negotiate and enter into international water agreements rests with the state of BiH, but the authority to implement those agreements lies solely with the entities and the Brčko District (FMAWMF, SRBDA, and ASRBD 2012).

---

[10] Articles 3.1 and 3.2 of annex 2 relate to the impact of both natural and artificial changes on rivers and streams at the interentity boundary line.

Legal frameworks of the political units

Pursuant to the constitution, the entities and Brčko District have established their own laws on water management. The Federation of BiH and the Republic of Srpska adopted their first water laws in 1998.[11] The laws, which were designed to reflect social changes and to ensure consonance with the new constitution, replaced outdated executive instruments. Yet both laws failed to explicitly eliminate all of the socialist-era legal provisions pertaining to water, leaving a convoluted regulatory system and institutional framework (FMAWMF, SRBDA, and ASRBD 2012; IMF 2004).[12] Given this "extremely complicated and ill-defined division of competencies . . ." (IMF 2004, 200),[13] it is unsurprising that the internationally supported project Institutional Strengthening of the Water Sector in BiH found that the 1998 water laws and implementing regulations were insufficiently reflective of the realities of the new BiH (Bogdanovic 2000, 2001).[14]

---

[11] Water Law of the Federation of Bosnia and Herzegovina (Federation of BiH) (*Official Gazette F BiH* No.18/98), 1998; Water Law of the Republic of Srpska (*Official Gazette RS* No. 10/98), 1998.

[12] The transition from the socialist-era system to an institutional framework consistent with EU policies and requirements "is a process that must be implemented progressively, over a longer period of time, simultaneously with the changes taking place in other segments of society, because this is an exceptionally complex management system . . ." (FMAWMF, SRBDA, and ASRBDF 2012, 88–89). The regulatory system has been further complicated by the entities' failure, during the transitional period between the adoption of new laws and their entry into force, to set aside a time during which all former bylaws had to be replaced by new legislation designed to implement the new laws (FMAWMF, SRBDA, and ASRBD 2012).

[13] Under the 1998 Federation of BiH water law, the entities that were responsible for water management included the Federation of BiH Ministry of Agriculture, Water Management and Forestry; multiple *vodopriveda* organizations (vodopriveda are departments of the Ministry of Agriculture, Water Management and Forestry); cantonal ministries of agriculture, water management, and forestry; and municipal water management authorities. Municipal and town councils were responsible for water supply, sewage, and wastewater treatment (IMF 2004). Under the 1998 Republic of Srpska water law, water management was the responsibility of the Ministry of Agriculture, Forestry and Water Management, while municipalities were in charge of water supply and sewage, and the Ministry of Regional Planning, Construction and the Environment oversaw public utility administration (IMF 2004).

[14] The Institutional Strengthening of the Water Sector project in BiH was initiated in 1998, in response to the perceived need for the development of legal and institutional frameworks to support a sustainable water sector (IMF 2004). After the first phase yielded little progress, the IMF recommended a number of reforms for the second phase, including water management on the river-basin level, funding and regulatory mechanisms, and the establishment of state-level mechanisms to allow BiH to meet its international obligations and participate in cooperative water management strategies with other countries (IMF 2004). The next wave of water legislation, finalized in 2006, came about in large part through the project, which was supported by the EU CARDS (Community Assistance for Reconstruction, Development and Stabilisation) initiative in the Western Balkans (Fejzibegović 2008). For more information on the EU CARDS initiative, see Bruch, Wolfarth, and Michalcik (2012).

368 Water and post-conflict peacebuilding

In 2005, the Brčko Supervisor abolished the Federation of BiH and Republic of Srpska water laws that had previously been in force in the Brčko District and adopted the 1998 Water Law of the Republic of Srpska as the official water law of the Brčko District (PM Group 2011).[15] In 2006, in response to existing institutional inadequacies and the further complications that had arisen when both entities passed additional water protection laws in 2002 (Republic of Srpska) and 2003 (Federation of BiH), the entities adopted new water laws that superseded all previous water laws and any other conflicting legislation (IMF 2004); these legal instruments now provide the framework under which the water regulatory systems are being modernized.[16] In addition to the new water laws, other norms and legal instruments directly affect the management of water resources—in particular, legislation pertaining to environmental protection, spatial planning, forestry, agricultural land, and public revenues.

The Federation of BiH must also coordinate its regulatory framework with those of its ten political subunits (cantons),[17] which have the authority to manage water within their borders.[18] Under article 3, section 3, of the Federation of BiH constitution, when exercising the water management competency of the Federation of BiH, the Ministry of Agriculture, Water Management and Forestry must demonstrate flexibility—by, for example, taking into account cantonal competencies and the different conditions among the cantons.[19] The 2006 Federation of BiH water law required the cantons to coordinate their regulatory structure with that of Federation of BiH,[20] but the law failed to provide either procedures to achieve such coordination or methods of verifying and reporting on how coordination was being achieved.

The Brčko District and entity water laws (adopted in 2005 and 2006, respectively) also distributed water management authority among several different institutions. In the Brčko District, the utilities department is the main authority for all natural resources, including water (Skejović-Hurić 2009). In both the Federation of BiH and the Republic of Srpska, the respective ministries of agriculture, water management, and forestry have general responsibility for water

---

[15] In 2006, when interentity boundaries within the Brčko District ceased to be legally significant, all entity laws stopped having any legal effect in the district (OHR Brčko Supervisor 2006), so the district elected to adopt the Water Law of the Republic of Srpska as its own.

[16] Water Law of the Federation of BiH (*Official Gazette of F BiH* No. 70/06), 2006; Water Law of the Republic of Srpska (*Official Gazette of RS* No. 50/06), 2006.

[17] Known in Bosnian as *kantoni* and in Croatian as *zupanije*.

[18] See, for example, article 3, section 2, of the Federation of BiH constitution; see also article 19 of the constitution of Canton Središnja Bosna. In both constitutions, waters (among other things) are included under the heading of environment.

[19] The Federation of BiH water law divides the federation's surface waters (such as watercourses, reservoirs, lakes, or wetlands) into two categories. The vodoprivredas have jurisdiction over Category 1 waters, and towns and municipalities are granted jurisdiction over Category 2 waters. See Water Law of the Federation of BiH (arts. 5–9).

[20] See Water Law of the Federation of BiH (art. 222).

Management of waters in Bosnia and Herzegovina   369

management. In addition, each entity has two distinct water management agencies, each of which serves either the Adriatic or the Black Sea river basin in the respective entity.

In other words, four separate agencies (two in the Federation of BiH and two in the Republic of Srpska) and one Brčko District department are responsible for water management in BiH. But under the Dayton Peace Agreement, the state of BiH has no means of coordinating the work of the five authorities or harmonizing the management of national water resources. Had such coordination and harmonization been possible, the state of BiH might have implemented a system in line with the model that professionals and scientists in the field accept as necessary for effective and efficient water management. This model is described in the Federation of BiH water management strategy as one that (1) conforms with the principle of managing on the river-basin level and (2) allows for the development of cooperative management systems across administrative and interstate borders (FMAWMF, SRBDA, and ASRBD 2012).[21]

European Union requirements

EU legislation includes a number of goals for the management of waters that are within and shared among its member states, many of which are designed to preserve the environmental integrity of aquatic ecosystems. The EU Water Framework Directive (WFD), the legal framework that underpins EU water policy, covers the management of fresh surface and groundwater, transitional (estuary) waters, and coastal waters (European Parliament and the Council of the European Union 2000). The goals of the WFD are defined in general terms— but, taken collectively, they reflect a complex set of intentions:

- Prevention of further damage.
- Protection and improvement of aquatic ecosystems and the terrestrial ecosystems and wetlands that depend on them.
- Increasing the sustainability of water use through long-term protection of water resources.
- Strengthening the protection and improvement of the aquatic environment by gradually decreasing groundwater pollution (for example, decreasing or eliminating the emission of certain harmful substances).
- Mitigating the effects of floods and droughts.[22]

---

[21] The EU Water Framework Directive refers to the principle of managing on the river-basin level as the "correct geographical scale" principle and mandates institutional cooperation between member states (European Parliament and the Council of the European Union 2000).

[22] See also Commission of the European Communities (2007a, 2007b).

370 Water and post-conflict peacebuilding

For BiH to obtain EU membership status, its national water legislation must incorporate the WFD and include an implementation and enforcement plan. In addition, BiH legislation must incorporate the aims and time frames of a number of other EU legal instruments that are directly connected (or unavoidably related) to water management (EC 1998); moreover, these aims and time frames must be included in the legislation of the Federation of BiH, the Republic of Srpska, and the Brčko District. In practical terms, the implementation of the acquis communitaire in each political unit will mean that all of BiH will share a single water policy.

Under the Stabilization and Association Agreement (SAA) concluded in 2008 between the European Communities, the European Communities' member states, and BiH, BiH will gradually become more closely associated with the EU, over a transitional period of no more than six years.[23] The progress of this association will be checked annually by the Stabilization and Association Council (European Parliament and the Council of the European Union 2008),[24] and a thorough review of the ongoing application of the SAA will be conducted before the end of the third year after the SAA enters into force (FMAWMF, SRBDA, and ASRBD 2012). As part of this process, BiH is required to focus on clearly established short- (two to four years) and medium-term (four to six years) priorities for the adoption and implementation of new legislation, including water regulations that are consistent with the WFD (FMAWMF, SRBDA, and ASRBD 2012; European Parliament and the Council of the European Union 2008).[25] Among the priorities that apply to water management are (1) strengthening administrative capacities and procedures for ensuring strategic planning and coordination between relevant actors, (2) focusing on the alignment of BiH legislation with the acquis communitaire, and (3) developing strategies to significantly reduce water pollution (FMAWMF, SRBDA, and ASRBD 2012).

International and regional frameworks for water resource management

Apart from the requirements of the EU, BiH is involved in other multilateral efforts focused on the management of (1) fresh surface and underground waters and (2) coastal marine areas in BiH's two international watersheds. A number of international legal frameworks—including the United Nations Economic Commission for Europe (UNECE) Water Convention, the Danube River Protection

---

[23] Stabilization and Association Agreement between the European Communities and Their Member States, of the One Part, and Bosnia and Herzegovina, of the Other Part, Luxembourg, June 16, 2008.

[24] The Stabilization and Association Council is composed of members of the Council of the European Union, members of the European Commission, and members of the BiH Council of Ministers.

[25] The priorities establish broad goals (for example, "adopting a State environmental law to create the framework for nationwide harmonised environmental protection"), and BiH is required to both adopt and implement legislation in furtherance of these goals (FMAWMF, SRBDA, and ASRBD 2012, 9).

Convention (DRPC), the Framework Agreement on the Sava River Basin (FASRB), and the Protocol on Navigation Regime to the FASRB—were established to facilitate and support sustainable water management at the basin level through the preservation and improvement of freshwater resources, and their rational and equitable use.[26] In addition, permanent international river-basin commissions—primarily the International Commission for the Protection of the Danube River (located in Vienna, Austria) and the International Sava River Basin Commission (located in Zagreb, Croatia)—have been developing multilateral cooperation in the Danube River basin (FMAWMF, SRBDA, and ASRBD 2012).

The state of BiH has clear duties to fulfill in the international arena, including those articulated in the UNECE Water Convention, the DRPC, the FASRB, and the Protocol on Navigation Regime to the FASRB, as well as duties connected to BiH commitments in the Mediterranean, including the Convention for the Protection of the Mediterranean Sea against Pollution (known as the Barcelona Convention) (FMAWMF, SRBDA, and ASRBD 2012).[27] As a party to these agreements and as a participant in the two principal river-basin commissions in the region, the BiH is being pushed to identify integrated and cooperative solutions for its water management issues at the state level, despite the fact that the Dayton Peace Agreement created three distinct water management systems. In the future, BiH's international duties will continue to broaden, partly because BiH is expected to become a party to new international treaties, and partly because integration into the EU will expand BiH's obligations.[28]

WATER MANAGEMENT STRATEGIES IN BIH

The dissolution of the SFRY and the subsequent war changed BiH society and the structure of the state in such a way as to necessitate wholesale reform of water management, including water legislation and the public institutions responsible for water resource management and service provision. The current water laws of both entities provide for the adoption of water management strategies that will (1) describe or assess the current state of the water management sector; (2) set goals and determine the time frames and priorities for their achievement;

---

[26] Convention on the Protection and Use of Transboundary Watercourses and International Lakes (Helsinki, Finland, 1992); Convention on Cooperation for the Protection and Sustainable Use of the Danube River (Sofia, Bulgaria, 1994); Framework Agreement on the Sava River Basin (Kranjska Gora, Slovenia, 2002); Protocol on the Navigation Regime to the FASRB (Kranjska Gora, Slovenia, 2002). For more information on post-conflict management of the Sava River Basin, see Amar Čolakhodžić, Marija Filipović, Jana Kovandžić, and Stephen Stec, "The Sava River: Transitioning to Peace in the Former Yugoslavia," in this book.

[27] Convention for the Protection of the Mediterranean Sea against Pollution (Barcelona, Spain, February 16, 1976).

[28] When the EU becomes a party to an international treaty, it automatically incorporates the treaty into the acquis communitaire; member states are then obligated to integrate the terms of the treaty into their national legal systems.

372 Water and post-conflict peacebuilding

(3) develop the necessary programs and projects to meet the goals; and (4) determine the level of resources that will be required for such efforts.[29] In addition to the SAA itself, the program for implementing the SAA and the deadlines that will be determined through negotiations between BiH and the European Commission will have a decisive influence on how the water management strategies of the Federation of BiH and the Republic of Srpska are implemented.

There are also ongoing efforts to adopt the comprehensive, overarching BiH water strategy that was drafted in late 2011 as a result of the Support to BiH Water Policy program, an EU-funded project (EuropeAid 2008; PM Group n.d.). According to the procedure set out by the BiH Ministry of Foreign Trade and Economic Relations (the project beneficiary), the comprehensive strategy should have been adopted by the BiH Council of Ministers (MOFTER 2010); at the time of writing, however, this had yet to occur.

The Federation of BiH

In addition to providing for the adoption of the Federation of BiH water management strategy, the 2006 Federation of BiH water law assigns competencies for implementing the strategy and describes procedures for drafting and adopting future iterations of the strategy. The current strategy, which was published in its final form in 2012 and is designed to be valid from 2010 to 2020, addresses two principal goals: (1) policy, legal, and institutional reform of water management to respond to social change; and (2) harmonization of national water management legislation with the water-related provisions of the acquis communitaire, a task that is both a part of the stabilization process and a requirement for eventual membership in the EU.

In accordance with the SAA, the time limits set in the Federation of BiH strategy for the adoption of the more than forty regulatory instruments that are required to bring the Federation of BiH into compliance with the acquis communitaire are more flexible than those in the 2006 water law. The strategy also articulates a clear commitment, on the part of the Federation of BiH, to be flexible in future negotiations with the European Commission, to prevent the strategy from obstructing further development or the adoption of legal and institutional reforms (FMAWMF, SRBDA, and ASRBD 2012).

Finally, the water management strategy must be in accord with the larger environmental protection strategy of the Federation of BiH. With respect to environmental protection and water management, the two strategies are meant to function as a coherent whole (FMAWMF, SRBDA, and ASRBD 2012).

---

[29] For example, article 24 of the Federation of BiH water law states that the federal water management strategy shall include "assessment of the current situation in water management," "goals and objectives relating to water . . . ," "priorities for achievement of water management goals," and "estimated resources needed to implement the program and deadlines for achieving goals." (An English translation of the Federation of BiH water law is available at www.fmpvs.gov.ba/texts/276_287_e.pdf.)

Management of waters in Bosnia and Herzegovina 373

From a broader perspective, the Federation of BiH water management strategy can be viewed as a powerful policy instrument that is fully in line with the Dayton Peace Agreement and strongly supports both local and national peace-building efforts in BiH. By focusing on reforming the water sector to match new realities and achieve integration into the EU, the strategy is intended to overcome the consequences of war—and, through national development and cooperative international mechanisms supporting sustainable resource management, to contribute to peacebuilding.[30]

Republic of Srpska

Under the 2006 water law of the Republic of Srpska, a strategy for integrated water resource management of the Republic of Srpska is designed to be a comprehensive sectoral policy; it contains the following elements (DW 2006):

- Specific measures to control surface water pollution.[31]
- Specific measures to prevent and control the pollution of groundwater, with the aim of achieving "good" status (as defined under the EU WFD).
- General descriptions of the condition of various aspects of the water management system.
- General goals and directions for the use and protection of waters, and for protection against harmful effects from waters.

Two documents, in addition to the water law, address water management in the Republic of Srpska: the Framework Plan for the Development of the Water Management of the Republic of Srpska, which was developed in 2006 by the

---

[30] For example, the strategy discusses funding that will be necessary "to bring the water supply system back to the pre-war level" (FMAWMF, SRBDA, and ASRBD 2012, 115n65). The strategy highlights the importance of supplying water to the population to ensure that a basic standard of living is achieved, and that the "intensive post-war activities on reconstruction and expansion of water supply systems" that are required to achieve such standards have been undertaken (F BiH 2012, 126). Thus, the strategy builds on the efforts undertaken by the international community immediately after the war, which assigned priority to rehabilitating the water sector (USAID and BiH 1999). In addition, the strategy addresses the need to remedy war-related damage to infrastructure associated with irrigation, and flood control (F BiH 2012). The strategy also emphasizes that "[n]either economic nor social development may be enabled without a secure access to water resources and it is evident that the accomplishment of the majority of [the UN Millennium Development Goals] depends on the way water is managed" (F BiH 2012, 177). The eight Millennium Development Goals, set out in the Millennium Declaration in September 2000, include ensuring environmental sustainability, developing a global partnership for development, combating disease, and eradicating poverty and hunger (F BiH 2012).

[31] The government of the Republic of Srpska determines the level of risk associated with various pollutants.

374   Water and post-conflict peacebuilding

Directorate for Water of the Ministry for Agriculture, Forestry and Water Management, and the Action Plan for the Implementation of the Framework Plan for the Development of the Water Economy of the Republic of Srpska, which was drafted in 2007 by the same ministry. The framework plan states that it was intended to serve as the first phase in the development of a strategy for integrated water resource management of the Republic of Srpska (Bratić et al. 2006; DW 2006). The action plan, which is valid from 2007 to 2016, acknowledges the need for regional cooperation between BiH and river-basin states that are parties to the DRPC and FASRB. The action plan also states that its goal is to align water management in the Republic of Srpska with the requirements of the EU WFD (MAFWM 2007). Neither the framework plan nor the action plan, however, is regulated by the Water Law of the Republic of Srpska; moreover, the water law requires the adoption of a strategy for integrated water resource management, but the relationship between that strategy, the framework plan, and action plan remains unclear.

IMPACT OF THE DAYTON PEACE AGREEMENT

In BiH in 2002, the author conducted a comparative analysis that assessed the regulation of water resources shared by federal or regional units in complex constitutional states. The goal of the analysis was to formulate a possible proposal for "an adequate legal framework for inter-Entity co-operation based on the present constitutional solutions" (Royal Haskoning 2001, 6). In the author's view, the development of such a framework is essential to the success of water resource management in BiH. The study investigated constitutional and legal aspects of shared water resources in Australia, India, Mexico, the SFRY, and the United States (Bogdanovic 2002).[32]

The analysis revealed certain gaps in the BiH legal system—in particular, (1) a lack of legal provisions regarding waters shared among the entities and (2) a lack of effective interentity dispute resolution mechanisms. These regulatory

---

[32]   The most well-known Australian agreement concerned the Murray and Darling rivers and was made in 1915, between four members of the Federation of Australia. In 1956, India adopted the federal Inter-State River Disputes Act, which was unique in that it attempted to provide a federal mechanism for the resolution of interstate water disputes. More recently, during the 1980s and 1990s, the federal government of Mexico—on the basis of legal grounds established by the federal water laws of 1972 and 1992— began the practice of signing agreements with individual Mexican states. The SFRY had strong constitutional and legal grounds for regulating relations between its federal republics, with respect to waters that formed or crossed the borders between republics. All three legal options in use in the United States (litigation before the Supreme Court, national legislation designed to resolve conflicts or address confusion, and interstate compacts and agreements) were investigated. Although European law—specifically, the constitutional and legal systems of Austria, Germany, the Netherlands, Spain, and Switzerland—was noted as being of potentially great significance for the analysis, it was not investigated (Bogdanovic 2002).

The search for viable cooperative grounds: Memorandums of understanding

Memorandums of understanding (MOUs) are formal, nonbinding agreements that express an agreed-upon intent but do not impose any consequences for failure to comply. Since the late 1990s, the entities have used MOUs, which are signed by their executive authorities, to regulate interentity relations and address gaps in the legal and constitutional systems. In other words, MOUs have made it possible to regulate cooperation within the existing constitutional framework (Bogdanovic 2000).

In the water sector, MOUs have been signed between entity governments, between entity ministers responsible for water management, and between entity governments and the European Commission. However, because MOUs signed by executive authorities have not been confirmed by any parliament—whether entity, Brčko District, or state—they were not binding legal instruments (FMAWMF, SRBDA, and ASRBD 2012). By their legal nature, MOUs cannot contradict constitutional provisions; thus, they could be instrumental in achieving wider and more complex regulation of interentity relations and relations between the state of BiH and the entities and Brčko District—but only if the state and its constitutional units adopt legislation to create a satisfactory legal framework for such agreements (Bogdanovic 2002).

On June 4, 1998, recognizing the need to (1) facilitate interentity cooperation regarding water management and (2) inform BiH institutions of international cooperation regarding transboundary waters, the Federation of BiH and the Republic of Srpska signed an MOU that established the Inter-Entity Commission for Coordination of Issues in the Field of Water Economy (Inter-Entity Commission) and defined the commission's scope and duties. The commission's scope encompasses many areas, including international watercourses; projects and treaties associated with water management; harmonization of water quality, legislation, and data exchange; and the construction and harmonized regulation of interentity hydraulic structures. Among the commission's general duties is ensuring that the interests of both entities are taken into account in the course of water use planning, particularly where such interests may be in opposition. The commission has the power to adopt decisions by consensus; where consensus cannot be achieved, the MOU provides for an alternative mechanism to resolve the dispute (FMAWMF, SRBDA, and ASRBD 2012).

An MOU signed in late 2000—by the Federation of BiH and the Republic of Srpska on one side, and by the European Commission on the other—expressed the desire of all parties for continued institutional reforms in the BiH water sector. Specifically, the agreement is intended to support the adoption of sound and

376 Water and post-conflict peacebuilding

transparent legislation addressing river-basin management in accordance with the acquis communitaire and multilateral treaties. This MOU helped obtain international donor support for a multiyear project that strengthened the institutional components of the BiH water sector and eventually led to the adoption of the 2006 water laws (Bogdanovic 2002; FMAWMF, SRBDA, and ASRBD 2012).

In 2001, the Federation of BiH and Republic of Srpska ministries of agriculture, forestry, and water management signed an MOU that committed them to cooperating in a number of areas, including water management. The MOU was intended to (1) strengthen cooperation between the two ministries and the European Commission and (2) foster comprehensive implementation of the 1998 MOU on water management. Ultimately, this MOU was concluded to provide broader support for the Inter-Entity Commission. The ministries agreed to harmonize and intensify the enforcement of water quality legislation—in particular, provisions regarding pollution and flood mitigation; they also committed to jointly develop a legal instrument to guide authorization and permitting of the construction of infrastructure on shared watercourses or in aquatic areas between the two entities. Finally, the MOU required the entities to establish an agreed-upon time frame to implement their obligations (FMAWMF, SRBDA, and ASRBD 2012).[33]

Though extensive, MOUs have not yielded the necessary changes in BiH and its political units. MOUs are generally policy instruments—or, at best, instruments of soft law—that express the intention to move forward in defined ways. Unlike contracts, legislation, or interstate compacts, such as those used in the United States, MOUs are not binding legal instruments. As a result, there are no consequences of the sort that would arise from breaching contractual duties or legal obligations. Given the nature of MOUs, it is not surprising that they have failed to achieve some of the goals that are either resource intensive or politically sensitive, such as harmonized legislation.

But the legal weakness of the MOUs is only part of the problem. Generally speaking, the entities lack the political will that is needed to meet the obligations specified in the MOUs. For example, the Inter-Entity Commission has failed, for several years, even to hold meetings—and has therefore been unable to achieve the goals articulated in the MOU that created it (FMAWMF, SRBDA, and ASRBD 2012).

The entities' 2006 water laws codified their political will to cooperate: both laws include weak commitments to harmonize water management strategies and river-basin management plans during the drafting and adoption phases (under the water laws, both harmonization and the drafting and adoption phases must occur within established time frames).[34] The effectiveness of such provisions

---

[33] There is no publicly available information regarding whether attempts have been made to implement the MOU (Bogdanovic 2002); and, as of mid-2012, no time frame had been established (F BiH 2012).

[34] See Water Law of the Federation of BiH, article 24, which sets 2009 as the deadline for the adoption of a water management strategy; and Water Law of the Republic of Srpska, article 31, which sets 2015 as the deadline for the adoption of a water management strategy.

Management of waters in Bosnia and Herzegovina   377

will become clear in the future, as the deadlines approach for the adoption of water management strategies and river basin management plans.[35]

Although the intent of the MOUs was to move the region forward—in particular, to strengthen cooperation and coordination in the realm of water resource management—progress has so far been illusory (for example, the creation of the Inter-Entity Commission) or incomplete. Ultimately, the inherent weakness of the MOUs is postponing peacebuilding and preventing stabilization in the region.

Strengthening the authority of the state of BiH

Since the late 1990s, ongoing attempts to create a consolidated, functional state that can meet EU membership requirements have been designed to build the political will to implement the necessary changes in the BiH constitution, but consensus is not yet in sight. Some observers have argued that such initiatives will lead to a breach of the Dayton Peace Agreement.[36] In the meantime, the state faces growing pressure from the EU requirements, particularly the SAA-based obligations. In the process of EU integration, only the state of BiH—not its constitutional subunits—is the EU's partner. BiH is responsible for transposing, implementing, and enforcing the acquis communitaire. Paradoxically, however, because of the Dayton Peace Agreement, transposition, implementation, and enforcement are within the competencies of the BiH constitutional subunits—the entities and the Brčko District—and can be realized only by them, not by the state of BiH. Thus, in practical terms, the state of BiH can perform only a coordinating role with respect to transposition, implementation, and enforcement. Certain measures designed to strengthen the authority of the state have been adopted but have yet to be fully implemented: the Support to BiH Water Policy program, for example, focuses on improving the capacity of the BiH institutions that are responsible for implementing international treaties and agreements (EuropeAid 2008). The obvious need for the development of a capable, coordinating state of BiH mechanism enhances the growing importance of the Ministry of Foreign Trade and Economic Relations. Proposals for the establishment of a state of BiH environmental protection agency, which were supported by the Federation of BiH water management strategy and also by the European Commission, remain unrealized (EC 2011; FMAWMF, SRBDA, and ASRBD 2012).

---

[35] The Federation of BiH strategy was adopted in 2011, two years after the deadline set by the law. The deadline for the adoption of the river basin management plans (which were designed to implement the water policies set out in the water management strategy) was 2012. The deadline for the adoption of the Republic of Srpska strategy and river basin management plans is 2015. At the time of writing, neither of the entities, nor the Brčko District, had adopted river basin management plans.

[36] See, for example, the dissenting opinion of Judge Bonello in *Sejdic and Finci* v. *Bosnia and Herzegovina*, European Court of Human Rights, *Sejdic and Finci* v. *Bosnia and Herzegovina* [GC], Nos. 27996/06 and 34836/06, ECHR 2009. December 22, 2009.

378 Water and post-conflict peacebuilding

CONCLUSION

With respect to water resources, the current organization of BiH is unique among complex world states. Water management is completely decentralized, to the point where there is no coordination between the political units of BiH with respect to policy, legislation, resolution of disputes over shared waters, or other areas. Nor does the constitution of BiH clearly define the role of the state of BiH and its political units or assign a duty—or even a procedure—for cooperation regarding water management. Efforts to address practical needs (including upstream-downstream relations) have yielded a number of MOUs and the creation of a cooperative institution, none of which have proven effective. More recent attempts to regulate interentity cooperation have taken the form of provisions in the water laws that address the development and adoption of water management strategies. It remains to be seen whether this approach will provide the cooperation necessary for sustainable water management in BiH.

The integration of BiH into the EU has become the driving force for a number of changes, including efforts to strengthen BiH institutions, to adopt requisite legislation, and to modernize the constitution.[37] BiH's commitment, through the SAA, to formally integrate into the EU necessitates a clearly defined role for the state of BiH and its administrative authority—not only with respect to water management, but other areas as well.

Parallel efforts, primarily through programs put in place by the international community, have incorporated BiH into various regional and international water-management initiatives, including (1) international treaties that have established cooperative water management bodies for countries having territory within the Danube and Sava river basins and (2) Mediterranean and Adriatic Sea initiatives (for example, the Barcelona Convention and the National [BiH] Mediterranean Action Plan for 2001–2005).[38] The institutions of the state of BiH must be strengthened and upgraded if they are to fully participate in such cooperative processes, but the inflexible provisions of the Dayton Peace Agreement are inhibiting the necessary changes, and there is no clear way to overcome the impediments. Establishing a modern, integrated, and sustainable system based on EU policies for water management would undoubtedly be a significant contribution to the lasting stability of BiH and help to solidify peacebuilding in the nation.

---

[37] As noted earlier, efforts to modernize the constitution may conflict with the Dayton Peace Agreement.

[38] The BiH Mediterranean Action Plan was among the national plans that resulted from the Mediterranean Conference of Water Stakeholders and Decision-Makers, Athens, Greece, November 2–4, 2000. For a summary of the core of the action plan based on materials from the Global Water Partnership, see www.gwp.org/Documents/The%20 Library/Note%20Briefings/GWP%20Med%20Core%20for%20Action%202001.pdf.

REFERENCES

Bogdanovic, S. 2000. Water law after Dayton: The current state of regulation in Bosnia and Herzegovina. *Water International* 25 (4): 534–543.

———. 2001. Constitutional aspects of inter-entity co-operation relating to BiH water resources. Paper presented at "Legal Aspects of Sustainable Water Resources Management," Teslic, Bosnia and Herzegovina, May 14–18.

———. 2002. Study of possibilities for inter-entity co-operation in shared water resources management: Constitutional-legal aspect. Unpublished report. Sarajevo, Bosnia and Herzegovina: Haskoning B.V. Consulting Engineers and Architects. On file with author.

Bratić, R., U. Hrkalović, B. Đorđević, S. Čubrilo, M. Stevanović, and B. Blagojević. 2006. Okvirni plan razvoja vodoprivrede Republike Srpske. *Vodoprivreda* 38 (1–3): 119–129.

Bruch, C., R. Wolfarth, and V. Michalcik. 2012. Natural resources, post-conflict reconstruction, and regional integration: Lessons from the Marshall Plan and other reconstruction efforts. In *Assessing and Restoring Natural Resources in Post-Conflict Peacebuilding*, ed. D. Jensen and S. Lonergan. London: Earthscan.

CD&M (Camp Dresser & McKee International) and HEIS (Hydro-Engineering Institute Sarajevo). 1999. Water and wastewater sector: Plan for institutional strengthening; Ten selected pilot vodovods. Final report. October 6. Sarajevo, Bosnia and Herzegovina: United States Agency for International Development. http://pdf.usaid.gov/pdf_docs/PNACP930.pdf.

Commission of the European Communities. 2007a. Accompanying document to the communication from the Commission to the European Parliament and the Council: "Towards sustainable water management in the European Union"; First stage in the implementation of the Water Framework Directive. Commission Staff Working Document. 2000/60/EC [COM(2007)128 final] [SEC(2007)363]. March 22. Brussels, Belgium. http://eur-lex.europa.eu/LexUriServ/LexUriServ.do?uri=SEC:2007:0362:FIN:EN:HTML.

———. 2007b. Annex to the communication from the Commission to the European Parliament and the Council: "Towards sustainable water management in the European Union"; First stage in implementation of the Water Framework Directive 2000/60/EC. 4th Commission report (executive summary) on implementation of the urban waste water treatment directive. [COM(2007)128 final] [SEC(2007)362]. March 22. Brussels, Belgium. http://ec.europa.eu/environment/water/water-framework/implrep2007/pdf/sec_2007_0363_en.pdf.

DW (Directorate for Water, Ministry of Agriculture, Forestry and Water Management, Republic of Srpska). 2006. Framework plan on the Republic of Srpska water management [in Serbian]. Bijeljina. www.voders.org/images/stories/OkvirniPlanRazvoja Vodoprivrede.pdf.

EC (European Commission). 1998. Guide to the approximation of European Union environmental legislation. 2nd ed. SEC(97) 1608. January. http://ec.europa.eu/environment/archives/guide/preface.htm.

EU (European Union). 2012. Acquis communitaire. http://europa.eu/legislation_summaries/glossary/community_acquis_en.htm.

EuropeAid. 2008. Service procurement notice: Support to BiH water policy Bosnia and Herzegovina. EC/BiH/08/012. Sarajevo: Delegation of the European Commission to Bosnia and Herzegovina. http://ec.europa.eu/europeaid/tender/data/d44/AOF88044.htm.

380 Water and post-conflict peacebuilding

EC (European Commission). 2011. Bosnia and Herzegovina 2011 progress report. Commission Staff Working Paper No. SEC(2011) 1206. Brussels, Belgium. http://ec.europa.eu/enlargement/pdf/key_documents/2011/package/ba_rapport_2011_en.pdf.

European Parliament and the Council of the European Union. 2000. Directive 2000/60/EC of the European Parliament and the European Council of 23 October 2000 establishing a framework for Community action in the field of water policy. *Official Journal of the European Communities* L (327): 1–21.

———. 2008. Council decision of 18 February 2008 on the principles, priorities, and conditions contained in the European Partnership with Bosnia and Herzegovina and repealing decision 2006/55/EC. (2008/211/EC.) *Official Journal of the European Union* L 80/18. March 19. http://eur-lex.europa.eu/LexUriServ/LexUriServ.do?uri=OJ:L:2008 :080:0018:0031:EN:PDF.

Fejzibegović, S. 2008. Legal and institutional framework of water resources management. Presented at a workshop sponsored by the United Nations Educational, Scientific, and Cultural Organization, Thessaloniki, Greece, June 27–28.

FMAWMF (Federal Ministry of Agriculture, Water Management and Forestry, Federation of Bosnia and Herzegovina), SRBDA (Sava River Basin District Agency), and ASRBD (Adriatic Sea River Basin District). 2012. Water management strategy of the Federation of Bosnia and Herzegovina. Sarajevo. http://jadran.ba/strategija/SUV_FBiH_eng.pdf.

Hitchner, B. 2011. Change course, overhaul Dayton, fix Bosnia. Peacefare.net. August 1. www.peacefare.net/?p=4128.

IMF (International Monetary Fund). 2004. Bosnia and Herzegovina: Poverty reduction strategy paper; Mid-term development strategy. IMF Country Report No. 04/114. April. Washington, D.C.

MAFWM (Ministry of Agriculture, Forestry and Water Management, Republic of Srpska). 2007. Plan of action for realisation development frame plan of Republika Srpska water industry sector: Period of plan 2007–2016. March. Bijeljina. www.voders.org/images/stories/Plan_action.pdf.

MOFTER (Ministry of Foreign Trade and Economic Relations, Federation of Bosnia and Herzegovina). 2010. Department of environmental protection. www.mvteo.gov.ba/org_struktura/sektor_prirodni_resursi/odjel_zastita_okolisa/?id=2034.

OHR Brčko Supervisor (United Nations Office of the High Representative Supervisor of Brčko). 2006. Supervisory order abolishing entity legislation within Brčko District and declaring the inter-entity boundary line to be of no further legal significance within the district. August 4. Sarajevo, Bosnia and Herzegovina: United Nations Office of the High Representative. www.ohr.int/ohr-offices/brcko/bc-so/default.asp?content _id=37764.

OSCE (Organization for Security and Co-operation in Europe). 2007. A look at water management in Bosnia and Herzegovina. Briefing paper presented at the second preparatory conference to the 15th OSCE Economic and Environmental Forum, Zaragoza, Spain, March 12–13.

PM Group. 2011. Support to BiH water policy: "Technical note"; Sub-strategy for implementation of EU directive on assessment and management of flood risks (2007/60/EC). September. Sarajevo, Bosnia and Herzegovina: European Union IPA Programme. www.fmpvs.gov.ba/texts/313_541_1032_e.pdf.

———. n.d. Support for water policy, Bosnia and Herzegovina. www.pmgroup-global .com/sectors/International-financial-Institutions/IFI-Featured-Projects/support-for-water -policy-bosnia.aspx.

Management of waters in Bosnia and Herzegovina 381

Redžić, Sulejman S. 2007. The ecological aspect of ethnobotany and ethnopharmacology of population in Bosnia and Herzegovina. *Collegium Antropologicum* 31(3): 869–890.

Royal Haskoning. 2001. River-basin bodies of inter-entity watercourses: Study of legal status. In *Water institutional strengthening of Bosnia and Herzegovina*. PHARE Project No. EC/BiH/99/045. Unpublished report. Sarajevo, Bosnia and Herzegovina. On file with author.

Sahovic, M. 1996. Ustav Bosne I Hercegovine prema Dejtonskom sporazumu. *Medjunarodni Problemi* 48 (1–2): 33–42.

Sarajevo Vodoprivreda. n.d. Geographic information system database of the Sarajevo Vodoprivreda. Data on file with author.

Schreuer, C. 1999. The Brčko Final Award of 5 March 1999. *Leiden Journal of International Law* 12 (3): 575–581.

Skejović-Hurić, N. 2009. Državna strategija, institucionalni i zakonski okvir u vodenom sektoru avna Budu e reforme u sektoru kori tenja voda Buduće koriš. Presented at "Developing Environmental Infrastructure Projects in the Water Sector in BiH," Sarajevo, Bosnia and Herzegovina, February 19. http://web.rec.org/documents/peip/docs/national _workshop_2009_feb19/presentations/13_PEIP_BIH_19022009_MOFTER_EN.pdf.

Sparavalo, Z. 1982. Zbirka saveznih i republickih propisa o vodama sa komentarom i tipskim primjerima sprovedenih akata. Sarajevo, Bosnia and Herzegovina: Vodoprivreda Bosne i Hercegovine.

Stoett, P. 2005. Environmental security in post-Dayton Bosnia and Herzegovina. No. 29. October. Montreal, Quebec: Centre d'Études des Politiques Étrangères et de Sécurité. www.er.uqam.ca/nobel/cepes/pdf/Bosnia_and_envifinal3.pdf.

Tuathail, G. O., J. O'Loughlin, and D. Djipa. 2006. Bosnia and Herzegovina ten years after Dayton: Constitutional change and public opinion. *Eurasian Geography and Economics* 47 (1): 61–75. www.colorado.edu/ibs/pec/johno/pub/Dayton10yrsafter.pdf.

USAID (United States Agency for International Development) and BiH (Bosnia and Herzegovina) 1999. Water and wastewater sector: Plan for institutional strengthening; Ten selected pilot vodovods. Final report: 6 October 1999. http://pdf.usaid.gov/pdf_docs/ PNACP930.pdf.

———. 2012. Assistance in BiH: What did it achieve? http://transition.usaid.gov/ba/about/ history.htm.

YLI (Yugoslav Lexicographical Institute). 1979. Opća enciklopedija Jugoslavenskog Leksikografskog Zavoda. Zagreb.

The right to water and sanitation in post-conflict legal mechanisms: An emerging regime?

Mara Tignino

On July 26, 2010, the United Nations General Assembly (UNGA) formally recognized a human right to water and sanitation by adopting Resolution 64/292, which states that water and sanitation are "essential for the full enjoyment of life and all human rights" (UNGA 2010, 2). The resolution relied on the definition of a right to water and sanitation in General Comment 15, adopted by the UN Committee on Economic, Social and Cultural Rights (CESCR) in 2002: "The human right to water entitles everyone to sufficient, safe, acceptable, physically accessible and affordable water for personal and domestic uses. . . . These uses ordinarily include drinking, personal sanitation, washing of clothes, food preparation, personal and household hygiene" (ECOSOC 2002, paras. 2, 12(a)). The right has since been affirmed by the UN Human Rights Council in Resolution A/HRC/15/L.14, which declared that "the human right to safe drinking water and sanitation is derived from the right to an adequate standard of living and inextricably related to the right to the highest attainable standard of physical and mental health, as well as the right to life and human dignity" (UNHRC 2010, 2). Thus the human right to water is contained within existing human rights treaties and is legally binding on the states that are party to those treaties.

The right to water and sanitation cannot be realized in isolation from other socioeconomic rights, such as the right to food and the right to health. After an armed conflict, lack of access to water and sanitation services undermines a state's ability to achieve sustainable development.[1] Principles and norms drawn

---

Mara Tignino is a senior researcher for the Platform for International Water Law, with the University of Geneva's Faculty of Law.

[1] The linkages between water and sustainable development are noted in Agenda 21, adopted at the UN Conference on Environment and Development (also known as the Earth Summit) held in 1992 in Rio de Janeiro, Brazil. Agenda 21 notes that "the extent to which water resources development contributes to economic productivity and social well-being is not usually appreciated, although all social and economic activities rely heavily on the supply and quality of freshwater" (UN 1992, sec. 18.6). Since the 1990s, the linkages between development and human rights have been affirmed by additional international meetings, including the 1993 World Conference on Human Rights, held in Vienna, Austria, and the 2000 UN Millennium Development Conference (Wolfensohn 2004).

384 Water and post-conflict peacebuilding

from human rights law can serve as a reference point in such situations, supplying standards for the provision of water and sanitation during socioeconomic reconstruction. Some post-conflict states, such as South Africa, have included the right to water and sanitation in domestic laws as well as in peace agreements. Moreover, some transitional justice mechanisms have addressed the impacts of armed conflict on socioeconomic rights, including access to water.[2]

This chapter argues that socioeconomic rights, including the right to water and sanitation, should be understood as an integral part of the peacebuilding process, and it focuses on legal mechanisms for and international practices in the protection of these rights.[3] It views protection of the right to water through the lens of the concept of a "regime," understood as a "system of rules or regulations" (Black 1990, 1283).

The right to water and sanitation is established by various mechanisms, ranging from norms enshrined in constitutions and peace agreements to obligations contained in human rights law instruments ratified by post-conflict states. There is also a wide spectrum of mechanisms capable of enforcing the right to water and sanitation, including international criminal tribunals, human rights bodies, and truth commissions.

This chapter considers the implications of taking a human rights–based approach to water and sanitation management in post-conflict settings. First, it focuses on the value of taking such an approach. Second, it examines some of the features of the right to water and sanitation that are relevant in post-conflict situations. Third, it discusses the modalities through which access to water might be addressed in the reconciliation efforts of a state emerging from armed conflict. Specifically, it explores the mechanisms available for implementing and enforcing the right to water and sanitation in a post-conflict setting. Finally, it highlights some obstacles to the establishment of the right to water and sanitation in post-conflict situations.

THE VALUE OF A RIGHTS-BASED APPROACH

Awareness is growing regarding the importance of improving access to safe water supplies as part of development and poverty reduction efforts (Lenton, Wright, and Lewis 2005). It is becoming clear that water scarcity is a problem not only

---

[2] According to the United Nations Security Council's report the *Rule of Law and Transitional Justice in Conflict and Post-Conflict Societies*, *transitional justice* includes "the full range of processes and mechanisms associated with a society's attempts to come to terms with a legacy of large-scale past abuses, in order to ensure accountability, serve justice and achieve reconciliation. These may include both judicial and non-judicial mechanisms, with differing levels of international involvement (or none at all) and individual prosecutions, reparations, truth-seeking, institutional reform, vetting and dismissals, or a combination thereof" (UNSC 2004, para. 8).

[3] See Tignino (2011) for more on this topic.

The right to water and sanitation in post-conflict legal mechanisms 385

of supply but also of uneven distribution of water resources and of competition among its multiple uses as population grows. Water scarcity has a direct impact on poverty and inequality, and solutions to it are undermined by weak governance (Falkenmark et al. 2007; UNDP 2006).

Meeting human needs for water and basic sanitation is one of the most pressing challenges in many post-conflict states. Combined with the ongoing and future impacts of climate change, the direct consequences of armed conflict on water infrastructure pose great risks to long-term access to water supplies. For example, in 2003, after two decades of armed conflict, the water network in Kabul, Afghanistan, was found to be losing up to 60 percent of its supply because of leaks and illegal use. Moreover, a drought had caused a catastrophic drop in the groundwater level in the Afghan capital between 2000 and 2003 (UNEP 2003a). Water facilities were also damaged or destroyed in Iraq during the 1990–1991 Gulf War, and by Israel's military operations in Lebanon in 2006 and in Gaza between December 2008 and January 2009 (UNEP 2003b; UNGA 2006; UNHRC 2009).

Damage to water infrastructure, sanitation services, and relevant governance structures is an obstacle to short-term recovery and long-term sustainable development when that damage is coupled with inequitable access to services. It is no surprise then that over the years the linkages between sustainable development and human rights have been recognized (Boisson de Chazournes 2007).

Sustainable development rests on three interdependent pillars: environmental protection, economic development, and social development (UNDESA 2002). Access to water and sanitation is a critical aspect of all three pillars. From an environmental point of view, access to safe water supplies requires that water be free from dangerous and toxic substances (ECOSOC 2002). Access to safe water supplies and sanitation services is also an important dimension of a state's socioeconomic development, supporting livelihoods and economic revitalization and contributing to poverty reduction (UN 2000).

Taking a rights-based approach to defining, implementing, and ultimately enforcing access to water and sanitation can help to produce more equitable short-term and more sustainable long-term development results (de Albuquerque 2010), thus alleviating some of the critical underlying causes of conflict at a local, national, and even international level. From a governance perspective, taking a rights-based approach provides a basis for integrating the right to water and sanitation into the policies and laws of post-conflict states, as well as for the development of the judicial mechanisms necessary to assess and ensure states' compliance (Arbour 2006).

Peace agreements often constitute the basis on which a constitution and legal framework are drafted in post-conflict states, and they can thus provide the first opportunity for enshrining a rights-based approach in a post-conflict state's policy and legal framework (Arbour 2006). Even without expressly ensuring a right to water and sanitation, peace agreements can emphasize the centrality of access to these services in post-conflict reconstruction and development.

386 Water and post-conflict peacebuilding

Realization and protection of the right to water and sanitation requires legal systems based on the rule of law, nondiscrimination, accountability for violations, and specific attention to the interests of vulnerable groups. When a post-conflict situation is approached from a human rights perspective, the governance structure of the post-conflict state will be built in accordance with the principles of human rights law. Some post-conflict states have underscored their commitment to this perspective. For instance, the Comprehensive Peace Agreement of 2005 between the government of Sudan and the Sudan People's Liberation Movement/Army affirms that the government of Sudan "shall comply fully with its obligations under the international human rights treaties to which it is or becomes a party" and "should endeavor to ratify other human rights treaties which it has signed."[4] Under the agreement, Sudanese law is required to be in accord with the obligations in those treaties. One of the instruments ratified by Sudan is the International Covenant on Economic, Social and Cultural Rights (Covenant on ESCR), which includes the right to water and sanitation as part of the right to an adequate standard of living and the right to the highest attainable standard of health (ECOSOC 2002).[5]

The establishment of a legal right to water and sanitation does not automatically resolve the difficult policy issues that invariably arise regarding the financing and regulation of those services. However, it does provide international standards to which political and economic decision makers may refer when creating water policies and making decisions regarding allocation of resources with respect to the rebuilding or creation of access to these services. In addition, the recognition of access to water and sanitation as a legal entitlement, rather than just another government service, can help post-conflict institutions establish legitimacy and credibility. The evolving international standards for implementing the right to water and sanitation support the rule of law, accountability for the delivery of water and sanitation, and participation of communities in the decision-making process. These are all critical aspects of post-conflict governance reforms.

Recognition of a right to safe drinking water and sanitation can contribute to the realization of the whole bundle of human rights. Human rights law takes the indivisibility of human rights as a fundamental precept. Civil, political, economic, social, and cultural rights are all interconnected (UN 1993). The human rights perspective that access to water and sanitation are a prerequisite for the realization of other social and economic rights, and even civil and political rights, may act as a point of leverage to bolster efforts to prioritize human water needs.

---

[4] Art. 1.6.1, chap. II, Power Sharing. For the complete text of the Comprehensive Peace Agreement, see http://unmis.unmissions.org/Portals/UNMIS/Documents/General/cpa-en.pdf.

[5] The Covenant on ESCR was adopted by the UNGA on December 16, 1966. For its full text, see www.ohchr.org/Documents/ProfessionalInterest/cescr.pdf.

The right to water and sanitation in post-conflict legal mechanisms 387

According to articles 2.1 and 23 of the Covenant on ESCR, post-conflict states themselves have the primary responsibility, to the degree made possible by the available resources, to realize the right to water and sanitation, but other states also have a responsibility: to extend international assistance, whether bilaterally or collectively. A rights-based approach might support the view that states that finance water projects to improve sanitation and access to water are complying with a legal obligation. Although states may be reluctant to consider financial assistance under human rights treaties to be mandatory, such commitments, especially within a treaty framework, may create shared expectations among stakeholders and thus may become legal obligations (Boisson de Chazournes 2007). Technical and financial assistance can be a significant incentive to promote compliance with the right to water and sanitation.

MAIN FEATURES OF THE RIGHT TO WATER AND SANITATION

The right to water and sanitation is recognized either expressly or implicitly by a number of universal and regional human rights law instruments, including but not limited to the 1966 Covenant on ESCR, the 1979 Convention on the Elimination of All Forms of Discrimination against Women (CEDAW), and the 1989 Convention on the Rights of the Child (which is overseen by the Committee on the Rights of the Child (CRC)).[6] These universal instruments are among the most ratified treaties. Many post-conflict states, including Afghanistan, Guatemala, Iraq, Nepal, Sudan, and Timor-Leste, are parties to them.[7]

The right to water encompasses an amount of water sufficient for personal and domestic uses; the right to sanitation encompasses the collection, transport, treatment and disposal or reuse of human excreta and associated hygiene (de Albuquerque 2010). Proper sanitation services are necessary to prevent contamination of drinking-water supplies and the resulting negative impacts on health. Various publications provide guidance on the amount of water that is necessary per person per day to sustain life. For example, *Domestic Water Quantity, Service Level and Health*, a paper published by the World Health Organization surveying the literature, suggests that intermediate level of access to water requires approximately 50 liters per person per day, which includes water for consumption and basic hygiene; this amount is necessary to ensure that health concerns are

---

[6] Although CEDAW (art. 14.2(h)) and the Convention on the Rights of the Child (art. 24.2(c)) expressly provide for a right to water, under the Covenant on ESCR (arts. 11.1 and 12.2), the right to water is part of the right to an adequate standard of living and the right to the highest attainable standard of health. CEDAW was adopted by the UNGA on December 18, 1979. For the complete text of CEDAW, see www.un.org/womenwatch/daw/cedaw/text/econvention.htm. The Convention on the Rights of the Child was adopted by the UNGA on November 20, 1989. For the complete text of that convention, see www.ovcsupport.net/libsys/Admin/d/DocumentHandler.ashx?id=123.

[7] Information on the status of ratification is available from the UN treaty collection at http://treaties.un.org/Pages/Treaties.aspx?id=4&subid=A&lang=en.

388   Water and post-conflict peacebuilding

"low" (Howard and Bartram 2003, 22).[8] Water also has to be free of substances that constitute a threat to a person's health. Provision of basic sanitation services is one of the main ways to protect the quality of drinking water (de Albuquerque 2010).

The right to water and sanitation contains some core obligations, such as "to ensure access to the minimum essential amount of water," "to ensure the right of access to water and water facilities and services on a non-discriminatory basis," and "to adopt relatively low-cost targeted water programs to protect vulnerable and marginalized groups" (ECOSOC 2002, para. 37). Some obligations are immediate, and others are progressive. For example, states have an immediate obligation to avoid engaging in any activity that denies or limits access to safe drinking water and sanitation. Obligations of a progressive nature include the requirement that states "take steps"—for instance, by adopting legislative and administrative policies and programs related to water and sanitation (UNOHCHR 2007).

Post-conflict states should move toward the goal of realizing the right to water and sanitation within the limits of available resources and within the framework of international cooperation and assistance.[9] A state must not attribute failure to meet its minimum core obligations to a lack of resources unless it can demonstrate that "every effort has . . . been made to use all available resources at its disposal in order to satisfy, as a matter of priority, those [minimum] obligations . . . " (ECOSOC 2002, para. 41).

The link between water and sanitation and the privatization of water services is a matter of concern when post-conflict states conclude concession contracts with private companies for the reconstruction of water infrastructure. Such privatization can increase water tariffs and raises the risk that water will be unaffordable for the poor (Salman and McInerney-Lankford 2004). The CESCR has pointed

---

[8] Guy Howard and Jamie Bartram do note that minimum requirements for water following disasters and other emergencies may be lower; for example, the Sphere Project suggests "15 litres of water used per capita per day as being a key indicator in meeting minimum standards for disaster relief" (Howard and Bartram 2003, 1). The 2011 Sphere Handbook provides that a minimum of 7.5 to 15 liters per person per day is necessary for survival needs (drinking and food preparation), basic hygiene practices, and basic cooking needs (Sphere Project 2011). However, there are "medium" concerns over health with less than 20 liters per person per day, as not all needs are met and quality is uncertain (Howard and Bartram 2003, 22). Accordingly, 50 liters per person per day provides a more appropriate standard for a post-conflict state aiming at setting more stable and long-term frameworks.

[9] In this regard, the CESCR "require[s] that States parties recognize the essential role of international cooperation and assistance and take joint and separate action to achieve the full realization of the right to water" (ECOSOC 2002, para. 30). In addition, the CESCR points out that "[d]epending on the availability of resources, States should facilitate realization of the right to water in other countries, for example through provision of water resources, financial and technical assistance, and provide the necessary aid when required" (ECOSOC 2002, para. 34).

The right to water and sanitation in post-conflict legal mechanisms   389

out some measures that governments must take if water services are privatized (McCaffrey 2005). States must ensure that third parties controlling or operating water services do not compromise equitable access to sufficient and safe water and sanitation services. This requires the adoption of an adequate legal framework that includes "independent monitoring, genuine public participation and imposition of penalties for non-compliance" (ECOSOC 2002, para. 24). Furthermore, when investments are made in water and sanitation, whether private or public, they should benefit as much of the population as possible; in particular, states should take steps to ensure access to water for vulnerable groups such as those living in rural areas, indigenous communities, internally displaced persons, and refugees (ECOSOC 2002).

A post-conflict state should pay special attention to ensuring that the population has access to water on an equitable basis. Post-conflict states often have to deal with practices that lead to inequitable and discriminatory access to water. Those practices may be among the ways a population was targeted during the armed conflict, and they may be a contributing cause of internal displacement of populations and the movement of refugees. The principle of nondiscrimination is recognized in all human rights instruments, and states must not deviate from this rule.[10]

In the past decade the conceptual links between water and human rights law have been strengthened, with numerous judgments being adopted by international and national courts since 2002. In two judgments—from June 17, 2005, and March 29, 2006, respectively—the Inter-American Court of Human Rights determined that the indigenous Paraguayan communities of Yakye Axa and Sawhoyomaxa had lacked access to sufficient drinking water (an element of the right to life) and referred for that purpose to General Comment 15, which establishes the right to water in the Covenant on ESCR.[11] Additionally, in the *Sawhoyomaxa* case, the court decided that the government of Paraguay must make reparations by creating a community development fund to provide sanitation infrastructure and a supply of drinking water to the members of that community.

MECHANISMS FOR REALIZING THE RIGHT TO WATER AND SANITATION IN POST-CONFLICT SETTINGS

Multiple mechanisms and institutions are available to aid in the realization of the right to water and sanitation in post-conflict settings. These include constitutions,

---

[10]   Judicial Conditions and Rights of Undocumented Migrants, Inter-American Court of Human Rights, Ser. A, No. 18, Advisory Opinion, September 17, 2003.

[11]   Although in both cases the court affirmed positive duties concerning the right to life, it was only in *Sawhoyomaxa Indigenous Community v. Paraguay* that the court found enough evidence to hold the state liable for violation of the right to life. *Yakye Axa Indigenous Community v. Paraguay*, Inter-American Court of Human Rights, Ser. C, No. 125, Judgment, June 17, 2005; *Sawhoyomaxa Indigenous Community v. Paraguay*, Inter-American Court of Human Rights, Ser. C, No.146, Judgment, March 29, 2006.

390 Water and post-conflict peacebuilding

legislation, and peace agreements; UN treaty bodies; international criminal tribunals; regional human rights institutions; and truth commissions.

Constitutions, legislation, and peace agreements

Inclusion of the right to water and sanitation in constitutions provides a way to anchor this right in the domestic legal system; therefore, constitutions are a fundamental mechanism for redressing social and economic inequalities related to access (Gowlland-Gualtieri 2007). The Constitution of the Republic of South Africa was one of the first national constitutions to guarantee a right to water (in section 27(1)(b)) and to adopt a legal framework for ensuring access to water services by communities that had historically faced discrimination (section 9 addresses the equality of rights and nondiscrimination).[12] South Africa's National Water Act, concluded in 1998, embraces human rights principles such as nondiscrimination, recognizing in the preamble that "the ultimate aim of water resource management is to achieve the sustainable use of water for the benefit of all users."[13]

The right to water was addressed in *City of Johannesburg v. Mazibuko* on March 25, 2009, in which the Constitutional Court of South Africa made reference to General Comment 15.[14] Relying on General Comment 15, the court determined (in paragraph 17) that "a right of access to sufficient water cannot be anything less than a right of access to that quantity of water that is required for dignified human existence." The case demonstrates how the UN definition of a right to water can serve as guidance to courts as they interpret provisions on the right to water that are enshrined in domestic legislation.

There are few examples of peace agreements that include socioeconomic rights. The Darfur Peace Agreement, concluded between the government of the Sudan, the Sudan Liberation Movement/Army, and the Justice and Equality Movement in 2006, is an example. The agreement recognizes that "competition for pasture and water by nomadic herders and settled agricultural producers is an important problem" and points to the need to develop "a framework for an

---

[12] For the complete text of the Constitution of the Republic of South Africa, approved on December 4, 1996, see www.info.gov.za/documents/constitution/. Other post-conflict states whose constitutions have incorporated the right to safe drinking water include Colombia and Democratic Republic of the Congo, in articles 366 and 48, respectively. For the Political Constitution of the Republic of Colombia of 1991 with Reforms through 2005, adopted on July 27, 2005, see http://pdba.georgetown.edu/Constitutions/Colombia/col91.html. For the Constitution of the Democratic Republic of the Congo, adopted on February 18, 2006, see www.wipo.int/wipolex/en/details.jsp?id=7449.

[13] For the complete text of the National Water Act of South Africa, see www.info.gov.za/view/DownloadFileAction?id=70693.

[14] *City of Johannesburg v. Mazibuko*, Constitutional Court of South Africa, Case No. 489/08, para. 17, March 25, 2009.

The right to water and sanitation in post-conflict legal mechanisms **391**

equitable access by different users" of water resources.[15] The agreement also extends special protection for access to potable water to internally displaced persons and refugees who are returning to their homes, restarting their livelihoods, and commencing reintegration.[16]

The Agreement on Social and Economic Aspects and Agrarian Situation, concluded in 1996, between the Presidential Peace Commission of the Government of Guatemala and the Unidad Revolucionaria Nacional Guatemalteca, spells out several targets for the achievement of socioeconomic rights, especially in relation to indigenous communities.[17] The Guatemalan agreement recognizes that socioeconomic rights and social justice are necessary to peace and security: "A firm and lasting peace must be consolidated on the basis of social and economic development directed towards the common good, meeting the needs of the whole population."[18] Ensuring access to water for indigenous communities is listed as an explicit part of this objective.[19]

The inclusion of socioeconomic rights in constitutions and peace agreements goes hand in hand with the development of the legislative and judicial mechanisms necessary for their implementation. Realization of the right to water and sanitation often depends on well-functioning national institutions and well-designed legislation. UN treaty bodies such as the CESCR and the CRC can assist in the development of legislation and institutional frameworks at the domestic level in post-conflict states (Chinkin 2006).

United Nations treaty bodies

States party to UN human rights treaties are required to regularly submit reports on the measures they have adopted and the progress they have made toward realizing the relevant rights, including the right to water and sanitation. The reporting obligations are the minimum duties under several of these human rights treaties. The UN treaty bodies also make general recommendations on ways to improve national frameworks for the protection of such rights. Although human rights treaty bodies do not often have any enforcement mechanisms at their disposal and thus have limited capacity to bring about change, those bodies can be a forum for dialogue between a post-conflict state and an international body of experts—particularly when the state has limited resources for realizing a broad range of socioeconomic rights. The reporting procedure itself is an opportunity to reaffirm a government's commitment to respect the human rights of its citizens and to reassert that commitment in the domestic political forum (Alston 1997).

---

[15] Art. 21, para. 149, chap. II, Wealth Sharing.
[16] Art. 21, paras. 179 and 187, chap. II, Wealth Sharing.
[17] For the complete text of the Agreement on Social and Economic Aspects and Agrarian Situation, see www.incore.ulst.ac.uk/services/cds/agreements/pdf/guat6.pdf.
[18] Preamble.
[19] Art. 34 (f).

392   Water and post-conflict peacebuilding

Through increasing cooperation between treaty bodies and national governments, the reporting process may also contribute to the identification of needs and priorities for the provision of humanitarian and technical assistance (ECOSOC 1990).

The effectiveness of the reporting procedure depends on the information submitted by the state party. When a state provides insufficient information on the realization of its obligations, human rights treaty bodies may request additional information (Sepúlveda 2003). This was the case with Israel when it submitted its first periodic report to the CESCR in 1998. The report did not contain information on the West Bank and Gaza. The committee asked Israel "to provide additional information on the realization of economic, social and cultural rights in the occupied territories, in order to complete the State party's initial report and thereby ensure full compliance with its reporting obligations" (UNCESCR 1998, para. 32).

A lack of technical and human resources may affect a post-conflict state's ability to submit national reports on a timely basis (O'Flaherty 2003). This was the case with Sudan, which did not submit its second and third periodic reports to the CESCR (Samar 2009). Moreover, damage to water infrastructure and sewage systems during an armed conflict, as well as restrictions on access to water during a regime of occupation, can hamper the capacity of a state to ensure access to water and sanitation.

In addition, human rights treaty bodies may underline existing gaps in national legislative and judicial mechanisms for ensuring equitable access to sufficient water and sanitation. They may also indicate areas where technical assistance and development cooperation is needed (ECOSOC 1990). In its concluding observations for Uganda, the CRC noted its concerns regarding the "increasingly large numbers of children who do not enjoy the right to an adequate standard of living, including access to food, clean drinking water, adequate housing and latrines" (UNCESCR 2005, para. 57). The CRC recommended that Uganda "reinforce its efforts to provide support and material assistance, with a particular focus on the most marginalized and disadvantaged families, and to guarantee the right of children to an adequate standard of living" (UNCESCR 2005, para. 58).

In a similar way, the 2006 CRC country report on Peru indicated that lack of access to water posed a barrier to the attainment of an adequate standard of living. Concern focused particularly on the disparity in access to water between rural and urban areas, as only 34 percent of rural families had access to water, compared to 74 percent of those living in urban areas. The CRC also expressed concern about "environmental health problems arising from a lack of access to safe drinking water, inadequate sanitation and contamination by extractive industries . . . ," and it recommended an increased state effort "to provide sanitation and safe drinking water to all the population . . ." (UNCESCR 2006, paras. 50, 51).

Reporting procedures can play a specific function in the realization of socioeconomic rights included in peace agreements. For example, the CESCR

The right to water and sanitation in post-conflict legal mechanisms 393

noted that Guatemala had made "insufficient progress" toward the realization of the socioeconomic rights contained in that country's 1996 peace agreement. It affirmed that the lack of implementation had led "to persistent serious problems, such as violence at the national level, intimidation, corruption, impunity and lack of constitutional, fiscal, educational and agrarian reforms. All these have impacted adversely on the full realization of economic, social and cultural rights enshrined in the Covenant, particularly with regard to indigenous peoples" (UNCESCR 2003, para. 10). Other human rights treaty bodies, such as the UN Committee on the Elimination of Discrimination against Women, have dealt with gaps in national legislation addressing discrimination against women—gaps that existed even though a peace agreement had provided for legal reforms (UNCESCR 2008).

Beyond reporting obligations, there are several special procedures of the UN Human Rights Council that have the specific purpose of addressing post-conflict situations (O'Flaherty 2003). Experts—designated as special rapporteurs, special representatives, or independent experts—are assigned to monitor, assess, and offer recommendations on the situation in specific countries and territories, currently including Cambodia, Haiti, Myanmar, Palestine, Somalia, and Sudan. The effectiveness of the recommendations made by these reports at the national level depends on the level of cooperation of the concerned states and on the receipt of international assistance.

The Commission of Inquiry on Lebanon and the UN Fact Finding Mission on the Gaza Conflict are examples of special investigating bodies addressing human rights violations committed during armed conflicts. Such bodies may recommend that assistance be given for the operation of national human rights mechanisms or that independent and appropriate investigation mechanisms be established at the national level (UNOHCHR 2006a, 2009). These recommendations may strengthen the capacity and legitimacy of national human rights institutions, which in turn could enhance local efforts to promote and respect human rights—including the right to water and sanitation.

Transitional justice mechanisms

After a conflict, transitional justice mechanisms can also play an important role in setting the stage for long-term peacebuilding (Türk 2009).[20] Such mechanisms, which include international criminal tribunals, human rights courts, and truth commissions, are crucial for strengthening the rule of law in post-conflict settings (UNSC 2004). Peace and reconciliation demand comprehensive societal transformation that should embrace a broad notion of justice. The former UN High Commissioner for Human Rights, Louise Arbour, indicated that transitional justice mechanisms established after an armed conflict should seek to more comprehensively address the root causes of conflicts and to promote respect for all

---

[20] For an analysis of consideration of environmental and natural resource issues in transitional justice mechanisms, see Harwell (2014) and Vialle et al. (2014).

394 Water and post-conflict peacebuilding

human rights (Arbour 2006). These mechanisms, especially human rights courts, are an emerging place for the right to water to be recognized in post-conflict situations.

International criminal tribunals

To restore peace and create stability, it is critical to guarantee credibility and legitimacy to the political and judicial institutions of post-conflict societies. International criminal tribunals help to ensure more credible reconstruction and peacebuilding in part because they offer a vital opportunity to redress wartime activities related to access to water and sanitation.

Intentional starving of civilians as a method of warfare, including willfully impeding relief supplies, is recognized as a war crime in the Statute of the International Criminal Court (ICC).[21] Intentional attacks against civilian objects, such as drinking-water supplies and installations, and the use of poison are also crimes within ICC jurisdiction.[22] In other words, international criminal law links violations of the law of war directly to the protection of the right to water and sanitation.

The judgments of international criminal courts have historically been centered on deliberate and systematic killing, torture, and rape. Such judgments rarely address crimes involving violations of socioeconomic rights. There have, however, been some exceptions. For example, in the *Kupreskic* case, the International Criminal Tribunal for the Former Yugoslavia (ICTY), on January 14, 2000, addressed the issue of whether "economic rights can be considered so fundamental that their denial is capable of constituting persecution," which is a crime against humanity.[23] Relying on the jurisprudence of the post–World War II Nuremberg Tribunal, which convicted several defendants of economic discrimination, the trial chamber of the ICTY recognized that the comprehensive destruction of homes and property constitutes a crime against humanity when committed with the requisite intent.

The *Kupreskic* judgment illustrates that violation of socioeconomic rights are an underlying element relevant to the crime of persecution. The measures offenders take against a national group may range from direct attacks on persons to discriminatory withdrawal of political, social, and economic rights. Discriminatory practices also take the form of attacks against essential resources for survival, such as water supplies. This point was underlined in the conclusions reached by the UN Fact Finding Mission on the Gaza Conflict:

---

[21] Art. 8(2)(b)(xxv).

[22] Art. 8(2)(b)(ii) and (xvii).

[23] *Prosecutor of the International Tribunal for the Former Yugoslavia v. Kupreskic*, International Tribunal for the Prosecution of Persons Responsible for Serious Violations of International Humanitarian Law Committed in the Territory of the Former Yugoslavia since 1991 Jan. 2000, IT-95-16-T, para. 630, Judgment, January 14, 2000. See www.icty.org/x/cases/kupreskic/tjug/en/kup-tj000114e.pdf.

The right to water and sanitation in post-conflict legal mechanisms 395

> [T]he series of acts that deprive Palestinians in the Gaza Strip of their means
> of sustenance, employment, housing and water . . . could amount to persecution,
> a crime against humanity. From the facts available to it, the Mission is of the
> view that some of the actions of the Government of Israel might justify a
> competent court finding that crimes against humanity have been committed
> (UNOHCHR 2009, para. 75).

The implication of the mission's conclusions is that attacks against water supplies aimed at depriving an identifiable group of people of the essential means of survival can constitute a crime against humanity.

The indictment brought by the ICC prosecutor against President Omar al Bashir of Sudan also illustrates these linkages. The prosecutor invited the judges to recognize that destruction, pollution, and poisoning of water resources in Darfur constituted an act underlying the crime of genocide. In the court's decision of March 4, 2009, issuing the first arrest warrant against al Bashir, a majority of the pretrial chamber judges dismissed the charge of genocide.[24] In a dissenting opinion, which was attached to the arrest warrant, Judge Anita Ušacka highlighted the large amount of evidence regarding the destruction of essential resources for survival. She stated that she would recognize the charge of genocide on basis of article 6 (c) of the ICC statute. Ušacka's opinion accepts the argument put forward by the prosecutor, stipulating that destruction of water sources and the resulting deprivation of the population's means of survival was an act underlying the crime of genocide.[25]

One of the theoretical bases for international criminal law encompasses restorative justice and reconciliation (Keller 2008). Restorative justice requires that victims have access to compensation. The ICC statute confers on victims the right to participate in ICC proceedings and to have access to compensation through a trust fund.[26] Condemnation from an international criminal tribunal and compensatory liability for restricting water access would act as a deterrent during

---

[24] *Prosecutor of the International Criminal Court v. Al Bashir*, International Criminal Court, ICC-02/05-01/09, Decision on the Prosecution's Application for a Warrant of Arrest against Omar Hassan Ahmad al Bashir, March 4, 2009.

[25] In a decision of February 3, 2010, the appeals chamber reversed the pretrial chamber's decision regarding the crime of genocide and remanded the matter to the chamber to reevaluate it on the basis of the correct standard of proof. On July 12, 2010, the pretrial chamber issued a second warrant of arrest including the charge of genocide. *Prosecutor of the International Criminal Court v. Omar Hassan Ahmad Al Bashir*, International Criminal Court, ICC-02/05-01/09, Appeals Chamber, Judgment on the Appeal of the Prosecutor against the "Decision on the Prosecution's Application for a Warrant of Arrest against Omar Hassan Ahmad Al Bashir," February 3, 2010 (see www.icc-cpi.int/iccdocs/doc/doc817795.pdf); *Prosecutor of the International Criminal Court v. Omar Hassan Ahmad Al Bashir*, International Criminal Court, ICC-02/05-01/09, Pre-Trial Chamber Judgment, Second Warrant of Arrest for Oman Hassan Ahmad Al Bashir, July 12, 2010 (see www.icc-cpi.int/iccdocs/doc/doc907140.pdf).

[26] Arts. 68, 75, and 79.

396 Water and post-conflict peacebuilding

conflict and a mechanism for redress during reconstruction, and be recognition that individuals must be ensured access to water.

Regional human rights tribunals

Regional human rights courts provide the most interesting examples of judicial enforcement of socioeconomic rights. The case *Social and Economic Rights Action Center and the Center for Economic and Social Rights v. Nigeria*—brought before the African Commission on Human and Peoples' Rights by two nongovernmental organizations on behalf of the Ogoni people—illustrates how the African commission has dealt with violations of socioeconomic rights.[27] The case concerned attacks perpetrated against the Ogoni people by both private actors and the military government of Nigeria. In finding the Nigerian government in violation of the right to a healthy environment and the right to health, the commission implicitly considered issues related to the right to water, specifically the contamination of water supplies. The commission dealt particularly with the disposal of toxic waste in the Niger Delta area, the resulting environmental degradation, and the consequent health problems among the Ogoni people.

In its conclusions, the commission requested that the government of Nigeria take several measures to ensure protection of the environment and of the health of the Ogoni people. It appealed to Nigeria to undertake "a comprehensive cleanup of lands and rivers damaged by oil operations," to ensure "that appropriate environmental and social impact assessments are prepared for any future oil development . . ." and to provide "information on health and environmental risks and meaningful access to regulatory and decision-making bodies to communities likely to be affected by oil operations."[28] Despite these appeals, the adverse environmental effects of oil development activities in the Niger Delta region, particularly in Ogoniland, have remained an issue of concern to UN treaty bodies (UNCERD 2007).

The commission also rendered an important decision in May 2009 dealing with the right to water and the role that water plays during and after an armed conflict.[29] Indicating that the poisoning of wells and denying access to water sources during the Darfur conflict amounted to a violation of the African Charter on Human and Peoples' Rights, the commission recommended several measures related to water resources. In one of these, regarding the rehabilitation of economic and social infrastructure in the Darfur states, it specifically referred to

---

[27] *Social and Economic Rights Action Center and the Center for Economic and Social Rights v. Nigeria*, African Commission on Human and Peoples' Rights, Communication No. 155/96, October 13–27, 2001.

[28] *Social and Economic Rights Action Center and the Center for Economic and Social Rights v. Nigeria*, African Commission on Human and Peoples' Rights, Communication No. 155/96, paras. 52–54, October 13–27, 2001.

[29] *Centre on Housing Rights and Evictions v. The Sudan*, African Commission on Human and Peoples' Rights, Communication Nos. 279/03 and 296/05, May 2009.

The right to water and sanitation in post-conflict legal mechanisms **397**

water services as necessary to support the dignified and safe return of internally displaced persons and refugees. It called for the establishment of a National Reconciliation Forum to address the long-term sources of the conflict, and in doing so it identified the resolution of issues related to water rights as a particularly important way to prevent future conflict.

Cases concerning armed conflict have also been addressed through the Inter-American human rights system, which includes both a court and a commission. In the *Plan de Sánchez* case, the Inter-American Court of Human Rights called for monetary and infrastructure reparations as compensation to the victims of the 1982 massacre that destroyed the village of Plan de Sánchez in central Guatemala. The state of Guatemala subsequently implemented development programs in the water sector to maintain and improve the sewage system and potable water supplies for the Plan de Sánchez villagers affected by armed conflict.[30] This form of reparation was seen as necessary for effective implementation of post-conflict reconstruction and social development.

Truth commissions

The right to water and sanitation in post-conflict settings can also be analyzed through the lens of the practice of truth commissions. Former UN High Commissioner Arbour has emphasized that truth commissions are particularly well suited for investigating violations of socioeconomic rights and for promoting protection of those rights, given that a truth commission's mandate often includes redress for the causes and the consequences of a conflict (Arbour 2006; UNOHCHR 2006b). This approach is exemplified in the final report of the Timor-Leste Commission for Reception, Truth and Reconciliation, which dedicates an entire chapter to the effects of the Indonesian occupation on the socioeconomic rights of the people of Timor-Leste.[31]

In the reparation program recommended to the government of Sierra Leone, the Sierra Leone Truth and Reconciliation Commission dealt with several socioeconomic rights, including health and education. It noted, for instance, that social services such as health care "should be universally provided," particularly to vulnerable people whose needs require prioritization (SLTRC 2004, 235). Furthermore, it was recommended that services be extended to people throughout Sierra Leone: "The government must be seen to be establishing infrastructure

---

[30] *Plan de Sánchez Massacre v. Guatemala*, Inter-American Court of Human Rights, Ser. C, No. 116, Reparation, November 19, 2004.

[31] In its report, the commission in Timor-Leste noted that the conflict's effect on socioeconomic conditions "was equally damaging and possibly more long-lasting" than the threats to civil and political rights (CAVR 2005, 140). The commission found that Indonesia had failed to "meet the basic needs of the population for food, shelter and essential medicines" and had caused "their economic and social situations to deteriorate . . ." (CAVR 2005, 141–142).

398   Water and post-conflict peacebuilding

and delivering health, education, justice and security . . ." (SLTRC 2004, 123). Those recommendations may be interpreted as including improved access to water facilities as part of the process of national reconciliation.

Another example is provided by the Moroccan Equity and Reconciliation Commission, which was established to inquire into human rights violations that had occurred between 1956 and 1999, the most serious having occurred in the Western Sahara conflict with the Polisario Front (Amnesty International 2008). The commission recommended "communal reparations" to strengthen the economic and social development of specific regions that had been particularly affected by political violence and had been marginalized and excluded (ICTJ 2005). In this case as well, economic and social development may be interpreted to include access to safe drinking-water supplies and basic sanitation services.

To date, no truth commission has expressly addressed the right to water and sanitation or the topic of legislative and institutional reforms in the water sector. However, the recognition of the right to water and sanitation by the UNGA and the Human Rights Council in 2010 strengthens the importance of the right to water and sanitation among socioeconomic rights. Moreover, the scarcity of water and risks related to the degradation of water resources underscore the need to enhance legislation on water in post-conflict states. Truth commissions may stimulate the creation of new domestic legislation by recommending measures to protect the right to drinking-water supplies and basic sanitation services.

Restoring the rule of law in post-conflict situations is a problem with many potential solutions. Approaches should be adapted to the specificities of each conflict and each affected society (Stromseth 2009). Criminal trials, human rights tribunals, and truth commissions are among the many means by which peace can be pursued in post-conflict states, and each of these mechanisms has the potential to interact with the right to water and sanitation.

OBSTACLES AND THE WAY FORWARD

The right to water and sanitation has been explicitly referenced less often than other socioeconomic rights in post-conflict arrangements, but that is beginning to change. Many aspects of the right to water and sanitation are implicated in the realization and protection of other socioeconomic rights, such as the right to health and the right to food and housing, but reliance on this implication alone undermines consideration of the right to water as an autonomous right (Cahill-Ripley 2005). When dealing with deliberate destruction of water installations, discriminatory practices, or the denial of access to drinking-water aid, international criminal courts, human rights bodies, and truth commissions must address the right to water and sanitation separately from other human rights obligations.

Post-conflict states are often reluctant to integrate the right to water and sanitation into legislation. One explanation for this reluctance might be a perceived incompatibility between the short- and long-term investments demanded by the right and the inadequate financial, technical, and human resources many

The right to water and sanitation in post-conflict legal mechanisms 399

post-conflict states possess. However, such resources are a necessary precondition for compliance with all of a state's human rights obligations, not only the right to water and sanitation. For example, the establishment of a criminal justice system with fair trials and humane conditions of detention may also require a large amount of financial and human resources (Arbour 2006).

In the aftermath of a conflict, the first concerns of international institutions are to provide security and to establish functioning and accountable legal and administrative institutions, so few post-conflict constitutions and peace agreements have thus far included an explicit reference to a right to water and sanitation. However, the UN and other international organizations assisting in the drafting of post-conflict arrangements can promote the inclusion of this right and can help mobilize financial resources for water and sanitation projects. United Nations Security Council Resolution 1272, on Timor-Leste, provides an example. According to the resolution, the objectives of the UN administration in Timor-Leste included assisting in the "development of civil and social services" and ensuring "the delivery of humanitarian assistance" (UNSC 1999). Although it does not deal with the satisfaction of human water needs as a legal entitlement, the resolution may be considered to include provision of water services under the umbrella of "humanitarian assistance."

Ensuring access to water is often considered a task of humanitarian agencies that does not have any significant implications for human rights law. Now that the UNGA and the Human Rights Council have recognized the right to water and sanitation, mechanisms—such as international criminal tribunals, regional human rights courts, and national truth commissions—must assess violations of the right to water and sanitation. This is a requisite of long-term peace and justice in post-conflict states.

REFERENCES

Alston, P. 1997. Final report on enhancing the long-term effectiveness of the United Nations human rights treaty system. Expert report to the United Nations. E/CN.4/1997/74. March 27.

Amnesty International. 2008. *Broken promises: The equity and reconciliation commission and its follow-up*. London.

Arbour, L. 2006. *Economic and social justice for societies in transition.* Working Paper No. 10. New York: New York University School of Law Center for Human Rights and Global Justice. www.unhchr.ch/huricane/huricane.nsf/424e6fc8b8e55fa6802566b0004083d9/40032f0dc00bf784c12572140031760a/$FILE/TransitionalJustice.pdf.

Black, H. C. 1990. *Black's Law Dictionary*, 6th ed. St. Paul, MN: West.

Boisson de Chazournes, L. 2007. The Bretton Woods institutions and human rights. In *Economic globalisation and human rights*, ed. W. Benedek, K. De Feyter, and F. Marrella. Oxford, UK: Oxford University Press.

Cahill-Ripley, A. 2005. The human right to water—a right of unique status: The legal status and the normative content of the right to water. *International Journal of Human Rights* 9 (3): 389–410.

400 Water and post-conflict peacebuilding

CAVR (Commission for Reception, Truth and Reconciliation in Timor-Leste). 2005. *Chega!* Dili.

Chinkin, C. 2006. The protection of economic, social and cultural rights post-conflict. www2.ohchr.org/english/issues/women/docs/Paper_Protection_ESCR.pdf.

de Albuquerque, C. 2010. Human rights obligations related to access to safe drinking water and sanitation. Expert report to the United Nations. A/65/254. August 6. www.ohchr.org/Documents/Issues/Water/MDGReportA6524.pdf.

ECOSOC (Economic and Social Council, United Nations). 1990. General Comment No. 2. E/1990/23. February 2.

————. 2002. General Comment No. 15. E/C.12/2002/11. January 20.

Falkenmark, M., A. Berntell, A. Jägerskog, J. Lundqvist, M. Matz, and H. Tropp. 2007. *On the verge of a new water scarcity: A call for good governance and human ingenuity.* SIWI Policy Brief. Stockholm, Sweden: Stockholm International Water Institute. www.siwi.org/documents/Resources/Policy_Briefs/PB_Water_Scarcity_2007.pdf.

Gowlland-Gualtieri, A. 2007. *South Africa's water law and policy framework: Implications for the right to water.* Geneva, Switzerland: International Environmental Law Research Center.

Harwell, E. E. 2014. Building momentum and constituencies for peace: The role of natural resources in transitional justice and peacebuilding. In *Governance, natural resources, and post-conflict peacebuilding*, ed. C. Bruch, C. Muffett, and S. S. Nichols. London: Earthscan.

Howard, G., and J. Bartram. 2003. *Domestic water quantity, service level, and health.* Geneva, Switzerland: World Health Organization.

ICTJ (International Center for Transitional Justice). 2005. Kingdom of Morocco: The Moroccan Equity and Reconciliation Commission: Three-part summary of the final report. New York.

Keller, L. M. 2008. The false dichotomy of peace versus justice and the International Criminal Court. *Hague Justice Journal* 3 (1): 12–47.

Lenton, R., A. Wright, and K. Lewis. 2005. *Health, dignity, and development: What will it take?* UN Millennium Project Task Force on Water and Sanitation Report. London: Earthscan. www.unmillenniumproject.org/documents/WaterComplete-lowres.pdf.

McCaffrey, S. C. 2005. The human right to water. In *Freshwater and international economic law*, ed. E. Brown Weiss, L. Boisson de Chazournes, and N. Bernasconi-Osterwalder. Oxford, UK: Oxford University Press.

O'Flaherty, M. 2003. Future protection of human rights in post-conflict societies: The role of the United Nations. *Human Rights Law Review* 3 (1): 53–76.

Salman, S. M. A., and S. A. McInerney-Lankford. 2004. *The human right to water: Legal and policy dimensions.* Washington, D.C.: World Bank.

Samar, S. 2009. Report of the Special Rapporteur on the situation of human rights in the Sudan. Independent report to United Nations Human Rights Council. A/HRC/11/14. June. www2.ohchr.org/english/bodies/hrcouncil/docs/11session/A.HRC.11.14_AUV.pdf.

Sepúlveda, M. 2003. *The nature of the obligations under the International Covenant on Economic, Social and Cultural Rights.* Utrecht, Netherlands: Intersentia.

Sphere Project. 2011. *Humanitarian charter and minimum standards in humanitarian response.* Geneva, Switzerland. www.sphereproject.org/handbook/.

SLTRC (Sierra Leone Truth and Reconciliation Commission). 2004. *Witness to Truth: Report of the Sierra Leone Truth and Reconciliation Commission.* Vol. 2. Accra, Ghana: Graphic Packaging Ltd. www.sierra-leone.org/Other-Conflict/TRCVolume2.pdf.

The right to water and sanitation in post-conflict legal mechanisms 401

Stromseth, J. E. 2009. Rule of law symposium: Strengthening demand for the rule of law in post-conflict societies. *Minnesota Journal of International Law* 18:415–424.

Tignino, M. 2011. *L'eau et la guerre: Éléments pour un régime juridique.* Brussels, Belgium: Bruylant.

Türk, V. 2009. Capacity-building. In *Post-conflict peacebuilding: A lexicon*, ed. V. Chetail. Oxford, UK: Oxford University Press.

UN (United Nations). 1992. *21: Earth Summit; The United Nations Programme of Action from Rio.* Geneva, Switzerland.

———. 1993. Vienna declaration and programme of action. World Conference on Human Rights. A/CONF.157/23. June 25.

———. 2000. United Nations Millennium Declaration. A/55/L.2. September 8.

UNCERD (United Nations Committee on the Elimination of Racial Discrimination). 2007. *Concluding observations: Nigeria.* CERD/C/NGA/CO/18. March 27.

UNCESCR (United Nations Committee on Economic, Social and Cultural Rights). 1998. *Concluding observations of the Committee on Economic, Social and Cultural Rights: Israel.* E/C.12/1/Add.27. December 4.

———. 2003. *Concluding observations of the Committee on Economic, Social and Cultural Rights: Guatemala.* E/C.12/1/Add.93. December 12.

———. 2005. *Concluding observations of the Committee on Economic, Social and Cultural Rights: Uganda.* CRC/C/UGA/CO/2. November 23.

———. 2006. *Concluding observations of the Committee on Economic, Social and Cultural Rights: Peru.* CRC/C/PER/CO/3. March 13.

———. 2008. *Concluding observations of the Committee on Economic, Social and Cultural Rights: Burundi.* CEDAW/C/BDI/CO/4. April 8.

UNDESA (United Nations Department of Economic and Social Affairs). 2002. Johannesburg declaration on sustainable development. September 4. www.un.org/esa/sustdev/documents/WSSD_POI_PD/English/POI_PD.htm.

UNDP (United Nations Development Programme). 2006. *Beyond scarcity: Power, poverty and the global water crisis.* New York: Palgrave Macmillan.

UNEP (United Nations Environment Programme). 2003a. *Afghanistan post-conflict environmental assessment.* Geneva, Switzerland.

———. 2003b. *Desk study on the environment in Iraq.* Geneva, Switzerland.

UNGA (United Nations General Assembly). 2006. *Implementation of General Assembly Resolution 60/251 of 15 March 2006 entitled "Human Rights Council."* A/HRC/3/2. November 23.

———. 2010. Resolution 64/292. A/RES/64/292 (2010). August 3.

UNHRC (United Nations Human Rights Council). 2009. *Human rights in Palestine and other occupied Arab territories.* A/HRC/12/48. September 15.

———. 2010. *Human rights and access to safe drinking water and sanitation.* A/HRC/15/L.14. September 24.

UNOHCHR (United Nations Office of the High Commissioner on Human Rights). 2006a. *Commission of inquiry on Lebanon.* A/HRC/3/2. November 23.

———. 2006b. *Rule-of-law tools for post-conflict states: Truth commissions.* New York. www.ohchr.org/Documents/Publications/RuleoflawTruthCommissionsen.pdf.

———. 2007. *Report of the United Nations High Commissioner for Human Rights on the scope and content of the relevant human rights obligations related to equitable access to safe drinking water and sanitation under international human rights instruments.* A/HRC/6/3. August 16.

402 Water and post-conflict peacebuilding

———. 2009. *Fact finding mission on the Gaza conflict.* A/HRC/12/48. September 25.

UNSC (United Nations Security Council). 1999. Resolution 1272 (1999). S/RES/1272. October 25.

———. 2004. The rule of law and transitional justice in conflict and post-conflict societies. S/2004/616. August 23.

Vialle, A-C., C. Bruch, R. Gallmetzer, and A. Fishman. 2014. Peace through justice: International tribunals and accountability for wartime environmental wrongs. In *Governance, natural resources, and post-conflict peacebuilding*, ed. C. Bruch, C. Muffett, and S. S. Nichols. London: Earthscan.

Wolfensohn, J. D. 2004. Some reflections on human rights and development. In *Human rights and development: Towards mutual reinforcement,* ed. P. Alston and M. Robinson. Oxford, UK: Oxford University Press.

PART 5

Lessons learned

Harnessing water management for more effective peacebuilding: Lessons learned

Jessica Troell and Erika Weinthal

Water resources play an important and multifaceted role in post-conflict peacebuilding. Immediately after conflict ceases, access to water and sanitation is vital for meeting basic human needs. In the longer term, effective water resource management can provide critical peace dividends by rebuilding livelihoods and promoting reconciliation. However, despite an increasing recognition of the value of integrating assessment and management of water and other natural resources into the planning and implementation of recovery and post-conflict peacebuilding, there is still little guidance on how this integration should take place.

To fill this gap with respect to the role that water management can play in promoting sustainable peacebuilding, three broad questions must be addressed: What are the risks to peacebuilding if water management issues are not appropriately addressed at war's end? How can local, national, and international actors capitalize on the shared experiences of practitioners, academics, and policy makers to more effectively harness water management for peacebuilding? How can these experiences and lessons be operationalized?

Given the diversity and complexity of post-conflict situations, there is no single blueprint for achieving water management that both promotes and supports recovery and peacebuilding. Prioritizing and sequencing interventions and coordinating those activities among multiple actors with diverse objectives present a number of context-specific challenges. However, the experiences documented here, coupled with the broader experiences with integrating natural resource management into peacebuilding efforts, point to an emerging framework that focuses on four post-conflict peacebuilding objectives and their respective activities: (1) establishing security; (2) restoring basic services; (3) revitalizing the economy and enhancing livelihoods; and (4) rebuilding governance and inclusive political processes.[1]

Jessica Troell is a senior attorney and director of the International Water Program at the Environmental Law Institute. Erika Weinthal is an associate professor of environmental policy at the Nicholas School of the Environment at Duke University.

[1] This framework follows that of Bruch et al. (2014), drawing substantially on the *Report of the Secretary-General on Peacebuilding in the Immediate Aftermath of Conflict* (UNSG 2009), although the activities have been regrouped and supplemented by activities articulated by USIP and U.S. Army PKSOI (2009) and the Sphere Project (2004).

406 Water and post-conflict peacebuilding

Efficient and equitable water resource management and service delivery play a central role in achieving each of these objectives. Immediately after the end of a conflict, water must be available and of sufficient quality to support basic human needs and to restart local livelihoods for civilians, including excombatants, refugees, and internally displaced persons (IDPs). Access to safe water is also essential for maintaining public health and avoiding increased morbidity and mortality both during and following conflict (Kruk et al. 2009). As countries move beyond crisis into peace consolidation and toward development, water is key to sustaining food security, promoting poverty alleviation, and supporting broader economic recovery and development. To realize the benefits of effective water management, countries emerging from conflict must also rebuild (or build anew) water governance frameworks that have the human, technical, and institutional capacity to manage complex issues related to allocation, service provision, and resource sustainability. Moreover, many water resources are shared across national boundaries, adding a complex dimension to the governance and management of the shared waters while also providing an opportunity for water to play a crucial role in fostering regional cooperation.

Post-conflict conditions are complex and fluid. Of the many practical lessons learned over the years about the role of water in post-conflict peacebuilding, perhaps the most important is the need for programming to be deliberately adaptive in its approach. Dealing with the uncertainty and rapid change in post-conflict situations requires a flexible approach that can respond to the evolving reality on the ground. Water resource management more broadly will benefit from such an approach, which can help to address social, economic, environmental, and climate-related drivers of change that are affecting both water quality and quantity around the world. Thus policies and approaches—even those successful in other situations—must be capable of supporting the elements of adaptive water governance and management. These elements are (1) meaningful participation of stakeholders in decision making, implementation, and monitoring and evaluation; (2) support for governance mechanisms that are flexible and can better cope with uncertainty and change; (3) a focus on intersectoral, intergovernmental, and interinstitutional coordination and cooperation; and (4) programming that fosters learning and knowledge exchange. These elements are highlighted in the cases throughout this book.

In order to cover the various ways in which water plays a critical role along the post-conflict continuum, this chapter organizes the lessons related to water management in post-conflict peacebuilding along the timeline of peacebuilding more broadly—from the immediate aftermath of conflict to peace consolidation and on to development—while acknowledging that these categories are not distinct, but rather are intimately connected and often overlap. Thus, the first section discusses humanitarian interventions related to water and sanitation that begin to take place in the direct aftermath of conflict (or continue to evolve from interventions that began during conflict). The second section discusses the role of water in supporting post-conflict recovery of livelihoods and the broader

Harnessing water management for more effective peacebuilding   407

economy throughout the peacebuilding process. The third section examines the various ways in which water management has been and can be leveraged to foster local and regional cooperation. The fourth section considers several cross-cutting issues, including water governance at the local and national levels, the need for broad-based stakeholder and public engagement in planning and implementation, the critical role of women in post-conflict water interventions, and donor commitment. The fifth section addresses the challenges of coordinating and sequencing water-related interventions. The final section explores three key emerging issues and their impact on water and post-conflict peacebuilding, including the implications of climate change, large-scale land acquisitions, and the development of large mining operations.

WATER MANAGEMENT IN THE IMMEDIATE AFTERMATH OF CONFLICT: MEETING BASIC HUMAN NEEDS

During and immediately following conflict, humanitarian interventions focus on saving lives. As a basic human need, the provision of safe water (and basic sanitation) is invariably among the highest priorities. The 2009 *Report of the Secretary-General on Peacebuilding in the Immediate Aftermath of Conflict* highlights water and sanitation services as one of five recurring priorities for peacebuilding in the immediate post-conflict context (UNSG 2009).[2]

There is a growing body of evidence that water and sanitation services, as part of the broader delivery of social and administrative services, contributes positively to peacebuilding by reducing social tensions, by creating necessary services, and by reaching out to the population and rebuilding systems of legitimacy and accountability (UN PBSO 2012). It symbolizes a return to normality and builds both confidence and credibility in the intentions and capacity of government, thus creating important peace dividends—timely and tangible results that are associated with social cohesion and stability and can promote trust in the peace process (UN PBSO 2012).

In the absence of immediate improvements to their social welfare, populations may become disillusioned with the slow pace of recovery and lose confidence in the peace process and in the government. At times, support for insurgents in Iraq has been linked to areas where populations experienced a sharp decline in environmental and health conditions owing to disruptions in the supply of water and other key public services (Briggs and Weissbecker 2012).

Because governments frequently lack the technical, financial, and institutional capacity to provide basic water services in the immediate aftermath of conflict,

---

[2] The United Nations, following the 2009 *Report of the Secretary-General on Peacebuilding in the Immediate Aftermath of Conflict*, defines *immediate aftermath* as the first three years following the signing of a peace agreement. Longer-term peacebuilding, or *peace consolidation*, follows this period, and the length of peace consolidation is context-driven (UN PBSO 2012).

408   Water and post-conflict peacebuilding

aid delivery remains critical during this time. Humanitarian organizations, donors, and nongovernmental organizations (NGOs) must step in to build the capacity of those governments while implementing interim solutions that help avoid dire public health outcomes and enable people to begin to rebuild their lives. Effective coordination among those organizations presents an ongoing challenge for peacebuilding. Such coordination is critical not only for achieving immediate programming goals but also in building the necessary state ownership and capacity to take over provision of services.

Challenges in providing water for refugees and internally displaced persons

As refugees and IDPs seek to return home as soon as a conflict abates, their ability to restart their lives often depends upon access to basic services such as water. Humanitarian interventions that prioritize basic human needs such as the provision of safe water and sanitation can generate critical peace dividends.

At the end of 2012, a total of 15.4 million people worldwide were refugees and 28.8 million were internally displaced (UNHCR 2012). An estimated 7.6 million of those people were newly displaced by conflict or persecution in 2012, including 1.1 million refugees—the highest number of newly displaced in one year since 1999. While the numbers of people displaced have varied by conflict, more than half of all newly displaced persons (IDPs and refugees) worldwide in 2012 came from only five countries: Afghanistan, Iraq, Somalia, Sudan, and Syria. Over 50 percent of the more than half-million refugees repatriated in 2012 were resettled in post-conflict Afghanistan, Côte d'Ivoire, or Iraq (UNHCR 2012).

After nearly three decades of conflict, Afghanistan is one of the countries most affected by protracted population displacement. In the early 1990s, approximately 7.5 million people were forced to leave their homes. Approximately 3.2 million registered as refugees in Pakistan, 2.4 million in Iran, and 2 million of them remained in Afghanistan as IDPs (World Bank and UNHCR 2011). At the end of 2011, 2.7 million Afghan people were still refugees (UNHCR 2011), and the ongoing conflict had led to new forms of internal displacement as many people moved to informal settlements in urban areas with low or nonexistent levels of basic services, not to camps (World Bank and UNHCR 2011). Likewise, the conflict in Somalia has resulted in one of the highest instances of displaced persons: 2.2 million (1.1 million refugees and 1.1 million IDPs), nearly one-quarter of the country's population (UNHCR 2011).

The vast numbers of people living in camps, as well as resettling in areas with little or no infrastructure, present a daunting challenge to those tasked with providing basic water and sanitation services. Because post-conflict governments often lack the institutional, technical, and financial capacity to achieve such access, others must step in, including humanitarian organizations, donors, and NGOs. In situations of continued violence, even militaries are playing an important role. However, the ability of these organizations to meet the basic water needs

Harnessing water management for more effective peacebuilding **409**

of refugees and IDPs in post-conflict situations is limited. A study by the United Nations High Commissioner for Refugees (UNHCR) using data from 2003 through 2005 showed that, out of the seventy to ninety camps studied,[3] over 40 percent were not able to meet the UNHCR standard of twenty liters of water per person per day (Cronin et al. 2008).

The public health consequences of inadequate water and sanitation services in these situations are evidenced by the recurring cholera outbreaks that have plagued populations from Guinea-Bissau to Iraq to southern Sudan (Colombatti et al. 2009; WHO 2008; Wakabi 2008). During the 1994 Rwandan crisis, more than 1 million Rwandans fled to the neighboring Democratic Republic of the Congo (DRC), where up to 60,000 people died from water shortages and cholera (Cronin et al. 2008). While simple measures to reduce contamination of water sources (such as bucket chlorination, designated defecation areas, and oral rehydration) significantly reduced death rates from cholera, the global acute malnutrition rates among refugees under five years of age and those in female-headed households were still extremely high and correlated closely with those who had a history of waterborne dysentery.

Access to clean water is also essential to prevent the malnutrition that results from infection with many waterborne diseases (Briggs and Weissbecker 2012). An estimated 50 percent of malnutrition is due to repeated diarrhea or intestinal nematode infections that result from unsafe water and insufficient sanitation and hygiene (Prüss-Üstün et al. 2008). Diarrheal disease not only causes malnutrition directly but also weakens an individual's resistance to subsequent infections, increasing overall morbidity and mortality (Dewey and Brown 2003).

In many parts of the world, water scarcity further complicates the provision of the minimum necessary even for survival, much less disease prevention. Due to fighting along the Sudan-South Sudan border, some Sudanese refugees arriving in the Doro and Jammam refugee camps in South Sudan were only receiving between five and seven liters of water a day, less than any of the minimum humanitarian standards, and are consequently suffering high rates of diarrheal disease (Amnesty International 2012). IDPs in Afghanistan, moreover, are less likely to have access to water and sanitation than the urban poor and more likely to experience diarrhea and other forms of waterborne and water-washed diseases (World Bank and UNHCR 2011).[4]

When host and camp communities must compete for water, the difficulties of achieving equitable allocation become greater, and the risk of disputes increases.

---

[3] The number of camps with available data varied across the study years: in 2003, 92 camps provided data; in 2004, 73 camps; and in 2005, 93 camps (Cronin et al. 2008).

[4] There are two types of water-related illness—those that people get because water contains bacteria or other infectious agents and those that people get because they do not have enough clean water to prevent oral-fecal transmissions. For the latter, *water-washed* is a term of art within the WASH (water, sanitation, and hygiene) and public health communities.

410   Water and post-conflict peacebuilding

The recent influx of Syrian refugees into neighboring countries, such as Jordan, has put increasing stress on already scarce local water supplies (IRIN 2013). The Jordanian government has been forced to dig new and deeper boreholes for Jordanians and the tens of thousands of refugees now sharing the resource, with resulting spikes in prices for delivered water and an increasing resentment by the local population (Warrick 2013). In Jordan, where water scarcity is also compounded by low water efficiency rates, donors should work with host governments to enhance water supply, not only through trucking in water, but more so through refurbishing dilapidated water systems in the host communities to prevent leakage and improve efficiency (Baker 2013).

The time necessary to collect water and the distances that people must travel to sources also present various risks to those living in camps. A survey conducted in eastern Chad reported that the average time people in camps spent to collect water was almost six hours per day, and that most households still used unsafe sources and had high rates of diarrheal disease and child malnutrition (UNHCR 2006). In northern Uganda, those searching for water outside camps were exposed to attacks by the Lord's Resistance Army and thus resorted to using unsafe sources.

Militaries and peacekeeping forces also place demands on local water resources. It is essential that they take into account the potential for competition with surrounding communities for scarce water resources and to adhere to best practices for water conservation so as not to cause harm to the water supplies of the local populations (Waleij et al. 2014; UNEP 2012). For example, even in water scarce environments, the UN Department of Peacekeeping Operations attempts to provide each soldier with approximately eighty-four liters of water per day (UNEP 2012). This high level of use can spark community resentment, leading some UN peacekeeping operations to take measures to reduce their water consumption while improving water conservation and reuse. For example, the United Nations Mission in Sudan introduced water conservation technologies, including rainwater harvesting (Waleij et al. 2014). The Sudan operations also established rules for groundwater extraction; adopted low-level technology such as flow regulators, shower timers, and water meters; used nonpotable water; and recycled wastewater. Swedish troops in Afghanistan are conserving water by using groundwater injection, a process that removes contaminants from wastewater and injects the treated water into an aquifer. Similarly, the U.S. Army Corps of Engineers has worked with Afghan soldiers to develop an irrigation scheme that recycles wastewater at an Afghanistan National Army base in Herat Province so Afghan soldiers can continue to water their trees and flowers on the base, while providing troops with ample potable water.

Too much water, in the form of floods, can also be a daunting challenge for humanitarian operations. Flooding in camps in Jordan (with Syrian refugees), South Sudan (with South Sudanese IDPs), and Thailand (with Burmese refugees) has destroyed shelters and other structures, washed out roads, prevented delivery of food and other aid, and promoted the spread of disease (*New York Times* 2013;

Harnessing water management for more effective peacebuilding **411**

Guardian 2012; Sai and Saw 2011). This indicates the need for more effective assessment of the hazard vulnerability of proposed camp locations and more effective integration of disaster risk reduction (DRR) into planning and implementation of operations.[5]

The challenges of providing water immediately after conflict are not limited to refugee and IDP camps. In urban centers, the destruction of infrastructure and capacity to provide basic services frequently results in severe public health impacts for returning and conflict-affected populations. For example, because the sewage treatment plants in Baghdad, Iraq, remained nonoperational for years following the violence of 2003, cholera and typhoid outbreaks became rampant (Briggs and Weissbecker 2012). These impacts are exacerbated by the rapid urban population growth experienced by many post-conflict cities, which puts major stress on insufficient or damaged water service infrastructure and institutions. In Liberia, the population of the capital city of Monrovia increased from 400,000 in 1988 to approximately 1 million in 2003 as Liberians fled conflict and devastation in the countryside and settled in the capital and the camps surrounding it (Pinera and Reed 2014*).[6] Similarly, in less than two years, the population in Kabul, the capital of Afghanistan, grew from approximately 1.8 million under the Taliban to approximately 2.8 million in 2004, and an estimate of more than 3.5 million in 2008 (Pinera and Reed 2014*). In both Monrovia and Kabul, it took several years to rehabilitate the infrastructure necessary to meet even a portion of this increased demand for water.

Thus one of the most important challenges that face policy makers and practitioners in the immediate post-conflict context is providing water services to the large number of displaced persons and resettling populations. It is critical that peacekeepers, governments, and communities understand as best they can how to do this in a way that both meets short-term needs of conflicting user groups and also enables sustainable management of water resources over the long term in often water-scarce environments. The water-usage footprint of refugee and IDP camps, and of peacekeeping forces in the area, must be minimized to limit competition for water with surrounding communities. Moreover, assessment of water resources prior to undertaking interventions can provide important data on where and how to site camps to minimize adverse impacts on water resources and provide sustainable access to those in need.

Standards for water services and delivery

The international humanitarian community tries to meet the challenges of providing water for basic human needs in post-conflict situations by setting and monitoring

---

[5] Guidance on DRR mainstreaming into the emergency management cycle of WASH programming (including in post-conflict situations) was developed by the Global WASH Cluster, discussed later within this chapter, in 2011 (GWC 2011a).

[6] Citations marked with an asterisk refer to chapters within this book.

412 Water and post-conflict peacebuilding

standards, and through efforts to better coordinate activities. The "cluster approach"—a system of sectoral coordination—was introduced as part of humanitarian reforms following a UN humanitarian response review's critical reflection on the coherence, efficacy, and accountability of the responses in Darfur in 2004 (Sistenich 2012). Clusters were defined by sector in 2005, and a lead organization was appointed to oversee implementation and capacity building in each sector. The United Nations Children's Fund (UNICEF) was designated as both the global water, sanitation, and hygiene (WASH) cluster lead and the default lead on coordination efforts at the country level, unless another organization is better positioned to do so (Steets et al. 2010; GWC 2011b). Membership in the Global WASH Cluster (GWC) is open to and includes humanitarian organizations, NGOs, and donors, as well as other stakeholders (including the private sector and academic institutions), with research institutions, governments, other clusters, and donors having various levels of involvement below a voting membership (GWC 2011b).

The GWC strategic plan for 2011–2015 identifies a number of improvements in practice that are attributable to the work of the cluster, including enhanced coordination at both the global and national levels; better identification of gaps and reduced duplication of efforts; improved guidance and formalization of practice (including information management and national-level coordination models); improved partnerships among UN and partner organizations; and enhanced ability and performance in mobilizing funding and resources (GWC 2011b). The plan also highlights several critical issues, including the lack of appropriate levels of inclusion of national and local actors, a focus on cluster processes rather than humanitarian actions, and inadequate attention to cross cutting and intersectoral issues.

The GWC and the institutions involved in national coordination efforts under the cluster approach are also key participants in an ongoing initiative to improve and integrate humanitarian standards and indicators of success. Perhaps the most widely referenced set of current standards is the *Humanitarian Charter and Minimum Standards in Humanitarian Response*, also known as the Sphere Handbook. The handbook was first drafted in 1997 by a number of NGOs and the International Federation of the Red Cross and Red Crescent Societies in order to establish a set of universal minimum standards of quality and accountability in core areas of humanitarian response (Sphere Project 2011). First published in 2000, then revised in 2004 and again in 2011, the handbook sets forth core principles in the form of a humanitarian charter, a set of principles that translate international humanitarian legal obligations into actions from a protection perspective, and a set of four technical areas of minimum standards, including standards for WASH interventions in a humanitarian context. The technical standards are evidence-based and represent sector-wide consensus on best practices. Minimum standards are followed by practical suggestions for action and a set of indicators to measure progress in achieving the standards. Guidance notes provide practical advice on application of the standards. With respect to water,

Harnessing water management for more effective peacebuilding **413**

the Sphere Handbook sets a standard of at least fifteen liters per person per day, available within 500 meters of the household, with a waiting time of less than thirty minutes to obtain that water (Sphere Project 2011). UNHCR, in contrast, sets a higher standard for its operations at twenty liters per person per day (following the World Health Organization recommendations) available less than 200 meters from dwellings (UNHCR 2006).

Despite the comprehensive nature of the Sphere Handbook, several sets of standards are used in practice by various governments and international organizations. To address this issue, the Humanitarian Accountability Partnership, the Sphere Project, and People in Aid have come together to form the Joint Standards Initiative that will involve UN agencies, affected governments and populations, and others in an attempt to create a universal set of standards and indicators to facilitate integrated aid operations at the local and country levels (SDC 2013). While the Sphere Project (including the Sphere Handbook) has been criticized for attempting to universalize standards that should be uniquely tailored, it should be noted that the 2011 version of the Sphere Handbook recognizes that its standards cannot be met in many situations and stresses the need for analysis of vulnerability and capacity in order to understand the local context and to tailor responses accordingly (Sphere Project 2011).

The Sphere standards also promote a rights-based approach to WASH-related humanitarian interventions. Rights-based approaches to development more broadly have emerged in recent years, emphasizing social and economic rights as the basis for poverty alleviation and exerting more pressure on national governments to promote, fulfill, and protect human rights (SIDA 2012; Nyamu-Musembi and Cornwall 2004). These approaches also prioritize empowerment of the poorest and most marginalized populations in post-conflict situations, thus attempting to redress inequities that can undermine peacebuilding. Rights-based approaches set high standards and can improve the basis for state accountability when rights are not realized. They also emphasize the process through which rights are realized, focusing on inclusive decision making (Boesen and Martin 2007).

Critics of rights-based approaches point to the fact that in water-scarce or resource-constrained contexts, rights-based language makes little difference in implementation and can actually discourage the kind of practical actions that may be necessary under emergency circumstances. The basis for claims against governments is also arguably counterproductive and open to abuse where government capacity is still weak and being built to promote, protect, and fulfill the right to water. The notion of a rights-based approach also highlights the challenge of physical water scarcity and the difficult decisions that must be made about allocation, particularly where communities and refugee or IDP camps must compete for scarce water resources. In Darfur, for example, rights-based approaches led to the drilling and establishment of hundreds of wells and water points in or near camps for displaced persons in arid regions where groundwater is the only reliable source of water most of the year (Phillips 2008). Meanwhile, local communities were not supplied with the same minimum amounts, and in some

414   Water and post-conflict peacebuilding

instances IDPs were selling the water received from international organizations to nearby cities, as the amount received in the camps was often more than many IDPs were accustomed to receiving before the crisis (UNEP 2013c). Rights-based approaches must therefore take sustainable yield of the resource into account, whether through integrating impact assessment processes into planning or by other means. Mechanisms for improving water harvesting and conservation are also important means for minimizing impacts on the resource and tensions among users.

Despite criticisms of various attempts to establish standards for water services—whether the Sphere Project or a rights-based approach—it is essential that standards be set in order to ensure effective delivery of water and sanitation services. At the same time, it is important to recognize that a single set of standards cannot apply to all circumstances. Water standards and policies must be tailored to specific situations and needs.

The diversified institutional landscape governing post-conflict water management

In post-conflict countries, interventions take place across different levels of scale, ranging from the community to the national and transboundary levels as well as across urban and rural areas and with different levels of danger (Burt and Keiru 2014*). Whereas water interventions in the immediate aftermath of conflict often have been implemented by humanitarian organizations, mounting insecurity in some post-conflict countries such as Afghanistan and Iraq has also caused some organizations to limit their interventions. When that happens, militaries that often are not trained in the basics of water governance and service delivery have had little choice but to oversee the provision of water. In Afghanistan, the U.S. military has begun to incorporate water delivery and services into its counterinsurgency operations and provincial reconstruction teams to both generate visible health and economic benefits as well as to garner local support (Palmer-Moloney 2014*; Mosher et al. 2008); Finland, Sweden, the United Kingdom, and other countries have subsequently deployed provincial reconstruction teams.

In highly insecure situations, humanitarian actors may need to rely on coordination with military forces in order to carry out water delivery. However, there can be long-term risks in blurring the line between humanitarian work and military engagement. Humanitarian actors can be put at risk if their work is too closely associated with military programs, and long-term development goals can be compromised by placing too much emphasis on short-term security objectives if programs are not integrated with other national programs (Civic 2014). Close cooperation in program design and funding mechanisms across organizations is thus required to minimize the risks to the long-term sustainability of water service programs while also balancing military objectives (Civic 2014).

As countries move away from immediate humanitarian interventions toward broader consolidation in water access and sanitation, there is also increasing

Harnessing water management for more effective peacebuilding   415

recognition of the important role that informal service providers are playing. During or immediately following conflict, an informal market of water sellers and transporters tends to emerge to fill service gaps in water provision. This is especially true in urban and peri-urban settings, as was the case in Luanda, Angola (Cain 2014*). There, the informal sector became highly developed during the country's long conflict, creating an informal system that could be harnessed in formalizing service networks and creating livelihood opportunities after the conflict. At the same time, the informal sector can also present challenges related to equity in access (often due to unregulated tariffs) and to the lack of regulation of the quality of the resource and service.

Experience from Liberia illustrates how informal service provision can be integrated into the formal water service sector. Criminal gangs controlled illegal water vendors, which hampered donor and government efforts to rebuild more formal structures (Pinera and Reed 2014*). Instead of setting up an adversarial situation with the informal sector, Oxfam, which has had a local presence for several years, was able to broker an agreement between the vendors and the Liberia Water and Sewer Corporation to recognize the vendors as legitimate and to provide them with tanks to improve their capacity; the agreement also provided for testing the quality of the water they were selling. Such arrangements can provide an interim mechanism for breaching the service gap over the short to medium term after conflict.

The diversity of institutions working on post-conflict water management requires specific mechanisms for coordination and cooperation, such as those being developed by the Global WASH Cluster and the Joint Standards Initiative described above. Emerging actors, such as informal service providers and militaries, are playing increasingly important roles, but both also call into focus the need for accountability and the importance of effective water governance to ensure that humanitarian and resource management goals are achieved.

Beyond humanitarian assistance: Laying the foundations for peace consolidation and sustainable development

Rapid restoration of water services immediately after conflict must also lay the foundation for sustainable recovery and a transition to peace consolidation and development. A number of experiences around the world point to key features of immediate and early post-conflict interventions in the water sector that will ensure this longer-term sustainability. It is critical to balance the humanitarian focus on the emergent needs of a post-conflict population with these factors impacting the medium- to long-term sustainability of the natural resource, even where this might require greater initial financial and technical investments in assessments and longer planning cycles, which in turn might require even higher levels of coordination among humanitarians, donors, and post-conflict governments and civil society.

Perhaps the most commonly cited factor for ensuring sustainability is the ongoing involvement of different users in planning, developing, and implementing

416 Water and post-conflict peacebuilding

water sector interventions. Involvement of diverse stakeholders has the potential to ensure that the needs, priorities, and concerns of all are taken into consideration when developing and implementing water services and management interventions. This can be critically important in areas where competition over natural resources has contributed to conflict or has the potential to spark renewed conflict by exacerbating other tensions.

In Somalia, for example, UNICEF was forced to rethink its water and sanitation programming by first enabling negotiations to resolve historic conflicts over access to scarce water. Once existing tensions were addressed through a facilitated process that brought together all of the relevant stakeholders, an agreement was reached among local leaders on the construction of water systems and monitoring mechanisms, and water was provided to IDP camps while also creating mechanisms for longer-term management of the natural resource (UN PBSO 2012).

Similarly, in Kyrgyzstan, water access has been a key factor in ethnic tensions between Kyrgyz and Uzbek populations. Uzbek communities in southern Kyrgyzstan perceived their Kyrgyz neighbors to have better access both during and following the ethnic conflict in 2010 that killed 200 people and displaced thousands, deepening feelings of discrimination and intercommunal grievances. However, World Food Programme activities that focused on building irrigation channels were able to serve as platforms for bringing stakeholders together to air these grievances and develop trust (UN PBSO 2012). Because these communities saw that together they could work toward creating mutual benefits from the project activities, it was possible to harness that cooperation to support more effective water management.

The work of the NGO Tearfund in building community-based water management schemes has been notably successful and even brought to scale in the DRC by the national government (Burt and Keiru 2014*). This is largely due to the long-term involvement of local and government stakeholders in the planning, implementation, and monitoring and evaluation of the schemes. In particular, women from communities that previously suffered from high levels of mistrust played a leadership role in decision making and implementation throughout the process, which was key in building trust and ensuring the schemes' sustainability.

Similarly, during reconstruction in Kurdistan, the high level of community involvement facilitated a negotiating process to determine how decisions regarding water resources would be made, including timing and quantities of abstraction, allocation, and monitoring (Barwari 2013). However, while this resulted in sustainable management of irrigation water, it notably excluded women from the negotiations and failed to prioritize the domestic water needs that is the purview of the females running the households. Care must be taken to provide specific mechanisms for involvement of traditionally marginalized populations, such as women and the very poor, in order to ensure equitable outcomes.

In their chapter, Murray Burt and Bilha Joy Keiru highlight another key aspect of sustainable interventions: effective engagement with national and local

Harnessing water management for more effective peacebuilding **417**

governments. When a government lacks the capacity to provide immediate access to water services, to manage aid packages, or to coordinate all of the activities within the sector, donors and other international institutions may turn to NGOs or the private sector to fill this role. While sometimes an effective short-term practice, bypassing government completely fails to build the necessary foundation for sustainability of these services. Tearfund's work emphasizes the importance of early and ongoing engagement of relevant government stakeholders to build their capacity and ensure the generation of political will to sustain these interventions.

For countries to reap the peace dividends associated with provision of water services, donors and governments must emphasize basic services in their funding allocations. Yet spending on water services is often a much lower priority than other areas. From 1977 to 1997, only 4.2 percent of World Bank lending in post-conflict reconstruction went to the water and sanitation sectors (Kreimer et al. 1998).[7] In Uganda, lending for water and sanitation services comprised only 6 percent of all post-conflict lending throughout the 1980s and 1990s (Kreimer et al. 2000). This general trend still continues in some post-conflict countries: from 2001 to 2009 in Afghanistan, for example, international, bilateral, and multilateral aid to the country reached US$24 billion, yet only US$1.2 billion, or 5 percent, went to the water sector (CPHD 2011).

Another challenge is the lack of information required for decision making that promotes sustainable interventions. Water quantity, quality, and allocation data, as well as the mechanisms for managing the water resources (and how these have been impacted by conflict) should inform sectoral activities, but are often missing because the baseline and monitoring data never existed, or they were destroyed during conflict. In Afghanistan's Helmand Province, for example, there is no comprehensive record of the number of wells that have been dug or drilled; no documentation of changes in the water table over time; and no ongoing collection and sharing of data on groundwater quality (Palmer-Moloney 2014*). Groundwater levels are dropping because of drought conditions and water withdrawn from wells, but lack of data has hampered effective responses. Environmental assessments can provide a tool for filling some of this data gap, but must be complemented by ongoing monitoring, which can be challenging in a post-conflict environment where equipment maintenance and human capacity are limited (Jensen and Lonergan 2012).

Experiences in Liberia and the DRC demonstrate how communities can generate such information—highlighting again the importance of community involvement in decision making (Pinera and Reed 2014*; Burt and Keiru 2014*). In the absence of such local knowledge, early interventions might inadvertently damage broader recovery efforts to restore livelihoods and sustain peace. Uncontrolled and uninformed digging of deep wells to meet immediate humanitarian needs in Afghanistan inadvertently undermined the traditional *karez* water

---

[7] There is limited data on water and sanitation lending.

418   Water and post-conflict peacebuilding

system of underground canals, disrupting local livelihoods and engendering new conflicts over access to water (UNEP 2003). A similar experience occurred in Darfur: from 2003 until 2006, a number of humanitarian actors drilled and constructed hundreds of wells and water points to provide displaced persons with water, without monitoring extraction rates from the groundwater or assessing how much water can be withdrawn (UNEP 2007). A 2007 assessment by United Nations Environment Programme (UNEP) made it clear that some of the extraction rates were unsustainable, and had led to five of twelve boreholes running dry in the Abu Shouk camp in southern Darfur. This points to the importance of baseline resource assessments and adequate monitoring programs to prevent overuse of the resource and renewed conflict as access dwindles over time.

While immediate post-conflict interventions focus on meeting urgent needs, the restoration of water and sanitation services to meet those needs also lays the foundation for long-term recovery and peace consolidation. How those services are developed and provided can have an important impact on the options for sustainable natural resource management. Stakeholder engagement and effective data collection and management are important tools to ensure that this foundation is strong and avoids unnecessary damage to the natural resource.

Peacebuilding and water infrastructure development

The building (or rebuilding) of water infrastructure is critical to post-conflict peacebuilding efforts, especially as countries move away from immediate humanitarian interventions toward recovery and peace consolidation. Water and sanitation infrastructure not only provides access to potable water and hygienic living conditions for concentrated populations, but investments in infrastructure also correlate positively with overall economic development rates (Mardirosian 2010). Moreover, infrastructure reconstruction is an important demonstration of legitimate state building, and the absence of basic services can be a flashpoint for public protest against authorities, as happened in Iraq during frequent water service interruptions in 2010.

Rebuilding of infrastructure requires large amounts of capital investment, high levels of technical and administrative capacity, and effective regulatory oversight. Whether the infrastructure never existed or suffered damage during conflict, rebuilding can take years, depending on the level of deterioration. For example, while the DRC is considered to be a water-abundant country, the water use in 2000 in the DRC, at seven cubic meters per capita (approximately nineteen liters per day), was much lower than in many water-scarce countries in the Sahel (UNEP 2011). In Liberia, by 2006 (three years after the end of Liberia's second civil war), the "percentage of people with access to basic social services such as clean and safe drinking water, averaged about 40 percent of their pre-war levels" (ROL and UNDP 2006, 40). Prior to the first Liberian civil war, in 1989, 45 percent of the urban population and 23 percent of the rural population had access to pipe-borne water; by 1999 only 25 percent of the urban population and

Harnessing water management for more effective peacebuilding **419**

4.1 percent of the rural households had that access. By the end of the second civil war in 2003, pipe-borne water was almost entirely absent, leaving the population dependent upon (often untreated) wells, ponds, and rivers for their primary sources of drinking water. In Kabul, Afghanistan, where institutional reforms progressed more rapidly than in Liberia, it still took three years to develop a vision for the institutional development of the metropolitan water utility (Pinera and Reed 2014*).

In countries with continued violence, such as Iraq and Afghanistan, delays are often directly attributable to the physical risks to government staff and contractors. In Iraq, government contractors were forced to hire private mercenaries to protect infrastructure assets, but the costs had to be drawn from a budget for other infrastructure projects (Mardirosian 2010). The costs of protecting water infrastructure can be high: in 2004, half of the budget for the water sector from the Iraq Relief and Reconstruction Fund was reallocated from technical support to security, resulting in only forty-nine out of 136 water projects being completed by 2006.

While there has been a global debate on the role that privatization can play in increasing access to water services (Allouche 2014*), private investment in the water sector is rarely undertaken in post-conflict situations, particularly in the first few years following the end of armed conflict (Schwartz and Halkyard 2006). Private investors perceive several risks in post-conflict countries: physical risks to investments; little assurance of return on investment; and economic, political, and legal frameworks conducive to corruption (Hoeffler 1999). The countries also lack markets, and cost recovery is not viable without government subsidies, which are rarely possible in post-conflict situations (Mardirosian 2010). Accordingly, donors and development banks most often step in to work with national governments to rebuild conflict-damaged infrastructure. Only in a few cases have private investors entered the water sector; one exception was in Kosovo, where a management contract was signed with a foreign operator in 2001 that led to successful reinvigoration of water services and capacity building of national staff that took over when the management contract ended (Marin, Mugabi, and Mariño 2010).

A United Nations Development Programme (UNDP) project implemented in Lebanon following the 2006 conflict with Israel demonstrates how international actors can integrate local government capacity-building efforts in a decentralized water services governance framework. During the early recovery process, local governments in Lebanon engaged in deliberative problem solving, planning, decision making, and the conclusion of service delivery contracts, work plans, and timetables in a learning-by-doing approach (Hamill and Ali-Ahmad 2007). One of the challenges identified in this approach was the need to balance urgent response mechanisms with a participatory approach that is slower but results in more-sustainable solutions. As far as possible, local municipal councils were engaged in local planning and decision making. The mayor of each municipality had to obtain the approval of the relevant council when making project decisions,

420 Water and post-conflict peacebuilding

and one council member was charged with day-to-day project administration. UNDP field officers undertook assessments of local stakeholder needs to feed into the project work plan, implemented by the council. With careful planning, speed and participation appear not to have been mutually exclusive. This UNDP project demonstrates the importance of building on existing institutional capacities, as the municipal governments were well positioned and had the underlying legal mandate for service provision, but lacked the financial and technical capacity to deliver on that mandate (Hamill and Ali-Ahmad 2007).

Coordination is critical among those investing in post-conflict infrastructure redevelopment. A World Bank evaluation of water and sanitation projects undertaken in Bosnia and Herzegovina during the first phase of reconstruction from 1991 to 1995 found that it was difficult to attain the projects' objectives because most of the funding agencies opted to work on their own, using different operational policies and procedures, causing confusion during project implementation and overlaps in donor activities (World Bank 2003). Similarly, Jean-François Pinera and Robert A. Reed highlight the high number of donors, humanitarians, members of civil society, and national governments participating in the rehabilitation of water and sanitation infrastructure in the urban areas of post-conflict Kabul, Afghanistan, and Monrovia, Liberia (Pinera and Reed 2014*). Large-scale rehabilitation projects (often coupled with institutional reforms to support government capacity building) by multilateral development banks, international humanitarian organizations, and donors were accompanied by smaller NGO-led projects to avoid communicable disease outbreaks in underserved populations where the network is not likely to reach (Pinera and Reed 2014*). In Kabul, for example, at least seven institutions had separate initiatives on large water works projects alone, resulting in duplications in investments and a need for improved coordination.

It is also critical that infrastructure investments do not inadvertently increase social inequities that may spark renewed tensions. Following the end of the first civil war in Sudan in 1972, the government in Khartoum began construction of the Jonglei Canal to drain the Sudd marshes of the White Nile and convey water from Bahr el Jebel in the south to north Sudan and Egypt for commercial farming. In failing to consider the negative impacts on the ecosystem or the adverse effects on the livelihoods of local communities, the plan sparked protest riots in southern Sudan (Salman 2014*).

In Zimbabwe, access to water services was leveraged to reinforce disparities among religious sects, ethnic groups, and the political opposition. Following independence in Zimbabwe in 1980, the new government sought to strengthen its political legitimacy by addressing inequalities in service provision. By 1988, as a result of the party's efforts to improve water services, 84 percent of the population had access to safe drinking water (Allouche 2014*). However, closer inspection of the government programs reveals that Matabeleland—a region that was a center of opposition to the government party during the conflict—was purposefully excluded from infrastructure and service improvements (Allouche 2014*). Intentional neglect of certain areas in order to disadvantage particular

Harnessing water management for more effective peacebuilding   421

political or ethnic groups may strengthen state control in the short term, but an imbalanced approach fosters grievances that can undermine state legitimacy and the peace process over the long term.

Rehabilitation of water services infrastructure plays a critical role in transitioning from immediate humanitarian assistance to sustainable development and peace consolidation, but faces many challenges related to the high levels of investment and capacity (technical and regulatory) that are necessary. Lessons from specific experiences highlight the need for careful coordination among donors, effective stakeholder engagement, conflict-sensitive approaches that avoid perpetuating inequities in allocation of services, avoidance of duplication or overlap, and support for meaningful livelihoods recovery and broader reconstruction.

WATER FOR LIVELIHOODS AND ECONOMIC RECOVERY

Armed conflicts tend to exacerbate poverty and destroy livelihoods (World Bank 2004). Countries that were immersed in violence between 1981 and 2005 are likely to have a poverty rate as much as 21 percent higher than a country that did not experience such violence (World Bank 2011). Armed conflict undermines economic growth by disrupting labor markets, obliterating infrastructure that provides access to markets (such as roads, bridges, shipping ports, and airports), and weakening the capacity of state institutions (Collier 1999). The World Bank estimates that the economic costs of lost production during civil war ranges from 2 to 3 percent of global domestic product over the course of a conflict (World Bank 2011).[8]

The durability of peacebuilding efforts thus depends substantially on the ability of governments to demonstrate the benefits of peace, especially so that former combatants and other conflict-affected groups, including returnees, will continue to have a stake in the political process (del Castillo 2008). One way to generate immediate material gains is to assist former combatants and others to build sustainable livelihoods and income-generating options (Doyle and Sambanis 2006). Providing access to water and other natural resources is often essential in supporting these activities. For post-conflict societies to reap the material gains of peacebuilding, water must invariably be mainstreamed into economic and development decision making.

Restoring trust among communities and in national institutions governing water is a core component of improving livelihoods. At war's end, there are high expectations that livelihoods will improve almost immediately, but the reality of fractured societies, weakened political institutions, and dilapidated infrastructure make it challenging to deliver these benefits quickly. As Jennifer McCarthy and Daanish Mustafa show in their analysis of experiences in Faryab Province,

---

[8] The World Bank notes that these numbers do not include the destruction or loss of assets (World Bank 2011). For further analysis on the economic costs of violence, see Skaperdas et al. (2009).

422   Water and post-conflict peacebuilding

Afghanistan, poor implementation of national water management policies at the local level weakened trust in government institutions despite the emphasis on participatory development under the National Solidarity Programme (McCarthy and Mustafa 2014*). McCarthy and Mustafa argue that this distrust is due to the failure of post-conflict interventions to incorporate village- and household-level experiences and knowledge regarding water management.

Post-conflict planning must therefore focus on restoring both agricultural and nonagricultural livelihoods, improving intersectoral coordination, relying on existing social capital and water management institutions where they exist, and assuring that all steps toward economic recovery are conflict sensitive. These are discussed in turn below.

Agricultural livelihoods

In the immediate aftermath of conflict, humanitarian organizations and other actors focus their water-related interventions on securing safe water and sanitation to prevent the spread of infectious disease and to bring back a sense of normality to those displaced by conflict. Over the longer term, providing access to safe and reliable sources of water is necessary for the restoration of agricultural livelihoods and food security. While a wide range of livelihoods depends on access to water, the agricultural sector is responsible worldwide for 70 percent of water withdrawals (FAO 2010). The remaining 30 percent of water withdrawal goes to the industrial (19 percent) and municipal (11 percent) sectors. In sub-Saharan Africa, the balance shifts even further to agriculture, with 87 percent of water withdrawal going to agriculture, 3 percent to industrial uses, and 10 percent to municipal purposes.

Despite these global trends, there is wide variation in water usage in post-conflict countries. In post-conflict Sierra Leone, for example, agriculture consumes the largest percentage of water (UNEP 2010); likewise, agriculture (mostly irrigated) uses 95 percent of water resources in Afghanistan (CPHD 2011). In contrast, in Burundi only 0.9 percent of land area is irrigated. Similarly, in Angola and Liberia only 0.6 and 0.3 percent of land is irrigated, respectively (AFDB 2012).

Because agriculture in many post-conflict countries employs the largest percentage of the population, many countries invest in the sector to create jobs and simultaneously improve food security at war's end, especially where the service and manufacturing sectors are absent. Even in mineral-rich countries, agriculture often provides the main source of employment; in Angola, for example, approximately 85 percent of the labor force is employed in agriculture (USAID 2012). In rural areas where most of the population was previously employed in agriculture, as in post-conflict northern Uganda, restoring agriculture during early recovery efforts helps to absorb demobilized excombatants and returning IDPs, ultimately providing a key link between humanitarian assistance and development (Birner, Cohen, and Ilukor 2011; USAID 2009). Moreover, water in countries

Harnessing water management for more effective peacebuilding   423

like Afghanistan is what makes agricultural land valuable; UNEP has found that irrigated land with a reliable water source is four to fourteen times more valuable than that of rain-fed land (UNEP 2013a). Thus investments in sustainable water management are critical in supporting reinvigoration of an agricultural economy.

In many post-conflict countries, food insecurity is compounded by the widespread destruction of irrigation infrastructure. Experience from Afghanistan, Liberia, and Timor-Leste (among other countries) shows that irrigation infrastructure can be both deliberately and incidentally harmed by conflict. As a result, it is essential in the aftermath of conflict to restore irrigation systems as a step toward rebuilding agriculture-based livelihoods. In the Afghan village of Bako Kham, in Kapisa Province, food security depends entirely upon restoring an irrigation system that had fallen into disrepair during the conflict (Burt and Keiru 2014*). Yet, in restoring the irrigation system, it was necessary to look at the linkages between irrigation and drinking-water systems because the canals used for irrigation would pass through residential areas and would also be used as the main source of drinking water. This points to the need for a multiuse perspective in post-conflict water management.

One of the main tasks facing governments and the international community when seeking to jump-start agriculture is to use irrigation both to ensure food security and to incentivize the return of refugees, displaced persons, and demobilized soldiers. Indeed, this was the case in post–World War II Japan; in order to enhance its food security to feed returning soldiers, the government made the construction of irrigation projects a central component of its early recovery efforts (Sugiura, Toguchi, and Funiciello 2014*). Likewise, following the communal violence that engulfed India and Pakistan at independence and partition, the government of India was faced with the resettlement and rehabilitation of millions of refugees who had entered eastern Punjab. With more than 80 percent of India's population dependent upon subsistence agriculture that was fed by the waters from monsoons, the government developed irrigation systems to increase food production and establish an agrarian economy in eastern Punjab as part of its recovery efforts (Zawahri 2014*).

A lack of reliable hydrological data and functioning hydrological infrastructure is a challenge facing international actors and governments in many post-conflict countries as they seek to restore the economy, including the agricultural sector, and build government capacity. Three decades of war and instability in Afghanistan weakened its capacity for hydrological data collection, and the thirty-year gap in hydrometerological data and equipment has made the restoration of the country's irrigation infrastructure even more difficult (Dehgan, Palmer-Moloney, and Mirzaee 2014*; IRIN 2006; IDMC 2005). Without baseline hydrological data, donors and governments often must make decisions without knowledge about how the quality and quantity of the water resources are changing across Afghanistan's water basins.

Lack of historical data on water quality, quantity, abstraction rates, and rights for abstraction is common across post-conflict countries. This points to the

424   Water and post-conflict peacebuilding

need for strong baseline assessment processes, as well as adaptive management approaches that focus on data gathering and regular monitoring and review of management approaches and resource status so interventions can be adjusted as new information becomes available. The post-conflict period can provide an important window of opportunity for instituting valuable programs for information collection and management and adaptive governance approaches that utilize this information as it becomes available to inform more effective planning and decision making.

The revival of the agricultural sector will be vital for reintegration of people displaced by armed conflict in the short term, and for stabilizing post-conflict societies over the long term by generating employment, providing sustainable livelihoods, and improving social welfare. To that end, donors have promoted agricultural development in Afghanistan as a bulwark against insurgency; the success of these activities is, however, heavily dependent upon securing sufficient water resources for water-intensive crops such as wheat (Dehgan, Palmer-Moloney, and Mirzaee 2014*). At times, segments of the population have quickly reverted to growing opium poppy instead of food crops because opium poppy requires less water and provides a higher financial return than staple crops (Goodhand 2005; Catarious and Russell 2012). In water-scarce Yemen, khat production, which consumes approximately 37 percent of all water for irrigation, has not only contributed to the country's growing water crisis—Yemen's capital, Sana'a, may be the first city in the world to run out of water—but has reduced the amount of agriculture devoted to food production, weakening food security (Lichtenthaeler 2010).[9]

Because agriculture is often the largest sector in a post-conflict country, restoration of irrigation systems is critical, as land values and productivity are tightly linked to access to water. But to do so, baseline hydrological data must be developed in order to maximize investment in irrigation systems.

Nonagricultural livelihoods

Water is also a critical resource for nonagricultural livelihoods. In post-conflict DRC, given the population's reliance on rain-fed agriculture and minimal irrigation, only 32 percent of water withdrawals are for agriculture while domestic water consumption accounts for 52 percent (16 percent is used by industry)

---

[9] In a similar manner, protracted drought in Syria from 2006 to 2010 amplified poor water management and agricultural policies that promoted self-sufficiency in food staples and water-intensive cash crops such as cotton. While there are a number of causes underlying the Syrian uprising, the social costs of the drought compounded by ineffective government policies contributed to societal grievances, as rural people were forced to migrate in large numbers to urban centers in the face of widespread crop failure, which in turn placed additional stress on overly stretched government resources (Dahi 2013; Mohtadi 2012).

(UNEP 2011). Water is important for other economic sectors in the DRC, including hydropower generation, fisheries, and navigation.

Pastoralists, especially in post-conflict and conflict-affected regions, are heavily dependent upon water for their livelihoods. In the Sahel, access to water points is vital for managing grazing lands and livestock (Thébaud, Vogt, and Vogt 2006). Shifting rainfall patterns and destruction of water points during conflict often force transhumant pastoralists to change migration patterns and use the same water sources as settled farming communities. In the Karimojong Cluster—an area that stretches from northeastern Uganda to southeastern South Sudan across northwestern Kenya and into Ethiopia—pastoralists have been forced to cover increasing distances to access water and grazing grounds they rely upon as drought and climate fluctuations drive resource scarcity (Lind 2014). Delineating access to water is also an important issue for pastoralists residing along the border between Sudan and South Sudan.

Water is also vital for supporting the livelihoods and ecosystem services for marshland families in Iraq, including wild and cultivated sources of food, livestock, fisheries, reeds for housing, transportation, and climate regulation. In the late 2000s, drought combined with upstream water diversions in Iraq and Turkey reduced the amount of water in the Iraqi marshlands; without water to support their livestock (primarily buffalos and cattle), families were forced to move away from the marshlands (IRIN 2009).

While conflict can arise between ethnic groups as they seek water for their livelihoods, those disputes also present an opportunity to reach water-sharing agreements that further peacebuilding efforts. In the state of South Kordofan, in Sudan, the British government and the international NGO PACT have developed an integrated approach that provides drinking water and water for livestock as a means to mitigate historical tensions between Misseriya herders and the Ngok Dinka; conflict between the two groups has often broken out during the dry season when cattle migrate over farmlands. Since the development of the new water sources and the social institutions to maintain them, a potentially difficult migration by the Misseriya was completed without incident in 2011. Unfortunately, these crossings were later stymied in 2012 by border closures and clashes (Craze 2013). Nevertheless, this is a positive example where water was successfully used, at least initially, as a platform for peacebuilding and cooperation between these two groups.

Water is thus critical for restarting and sustaining diverse nonagricultural livelihoods. While disputes can arise over water resources for livelihoods in post-conflict situations, those tensions can also provide opportunities for conflict-sensitive approaches that promote reconciliation and peacebuilding.

Intersectoral coordination

After Mozambique's civil war ended in 1992, peacebuilding was adversely affected by a combination of land and water shortages (Myers 1994). The absence

426 Water and post-conflict peacebuilding

of coordinated reforms in land tenure and water rights caused many refugees and displaced persons to return to places other than their areas of origin, mostly moving to peri-urban and urban areas, placing new pressures on the already taxed water infrastructure (Myers 1994).

One of the main lessons for reviving the broader economy is mainstreaming water into the development processes among the land, water, agricultural, and energy sectors. Land tenure issues are a primary example where the failure to account for water rights and management can impact the utility and equity of reform. Despite this, there is little evidence of effective coordination among ministries and donors focused on various sectoral programs related to the impacts on and need for access to water in post-conflict programming.

As with land rights (that often combine both customary and statutory governance mechanisms), water rights vary across a spectrum from customary practices to statutory rights or authorizations for use. In practice, all of these rights systems can be influenced by the power distortions and coping mechanisms that emerged during the conflict. Transitioning to more formal systems of water rights can be a long process and requires a careful understanding of the various systems for allocating rights that often exist simultaneously within a post-conflict country, and the ways in which those rights may be linked to other natural resource tenure systems, particularly landownership. In Kurdistan, land allocation and water access were viewed as integrally connected in the design of community-based initiatives to support resettlement of displaced families (Barwari 2013). Because land and water were considered together, communities were better able to utilize traditional means of dispute resolution for conflicts that might ensue over reconstruction programs and the return of refugees and IDPs.

The importance of intersectoral coordination can also be seen in the post-partition economic reconstruction in eastern Punjab. Here, the Indian government's understanding of the importance of multilevel and intersectoral coordination led not only to efforts to coordinate water and land access but also to work across levels of government to integrate refugees and rebuild livelihoods. The Indian government from the outset was cognizant of the need to provide Punjabi farmers with both defined property rights and access to water (Zawahri 2014*). Specifically, it allocated land to refugees to assist with resettlement and economic recovery at the same time it made irrigation water available from canals and wells; it also undertook extensive investments in hydrological infrastructure, including the multipurpose Bhakra-Nangal Dam along the Sutlej River. Intersectoral coordination resulted in both short-term and long-term welfare gains accruing to the population at large. The construction of the hydrological infrastructure and cleaning of existing irrigation systems provided much needed employment for the refugee population in the short term, helping to stabilize the post-conflict economy.

Water-related policies, programs and decision making must therefore be integrated into or, at the very least coordinated with, other relevant sectoral programs and policies—particularly land reform initiatives, agriculture, and

Harnessing water management for more effective peacebuilding   427

broader development planning—so as to facilitate post-conflict economic reconstruction.

Social capital and water management institutions

Donor and government interventions to improve livelihoods and foster economic recovery are more effective when they consider how best to build upon existing social capital and local water governance practices. Social capital was critical to water management in post–World War II Japan (Sugiura, Toguchi, and Funiciello 2014*). Much of the country's post-war success at revitalizing the agricultural security and attaining food security was due to the persistence of social structures in Japan throughout the war. Japanese government policy makers fostered communication between local villages and central authorities over water allocation and use—that is, they sought to build on existing institutions and capacities, and not try to establish new institutions that would be at odds with community institutions in the irrigation sector.

In urban and peri-urban areas of Angola, a community-based approach helped identify a balanced approach that built on existing social capital and increased capacity for improved water services (Cain 2014*). The focus in Angola was on the social capital and employment generated by the evolution of an informal water service sector during conflict. This informal sector was able to reach individuals not covered by the failing state infrastructure, but was also plagued with inconsistencies in availability and quality (Cain 2014*). Building community-based institutions was ultimately the key to linking the formal and informal sectors to enable increasing levels of oversight and regulation without destroying the social capital inherent in the relations formed by the informal market.

Informal institutions should not be viewed as either a challenge to the consolidation of the state or as a barrier to economic recovery, because they can support the reconstruction of the institutions vital for economic recovery (Allouche 2014*). Often, governments and international actors will give preference to the rebuilding of formal, state-based institutions for water services because the restoration of state institutions is seen as a way to enhance the legitimacy and authority of the government as part of a formal, bureaucratic concept of state formation (Allouche 2014*). Viewed through this lens, the state serves as the main provider of public goods, and the informal sector is seen as a challenge to the government's authority. Yet, as Jeremy Allouche argues, during conflict it is often the informal sector and small-scale providers that fill the void for water service provision, and harnessing the capacity of the informal sector after conflict may provide an alternative and viable means to complement more traditional state building and reach more of the population at a faster pace.

Water user associations (WUAs) are an institutional mechanism for groups of users (usually farmers) to come together to manage their shared water resources, often with the intended purpose of providing and maintaining irrigation schemes. WUAs are often more effective where social capital is present or where the

428   Water and post-conflict peacebuilding

associations are built upon local governance structures (Sauer et al. 2010). In a few post-conflict situations, donors such as the Belgian Development Agency in the DRC have succeeded in establishing WUAs in rural areas to manage small-piped water networks; that these WUAs were designed to function as small-scale enterprises have enabled them to monitor water usage and collect payments for water sold (UNEP 2011).

Ultimately, whether building new institutions or revitalizing existing mechanisms, it is important to recognize that post-conflict water management does not take place on a blank slate. Customary and informal mechanisms for management that may have emerged or been impacted by conflict can provide significant sources of social capital for building effective water management regimes. It is therefore critical for those involved in peacebuilding efforts to understand the existing institutional (and practical) water management landscape and the ways it has been shaped by conflict.

Conflict-sensitive economic recovery

Investment in infrastructure and governance to facilitate economic recovery can—if not undertaken appropriately—exacerbate inequities in access to natural resources and impact communities and the environment quite severely, undermining both economic recovery and reconciliation. Many conflicts have a long history of poor governance and government corruption, including rent-seeking behaviors related to public services (Gaigals and Leonhardt 2001). One way to ensure that programs to remediate water infrastructure and service provision are conflict-sensitive is to ensure that they meaningfully involve local stakeholders in a thorough assessment of the local context to understand the political economy of the conflict and its impacts on resource-related interventions. It is particularly important to recognize the relationship between national-level investments—for example, in reinvigorating agriculture—and the various local contexts in which they will be implemented.

Job creation at the local level is not only essential for economic recovery in post-conflict societies, but also an important indicator of policies that successfully take into account the local context. Because state capacity to manage water and build water infrastructure was limited in rural Afghanistan, the NGO Tearfund played an important role in helping to build the local capacity to manage water in Bako Kham village, in Kapisa Province, by stimulating demand for a household water treatment system, a bio-sand filter, that could be produced by local artisans. Through working with the government, the community development council, and communities, Tearfund contributed to local livelihoods by training local artisans to produce the filters and by holding training sessions on how to operate and maintain the filters (Burt and Keiru 2014*). As a result of their efforts, several trained technicians opened bio-sand filter shops in Bako Kham village.

Examining experiences in South Sudan, Sam Huston points to two principles —equity and consensus building at the local level—that can foster conflict-sensitive

Harnessing water management for more effective peacebuilding   **429**

approaches in the water sector (Huston 2014*). While certain regions or populations may have greater needs within the water sector at conflict's end, experience in South Sudan shows that in the absence of data about where to target financial and technical resources, government decisions to equitably distribute the benefits from natural resources across its ten states has served to prevent and mitigate conflict within the allocation process. Consensus building helps to ensure that local authorities and communities have a voice in decisions to allocate natural resources and their benefits, helping to mitigate the likelihood for conflict. Huston describes how local authorities, traditional leaders, peace committees, and community organizations in Southern Sudan collectively decided where to situate new water points. An emphasis on transparency in decision making further strengthened communities' ownership over the process and contributed to the sustainability and management of these water points.

If post-conflict investment is not sensitive to inequities in access to water resources, there is a danger of relapsing into conflict. It is therefore important to assure equity and consensus at the local level, where disputes over access are most likely to arise.

TRANSBOUNDARY COOPERATION

Cooperative transboundary water management practices can play a critical role in peacebuilding between countries and at the regional level. Of the fifty-five countries affected by major conflict during or since 1990, fifty-one share at least one basin with one or more nations.[10] This hydrological interdependence has the potential to fuel competition and spark tensions between riparian states, but it also offers a unique set of opportunities to unite them. Indeed, research has shown that from 1948 to 1999, of 1,831 state-to-state water interactions in a transboundary basin, approximately two-thirds of the events were cooperative and none led to formal war (Wolf, Yoffe, and Giordano 2003). Violent conflict over water is more common at the subnational level than among countries (Wolf 2007).

The institutions created to enable countries to jointly manage shared waters have proven resilient, even during periods of acute conflict. The Mekong Committee, for example, was founded in 1957 and remained active through the Viet Nam War and internal upheavals in Cambodia and Laos (Wolf 2007; Nakayama 2011). Likewise, the Indus River Commission has endured two wars between India and Pakistan (Wolf 2007; Zawahri 2014*). This indicates that the complex interdependencies among countries created by sharing international waters can also provide powerful incentives for collective action and cooperation (Kramer 2008). These incentives can be harnessed to rebuild trust and confidence among former adversaries following interstate conflict and facilitate reconciliation and peacebuilding.

---

[10]   See table 1 on page 3 of this book for a listing of these fifty-five countries.

430   Water and post-conflict peacebuilding

Water in negotiated agreements

For centuries, states have successfully managed to negotiate agreements over shared water resources; the International Freshwater Treaties Database includes more than 400 international freshwater agreements from 1820 to 2007. Today, more peace agreements are beginning to recognize the importance of including natural resources, such as water, within the treaty framework. Whereas between 1989 and 2004 natural resources were mentioned in approximately half of all agreements, from 2005 to 2010 natural resource provisions were included in all major peace agreements (Bruch et al. 2014). Table 1 lists countries affected by major conflict that have explicitly addressed water in peace agreements from 1990 through 2013.

How water is addressed in peace agreements has a significant impact on the overall peacebuilding process. The 2006 Abuja Agreement between the government of Sudan and Darfur insurgents, for example, recognized certain rights of all Sudanese citizens, including a right to safe drinking water. Peace agreements for ten other major conflicts also contain provisions explicitly addressing water resources. These include provisions addressing water supplies for former combatants, returning refugees, and IDPs; provisions on international cooperation over water resources; provisions on drinking water and navigation; and provisions covering water resource management and governance in general.[11]

When water is explicitly addressed in a peace agreement, especially where water was a contributing source of tension between the involved countries, the explicit nature of the commitment to jointly address water-related issues can facilitate the peacebuilding process. A primary example is the 1994 peace treaty between Israel and Jordan. Conflict over water had festered between the two countries since the failure of the Johnston mission in the 1950s to devise a water-sharing plan for the Jordan River Basin. Indeed, water was so contentious that it ended up being the last issue resolved, allowing for the successful conclusion of the 1994 treaty (Haddadin 2014*). Article 6, annex II of the treaty outlines the details of a water-sharing agreement; commits the parties to joint planning, development, and monitoring; requires the countries to notify each other of any proposed project that could modify the flow of their shared waters; and establishes the Joint Water Commission to undertake and manage the commitments in the treaty.[12] While somewhat skeletal in comparison to more comprehensive basin-level

---

[11]   In addition to the peace agreements noted in table 1, some other peace agreements—including those between Georgia and Russia; Indonesia and the Free Aceh Movement; Indonesia and Timor-Leste; Iraq and U.S.-led coalition forces; and the Philippines and Muslim Mindanao—refer broadly to natural resources and the environment, implicitly addressing water resources. Peace agreements between Bangladesh and United People's Party of the Chittagong Hill Tracts and between Sri Lanka and the Liberation Tigers of Tamil Eelam address fisheries.

[12]   Treaty of Peace between the Hashemite Kingdom of Jordan and the State of Israel, October 26, 1994.

Table 1. Objectives of water provisions in peace agreements, 1990–2013

Conflict and date of agreement[†]	DDR*	Basic services	Infrastructure and navigation	Resettlement	Livelihoods	Governance	Cooperation
Israel/occupied Palestinian territories (1993)			Desalination, infrastructure development			Water resource management	Water rights; equitable utilization
Rwanda (1993)	Water for troop assembly points			Water at resettlement sites			
Croatia/Serbia (1996)			Navigation				International river traffic
Guatemala (1996)		Drinking water	Water infrastructure			Management, water rights	
Sierra Leone (1996)		Drinking water					
United Kingdom/ Northern Ireland (1998)							Inland waterways; water quality
Burundi (2000)						Water management	
Sudan/Southern Sudan (2005)	Water supply for excombatants		Navigation			Federal-state concurrent competencies	Nile Commission, transboundary dispute resolution
Sudan/Darfur (2006)	Water supply for excombatants	Drinking water, water services	Development of water resources	Access to water en route to and at resettlement sites; return of historic water rights	Access to water resources for agriculture and herds	Management, allocation, water rights	
Democratic Republic of the Congo (2009)				Water in return areas			
Myanmar (2012)				Water for resettlement			

Source: Compiled by the Environmental Law Institute.

Notes: This table includes peace agreements for countries affected by major conflict between 1990 and 2013, with *major conflict* defined as a conflict resulting in more than 1,000 battle deaths (Bruch et al. 2014).

[†]The date provided is the date of the agreement that addressed water; in protracted conflicts, there often are multiple peace agreements.

*DDR: disarmament, demobilization, and reintegration of excombatants.

432 Water and post-conflict peacebuilding

treaties (not peace treaties), the inclusion of these water-related provisions in the peace treaty has provided a legal and institutional basis for sustaining cooperative interactions between Israel and Jordan. Even as political tensions have increased between Israel and Jordan, the countries have continued to abide by the spirit of the water agreement.

The inclusion of provisions on water management in a peace agreement can also serve as a preliminary confidence-building measure (Conca and Dabelko 2002). Following the conflict between Israel and the Palestinian Authority, the inclusion of water issues in the Oslo Accords offered a mechanism for technical cooperation that enabled the parties to begin to work together to build confidence before more controversial issues were addressed. Mara Tignino argues that the states must redress the "deliberate destruction of water installations, discriminatory practices, [and] the denial of access to drinking-water aid" through both institutional and pecuniary means if there is to be real reconciliation and sustained peacebuilding (Tignino 2014, 398*). Recognizing this kind of discrimination at the onset of post-conflict peacebuilding can provide accountability for past injustices and help initiate appropriate trust-building measures (Tignino 2014*; Weinthal and Marei 2002). Thus the Permanent Status Agreement between Israel and Palestine included provisions on Palestinian water rights, as well as an agreement that additional water must be developed in order to meet the needs of "various uses" in the two countries. These provisions provided a foundation upon which to deal with the inequitable use of water resources during the Israeli occupation of the West Bank and Gaza that had restricted Palestinian agriculture. Yet, because the Palestinians were not allowed to implement water infrastructure projects as anticipated, the inequalities in water access became entrenched. Furthermore, restrictions on Palestinian access to water resources have remained in place despite the Oslo Accords. Consequently, the initial peace benefits of including water in the peace process have been undermined over time as the concrete steps to remedy water-related grievances have not been taken (Selby 2013).

When South Sudan became an independent nation in 2011, waters that were previously domestic became transboundary. The country also became the newest member of the Nile Basin Initiative, and appears poised to sign the Cooperative Framework Agreement of the Nile Basin countries, which would replace colonial-era treaties that allocated the basin's water to Egypt and Sudan. The experience of then-Southern Sudan in negotiating when and how to address water as part of the peace process is informative. In concluding the 2005 Comprehensive Peace Agreement (CPA) with Sudan, Southern Sudan ceded all authority for both broader regional water cooperation in the Nile Basin and economic development to the north (Salman 2014*). This was especially remarkable given the central role of natural resource management (particularly oil and gas) laid out in the Wealth Sharing Agreement under the CPA. However, by placing management of the Nile waters under the exclusive jurisdiction of the Sudanese national government, at least for the period 2005–2011, the CPA process avoided getting mired in Nile politics. Thus, while South Sudan did claim status as a new Nile riparian post-independence, the CPA's management structure maintained regional stability in the Nile Basin prior to the independence of South Sudan. Over the longer term, conflicts over the management and use of the tributaries of the Nile that flow through South Sudan could precipitate a new set of disputes between Sudan and South Sudan (Salman 2014*).

Treatment of water issues in peace agreements can significantly affect the level of cooperation between governments. Collaboration over water can build confidence between governments that otherwise have little formal communication or which have experienced a high degree of tension. Such water treaties thus offer a concrete mechanism for not only institutionalizing interactions among countries previously in conflict, but also for initiating steps toward joint management of a shared resource.

Third-party intervention and technical cooperation

Addressing transboundary water management in post-conflict peacebuilding often hinges on the involvement of third parties that can help to promote conflict resolution and foster reconciliation among state and nonstate actors. Third-party facilitators, which may include local stakeholders, international NGOs, international organizations, or other national governments, play an important role throughout the conflict cycle—that is, from bringing governments to the table to negotiate a water agreement, to providing incentives for keeping parties at the table, to assisting with the implementation of an agreement and providing support for dispute resolution (Nakayama 1997; Weinthal 2000, 2002; Zawahri 2009).

The Indus River and Jordan River experiences illuminate the role of third-party support for conflict resolution and reconciliation in post-conflict peacebuilding. Partition created fundamental economic and political divisions between India and Pakistan. In recognition of the fact that a third party would be necessary to facilitate discussion over shared waters, the World Bank stepped in to facilitate the negotiation of the 1960 Indus Waters Treaty between the two countries. The Bank helped to define the agenda, used incentives and pressure to mediate disputes (for example, through the granting or threatening to withhold financial assistance), and coordinated the donor community in underwriting the construction of hydrological infrastructure to facilitate the treaty's implementation (Zawahri 2009, 2014*).

In the Jordan Basin, civil society has facilitated cooperation and peacebuilding. Through sustained engagement at the grassroots level in environmental education and public awareness, Friends of the Earth Middle East (FoEME) has been instrumental in pushing Israel and Jordan to commit to restoring the water quality of the Lower Jordan River (Mehyar et al. 2014*). As a result of these efforts, the Israeli Water Authority announced in May 2013 that it would begin for the first time to pump water regularly from the Sea of Galilee into the Lower Jordan River in order to begin to rehabilitate the river (Rinat 2013).

434 Water and post-conflict peacebuilding

Cooperation over the Sava River Basin in the period following the breakup of Yugoslavia was greatly facilitated by the sustained intervention of the European Union (EU) (Čolakhodžić et al. 2014*). Confronting the transformation of a domestic river system into an international one, in 2001 the EU designated the Sava River Basin as one of thirteen European pilot projects to implement the EU Water Framework Directive, which supported the negotiation and conclusion of the international Framework Agreement on the Sava River Basin, a protocol on navigation, and the establishment of the International Sava River Basin Commission in 2006.

Impartial third parties can also mitigate asymmetries in information and power among riparian states—imbalances that can lead to misunderstanding and perpetuate conflict. This is particularly true in cases where a party emerging from conflict is faced with negotiating and implementing a water agreement with one or several other parties that have greater scientific knowledge about the water basin and possess stronger institutional capacity. During the Oslo Accords negotiations between the Israelis and Palestinians, for example, there was an acute asymmetry of power caused by the fact that the Israeli military administration had controlled all data on the West Bank aquifers since 1967. Accordingly, bilateral donors, including U.S. Agency for International Development (USAID) and the Norwegian Ministry of Foreign Affairs, focused on the creation of databases that would both provide greater information to the newly created Palestinian Water Authority and support more effective and balanced cooperation between the parties (Kramer 2008; Claussen et al. 2004).

Problems can arise when donors or other international organizations promote regional projects without addressing the priorities of each country. This was the case with the program sponsored by the Centre for Environmental Studies and Resource Management to build a regional computerized library system, called Waternet, that would have enabled Israel, the Palestinian Authority, and Jordan to share information (Claussen et al. 2004). Because the parties all sought to gain different benefits from the Waternet program, each country pursued their own local data project rather than integrating their databases into a regional one, ultimately fragmenting cooperative efforts. Israel, for instance, was able to concentrate previously unpublished reports into one network. Jordan sought to make water information electronically available to local water users. In contrast, the Palestinian Authority sought access to Israeli water data, but the unpredictable political climate impeded any chance of the program's implementation.

When managed appropriately, donor efforts to address weak and missing hydrological data can build domestic institutional capacity to participate in regional water management. Following the collapse of the Taliban regime in Afghanistan in 2001, there was almost no reliable, up-to-date hydrological data for the country. In fact, a World Bank baseline study of the Amu Darya Basin had to rely upon river flow data from before the Soviet invasion in 1979 (Ahmad and Wasiq 2004). Matthew King and Benjamin Sturtewagen argue that the absence of technical knowledge and limited hydrometeorological data greatly hampered

Harnessing water management for more effective peacebuilding **435**

Afghanistan's ability to pursue regional cooperation (King and Sturtewagen 2010). UNEP sought to fill this void in the Sistan Basin wetlands (shared by Afghanistan and Iran) by commissioning a survey of satellite images of environmental change in the basin from 1976 to 2005 (UNEP 2006).

Helping to build up institutional capacity and technical knowledge may not be sufficient to foster broader regional cooperation in the absence of strong negotiating capacity. Thus, despite UNEP's efforts to broker a dialogue over the Sistan Basin, negotiations ultimately came to a standstill in 2007 because Afghanistan was wary of moving forward too quickly with any regional agreement for fear that they lacked the technical and negotiating capacity to make an optimal deal.

Donors have played a role in supporting technical cooperation around water in the South Caucasus (Vardanyan and Volk 2014*). There, USAID supported a regional program to promote capacity building for integrated water resource management in the Kura-Araks Basin, which was meant to provide a foundation for broader regional cooperation during a protracted conflict. USAID assisted with the collection and sharing of data on water quality and quantity in the South Caucasus as a first step toward restoring relations between decision makers and civil society. While the participation in data sharing promoted better understanding of the causes and severity of water issues and highlighted the need for regional cooperation, the political tensions in the region have forestalled more comprehensive cooperative efforts.

The role of third parties as mediators in regional post-conflict reconciliation is thus a key lesson from a number of transboundary basins. In addition to providing a neutral forum for negotiations, third parties (particularly donors) can provide important resources to mitigate power differentials that arise when riparians have uneven access to data and technical information. Such technical cooperation can be an important first step in regional cooperation over shared water resources, although much still hinges on the broader political climate.

Basin treaties and institutions

As with peace agreements, agreements on shared waters can also provide an important legal mechanism for confidence building and conflict resolution among riparian states. For example, the inclusion of information sharing and joint monitoring can provide the transparency and accountability to shore up confidence and build trust between countries (Hamner and Wolf 1998; Conca, Wu, and Mei 2006). Neda A. Zawahri argues that the clear rules pertaining to conflict resolution and monitoring set forth in the Indus Waters Treaty were critical in enabling India and Pakistan to resolve disputes over water despite the fact that the two countries continue to be enmeshed in broader political disputes (Zawahri 2014*). Undoubtedly, the fact that the treaty was also able to divide the six rivers shared between India and Pakistan (the Indus River and the two westernmost tributaries to Pakistan and the three easternmost tributaries to India) and ultimately break down the physical interdependence of the water system was also important.

436   Water and post-conflict peacebuilding

Treaties that include provisions for the establishment of a joint water management institution are more apt to build confidence and trust, resolve conflicts, and hence promote cooperation and peacebuilding over the long term (Wolf et al. 2005). Most international freshwater treaties establish a permanent basin organization to oversee implementation and enforcement of the treaty's provisions.[13] Permanent basin organizations help to institutionalize cooperation and build trust among the parties by convening regular meetings among representatives of the riparian countries and, more and more frequently, facilitating joint data collection and monitoring and even joint development and resource protection projects. They also provide a venue for dispute resolution. Mechanisms for jointly monitoring and verifying members' activities (for example, through field visits or submission of annual reports) help to rein in opportunities for noncompliance and build confidence through increased accountability (Zawahri 2009). Regular meetings can also build trust by providing direct communication between representatives of the basin governments through the exchange of hydrological and meteorological data, which over time can help to build a community of likeminded experts concerned with management of the water system.

Both the Indus Waters Treaty and the Jordan-Israel peace treaty established institutional interdependence by committing the water managers to meet regularly to ensure its implementation. Throughout the second half of the twentieth century, the existence of the Permanent Indus Commission mitigated the possibility that water might be a significant source of tension, despite decades of otherwise mounting political tension between the two countries, and in many ways has provided a lifeline for maintaining some measure of communication between the states (Zawahri 2014*). In contrast, the lack of provisions regarding water resources, including dispute resolution over shared waters, in the Dayton Peace Agreement has negatively affected the post-conflict peacebuilding process in Bosnia and Herzegovina. The Dayton Peace Agreement focused on a division of authority over natural resources based on ethnic lines, creating three separate political entities that have overlapping control over shared water resources. It has proven difficult for the jurisdictions to establish appropriate legal mechanisms to foster the necessary cooperation for effective management (Bogdanovic 2014*).

Basin treaties and institutions are thus important mechanisms for fostering regional cooperation and trust among states sharing water resources. Much hinges, however, on the inclusion of effective provisions within the relevant treaty and the ongoing commitment to implementation on the part of the countries. This, in turn, depends heavily on the competence and capacities of the basin institution, which often requires significant and long-term technical support.

---

[13] Ken Conca, Fengshi Wu, and Ciqi Mei found that this was indeed the case in forty-five out of sixty-two (73 percent) international river treaties concluded from 1980 until 2000 (Conca, Wu, and Mei 2006).

Regional stability and post-conflict water management at the national level

Post-conflict reconstruction and development of water resources at the national level has the potential to undermine regional stability and peacebuilding if undertaken unilaterally and without consideration for transboundary consequences. Afghanistan's plans for developing and upgrading water infrastructure in each of its major river basins are crucial to the country's social and economic development (Deghan, Palmer-Moloney, and Mirzaee 2014*). However, these actions will also affect transboundary water flows and the ability of Iran in the Helmand Basin and the Central Asian states in the Amu Darya Basin to address their own increasingly pressing water needs. Afghanistan claimed that it was unable to enter into bilateral negotiations with Iran, for example, because it lacks the expertise, capacity, and data necessary to negotiate. Failure to engage, however, may be pushing some neighboring countries, such as Iran, to intentionally undermine water development projects in Afghanistan and even contribute to the rationale for Iran's support for factions of the Taliban in western Afghanistan (Deghan, Palmer-Moloney, and Mirzaee 2014*).

Afghanistan's economic development must be understood within its regional context if it is to avoid backlash from neighboring countries (Dehgan, Palmer-Moloney, and Mirzaee 2014*; Palmer-Moloney 2014*). Donors in the water sector must look beyond the local and national levels and incorporate regional water strategies into policy development and aid programming that promote joint data collection and monitoring and establish some sort of institutional mechanism for coordination, such as a basin organization. Such an organization could initially be guided by a neutral third party to provide a baseline assessment of the Helmand Basin and make recommendations for bilateral management initiatives. Likewise, any decisions undertaken by South Sudan to develop the White Nile will have implications for economic development downstream in Sudan and Egypt (Salman 2014*). South Sudan's entry into the Nile Basin Initiative signals its willingness to engage on the basis of this regional interdependence (*Sudan Tribune* 2013).

While the establishment of basin organization and the mandating of data sharing in treaties can facilitate increased levels of cooperation, these alone are not sufficient to promote reconciliation and sustain peacebuilding in post-conflict basins. Often overlooked is the importance of how critical the dissemination of data is for restoring trust in government agencies and for coordination among donors and policy makers to ensure implementation of projects (Palmer-Moloney 2014*). It is common for donors to undertake project assessments and make them publicly available; however, many other agencies, including the United Nations, militaries, and NGOs, should share and disseminate unclassified data. This would also allow for better coordination among governments, donors, militaries, and local communities in integrated water resource management.

If undertaken without consideration of its regional impact, national water policies can endanger regional stability. Domestic decision making must be

438   Water and post-conflict peacebuilding

based on engagement in bilateral negotiations and cooperation with neighboring governments when policies have a transboundary effect. Joint data collection and monitoring are two functions on which governments can collaborate.

CROSSCUTTING ISSUES

Many of the lessons related to post-conflict interventions in the water sector fall within the main thematic areas in post-conflict peacebuilding: humanitarian interventions, livelihoods, economic recovery, and transboundary cooperation. Additional lessons derived from the chapters in this book and the broader experiences of those implementing post-conflict water management cut across the timeline and sector-specific issues of post-conflict recovery and apply to diverse aspects of water interventions. Four crosscutting issues are particularly important to the effectiveness of water management in peacebuilding: rebuilding water governance regimes, facilitating stakeholder and public engagement, mainstreaming gender considerations, and sustaining donor commitment.

Rebuilding water governance

Experiences in post-conflict peacebuilding and water management from around the world—including those analyzed in this book—stress the integral role of water resources in peacebuilding. Indeed, of the fifty-five countries affected by major conflict between 1990 and 2013, thirty addressed water in their post-conflict constitutions (see table 2).

Governments and other institutions that are charged with post-conflict peacebuilding are faced with multiple, often competing, priorities with limited resources and time to address them. Sustaining access to water for livelihoods, economic growth, and development over time requires a governance framework that can balance competing demands for an increasingly scarce resource, prevent and manage pollution and other adverse impacts, regulate service provision, and maintain infrastructure. Additionally, there are tensions between technical efforts that have concrete outcomes on an immediate or short-term basis and the need to allocate resources to institutional and governance capacity building that can sustain interventions over the long run. These tensions present difficult questions. At what points along the post-conflict continuum must water policies, laws, and institutions be built to ensure sustainability and prevent inequitable and unaccountable decision making? What levels of governance are most effective at these various points? When will failure to invest in governance frameworks—policies, laws, and institutions—undermine the sustainability of post-conflict investments?

Importance of context

The history of every post-conflict country includes coping mechanisms used by different factions and the civilian population during the conflict to obtain access

Table 2. Countries affected by major conflict between 1990 and 2013 that adopted constitutional provisions related to water

Country	Constitution year (amended)	Legislative power	Public domain/ interest	State responsibility/ management	Local authority or federalism	Transboundary waters	Development	Protection of water resources	Other
Algeria	1996	✓							
Angola	2010		✓		✓				
Chad	1995 (2005)	✓	✓						
Congo, Republic of (Brazzaville)	2001	✓							
Democratic Republic of the Congo	2005				✓				Criminal law, water pollution
Eritrea	1997			✓	✓				Sustainability, future generations
Ethiopia	1994					✓			
Guatemala	1985 (1993)	✓	✓	✓				✓	Water pollution
Guinea-Bissau	1984 (1996)	✓	✓						
India	1949 (2007)	✓					✓	✓	Duties
Indonesia	1945 (2002)		✓	✓					
Iraq	2005				✓	✓			
Kosovo	2010							✓	
Laos	1991 (2003)				✓			✓	Duties
Mozambique	2004		✓						
Myanmar	2008	✓	✓	✓	✓		✓		
Nepal	2007 (2010)		✓	✓					
Pakistan	1973 (2004)				✓				
Peru	1993	✓		✓					

Table 2. (*Cont'd*)

Country	Constitution year (amended)	Legislative power	Public domain/ interest	State responsibility/ management	Local authority or federalism	Transboundary waters	Development	Protection of water resources	Other
Philippines	1946 (2011)	✓	✓	✓			✓		Rights
Russia	1993	✓	✓	✓					
Serbia	2006	✓	✓		✓				
Somalia	2012			✓					Rights
South Sudan	2011	✓		✓	✓	✓			
Sri Lanka	1978 (2010)				✓		✓		Floods
Sudan	2005	✓			✓	✓			
Tajikistan	1994 (2003)		✓	✓					
Thailand	2007		✓	✓				✓	Sustainability
Turkey	1982 (2010)		✓						
Uganda	1995 (2005)		✓	✓	✓				

Source: Compiled by the Environmental Law Institute.

Notes: This table includes constitutional provisions on water for countries affected by major conflict between 1990 and 2013, with major conflict being a conflict resulting in more than 1,000 battle deaths (Bruch et al. 2014). The constitutions of Iran (1979, amended 1989) and Nicaragua (1986)—whose conflicts extended into the period of analysis—include multiple provisions related to water.

Many constitutions also refer to fisheries, including those of Chad, Republic of Congo, India, Myanmar, Philippines, Serbia, and Sri Lanka.

Legislative power: Constitution gives a mandate to regulate water resources.

Public domain/interest: Constitution states that water resources are in the public domain, are public property, or to be managed in the public interest, giving an implicit constitutional mandate to the state to regulate and manage water resources.

State responsibility/management: Constitution provides for broad state responsibility over water resources.

Local authority or federalism: Constitution provides that local authorities or provinces (in nonfederal states) have responsibilities related to water resources; in federal states, constitution provides explicit responsibilities of subnational units in water management.

Transboundary waters: Constitution allocates responsibility for transboundary waters.

Development: Constitution notes importance of water for development or provides a mandate for using water for development.

Protection of water resources: Constitution provides for the protection of water resources.

to and control water. Understanding the role that water may have played during the conflict is an important starting point in strengthening its contribution to peacebuilding. This is a complicated picture, however, with multiple levels of formal and customary water governance that can be difficult for peacebuilders to discern without involvement of diverse stakeholders in program planning and implementation.

More broadly, conflict-sensitive and participatory approaches must be employed to avoid undermining societal confidence in the process and inadvertently creating new drivers of conflict. As noted above, water scarcity has played a role in perpetuating local conflict among ethnic groups and subgroups in South Sudan (Huston 2014*). Such scarcity is a critical factor in structuring decision making that focuses on issues of equity and consensus building at the local level. Recognizing these underlying tensions and involving relevant stakeholders—particularly local government and community leaders—in decisions on water management is critical for preventing new conflicts over access to water in South Sudan and elsewhere.

Post-conflict water governance regimes are characterized by complexity. In Afghanistan, local water governance has traditionally been undertaken by community-based management structures with elected or, more often, selected water masters (called *mirabs*), who oversee water infrastructure construction and maintenance, enforcement of local norms, and conflict resolution (McCarthy and Mustafa 2014*). Community-level water rights and allocation regimes are based primarily on landownership and levels of contribution to water infrastructure maintenance, and the state's role has been largely absent at the local level. During the conflict, however, warlords often replaced local mirabs and violated customary water agreements to divert resources for their benefit, including poppy production. McCarthy and Mustafa suggest that a lack of thorough understanding of local conditions, particularly of power structures and contemporary social dynamics as influenced by the conflict, appear to be hindering effective progress of water interventions in some Afghan communities. More broadly, while customary water management practices and traditional leadership can provide an important foundation for fashioning locally appropriate water governance responses, it is also important to recognize that traditional structures are not necessarily inclusive and can often be subject to elite capture.

Governance and political economy assessment tools geared toward the water sector can support the development of the broad and deep understanding necessary to determine whether to build on existing governance structures or use the window of opportunity of post-conflict rebuilding to reassess critical issues of equity, representation, and capacity building. For example, strategic environmental assessment (SEA), which can be applied at the sectoral level, is a tool increasingly being used to support development decision making. An SEA analyzes the potential environmental and social consequences of proposed policies, plans, and programs. David Jensen has noted that although a lack of robust regulatory regimes, low levels of baseline information, and insufficient technical capacity

442   Water and post-conflict peacebuilding

can provide substantial obstacles to carrying out an SEA, the assessments have proven effective at the sectoral level, particularly in the early phases of post-conflict reconstruction (Jensen 2012). Jensen points to the importance of leveraging the SEA process to identify peacebuilding opportunities from natural resources, in addition to increasing aid effectiveness between related donor projects. An SEA can also provide an opportunity to engage with diverse stakeholders—from identifying potential impacts to implementing mitigation measures.

Role of local governance

Over the past decades, many countries have attempted to decentralize water resource management authority and strengthen local government capacity to undertake these responsibilities. Decentralization recognizes that water management and service delivery is inherently a local process that requires the participation of users and other stakeholders. Bringing water governance to a local level can facilitate such participation and enable more effective and responsive resource management.

Moreover, strong local government and inclusive local governance are important pieces of the peacebuilding process. Local governments are key actors in bringing formal state institutions into direct contact with citizens and in giving them a voice in decision making. Water management provides an important platform for rebuilding community trust in the local administration, as well as reconnecting local governments to the national level. Where the state lacks the capacity to govern water or other natural resources throughout a country, local governance mechanisms can provide important peace dividends. Tailored approaches at the local level can also more readily address the often vast differences between urban and rural needs and challenges (Pinera and Reed 2014*). Active participation of stakeholders and cooperative planning are key aspects of such approaches.

Burt and Keiru demonstrate the importance of building local water governance in rural areas to bridge the gaps at the state level in post-conflict Afghanistan, the DRC, and Liberia. Because institution building at the national level can take years, Tearfund invested in building community-based management institutions that focused on inclusivity and local peacebuilding while successfully expanding water and sanitation services to multiple rural communities (Burt and Keiru 2014*).

Linking local water governance with national processes is important to ensure that local initiatives contribute to the national objectives for integrated water resource management and support a unified and coordinated approach to nation building in post-conflict situations (Burt and Keiru 2014*). Providing the appropriate linkages between local and national governance building can also prevent overreliance of communities on NGOs and help develop an understanding of the role of the government in ensuring the right to basic services. In Afghanistan, the DRC, and Liberia, these linkages were established via institutions that purposefully engaged civil society, communities, and the central government in local water management and oversight.

Harnessing water management for more effective peacebuilding 443

While important, decentralization is not necessarily a panacea for effective post-conflict service provision. Decentralization of responsibilities without the necessary resources and capacity building of local institutions to carry out those responsibilities (that is, an unfunded mandate) can further undermine governmental legitimacy in the eyes of the public. It can also stunt the rebuilding of necessary linkages between the state and society if management authority is devolved to local communities before the lines of responsibility are delineated between the central and local authorities. Moreover, effective integration of post-conflict assistance into the local institutional landscape can be challenging. As noted above, local institutions rarely escape conflict unscathed, and it can be difficult for outside organizations to penetrate the complexities of such impacts and the ways in which they affect inclusiveness, accountability, and equity.

Adaptive governance for a rapidly changing context

Water governance in the wake of conflict is characterized by complex and uncertain conditions. Multiple levels of formal and informal governance often coexist and continue to evolve as peacebuilding and reconstruction efforts foster new institutions, activities, and policies. Data on which to make informed decisions may be limited or missing altogether. Dealing with uncertainty and change of this kind requires governance tools that are flexible enough to incorporate data as they become available and to adapt to new circumstances as they arise.

That complexity is illustrated by the attempts to improve access to water in South Sudan. Since southern Sudan and Sudan signed the Comprehensive Peace Agreement in 2005, large numbers of South Sudanese have returned from areas in the north and neighboring countries (UNEP 2007). Between 2007 and 2012, over 1.8 million people returned to South Sudan, with 155,000 reaching their final destination in 2012 (International Office of Migration 2012). As Huston underscores, meeting the expectations of these returnees for basic water services is an "overwhelming task," given the destroyed or dilapidated infrastructure, lack of hydrological data to develop and manage the resource sustainably, and weak institutional capacity in South Sudan for water governance (Huston 2014*, 85).

The ability to adapt to changing circumstances is particularly relevant in the water sector, as water resources are subject to seasonal, annual, and decadal variability. Demands on water will continue to evolve with changes in development levels, population growth, and urbanization, among other pressures. Climate variability and change is already influencing various aspects of the hydrological cycle, including the amount and timing of precipitation, presenting increased uncertainty and the need for adaptive approaches to water governance. Management constraints in post-conflict situations further contribute to uncertainty, as institutions, policies, and laws and the capacities to implement and enforce them evolve over time.

In Afghanistan, Angola, the DRC, and Liberia, interim solutions tailored to local needs have achieved pockets of success in sustainable water management

444 Water and post-conflict peacebuilding

(Cain 2014*; Burt and Keiru 2014*; Pinera and Reed 2014*). Yet these experiences also highlight common challenges, including continued lack of capacity and resources for scaling up and failures in coordination among levels of government or peacebuilding actors. Accepting change as an inherent aspect of rebuilding water governance requires periodic review of policies, plans, and programs to ensure that responses are still appropriate as new data become available, capacities are built, and interventions mature. Iterative assessment processes, especially SEAs that look more broadly at the potential impacts of policies, plans, and programs provide one mechanism for operationalizing an adaptive management approach. Assessment processes, when structured appropriately, also provide an entry point for stakeholder and public involvement in decision making.

Public and stakeholder participation

One of the most critical and consistent lessons from experiences around the world in post-conflict peacebuilding and water management is the importance of meaningful stakeholder engagement and public participation in decision making. Stakeholder engagement is essential to understanding the often-competing water needs and priorities of various users, from community members to the private sector. It also uncovers issues among users or communities that could reignite conflict; the dialogue that meaningful participation facilitates can be an important mechanism for fostering trust and mutual understanding. As noted above, post-conflict governance is often characterized by multiple (polycentric or hybrid) coexisting systems of water governance, which are likely to have been impacted by conflict. Numerous experiences examined in this book point to the importance of understanding these various systems and their evolution to ensure that new policies and institutions respect and undergird functional systems and the social equity they foster, while also avoiding the entrenchment of existing inequities in power and access.

In their chapter on post-conflict water management in northern Afghanistan, McCarthy and Mustafa highlight the risks of ineffective involvement of local stakeholders. The National Solidarity Programme in Afghanistan sought to improve rural infrastructure, create robust local governance mechanisms, and alleviate poverty throughout the country. It specifically aimed to devolve decision making over water and other natural resources to the local level through community development councils and implementing partners (including local and international NGOs). The authors found, however, that in certain communities this process did not account for customary water management arrangements or address the power differentials that had been created or reinforced during conflict through water management practices (McCarthy and Mustafa 2014*). Failure to engage effectively with these communities led to a perception that the government was ignoring their needs for improved water sources.

The lack of data that plagues post-conflict water interventions can also be mitigated by engaging broadly with stakeholders who may hold important local or technical knowledge about water resources. By broadening the available information, data, and knowledge, stakeholder engagement can significantly enhance both the legitimacy and the quality of decisions—revealing hidden assumptions and increasing the likelihood of effective solutions. Engaging with stakeholders also contributes to their knowledge base, increasing capacity for more effective and sustainable water management over the long term. Incorporating stakeholder priorities, needs, and feedback into decision making also builds trust in decision makers and contributes to the legitimacy of the decision-making process, contributing to the reestablishment of sound governance and peacebuilding overall.

Water management needs to be integrated into and support national, local, and sectoral development plans and projects. This requires effective engagement of local institutions—formal, informal, and customary—to ensure that policies, strategies, and activities consider the competing priorities for and impacts on water resources. Governance tools that foster access to relevant information and access to decision making can be used to support stakeholder engagement. Transparency and accountability must also be centerpieces of resilient water governance interventions. This is particularly important given the need to strengthen lines of communication and accountability between the central government and local governments in post-conflict situations.

The rehabilitation of the Iraqi marshlands, for example, requires a complex mix of domestic efforts to promote both community stewardship and regional consensus and cooperation with Syria and Turkey over the sharing of the waters of the Tigris and Euphrates rivers (Lonergan 2012). Given these constraints on restoring the Iraqi marshlands, Chizuru Aoki and colleagues highlight how important it is for donors and public authorities to narrow the scope of their work with local communities in such complicated settings (Aoki, Al-Lami, and Kugaprasatham 2014*). They demonstrate how continuous consultations between the national coordinator and local partners, including tribal chiefs and religious leaders, thus facilitated a transparent process for carrying out a project to improve water supply in the marshlands.

If undertaken appropriately, interventions to provide access to water and sanitation provide an opportunity to build important relationships among government institutions, civil society, communities, and the private sector, promoting cooperation and supporting peacebuilding (UNEP 2013b). Experiences in the DRC and elsewhere demonstrate how active involvement of all relevant stakeholders at both the community level and within the government can lead to practical solutions while building both capacity and stakeholder relations (Burt and Keiru 2014*). Often, however, these opportunities are missed and rebuilding government capacity to resume basic functions, such as water service provision, takes several years.

While there has been a consistent push by the international community to engage stakeholders broadly in projects, these forms of civic engagement and public participation must also engage the informal sector broadly (Allouche 2014*). By engaging the informal sector—for example, through programs that

446 Water and post-conflict peacebuilding

train mechanics to repair water systems, rehabilitate private latrines, and establish water committees—there is a greater likelihood that populations outside of the reach of the main water network will gain access to improved water (Pinera and Reed 2014*). Top-down approaches that seek to enhance the institutional capacity of the government water providers over the long term through large-scale rehabilitation projects often do not have the capacity in the short-term to reach marginalized populations. Thus, direct engagement of illegal vendors in Monrovia and signing agreements with the Liberia Water and Sewer Corporation not only ensured that populations unconnected to the water network could buy water, but also provided some degree of water quality control by connecting the vendors to the network of treated water (Pinera and Reed 2014*).

Public participation also plays a vital role in enhancing regional cooperation around water.[14] Treaties negotiated by political leaders are unlikely to sustain the peace if there is no societal support for their implementation. Civil society engagement can help to foster this support by enabling organizations and individuals to become vested in the outcomes of decision-making processes in which they took part. Indeed, regional cooperation in the Jordan River Basin has been strengthened since the mid-1990s by Track II diplomacy.[15] Focusing on the mutual dependence of shared water resources, the Good Water Neighbors project of FoEME has brought together a range of community activists to undertake community-level projects in Israel, Jordan, and Palestine to build trust through community participation (Mehyar et al. 2014*). Just as donor projects require long-term and sustained commitments to generate political benefits, fostering trust and confidence among communities also requires a long-term and active commitment.

Within the Sava River Basin, regional regimes such as the 1998 Aarhus Convention have helped to strengthen domestic governance by mandating the creation of domestic mechanisms for citizen participation in decision making on environmental matters.[16] The Aarhus Convention, related regional treaties (including the Espoo Convention on transboundary environmental impact assessment), and accompanying guidance developed by the treaties' secretariats assist its members, including the riparians on the Sava Commission, on fostering public participation in its decisions (Čolakhodžić et al. 2014*).

---

[14] On public participation in international water management generally, see Bruch et al. (2005).

[15] In contrast to state-to-state diplomacy (Track I diplomacy), Track II diplomacy focuses on civil-society-to-civil-society engagement. See Davidson and Montville (1981–1982); McDonald and Bendhamane (1987).

[16] The Aarhus Convention's formal name is the United Nations Economic Commission for Europe Convention on Access to Information, Public Participation in Decision-making and Access to Justice in Environmental Matters.

Gender and water

Because girls and women in most post-conflict countries are usually charged with collection and management of water for household use, they usually suffer the greatest impact from water scarcity and lack of sanitation (ROL and UNDP 2006). Where water is not readily accessible, it can take up to six hours daily to collect water for household needs (WASH Advocates 2013). The burden is even greater for displaced populations. In Kyangwali camp in Uganda, for example, 42 percent of school-age children were regularly kept from school to help their mothers collect water (AAH 2004). The time that women spend collecting water can severely undermine their ability to spend time on income-generating activities or on growing food for their families. It also results in high energy expenditures: a woman collecting water for a family of four only 200 meters from her home spends on average 15 percent of a standard ration of 2100 kilocalories per day (Shrestha and Cronin 2006).

The lack of safe water and sanitation for girls and women inhibits not only their livelihood opportunities but also the overall economic recovery. In eastern Uganda, women have to spend as much as seventeen hours per week collecting water (UNDP 2006). Because it is so time-consuming, girls are also likely to miss school, have higher rates of illiteracy, and lower income-generation potential. It is also common for girls to stop attending school once they begin to menstruate owing to the lack of sanitary facilities (UNDP 2006); the International Rescue Committee has estimated that there is likely to be a 10–20 percent school absenteeism rate for girls who have reached puberty and begun to menstruate (IRC 2005). On the contrary, for every 10 percent increase in female literacy, it is estimated that a country's economy can grow by 0.3 percent (UNICEF n.d.).

Where women and girls have to leave their villages and camps to secure water, they are often exposed to gender-based violence. The farther they have to travel, the more at risk they are. Addressing these concerns is challenging, because women are often reluctant to speak about their fears (Burt and Keiru 2014*). With the use of participatory techniques, the NGO Tearfund, in conjunction with its partner Association of Evangelicals of Liberia, created a safe space for women in Henry Town, Liberia, to raise these issues and to engage the broader community in developing solutions that enabled women to play a larger role in water resource management. In this case, representation on the community development council was changed to require equal representation of men and women. By empowering women and institutionalizing their role in water-related decision making, new construction of hand-pump wells was completed in safe locations close to town. The installation of these wells led to a reduction in water-related diseases by 48 percent for adults and 30 percent for children, while also greatly reducing instances of gender-based violence (Burt and Keiru 2014*). Thus, changes in governance mechanisms during the post-conflict period can capitalize on changing social and policy dynamics and provide a window of opportunity to strengthen women's voices in water-related decision making.

448 Water and post-conflict peacebuilding

Including women in decision making also has broader implications for restoring livelihoods, as was the case in Kurdistan where women were allowed to partake in the negotiations over water allocations, albeit indirectly (Barwari 2013). Men in the community focused on water for irrigation and its relevance to land use; women, on the other hand, needed sufficient water for domestic purposes. The government held separate meetings for women so that they had a culturally appropriate forum in which they felt comfortable voicing their concerns about water issues. Similarly, when women returning from refugee camps were able to play a role in leadership and decision making in South Kivu in eastern DRC, they identified rehabilitation of the water system as a high priority (Burt and Keiru 2014*). From their experience living in refugee camps during the conflict, they understood the link between water quality and health. Moreover, because many of these women returned as widowed heads of household, they were forced to assume leadership roles and to resolve conflicts with the neighboring village so as to share a water source between the two communities.

Gender-specific or gender-differentiated interventions in the water sector can help to ease the burden on women and enhance their personal security. One notable intervention by the African Union–United Nations Mission in Darfur has been the introduction of rolling water containers known as "water hippos," which has made it safer and easier for women and girls to transport larger quantities of water (IRIN 2011). Increasing the peacekeeping patrols in areas where women and girls go out alone to collect water has also enhanced their security (UNEP 2012).

Donor commitment

Sustained donor commitment is necessary to ensure the long-term viability of interventions, whether constructing water and sanitation delivery systems, reviving agriculture and ecosystems, reinvigorating water governance regimes, or rebuilding infrastructure for irrigation, flood control, storm drainage, and wastewater treatment. The lack of investment in water and other infrastructure at the end of armed conflict becomes a formidable impediment in the early phases of the peacebuilding process (del Castillo 2008), compounded by post-conflict governments' lack of financial resources and institutional capacity.

While donor assistance is clearly necessary for post-conflict economic recovery, the great variation among donor policies and approaches makes it difficult to distill generalized lessons. For the most part, investments come from a mix of donations and lending from multilateral development banks, bilateral organizations, and NGOs, and are intended for different purposes. Following the Israeli-Palestinian and Israeli-Jordanian peace processes, many international and bilateral donors' concentrated their initial efforts on national-level projects; since 2001 in Afghanistan, in large response to the National Solidarity Programme, donors have instead introduced water resource initiatives at the local level (McCarthy and Mustafa 2014*).

Aid to post-conflict countries often peaks right after conflict and then declines —ironically—at the point when post-conflict countries are better able to absorb

Harnessing water management for more effective peacebuilding **449**

it (Schwartz and Halkyard 2006). In the water sector, investments are channeled into the immediate provisioning of basic services and jump-starting the economy. But in order to sustain peacebuilding efforts and foster environmental restoration in conflict-affected countries, experience shows that donors must take a longer and wider perspective on water management that looks beyond rehabilitation of delivery infrastructure and considers integrated management of the resource at the level of the watershed. This requires elongating the time horizons of planning and donor commitments as well as adhering to an integrated water resource management approach that incorporates mechanisms for coordination across sectors and among levels of government. Short-term funding cycles are, however, all too common and pose numerous challenges, as has been the case with watershed planning in Haiti. Owing to USAID's three-year funding cycle, which is dependent on congressional allocation, a failure to renew the Economic Development for a Sustainable Environment project in Haiti resulted in the cessation of the watershed program (Fischer and Levy 2011).[17] In addition, the focus predominately on short-term infrastructure projects in the lower watershed areas, rather than taking a longer-term approach that takes into account the entire catchment area, has limited the project's ability to address the underlying causes of Haiti's environmental vulnerabilities (Fischer and Levy 2011).

Wetland restoration, in particular, requires longer donor time and investment commitment. In Iraq, where it was difficult for international donors to work on the wetlands owing to security conditions, investments in local capacity building and training activities were important small steps for enhancing the expertise of Iraqi personnel and institutions (Aoki, Al-Lami, and Kugaprasatham 2014*).[18] Moreover, balancing longer-term goals with more visible short-term projects such as drinking-water provision that are highly visible to local communities were considered important for reestablishing local livelihoods in the marshlands.

In the case of the Indus Waters Treaty, the World Bank mobilized financial resources to underwrite large-scale water reconstruction projects and sustain those commitments over a long period. The Indus Waters Treaty is hailed as a success because the World Bank was responsible for operating the Indus Basin Development Fund, to support infrastructure development, and as such was able to coordinate funding from the broader donor community and allocate aid to India and Pakistan for adhering to the agreement (Zawahri 2009, 2014*).[19]

Where multiple donors are involved in implementing projects with different objectives, coordination is necessary to ensure that donors do not work at counter

---

[17] For further discussion on integrated resource management and other lessons drawn from restoration projects in Haiti, see Gingembre (2012).

[18] For additional perspectives on restoration of the Iraqi marshlands, see Lonergan (2012); Suzuki and Nakayama (2011).

[19] In 1960, the year the treaty was signed, US$893.5 million was raised. In 1964, the Indus Basin Supplemental Agreement raised an additional US$315 million (Wolf and Newton n.d.; World Bank n.d.).

450   Water and post-conflict peacebuilding

purposes. This has become increasingly important with donors, such as militaries, that are subject to funding and operation cycles. In Afghanistan, water projects carried out under the auspices of the U.S. military had to follow the civilian-military command cycles (Palmer-Moloney 2014*; Civic 2014). A change in command—from the regional military to civilian leaders at the provincial or district level—could cause water projects to fail unless more guidance and training of civilian and military leadership at the command and control levels is introduced.

Donors—whether bilateral organizations, multilateral development banks, or NGOs—play a central role in post-conflict peacebuilding, especially in the immediate aftermath of conflict. But there is often an irony in that role: their aid often drops off just when a post-conflict country has stabilized enough to absorb it usefully. To overcome this, it is important for donors to take a longer view of the recovery process.

SEQUENCING INTERVENTIONS AND COORDINATION

While humanitarian assistance is usually short term, it can persist for much longer than anticipated, extending well beyond the immediate aftermath of conflict (Bruch et al. 2014). It therefore both coexists with and shapes development and other post-conflict peacebuilding activities. A critical lesson that emerges in post-conflict countries regarding sequencing in the water sector is that donor commitments must be sustained and cannot be parceled into neatly defined time frames with clearly delineated transitions from humanitarian assistance to development, especially since peacebuilding transcends both of these periods.

Despite the emphasis in post-conflict recovery on sequencing humanitarian, security, and economic interventions (Doyle and Sambanis 2006), there is no fixed sequence of how water interventions should progress beyond the humanitarian demands immediately following armed conflict. Emergency interventions to provide basic services quickly for stabilization purposes often end up not being maintained because they are not designed to be sustainable and hence fail to contribute to long-term development (Huston 2014*).

Rather than conceptualizing post-conflict interventions linearly, more flexible funding mechanisms are necessary to allow donors to emphasize long-term sustainability so interventions can achieve both stabilization and development. Post-conflict needs assessments that evaluate water systems and infrastructure remain vital for providing not only an initial baseline for humanitarian interventions, but also for influencing subsequent development interventions (Jensen 2012). Likewise, delaying institution building in the water sector until security is stabilized and human needs are met can impede both short-term and long-term economic recovery, as well as regional cooperation. Table 3 presents approaches to post-conflict water management thematically, reflecting the wide variety of considerations that must be taken into account in interventions.

The perspective of humanitarian organizations—often focused on short-term impacts—can be at odds with longer-term governance and sustainable planning

Table 3.   Approaches to managing water in post-conflict situations

	Immediate aftermath	*Peace consolidation*
Drinking-water and sanitation provision	Conduct assessments of: – Baseline hydrological data (and initiate collection of baseline data). – WASH in refugee and IDP camps to help define priority areas for interventions. – Damage to water infrastructure from conflict. – Institutional capacity and governance mechanisms for drinking-water and sanitation provision, using participatory methods. Introduce monitoring of water withdrawals and quality in camps, rural areas, and urban areas. Include a rights-based approach in water and sanitation interventions. Invest in coordination among actors involved in humanitarian provision of assistance (likely under existing cluster approach). Identify projects that can be completed rapidly to produce visible peace dividends, such as purification systems for reducing contamination of water sources; conduct rapid EIAs for such projects. Carry out SEAs of sector-wide policies, plans, and programs. Provide immediate support for provision of basic services (particularly drinking water and sanitation) to ensure the return and reintegration of refugee populations and IDPs. Adhere to codes of conduct or standards for humanitarian interventions in water and sanitation. Introduce conflict sensitivity in programming so that humanitarian and military operations do not place additional stress on limited water supplies.	Build capacity to monitor water quality and maintain databases. Invest in infrastructure rehabilitation to support (1) the return of refugee populations and IDPs, and (2) the broader population. Carry out EIAs in the rehabilitation and construction of infrastructure. Engage both the informal sector and private sector to ensure that service is effectively regulated. Build capacity of institutions and governance mechanisms for effective water and sanitation provision, including legal and regulatory frameworks.
Livelihoods and economic recovery	Conduct assessments of: – Livelihoods uses and users that depend on water (may be integrated into SEA). – Competing demands from different sectors on access to water. – Availability and quality of hydrometerological data. – Water infrastructure. – Linkages between water uses and users across sectors. Invest in measures to promote food security. Take into account local knowledge and mechanisms for water use and allocation. Invest in projects to rebuild water infrastructure that also provide short-term employment, including food-for-work projects.	Mainstream water into economic development policy and decision making pertaining to livelihoods recovery. Promote intersectoral coordination, especially pertaining to (1) land and water, and (2) drinking water and irrigation. Promote coordination among levels of governance (community, local, regional, national, and transboundary) and incorporate into framework water legislation. Invest in irrigation rehabilitation and infrastructure construction. Build capacity to collect and share water-related data. Adopt a conflict-sensitive approach for infrastructure development, taking into account equity and consensus-building principles.

Table 3. *(Cont'd)*

	Immediate aftermath	*Peace consolidation*
Transboundary water	Conduct assessments of: – How water sharing may have changed during conflict. – Available data for transboundary waters. Identify conflicts that may have existed or exist between upstream and downstream water users. Provide training to water negotiators.	Establish formal water negotiation teams as part of line ministry or across relevant departments, and build negotiation skills. Negotiate water-sharing treaties that include best practices such as establishing a water basin commission, data sharing, conflict resolution mechanisms, and adaptive management. Create a mechanism for states to resolve potential conflicts between upstream and downstream water users. Ensure an inclusive approach to negotiating and implementing agreements that draws upon civil society and its linkages both within society and across borders.
Governance	Identify and assess the types of institutions governing water—including both customary and formal—and the ways in which they have been impacted by the conflict and their effectiveness. Use an institutional assessment to determine whether to build on existing water governance arrangements or integrate new approaches to achieve policy goals. Promote institutions that take into account inclusion, equity, and justice, including water affordability and water quality. Include local and national organizations and civil society in designing water policies and programs. Include water rights in the design of international peace agreements and constitutions, especially where water was a source of tension during conflict.	Undertake water reform so that water institutions across the formal, informal, and customary sectors are connected and harmonized in a mutually reinforcing manner. This should be reflected in any legal reforms. Update or develop new water legislation, regulations, and institutional arrangements that: – Reflect best international practice tailored to national and local circumstances and priorities. – Implement and enforce national obligations under international agreements pertaining to water management. – Promote integrated water resource management and adaptive water governance approaches.

Table 3. (Cont'd)

	Immediate aftermath	Peace consolidation
Public engagement	Undertake iterative stakeholder analyses to account for a changing institutional and actor landscape across sectors. Include civil society and informal-sector groups in assessments. Include civil society and informal sector in planning meetings to present and discuss options for water management. Assess local grievances over water use and allocation. Integrate gender considerations across all water resource management work and analyze the gender-specific aspects of water provision and use. Include women in high-level negotiations over water to ensure that domestic water needs are addressed.	Include civil society (including the informal sector) in implementation of projects and monitoring. Create institutionalized mechanisms for ensuring transparent, participatory, and accountable decision making and policy making related to water management. Design mechanisms for continued feedback from civil society on water and sanitation services provision. Create a forum for community actors to raise potential sources of conflict over water resources. Provide for a larger role and greater representation for women in water resource management at all levels. Design gender-specific interventions in the water sector to ease the burden on women and enhance their personal security.
Donor commitment	Establish mechanisms to coordinate water-related interventions. Such coordination is often undertaken as part of the WASH cluster approach, but broader coordination across WASH and water resource management interventions should be considered.	Leverage private-sector investment. Encourage projects that take a long-term approach by focusing on the entire watershed or catchment area.
Emerging issues	Integrate climate change concerns into planning and implementation of water sector planning and projects. Carry out vulnerability assessment and adaptation planning at the sectoral level. Take into account intersectoral impacts.	Ensure that projects are sensitive to impacts of climate change. Build resilience mechanisms and adaptation planning into projects. Encourage transparency and best practices in foreign investment in mining and large-scale land acquisitions, especially regarding impacts on the water sector. Carry out EIAs and SEAs on emerging projects such as large-scale agricultural developments and extractive industries.

Notes: EIA: environmental impact assessment; IDP: internally displaced person; SEA: strategic environmental assessment; WASH: water, sanitation, and hygiene.

454   Water and post-conflict peacebuilding

for the development of water resources. Coordination among multiple actors and simultaneous interventions presents a daunting challenge. But who can play such a coordinating role? In the area of municipal water, one option is the establishment of dialogues among stakeholders under the auspices of the relevant water utility (Pinera and Reed 2014*). However, there are few post-conflict situations in which utilities have the capacity to play that role, at least at the outset, leaving donors to fill the gap. Without integration and coordination, there are higher risks of unsustainable results, such as the potential socioeconomic impacts from drilling wells in areas of Afghanistan with dropping water tables (Palmer-Moloney 2014*).

Table 3 outlines various approaches to managing water in post-conflict situations. These approaches are organized thematically to capture critical entry points for governments, donors, and communities to intervene: drinking-water and sanitation provision, livelihoods and economic recovery, and transboundary water management. Because there is no single formula for integrating water into post-conflict peacebuilding, approaches must also take into account overarching, crosscutting issues that include governance, public engagement, and donor commitment. Managing water resources is particularly susceptible to emerging issues and uncertainty, especially in light of climate variation and change. In all these approaches, policy makers must devise solutions that are adaptive.

A great deal of thinking has been devoted to describing the stages of the post-conflict period, from immediate humanitarian and security needs to long-term recovery and development. While it is important to understand how the stages, in theory, fall into a general order, it is more important to understand that post-conflict recovery is not a linear progression that unfolds in discrete, clearly defined phases. It is therefore important to exercise flexibility in sequencing interventions, not simply to follow a set playbook. It is also important to understand how short-term interventions can lay the groundwork for longer policies that can achieve stability, sustainability, and governance.

EMERGING CHALLENGES

Post-conflict countries not only face humanitarian, security, and development challenges, but also are often characterized by an ever-changing institutional landscape. The fluid conditions complicate the design of adaptive, inclusive, and conflict-sensitive water resource management policies. Three emerging issues are likely to significantly affect future water resource management and post-conflict peacebuilding: climate change, large-scale land acquisitions, and the development of large mining operations.

Building climate resilience into post-conflict water management

Looming in the background of many post-conflict programs are the uncertain impacts that climate variability and change will have on water management over the long term and the potential implications of these impacts on food security and peacebuilding. Climate change, especially as experienced through its effects on water quantity and quality, is likely to influence the effectiveness of water interventions for restoring basic human security, strengthening livelihoods, and fostering cooperation. Changing weather patterns that increase the intensity and occurrence of floods, droughts, and storms are likely to exacerbate already existing development problems and human vulnerabilities that have already been aggravated due to conflict (Matthew and Hammill 2012). If the challenges posed by climate variability and change are not effectively addressed in post-conflict recovery planning, the international community's efforts in the water sector to rebuild sustainable livelihoods and provide security could be seriously undermined. Notwithstanding these challenges, the post-conflict period can be a window of opportunity to introduce adaptive and responsive water governance structures that are capable of coping with the uncertainties and impacts of climate variability and change and, in turn, build a sector that is less prone to conflict over water availability and quality.

Many discussions surrounding adaptation have focused on water resources and have become a central component in the policy discussions on climate change and conflict (Clausen and Bjerg 2010; Stark, Mataya, and Lubovich 2009). One of the sectors most vulnerable to water variability and rising temperatures is agriculture, where changing water availability and temperature could result in greater food insecurity and food shortages worldwide (Smith and Vivekananda 2007). In Côte d'Ivoire, for example, recurring drought compounded by conflict resulted in a 27 percent drop in cereal harvests in 2003 from the previous year (IRIN 2007). Drought in the late 2000s in Iraq undermined the country's economic recovery, damaging its wheat harvest (Ryan 2009). Pastoralism in many post-conflict countries is similarly vulnerable to fluctuations in water availability, as pastoralists will have to travel farther to look for water sources or compete with other communities at the local level over water points, potentially causing conflict (Stark, Terasawa, and Ejigu 2011).

It therefore is important for post-conflict water interventions to account for the fact that economies heavily dependent on agriculture (and perhaps also experiencing rapid population growth, unregulated economic development, and poor health levels) are more likely to be sensitive to climate impacts (Stern 2007). Laura Palmer-Moloney underscores, for example, the immediacy of climate impacts on water resources for Afghanistan's economic recovery. From 1998 to 2008, severe drought contributed to dropping groundwater tables, diminishing agricultural productivity and increasing scarcity of surface water and contamination in the water supply (Palmer-Moloney 2014*). At the other extreme, it is expected that climate change will influence glacial melt patterns, thus increasing the risk of flooding (UNEP 2013a). And because conflict-affected countries experience high levels of poverty, inequality, and weak governance, climate change may also exacerbate the risk of relapse into armed conflict (Smith and Vivekananda 2007).

456   Water and post-conflict peacebuilding

Post-conflict development strategies can better manage climate risk through enhanced disaster planning that takes climate data into account (Matthew and Hammill 2012). Marginalized and rural communities are often the first to experience the effects of climate change on the water sector because of their heightened vulnerability to external stressors; as such, they should be included in decisions that shape development pathways (Matthew and Hammill 2012).

Because the impacts of climate change on water may overwhelm the capacity of weak institutions, as well as of informal coping mechanisms, how a government responds to the stresses of climate change will determine whether local disputes over water, pasturage, and other natural resources escalate into local conflicts and then into national or international conflicts (Kevane and Gray 2008; Hsiang, Burke, and Miguel 2013). Adaptation planning will need to be a central component of humanitarian and development policies in post-conflict countries, both to ensure food security and to absorb populations in urban centers that migrate owing to protracted drought or recurring floods. Within the water sector such policies have focused on demand control, water reuse, and loss reduction (Hallegatte 2009).

Even for countries that have successfully negotiated agreements over shared water after conflict, climate change introduces new constraints on the robustness of these agreements. For example, changing precipitation patterns and sustained droughts in 1999 led to tension between Israel and Jordan when Israel indicated that it would be unable to deliver water to Jordan per its treaty obligations; likewise, Jordan has had problems delivering water to Israel from the Yarmouk River per its treaty obligations, most likely due to upstream extraction by Syria (Freimuth et al. 2007). And climate change has the potential to complicate negotiations by providing a plausible reason (or excuse) for water problems, when a source of the problem has to do with overextraction. In the case of the Yarmouk River, for example, Jordan has argued that decreases in the flow of the Yarmouk are because of Syrian water use, whereas Syria has argued that these reductions are a result of climate change (Haddadin 2014*). More recently, treaties governing transboundary waters have begun to recognize the need for flexibility and have ceased to allocate on the basis of fixed quantities, instead adaptively managing allocations in response to changes in flows. Tools used to implement this flexibility include mandatory or triggered review processes, drought response provisions, and institutional procedural requirements for monitoring and evaluation of allocation strategies (Kistin and Ashton n.d.).

Large-scale land acquisitions

An emerging issue for post-conflict countries is threats to food security, threats that can arise both from within and also from abroad. In many instances, foreign investment in post-conflict countries is being devoted both to developing large-scale agriculture to feed domestic populations in post-conflict countries and to growing food for populations elsewhere in the world that are facing diminishing

Harnessing water management for more effective peacebuilding **457**

water supplies, reduced arable land, rising food prices, and growing populations (Paul, Weinthal, and Harrison 2012). Countries such as Brunei, China, Kuwait, Oman, Pakistan, and Saudi Arabia have sought to enhance their food supply, for example, by purchasing or leasing large swatches of farmland abroad in Ethiopia, the Philippines, and Sudan (Cotula et al. 2009; Woertz 2011; Pulhin and Ramirez 2013). While the full scope of countries seeking to enhance their food security through purchasing or leasing large swatches of farmland abroad is not entirely known, studies have documented an increasing trend since the 2007–2008 global food crisis in such countries as Ethiopia, Liberia, Mali, Madagascar, Sierra Leone, and Sudan (Jägerskog et al. 2012; Cotula 2011; De Schutter 2011; Provost and McClanahan 2012). One impact is that large-scale agricultural acquisitions often compete with small-scale subsistence farming, resulting in new conflicts over access to land and livelihoods viability (Unruh and Williams 2013).

One issue in discussions about large-scale land acquisitions is weighing the advantages and disadvantages for revenue and employment generation. An often-overlooked question, however, is the impact of these operations on the water sector, as substantial amounts of water are required to support agricultural plantations. As a result, industrial farming often brings the construction of large irrigation projects, which may have an impact on the recharge capacity of surrounding groundwater supplies, as well as on the sustainability of surface water sources. Water quality may also be degraded when runoff from these developments and operations are not sufficiently regulated. Despite the risks, most concession contracts with foreign investors do not take into account water issues (Cotula 2011). For example, agricultural concession contracts in Liberia have failed to adequately address water, whereas some contracts in Mali grant investors the right to use water with few, if any, restrictions during the wet season (Cotula 2011). Large-scale land acquisitions may also affect transboundary water resources, especially where irrigation schemes require energy sources from hydropower (Jägerskog et al. 2012). Water usage for large-scale agriculture in Ethiopia and Mali, for example, could potentially add another layer of complexity to transboundary water management in the Nile and Niger River basins, respectively (Jägerskog et al. 2012).

In order to prevent large-scale land acquisitions from undermining access to water and damaging livelihoods, foreign investment in post-conflict countries must be sensitive to local interests and must address water in any land transaction. In addition to mitigating potential impacts on subsistence agriculture, investors and governments will need to take into account the ways in which large-scale land acquisitions might restrict pastoralists' ability to access commonly owned watering holes for their cattle.

Mining and water in post-conflict peacebuilding

Investments in the mining sector hold the potential to help countries such as Afghanistan, Angola, the DRC, Liberia, and Sierra Leone to foster economic

458   Water and post-conflict peacebuilding

recovery (Rustad, Lujala, and Le Billon 2012).[20] Much attention has been paid to the management of resource extraction and revenue generation to ensure that local populations benefit from high-value natural resources. Less attention has been paid, however, to the impacts of mining on the water sector.

Mining operations in Katanga, in the DRC, have reduced surface water availability and contaminated surface and groundwater sources (UNEP 2011). Similar effects of mining operations on water quality and quantity are seen across the globe. Countries emerging from conflict need to balance the immediate needs for economic recovery with sustainable water management, especially for drinking water in surrounding communities.

Water consumption is also an important component of mining. Major investments in the mining sector, such as the Aynak copper mine in Afghanistan, will require large quantities of water to process the copper ore; one estimate is that the mine will use 43 million cubic meters of water annually by 2020 (UNEP 2013a).[21] For Afghanistan, this will be critical given that water demand for Kabul, approximately thirty miles from Aynak, is expected to increase six-fold over the next forty years (UNEP 2013a).

CONCLUSION

Experiences from numerous conflict-affected countries demonstrate that water interventions are integral to all stages of the post-conflict process, from the end of conflict through recovery and rebuilding, to long-term sustainable development. At conflict's end, the provision of safe drinking water and sanitation is an utmost priority to maintain public health and support basic human needs. Unfortunately, many decisions concerning the provision of basic services are made while countries have yet to fully emerge from conflict, and as a result, decisions must be made before full accounting of local conditions and data have been taken. To generate crucial peace dividends under such conditions, donors and governments must coordinate programming goals and adhere to widely accepted standards for provision of water and sanitation services. And in situations where governance mechanisms are in flux, informal service providers can play a critical role in service provision.

In post-conflict countries, efforts to restore livelihoods, revive the economy, and foster cooperation are all likely to require data collection and infrastructure development. Here too, coordination and sequencing becomes imperative to

---

[20] While significant water is also used in oil and gas exploration, especially for non-conventional sources of energy, this section highlights cases of minerals and metals.

[21] A lack of water metering precludes exact comparison between the water demands of the mine and the current water footprint of Kabul; however, Thomas J. Mack and colleagues report an estimated per capita domestic water-use rate of 40 liters per day in the city of Kabul (Mack et al. 2010). With a metropolitan population of 3,289,000 (Central Statistics Office Afghanistan 2012), this would put annual domestic water withdrawals for the city at 48 million cubic meters.

ensure that such activities contribute to local capacity building and do not engender societal inequities. It is important to incorporate strategic environmental assessments and meaningful local input into program design. An overarching challenge that confronts most conflict-affected countries, however, is ensuring long-term investment in the water sector, especially since priorities and time horizons of funding agencies and the private sector may not comport with the timelines needed for infrastructure investments for longer-term economic recovery.

Throughout the post-conflict peacebuilding process, local involvement through inclusion of the informal sector, broad stakeholder and public engagement, and mainstreaming of gender issues can also help to support the rebuilding of governance and institutional mechanisms that undergird efforts to restore livelihoods, rebuild the economy, and foster cooperation. A holistic focus on governance mechanisms (for example, integrated water resource management) rather than compartmentalizing governance interventions, in particular, is important for designing interventions to manage shared river basins or fragile ecosystems like wetlands that provide numerous services to local populations. By not overlooking the role of local governance, donors and governments may further avoid aggravating tensions between local and national water institutions that often exist in conflict-affected or weakly institutionalized countries.

While there are multiple pathways by which water can be harnessed to address humanitarian crises, promote economic recovery, and foster regional cooperation, it is equally true that there is no overarching template that can be applied to all countries emerging from conflict. Rather, attention should be paid to the specific context in which these interventions are taking place with an emphasis on fostering a nuanced, coordinated, participatory, flexible, and conflict-sensitive approach to managing water and its natural variability. Such an adaptive approach will be especially important as water governance institutions respond to unprecedented changes in the global climate.

REFERENCES

AAH (Aktion Afrika Hilfe). 2004. Impacts of inadequate safe water resources in the "Acholi-Pii caseload" refugees in Kyangwali refugee settlement, Hoima District, Uganda, Aktion Afrika Hilfe. Munich, Germany.

AFDB (African Development Bank Group). 2012. AfDB socio economic database. May. http://opendataforafrica.org/xpcbgic.

Ahmad, M., and M. Wasiq. 2004. *Water resource development in northern Afghanistan and its implications for Amu Darya Basin.* World Bank Working Paper No. 36. Washington, D.C.: World Bank.

Allouche, J. 2014. The role of informal service providers in post-conflict reconstruction and state building. In *Water and post-conflict peacebuilding,* ed. E. Weinthal, J. Troell, and M. Nakayama. London: Earthscan.

Amnesty International. 2012. *"We can run away from bombs, but not from hunger": Sudan's refugees in South Sudan.* London. www.amnestyusa.org/sites/default/files/3919_s_sudan_report_final_2.pdf.

460 Water and post-conflict peacebuilding

Aoki, C., A. Al-Lami, and S. Kugaprasatham. 2014. Environmental management of the Iraqi marshlands in the post-conflict period. In *Water and post-conflict peacebuilding*, ed. E. Weinthal, J. Troell, and M. Nakayama. London: Earthscan.

Baker, A. 2013. Will Syria's refugee crisis drain Jordan of its water? *Time Magazine*, April 4. http://world.time.com/2013/04/04/how-syrias-refugee-crisis-is-draining-jordans -scarce-water-supply/.

Barwari, N. 2013. Rebuilding peace: Land and water management in the Kurdistan Region of northern Iraq. In *Land and post-conflict peacebuilding*, ed. J. Unruh and R. C. Williams. London: Earthscan.

Birner, R., M. J. Cohen, and J. Ilukor, with T. Muhumuza, K. Schindler, and S. Mulligan. 2011. Rebuilding agricultural livelihoods in post-conflict situations: What are the governance challenges? The case of northern Uganda. Uganda Strategy Support Program (USSP). USSP Working Paper No. 7. Kampala, Uganda and Washington, D.C.: International Food Policy Research Institute. www.ifpri.org/sites/default/files/publications/usspwp07.pdf.

Boesen, J. K., and T. Martin. 2007. *Applying a rights-based approach: An inspirational guide for civil society*. Copenhagen, Denmark: Danish Institute for Human Rights. www.humanrights.dk/files/pdf/Publikationer/applying%20a%20rights%20based%20 approach.pdf.

Bogdanovic, S. 2014. Management of waters in post-Dayton Bosnia and Herzegovina: Policy, legal, and institutional aspects. In *Water and post-conflict peacebuilding*, ed. E. Weinthal, J. Troell, and M. Nakayama. London: Earthscan.

Briggs, C., and I. Weissbecker. 2012. Salting the Earth: Environmental health challenges in post-conflict reconstruction. In *Assessing and restoring natural resources in post-conflict peacebuilding*, ed. D. Jensen and S. Lonergan. London: Earthscan.

Bruch, C., L. Jansky, M. Nakayama, and K. A. Salewicz, eds. 2005. *Public participation in the governance of international freshwater resources*. Tokyo: United Nations University Press.

Bruch, C., D. Jensen, M. Nakayama, and J. Unruh. 2014. *Post-conflict peacebuilding and natural resources: The promise and the peril*. New York: Cambridge University Press.

Burt, M., and B. J. Keiru. 2014. Community water management: Experiences from the Democratic Republic of the Congo, Afghanistan, and Liberia. In *Water and post-conflict peacebuilding*, ed. E. Weinthal, J. Troell, and M. Nakayama. London: Earthscan.

Cain, A. 2014. Conflict and collaboration for water resources in Angola's post-war cities. In *Water and post-conflict peacebuilding*, ed. E. Weinthal, J. Troell, and M. Nakayama. London: Earthscan.

Catarious, D. M., Jr., and A. Russell. 2012. Counternarcotics efforts and Afghan poppy farmers: Finding the right approach. In *High-value natural resources and post-conflict peacebuilding*, ed. P. Lujala and S. A. Rustad. London: Earthscan.

Central Statistics Office Afghanistan. 2012. Population of Kabul City by district and sex 2012-13. http://cso.gov.af/Content/files/Population%20of%20Kabul%20City%20by%20 District%20and%20Sex.pdf.

Civic, M. A. 2014. Civil-military coordination and cooperation in peacebuilding and natural resource management: An enabling framework, challenges, and incremental progress. In *Governance, natural resources, and post-conflict peacebuilding*, ed. C. Bruch, C. Muffett, and S. S. Nichols. London: Earthscan.

Clausen, T. J., and C. Bjerg. 2010. The blue revolution: Adapting to climate change. Thought Leadership Series No. 6. Copenhagen, Denmark: Copenhagen Climate Council.

Harnessing water management for more effective peacebuilding 461

Claussen, J., F. Daibes, J. Halwani, S. Hansen, E. Salameh, and E. Weinthal. 2004. Evaluation of CESAR's activities in the Middle East funded by Norway. A report prepared by Nordic Consulting Group, Evaluation Report No. 3/2004. Oslo: Norwegian Ministry of Foreign Affairs.

Čolakhodžić, A., M. Filipovič, J. Kovandžič, and S. Stec. 2014. The Sava River: Transitioning to peace in the former Yugoslavia. In *Water and post-conflict peacebuilding*, ed. E. Weinthal, J. Troell, and M. Nakayama. London: Earthscan.

Collier, P. 1999. On the economic consequences of civil war. *Oxford Economic Papers* 51:168–183.

Colombatti, R., C. S. Vieira, F. Bassani, R. Cristofoli, A. Coin, L. Bertinato, and F. Riccardi. 2009. Contamination of drinking water sources during the rainy season in an urban post-conflict community in Guinea Bissau: Implications for sanitation priority. *African Journal of Medicine and Medical Sciences* 38 (2): 155–161.

Conca, K., and G. D. Dabelko, eds. 2002. *Environmental peacemaking*. Washington, D.C.: Woodrow Wilson Center Press; Baltimore, MD: Johns Hopkins University Press.

Conca, K., F. Wu, and C. Mei. 2006. Global regime formation or complex institution building? The principled content of international river agreements. *International Studies Quarterly* 50:263–285.

Cotula, L. 2011. *Land deals in Africa: What is in the contracts*. London: International Institute for Environment and Development.

Cotula, L., S. Vermeulen, R. Leonard, and J. Keeley. 2009. *Land grab or development opportunity? Agricultural investment and international land deals in Africa*. London: International Institute for Environment and Development; Rome: Food and Agriculture Organization of the United Nations International Fund for Agricultural Development.

CPHD (Centre for Policy and Human Development). 2011. *Afghanistan human development report 2011: The forgotten front; Water security and the crisis in sanitation*. Kabul, Afghanistan: Kabul University.

Craze, J. 2013. Dividing lines: Grazing and conflict along the Sudan–South Sudan border. Geneva, Switzerland: Graduate Institute of International and Development Studies.

Cronin, A. A., D. Shrestha, N. Cornier, F. Abdalla, N. Ezard, and C. Aramburu. 2008. A review of water and sanitation provision in refugee camps in association with selected health and nutrition indicators—The need for integrated service provision. *Journal of Water and Health* 6 (1): 1–13.

Dahi, O. S. 2013. The Syrian cataclysm. Middle East Research and Information Project, March 4. www.merip.org/syrian-cataclysm.

Davidson, W. D., and J. V. Montville. 1981–1982. Foreign policy according to Freud. *Foreign Policy* 45:145–157.

Dehgan, A., L. J. Palmer-Moloney, and M. Mirzaee. 2014. Water security and scarcity: Potential destabilization in western Afghanistan and Iranian Sistan and Baluchestan due to transboundary water conflicts. In *Water and post-conflict peacebuilding*, ed. E. Weinthal, J. Troell, and M. Nakayama. London: Earthscan.

del Castillo, G. 2008. *Rebuilding war-torn states: The challenge of post-conflict economic reconstruction*. Oxford, UK: Oxford University Press.

De Schutter, O. 2011. The green rush: The global race for farmland and the rights of land users. *Harvard International Law Journal.* 52 (2): 504–559.

Dewey, K., and H. Brown. 2003. Update on technical issues concerning complementary feeding of young children in developing countries and implication for intervention programs. *Food Nutrition Bulletin* 24 (1): 5–28.

462   Water and post-conflict peacebuilding

Doyle, M. W., and N. Sambanis. 2006. *Making war and building peace.* Princeton, NJ: Princeton University Press.

FAO (Food and Agriculture Organization of the United Nations). 2010. Aquastat: Water withdrawal by sector, around 2003. www.fao.org/nr/water/aquastat/dbase/AquastatWorld DataEng_20101129.pdf.

Fischer, A., and M. A. Levy. 2011. Designing environmental restoration programs in politically fragile states: Lessons from Haiti. In *Harnessing natural resources for peacebuilding: Lessons from U.S. and Japanese assistance,* ed. C. Bruch, M. Nakayama, and I. Coyle. Washington, D.C.: Environmental Law Institute.

Freimuth, L., G. Bromberg, M. Mehyar, and N. Al Khateeb. 2007. Climate change: A new threat to Middle East security. EcoPeace/Friends of the Earth Middle East.

Gaigals, C., and M. Leonhardt. 2001. *Conflict-sensitive approaches to development: A review of practice.* London: International Alert, Saferworld, and International Development Research Centre. http://web.idrc.ca/uploads/user-S/10596649641conflict-sensitive -develop.pdf.

Gingembre, L. 2012. Haiti: Lessons learned and way forward in natural resource management projects. In *Assessing and restoring natural resources in post-conflict peacebuilding,* ed. D. Jensen and S. Lonergan. London: Earthscan.

Goodhand, J. 2005. Frontiers and wars: The opium economy in Afghanistan. *Journal of Agrarian Change* 5 (2): 191–216.

Guardian. 2012. South Sudan's refugee camps flooded. September 27. www.theguardian.com/ global-development/gallery/2012/sep/27/south-sudan-refugee-camps-flooded.

GWC (Global WASH Cluster). 2011a. Disaster risk reduction and water, sanitation and hygiene . . . comprehensive guidance: A guideline for field practitioners planning and implementing WASH interventions. New York: CARE International.

———. 2011b. Global WASH Cluster strategic plan 2011–2015. www.washcluster .info/?q=content/gwc-2011-%E2%80%93-2015-strategic-plan.

Haddadin, M. J. 2014. The Jordan River Basin: A conflict like no other. In *Water and post-conflict peacebuilding,* ed. E. Weinthal, J. Troell, and M. Nakayama. London: Earthscan.

Hallegatte, S. 2009. Strategies to adapt to an uncertain climate change. *Global Environmental Change* 19 (2): 240–247.

Hamill, K., and Z. Ali-Ahmad. 2007. Local government in post-conflict situations: Lebanon case study. Paper prepared for the United Nations Development Programme's "Workshop on Local Government in Post-Conflict Situations: Challenges for Improving Local Decision-Making and Service Delivery Capacities," Oslo, Norway, November 28–29. www.gsdrc.org/go/display&type=Document&id=3494.

Hamner, J. H., and A. T. Wolf. 1998. Patterns in international water resource treaties: The transboundary freshwater dispute database. *1997 Yearbook of the Colorado Journal of International Environmental Law and Policy* 9:157–177.

Hoeffler, A. 1999. Challenges of infrastructure rehabilitation and reconstruction in war-affected economies. Economic Research Papers No. 48. African Development Bank. www.afdb.org/fileadmin/uploads/afdb/Documents/Publications/00157630-FR-ERP-48.PDF.

Hsiang, S. M., M. Burke, and E. Miguel. 2013. Quantifying the influence of climate on human conflict. *Science,* August 1.

Huston, S. 2014. Thirsty for peace: The water sector in South Sudan. In *Water and post-conflict peacebuilding,* ed. E. Weinthal, J. Troell, and M. Nakayama. London: Earthscan.

IDMC (Internal Displacement Monitoring Center). 2005. Water is a main source of conflict in Afghanistan. September. www.internal-displacement.org/idmc/website/countries.nsf/(httpEnvelopes)/708ABC4712532B7B802570B8005A7535?OpenDocument.

International Office of Migration. 2012. IOM South Sudan annual report 2012. www.iom.int/files/live/sites/iom/files/Country/docs/IOM_South_Sudan_Annual_%20Report_2012.pdf.

IRC (International Rescue Committee). 2005. School sanitation and hygiene notes and news. May. www.irc.nl/page/22824.

IRIN (Integrated Regional Information Networks). 2006. Running dry: The humanitarian impact of the global water crisis; Afghanistan: Water crisis a growing human tragedy. September 8. www.irinnews.org/InDepthMain.aspx?InDepthId=13&ReportId=60533&Country=Yes.

————. 2007. Côte d'Ivoire: Drought and poor infrastructure spell water shortage in the west. March 19. www.irinnews.org/report/70777/cote-d-ivoire-drought-and-poor-infrastructure-spell-water-shortage-in-the-west.

————. 2009. Iraq: Marshland livelihoods again under threat. March 10. www.irinnews.org/report/83391/iraq-marshland-livelihoods-again-under-threat.

————. 2011. Sudan: North Darfur water project helps protect women from sexual violence. April 27. www.irinnews.org/Report.aspx?ReportID=92597.

————. 2013. Containing disease in a Syrian refugee camp in Iraq. July 3. www.irinnews.org/report/98349/containing-disease-in-a-syrian-refugee-camp-in-iraq.

Jägerskog, A., A. Cascão, M. Hårsmar, K. Kim. 2012. Land acquisition: How will they impact transboundary waters? Report No. 30. Stockholm, Sweden: Stockholm International Water Institute.

Jensen, D. 2012. Evaluating the impact of UNEP's post-conflict environmental assessments. In *Assessing and restoring natural resources in post-conflict peacebuilding*, ed. D. Jensen and S. Lonergan. London: Earthscan.

Jensen, D., and S. Lonergan. 2012. Natural resources and post-conflict assessment, remediation, restoration, and reconstruction: Lessons and emerging issues. In *Assessing and restoring natural resources in post-conflict peacebuilding*, ed. D. Jensen and S. Lonergan. London: Earthscan.

Kevane, M., and L. Gray. 2008. Darfur: Rainfall and conflict. *Environmental Research Letters* 3 (034006): 1–10. http://iopscience.iop.org/1748-9326/3/3/034006.

King, M., and B. Sturtewagen. 2010. Making the most of Afghanistan's river basins: Opportunities for regional cooperation. New York: EastWest Institute.

Kistin, E., and P. Ashton. n.d. Adapting to change on transboundary rivers: An analysis of treaty flexibility on the Orange-Senqu River. www.orangesenqurak.com/UserFiles/File/OtherV2/Adapting%20to%20Change%20on%20Transboundary%20Rivers%20CSIR%202008.pdf.

Kramer, A. 2008. *Regional water cooperation and peacebuilding in the Middle East*. Brussels, Belgium: Adelphi Research.

Kreimer, A., P. Collier, C. S. Scott, and M. Arnold. 2000. *Uganda: Post-conflict reconstruction*. Washington, D.C.: World Bank.

Kreimer, A., J. Eriksson, R. Muscat, M. Arnold, and C. Scott. 1998. *The World Bank's experience with post-conflict reconstruction*. Washington, D.C.: World Bank.

Kruk, M. E., P. C. Rockers, E. H. Williams, S. T. Varpilah, R. Macauley, G. Saydee, and S. Galea. 2009. Availability of essential services in post-conflict Liberia. *Bulletin of the World Health Organization*. www.who.int/bulletin/volumes/88/7/09-071068/en/.

464   Water and post-conflict peacebuilding

Lichtenthaeler, G. 2010. Water conflict and cooperation in Yemen. *Middle East Report* 40 (Spring): 30–36. www.merip.org/mer/mer254/water-conflict-cooperation -yemen.

Lind, J. 2014. Manufacturing peace in "no man's land": Livestock and access to natural resources in the Karimojong Cluster of Kenya and Uganda. In *Livelihoods, natural resources, and post-conflict peacebuilding*, ed. H. Young and L. Goldman. London: Earthscan.

Lonergan, S. 2012. Ecological restoration and peacebuilding: The case of the Iraqi marshes. In *Assessing and restoring natural resources in post-conflict peacebuilding*, ed. D. Jensen and S. Lonergan. London: Earthscan.

Mack, T. J., M. A. Akbari, M. H. Ashoor, M. P. Chornack, T. B. Coplen, D. G. Emerson, B. E. Hubbard et al. 2010. *Conceptual model of water resources in the Kabul Basin, Afghanistan.* Scientific Investigations Report No. 2009–5262. Reston, VA: United States Geological Survey. http://pubs.usgs.gov/sir/2009/5262/.

Mardirosian, R. C. 2010. Infrastructure development in the shadow of conflict: Aligning incentives and attracting investment. Working Paper No. 57. Stanford, CA: Collaboratory for Research on Global Projects.

Marin, P., J. Mugabi, and M. Mariño. 2010. Improving water services in a postconflict situation: The case of the management contract in Kosovo. *Gridlines* No. 52. www.ppiaf.org/ ppiaf/sites/ppiaf.org/files/publication/52-water-postconflict-situation.pdf.

Matthew, R., and A. Hammill. 2012. Peacebuilding and adaptation to climate change. In *Assessing and restoring natural resources in post-conflict peacebuilding*, ed. D. Jensen and S. Lonergan. London: Earthscan.

McCarthy, J., and D. Mustafa. 2014. Despite the best intentions? Experiences with water resource management in northern Afghanistan. In *Water and post-conflict peacebuilding*, ed. E. Weinthal, J. Troell, and M. Nakayama. London: Earthscan.

McDonald, J. W., and D. B. Bendhamane, eds. 1987. *Conflict resolution: Track two diplomacy.* Washington, D.C.: Foreign Service Institute, United States Department of State.

Mehyar, M., N. Al Khateeb, G. Bromberg, and E. Koch-Ya'ari. 2014. Transboundary cooperation in the Lower Jordan River Basin. In *Water and post-conflict peacebuilding*, ed. E. Weinthal, J. Troell, and M. Nakayama. London: Earthscan.

Mohtadi, S. 2012. Climate change and the Syrian uprising. *Bulletin of the Atomic Scientists*, August 16.

Mosher, D. E., B. E. Lachman, M. D. Greenberg, T. Nichols, B. Rosen, and H. H. Willis. 2008. Green warriors: Army environmental considerations for contingency operations from planning through postconflict. Santa Monica, CA: Rand Arroyo Center. www .rand.org/pubs/monographs/2008/RAND_MG632.pdf.

Myers, G. W. 1994. Competitive rights, competitive claims: Land access in post-war Mozambique. *Journal of Southern African Studies* 20 (4): 603–632.

Nakayama, M. 1997. Successes and failures of international organizations in dealing with international waters. *Water Resources Development* 13 (3): 367–382.

———. 2011. Support by Australia, European countries, and Japan to the Interim Mekong Committee during post-conflict periods in Laos and Vietnam. In *Harnessing natural resources for peacebuilding: Lessons from U.S. and Japanese assistance*, ed. C. Bruch, M. Nakayama, and I. Coyle. Washington, D.C.: Environmental Law Institute.

New York Times. 2013. Heavy rains flood U.N. camp for Syrian refugees in Jordan. Jan. 8. http://projects.nytimes.com/watching-syrias-war/heavy-rains-flood-syrian-refugee -camp-in-jordan.

Harnessing water management for more effective peacebuilding **465**

Nyamu-Musembi, C., and A. Cornwall. 2004. What is the "rights-based approach" all about? Perspectives for international development agencies. IDS Working Paper No. 234. Sussex, UK: Institute for Development Studies.

Palmer-Moloney, L. J. 2014. Water's role in security and stability in Helmand Province, Afghanistan. In *Water and post-conflict peacebuilding*, ed. E. Weinthal, J. Troell, and M. Nakayama. London: Earthscan.

Paul, C., E. Weinthal, and C. Harrison. 2012. Climate change, foreign assistance, and development: What future for Ethiopia? Washington, D.C.: Transatlantic Academy.

Phillips, D. L. 2008. Darfur early recovery and development dossier. New York: Columbia University Center for the Study of Human Rights. http://hrcolumbia.org/darfur/dossier.pdf.

Pinera, J.-F., and R. A. Reed. 2014. A tale of two cities: Restoring water services in Kabul and Monrovia. In *Water and post-conflict peacebuilding*, ed. E. Weinthal, J. Troell, and M. Nakayama. London: Earthscan.

Provost, C., and P. McClanahan. 2012. Sierra Leone: Local resistance grows as investors snap up land. *Guardian*, April 11.

Prüss-Üstün, A., R. Bos, F. Gore, and J. Bartram. 2008. *Safer water, better health: Costs, benefits and sustainability of interventions to protect and promote health*. Geneva, Switzerland: World Health Organization.

Pulhin, J. M., and M. A. M. Ramirez. 2013. National updates on agribusiness large scale land acquisitions in Southeast Asia—Brief #4 of 8: Republic of the Philippines. In *Agribusiness large-scale land acquisitions and human rights in Southeast Asia: Updates from Indonesia, Thailand, Philippines, Malaysia, Cambodia, Timor-Leste and Burma*, ed. S. Chao. Moreton-in-Marsh, UK: Forest Peoples Programme. www.forestpeoples.org/sites/fpp/files/publication/2013/08/lsla-briefings.pdf.

Rinat, Z. 2013. For first time, Israel's Water Authority to pump Kinneret water into Jordan River. *Haaretz*, May 17.

ROL (Republic of Liberia) and UNDP (United Nations Development Programme). 2006. *National human development report 2006 Liberia: Mobilizing capacity for reconstruction and development*. Monrovia. http://hdr.undp.org/en/reports/national/africa/liberia/LIBERIA_2006_en.pdf.

Rustad, S. A., P. Lujala, and P. Le Billon. 2012. Building or spoiling peace? Lessons from the management of high-value natural resources. In *High-value natural resources and post-conflict peacebuilding*, ed. P. Lujala and S. A. Rustad. London: Earthscan.

Ryan, M. 2009. Drought takes toll on Iraq revival efforts. Reuters, July 23. www.reuters.com/article/2009/07/24/us-iraq-water-idUSTRE56N01Q20090724.

Sai, Z. H., and Y. N. Saw. 2011. Floods in northern Thailand hit Burmese refugee camps. *Irrawady*, August 5. www2.irrawaddy.org/article.php?art_id=21844.

Salman, S. M. A. 2014. Water resources in the Sudan North-South peace process and the ramifications of the secession of South Sudan. In *Water and post-conflict peacebuilding*, ed. E. Weinthal, J. Troell, and M. Nakayama. London: Earthscan.

Sauer, J., M. Gorton, M. Peshevski, D. Bosev, and D. Shekerinov. 2010. Social capital and the performance of water user associations: Evidence from the Republic of Macedonia. *Journal of International Agricultural Trade and Development* 59 (1): 30–39.

Schwartz, J., and P. Halkyard. 2006. Post-conflict infrastructure: Trends in aid and investment flows. Public Policy for the Private Sector Note No. 305. Washington, D.C.: World Bank.

SDC (Swiss Agency for Development and Cooperation). 2013. Humanitarian standards forum 2013. Geneva, Switzerland.

466   Water and post-conflict peacebuilding

Selby, J. 2013. Cooperation, domination and colonisation: The Israeli-Palestinian Joint Water Committee. *Water Alternatives* 6 (1): 1–24.

Shrestha, D., and A. A. Cronin. 2006. The right to water and protecting refugees. *Waterlines* 24 (3): 12–14. www.unhcr.org/4add73269.pdf.

SIDA (Swedish International Development Cooperation Agency). 2012. A human rights based approach to peace building. Stockholm.

Sistenich, V. 2012. UN integration and humanitarian coordination: Policy considerations towards protection of the humanitarian space. Briefing note. Cambridge, MA: Program on Humanitarian Policy and Conflict Research, Harvard University. www.hpcrresearch.org/blog/vera-sistenich/2012-07-06/briefing-note-un-integration-humanitarian-coordination-policy-conside.

Skaperdas, S., R. Soares, A. Willman, and S. C. Miller. 2009. *The costs of violence.* Washington, D.C.: World Bank.

Smith, D., and J. Vivekananda. 2007. *A climate of conflict: The links between climate change, peace and war.* London: International Alert. www.international-alert.org/resources/publications/climate-conflict.

Sphere Project. 2004. *Humanitarian charter and minimum standards in disaster response.* Geneva, Switzerland. http://ocw.jhsph.edu/courses/refugeehealthcare/PDFs/SphereProject Handbook.pdf.

———. 2011. *Humanitarian charter and minimum standards in humanitarian response.* Geneva, Switzerland. www.sphereproject.org/resources/download-publications/?search =1&keywords=&language=English&category=22.

Stark, J., C. Mataya, and K. Lubovich. 2009. Climate change, adaptation, and conflict: A preliminary review of the issues. CMM Discussion Paper No. 1. Washington, D.C.: United States Agency for International Development. http://pdf.usaid.gov/pdf_docs/PNADR530.pdf.

Stark, J., K. Terasawa, and M. Ejigu. 2011. Climate change and conflict in pastoralist regions of Ethiopia: Mounting challenges, emerging responses. CMM Discussion Paper No. 4. Washington, D.C.: United States Agency for International Development. www.fess -global.org/Publications/Other/Climate_Change_and_Conflic_%20in_Ethiopia.pdf.

Steets, J., F. Grünewald, A. Binder, V. de Geoffroy, D. Kauffmann, S. Krüger, C. Meier, and B. Sokpoh. 2010. *Cluster approach evaluation report 2: Synthesis report.* Berlin, Germany: Global Public Policy Institute; Plaisans, France: Groupe URD. www.humanitarianinfo.org/iasc/pageloader.aspx?page=content-products-common&tempid=99.

Stern, N. 2007. *The economics of climate change: Stern review.* London: Cambridge University Press.

Sudan Tribune. 2013. South Sudan cabinet endorses joining Nile Basin Initiative. August 17. www.sudantribune.com/spip.php?article47686.

Sugiura, M., Y. Toguchi, and M. Funiciello. 2014. Irrigation management and flood control in post–World War II Japan. In *Water and post-conflict peacebuilding,* ed. E. Weinthal, J. Troell, and M. Nakayama. London: Earthscan.

Suzuki, T., and M. Nakayama. 2011. Post-project evaluation of UNEP-IETC's Iraqi Marshland Project. In *Harnessing natural resources for peacebuilding: Lessons from U.S. and Japanese assistance,* ed. C. Bruch, M. Nakayama, and I. Coyle. Washington, D.C.: Environmental Law Institute.

Thébaud, B., G. Vogt, and K. Vogt. 2006. The implication of water rights for pastoral land tenure: The case of Niger. In *Land and water rights in the Sahel: Tenure challenges of improving access to water for agriculture,* ed. L. Cotula. London: International Institute for Environment and Development.

Tignino, M. 2014. The right to water and sanitation in post-conflict legal mechanisms: An emerging regime? In *Water and post-conflict peacebuilding*, ed. E. Weinthal, J. Troell, and M. Nakayama. London: Earthscan.

UNDP (United Nations Development Programme). 2006. *Human development report 2006*: Beyond scarcity; Power, poverty and the global water crisis. New York.

UNEP (United Nations Environment Programme). 2003. *Afghanistan: Post-conflict environmental assessment*. Geneva, Switzerland. http://postconflict.unep.ch/publications/afghanistanpcajanuary2003.pdf.

———. 2006 *History of environmental change in the Sistan Basin based on satellite image analysis: 1976–2005*. Geneva, Switzerland. http://postconflict.unep.ch/publications/sistan.pdf.

———. 2007. *Sudan: Post-conflict environmental assessment*. Kenya, Nairobi. http://postconflict.unep.ch/publications/UNEP_Sudan.pdf.

———. 2010. *Sierra Leone: Environment, conflict and peacebuilding assessment*. Geneva, Switzerland. http://postconflict.unep.ch/publications/Sierra_Leone.pdf.

———. 2011. *Water issues in the Democratic Republic of the Congo: Challenges and opportunities*. Nairobi, Kenya. http://postconflict.unep.ch/publications/UNEP_DRC_water.pdf.

———. 2012. *Greening the blue helmets: Environment, natural resources and UN peacekeeping operations*. Nairobi, Kenya. http://postconflict.unep.ch/publications/UNEP_greening_blue_helmets.pdf.

———. 2013a. *Natural resource management and peacebuilding in Afghanistan*. Nairobi, Kenya. www.unep.org/disastersandconflicts/portals/155/countries/Afghanistan/pdf/UNEP_Afghanistan_NRM.pdf.

———. 2013b. Relationships and resources. June 24.

———. 2013c. Governance for peace over natural resources: A review of transitions in environmental governance in Africa as a resource for peacebuilding and environmental management in Sudan. Nairobi, Kenya. www.unep.org/disastersandconflicts/Portals/155/countries/sudan/pdf/Governance%20for%20Peace_Sudan_Web.pdf.

UNHCR (United Nations High Commissioner for Refugees). 2006. Practical guide to the systematic use of standards and indicators in UNHCR Operations. 2nd ed. Geneva, Switzerland. www.unhcr.org/cgi-bin/texis/vtx/home/opendocPDFViewer.html?docid=40eaa9804&query=refugee%20protection.

———. 2011. *UNHCR statistical yearbook 2011: Trends in displacement, protection and solutions*. Geneva, Switzerland. www.unhcr.org/516282cf5.html.

———. 2012. *UNHCR global trends 2012—Displacement: The new 21st century challenge*. Geneva, Switzerland. www.unhcr.org/51bacb0f9.html.

UNICEF (United Nations Children's Fund). n.d. Water, sanitation and hygiene. www.unicef.org/media/media_45481.html.

UN PBSO (United Nations Peacebuilding Support Office). 2012. *Peace dividends and beyond: Contributions of administrative and social services to peacebuilding*. New York. www.un.org/en/peacebuilding/pbso/pdf/peace_dividends.pdf.

Unruh, J., and R. C. Williams. 2013. Land: A foundation for peacebuilding. In *Land and post-conflict peacebuilding*, ed. J. Unruh and R. C. Williams. London: Earthscan.

UNSG (United Nations Secretary-General). 2009. *Report of the Secretary-General on peacebuilding in the immediate aftermath of conflict*. A/63/881-S/2009/304. June 11. New York. www.refworld.org/docid/4a4c6c3b2.html.

USAID (United States Agency for International Development). 2009. A guide to economic growth in post-conflict countries. Washington, D.C. http://pdf.usaid.gov/pdf_docs/PNADO408.pdf.

468   Water and post-conflict peacebuilding

———. 2012. Angola desk review. FEWS NET, October. www.fews.net/docs/Publications/AO_DeskReview_2012_10.pdf.

USIP (United States Institute of Peace) and U.S. Army PKSOI (United States Army Peacekeeping and Stability Operations Institute). 2009. *Guiding principles for stabilization and reconstruction.* Washington, D.C.: Endowment of the United States Institute of Peace.

Vardanyan, M., and R. Volk. 2014. Transnational cooperation over shared water resources in the South Caucasus: Reflections on USAID interventions. In *Water and post-conflict peacebuilding*, ed. E. Weinthal, J. Troell, and M. Nakayama. London: Earthscan.

Wakabi, W. 2008. Health situation remains grave in southern Sudan. *Lancet* 372 (9633): 101–102.

Waleij, A., T. Bosetti, R. Doran, and B. Liljedahl. 2014. Environmental stewardship in peace operations: The role of the military. In *Governance, natural resources, and post-conflict peacebuilding*, ed. C. Bruch, C. Muffett, and S. S. Nichols. London: Earthscan.

WASH Advocates. 2013. Water, sanitation and hygiene (WASH) and women and girls. Washington, D.C.

Warrick, J. 2013. Influx of Syrian refugees stretches Jordan's water resources even more thinly. *Washington Post*, June 15.

Weinthal, E. 2000. Making waves: Third parties and international mediation in the Aral Sea Basin. In *Words over war: Mediation and arbitration to prevent deadly conflict*, ed. M. C. Greenberg, J. H. Barton, and M. E. McGuinness. Lanham, MD: Rowman and Littlefield.

———. 2002. *State making and environmental cooperation: Linking domestic and international politics in Central Asia.* Cambridge, MA: MIT Press.

Weinthal, E., and A. Marei. 2002. One resource, two visions: The prospects for Israeli-Palestinian water cooperation. *Water International* 27 (4): 460–467.

WHO (World Health Organization). 2008. Cholera in Iraq. Sept. 10. www.who.int/csr/don/2008_09_10a/en/.

Woertz, E. 2011. Arab food, water, and the big landgrab that wasn't. *Brown Journal of World Affairs* 18 (1): 119–132.

Wolf, A. 2007. Shared waters: Conflict and cooperation. *Annual Review of Environment and Resources* 32:241–269.

Wolf, A. T., A. Kramer, A. Carius, and G. D. Dabelko. 2005. Managing water cooperation and conflict. In *State of the world 2005: Redefining global security.* Washington, D.C.: Worldwatch Institute. http://tbw.geo.orst.edu/publications/abst_docs/wolf_sow_2005.pdf.

Wolf, A. T., and J. T. Newton. n.d. *Case study of transboundary dispute resolution: The Indus Water Treaty.* www.transboundarywaters.orst.edu/research/case_studies/Indus_New.htm.

Wolf, A. T., S. B. Yoffe, and M. Giordano. 2003. International water: Identifying basins at risk. *Water Policy* 5 (1): 29–60.

World Bank. 2003. Project performance assessment report Bosnia and Herzegovina: Water, sanitation and solid waste urgent works projects (TF-24032). www-wds.worldbank.org/external/default/WDSContentServer/WDSP/IB/2004/01/08/000160016_20040108172120/Rendered/INDEX/274920BA.txt.

———. 2004. *The role of the World Bank in conflict and development: An evolving agenda.* Washington, D.C. http://siteresources.worldbank.org/INTCPR/214578-1112884026494/20482669/ConflictAgenda2004.pdf.

———. 2011. *World development report 2011: Conflict, security, and development.* Washington, D.C. http://tbw.geo.orst.edu/publications/abst_docs/wolf_sow_2005.pdf.

———. n.d. Indus Basin Supplemental Agreement becomes effective. http://go.worldbank.org/2RW90WESZ0.

World Bank and UNHCR (United Nations High Commissioner for Refugees). 2011. *Research study on IDPs in urban settings—Afghanistan.* Kabul, Afghanistan. http://siteresources.worldbank.org/EXTSOCIALDEVELOPMENT/Resources/244362-1265299949041/6766328-1265299960363/WB-UNHCR-IDP_Full-Report.pdf.

Zawahri, N. A. 2009. India, Pakistan and cooperation along the Indus River. *Water Policy* 11 (1): 1–20.

———. 2014. Refugee rehabilitation and transboundary cooperation: India, Pakistan, and the Indus River system. In *Water and post-conflict peacebuilding*, ed. E. Weinthal, J. Troell, and M. Nakayama. London: Earthscan.

APPENDIX 1
List of abbreviations

ABC: Abyei Boundaries Commission (Sudan)
AEL: Association of Evangelicals of Liberia
AGC-HAT: Army Geospatial Center's Hydrologic Analysis Team (United States)
ANDS: Afghanistan National Development Strategy
bcm: billion cubic meters
BiH: Bosnia and Herzegovina
CAWSS: Central Authority for Water Supply and Sewerage (Afghanistan)
CCI: Compagnie de Constructions Internationales
CDC: community development council
CESCR: (United Nations) Committee on Economic, Social and Cultural Rights
CEDAW: Convention on the Elimination of All Forms of Discrimination against Women
CFA: (Nile River Basin) Cooperative Framework Agreement
CLTS: community-led total sanitation
CMO-HEI: Civil Military Operations–Human Environment Interaction
COIN: counterinsurgency
CPA: Comprehensive Peace Agreement
CRC: (United Nations) Committee on the Rights of the Child
CRIM: Center for Restoration of the Iraqi Marshlands
DACAAR: Danish Committee for Aid to Afghan Refugees
DRC: Democratic Republic of the Congo
DRPC: Danube River Protection Convention
DRR: disaster risk reduction
EcoGov: Environmental Governance Project (Philippines)
EPAL: Luanda Provincial Water Company (Empresa de Aguas de Luanda) (Angola)
ESCR: economic, social, and cultural rights
EST: environmentally sound technologies
EU: European Union
EU-CARDS: European Union Community Assistance for Reconstruction, Development and Stabilization

472 Water and post-conflict peacebuilding

FDA: Forestry Development Authority (Liberia)
FASRB: Framework Agreement on the Sava River Basin
FoEME: Friends of the Earth Middle East
FPOs: field program officers
GAM: global acute malnutrition
GDP: gross domestic product
GEF: Global Environment Facility
GIZ: German Society for International Cooperation (Deutsche Gesellschaft für Internationale Zusammenarbeit)
GOIRA: government of the Islamic Republic of Afghanistan
GOS: government of the Sudan
GOSS: government of Southern Sudan (prior to July 9, 2011); government of South Sudan (as of July 9, 2011)
GRET: Group for Research and Technology Exchanges (Groupe de Recherche et d'Echanges Technologiques)
GTZ: German Technical Cooperation (Deutsche Gesellschaft für Technische Zusammenarbeit)
GWC: Global WASH Cluster
HAVA: Helmand-Arghandab Valley Authority (Afghanistan)
HDI: Human Development Index
HN: host nation
ICC: International Criminal Court
ICRC: International Committee of the Red Cross
ICPDR: International Commission for the Protection of the Danube River
ICTY: International Criminal Tribunal for the Former Yugoslavia
IDP: internally displaced person
IGAD: Intergovernmental Authority on Development
IRBM: integrated river basin management
IRC: International Rescue Committee
IRFFI: International Reconstruction Fund Facility for Iraq
IRRF: Iraq Relief and Reconstruction Fund
ISAF: International Security Assistance Force
ISRBC: International Sava River Basin Commission
IT: information technology
KfW: Reconstruction Credit Institute (Kreditanstalt für Wiederaufbau)
KMS: Committee for Clean Water (Kamati ya Maji Safi) (DRC)
KRBP: Kunduz River Basin Programme (Afghanistan)
LFI: Liberia Forest Initiative
LOCP: Lake Ohrid Conservation Project
LRA: Lord's Resistance Army
LUPP: Luanda Urban Poverty Programme (Angola)
LWSC: Liberia Water and Sewer Corporation
MDG: Millennium Development Goal
MFA: Ministry of Foreign Affairs

List of abbreviations **473**

MOU: memorandum of understanding
MRRD: Ministry for Rural Rehabilitation and Development (Afghanistan)
MSF: Doctors without Borders (Médecins Sans Frontières)
MW: megawatt
MZWP: Matabeleland-Zambezi Water Project
mcm: million cubic meters
NAIADES: Navigation and Inland Waterway Action and Development in Europe
NATO: North Atlantic Treaty Organization
NBI: Nile Basin Initiative
NCP: National Congress Party (India)
NGO: nongovernmental organization
Nil-COM: Nile Council of Ministers (of Water)
NRC: Norwegian Refugee Council
NSP: National Solidarity Programme (Afghanistan)
OSCE: Organization for Security and Co-operation in Europe
PCA: Permanent Court of Arbitration
PCBs: polychlorinated biphenyls
PIC: Permanent Indus Commission
PLO: Palestine Liberation Organization
PPP: public-private partnership
PRT: provincial reconstruction team
RC: Regional Command
RBA: rights-based approach
REC: Regional Environmental Center for Central and Eastern Europe
SAA: Stabilization and Association Agreement
SCWP: South Caucasus Water Program
SFRY: Socialist Federal Republic of Yugoslavia
SGBV: sexual and gender-based violence
SNHR: National Rural Water Service (Service National d'Hydraulique Rurale)
    (DRC)
SPLA: Sudan People's Liberation Army (South Sudan)
SPLM: Sudan People's Liberation Movement (South Sudan)
STIM: sustainable triangle for irrigation management
SWSS: sustainable water supply and sanitation
TCAPF: Tactical Conflict Assessment and Planning Framework
U.S.: United States
UK: United Kingdom
UN: United Nations
UNAMA: United Nations Assistance Mission in Afghanistan
UNAMID: United Nations/African Union Mission in Darfur
UNDAF: United Nations Development Assistance Framework
UNDP: United Nations Development Programme
UNECE: United Nations Economic Commission for Europe
UNEP: United Nations Environment Programme

474 Water and post-conflict peacebuilding

UNESCO: United Nations Educational, Scientific and Cultural Organization
UNGA: United Nations General Assembly
UNICEF: United Nations Children's Fund
UNITA: National Union for the Total Independence of Angola (União Nacional para a Independência Total de Angola)
UNHCR: United Nations High Commissioner for Refugees
UNMIS: United Nations Missions in Sudan
UNRWA: United Nations Relief and Works Agency for Palestinian Refugees
UNSC: United Nations Security Council
UNTSO: United Nations Truce Supervision Organization
USACE-ERDC: United States Army Corps of Engineers Engineer Research and Development Center
USAID: United States Agency for International Development
WASH: water, sanitation, and hygiene
WFD: Water Framework Directive
WFP: World Food Programme
WHO: World Health Organization
WRAPP: Water for Recovery and Peace Program (Sudan)
WRMA: Water Resources Management Agency (Armenia)
WUA: water user association
ZANU: Zimbabwe African National Union
ZAPU: Zimbabwe African People's Union

APPENDIX 2
Author biographies

Ali Al-Lami is a minister's advisor in Iraq's Ministry of Environment. From 2005 to 2008 he was the national coordinator for the Iraqi Marshlands Project of the United Nations Environment Programme. Al-Lami's academic experience includes serving as an assistant professor and chief researcher in aquatic ecology at Iraq's Fish Research Center. He has published more than one hundred papers, in both Arabic and English, in the field of aquatic ecology, in journals that include *Marina Mesopotamica*, *Journal of Environmental Science and Health*, and *Journal for Pure and Applied Sciences*. Al-Lami holds a B.Sc. in aquatic ecology and an M.Sc. in algal ecology, both from Basrah University, Iraq, and a Ph.D. in freshwater ecology from Al-Mustansiriyah University, Iraq.

Jeremy Allouche is a research fellow at the Institute of Development Studies, University of Sussex, United Kingdom. He previously worked at the University of Oxford; the Massachusetts Institute of Technology; the École Polytechnique Fédérale de Lausanne, where he was the director of the Water Institutions and Management Competence Centre, at the Swiss Graduate Institute of Public Administration; and the Graduate Institute of International and Development Studies, Geneva. Allouche's fields of interests are public-private partnerships, the governance and regulation of water supply and sanitation systems, service delivery and post-conflict reconstruction, water security, and transboundary water conflicts. Among the books that Allouche has written or edited are *Water Privatisation: Transnational Corporations and the Re-Regulation of the Water Industry* (Spon Press, 2001), *The Multi-Governance of Water* (SUNY Press, 2006), and *Water and Liberalisation: European Water Scenarios* (International Water Association Publishing, 2007).

Chizuru Aoki is coordinator of the Climate Mitigation Program and senior technology transfer officer at the secretariat of the Global Environment Facility (GEF). Before joining the GEF in 2010, she was senior program officer at the United Nations Environment Programme (UNEP), where she led a program that facilitated the transfer of environmentally sound water and sanitation technologies and coordinated UNEP's project for the environmental management of the Iraqi

476 Water and post-conflict peacebuilding

marshlands. Aoki first joined UNEP in 1993, helping to initiate the National Cleaner Production Centre network. In 1997, she left UNEP to become a Fulbright Fellow at the Massachusetts Institute of Technology (MIT), where she earned a Ph.D. in technology, management, and policy. Before returning to UNEP, in 2003, Aoki was a researcher at MIT. In addition to her Ph.D., she holds a B.S. in civil engineering from Rice University and an M.S. in environmental and water resources engineering from the University of Texas at Austin.

Slavko Bogdanovic is a professor of environmental law and water law at the Faculty of Law of the University Business Academy in Novi Sad, Serbia. He has written or coauthored more than 130 research papers on water law and environmental law at the national and international levels. He has also edited or coedited more than twenty-five books, the most recent of which are *Water Law and Policy in the Mediterranean: An Evolving Nexus* (Faculty of Law of the University Business Academy in Novi Sad and Faculty of Sciences of the University of Novi Sad, in collaboration with the Potential Conflict to Cooperation Potential program of the United Nations Educational, Scientific and Cultural Organization, 2011) and *Environmental Security in South-Eastern Europe: International Agreements and Their Implementation* (Springer, NATO Science for Peace and Security Series, 2011). Bogdanovic has also served as a legal expert, project team leader, and project coordinator in numerous research projects implemented by international organizations, international consultancy companies, and scientific organizations. He holds an LL.D. from the Faculty of Law of the University of Novi Sad.

Gidon Bromberg is the Israeli codirector of EcoPeace/Friends of the Earth Middle East. He has presented before the United Nations Commission on Sustainable Development, the U.S. House Committee on Foreign Affairs, the European Parliament, and the advisory committee of the UN High-Level Panel on Security. Bromberg is a member of the Israeli Inter-Ministerial Committee on the Future of the Dead Sea, the Israel UNESCO World Heritage Committee, and the Inter-Ministerial Committee for Sustainable Development in Israel; he is also a World Fellow of Yale University. In 2008, Bromberg and his codirectors were honored by *Time* magazine as Heroes of the Environment; in 2009, they received the prestigious Skoll Award for Social Entrepreneurship. Bromberg holds a B.Ec. and a law degree from Monash University, in Australia. As a fellow of the New Israel Fund, he earned a master's degree in international environmental law at American University, Washington, D.C.

Murray Burt, a chartered civil engineer in the United Kingdom and New Zealand, is the global water, sanitation, and public health program manager for Tearfund United Kingdom. He has extensive field experience working within commercial engineering consultancies and nongovernmental organizations in Africa, Asia, and New Zealand. Burt is the author of several publications focused on water and environmental management, and received the Arthur Mead Award from the

Institute of Professional Engineers New Zealand for promoting environmental sustainability principles. Burt's current work focuses primarily on conflict and post-conflict regions in Africa and Asia. He holds a B.S. in civil engineering from the University of Auckland, New Zealand, and an M.S. in water and environmental management from Loughborough University, United Kingdom.

Allan Cain is the director of Development Workshop and the cofounder and president of KixiCrédito, Angola's first nonbank microfinance institution. He is an architect and specialist in project planning and urban development with more than thirty-five years of professional experience in developing countries, many of those years in conflict and post-conflict Angola, where he pioneered housing microfinance. Cain has published widely in international journals; has consulted for a number of international organizations, including the World Bank, United Nations Habitat, and the European Union; is a member of the boards of several development institutions; and has lectured at universities in Angola, Canada, China, Norway, South Africa, the United Kingdom, and the United States. He is also a member of the international board of directors of BPD Water and Sanitation, where he represents the civil society sector. Cain holds a bachelor's degree in environmental studies from the University of Waterloo and did his graduate studies at the Architectural Association in London. He undertook further studies at Harvard Business School (in microfinance) and the University of Colorado-Boulder (in housing finance).

Amar Čolakhodžić is an environmental and sustainability consultant who assesses sustainable real estate developments to ensure conformity to green building standards, primarily in the Gulf Cooperation Council region but also internationally. He has undertaken a number of eco-friendly projects, including the development of a green project-investment pipeline and the establishment of a regional sustainability information center for Southeastern Europe. He has also served as an independent environmental policy analyst and environmental impact assessment evaluator in Bosnia and Herzegovina. Čolakhodžić holds a B.S. in business and project management and an M.S. in environmental sciences and policy from Central European University, where his thesis was a comparative assessment of the capacity of the International Sava River Basin Commission to prevent water use conflicts and foster cooperation.

Alex Dehgan is the chief scientist for the U.S. Agency for International Development (USAID). Before joining USAID, Dehgan held various positions at the U.S. Department of State, where he developed a science diplomacy strategy to help address foreign policy issues in Afghanistan, Iran, and Iraq. While serving as the founding country director for the Afghanistan Biodiversity Conservation Program of the Wildlife Conservation Society (WCS), Dehgan led WCS efforts to help create Afghanistan's first national park and conduct the first comprehensive biological surveys of the country in thirty years. In 2005, *Seed Magazine* included Dehgan on its list of Icons of Science; in 2011, he received the World Technology

478 Water and post-conflict peacebuilding

Award for Policy. Deghan has also received awards from USAID, the U.S. Department of State, and the U.S. Department of Defense. He holds a B.S. in zoology and political science from Duke University, an M.Sc. and a Ph.D. from the Committee on Evolutionary Biology at the University of Chicago, and a J.D. from the University of California, Hastings College of the Law.

Marija Filipović is an environmental policy professional whose past experience includes provision of the climate change adaptation portfolio for the Gateway National Recreation Area in the New York–New Jersey metropolitan area. Filipović has also researched design and implementation of U.S. climate policies on the federal and state levels. Currently, her main interests are the environmental impact of meat production on land, water, and air quality; the impact of livestock production on climate change, wildlife, and aquatic ecosystems; the implications of genetically modified organisms for the environment, and for human and animal health; world food crises; agronomics; and future trends in meat production. Filipović holds an M.P.A. in environmental science and policy from Columbia University's School of International and Public Affairs.

Mona Funiciello is a Climate Policy Fellow at GlobalSolutions.org. She was previously a research intern at the Environmental Law Institute, where she focused on post-conflict natural resource management. In 2011, a paper Funiciello wrote— "Expanding the Role and Function of Science Advisory Panels: A New Way to Bridge Science and Policy in Environmental Treaty Regimes"—appeared in volume 18 of *Papers on International Environmental Negotiation*, a series published by the Program on Negotiation at Harvard Law School. Before entering graduate school, Funiciello spent eight years working as a fundraiser for the Massachusetts Audubon Society. She holds a B.A. in English from the University at Albany, State University of New York, and an M.A. in urban and environmental policy and planning from Tufts University, where she studied international environmental policy; international planning; and sustainable development, with a focus on the Asia-Pacific region. Her master's thesis focused on building capacity for forest carbon monitoring in Indonesia.

Munther J. Haddadin is a consultant based in Amman, Jordan. He has served as minister of water and irrigation in the Jordan cabinet (1997–1998); as a senior negotiator in charge of water, energy, and the environment in Jordan's delegations to the Middle East peace process (1991–1995); and as a courtesy professor at Oregon State University (since 2001), the University of Oklahoma (since 2003), and the University of Central Florida (since 2007). He holds a Ph.D. in civil engineering from the University of Washington, in Seattle.

Sam Huston is a water sector expert with more than eight years of experience working on water and sanitation projects in Afghanistan, the Dominican Republic, Ethiopia, Kenya, Mozambique, South Sudan, Sudan, and Uganda. Huston worked in the water sector in South Sudan for more than three years, first as the program coordinator for the Water for Recovery and Peace Program, which was developed by Pact and funded by the U.S. Agency for International Development (USAID) and the World Bank; he then worked as the water and sanitation advisor for USAID in South Sudan. In addition, Huston helped establish and served as the chair of the Water, Sanitation and Hygiene Donor Group for South Sudan. Huston holds a B.S. in civil engineering from the University of Minnesota and an M.A. in conflict resolution from the University of Bradford, United Kingdom.

Bilha Joy Keiru, a development practitioner with more than eight years of experience in the humanitarian and development fields, is currently working for Tearfund United Kingdom as a policy and learning officer in a water, sanitation, and hygiene program being conducted in conflict-affected and post-conflict zones in Africa, Asia, and Haiti; the program is funded by the United Kingdom's Department for International Development. In 2009, two papers that Keiru coauthored were presented at international conferences: "Innovative Rainwater Harvesting Techniques for Emergencies: Lessons from the Field" (presented at the 34th Water, Engineering and Development Centre International Conference) and "Strengthening Community Management of Water Schemes in the Post Conflict Context of Eastern DRC" (presented at World Water Week). Keiru holds a B.A. in communications and an M.A. in development studies from the University of Leeds, United Kingdom.

Nader Al Khateeb has more than thirty years of experience in the water and environmental sectors, and has served as the Palestinian director of EcoPeace/Friends of the Earth Middle East (FoEME) since 2001. FoEME is the only regional organization with offices in Palestine, Jordan and Israel. From 1984 to 1993, Al Khateeb served as chief engineer for the Bethlehem, Beit Jala, and Beit Sahour Water Authority. From 1994 to 1997, he was a senior water resource engineer with the Water Resources Action Program of the United Nations Development Programme, consulting on the effort to formulate and establish the Palestinian Water Authority. In 1998, he joined the newly established Water and Environmental Development Organization (WEDO); in 2001, WEDO became the base for the Palestinian branch of FoEME. In 2008, Al Khateeb and his two codirectors were honored by *Time* magazine as Heroes of the Environment; in 2009, they were awarded the prestigious Skoll Award for Social Entrepreneurship.

Elizabeth Koch-Ya'ari is the Israeli Jordan River Rehabilitation Project coordinator of EcoPeace/Friends of the Earth Middle East. Koch-Ya'ari holds a B.A. in international relations and an M.A. in government, diplomacy, and strategy and has extensive experience managing regional and international projects in the fields of peacebuilding, environmental peacemaking, and cultural heritage.

Jana Kovandžić works in the environmental consultancy of Schneider Electric. Previously, she worked for the Earth Charter Youth Leadership Team and undertook environmental education projects for the United Nations Association of Serbia. Among her interests is exploring the potential for renewable energy in

480   Water and post-conflict peacebuilding

the Balkans. As a member of Rotaract Club, Kovandžić leads a project supporting children with albinism in East Africa. She holds a B.A. in political science from the University of Belgrade and an M.Sc. in environmental science, policy, and management from Central European University, Lund University, and Manchester University.

Sivapragasam Kugaprasatham has specialized in water supply, sanitation, environmental assessment, and project management in developing countries since the mid-1990s. From 2004 to 2009, he served as project officer at the International Environmental Technology Center, a branch of the United Nations Environment Programme; in that capacity, he provided technical and implementation support for drinking water and sanitation projects; worked on marshland management pilot projects; and collected and analyzed data on marshland conditions and the capacity building of the Iraqi partners. Kugaprasatham's research work on biofilms has been published in *Water Research* and *Water Science and Technology*. He holds a B.S. in civil engineering from the University of Peradeniya, Sri Lanka; an M.S. in environmental engineering from the Asian Institute of Technology (AIT), Thailand; and a Ph.D. in urban engineering from the University of Tokyo. He was among the recipients of a UN21 Award for the Iraqi Marshlands Project and received the Hisamatsu Prize for outstanding academic performance at AIT.

Jennifer McCarthy is a Canadian national who works for a British nongovernmental organization (NGO) that implements programs focused on gender equity and rural livelihoods in partnership with civil society groups in Afghanistan, Pakistan, and the Middle East. McCarthy has also worked with the United Kingdom Stabilisation Unit, as well as with NGOs in Burma, Canada, and Indonesia. She holds a Ph.D. in geography from King's College London, and her research focuses on the connections between participatory development, village-level power structures, and vulnerability in rural northern Afghanistan.

Munqeth Mehyar is president of and the Jordanian director of EcoPeace/Friends of the Earth Middle East (FoEME), a unique regional organization that brings together Jordanian, Palestinian, and Israeli environmentalists to promote sustainable development and advance peace efforts in the Middle East. As Jordanian director, Mehyar leads FoEME activities related to the Jordan River, the Dead Sea, and the Good Water Neighbors project. He has organized dozens of conferences, workshops, and study tours; supervised research on shared ecosystems; and coauthored reports and policy papers; he also speaks regularly on water, peace, and security issues. In addition to his role at FoEME, he is vice president of the Jordan Society for Sustainable Development. In 2000, Mehyar received the Al Houssain Distinguished Giving medal for his entrepreneurial activities. In 2008, he and his codirectors were honored by *Time* magazine as Heroes of the Environment; in 2009, they were awarded the prestigious Skoll Award for Social Entrepreneurship. Mehyar holds a degree in regional planning and architecture from the University of Louisiana.

Author biographies **481**

Mehdi Mirzaee is an assistant professor at the School of Civil Engineering, Islamic Azad University (Central Tehran Branch), Iran, and courtesy faculty in the Department of Geosciences, Oregon State University. He is a water resource management and policy expert and has worked in many national water resource projects since 1994. In 2007, he published the first Iranian book on integrated water resource management (IWRM) and has since tried to further define and apply this approach to water development projects in Iran. His areas of interest and study include IWRM, water policy and management, transboundary watersheds, and conflict resolution, particularly in the Middle East. Although a civil engineer by profession, Mirzaee is also interested in the interaction between development and sociopolitical issues. He holds a bachelor's degree from Islamic Azad University, Iran, and a master's degree from Amirkabir University of Technology–Tehran, both in civil engineering and water resources, and a Ph.D. from K.N. Toosi University of Technology, Iran, in hydrology and water resources.

Daanish Mustafa is a reader in politics and environment at the Department of Geography, King's College London. A majority of his research has focused on the intersection of water resources, environmental hazards, and development geography. Mustafa has published scholarly articles on the critical geographies of violence and terror—focusing mostly on Pakistan, but also on South Asia in general, Central America, and the United States. He has extensive experience in the nonprofit and development sectors in Pakistan. In 1998, Mustafa became the first recipient of the Gilbert F. White Award of the Association of American Geographers. He holds a B.A. from Middlebury College, an M.A. from the University of Hawaii–Manoa, and a Ph.D. from the University of Colorado–Boulder.

Mikiyasu Nakayama is a professor in the Department of International Studies, Graduate School of Frontier Sciences, University of Tokyo. Nakayama's research subjects include the application of satellite remote-sensing data for environmental monitoring of lake basins, the use of geographic information systems for the environmental management of river and lake basins, environmental impact assessment methodologies applicable to involuntary resettlement caused by dam construction, and the involvement of international organizations in the management of international water bodies. Nakayama holds a B.A., an M.Sc., and a Ph.D., all in agricultural engineering, from the University of Tokyo.

Laura Jean Palmer-Moloney is a senior research geographer at the Engineer Research and Development Center (ERDC) of the U.S. Army Corps of Engineers, a post she has held since 2009. During 2011and 2012 she deployed to Afghanistan, where she served as senior advisor on watershed management, reporting to the Commanding General of Regional Command Southwest Camp Leatherneck, Helmand Province. Palmer-Moloney has also served as the principal investigator of the ERDC Civil-Military Operations–Human Environment Interaction research effort and as a subject matter expert for the Helmand Deep Dive initiative, sponsored by the Office of the U.S. Secretary of Defense Strategic Multilayer

482   Water and post-conflict peacebuilding

Assessment Office. Palmer-Moloney is the author or coauthor of numerous publications, including her 2012 Ph.D. dissertation titled *Human-Environment Interaction and Water Complexities: Mustering Science and Policy for a Coastal Resources Management Approach to Counterinsurgency (COIN) Operations* and "Water as Nexus: Linking U.S. National Security to Environmental Security" (*Journal of Military Geography*, 2011). She holds a Ph.D. in coastal resources management, with an emphasis in wetlands ecology and hydrology, from East Carolina University, Greenville, North Carolina.

Jean-François Pinera, a water and sanitation specialist with more than twenty years of experience in project management, emergency operations, and research in Africa, Asia, the Caribbean, and the Caucasus, is currently employed by the International Committee of the Red Cross. His interests include emergency response (especially in urban areas) and water supply and sanitation for low-income urban communities. He has worked with a wide range of organizations, including Médecins Sans Frontières, Action Contre la Faim, and the United Nations Children's Fund. Pinera also spent three years as a research scholar at the Water, Engineering and Development Centre, which is part of Loughborough University, United Kingdom. Pinera holds a Ph.D. from Loughborough University; his Ph.D. research focused on cities affected by armed conflicts.

Robert A. Reed is a senior lecturer at the Water, Engineering and Development Centre, part of the School of Civil and Building Engineering, Loughborough University, United Kingdom. A public health engineer with more than thirty years of experience in emergency water supply and sanitation, Reed has participated in emergency field operations in Africa and Asia; conducted research to improve technology and management in the fields of emergency water supply and sanitation; taught at the undergraduate, postgraduate, and professional development levels; and initiated a new master's program, focused on engineering in emergencies.

Salman M. A. Salman is an academic researcher and consultant on water law and policy. He is also a fellow with the International Water Resources Association. Until December 2009, he worked as lead counsel and water law adviser with the legal vice presidency of the World Bank. Before joining the World Bank, he was a legal officer with the United Nations International Fund for Agricultural Development. Prior to that, he was a lecturer at the Law School of the University of Khartoum, Sudan. Salman is the author, coauthor, or editor of ten books and has published more than sixty articles and book chapters on various issues in water law and policy. Some of his books have been translated into and published in Arabic, Chinese, French, and Russian. In 2001, he was selected as the director of the English-speaking section of the Hague Academy of International Law session on water resources and international law. Salman obtained his LL.B. from the University of Khartoum Law School and holds an LL.M. and a J.S.D. from Yale Law School.

Author biographies 483

Stephen Stec is an adjunct professor at Central European University, Hungary, and a fellow of the Institute for East European Law and Russian Studies at Leiden University, in the Netherlands. In 2009 and 2011–2012, he was Visiting MESPOM Scholar-in-Residence at Middlebury College and the Monterey Institute of International Studies. He has worked in countries in transition for two decades, establishing the environmental law programs of the American Bar Association/Central European and Eurasian Law Initiative and the Regional Environmental Center for Central and Eastern Europe (REC). While at REC, he directed a U.S. government–funded project to support the establishment of the International Sava River Basin Commission. From 2006 to 2008, Stec served on the managing board of the Environment and Security Initiative. In 2007, he was awarded the Rule of Law Award by the American Bar Association.

Mikiko Sugiura is a lecturer at the Graduate University of Advanced Studies, more commonly known as Sokendai. Her field-based research focuses on water resources management—in particular, the management of water scarcity and conflict. She holds a B.A. in law from the University of Tokyo, and an M.A. and Ph.D., both in international relations, also from the University of Tokyo.

Mara Tignino is a senior researcher at the Platform for International Water Law at the University of Geneva School of Law. Her areas of expertise include the protection of water during armed conflict, the rights and duties of nonstate actors with respect to water resource management, and the settlement of water disputes. In addition to working as a consultant to governments, the private sector, international agencies, and nongovernmental organizations, Tignino has served as a visiting scholar at the George Washington University School of Law, Washington, D.C., and is the author of *L'Eau et la Guerre: Éléments pour un Régime Juridique* in the collection of the Geneva Academy for International Humanitarian Law and Human Rights (Bruylant, 2011). She holds a B.A. in political science from the Libera Università Internazionale degli Studi Sociali, in Rome, and an M.A. and Ph.D. in international law from the Graduate Institute of International and Development Studies, Geneva.

Yuka Toguchi is a graduate student in the Department of International Studies, Graduate School of Frontier Sciences, University of Tokyo. Her research subjects include flood control measures undertaken by governments and local populations, and resource management in post-conflict societies. She holds a B.A. in civil engineering from the College of Science and Technology, Nihon University, where she completed an undergraduate thesis titled "Analysis of Environmental International Agreements: Comparison of Water and Sanitation with Climate Change."

Jessica Troell is a senior attorney and director of the International Water Program at the Environmental Law Institute (ELI). She has extensive experience in international and comparative water law and policy, with a focus on participatory water governance, community-based resource management, transboundary water

484　Water and post-conflict peacebuilding

management, adaptation to climate change in the water sector, and institutional development and capacity building. At ELI, Troell works with nongovernmental organizations, governments, the private sector, and universities throughout the world to create, implement, and enforce sustainable water laws, policies, and management mechanisms. Before joining ELI, she was a law fellow at the Mandela Institute, Witwatersrand University, South Africa, and a Peace Corps volunteer in Morocco. She has also worked at the International Environmental Law Office of the U.S. Environmental Protection Agency and the Natural Resources Defense Council. Troell is a graduate of Oberlin College and the University of Virginia School of Law.

Marina Vardanyan is the leader of the water and energy portfolio of the U.S. Agency for International Development office in Armenia and the mission environmental officer. She also assists the European Commission as an independent expert, evaluating projects in the fields of global monitoring for environment and security, water management, biodiversity, and environmental management. Vardanyan has served as a visiting lecturer in environmental economics and water management at the American University of Armenia, and as an associate professor in environmental economics at the Yerevan State Institute of Economics, and at the Department of Ecology, Yerevan State University. Her publications include "Towards Integrated Water Resources Management in Armenia" (Wessex Institute, 2005) and "MIS Systems in Armenian Water Resources Management: A Case Study" (Wessex Institute, 2004), both coauthored, and "Recent Improvements in Armenian Water Governance." Vardanyan holds an M.S. in biophysics from Yerevan State University and a Ph.D. from the Institute of Agrochemical Problems and Hydroponics, National Academy of Sciences of the Republic of Armenia.

Richard Volk provides technical and managerial support for a variety of watershed and coastal resources management activities of the U.S. Agency for International Development (USAID) Office of Water, where he has worked since 1998. He also manages several coastal and aquatic resource management programs for USAID and provides technical assistance to USAID missions on the design and implementation of basin management and integrated coastal management initiatives worldwide. During his thirty years in natural resource management, he has worked in more than fifty countries, providing technical assistance to numerous programs addressing water and coastal resources management, fisheries, biodiversity conservation, climate adaptation, and environmental planning. Before joining USAID, Volk was executive director of the Corpus Christi Bay National Estuary Program, a five-year scientific assessment and consensus-building effort designed to develop a comprehensive conservation and management plan for three of the seven major estuaries on the Texas coast. Volk holds a B.S. in biology and an M.P.A. in development assistance.

Erika Weinthal is an associate professor of environmental policy and associate dean for international programs at the Nicholas School of the Environment, Duke

University. Her research focuses on water cooperation and conflict, the political economy of the resource curse, and climate change adaptation. Her book *State Making and Environmental Cooperation: Linking Domestic Politics and International Politics in Central Asia* (MIT Press, 2002) received the 2003 Chadwick Alger Prize and the 2003 Lynton Keith Caldwell Prize. She is the coauthor (with Pauline Jones Luong) of *Oil Is Not a Curse: Ownership Structure and Institutions in Soviet Successor States* (Cambridge University Press, 2010). She serves on the Executive Committee of the Faculty Advisory Board for the Duke Human Rights Center; is a member of the Expert Advisory Group on Environment, Conflict and Peacebuilding of the United Nations Environment Programme; and is an associate editor at *Global Environmental Politics*. Weinthal holds a Ph.D. from Columbia University.

Neda A. Zawahri is an associate professor in the Department of Political Science at Cleveland State University. Her research interests include the management of international river disputes; the role of international institutions in facilitating cooperation and environmental security; and the potential for conflict and co-operation between adversaries. Zawahri's research focuses on the Middle East and South Asia; she has conducted extensive field research in India, Israel, Jordan, Syria, and Turkey, and has published widely on the management of the Euphrates, Indus, Tigris, and Yarmouk rivers. Zawahri holds a Ph.D. from the University of Virginia.

APPENDIX 3

Table of contents for
Post-Conflict Peacebuilding and Natural Resource Management

This book is one of a set of six edited books on post-conflict peacebuilding and natural resource management, all published by Earthscan. Following is the table of contents for the full set. Titles and authors are subject to change.

HIGH-VALUE NATURAL RESOURCES AND POST-CONFLICT PEACEBUILDING
Edited by Päivi Lujala and Siri Aas Rustad

Foreword
Ellen Johnson Sirleaf

High-value natural resources: A blessing or a curse for peace?
Päivi Lujala and Siri Aas Rustad

Part 1: Extraction and extractive industries

Introduction

Bankrupting peace spoilers: Can peacekeepers curtail belligerents' access to resource revenues?
Philippe Le Billon

Mitigating risks and realizing opportunities: Environmental and social standards for foreign direct investment in high-value natural resources
Jill Shankleman

Contract renegotiation and asset recovery in post-conflict settings
Philippe Le Billon

Reopening and developing mines in post-conflict settings: The challenge of company-community relations
Volker Boege and Daniel M. Franks

488   Water and post-conflict peacebuilding

Diamonds in war, diamonds for peace: Diamond sector management and
kimberlite mining in Sierra Leone
Kazumi Kawamoto

Assigned corporate social responsibility in a rentier state: The case of Angola
Arne Wiig and Ivar Kolstad

Part 2: Commodity and revenue tracking

Introduction

The Kimberley Process at ten: Reflections on a decade of efforts to end the
trade in conflict diamonds
J. Andrew Grant

The Kimberley Process Certification Scheme: A model negotiation?
Clive Wright

The Kimberley Process Certification Scheme: The primary safeguard for the
diamond industry
Andrew Bone

A more formal engagement: A constructive critique of certification as a means
of preventing conflict and building peace
Harrison Mitchell

Addressing the roots of Liberia's conflict through the Extractive Industries
Transparency Initiative
Eddie Rich and T. Negbalee Warner

Excluding illegal timber and improving forest governance: The European
Union's Forest Law Enforcement, Governance and Trade Initiative
Duncan Brack

Part 3: Revenue distribution

Introduction

Sharing natural resource wealth during war-to-peace transitions
Achim Wennmann

Horizontal inequality, decentralizing the distribution of natural resource
revenues, and peace
Michael L. Ross, Päivi Lujala, and Siri Aas Rustad

The Diamond Area Community Development Fund: Micropolitics and
community-led development in post-war Sierra Leone
Roy Maconachie

Direct distribution of natural resource revenues as a policy for peacebuilding
Martin E. Sandbu

Part 4: Allocation and institution building

Introduction

High-value natural resources, development, and conflict: Channels of causation
Paul Collier and Anke Hoeffler

Petroleum blues: The political economy of resources and conflict in Chad
John A. Gould and Matthew S. Winters

Leveraging high-value natural resources to restore the rule of law: The role of
the Liberia Forest Initiative in Liberia's transition to stability
Stephanie L. Altman, Sandra S. Nichols, and John T. Woods

Forest resources and peacebuilding: Preliminary lessons from Liberia and
Sierra Leone
Michael D. Beevers

An inescapable curse? Resource management, violent conflict, and peacebuilding in the Niger Delta
Annegret Mähler

The legal framework for managing oil in post-conflict Iraq: A pattern of abuse
and violence over natural resources
Mishkat Al Moumin

The capitalist civil peace: Some theory and empirical evidence
Indra de Soysa

Part 5: Livelihoods

Introduction

Counternarcotics efforts and Afghan poppy farmers: Finding the right approach
David M. Catarious Jr. and Alison Russell

The Janus nature of opium poppy: A view from the field
Adam Pain

Peace through sustainable forest management in Asia: The USAID Forest
Conflict Initiative
Jennifer Wallace and Ken Conca

Women in the artisanal and small-scale mining sector of the Democratic
Republic of the Congo
Karen Hayes and Rachel Perks

490   Water and post-conflict peacebuilding

Forest user groups and peacebuilding in Nepal
Tina Sanio and Binod Chapagain

Lurking beneath the surface: Oil, environmental degradation, and armed conflict in Sudan
Luke A. Patey

Part 6: Lessons learned

Building or spoiling peace? Lessons from the management of high-value natural resources
Siri Aas Rustad, Päivi Lujala, and Philippe Le Billon

ASSESSING AND RESTORING NATURAL RESOURCES IN POST-CONFLICT PEACEBUILDING
Edited by David Jensen and Steve Lonergan

Foreword
Klaus Töpfer

Placing environment and natural resource risks, impacts, and opportunities on the post-conflict peacebuilding agenda
David Jensen and Steve Lonergan

Part 1: Post-conflict environmental assessments

Introduction

Evaluating the impact of UNEP's post-conflict environmental assessments
David Jensen

Environment and peacebuilding in war-torn societies: Lessons from the UN Environment Programme's experience with post-conflict assessment
Ken Conca and Jennifer Wallace

Medical and environmental intelligence in peace and crisis-management operations
Birgitta Liljedahl, Annica Waleij, Björn Sandström, and Louise Simonsson

Thinking back-end: Improving post-conflict analysis through consulting, adapting to change, and scenario building
Alexander Carius and Achim Maas

Part 2: Remediation of environmental hot spots

Introduction

Salting the Earth: Environmental health challenges in post-conflict reconstruction
Chad Briggs and Inka Weissbecker

Table of contents **491**

Remediation of polluted sites in the Balkans, Iraq, and Sierra Leone
Muralee Thummarukudy, Oli Brown, and Hannah Moosa

The risks of depleted uranium contamination in post-conflict countries:
Findings and lessons learned from UNEP field assessments
Mario Burger

Linking demining to post-conflict peacebuilding: A case study of Cambodia
Nao Shimoyachi-Yuzawa

Part 3: Restoration of natural resources and ecosystems

Introduction

Restoration of damaged land in societies recovering from conflict: The case of
Lebanon
Aïda Tamer-Chammas

Ecological restoration and peacebuilding: The case of the Iraqi marshes
Steve Lonergan

Haiti: Lessons learned and way forward in natural resource management projects
Lucile Gingembre

Peacebuilding and adaptation to climate change
Richard Matthew and Anne Hammill

Part 4: Environmental dimensions of infrastructure and reconstruction

Introduction

Addressing infrastructure needs in post-conflict reconstruction:
An introduction to alternative planning approaches
P. B. Anand

Mitigating the environmental impacts of post-conflict assistance: Assessing
USAID's approach
Charles Kelly

Challenges and opportunities for mainstreaming environmental assessment
tools in post-conflict settings
George Bouma

Environmental assessment as a tool for peacebuilding and development: Initial
lessons from capacity building in Sierra Leone
Oli Brown, Morgan Hauptfleisch, Haddijatou Jallow, and Peter Tarr

Natural resources, post-conflict reconstruction, and regional integration:
Lessons from the Marshall Plan and other reconstruction efforts
Carl Bruch, Ross Wolfarth, and Vladislav Michalcik

492 Water and post-conflict peacebuilding

Making best use of domestic energy sources: The Priority Production System for coal mining and steel production in post–World War II Japan
Mikiyasu Nakayama

Road infrastructure reconstruction as a peacebuilding priority in Afghanistan: Negative implications for land rights
Jon Unruh and Mourad Shalaby

Evaluating post-conflict assistance
Suppiramaniam Nanthikesan and Juha I. Uitto

Part 5: Lessons learned

Natural resources and post-conflict assessment, remediation, restoration, and reconstruction: Lessons and emerging issues
David Jensen and Steve Lonergan

LAND AND POST-CONFLICT PEACEBUILDING
Edited by Jon Unruh and Rhodri C. Williams

Foreword
Jeffrey D. Sachs

Land: A foundation for peacebuilding
Jon Unruh and Rhodri C. Williams

Part 1: Peace negotiations

Introduction

The Abyei territorial dispute between North and South Sudan: Why has its resolution proven difficult?
Salman M. A. Salman

Land tenure and peace negotiations in Mindanao, Philippines
Yuri Oki

Part 2: Response to displacement and dispossession

Introduction

The role of restitution in post-conflict situations
Barbara McCallin

Land issues in post-conflict return and recovery
Samir Elhawary and Sara Pantuliano

Return of land in post-conflict Rwanda: International standards, improvisation, and the role of international humanitarian organizations
John W. Bruce

Post-conflict land tenure issues in Bosnia: Privatization and the politics of reintegrating the displaced
Rhodri C. Williams

Angola: Land resources and conflict
Allan Cain

Refugees and legal reform in Iraq: The Iraqi Civil Code, international standards for the treatment of displaced persons, and the art of attainable solutions
Dan E. Stigall

Part 3: Land management

Introduction

Snow leopards and cadastres: Rare sightings in post-conflict Afghanistan
Douglas E. Batson

Community documentation of land tenure and its contribution to state building in Afghanistan
J. D. Stanfield, Jennifer Brick Murtazashvili, M. Y. Safar, and Akram Salam

Title wave: Land tenure and peacebuilding in Aceh
Arthur Green

Beyond land redistribution: Lessons learned from El Salvador's unfulfilled agrarian revolution
Alexandre Corriveau-Bourque

Institutional aspects of resolving land disputes in post-conflict societies
Peter Van der Auweraert

Rebuilding peace: Land and water management in the Kurdistan Region of northern Iraq
Nesreen Barwari

Transboundary resource management strategies in the Pamir mountain region of Tajikistan
Ian D. Hannam

Part 4: Laws and policies

Introduction

Title through possession or position? Respect for housing, land, and property rights in Cambodia
Rhodri C. Williams

494 Water and post-conflict peacebuilding

Land conflicts and land registration in Cambodia
Manami Sekiguchi and Naomi Hatsukano

Legal frameworks and land issues in Muslim Mindanao
Paula Defensor Knack

Unexplored dimensions: Islamic land systems in Afghanistan, Indonesia, Iraq, and Somalia
Siraj Sait

Customary law and community-based natural resource management in post-conflict Timor-Leste
Naori Miyazawa

Part 5: Lessons learned

Lesson learned in land tenure and natural resource management in post-conflict societies
Jon Unruh and Rhodri C. Williams

WATER AND POST-CONFLICT PEACEBUILDING
Edited by Erika Weinthal, Jessica Troell, and Mikiyasu Nakayama

Foreword
Mikhail Gorbachev

Shoring up peace: Water and post-conflict peacebuilding
Jessica Troell and Erika Weinthal

Part 1: Basic services and human security

Introduction

The role of informal service providers in post-conflict reconstruction and state building
Jeremy Allouche

A tale of two cities: Restoring water services in Kabul and Monrovia
Jean-François Pinera and Robert A. Reed

Conflict and collaboration for water resources in Angola's post-war cities
Allan Cain

Thirsty for peace: The water sector in South Sudan
Sam Huston

Community water management: Experiences from the Democratic Republic of the Congo, Afghanistan, and Liberia
Murray Burt and Bilha Joy Keiru

Environmental management of the Iraqi marshlands in the post-conflict period
Chizuru Aoki, Ali Al-Lami, and Sivapragasam Kugaprasatham

Part 2: Livelihoods

Introduction

Irrigation management and flood control in post–World War II Japan
Mikiko Sugiura, Yuka Toguchi, and Mona Funiciello

Refugee rehabilitation and transboundary cooperation: India, Pakistan, and the Indus River system
Neda A. Zawahri

Despite the best intentions? Experiences with water resource management in northern Afghanistan
Jennifer McCarthy and Daanish Mustafa

Water's role in measuring security and stability in Helmand Province, Afghanistan
Laura Jean Palmer-Moloney

Part 3: Peace processes, cooperation, and confidence building

Introduction

The Jordan River Basin: A conflict like no other
Munther J. Haddadin

Transboundary cooperation in the Lower Jordan River Basin
Munqeth Mehyar, Nader Al Khateeb, Gidon Bromberg, and Elizabeth Koch-Ya'ari

The Sava River: Transitioning to peace in the former Yugoslavia
Amar Čolakhodžić, Marija Filipović, Jana Kovandžić, and Stephen Stec

Transnational cooperation over shared water resources in the South Caucasus: Reflections on USAID interventions
Marina Vardanyan and Richard Volk

Water security and scarcity: Potential destabilization in western Afghanistan and Iranian Sistan and Baluchestan due to transboundary water conflicts
Alex Dehgan, Laura Jean Palmer-Moloney, and Mehdi Mirzaee

496   Water and post-conflict peacebuilding

Water resources in the Sudan North-South peace process and the ramifications
of the secession of South Sudan
Salman M. A. Salman

Part 4: Legal frameworks

Introduction

Management of waters in post-Dayton Bosnia and Herzegovina: Policy, legal,
and institutional aspects
Slavko Bogdanovic

The right to water and sanitation in post-conflict legal mechanisms: An
emerging regime?
Mara Tignino

Part 5: Lessons learned

Harnessing water management for more effective peacebuilding:
Lessons learned
Jessica Troell and Erika Weinthal

LIVELIHOODS, NATURAL RESOURCES, AND POST-CONFLICT PEACEBUILDING
Edited by Helen Young and Lisa Goldman

Foreword: Saving lives, losing livelihoods
Jan Egeland

Managing natural resources for livelihoods: Helping post-conflict
communities survive and thrive
Helen Young and Lisa Goldman

Part 1: Natural resource conflicts, livelihoods, and peacebuilding approaches

Introduction

Social identity, natural resources, and peacebuilding
Arthur Green

Swords into plowshares? Accessing natural resources and securing agricultural
livelihoods in rural Afghanistan
Alan Roe

Forest resources in Cambodia's transition to peace: Lessons for peacebuilding
Srey Chanthy and Jim Schweithelm

Post-tsunami Aceh: Successful peacemaking, uncertain peacebuilding
Michael Renner

Manufacturing peace in "no man's land": Livestock and access to natural resources in the Karimojong Cluster of Kenya and Uganda
Jeremy Lind

Resolving natural resource conflicts to help prevent war: A case from Afghanistan
Liz Alden Wily

Part 2: Innovative approaches to livelihoods in post-conflict situations

Introduction

Transboundary protected areas: Opportunities and challenges
Carol Westrik

A peace park in the Balkans: Cross-border cooperation and livelihoods creation through coordinated environmental conservation
J. Todd Walters

Mountain gorilla ecotourism: Supporting macroeconomic growth and providing local livelihoods
Miko Maekawa, Annette Lanjouw, Eugène Rutagarama, and Douglas Sharp

The interface between natural resources and disarmament, demobilization, and reintegration: Enhancing human security in post-conflict situations
Glaucia Boyer and Adrienne M. Stork

From soldiers to park rangers: Post-conflict natural resource management in Gorongosa National Park
Matthew F. Pritchard

Mitigating conflict in Sierra Leone through mining reform and alternative livelihoods programs for youth
Andrew Keili and Bocar Thiam

Linking to peace: Using BioTrade for biodiversity conservation and peacebuilding in Colombia
Lorena Jaramillo Castro and Adrienne M. Stork

Part 3: Institutions and policies

Introduction

Fisheries policies and the problem of instituting sustainable management: The case of occupied Japan
Harry N. Scheiber and Benjamin Jones

498   Water and post-conflict peacebuilding

Developing capacity for natural resource management in Afghanistan: Process, challenges, and lessons learned by UNEP
Belinda Bowling and Asif Zaidi

Building resilience in rural livelihood systems as an investment in conflict prevention
Blake D. Ratner

Improving natural resource governance and building peace and stability in Mindanao, Philippines
Cynthia Brady, Oliver Agoncillo, Maria Zita Butardo-Toribio, Buenaventura Dolom, and Casimiro V. Olvida

Commerce in the chaos: Bananas, charcoal, fisheries, and conflict in Somalia
Christian Webersik and Alec Crawford

Part 4: Lessons learned

Managing natural resources for livelihoods in post-conflict societies: Lessons learned
Lisa Goldman and Helen Young

GOVERNANCE, NATURAL RESOURCES, AND POST-CONFLICT PEACEBUILDING
Edited by Carl Bruch, Carroll Muffett, and Sandra S. Nichols

Foreword
Óscar Arias Sánchez

Natural resources and post-conflict governance: Building a sustainable peace
Carl Bruch, Carroll Muffett, and Sandra S. Nichols

Part 1: Frameworks for peace

Introduction

Reducing the risk of conflict recurrence: The relevance of natural resource management
Christian Webersik and Marc Levy

Stepping stones to peace? Natural resource provisions in peace agreements
Simon J. A. Mason, Damiano A. Sguaitamatti, and Pilar Ramirez Gröbli

Considerations for determining when to include natural resources in peace agreements ending internal armed conflicts
Marcia A. Dawes

Peacebuilding through natural resource management: The UN Peacebuilding Commission's first five years
Matti Lehtonen

Preparing for peace: A case study of Darfur, Sudan
Margie Buchanan-Smith and Brendan Bromwich

Part 2: Peacekeepers, the military, and natural resources

Introduction

Environmental experiences and developments in United Nations peacekeeping operations
Sophie Ravier, Anne-Cécile Vialle, Russ Doran, and John Stokes

Crime, credibility, and effective peacekeeping: Lessons from the field
Annica Waleij

Environmental stewardship in peace operations: The role of the military
Annica Waleij, Timothy Bosetti, Russ Doran, and Birgitta Liljedahl

Taking the gun out of extraction: UN responses to the role of natural resources in conflicts
Mark B. Taylor and Mike Davis

Military-to-military cooperation on the environment and natural disasters: Engagement for peacebuilding
Geoffrey D. Dabelko and Will Rogers

Civil-military coordination and cooperation in peacebuilding and natural resource management: An enabling framework, challenges, and incremental progress
Melanne A. Civic

Part 3: Good governance

Introduction

Burma's ceasefire regime: Two decades of unaccountable natural resource exploitation
Kirk Talbott, Yuki Akimoto, and Katrina Cuskelly

Taming predatory elites in the Democratic Republic of the Congo: Regulation of property rights to adjust incentives and improve economic performance in the mining sector
Nicholas Garrett

Stopping the plunder of natural resources to provide for a sustainable peace in Côte d'Ivoire
Michel Yoboue

500   Water and post-conflict peacebuilding

Post-conflict environmental governance: Lessons from Rwanda
Roy Brooke and Richard Matthew

Process and substance: Environmental law in post-conflict peacebuilding
Sandra S. Nichols and Mishkat Al Moumin

Corruption and natural resources in post-conflict transition
Christine Cheng and Dominik Zaum

Sartor resartus: Liberian concession reviews and the prospects for effective
internationalized solutions
K. W. James Rochow

Preventing violent conflict over natural resources: Lessons from an early
action fund
Juan Dumas

Part 4: Local institutions and marginalized populations

Introduction

Legal pluralism in post-conflict environments: Problem or opportunity for
natural resource management?
Ruth Meinzen-Dick and Rajendra Pradhan

The role of conservation in promoting sustainability and security in at-risk
communities
Peter Zahler, David Wilkie, Michael Painter, and J. Carter Ingram

Social benefits in the Liberian forestry sector: An experiment in post-conflict
institution building for resilience
John Waugh and James Murombedzi

Integrating gender into post-conflict natural resource management
Njeri Karuru and Louise H. Yeung

Indigenous peoples, natural resources, and peacebuilding in Colombia
Juan Mayr Maldonado and Luisz Olmedo Martínez

Part 5: Transitional justice and accountability

Introduction

Building momentum and constituencies for peace: The role of natural
resources in transitional justice and peacebuilding
Emily E. Harwell

Peace through justice: International tribunals and accountability for wartime
environmental wrongs
Anne-Cecile Vialle, Carl Bruch, Reinhold Gallmetzer, and Akiva Fishman

Legal liability for environmental damage: The United Nations Compensation Commission and the 1990–1991 Gulf War
Cymie Payne

Reflections on the United Nations Compensation Commission experience
Lalanath de Silva

Part 6: Confidence building

Introduction

Environmental governance and peacebuilding in post-conflict Central America: Lessons from the Central American Commission for Environment and Development
Matthew Wilburn King, Marco Antonio González Pastora, Mauricio Castro Salazar, and Carlos Manuel Rodriguez

Promoting transboundary environmental cooperation in Central Asia: The Environment and Security Initiative in Kazakhstan and Kyrgyzstan
Saba Nordström

The Perú and Ecuador peace park: One decade after the peace settlement
Yolanda Kakabadse, Jorge Caillaux, and Juan Dumas

Transboundary collaboration in the Greater Virunga Landscape: From gorilla conservation to conflict-sensitive transboundary landscape management
Johannes Refisch and Johann Jenson

Part 7: Integration of natural resources into other post-conflict priorities

Introduction

Natural resource management and post-conflict settings: Programmatic evolution in a humanitarian and development agency
Jim Jarvie

Consolidating peace through Aceh Green
Sadaf Lakhani

Using economic evaluation to integrate natural resource management into Rwanda's post-conflict poverty reduction strategy paper
Louise Wrist Sorensen

Mitigating natural resource conflicts through development projects: Lessons from World Bank experience in Nigeria
Sandra Ruckstuhl

502 Water and post-conflict peacebuilding

Mainstreaming natural resources into post-conflict humanitarian and development action
Judy Oglethorpe, Anita Van Breda, Leah Kintner, Shubash Lohani, and Owen Williams

Natural resources and peacebuilding: What role for the private sector?
Diana Klein and Ulrike Joras

Part 8: Lessons learned

Fueling conflict or facilitating peace: Lessons in post-conflict governance and natural resource management
Sandra S. Nichols, Carroll Muffett, and Carl Bruch

Index

NOTE: Page numbers with *f* indicate figures; those with *t* indicate tables.

Aarhus Convention, 286, 446
Abdullayev, Iskandar, 194
absolute water scarcity, 2n
Abyei Protocol, 331, 344–348, 352
access to water, 1–2, 4, 405–407, 447
  as a human right, xiii–xiv, 4, 17,
    359–360, 383–399
  immediate aftermath of conflict,
    407–421
  infrastructure development, 418–421
  intersectoral coordination, 29, 85–93,
    406, 412–414, 425–427
  sustainable development, 383n, 385
  universal access goals, 58, 60
  See also basic needs and services;
    Millennium Development Goals
adaptive governance, 6, 112–113, 405,
    406, 443–444
Adriatic Sea watershed, 363t
Afghanistan, 9
  adaptive governance, 443–444
  Afghan National Development Strategy
    (ANDS), 189–190, 193–194
  Afghan Sustainable Water Supply and
    Sanitation (SWSS) project, 224–225
  agriculture/irrigation systems, 6,
    101–105, 315–317, 321, 423
  Bonn Agreement, 307n
  capacity building, 321
  community development councils
    (CDCs), 194, 197–198, 202,
    203–204, 205, 207

conservation technologies, 410
counterinsurgency operations, 211–216,
    219–232, 414, 424
dam construction, 13
disputes and negotiations with Iran,
    305–318
drought and desertification, 312–313,
    315, 316f, 455
food security, 423
freshwater springs, 218f
government legitimacy perceptions,
    205–206
Hari Rud watershed, 312, 315, 318,
    319
Helmand-Arghandab Valley Authority
    (HAVA), 4, 192
Helmand River Basin, 216–232,
    305–322, 437
household-level water treatment,
    103–105
humanitarian assistance, 47, 101,
    193–194, 205–206, 220–221
hydrometeorological data, 131, 140,
    221–224, 226–230, 240–241, 305,
    315, 317, 319–321, 423, 434–435
integrated water resource management
    (IWRM), 195
Kunduz River Basin Programme
    (KRBP), 198–204, 207
local governance and power dynamics,
    140, 190, 196–198, 201–202,
    204–205, 441–444

504 Index

local water management programs, 28, 101–105, 140, 189–207, 441, 444
maps, 5*f*, 44*f*, 101*f*, 191*f*, 212*f*, 213*f*, 218*f*, 306*f*, 307*f*, 309*f*
marginalized households, 200–204
Millennium Development Goals, xvi, 193–194
mining sector, 457–458
Ministry of Irrigation and Water Resources, 192
national peacebuilding, 193–194, 198, 204–206, 213–215
National Solidarity Programme (NSP), 140, 189–190, 194–207, 444, 448
opium poppies, 232, 312, 424
provincial reconstruction teams, 11, 212n2, 222–224, 414
reconstruction goals, 214
refugees and internally displaced persons, 8, 102, 312–313, 408, 409
Soviet involvement, 6, 192–193
traditional water management systems, 190–194
transboundary water, 3*t*, 221, 240–241, 305–322, 437
UN Assistance Mission in Afghanistan (UNAMA), 320
urban water restoration, 28, 43–60, 411, 419, 420
violence and insecurity, 11, 43–44, 101, 191n, 193, 206–207, 211–232, 414
WASH program, 102–105
water complexity analysis, 215*t*, 226–230
water pollution, 102–105, 203, 217
water scarcity, 9, 201, 227
water security, 206–207, 219–232, 306, 312–313
watersheds, 307*f*
Water Strategy for Afghanistan, 2009–2014, 214–215
women's empowerment, 29–30
See also Kabul
African Commission on Human and Peoples' Rights, 396–397
African Union, 339, 351

agricultural sector, 12, 17, 139, 422–424
Afghanistan's irrigation programs, 101–105, 140, 189–207, 315–317, 321, 424
climate change, 455
Indus River Basin, 139–140, 163–184
Iran's water scarcity, 311–313
Japan's irrigation reforms, 139, 141–160
large-scale land development, 456–457
pastoralists/livestock, 29, 86–89, 332, 346–347, 425
subsistence-level farming, 457
Sudan, 349
transboundary land and water coordination, 139–140, 163–184
water rights, 12–13
See also food security; livelihoods
Albania, 276*t*, 279n
Algeria, 3*t*, 439*t*
Al Khateeb, Nader, 239–240
Al-Lami, Ali, 30, 407
Allouche, Jeremy, 27–28, 29, 139, 407, 427
Al Rifai, Zeid S., 254
Amu Darya Basin, 437
Angola, 28–29
adaptive governance, 443–444
agricultural sector, 422
Agua para Todos program, 68
cholera, 68
colonial-era management systems, 69
community-based projects, 64
constitutional provisions on water, 439*t*
inequitable distribution of resources, 63
informal settlements, 29, 66–70
informal water sector, 11, 63–64, 71–77, 415
maps, 5*f*, 65*f*
Millennium Development Goals/Water for All program, 67–68, 78, 80, 82
mining sector, 82n, 457–458
National Directorate for Water Supply and Sanitation, 80
private sector, 78
social capital, 427
transboundary water, 3*t*
urban water restoration, 63–83, 411
water services, 64–69
See also Luanda

Index 505

Aoki, Chizuru, 30, 407
Arab League, 247, 249, 252–253, 257
Araks River, 299
  See also Kura-Araks Basin
Aral Sea Basin, 15
Arbour, Louise, 393–394, 397
Armenia
  maps, 5*f*, 298*f*
  transboundary water management, 3*t*,
    297–303
  water availability, 300
  Water Resources Management Agency
    (WRMA), 300
Armitage, Richard, 252
Ayub Khan, Mohammed, 175
Azerbaijan
  maps, 5*f*, 298*f*
  Nagorno-Karabakh region, 297–299
  refugees and internally displaced
    persons, 298
  South Caucasus Water Program
    (SCWP), 300–303
  transboundary water management, 3*t*,
    297–303
  water availability, 299–300

Baghdad (Iraq), 411
Baker, James, 255
the Balkans. *See* Bosnia and Herzegovina;
    Croatia; Montenegro; Serbia
Bangladesh, 164n3
  informal water sector, 38–39
  transboundary water management, 3*t*,
    430n11
Ban Ki-Moon, x, 1
Barram, Jamie, 388n8
al-Bashir, Omar, 395
basic needs and services, 6, 9–11, 16,
    27–30, 360, 405–407
  capacity building, 98, 125–126, 132, 134
  civil society, 28, 32
  data collection requirements, 131–132,
    140, 417, 423–424, 437, 441–442
  fostering cooperation and trust, 27
  humanitarian and international
    standards, 387–388
  humanitarian assistance, 39–40, 47,
    49–55, 59, 123–124

human rights perspectives, xiii–xiv, 4,
    17, 359–360, 383–399, 451*t*
immediate aftermath of conflict,
    407–421
informal sector providers, 27–28,
    31–40, 73–74, 415
informal settlements, 28–29
infrastructure development, 418–421
intersectoral coordination, 29, 85–93,
    406, 412–414, 425–427
legitimacy of the state, 32, 34–37
private-sector investment, 38
refugees and internally displaced
    persons, 408–411
resistance movements, 38
sequencing of interventions, 451*t*
service delivery standards, 411–414
state-building process, 34–36
sustainability, 55–59, 64, 79–80,
    100–101, 105, 134
urban water restoration, 28–29, 43–60,
    63–83
violence and insecurity challenges, 30,
    85–86, 117–135, 414
women's empowerment, 29–30,
    98–100, 108–111
See also community-based projects
Bernauer, Thomas, 15–16
Black, Eugene, 174
Black Sea watershed, 363*t*
Blue Nile River, 334*f*, 335–336, 349, 350
  See also Nile River Basin
Boban, Mate, 274
Bogdanovic, Slavko, 359, 408
borders. *See* transboundary water
Bosnia and Herzegovina (BiH)
  constitutional competencies of the state,
    366, 377
  Dayton Peace Agreement, 274, 359,
    361, 365–366, 371, 374, 436
  Emergency Water Construction
    Program, 364
  ethnic divisions in governance, 280,
    282, 361–362, 363*f*, 365–366
  ethnic groups, 272n
  EU accession, 284n14, 292, 362,
    369–374, 378, 446
  humanitarian assistance, 364, 420

506 Index

hydropower potential, 288*t*, 289
institutional frameworks, 359, 361–378
Institutional Strengthening of the Water
Sector project, 367
inter-entity Memorandums of
Understanding (MOUs), 374–377
maps, 5*f*, 273*f*, 363*f*
Millennium Development Goals,
373n30
Mostar water and sewage system, 36
polluted water, 364
principles of unity, 365–366
regional water management agreements
and frameworks, 370–371, 378, 446
Sava River share, 276*t*, 280, 363
Stabilization and Association
Agreement (SAA), 370, 372, 377, 378
transboundary water, 3*t*, 240, 271–276
water management fragmentation,
367–369
water management reforms, 371–374
See also Sava River Basin
Boucart, Abraham, 245
Boutros Ghali, Boutros, 14
Bromberg, Gidon, 239–240, 408
Burt, Murray, 29–30, 408, 416–417, 442
Burundi, 3*t*, 350–351, 431*t*
Bush, George H. W., 255
Bush, George W., 262

Cain, Allan, 29, 409
Cambodia, 3*t*, 429
camps. *See* informal settlements; refugees
and internally displaced persons
capacity building
Afghanistan, 321
community-based projects, 98, 109,
112, 125–126, 132
Community Management Model, 80
governance, 30, 91–93, 446
Helmand River Basin, 321
Iran, 321
Iraq, 30, 125–126, 132, 134
Liberia, 109
South Caucasus, 299–303, 435
South Sudan, 91–93
transboundary water management,
240–241, 297–303, 435

carriers of water. *See* water collection
Caucasus. *See* South Caucasus
Chad, 3*t*, 439*t*
Chesterman, Simon, 33
children. *See* illness; women and girls
chlorine treatment, 72, 75
cholera, 27, 75
Angola, 68
Democratic Republic of the Congo, 96,
97, 409
Iraq, 411
*Civilian Capacity in the Aftermath of
Conflict*, x
Civil-Military Operations–Human
Environment Interaction
(CMO-HEI), 225–226
civil society, xiv, 17, 28, 32
climate change, xv–xvi, 316*f*, 453*t*
disaster planning, 456
disasters, xv, 146
environmental resilience, 12
glacial melt, 315
Global Environment Facility, 135
resilience, 454–456
water complexity analysis, 227,
231–232
water scarcity, 15–16
cluster approach to service delivery,
412–414
Čolakhodžić, Amar, 240, 409
Colombia, 3*t*
community-based projects, xiv–xv,
95–114, 415–418, 453*t*
accountability, 77
Afghanistan, 52–53, 101–105,
189–207, 441
Angola, 64, 68–69, 77–81
capacity building programs, 98, 109,
112, 125–126, 132
Democratic Republic of the Congo, 11,
96–101
grassroots engagement, 111–112
health and security, 110
household-level water treatment,
103–105
informal water sector, 28, 29
information and knowledge exchange,
417–418, 445

institutional framework, 98
Iraq, 122–123, 125, 130–131, 132, 445
Japan, 142, 144–145, 150–155
Lebanon, 419–420
Liberia, 54, 57, 105–110
management committees, 64, 130–131
nation building linkages, 112–113
needs-based response, 57–58
stakeholder participation, 79, 80,
  122–123, 125, 130–131, 132, 416,
  444–446
sustainability strategies, 64, 100–101,
  105, 113
urban water system restoration, 43–44,
  52–53, 64, 68–69, 77–81
women's leadership, 98–100, 108–111,
  447–448
Community Management Model, 68–69,
  77–81
  impact, 80–81
  low-cost technology, 78
  monitoring and maintenance systems, 79
  social capital, 81–83
  stakeholder and consumer engagement,
    79, 80
  sustainability strategies, 79–80
  training and capacity building, 80
conflict, 6–9, 27
  economic causes, 33
  informal settlements, 8, 16, 28–29
  informal water providers, 27–28
  infrastructure neglect, 8
  military targets, 7
  socioeconomic impact, 6
  water scarcity, 14–16, 441
  See also immediate aftermath of
    conflict; post-conflict period
conflict-sensitive approaches
  consensus building, 89–90
  economic recovery, 428–429
  South Sudan, 29, 85–93
conservation, 11, 410
constitutional provisions on water, 366,
  377, 390, 439–440t
contamination. See illness
Convention for the Protection of the
  Mediterranean Sea against Pollution
  (Barcelona Convention), 371

Convention on Biological Diversity, 133
Convention on the Elimination of All
  Forms of Discrimination against
  Women (CEDAW), 387, 393
Convention on the Law of the
  Non-Navigational Uses of
  International Watercourses of 1997,
  xv
Convention on the Protection and Use of
  Transboundary Watercourses and
  International Lakes (Helsinki
  Convention), 280, 281
Convention on the Rights of the Child
  (CRC), 387
Convention on Wetlands of International
  Importance (Ramsar Convention),
  133, 308, 343–344
cooperation, 17, 27, 29, 429–438
coordination. See intersectoral
  coordination
corruption, 181
cost of water, 8
  Community Management Model, 79
  distance to water sources, 73
  drought, 201
  informal urban settlements, 29
  privatized water supplies, 13–14,
    388–389
  profits, 74–75
  See also informal water sector
Côte d'Ivoire, 408, 455
counterinsurgency (COIN) operations,
  211–216, 219–232, 414
  Civil-Military Operations–Human
    Environment Interaction
    (CMO-HEI), 225–226
  Tactical Conflict Assessment and
    Planning Framework (TCAPF),
    223–224, 231
  water security, 206–207, 219–232, 424
Criddle, Wayne D., 248, 249
Croatia, 282
  EU membership goal, 284n14, 292
  hydropower potential, 288t, 289
  landmines, 274–275
  maps, 5f, 273f
  refugees and internally displaced
    persons, 277

508 Index

Sava River share, 276t, 280
transboundary water, 3t, 271–276, 431t
See also Sava River Basin

dams, 13, 425
Egypt, 336n23, 341–342
hydropower potential, 288t, 289
Japan, 153t, 157
Danube Basin
Convention on Co-operation for the
Protection and Sustainable Use,
281–282
Convention Regarding the Regime of
Navigation (Belgrade Convention), 281
Danube River Protection Convention
(DRPC), 370–371
International Commission for the
Protection of the Danube River, 371
UNDP/GEF Danube Regional Project,
285
See also Sava River Basin
Darfur, 396–397
Abuja Agreement, 390–391, 430
gender-based violence, 448
rights-based approaches, 413–414
water scarcity, 10
well construction, 418
Dayton Peace Agreement, 274, 359, 361,
365–366, 371, 374, 436
See also Bosnia and Herzegovina
Dehgan, Alex, 241, 409
Democratic Republic of the Congo
adaptive governance, 443–444
baseline and monitoring data, 417–418
cholera, 96, 97, 409
community-based water projects, 11,
96–101, 445
constitutional provisions on water, 439t
deaths from water pollution, 8
female-headed households, 98–99
infrastructure development, 418
local governance, 442
maps, 5f, 97f
mining sector, 457–458
Nile Basin Cooperative Framework
Agreement (CFA), 350–351
refugee return, 96
transboundary water, 3t, 431t

water-user associations (WUAs), 427–428
women's empowerment, 29–30,
98–100, 448
Dennys, Christian, 197, 202
Development Workshop
Angola, 29, 63–64, 68–69, 77–81
Community Management Model,
68–69, 77–81
Sustainable Community Service
Project, 77–81
value chain tools, 64, 70–73
diarrhea, 102–103, 203, 409, 410
disaster planning, 456
disaster risk reduction (DRR), 411
disease. *See* illness (waterborne and
water-washed)
displaced persons camps. *See* informal
settlements
disputes over water, 9
See also transboundary water
distribution of freshwater, 1–2
See also access to water
domestic violence. *See* gender; women
and girls
donor commitment, 448–450, 453t
drinking water, 1–2, 6, 9–11, 16, 27–30,
451t
as a human right, xiii–xiv, 4, 17,
359–360, 383–399
informal sector providers, 27–28,
31–40
Iraq's marshlands, 121–123
Millennium Development Goals, 4, 28,
121
Zimbabwe, 35
See also basic needs and services

eastern Punjab. *See* India; Indus River
System
economic development
India, 169–173, 178–180
industrial agriculture, 456–457
See also livelihoods
economic recovery
dams, 13, 153t, 157, 288t, 289, 425
large-scale agricultural development,
456–457
See also livelihoods

Index 509

education. *See* information and knowledge exchange
Egypt
  Aswan High Dam, 336n23, 341–342
  cotton production, 341
  land tenure reforms, 181
  Nile Basin Cooperative Framework Agreement (CFA), 350–351
  transboundary water agreements, 336–338
Eisenhower, Dwight D., 247
electricity, 13n
  See also basic needs and services
El Salvador, 3*t*
energy supply, 13
environmentally sound technologies (ESTs), 117, 120, 123, 131–132
Eritrea, 3*t*, 350–351, 439*t*
Espoo Convention, 446
Ethiopia
  constitutional provisions on water, 439*t*
  large-scale agricultural development, 457
  Nile Basin Cooperative Framework Agreement (CFA), 350–351
  Somali migrants, 16
  transboundary water, 3*t*
EU Community Assistance for Reconstruction, Development and Stabilisation (EU-CARDS), 285, 367n14
EU Flood Directive, 288
EU membership, 281, 284, 291, 292, 362, 446
  acquis communitaire, 362, 369–370, 371n28, 372
  Stabilization and Association Agreement (SAA) with BiH, 370, 372, 377, 378
  Support to BiH Water Policy program, 372, 377
  transition process, 367n12, 370
EU Water Framework Directive (WFD), 240, 280, 284–285, 287–288, 369–370, 374

Filipović, Marija, 240, 410
financial sustainability, 56

fisheries, 30, 117–135, 425
flooding/flood control, 269n, 410–411, 455–456
  damage and fatalities, 143, 145, 146, 157, 159
  disaster risk reduction (DRR), 411
  Helmand River Basin, 314
  Japan, 141–142, 146–149
  Kura-Araks Basin, 300
  Sava River Basin, 287–288, 289, 291
  See also dams
Food and Agriculture Organization of the United Nations, 1–2
food security, 145–146, 149–150, 151, 169–170, 423, 456–457
former Yugoslavia. *See* Bosnia and Herzegovina; Croatia; Sava River Basin; Serbia; Yugoslavia
Franjieh, George, 245
Free Aceh Movement, 430n11
Friends of the Earth Middle East (FoEME), 239–240, 265–270, 433, 446
Funiciello, Mona, 139, 410

Garstin, William, 341
gas industry, 458n20
gender, 447–448
  Afghanistan, 29–30
  community leadership, 98–100, 108–111, 447–448
  Convention on the Elimination of All Forms of Discrimination against Women (CEDAW), 387, 393
  Darfur, 448
  Liberia, 105–110
  See also water collection; women and girls
Georgia
  maps, 5*f*, 298*f*
  South Caucasus Water Program (SCWP), 300–303
  transboundary water management, 3*t*, 297–303, 430n11
  water availability, 299
Global Environment Facility, 135
global warming. *See* climate change
Global WASH Cluster (GWC), 102–105, 412–414, 451*t*

510 Index

GOIRA. *See* Afghanistan
Goodhand, Jonathan, 205
GOSS. *See* South Sudan
governance, 405–406, 438–444, 452*t*
  adaptability, 406, 443–444
  capacity building, 30, 91–93, 446
  corruption, 181
  human rights perspectives, 359–360,
    383–399
  inclusive processes, 6, 112–113, 405
  international donors, 39–40
  intersectoral coordination, 29, 85–93,
    406, 412–414, 425–427
  legitimacy considerations, 32, 34–37
  local levels, 130–131, 442–443
  public participation, 79, 80, 444–446
  reconstitution of institutions, 17, 27–28
  state building, 31–40
  See also community-based projects;
    constitutional provisions on water;
    legal and institutional frameworks;
    management of water resources;
    stakeholder participation;
    transboundary water
Green, Reginald Herbold, 46
Green Cross International, xiii, xiv, xv
Guatemala, 391
  constitutional provisions on water, 439*t*
  human rights obligations, 393, 397
  map, 5*f*
  transboundary water, 3*t*, 431*t*
Guinea-Bissau, 3*t*, 439*t*

Habib, Philip, 252
Haddadin, Munther J., 239, 240, 410
Haiti, 57–58, 449
Hamun wetlands, 308, 309*f*, 310*f*
Han, 310*f*
health and well-being, 38, 51
  chlorine treatment, 72, 75
  community-based programs, 110
  educational programs, xv
  household water treatment, 103–105
  malnutrition, 409, 410
  state building and regulation, 35,
    37–39, 68–69
  water requirements per day, 387–388
  See also illness

Helmand-Arghandab Valley Authority
    (HAVA), 192
Helmand Deep Dive, 219–232
Helmand River Basin, 4
  agriculture, 311–313
  baseline and monitoring data, 417
  capacity building, 321
  counterinsurgency projects, 216–232
  drought and desertification, 312–313,
    314, 315, 316*f*
  flood control, 314
  Hamun wetlands (Sistan Basin),
    308–311, 313, 435
  hydrometeorological data, 240–241,
    305, 315, 317, 319–321
  international donor community support,
    321–322
  joint management commission
    formation, 322
  maps, 307*f*, 309*f*
  regional stability, 437
  transboundary disputes and
    negotiations, 305–318
  water insecurity, 311–313
  well construction, 417–418
Helsinki Water Convention. *See*
    Convention on the Protection
    and Use of Transboundary
    Watercourses and International
    Lakes
Hendrix, Cullen, 15
Hildyard, Nicholas, 204
household water treatment systems,
    103–105
Hoveida, Amir Abbas, 314
Howard, Guy, 388n8
human capital, 9
humanitarian assistance, 6, 10, 12, 28,
    419–421
  Afghan water resource development,
    193–194, 205–206, 220–221
  basic service delivery, 39–40
  Bosnia and Herzegovina, 364
  coordination and sequencing of
    interventions, 449–454
  donor commitment, 448–450, 453*t*
  government capacity building, 91–93
  Helmand River Basin, 321–322, 435

Iraq's wetland restoration project, 123–124, 132–133
Jordan River Basin, 252
peacebuilding priorities, 95–96
Sava River Basin, 281–282, 284–285
transboundary water mediation, 434–435
urban water restoration projects, 43–60
Humanitarian Charter and Minimum Standards in Humanitarian Response. See Sphere Handbook
human need. *See* basic needs and services
human rights, 383–399, 413–414
  access to water, xiii–xiv, 4, 17, 359–360, 451*t*
  Convention on the Elimination of All Forms of Discrimination against Women (CEDAW), 387
  Convention on the Rights of the Child (CRC), 387
  International Covenant on Economic, Social, and Cultural Rights (ESCR), 386, 387, 388–389
  peace agreements, 385–386, 390–391
  principle of non-discrimination, 389
  socioeconomic rights, 394–395
  sustainable development, 383n, 385
  transitional justice mechanisms, 360, 367, 384n2, 393–398
  UN Resolution 64/292, xiv, 383, 398
  See also constitutional provisions on water; transitional justice mechanisms
Human Rights Council, 398, 399
human rights courts, 360
Hussein, Saddam, 117
  Kuwait invasion, 121n
  marshland destruction, 118–120
Hussein bin Talal, King of Jordan, 257
Huston, Sam, 29, 410, 428–429, 443
hydroelectric dams. *See* dams
hydrometeorological data, 14, 16, 423–424
  Afghanistan, 131, 140, 221–224, 226–230, 319–321, 434–435
  collection and monitoring programs, 131–132, 140, 417, 423–424, 437, 451*t*
  South Caucasus—Kura-Araks Basin, 299–303, 435

stakeholder participation, 444–445
strategic environmental assessment (SEA), 441–442, 451*t*, 453*t*
transboundary water management, 240–241

IDPs. *See* refugees and internally displaced persons
Ignatieff, Michael, 33
illness (waterborne and water-washed), 1, 8, 27, 409n4
  cholera, 27, 54, 68, 75, 96, 97, 409, 411
  conflict-related environmental pollution, 278
  diarrhea, 102–103, 203, 409, 410
  dissolved solids levels, 217
  illegal vendors, 54–55
  in refugee camps, 409
  typhoid, 27, 411
  See also health and well-being
immediate aftermath of conflict, 407–421
  community-based management, 415–418
  definition, 6, 407n
  human rights-based approaches, 413–414
  information and knowledge exchange, 417–418
  infrastructure development, 418–421
  international assistance, 419–421
  legal and institutional frameworks, 414–415
  private investors, 419
  refugees and internally displaced persons, 408–411
  sequencing of interventions, 451–453*t*
  service standards/Global WASH Cluster (GWC), 411–414
  urban water, 411
  water sustainability goals, 415–418
India
  Bhakra-Nangal Dam, 170–171
  constitutional provisions on water, 439*t*
  corruption, 181
  economic development, 169–173, 178–180
  farmland allocations, 168–169, 171–173, 178, 181–182
  food security, 169–170

512   Index

grain production, 171
hydrometeorological data, 423
informal water sector, 38–39
intersectoral coordination, 425
irrigation infrastructure, 170–172, 178
Kashmir disputes, 163, 164–165, 175,
   179, 180
livelihoods, 163–184
maps, 5*f*, 165*f*, 166*f*
partition, 163–168, 423, 433
transboundary water, 3*t*, 163, 173–180,
   433
water rights, 12–13
See also Indus River System
Indonesia
constitutional provisions on water, 439*t*
transboundary water management, 3*t*,
   430n11
Indus River System, 139–140, 163–184
components, 165–166
Delhi Agreement, 174
dispute mediation, 174–182, 433
hydrometeorological infrastructure,
   170–172, 174, 179, 435–436
Indus Basin Development Fund, 175,
   180, 183
Indus Waters Treaty (IWT), 163,
   175–176, 179, 183, 433
integrated water resource management
   (IWRM), 174–175, 184–185
international donors, 179, 182–183
maps, 166*f*
Permanent Indus Commission (PIC),
   176–178, 184, 429, 436
World Bank, 174–176, 179, 433, 449
industrial agriculture, 456–457
informal institutions, 32, 37, 427
See also informal water sector
informal settlements, 8, 16, 28
basic services, 28–29, 37–39, 59–60,
   408–411
community-based projects, 52–53
informal water sector, 29, 37, 64,
   66–70, 415
Kabul, 48, 52–53, 57, 411
Luanda, 64, 66–70, 70*f*
Monrovia, 50, 57, 411
waterborne illness, 409

informal water sector, 11, 16, 27–28, 31–
   40, 63–64, 415, 445–446
actors, 72
association and cooperation, 72, 73–74
community-based projects, 28, 29
criminality, 54–55
engagement, 73–81
health and safety, 72, 75
informal settlements, 29, 37, 64, 66–70
international donors, 39–40
profits, 74–75
regulatory controls, 38–39, 68–69
social capital, 75–77, 81–83
state building contexts, 31–40
value chain analysis, 70–73
information and knowledge exchange,
   406
community-based monitoring, 417–418
environment and health awareness, xv
stakeholder involvement, 444–445
transboundary water management, 435
infrastructure development, 8, 170–172,
   174, 178–179, 418–421, 451*t*
insecurity. *See* violence and insecurity
institutional frameworks. *See* legal and
   institutional frameworks
institutional sustainability, 56–57
integrated water resource management
   (IWRM), 11
Afghanistan, 195
capacity building, 240
data collection and sharing, 221
Indus River system, 174–175, 184–185
Iraq, 123, 132
Japan, 155, 159
Liberia, 108, 112
Sava River Basin, 282–290, 371, 373–
   374, 378
South Caucasus, 297, 301–303
Inter-American Court of Human Rights,
   389, 397
Intergovernmental Authority on
   Development, 327, 328n3
internally displaced persons. *See* refugees
   and internally displaced persons
International Covenant on Economic,
   Social, and Cultural Rights (ESCR),
   386, 387, 388–389, 392–393

Index   513

international criminal tribunals, 360, 394–396
International Freshwater Treaties Database, 430
international humanitarian assistance. *See* humanitarian assistance
International Reconstruction Fund Facility for Iraq (IRFFI), 120
International Sava River Basin Commission (ISRBC), 271–272, 281, 283–292, 371
International Security Assistance Force (ISAF). *See* Afghanistan
intersectoral coordination, 29, 85–93, 139–140, 163–184, 406, 412–414, 425–427
intestinal nematode infections, 409
Iran
  agricultural sector, 311–313, 321
  capacity building, 321
  drought and desertification, 312–313, 315, 316*f*
  Hari Rud watershed, 312, 318, 319
  Helmand River Basin, 4, 305–322, 437
  hydrometeorological data, 240–241, 305, 315, 317, 319–321
  land tenure reforms, 181
  maps, 306*f*, 309*f*
  nationalization of oil companies, 246
  political instability, 317
  Sistan Basin, 308–311, 313, 435
  transboundary water, 3*t*, 240–241
  water disputes with Afghanistan, 305–318
  water insecurity, 305, 311–313
Iraq
  capacity building programs, 30, 125–126, 132, 134
  Center for Restoration of the Iraqi Marshlands (CRIM), 124
  cholera and typhoid, 411
  Coalition Provisional Authority, 11
  constitutional provisions on water, 439*t*
  de-Baathification policy, 129
  drought, 455
  humanitarian assistance, 123–124, 132–133
  integrated water resource management (IWRM), 123, 132

  local governance, 130–131
  maps, 5*f*, 118*f*, 119*f*
  marshland destruction, 117–120, 425
  marshland restoration project, 30, 117–135, 445, 449
  Millennium Development Goals, 121, 125
  Ministry of Environment, 120–121, 124–125, 128, 133, 134
  multilateral environmental agreements, 133
  peacebuilding process, 129–131
  refugees and internally displaced persons, 126, 408
  safe drinking water, 121–123, 125, 129–130, 407
  stakeholder participation, 122–123, 125, 130–131, 132
  transboundary water, 3*t*, 135
  transboundary water management, 430n11
  urban water infrastructure, 411
  violence and insecurity, 11, 30, 124–125, 128–129, 407, 414
  water network damage, 6
  World Heritage sites, 134–135
Iraq Trust Fund, 120
irrigation. *See* agricultural sector
Israel
  Balfour Declaration, 243
  drought, 456
  human rights obligations, 392, 393, 394–395
  Jordan-Israel Peace Treaty, 239, 241, 244, 255–259, 266, 430–432, 436
  maps, 5*f*, 245*f*, 267*f*
  Oslo Accords, 432, 434
  Palestinian refugees, 244
  regional peace talks, 262
  Seven Year Plan of 1953, 246
  transboundary water disputes, 3*t*, 179–180, 183, 239–240, 243–262, 265–270
  violence and insecurity, 261–262
  water pipeline, 248, 250, 254–255, 259
  See also Palestinian Territories
Israeli-Jordanian Joint Water Committee, 179–180, 183

514   Index

Japan, 139–160
  Agriculture and Commerce Ministry, 148
  climate change, 146
  dams and storage capacity, 153*t*, 157
  flood damage and fatalities, 143, 145,
    146, 157, 159
  Flood Prevention Association Act, 146
  food security, 145–146, 149–150
  integrated water resource management
    (IWRM), 155, 159
  land reforms, 150
  local management of irrigation, 142,
    144–145, 150–155, 159–160
  maps, 5*f*, 143*f*, 151*f*
  national management of flood
    prevention, 141–142, 155–160
  natural resource reserves, 146n
  Ooi River National Agricultural Water
    Project, 142, 151–155
  post-war period, 141n, 144–147, 148*t*,
    149–160
  pre-war period, 142–144, 146–150,
    156
  San Francisco Peace Treaty of 1951,
    141n, 149
  social capital, 427
  tsunami of 2011, 157n
  water management legislation,
    143–144, 146–149, 155, 158–159
  water rights, 12–13
  water scarcity, 154
Jensen, David, 441–442
Johnson Sirleaf, Ellen, 10, 106–107
Johnston, Eric, 247–249, 252, 430
Joint Standards Initiative, 413
Jordan
  drought, 456
  floods, 410
  Ionedis Plan of 1939, 246
  Jordan-Israel Peace Treaty, 239, 241,
    244, 255–259, 266, 430–432, 436
  maps, 5*f*, 245*f*, 267*f*
  municipal drinking water, 252
  Palestinian refugees, 244, 250, 252
  Syrian refugees, 410
  Syrian relations, 253–255, 258, 259
  transboundary water disputes, 179–180,
    183, 239–240, 243–262, 265–270

Jordan River Basin, xiv–xv, 239–240,
  265–270
  community engagement, 239–240, 446
  drought, 456
  environmental rehabilitation, 265–270
  humanitarian assistance, 252
  Jordan-Israel Peace Treaty provisions,
    255–259, 266, 430–432, 436
  maps, 245*f*, 267*f*
  pollution, 265–266, 268
  Syrian relations, 253–255, 258, 259
  third-party mediation, 247–253,
    260–261, 433
  U.S. funding, 250, 251
  utilization conflicts, 245–251,
    254–255, 257, 260, 269
  violence and insecurity, 261–262
  water sharing plan, 248–251, 254–255,
    257–259, 266

Kabul (Afghanistan), 43–60, 411, 419
  Central Authority for Water Supply and
    Sewerage, 9, 46, 47, 52, 53
  community-based projects, 52–53, 57, 59
  informal settlements, 48, 52–53, 57
  institutional sustainability, 56
  international humanitarian
    organizations, 47, 51–52, 53, 59, 420
  large-scale rehabilitation projects,
    51–52, 58–59
  population, 46n, 48
  water network, 46, 47*f*, 48*t*, 52*t*
  See also Afghanistan
Karadžić, Radovan, 274
Karzai, Hamid, 193
Kashmir
  maps, 165*f*, 166*f*
  partition disputes, 163, 164–165, 175,
    179, 180
  water disputes, 174–175, 177
Keiru, Bilha Joy, 29–30, 411, 416–417, 442
Kenya
  droughts, 15–16
  Nile Basin Cooperative Framework
    Agreement (CFA), 350–351
  Somali migrants, 16
  transboundary water, 336–338
Khan, Akhtar Hamid, 202

Index 515

Khateeb, Nader Al, 411
King, Matthew, 434–435
Koch-Ya'ari, Elizabeth, 239–240, 411
Kosovo, 274, 278
  constitutional provisions on water, 439*t*
  private investors, 419
  transboundary water, 3*t*
Kovandžić, Jana, 240, 411
Kugaprasatham, Sivapragasam, 30, 412
Kunduz River Basin Programme (KRBP),
  198–204, 207
*Kupreskick, Prosecutor of the
  International Tribunal for the
  Formal Yugoslavia v.*, 394
Kura-Araks Basin, 297–303, 435
Kurdistan, 416, 425, 448
Kuwait, 3*t*
Kyrgyzstan, 15, 416

Lahoud, Salim, 249–250
land
  farmland allocation, 168–169,
    171–173, 178, 181–182
  large-scale land development, 456–457
  mining, 82n, 107–108, 457–458
  tenure reforms, 150, 181
  transboundary land and water
    coordination, 139–140, 163–184
  See also intersectoral coordination
Laos, 3*t*, 429, 439*t*
large-scale agricultural development,
  456–457
learning. *See* information and knowledge
  exchange
Lebanon
  community-based projects, 419–420
  human rights treaties, 393
  map, 5*f*
  transboundary water, 3*t*, 243–262
legal and institutional frameworks, 17,
  359–360, 414–415
  Bosnia and Herzegovina, 359,
    361–378, 446
  constitutional provisions on water, 390,
    439–440*t*
  Convention on the Elimination of All
    Forms of Discrimination against
    Women (CEDAW), 387

Convention on the Rights of the Child
  (CRC), 387
EU *acquis communitaire*, 362,
  369–370, 371n28, 372
human rights law, xiii–xiv, 4, 17,
  359–360, 383–399
institutional sustainability, 56–57
International Covenant on Economic,
  Social, and Cultural Rights (ESCR),
  386, 387, 388–389
international criminal tribunals,
  394–396
Japan, 141–142, 146–149
legislation, 390
Memorandums of Understanding
  (MOUs), 375–377, 378
peace agreements, 385–386, 390–391,
  430–433
regional human rights tribunals,
  396–397
regional treaties and institutions,
  15, 17, 163, 175–176, 183–184,
  239–241, 259–260, 370–371,
  435–436, 446
restorative justice and compensation,
  395–396
sequencing of interventions, 452*t*
transitional justice mechanisms, 360,
  367, 374n2, 393–398
truth commissions, 397–398
UN General Assembly Resolution
  64/292, xiv, 383, 398, 399
See also governance; management of
  water resources
legibility (definition), 28n
legitimacy of the state, 32, 34–37
liberal peacebuilding model, 31–32,
  33–34
Liberia
  access to water and sanitation, 6, 10
  adaptive governance, 443–444
  agriculture/irrigation systems, 423, 457
  baseline and monitoring data, 417–418
  civil wars, 6
  community-based projects, 28,
    105–110, 415
  gender-based violence, 105–110
  infrastructure development, 418–419

516 Index

integrated water resource management
(IWRM), 108, 112
international humanitarian
organizations, 49–50
local governance, 442
maps, 5*f*, 45*f*, 106*f*
mining sector, 107–108, 457–458
Poverty Reduction Strategy, 10
training and capacity building, 109
transboundary water, 3*t*
Truth and Reconciliation Commission,
106–107
urban water restoration, 28, 43–60,
420, 446
women's empowerment, 29–30
See also Monrovia
Libya, 3*t*
Lilienthal, David, 174
livelihoods, 6, 12–14, 16–17, 27,
139–140, 405, 421–429, 451*t*
agricultural sector, 17, 139, 141–160,
189–207, 422–424
conflict-sensitive approaches, 428–429
costs of water, 13
counterinsurgency operations, 211–232
donor contributions, 182
economic development, 169–173
cnergy supply, 13
environmental sustainability, 12, 139
fisheries, 425
hydrometeorogical data, 140, 221–224,
226–230, 423–424
hydropower, 288*t*, 289, 425
intersectoral coordination, 140,
425–427
mining sector, 457–458
nonagricultural livelihoods, 424–425
pastoralist communities, 15–16, 425
privatized water sector, 13–14
refugee resettlement, 139–140, 423
social capital, 427–428
state building models, 33
transboundary water, 139–140,
163–184
water rights, 12–13
women's decision-making, 447–448
local engagement. *See* community-based
projects

local governance, 130–131, 442–443
Afghanistan, 140, 190, 196–198,
201–202, 204–205, 441–444
Democratic Republic of the Congo,
442
Iraq, 130–131
Liberia, 442
See also governance
Luanda (Angola), 63n
ANGOMENHA filling station, 72,
73–74, 75
cholera, 68
community-based projects, 64, 68–69,
77–81
distance to water sources, 67*t*, 73
formal water sector, 72, 73
household water sources, 67*t*, 72
inequitable distribution of resources, 64
informal settlements, 64, 66–70
informal water sector, 71–77, 415
Luanda Provincial Water Company
(EPAL), 66, 69, 72–73, 75n, 77–80
population growth, 67*t*
social capital, 75–77, 81–83
Sustainable Community Service
Project, 77–81
water value chain analysis, 64, 70–73
See also Angola

Madagascar, 457
Main, Chas. T., 247
Malawi, 38
Mali, 457
malnutrition, 409, 410
management of water resources, 2, 4–5,
405–421
building cooperation and trust, 17, 27
capacity building programs, 240–241,
297–303
colonial-era systems, 69
community-based projects, 64, 95–114,
130–131, 140, 415–418
flexible programming, 406
human capital, 8–9, 47, 50
intersectoral coordination, 29, 85–93,
406, 412–414, 425–427
Japan's flood control system, 141–142,
146–149

Index   517

legal frameworks, 17
policy coherence, 12–13
power arrangements, 140
privatization options, 13–14, 55–57,
    388–389
rights-based approaches, xiv, 4, 17,
    359–360, 383–399
social capital, 427–428
sustainability goals, 50, 56–57, 59
transboundary water commissions,
    xiv–xv, 15, 17, 176–180, 183–184,
    239, 262, 271, 281–292, 322,
    429–438
women's leadership, 447–448
See also governance; legal and
    institutional frameworks
maps, 5*f*
Afghanistan, 44*f*, 101*f*, 191*f*, 212*f*,
    213*f*, 218*f*, 306*f*, 307*f*
Angola, 65*f*
Armenia, 298*f*
Azerbaijan, 298*f*
Bosnia and Herzegovina, 273*f*, 363*f*
Croatia, 273*f*
Democratic Republic of the Congo, 97*f*
Georgia, 298*f*
Helmand River Basin, 307*f*, 309*f*
India, 165*f*, 166*f*
Indus River System, 166*f*
Iran, 306*f*
Iraq, 118*f*, 119*f*
Israel, 245*f*
Japan, 143*f*, 151*f*
Jordan, 245*f*
Jordan River Basin, 245*f*, 267*f*
Kashmir, 165*f*, 166*f*
Liberia, 45*f*, 49*f*, 106*f*
Nile River Basin, 329*f*
Pakistan, 165*f*, 166*f*
Serbia, 273*f*
Slovenia, 273*f*
South Caucasus, 298*f*
South Sudan, 87*f*, 329*f*
Sudan, 87*f*, 329*f*
water availability, 2*f*
White Nile River Basin, 334*f*
Yugoslavia, 273*f*
marsh Arabs. *See* Iraq

Matabeleland-Zambezi Water Trust
    (MZWP), 36
McCarthy, Jennifer, 140, 196, 197n6, 199,
    412, 421–422, 441
McChrystal, Stanley, 219
MDGs. *See* Millennium Development
    Goals
Mehyar, Munqeth, 239–240, 412
memorandums of understanding (MOUs),
    375–377, 378
Middle East
    Cold War, 246–247, 250
    Israeli-Palestinian violence, 261–262
    Palestinian refugees, 244, 247, 250,
        252–253
    regional peace talks, 262
    wars and armistice agreements, 244,
        250, 251, 260
    water scarcity, 14
    See also Jordan River Basin;
        transboundary water; specific
        countries, e.g. Syria
Millennium Development Goals (MDGs),
    4, 28, 68, 121
    Afghanistan, xvi, 193–194
    Angola, 67–68, 78, 80, 82
    Bosnia and Herzegovina, 373n30
    Iraq, 121, 125
    South Sudan, 29, 86
    Sudan, xvi
Milošević, Slobodan, 273
mining sector, 82n, 107–108, 457–458
Mirzaee, Mehdi, 241, 413
Monrovia (Liberia), 43–60, 411
    community-based rehabilitation
        projects, 54, 57, 59
    informal settlements, 50, 57
    informal water sector, 50, 54–55, 446
    institutional sustainability, 56–57
    international humanitarian
        organizations, 49–50, 53–55, 59, 420
    large-scale rehabilitation projects, 54,
        58–59
    Liberia Water and Sewer Corporation,
        48–49, 50, 54, 55, 446
    population, 50, 51*t*
    water resources, 48–50, 51*t*, 53*t*
    See also Liberia

518   Index

Montenegro, 273f
  hydropower potential, 288t, 289
  map, 5f
  Sava River share, 276t, 279n, 280
Moorhead, Alan, 340
Morocco, 398
mortality rates, 1, 8, 27
  See also illness
Mozambique, 3t, 425–426, 439t
Mugabe, Robert, 35
multilateral environmental agreements,
    133
  See also transboundary water
Murphy, Richard, 252
Musemwa, Muchaparara, 35–36
Muslim Mindanao, 430n11
Mustafa, Daanish, 140, 204, 413,
    421–422, 441
Myanmar (Burma), 170
  constitutional provisions on water, 439t
  transboundary water management, 3t,
    431t

Nagorno-Karabakh region, 297–299
Najibullah, Mohammad, 192
Nakayama, Mikiyasu, 413
Nasser, Gamal Abdel, 247, 249
natural resources (definition), 6
Nehru, Jawaharlal, 164–165, 170, 175
Nepal, 3t, 38, 439t
New Eden Project, 123–125
Nicaragua, 3t
Nigeria, 5f, 39, 396
Nile River Basin, 15, 241, 327–352
  Abyei dispute, 331, 344–348, 352
  Agreement for the Full Utilization of
    the Nile Waters, 331n14, 337–338,
    349n49, 350
  Aswan High Dam, 336n23, 341–342
  Jonglei Canal Project, 340–344, 352
  large-scale agricultural development,
    457
  map, 329f
  Nile Basin Cooperative Framework
    Agreement (CFA), 350–351, 352,
    432–433
  Nile Basin Initiative (NBI), 338–339,
    350, 351

  political geography, 332–338, 352
  water allocation, 348–349, 352
Nissenbaum, Dion, 219
nonagricultural livelihoods, 424–425
Northern Ireland, 431t
Nyerere Doctrine, 337

Obama, Barack, 262, 312
oil industry, 458n20
Operation Enduring Freedom. *See*
    Afghanistan

Pact Sudan, 29
Pakistan, 12–13, 164n3
  constitutional provisions on water, 439t
  Kashmir disputes, 163, 164–165, 175,
    179, 180
  livelihoods, 163
  maps, 5f, 165f, 166f
  partition, 163–168
  transboundary water, 3t, 163, 173–180,
    433
  See also Indus River System
Palestinian Territories
  basic needs and services, 38
  human rights, 393, 394–395
  map, 5f
  Oslo Accords, 432, 434
  Palestine Liberation Organization
    (PLO), 256–257
  Palestinian Water Authority, 434
  partition, 243–244
  self-governance, 257
  transboundary water disputes, 3t,
    239–240, 243–262, 269
  violence and insecurity, 261–262
Palmer-Maloney, Laura Jean, 140, 241,
    413, 455
Pan-European Transport Corridors,
    286–287
participatory photography, 199
pastoralist communities, 15–16, 29,
    86–89, 332, 346–347, 425, 455
peacebuilding, 1–16, 405–407
  asset management, 6
  challenges, 6, 195–196
  counterinsurgency operations, 211–216,
    414

Index   519

definition, 6, 193n
human rights perspectives, xiii–xiv, 4,
17, 359–360, 383–399
immediate aftermath of conflict,
407–421
international mechanisms, 373
liberal model, 31–32, 33–34
livelihoods, 421–429
objectives, 6, 95
priorities for international support,
95–96, 193–194
sequencing of interventions, 450–454
top-down approaches, 193–194, 198,
204–206, 446
transboundary cooperation, 429–438
Peacebuilding Commission, ix–x
peace consolidation
definition, 6
sequencing of interventions, 451–453*t*
water sustainability, 415–418
peace dividends, 139, 417
peacekeeping, 11, 409
peacemaking, 6
Peel Commission, 243–244
peri-urban settlements. *See* informal
settlements
Permanent Indus Commission (PIC),
176–178, 184, 429, 436
Peru, 3*t*, 392, 439*t*
Philippines
constitutional provisions on water, 440*t*
informal water sector, 39
transboundary water management, 3*t*,
430n11
Pinera, Jean-François, 28, 29, 414, 420
Plan de Sánchez Massacre v. Guatemala,
397
political hydrology, 307–311, 317
Port-au-Prince, Haiti, 57–58, 59–60
post-conflict period, 5*f*, 6, 29–30
actors, 5
basic needs and services, 9–11, 16,
27–30
corruption, 181
definition, 6
economic development, 33
economies and livelihoods, 12–14,
16–17, 27

fostering cooperation, 17, 27, 29
humanitarian assistance, 10, 12, 28,
39–40
immediate aftermath of conflict, 6,
407–421
intersectoral coordination,
425–427
security and stability, 28,
29–30
state building, 31–40
transboundary water, 2–4
violence and insecurity, 10–11, 30
See also peacebuilding
potable water. *See* drinking water
private sector
Angola, 78
investment, 11, 38, 419
public-private partnerships, 14
See also informal water sector
privatized water supplies, 13–14, 55–57,
388–389
*Prosecutor of the International Tribunal
for the Formal Yugoslavia v.
Kupreskick*, 394
*Prosecutor of the International
Criminal Court v. Omar
Hassan Ahmad Al Bashir*,
395
*Provincial Reconstruction Team
Handbook*, 222
provincial reconstruction teams, 11,
212n2, 222–224, 414
public health. *See* health and well-being;
illness
public participation. *See* community-based
projects; governance; stakeholder
participation
public-private partnerships, 14

Rabin, Yitzhak, 261, 262
Radcliffe Award, 166
Rahman, Abdur, 191–192
rainfall variability, 15–16
Ramsar Convention on Wetlands, 133,
308, 343–344
rape. *See* women and girls
Reagan, Ronald, 255
Reed, Robert A., 28, 29, 414, 420

520 Index

refugees and internally displaced persons, 8, 16, 28–29, 408–411
  Afghanistan, 102, 312–313
  Azerbaijan, 298
  Croatia, 277
  flooding, 410–411
  food security, 423
  Iraq, 126
  Israel, 244
  livelihoods, 139–140, 163–184
  malnutrition, 409, 410
  Palestinians, 244, 247, 250, 252
  return, 96
  Serbia, 277
  waterborne illness, 409
  See also informal settlements
Regional Environmental Center for Central and Eastern Europe (REC), 281–282, 283–285
regional human rights tribunals, 396–397
regional treaties. *See* transboundary water
regional water management, 17
  See also transboundary water
rehabilitation (definition), 46
Report of the Secretary-General on Peacebuilding in the Immediate Aftermath of Conflict, x
Republic of Congo, 3*t*, 439*t*
Republic of South Sudan. *See* South Sudan
Republic of Srpska. *See* Bosnia and Herzegovina
resilience, 454–456
restoration of basic services. *See* basic needs and services
restorative justice and compensation, 395–396
rights-based approaches, 12–13, 413–414
  See also human rights
riparians, 15
Rubin, Barnett, 195
rural communities, 37–39
  See also agricultural sector
Russia, 3*t*, 430n11, 440*t*
Rwanda, 3*t*, 350–351, 431*t*

Salehyan, Idean, 15
Salman, Salman M. A., 241, 414

sanitation, 1, 407–421, 451*t*
  as a human right, xiii–xiv, 4, 17, 359–360, 383–399
  illness, 8
  informal providers, 37
  Millennium Development Goals (MDGs), 4, 28
  post-conflict delivery, 6, 9–11, 16, 27–30
  See also basic needs and services
Sava River Basin, 15, 240, 275–276, 289–290, 363, 431*t*
  conflict-related environmental impacts, 276–279
  conflict risk, 290–291
  development, 276
  environmental rehabilitation, 289–290
  EU-CARDS project, 285, 367n14
  EU membership goals, 281, 284, 291, 292
  flood control, 287–288, 289, 291
  former Yugoslav management, 278–279
  Framework Agreement on the Sava River Basin (FASRB), 271, 282–286, 290–291, 371, 434
  humanitarian assistance, 281–282, 284–285
  hydropower potential, 288*t*, 289
  incremental negotiations, 282–283, 285
  integrated water resource management (IWRM), 282–290, 371, 373–374, 378
  International Sava River Basin Commission (ISRBC), 271–272, 281, 283–292, 371
  Kosovo conflict, 274, 278
  landmines, 274–275, 277
  navigation goals, 278, 282–283, 286–287, 289–290, 292
  pollution, 276, 290–291, 364
  Protocol on the Navigation Regime, 271, 371
  Sava River Basin Management Plan, 287–288
  Yugoslav wars, 272–275
  See also specific countries, e.g. Croatia
Savimbi, Joseph, 65
Sawhoyomaxa Indigenous Community v. Paraguay, 389

Index   521

scarcity, 1–2, 9, 14–16, 385
  Afghanistan, 9, 201, 227
  climate change, 15–16
  Darfur, 10
  definitions, 2n
  Iran, 305, 311–313
  Japan, 154
  Middle East, 14
  Somalia, 16
  South Sudan, 441
schools, xiv–xv
Schultz, George, 255
security and stability, 6, 28, 405
  food security, 145–146, 149–150, 151,
    169–170, 423
  state building, 33–40
  transboundary water management,
    437–438
  water security, 206–207, 219–232,
    305, 306, 311–313
  See also violence and insecurity; water
    security
Sedra, Mark, 205
Senegal, 3*t*
sequencing of interventions, 450–454
  basic needs and services, 451*t*
  climate change, 453*t*, 454–456
  donor commitment, 453*t*
  governance after conflict, 452*t*
  livelihoods, 451*t*
  public engagement, 453*t*
  transboundary water, 452*t*
Serbia, 282
  constitutional provisions on water, 440*t*
  EU membership goal, 284n14, 292
  hydropower potential, 288*t*, 289
  Kosovo conflict, 274, 278
  maps, 5*f*, 273*f*
  refugee and internally displaced person
    populations, 277
  Sava River share, 276*t*, 279n, 280
  transboundary water, 3*t*, 240, 271–276,
    431*t*
  See also Sava River Basin
service delivery standards, 411–414
settlements. *See* informal settlements
sexual violence, 29–30, 105–110,
  447–448

Shafiq, Mohammad Musa, 314
Shah, Usman, 194, 199
shared water. *See* transboundary water
Siegfried, Tobias, 15–16
Sierra Leone
  large-scale agricultural development,
    457
  mining sector, 457–458
  transboundary water, 3*t*, 431*t*
  Truth and Reconciliation Commission,
    397–398
Singh, Maharaja Hari, 164–165
Slovenia
  EU membership, 282, 284n14
  hydropower potential, 288*t*, 289
  maps, 5*f*, 273*f*
  Sava River share, 276*t*, 280
  transboundary water, 271–276
  See also Sava River Basin
small-scale water providers, 37–39
*Social and Economic Rights Action
  Center and the Center for Economic
  and Social Rights v. Nigeria*, 396
social capital, 75–77, 81–83, 427–428
social marketing approach, 102–103
Solo, Tova Maria, 37
Somalia
  constitutional provisions on water, 440*t*
  refugees and internally displaced
    persons, 408
  stakeholder participation, 416
  transboundary water, 3*t*
  water scarcity and famine, 16
South Africa, 5*f*, 384, 390
South Caucasus, 240, 297–303
  integrated water resource management
    (IWRM), 297, 301–303
  map, 298*f*
  water management capacity building
    programs, 299–303, 435
South Sudan, 85–93
  Abyei dispute, 331, 344–348, 352
  basic needs and services, 29, 85–93
  Comprehensive Peace Agreement of
    2005, 29, 86, 241, 327–332,
    338–339, 352, 386, 432–433
  conflict-sensitive recovery, 428–429
  constitutional provisions on water, 440*t*

522   Index

floods, 410
government capacity building, 91–93
government water policy, 88, 91–92
humanitarian assistance, 91–93
intersectoral competition and
coordination, 85–93
intertribal fighting, 87–88
Jonglei Canal Project, 340–344, 352
maps, 5*f*, 87*f*, 329*f*
Millennium Development Goals,
29, 86
Ministry of Water Resources and
Irrigation, 91–92
Nile Basin Cooperative Framework
Agreement (CFA), 351, 432–433,
437
Nile water management, 338–339
oil reserves, 333, 345, 347, 349
pastoralists, 29, 86–89, 332, 346–347,
425
refugees and internally displaced
persons, 409, 443
transboundary water, 3*t*, 241, 327–352,
431*t*
water allocation, 348–349
Water for Recovery and Peace Program
(WRAPP), 88
water scarcity, 441
Sphere Handbook, 412–413
Sphere Project, 388n8, 413–414
Sri Lanka, 3*t*, 430n11, 440*t*
Stability Pact for South Eastern Europe,
281–282
Stack, Lee, 341
stakeholder participation, 79, 80,
122–123, 125, 130–132, 416,
444–446
See also governance
state building, 31–40
European approach, 31–32, 33, 40
health and well-being, 35, 37–39
international donors, 39–40
legitimacy considerations, 32
service delivery, 34–37
Stec, Stephen, 240, 415
strategic environmental assessment
(SEA), 441–442, 451*t*, 453*t*
Sturtewagen, Benjamin, 434–435

Sudan, 29n
Abuja Agreement, 390–391, 430
Abyei dispute, 331, 344–348, 352
agriculture and irrigation, 339, 349,
420
Comprehensive Peace Agreement of
2005, 29, 327–332, 338–339, 352,
386, 432–433
conservation technologies, 410
constitutional provisions on water,
440*t*
human rights obligations, 392, 395
maps, 5*f*, 87*f*, 329*f*
Millennium Development Goals, xvi
Nile Basin Cooperative Framework
Agreement (CFA), 350–351, 437
Nile Water Commission, 331
oil infrastructure, 333
oil revenues, 347, 349
refugees and internally displaced
persons, 408, 443
transboundary water, 3*t*, 241, 327–352,
431*t*
water allocation, 348–349
See also Darfur; South Sudan
Sugiura, Mikiko, 139, 415
sustainability, 12, 50, 383n, 385
basic needs and services, 55–59, 64,
79–80, 100–101, 105, 134
community-based projects, 64,
100–101, 105, 113
components of, 55–56
Iraq's marshland restoration, 134, 425
privatization, 55–57
urban water systems, 55–58, 59
See also livelihoods
Sustainable Development Goals, xvi
Sustainable Triangle for Irrigation
Management (STIM), 154n
Syria
drought, 456
map, 5*f*
refugees and internally displaced
persons, 408, 410
regional peace talks, 262
transboundary water, 3*t*, 243, 253–255,
258, 259, 445
See also Jordan River Basin

Index   523

Tactical Conflict Assessment and Planning Framework (TCAPF), 223–224, 231
Tajikistan, 3*t*, 318, 440*t*
Taliban, 43, 101, 191n, 193
  in Faryab Privince, 206–207
  in Helmand province, 211–216, 219–232
  Iranian policies, 313–314, 317–318
  water policies, 313
  See also Afghanistan
Tanzania, 336–338, 350–351
tariffs, 13–14
Taylor, Charles, 6, 43, 49
Tearfund, 29–30, 96
  Afghanistan, 101–105, 428
  capacity building programs, 109
  Democratic Republic of the Congo, 96–101
  Liberia, 107–110, 447
  social marketing approach, 102–105
  stakeholder participation, 416
technical sustainability, 56
Tennessee Valley Authority model, 192, 247
Thailand, 3*t*, 410, 440*t*
Thakur, Ramesh, 33
Tignino, Mara, 359–360, 415, 432
Tilly, Charles, 33
Timor-Leste
  Commission for Reception, Truth and Reconciliation, 397
  irrigation systems, 423
  map, 5*f*
  transboundary water management, 3*t*, 430n11
  UN Security Council Resolution 1282, 399
Toguchi, Yuka, 139, 415
transboundary water, 2–4, 135, 239–241, 406, 429–438, 452*t*
  capacity building, 240–241, 297–303, 435
  civil society roles, 17, 265–270
  conflict, 14–16
  environmental rehabilitation projects, 265–270
  Good Water Neighbors project, 239–240

Helmand River Basin, 240–241, 305–322
hydrometeorological data, 240–241, 305, 315, 317, 321, 437
Indus River System, 139–140, 163–184
information-sharing and monitoring programs, 435
international donor contributions, 182–183, 261
joint water management commissions, 176–180, 183–184, 239, 262, 271, 281–292, 322
Jordan River Basin, 179–180, 239–240, 243–262, 265–270, 430–432
livelihoods, 163–184
Nile River Basin, 241, 327–352, 437
peace agreements, 430–433
peacebuilding opportunities, 239–241, 260–262, 265–270, 283–286, 291–292, 315
regional stability, 437–438
regional treaties and institutions, 15, 17, 163, 175–176, 183–184, 239–241, 259–260, 435–436, 446
Sava River Basin, 240, 271–292
South Caucasus region, 240, 297–303
third-party mediation and intervention, 174–184, 251–253, 260–261, 433–435
transitional justice mechanisms, 360, 367, 384n2, 393–398
  international criminal tribunals, 394–396
  regional human rights tribunals, 396–397
  restorative justice and compensation, 395–396
  truth commissions, 397–398
Troell, Jessica, 415
truth commissions, 360, 397–398
tsunami of 2011, 157n
Tudjman, Franjo, 273
Turkey, 3*t*, 425, 440*t*, 445
Turkmenistan, 312
typhoid, 27, 411

524 Index

Uganda, 417
  agricultural sector, 422
  constitutional provisions on water, 440*t*
  human rights treaties, 392
  international donors, 39–40
  Nile Basin Cooperative Framework
    Agreement (CFA), 350–351
  Sector Wide Approach program, 39–40
  transboundary water, 3*t*, 336–338
  water carrying, 447
UN Assistance Mission in Afghanistan
  (UNAMA), 320
UN Children's Fund (UNICEF), 412
UN Convention on the Law of the
  Non-Navigational Uses of
  International Watercourses, xv,
  349–350
UN Development Assistance Framework
  (UNDAF) for Iraq, 135
UN Development Programme (UNDP)
  Global Environment Facility (UNDP/
    GEF), 285, 302
  Water Governance Facility, 315
UN Economic Commission for Europe
  (UNECE)
  Convention on Access to Information,
    Public Participation and Access to
    Justice in Environmental Matters
    (Aarhus Convention), 286, 446
  Convention on the Protection and Use
    of Transboundary Watercourses and
    International Lakes (Helsinki
    Convention), 280, 281, 370–371
UN Environment Programme (UNEP)
  Iraqi Marshlands Project, 30, 117–135
  monitoring and evaluation role,
    126–127
  staff safety, 128–129
UN Framework Convention on Climate
  Change, 133
UN General Assembly Resolution 64/292,
  xiv, 383, 398, 399
UN High Commissioner for Refugees,
  102
UN Human Rights Council, 393
UN human rights treaty bodies, 391–393
União Nacional para a Independência
  (UNITA), 65–66

United Kingdom, 3*t*, 431*t*
UN Millennium Development Goals
  (MDGs). *See* Millennium
  Development Goals
UN Peacebuilding Commission, ix–x
UN Relief and Works Agency for
  Palestinian Refugees (UNRWA), 247
UN Secretary-General, 95, 111
UN Truce Supervision Organization
  (UNTSO), 244, 246, 250–255
urban water services, 43–60, 63–83, 411
  community engagement, 43–44, 52–53,
    54, 57–58
  informal settlements, 8, 16, 28–29,
    37–39, 52–53, 59–60, 408–411
  international humanitarian
    organizations, 47, 51–52, 53, 59, 420
  leadership, 59
  needs-based response, 57–58
  piped water, 37
  private-sector participation, 56–57
  rehabilitation process, 51–55, 58–60
  sustainability goals, 55–58, 59, 64
  universal access, 58, 60
  value chain analysis, 64, 70–73
  See also Kabul; Luanda; Monrovia
Ušacka, Anita, 395
U.S. Agency for International
  Development
  Bosnia and Herzegovina projects, 364
  Helmand River Basins projects, 220,
    223–225, 230–231
  Pact Sudan's Water for Recovery and
    Peace Program (WRAPP), 88
  Palestinian Water Authority, 434
  South Caucasus projects, 240,
    297–303, 435
Uzbekistan, 15

value chain analysis, 64, 70–73
Vardanyan, Marina, 240, 416
Viet Nam, 39, 429
violence and insecurity, 30, 85–86,
  117–135, 414
  Afghanistan, 11, 43–44, 101, 191n,
    193, 206–207, 211–232, 414
  counterinsurgency operations, 211–232,
    414

Index 525

gender-based violence, 29–30,
105–110, 447–448
Iraq, 11, 30, 124–125, 128–129, 414
Jordan River Basin, 261–262
water complexity, 229
Volk, Richard, 240, 416

Wade, Robert, 153
WASH interventions, 102–105, 412–413
See also Global WASH Cluster (GWC)
water. *See* drinking water; sanitation
water availability, 2f, 299–300
waterborne illness, 409n4
See also illness
water carrying, 29, 76–77, 99, 105–110,
410, 447–448
water collection, 29, 76–77, 99, 410
gender-based violence, 105–110, 447–448
time requirements, 447
water complexity, 226–230
definition, 215t
groundwater withdrawal, 227–229
pollution, 229
spatial and temporal aspects, 226t, 230
violence and insecurity, 229
weather and climate change, 227,
231–232, 453t, 454–456
water data. *See* hydrometeorological data
water disputes, 9
See also transboundary water
water management. *See* management of
water resources
Waternet program, 434
water rights, 12–13
See also constitutional provisions on
water; human rights
water security
Afghanistan, 206–207, 219–232, 306,
312–313
Iran, 305, 311–313
schools, xiv–xv
See also climate change; scarcity
water stress, 2n
water use, 1–2
water-user associations (WUAs),
427–428
water-washed illness, 409n4
See also illness

Weber, Max, 31–32, 33
Weinthal, Erika, 416
White Nile River Basin, 333–337,
350n51, 351, 352, 420, 437
See also Nile River Basin
Wolf, Aaron T., 283
women and girls, 29–30, 447–448
community leadership, 98–100, 108–111
Convention on the Elimination of All
Forms of Discrimination against
Women (CEDAW), 387, 393
gender-based violence, 29–30,
105–110, 447–448
literacy and education, 447
water carrying, 29, 76–77, 99,
107–108, 410
See also gender
Woodhead Commission, 243–244
World Bank, x
Indus Basin Development Fund, 175,
180, 183
Indus River Basin dispute mediation,
174–176, 179–180, 182, 433, 449
World Heritage sites, 134–135

*Yakye Axa Indigenous Community v.
Paraguay*, 389
Yemen, 3t
Yugoslavia
dissolution, 271–275
map, 273f
Sava River share, 275–276
water management, 278–279
See also Sava River Basin

Zaman, Idrees, 197, 202
Zambia, 39
Zawahri, Neda A., 139–140, 417
Zimbabwe
map, 5f
Matabeleland-Zambezi Water Trust
(MZWP), 36
opposition to the government, 420–421
state building process, 34–36
Zimbabwe African National Union
(ZANU), 35
Zimbabwe African People's Union
(ZAPU), 35